SOVIET DISSENT

Translated by Carol Pearce and John Glad

 WESLEYAN UNIVERSITY PRESS
Middletown, Connecticut

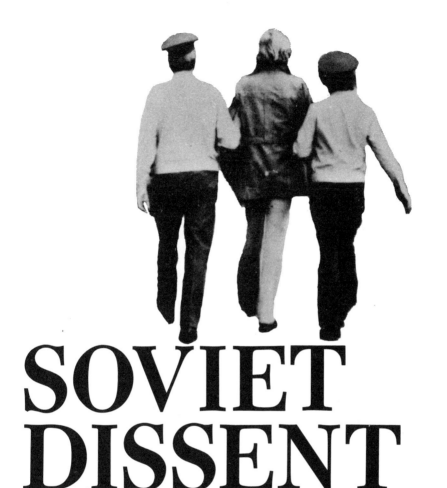

SOVIET DISSENT

Contemporary Movements for
National, Religious, and Human Rights

LUDMILLA ALEXEYEVA

Originally published in the United States in the Russian language and in some-what different form under the title ИСТОРИЯ ИНАКОМЫСЛИЯ В СССР (*History of Dissent in the USSR*), copyright © 1984 by Khronika Press.

Excerpts from *Letter to the Soviet Leaders* by Aleksandr I. Solzhenitsyn, translated from the Russian by Hilary Sternberg, copyright © 1974 by Aleksandr I. Solzhenitsyn (English translation copyright © 1974 by Writers and Scholars International Ltd.) reprinted by permission of Harper & Row, Publishers, Inc.

The following photographs are used by permission: Yuri Badzio © SMOLOSKYP, Organization for Defense of Human Rights in Ukraine; Victor Rtskheladze and Zviad Gamsakhurdia, Boris Talantov, and Andrey Tverdokhlebov, copyright © Peter Reddaway; Yakov Skornyakov, copyright © Open Doors; Anatoly Yakobson, copyright © A.C.E.R. All photographs other than the above, copyright © 1985 by Ludmilla Alexeyeva.

LIBRARY OF CONGRESS CATALOGING IN PUBLICATION DATA

Alekseeva, Liudmila, 1927–
    Soviet dissent.

Rev. translation of: Istoriia inakomysliia v SSSR.
    Includes index.
    1. Social movements—Soviet Union—History. 2. Dissenters—Soviet Union—History. 3. Civil rights—Soviet Union—History. 4. Soviet Union—Social conditions—1945–   . I. Title.
HN527.A4713   1985   303.4′84   84–11811
ISBN 0–8195–6176–2

All inquiries and permissions resquests should be addressed to the Publisher, Wesleyan University Press, 110 Mt. Vernon St., Middletown, Connecticut, 06457. Distributed by Harper & Row Publishers, Keystone Industrial Park, Scranton, Pennsylvania, 18512.

Manufactured in the United States of America

First printing, 1985
Wesleyan Paperback, 1987

To my husband, Nikolay Williams,
without whom this book could not have been written

Preface

This book is a mixture of my observations and understanding from inside the dissident movement in the USSR as well as my study of the movement from the outside. I view my work on the movement precisely as research, not as sketches based on mere personal impressions, although I am not a bystander, and I have an enthusiastic attitude toward it. For fifteen years, I was constantly occupied with typing *samizdat;* I took part in creating the mechanism for the distribution of *samizdat* and the collection of information for the *Chronicle of Current Events.* For ten years I was also engaged in aiding political prisoners and their families. I developed many friends and acquaintances, not only among human rights activists, but also among participants of other movements, thereby obtaining a direct knowledge of these other movements. The circle of my acquaintances was greatly widened during my work with the Moscow Helsinki Group—all sorts of people came to us with their problems from all over the Soviet Union.

I have attempted in this book to describe systematically the independent movements of dissent in the Soviet Union. Each movement is described separately, because each has its own shape and pursues its own purposes. My goal was to show the great variety of Soviet dissent and, at the same time, to demonstrate its internal unity—a unity evident in the application of peaceful means in the pursuit of human rights, which are now more and more coming into the foreground.

Personal experience, however, is not enough for a systematic description and history of all the dissident movements in the USSR from their inception to the present time. *Samizdat* completed the data necessary for this book. The source of essential information is the *Chronicle of Current Events,* which the academician Sakharov has called the principal achievement of the human rights movement. The anonymous editorial board that publishes *CCE* is renewed approximately every two years, generally because of the arrests of its editors. Since 1968, sixty-four issues of *Chronicle* have appeared; they contain an immense amount of material about the violation of human rights throughout the USSR and about the continuing struggle against these abuses. The excellent quality of the information from *Chronicle* has withstood investigation. At the trials for those involved in *Chronicle,* usually on charges of "slander," teams of KGB agents seeking grounds for these accusations on several occasions checked the reliability of the information of human rights activists. But even these diligent inspectors were able to find only a few inaccuracies.

CCE has been my major—although far from my only—source of information. In the thirty years of their existence, *samizdat* publications have grown into a huge library. In preparing this book I read through the *entire* library of *samizdat* that has reached the West. *Samizdat* is for the most part preserved in the *Samizdat* Archive of Radio Liberty in Munich, the archive of Khronika Press in New York, and in the files of Keston College in London.

My most valuable sources were:

1) The numerous information publications of various dissident movements and groups: *Chronicle of the Lithuanian Catholic Church; Ukrainian Herald;* information bulletins of the Ukrainian Helsinki Group and the Council of Relatives of Evangelical Christian Baptists; the independent trade union group SMOT; the Initiative Group for the Defense of the Rights of the Handicapped in the USSR; the Working Commission to Investigate the Abuse of Psychiatry for Political Purposes; the Right to Emigration group and others; the information publications of the Crimean Tartars and the German movements, of the Pentecostalists, and Adventists.

2) The documents of independent public associations—the Initiative Group for the Defense of Human Rights in the USSR; the Committee for Human Rights, the Helsinki groups, the Christian and Catholic Committees to Defend the Rights of Believers; the Free Trade Union, and many others.

3) *Samizdat* documents of appeals, open letters, and statements by Soviet citizens (collective and individual) to various Soviet and international bodies, usually complaints or protests against violations of the rights of individuals or groups. These documents contain a large amount of factual material and evaluations important for the study of the development of independent public opinion in Soviet society and for people's awareness of their own rights.

4) Works of *samizdat* authors and memoirs of participants in the various dissident movements, which are important sources for the study of the history of dissent and the evolution of its ideology.

5) Official documents distributed in *samizdat*—court sentences for political cases, as well as answers from officials to complaints and inquiries from Soviet citizens, and also unpublicized directives and instructions of various Soviet official agencies.

6) Interviews with well-known participants of the dissident movement, records of their statements at press conferences for foreign correspondents, and so on.

The study of all the documents of this rich archive became possible only after I had emigrated from the Soviet Union in 1977, under pressure from authorities and the possibility of arrest. The many years of contact with *samizdat* in my homeland did not give me, or my colleagues who are historians, the opportunity for traditional and exhaustive scholarly study. A complete collection of *samizdat* materials from the USSR does not exist, I imagine, even in the appropriate departments of the KGB, which cannot manage to find and confiscate everything. And dissidents in the Soviet Union can only acquaint themselves with current documents, since they cannot collect a huge archive, which would be difficult to keep from exposure and confiscation. It is for this reason that I, having come to the West and having access to *samizdat* archives, consider it my duty toward participants in dissent in the Soviet Union to study and publicize their collective experience, so dearly paid for.

My research work took six years. The first year, during the Carter Administration, I worked on a grant from the U.S. Department of State, compiling a handbook record on dissent in the USSR. My special thanks are due to the State Department and especially to Eric Willenz for the supporting grant that allowed me to begin the research on which this book was based.

My particular thanks are due to John Glad and Carol Pearce for translating the bulk of this book into English; to Cathy Cosman for translating the chapters on the Latvian National-Democratic Movement, the Socialists, and my conclusion; to Cathy Fitzpatrick for translating my introduction, and the chapters on the Estonian National-Democratic Movement, the concluding part of "The Movement for Human Rights," and for her work on the English publication of this book; to Peter Dornan, chairman of the *samizdat* department of Radio Liberty for allowing me to peruse materials and indices in his department; and to participants and experts in the movements described with whom I consulted: Nadia Svitlychna and Nina Strokata ("The Ukrainian National Movement"), Tomas Venclova ("The Lithuanian National Movement"), the late Aleksandr Malakhazyan ("The Armenian National Movement"), Ayshe Seytmuratova ("The Crimean Tartar

National Movement"), Roman Rutman and Lidiya Voronina ("The Jewish Emigration Movement"), The Reverend Georgy Vins ("The Evangelical Christian Baptists"), Arkady Polishchuk ("The Pentecostalists"), the Reverend Mihail Meerson-Aksyonov ("The Russian Orthodox Church"), Yury Gastev ("The Movement for Human Rights"), Ilya Levin and Yury Handler (Leningrad dissidents). I am also deeply grateful to Edward Kline and Peter Reddaway for their very valuable comments on the English publication.

Grateful acknowledgment is also due to the J. Roderick MacArthur Foundation for its assistance.

In early 1984, a Russian-language version of this book, in somewhat different form, was published by Khronika Press in New York. As a consequence, still more information has reached me through readers who are themselves exiles. I hope, in turn, that the *samizdat* will provide yet one more service—that through *samizdat* channels the book will reach my fellow countrymen. The English translation of my book was made possible by a grant from the Ford Foundation. Thanks to this, and also to the efforts of the U.S. Helsinki Watch Committee and of Wesleyan University Press, the readers of the free world can now familiarize themselves with the first such complete description of an amazing phenomenon of our time—an independent social movement of dissent in the USSR.

—Ludmilla Alexeyeva

Contents

Photographs

The Ukrainian National Movement   *Following page 42*

Leonid Plyushch, first *samizdat* liaison in the 1960s between Moscow and the Ukraine, before his arrest in 1970

Mykola Plakhotnyuk, physician, initiator of the 1967 Kiev demonstration, before his arrest in 1972

Ivan Svitlychny, philologist and 1960s activist, Kiev, 1968

Group of 1960s activists in Lvov, 1971

Yury Badzyo, whose *The Right to Live* was confiscated by the KGB, with his wife, Svetlana

Ivan Dzyuba, leading Ukrainian activist until his arrest in 1972

Levko Lukyanenko, and Ivan Kandyba, 1976, after release from prison term, founding members of the Ukrainian Union of Workers and Peasants and Ukrainian Helsinki Watch Group

Mykola Rudenko, leader of the Ukrainian Helsinki Watch Group, with his wife, Raisa, and Pyotr Grigorenko, founding member of Moscow and Ukrainian Helsinki Watch groups, with his wife, Zinaida, Moscow, 1976

The Lithuanian National Movement

Petras Paulaitis, member of the underground Union for the Struggle for a Free Lithuania and political prisoner, 1946–56, 1957–82, on his last release from prison in March 1982

Viktoras Petkus, founding member of the Lithuanian Helsinki Watch Group with Albertas Zilinskas

Nijole Sadunaite, activist for the *Chronicle of the Catholic Church in Lithuania,* 1977, in exile

xvii

The Soviet-German Emigration Movement   *Following page 170*

Soviet-German activist Friedrich Ruppel and his family, before emigration, Moscow train station, 1974, with Andrey Sakharov and his daughter, Tatyana

Soviet-German participants in Red Square demonstration, 1980

The Jewish Emigration Movement

Members of the Jewish refuseniks' scientific seminar, Moscow, 1973

Jewish refusenik Aleksandr Paritsky, founder of the independent university for young refuseniks, with his family before his arrest, Kharkov, 1981

Memorial Day, Minsk, 1975

The Evangelical Christian Baptists

Council of Relatives of Evangelical Christian Baptist Prisoners, 1980

Ivan I. Leven, manager of Baptists' underground printing press in the Leningrad area

Georgy Vins, founding member of the Initiative Group and Council Secretary, Independent Baptist Church, with his son Pyotr, member of the Ukrainian Helsinki Watch Group, who visited his father in Yakutsk camp, 1977

Yakov Skornyakov, Baptist minister, in camp with his two prisoner converts, c. 1980

The Pentecostalists

Vasily F. Patrushev, initiator of 1965 Pentecostal exodus, with his family

Pentecostal exodus leaders

Trial of Boris Perchatkin, 1980

Bishop Ivan Fedotov preaching at a Pentecostal service

The True and Free Seventh-Day Adventists

Vladimir Shelkov, in camp near Yakutsk, 1970, leader of the Independent Adventist church since 1949, who died in camp, 1980

The Reverend Rostislav Galetsky, baptizing an Adventist who is masked to conceal his identity

The Russian Orthodox Church   *Following page 298*

Boris Talantov in 1968, Orthodox layman who died in a labor camp in 1970

Father Gleb Yakunin, Moscow, 1978, initiator of defense of Orthodox church rights, and founder of the Christian Committee for the Defense of Human Rights of Believers, with his family

Father Sergy Zheludkov, active in Orthodox and human rights movements who died in 1984

Father Dmitry Dudko, popular Moscow preacher in the 1970s

Zoya Krakhmalnikova, Moscow, editor of the religious magazine *Hope*, before her arrest in 1983

The Movement for Social and Economic Justice

Vladimir Skvirsky, founding member of SMOT (Free Interprofessional Association of Workers) Moscow, 1978

Lev Volokhonsky, founding member of SMOT, Leningrad, 1978

Arkady Tsurkov, activist in group of young Social-Democrats in Leningrad, 1976

Aleksey Nikitin, fighter for independent trade unions, Dovetsk, 1980, who died in a psychiatric hospital in 1984

Yury Kiselyov, Moscow artist and founding member of Initiative Group for the Defense of the Rights of Invalids in the USSR, 1980

The Russian National Movement

Igor Ogurtsov, leader of All-Russian Social Christian Union for the People's Liberation, Leningrad, 1967

Gennady Shimanov, national-Bolshevik and *samizdat* writer, with his family in Moscow, 1973

Vladimir Osipov, editor of the Russian National Movement *samizdat* magazine *Veche*

The Movement for Human Rights   *Following page 362*

Larisa Bogoraz and Pavel Litvinov, authors of first open appeal of Soviet dissidents to Western opinion, 1968

Yuly Daniel, Moscow, 1971, after his release from a five-year sentence for publishing his novels abroad

Yulius Telesin, distributor of *samizdat* in the late 1960s

Vyacheslav Igrunov, after his release from 1976 sentence for possession of *samizdat* library in Odessa

Anatoly Marchenko, author of *My Testimony*, Moscow, 1980, between arrests

Natalya Gorbanevskaya, first editor of *Chronicle of Current Events*, with her children, 1973

Anatoly Yakobson, editor of *CCE* in 1970–72, Moscow, 1972

Ivan Kovalyov and Aleksandr Lavut, sentenced for work with *CCE* and Moscow Helsinki Watch Group

Irina Yakir, daughter of Pyotr Yakir and assistant of *CCE*, 1969–72, Moscow, 1980

Valery Abramkin, Moscow, 1972, who was sentenced in 1979 for participating in the independent *samizdat* magazine *Quest*

Vladimir Gershuni, Moscow, 1980, who was sentenced in 1983 for participating in *Quest* and the information bulletin of SMOT

Sergey Pisarev, initiator of struggle against psychiatric persecution for political reasons

Dr. Anatoly Koryagin, consultant for the Working Commission to Investigate the Abuse of Psychiatry for Political Purposes, with his family in Kharkov, 1979, before his arrest

Aleksandr Podrabinek, Irina Kaplun, Vyacheslav Bakhmin, founding members of the Psychiatric Commission

Ilya Rips, who tried self-immolation to protest invasion of Czechoslovakia

Dr. Valentin Turchin, first head of Soviet branch of Amnesty International

Members of Initiative Group for Defense of Human Rights in the USSR

The Moscow Trust Group, September 1982

Pyotr Yakir in 1979, active in human rights movement until his arrest in 1972

Andrey Tverdokhlebov, founding member of the Human Rights Committee, Group-73 and Soviet branch of Amnesty International, Moscow, 1974

Svetlana and Vladlen Pavlenkov, human rights activists, Gorky, 1974

Human rights activists of Kharkov, 1969

Yuliya Voznesenskaya and Tatyana Goricheva, activists of the "Second Culture" in Leningrad, 1980

Arseny Roginsky, sentenced in 1981 for participating in the underground publication *Memory*, Leningrad, 1979

Dr. Yury Orlov, leader of Moscow Helsinki Watch Group, in Moscow just before being taken prisoner, February 1977

A typical gathering outside the Moscow trial of Dr. Yury Orlov

MAPS

INTRODUCTION

SOVIET DISSENT

Soviet Dissent

Soviet dissent is little known to Westerners, but it is also little known to Soviet people as well. It resembles Soviet life in general in its diversity and variety and in the separation of its component parts. Nothing of what makes up real public life is visible on the surface.

The Soviet "dissident movement," as it is called, extends beyond the movement for human rights, although the two are sometimes equated. The movement encompasses various active civic communities that oppose official ideology or politics.

Among these, national and religious movements are the most widespread and active. In their present forms, these movements arose after the death of Stalin in 1953, but their roots extend back to pre-revolutionary periods. In the six decades of Soviet government, the state's unprecedented pressure on society rooted out public expression of ideas which the regime disliked, not only by suppression but often through physical destruction. As a consequence it is possible to view the appearance of these civic movements in the post-Stalinist period as a kind of rebirth.

Such revival and inception of new movements did not occur simultaneously. Each movement had its own process of development. In some cases years and even decades elapsed after the death of Stalin, before dissent was expressed. For a time after Stalin's death, which marked the end of total terror, society remained in a half-awake state of shock. The awakening was also slow because new awareness had to be hidden, not only because of fear—there have always been brave people among us—but because of the complete monopoly and control of the flow of information and ideas by the Party and the government. Literature of all kinds was controlled by the State: scientific as well as artistic, contemporary editions, reprints and translations, cinematography, the theater, painting (from the individual canvas to matchbox

3

labels), records and radio (from political to musical broadcasts), and the education system—from nursery school to doctoral programs.

The totality of ideological control created wholly new opportunities for the disinformation and manipulation of social opinion. As a result, the population of the enormous Soviet empire lost any real conception of its past and present history. History was replaced by the myths of official ideologues. History was rewritten to resemble the present state of uniformity: entire areas of ideas and facts, names, historical and philosophical schools were erased from memory. The official political program was constantly rewritten in accordance with fluctuating demands by governmental interests, and all opinion that differed from the official line was presented only in a "corrected" form that caricatured the original. Questions that had concerned many of our people were forgotten; the spiritual aspirations of the world outside the borders of the Soviet Union remained unknown.

The iron curtain separated the Soviet Union from the rest of world culture for at least two generations. One's knowledge of the world was limited to one's own observations, and knowledge of social processes was limited to one's own circle of personal acquaintances. Soviet society became atomized. In some of these tiny social units attempts were made to understand the new socioeconomic system, the new morality, and a new type of man. The spiritual and intellectual work of isolated individual and tiny groups was limited to miniature cells of humanity. In the words of the poet Osip Mandelshtam, "We live with no sense of the country beneath our feet / Our voices inaudible at ten paces."

The Party's complete control by the dissemination of ideas and information contributed to the explosive force of the Twentieth Party Congress in February 1956, which authorized a change in the world view that had been presented to Soviet citizens for decades. Stalin, previously deified, was now revealed as a cunning and bloody criminal. The exposures of Stalin's crimes, despite the will of the Party's elite, became the first impetus for the spiritual emancipation of society.

I believe that Nikita Khrushchev, the initiator of the exposure of Stalin, did not take this step simply out of political calculation. Along with others, he experienced a natural human urge to tear himself away from the ghostly, ahistorical world created by the official myth-makers and to enter the real world.

The Twentieth Party Congress lifted the veil from reality only slightly. The Party retained total control over the distribution of ideas and information. Although official Party line allowed criticism of the "personality cult," the official term for the horrors of the Stalinist period, it forbade any criticism of the Party that had implemented this "cult" for decades, or of the socioeconomic system that had made it

Western USSR

Eastern USSR

possible. Thus, criticism was limited strictly to the Stalinist period itself and was not permitted to extend backward to the Leninist period or ahead to the post-Stalin period, i.e., to the present moment.

But even such a limited enlarging of the boundaries of what was permitted, along with a refusal by the authorities to engage in mass terror, turned out to be sufficient for irreversible changes in the minds of people and in public life.

First Open Protest

The first to organize protest to the authorities were the outcasts of outcasts, nations that had been deported on Stalin's orders from their homelands to the eastern regions of the USSR and settled there in special settlements (reservations). After the death of Stalin, the Kalmyks, the Chechen, the Karacha, the Ingush, and the Balkars were permitted to return to their homelands. But the Crimean Tartars, who had been deported from the Crimea, the Meskhi, a national group from South Georgia; and the Volga Germans were denied such an opportunity. In 1956 representatives of the Crimean Tartars and the Meskhi went to Moscow to deliver petitions with thousands of signatures of their fellow countrymen. These were collective requests for permission to return to their homelands, addressed to the Central Committee of the Communist Party and to the Presidium of the Supreme Soviet of the USSR.

The Crimean Tartar movement to return to the Crimea is the only movement in the USSR that could be called an all-national movement. During the 1960s, more than three million signatures were affixed to Crimean Tartar petitions. Since the Crimean Tartar population is about 800,000, this means that every adult signed at least six or seven times.[1]

The movement of the Volga Germans to emigrate to West Germany and the movement of the Jews to emigrate to Israel are also movements of peoples who do not have their own territories and also aim to return to their historic homelands. But since West Germany and Israel are located beyond the borders of the USSR, the German and Jewish movements are essentially emigration movements.

Among the nations that live in their own territories with the status of republics within the Soviet Union, the first movement to emerge in the 1960s was the Ukrainian movement. Its aspiration was to resist the Russification of the republic and to insist on equal rights and democratization for the Ukraine. In the Baltic republics, independent civic life developed most fully in Lithuania, where, at the beginning of the 1970s, a widespread and well-organized Catholic movement developed. In Vilnius, the capital of Lithuania, there are frequent demonstrations, attended by many thousands of people, whose banners read "Russians, go home!" and "Freedom for Lithuania!" For Estonians and Latvians, the slogan "Russians, go home!" is accompanied by calls for "Freedom."

In the neighboring Caucasian republics of Armenia and Georgia, nationalists are separated from each other, possibly, in part, because of the widespread enmity between the Armenian and Georgian people, so deeply rooted in history that it is difficult to determine its origin.

The Russian national movement appeared in a definite form at the beginning of the 1970s. The Russian people have been declared in the Soviet empire to be the "first among equals," but only those Russians who make up the ruling class gain any real advantages from this ranking. Russian nationalism is increasingly found among those in power, both grafted on to Marxism or displacing it. Russians who are not part of this upper stratum hardly support the imperialist ambitions of the USSR; for them national sentiment is only natural patriotism. Only the more democratically inclined adherents of the Russian national movement recognize the right to self-determination for all the nationalities that make up the USSR, but they are in no hurry to promote its implementation. The majority of the Russian nationalists either do not speak definitively on this question or refuse to recognize the right at all. This creates a barrier between the Russian national movement and the other national movements that is difficult to surmount.

The religious movements in the USSR—Russian Orthodox, Catholic, and Protestant (Baptist, Pentecostal, and Seventh Day Adventist)—focus on the freedom to practice their faith and resistance to interference by the state in their internal affairs.

Both national and religious movements have had some success in working out an ideology, in consolidating their supporters, and in creating an organizational structure. But they have been less successful in unifying the diverse movements. Each movement is unique, but all have features in common and a common goal. Yet despite their commonality and the fact that the formation of a coalition would strengthen their overall chances for success, there are almost no connections among the dissenting movements.

The nationalist and religious movements lack information about each other. They have been unable to circumvent the strict ideological control of the mass media. They live in a society where everything from ABC books to historical and sociological research texts, to say nothing of the press, is manipulated to strengthen the propagandistic premise of the "unity and monolithic nature" of Soviet society and its "solidarity in supporting the Party and the Government." Thus, Lithuanians may be aware of their own national and religious problems, yet know nothing about the problems of Ukrainians, even though they resemble their own.

But it is not only a lack of information that divides the national movements of various peoples in the USSR. The national and religious sentiments that help such movements to cohere internally do not provide a basis for unification. Indeed they sometimes hinder unity. Nor are any of these movements in a position to play the catalytic role of uniting the others. The Russian national movement is the least likely to play such a role, because of the specific place of the Russian nation in the Soviet empire, and in view of the fact that Russification, that process whereby centralized power becomes more and more deeply rooted in the non-Russian republics, is possibly the most hated feature of subjugation by the nations settled with Russians. Whereas in Polish society, for example, which is homogeneous in nationality and religion, nationalist and religious feelings have rallied people to the democratic movement. In multi-national Soviet society, such feelings lead people to withdraw into their own national and religious communities. In such a heterogeneous society as the USSR, therefore, only the human rights movement can play a linking role for all other movements. The human rights movement has become a natural focus for all other movements, chiefly because of its universal orientation for all citizens, but also because of its neutrality with respect to religion, politics, and ethnic origin.

The human rights movement is considered to have a specific birthdate—December 5, 1965—when the first demonstration with the slogan "Respect the Soviet Constitution!" took place in Moscow's Pushkin Square.

At that time, another movement very similar in conception and spirit was growing in the United States of America—the civil rights movement. It is striking that in societies as different as the Soviet Union and America, similar social impulses arose independently at the same time. In both countries, oppressed citizens began to demand that the provisions of their constitution be observed. Many sacrificed their personal welfare to protest constitutional violations which had gone unnoticed by the majority. Such violations had existed since the adoption of their respective constitutions and were firmly entrenched in social and governmental tradition. In both countries, a handful of activists acting out of moral more than political considerations inspired large numbers of people to protest actively.

While demanding the right to free speech, proclaimed by the Soviet Constitution, the human rights movement activists also introduced a novel practice of publicizing facets of life in the USSR that are either hushed up or distorted by official information outlets and propaganda.

From the very beginning, the characteristic feature of the movement was its public nature; and adherence to the movement was determined first of all by open expression of one's opinion. Under Soviet conditions, which are hardly conducive to such openness, such a movement could not emerge all at once; people were not prepared for an open opposition to the regime, and there was no mechanism to obtain publicity without going over the heads of the authorities. The preparation of the necessary conditions for getting public exposure for independent civic positions took more than ten years after the death of Stalin.

The open movement was preceded by an era of underground circles (almost always made up of young people). Underground organizations had existed for at least a century in Tsarist Russia. In the Soviet era, underground groups operated even under Stalinist terror. A decision to go underground requires not only an organizational break, but an ideological and psychological break. In the flood of court cases fabricated by investigators concerning "anti-Soviet" and "terrorist" organizations, some were groups that really existed, usually clubs of a Marxist bent that aimed to "restore Leninist norms to public life," and so on.

During the second half of the 1950s, immediately after the Twentieth Congress, many such circles appeared, judging from their frequent exposure by investigative agencies. As before, their members remained few in number (usually three to seven). The people who became members of such groups were shaken by the revelations and did not trust the Soviet leadership to make substantial changes decisively and competently.

In the same year as the Twentieth Congress, Soviet tanks crushed the Hungarian revolution. Inside the USSR, Soviet leaders blamed Stalin for all the crimes of the past, while protecting themselves and the Party from blame. They did not admit to any faults in the Soviet system nor work to change it. This provoked the most courageous young people of the 1950s to search for others who thought as they did to join them in the struggle. Some discussed preparations to overthrow the regime, which, from their point of view, had betrayed the ideals of the revolution. They conceived of this coup as a new revolution. They could act in no other way except underground. Among them were many who would not have considered violent acts; they acted in secret because they had no reason to suppose that the peaceful nature of their independent activity would protect them from persecution. Marxist tradition itself doubtless played a crucial role in the spread of the underground. For decades, Soviet people knew nothing other than Marxism. Although they rebelled against the existing system in spirit, they continued, nevertheless, to evaluate it in Marxist terms, to analyze it using Marxist methods, and to search for ways to change it within the framework of a Marxist system.

But what had been possible under the Tsar was impossible under the Soviet system. Members of contemporary secret organizations could be saved from the KGB only through complete inactivity. None of the known underground organizations managed to survive for more than two years, and the majority were exposed after only a few months. One can tell from the composition of the political prisoner population of those years that underground clubs had been founded in various places, but most of them were organized in the Ukraine and in the Baltic republics. The forerunner of the Russian nationalist movement was also a secret organization. The All-Russian Social-Christian Union for the Liberation of the People (known by its Russian acronym VSKhSON) was exposed in Leningrad in 1967. The remaining underground activists from the Russian part of the USSR were, as previously, Marxists striving to correct the Soviet system by democratizing it.[2]

The Rise of Literary Expression

Underground circles were not the only, nor even the most effective, method of searching for an answer to the eternal questions in Russia: "Who is guilty?" and "What is to be done?" Since only criticism directed at the past was permitted, there were more opportunities for expression in literature and in retrospective journalism than in the daily press. During this period, writers and literary critics were at the forefront. The publication of Dudintsev's novel *Not by Bread Alone,* Ilya Ehrenburg's *The Thaw,* Valentin Ovechkin's sketches of village life, the *Literary Moscow* and *Pages from Tarusa* anthologies were all events of enormous political significance. But most important was the monthly literary and publicist journal *Novy mir* (New World), whose editor, Aleksandr Tvardovsky, brought together everything in Russian literature that showed talent and honesty.

The reading public was divided between advocates of the liberal *Novy mir* and advocates of the conservative *October* (a clear minority; for the most part those who took part in the crimes of the Stalin era, or those whose well-being and careers depended on preserving the Stalinist order). *Novy mir* not only helped in the spread of liberalism, but also in the solidarity of its readership. Carrying the current issues of *Novy mir* in one's pockets became a signal of liberal identity.

Tvardovsky's greatest achievement was in obtaining permission, with great difficulty, to publish Aleksandr Solzhenitsyn's "One Day in the Life of Ivan Denisovich." However, in February 1970, Tvardovsky was removed from the editorial board of *Novy mir,* and the journal soon lost its vigor. The repression of *Novy mir* was part of increasing censorship. Still, society did not sink back into its former spiritual and intellectual prostration. The temporary easing of censorship had an irreversible effect on the minds of people and on the social life of the country. Independent public opinion had been born and a consolidation of those forces that had been brought to life continued with the help of a method of unhindered dissemination of ideas and information now known by the term *samizdat,* which means literally "self-publishing." As Vladimir Bukovsky put it: "I write it myself, censor it myself, print and disseminate it myself, and then I do time in prison for it myself."[3]

There has always existed a more or less harsh system of censorship. In response, since the time of Aleksandr Radishchev in the eighteenth century, censored works have been passed around from hand to hand. But *samizdat* is unique as a *mass* phenomenon and as the *basic* means of self-knowledge and self-expression accessible to society in the post-Stalinist era in the Soviet Union (and in countries with similar socio-economic systems).

The mechanism of *samizdat* is very simple: the author types his work on a typewriter (the only means at the disposal of the average Soviet citizen), usually with four or five carbons, or photocopies it, and passes copies out to people he knows. If others are interested in the work, they make copies from their copy and distribute them among their friends. The more successful a work, the faster and further it is distributed. Of course, *samizdat* is extremely inefficient in terms of the time and effort expended, but it is the only possible way of overcoming the government monopoly on ideas and information. It has attracted talented writers, fearless and energetic distributors, and a readership that is continually growing. Those who hunger for a truthful picture of the world and for genuine knowledge are prepared to sacrifice time and energy and even endure persecution for its sake.

It was through *samizdat* that the Crimean Tartars first distributed petitions for signatures calling for a return to their homeland and accounts of representatives of the nation who had taken these petitions to Moscow. These materials, periodically distributed under the title *Information Bulletin,* were the earliest instances of the use of *samizdat* in organizing an independent citizens' movement. This method was also used in 1960 to distribute the *Fraternal Pamphlet* of the Initiative Group of Baptists, who launched an independent church of Evangelical Christian Baptists. *Fraternal Pamphlet* contained accounts of the work done by the Initiative Group and proposals to religious communities on how to act for future support of the Initiative Group. In

Lithuania *samizdat* was born through the effort to preserve in the national memory the history of the struggle against the German and Soviet occupations in the 1940s and 1950s. Thus appeared the multi-volumed "Lithuanian Archive," collections of documents and memoirs of those years.

The Ukrainian national movement began in the 1960s with uncensored and *samizdat* poetry and literature. In Armenia in 1966 an underground National Unification Party began to publish through *samizdat* a newspaper called *Paros* (Beacon).

Russian *samizdat* began with poetry, possibly because poetry is easier to reproduce—brief and easier to memorize. But there may be a deeper cause: spiritual emancipation begins in the area of simple human feelings. By the late 1950s and early 1960s, essays, short stories, and articles also were circulating in *samizdat*. At the time, Moscow and Leningrad were literally overflowing with poetry of the censored, forgotten, and persecuted poets from the pre-revolutionary and Soviet periods: Akhmatova, Mandelshtam, Voloshin, Gumilyov, Tsvetayeva, and many others who lived in the memory of the older generation. Contemporary poets were also read eagerly, even some who enjoyed official approval (Yevtushenko, Martynov), but through *samizdat*, unpublished poets were also read (Joseph Brodsky, Naum Korzhavin, and many, many others). Enthusiasm for poetry was the hallmark of the times. People who previously and subsequently had little interest in poetry or literature in general became avid fans.

The heightened hunger for self-expression in a society that had cast off its rigidity encouraged many people to write. According to estimates by Yury Maltsev, the works of more than 300 authors, most of them young people, were then circulating in *samizdat*.[4] Vladimir Bukovsky writes of that period that all the typewriters in Moscow offices and institutions were in constant demand; everyone who could type was copying poetry for himself or his friends. Verses were passed from hand to hand on separate sheets, then made into brochures for collections. A youth culture grew up whose password was knowledge of the poetry of Pasternak, Mandelshtam, and Gumilyov.

The print run of *samizdat* journals was small—from one typewritten edition of carbons (four to five copies) to two or three dozen copies. Although these journals were conceived as periodicals, most of them died after the second or third issue. They rarely spread outside the circle of the author's acquaintances. The most noted of such journals was *Syntax*,[5] three issues of which were published in 1960 by Aleksandr Ginzburg, a correspondence student of Moscow University. Its popularity is made evident by his arrest and by the Soviet press's condemnation of him after his arrest. Still, only Ginzburg's friends in Moscow and Leningrad could read *Syntax*. *Syntax* is often considered the first *samizdat* journal; however, Bukovsky writes in his memoirs that he took part in the publication of a handwritten journal while he was in elementary school in 1959,[6] and most likely not even that was the first underground journal.

The memoirs of Anatoly Krasnov-Levitin, Andrey Amalrik, Vladimir Bukovsky, General Pyotr Grigorenko, and others show that each memoirist is convinced that *samizdat* was born in his own circle. Each was unaware of activities beyond the confines of his own group of friends.[7] *Samizdat* did not originate in one group of friends, but in many, each with its own authors and *samizdat*.

People of all ages were drawn into *samizdat* activities, not only the young poetry lover but also the old lady pecking on her typewriter in a communal apartment. Among the older generation, memoirs were circulated as well as poetry. Memoirs were especially popular among former prisoners, millions of whom had returned from imprisonment after the death of Stalin. According to Khrushchev, by 1963 more than ten thousand manuscripts describing the camps had been received by the editorial boards of official journals.[8] They were published in *samizdat* as well.

As *samizdat* matured, it very quickly became politicized. Early *samizdat* issues contained essays on Khrushchev's removal from power and on the attempts of the new leadership to rehabilitate Stalin's image. News and discussion began to appear in regular columns: reviews of events for the month, news from literary life, memoirs, discussions on economics and on national problems.

From 1964 to 1970, dissident Marxist historian Roy Medvedev published articles monthly that later were published in the West as *A Political Diary*.[9] Medvedev later said that several of his friends compiled the material for *A Political Diary*, among them Yevgeny Frolov, a senior employee of the journal *Kommunist*—an official publication of the Central Committee of the Communist Party.[10] Frolov, who had access to unpublished Party documents, typed copies for the journal in the evening after his co-workers had gone. It took Frolov twelve hours to transcribe Khrushchev's Twentieth Party Congress speech.

A Political Diary was regularly read by about forty people whom Medvedev knew personally: Party employees, writers, scientists, and— for the most part—Party members. Medvedev himself printed five copies of each issue, but the more interesting documents and speeches were copied and circulated on a much larger scale (evidently from other sources). I myself remember seeing *samizdat* transcripts of a speech given at a closed meeting in the Institute of Marxism-Leninism about a proposed new edition of the history of the Communist Party of the Soviet Union, as well as the secret Khrushchev speech, even though I did not have access to *A Political Diary* and had not even heard of it until the *Chronicle of Current Events* mentioned its publication abroad. Considering the primitive methods available, the most notable *samizdat* works were distributed and copied with remarkable speed. Even lengthy works, which made retyping more difficult, found their way to persons unacquainted with the author and often to distant cities.

Few original books appeared in the early *samizdat*, which primarily consisted of books translated and typed by clandestine volunteers. Some of the more popular translations to appear were: Hemingway's *For Whom the Bell Tolls*, Koestler's *Darkness at Noon*, Orwell's *1984*, and Djilas's *The New Class*. Works printed in the USSR but not widely available either because they were printed in small editions or out of print for a long time were also distributed. I myself typed a collection of poems by Kipling that had appeared in Russian translation in 1927 and had become a bibliographic rarity by the end of the 1950s. Yugoslav dissident writer Mihajlo Mihajlov, visiting the Soviet Union in 1962, saw typed copies of Dudintsev's *Not by Bread Alone*, printed from the *Novy mir* text of 1956 that had been distributed in the provinces, where copies of *Novy mir* were unavailable.[11]

Pasternak's *Doctor Zhivago* (1958) was one of the first original works widely distributed in *samizdat*. It had been published abroad and brought into the Soviet Union illegally, a process that would later give rise to the term *tamizdat*, meaning "published over there." *Tamizdat* books and typed manuscripts were circulated, then copied photographically or retyped. As a rule, copies had a high readership ratio, since they were passed from hand to hand. A popular *samizdat* work was available to an individual for only a short time, usually one night, because of the long line of others waiting for it. Often entire families would stay up all night reading or would invite friends over for a collective reading: people would sit next to each other, passing the pages along, or would read the works aloud, or project microfilm copies onto the wall.

It was only by virtue of *samizdat* that the human rights movement itself was able to rise and spread.

The chief functions of the human rights movement are gathering and disseminating information on human rights violations and defending these rights, irrespective of citizens' nationality, religion, or social background. In this way contacts are established with other dissident movements. The movement's participants carry out their work with *samizdat* information journals, the best known of which is the *Chronicle of Current Events*,[12] as well as through open rights associations. The first contacts between human rights activists and the participants of the nationalist and religious movements came about through the *Chronicle*'s accounts of all human rights violations in the USSR known to its editorial staff, including those having to do with the equality of nationalities and freedom of religion. The participants in these movements, in turn, found their way to the *Chronicle* and began to supply it with information.

The Links Among Human Rights Associations

In May 1969, the first human rights association was formed in Moscow: it was known as the Initiative Group to Defend Human Rights in the USSR. Members appealed to the U.N. with complaints of severe violations of human rights in the USSR. The first document of this Group dealt with the persecution of participants in nationalist movements in the Ukraine and in the Baltic republics, of Crimean Tartars and Jews, and of religious believers tried because of their search for freedom of religious expression.[13] All of these problems were raised also by the Moscow Human Rights Committee, organized in 1970.[14] The Fund to Aid Political Prisoners in the USSR, founded in 1974, began to deal with all categories of prisoners sent to labor camps because of their dissident views (whether political, nationalistic, or religious in origin),* and this also facilitated unification among dissenting groups.

The next stage in the movement came about through the creation of the Moscow Helsinki Watch Group in May 1976. Similar groups were formed on the model of the Moscow Helsinki Group by activists in the most developed nationalist movements in the Ukraine, Lithuania, Georgia, and Armenia.

In January 1977 the Christian Committee for the Defense of the Rights of Religious Believers was created in Moscow to defend believers of any faith; its founders were Russian Orthodox human rights activists. It worked closely with the Moscow Helsinki Group. Using the Group's channels, the Committee established ties with activists of other religious movements and consequently engaged in

---

* According to Amnesty International, there are four categories of labor camp regimens regulating the conditions of imprisonment in Russia. They are, in order of increasing severity: standard, intensified, strict, and special. The regimens differ in the degree of punishment each imposes upon the prisoner, involving a progressive reduction in prisoners' rights to visits, receipt of correspondence, supplementary food purchases, etc. The type and amount of work required of a prisoner varies according to regimen. Prisoners held under "special regimen" are kept in cells. Extra-legislative regulations stipulate that food rations shall vary according to type of regimen.

some common activities.[15] Later human rights groups were formed by Adventists in 1978 and Pentecostalists in 1980. Like the Moscow Helsinki Group, they based their activities on the humanitarian provisions of the Helsinki Final Act. Thus, a common ideological basis for all these movements was formed—a demand that the signatory countries of the Helsinki accords observe the humanitarian provisions of the Final Act, which human rights activists viewed as the minimum obligatory civil rights for all countries that had signed this document.

In addition to this common ideological basis, the methods of fighting for these provisions were also the same—non-violent struggle within the framework of the Soviet Constitution and insistence on observation of international human rights obligations undertaken by the Soviet government. In this sense, all the various dissenting movements are human rights movements, in essence, by virtue of their demands and their methods. The way in which they differ from the human rights movement per se is in their emphasis on special goals, such as the equality of the nationalities or the freedom of religious expression.

All of these movements, beginning with the 1970s, can be viewed as the collective phenomenon of Soviet dissent.

Although the Ukrainian, Lithuanian, Georgian, and Armenian Helsinki groups were in no way "branches" of the Moscow Helsinki Group but operated independently, their activities under common platforms have brought them close to each other and to human rights activists generally. In an organizational sense, these groups had no direct contacts; they could communicate only through the Moscow Helsinki Group, with which they had been in contact since their formation. The Moscow Group announced the formation of these other groups at its press conferences (attended, of course, only by foreign correspondents); later, these groups sent their documents to Moscow and in this way they were distributed. Information on nationalist and religious movements usually followed the same route—through the human rights movement in Moscow. Several of the Moscow Helsinki Group's documents were issued jointly with the Ukrainian and Lithuanian Helsinki Groups.[16]

The authorities were so alarmed by this commonality of interests, which sprang up quickly and rapidly grew stronger, that even the loss of Soviet credibility in the West did not stop the regime from crushing Helsinki groups and other unifying centers. The suppression of open public associations in the early 1980s did not destroy the connections between different dissident movements and human rights activists, but it did greatly weaken these ties. From the beginning of the 1980s, one can speak of Soviet dissent as "unified" only to a degree: it is not so much what really exists, as what could be established if the persecution were to be eased. The experience of human rights associations has clearly shown that such unity, which in a variegated and complex society like that of the Soviet Union is a basic condition for success, can in fact be achieved.

PART ONE

THE MOVEMENTS FOR SELF-DETERMINATION

CHAPTER 1

The Ukrainian National Movement

The most popular expression of national sentiment in the 1960s in the Ukraine were the annual pilgrimages to the monuments of the great Ukrainian poet, Taras Shevchenko, on May 22, the anniversary of the day in 1861 when Shevchenko's ashes were brought back from Russia to his native village of Kanev on the Dnieper River. The date had been celebrated by Ukrainian intelligentsia before the revolution. Under the Soviets, Shevchenko's birth and death were celebrated but not on May 22. During the 1960s, however, it became customary on the old date to place flowers at the monuments to Shevchenko that had been erected in almost every city of the Ukraine. In Kiev people came with flowers all day long and, after the working day ended, the crowds grew large. Several hundred people, most of them students and young workers, gathered to read classical and modern Ukrainian poetry or sometimes their own poetry, and to sing Ukrainian folk songs.

The 1960s was a time of cultural revival in the Ukraine. This process was particularly notable among the intelligentsia, but it also evoked a deep response in other strata of the population. Bands of masked people went from house to house, singing ritual songs, in revival of an old custom of *kolyadki* (carolling). Carolling had always been a Christmas custom but under Soviet rule it had been celebrated at the New Year instead. Young people, especially liberal-arts students, wanted the old rite wholly revived, and sang at the houses of well-respected professors and writers, but sometimes, out of a sense of mischief, they carolled outside the homes of high-ranking officials.

The authorities, in an effort to prevent the renewal of such nationalist sentiment, each year postponed meetings scheduled on May 22 and Party and Komsomol officials warned politically suspect persons not to appear at the Shevchenko monuments. Those who did show up were unobtrusively photographed. They were subjected to public "criticism" and reprimanded by their superiors.

On May 22, 1967 in Kiev, according to the eyewitness account of
Nadia Svitlychna, several hundred persons had gathered at the monuments, where a mountain of flowers had been amassed. From time to
time someone would climb up on the base to recite poetry. After nine
o'clock in the evening several militia cars drove up. Militiamen, some,
judging by their uniforms' insignia, high ranking, made their way
through the crowd. The next speaker disappeared into the crowd and
the militia seized instead the first four or five persons in their path and
shoved them into the cars. The crowd did not disperse despite the
militiamen's demands. The searchlights the militia had set up near
the monument attracted an even larger crowd. Trolley traffic on the
street bordering the park was halted by the size of the throng. The
militia found themselves scattered throughout the crowd. One group
of demonstrators encircled a militiaman and shouted "Shame." Others
joined in and soon the militia were virtually surrounded. They made
their way out of the crowd with difficulty and left, taking their prisoners with them.

Mykola Plakhotnyuk, a physician who was in the crowd, suggested
that the demonstrators go to the Central Committee and insist that
those arrested be freed, that an apology be made for the gross insult
to the memory of Shevchenko, and that freedom of speech be honored.
About two to three hundred people made their way in a compact mass
to the Central Committee building. They agreed among themselves
not to sing or shout to avoid arrest for "violating public order." Fire
engines doused them with water, but they continued silently on their
way. About two hundred meters from their goal they found the street
blocked by cars and a human chain of Party and Komsomol workers
who had been summoned for emergency duty that Saturday evening.
The demonstrators, deciding to wait where they were and present their
demands when Central Committee staff arrived in the morning, formed
a tight column five across, interlocking their arms.

At 1:30 A.M. Minister of Public Order Ivan Golovchenko arrived
with an entourage that included the deputy minister of the Ukrainian
KGB, and inquired what the demonstrators were seeking. Oksana
Meshko, a teacher and former inmate of Stalin's camps, stepped forth.
Those arrested should be freed, she said. Golovchenko promised to
release them by morning. Would the demonstrators go home and send
a delegation to the Central Committee in the morning? About forty of
the crowd remained to witness the release of those arrested close to
3:00 A.M.

A few days later, some of the participants, including Plakhotnyuk,
were dismissed from their jobs.

In the years that followed until 1971, the authorities took no further

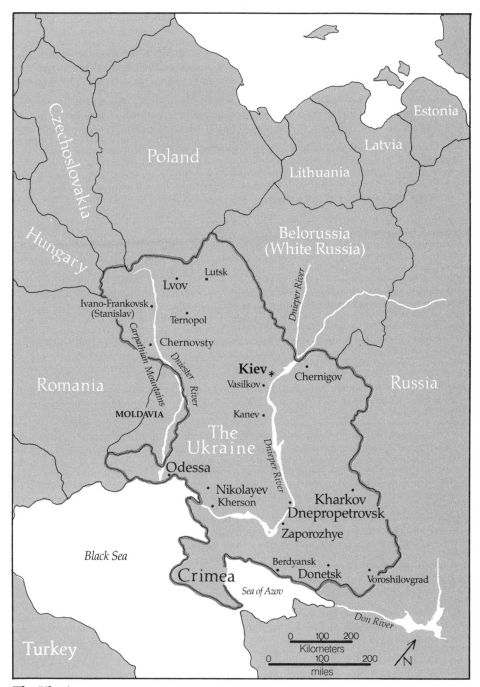

The Ukraine

police action against those who gathered at the Shevchenko monuments, although they warned "suspect persons" that if they appeared at the monuments they might face dismissal from their jobs. The authorities, in a countermove, began each May 22 to schedule official poetry festivals put on by Komsomol members, volunteer militia, and soldiers.[1] Nonetheless, the pilgrimages to the Shevchenko monuments continued until 1972, after repression and arrests had taken a heavy toll.

Russification of the Ukraine

The Ukraine has a larger land area than France (603,700 square kilometers as opposed to 551,600) with a population equal to France. Of a total population of more than 46 million, 36.4 million are native Ukrainians[2]—the largest European national ethnic group without an independent government. For a brief period in 1918 during the Ukrainian Rada, the Ukraine had its independence but since 1922 it has been a Union Republic of the USSR.

After Soviet power was established in the Ukraine, the peasantry strongly opposed collectivization and, as a result, in 1931 mass deportations of Ukrainians to the eastern regions of the Soviet Union began. Although there are no accurate statistics on the total number, 300,000 were deported in the first two months of 1931 alone.[3] The opposition to collectivization was crushed in 1932-33, after widespread starvation was created in the richest agricultural regions of the Ukraine. After the fall harvest had been gathered, the grain was requisitioned from the peasants. No grain was left for food or seed. Some of the requisitioned grain was exported at low prices and the foreign currency earned was used to buy heavy equipment, essential to the rapid industrialization of the Soviet Union. The approaches to cities that were stocked with food were manned by guard detachments to keep the starving villagers from entering. No official statistics exist on those who perished from starvation, because the government kept that tragedy a secret, but figures published in Ukrainian samizdat, based on the population decrease reported in the census figures, estimated that approximately 6 million people died in the Ukraine from 1932 to 1933.[4]

The depletion of the Ukrainian peasantry, which had made up the greater part of the population of the Ukraine or 23.8 million in 1926, made collectivization possible and simultaneously undermined the potential of the Ukrainian national movement. The cities, whose inhabitants numbered only 5.7 million,[5] and industrial centers were peopled chiefly by Russians. The industrialization of the Ukraine did not draw workers from the villages located around the new factories, as is normal during the industrialization process, but newcomers, for the most part from Russian areas of the USSR. This tended to preserve the gap between rural and urban populations, a condition that exists to this day.

Beginning in the 1930s, a consistent policy of Russification has been conducted in the Ukraine. Its basic form of expression is the almost complete displacement of the Ukrainian language by Russian. According to the 1970 general census, 3,017,000 Ukrainians living in the Ukraine, or 8.5 percent of the population, considered Russian their native language, or 942,000 and 2.6 percent more than in 1959. By way of comparison, only 135,000, or 2 percent of the 9.1 million Russians living in the Ukraine considered Ukrainian their native language, and only 2.5 percent of those Russians speak Ukrainian fluently. From 1970 to 1979, the Russian-speaking population of the Ukraine increased from 13.3 million to 15.5 million. Ukrainian speakers increased only from 32.7 million to 32.9 million.[6]

The Russian language has replaced Ukrainian in all spheres of life. Although Ukrainian is considered the official language of the Ukrainian republic, in fact, it is only used in the villages and by a small portion of the intelligentsia in the cities. Uneducated city dwellers use a mixture of vulgarized Russian and Ukrainian.

This displacement of Ukrainian by Russian is brought about by an entire complex of official measures controlling the demographic processes of the Ukraine:

1. The emigration of Ukrainians to underpopulated regions of the Soviet Union—Kazakhstan, Siberia, the Urals, and the Far East—is encouraged by economic incentives. At the same time, the emigration of Russians to the Ukraine is encouraged. From 1959 to 1970 the Ukrainian population in the Ukraine increased by only 3.1 million, or 9 percent, while the Russian population increased by 2 million, or 28 percent.

In 1972 there were 9.1 million Russians and 35.2 million Ukrainians in the Ukraine. By 1979 the number of Ukrainians grew by 1.2 million, or less than 4 percent, while the Russian population grew by 1.3 million, or 14 percent; as noted earlier, the Russian population was concentrated in cities and industrial centers. In 1970, 84.6 percent of the Russian population, or 7,000,712 people, lived in cities; Ukrainians made up only 30 percent of the population in industrial areas and 29.4 percent in the cities.[7]

2. The inculcation of Russian language and culture begins in preschool institutions. Russian nurseries and kindergartens predominate

throughout the Ukraine. Even those schools considered Ukrainian are, for the most part, Russified, because preference in staffing these institutions is given to Russians and Russified Ukrainians.

3. Most institutions of higher education in the Ukraine are Russified. Entrance examinations and the beginning stages of instruction are conducted in Russian. In Kiev, the capital of the Ukraine, only in the university—and not in all departments—are courses taught in Ukrainian. With the exception of certain western areas, the language of instruction is Russian in most Ukrainian institutions of higher learning. In 1970, of the 1,583,000 specialists with a higher degree working in the Ukraine, 601,000, or more than a third, were Russian. By way of comparison, in the Russian republic of the USSR, seventy-three of every thousand Ukrainians and forty-three of every thousand Russians hold a higher degree.[8]

4. The organization of higher education strongly influences the language of instruction in the secondary school system. A student who knows Russian has a distinct advantage when applying to an institution of higher education. This, in turn, fosters a movement away from Ukrainian to Russian and permits the network of Russian schools to grow at the expense of Ukrainian schools "in accordance with the wishes of the parents." Any student and parent who persists in advocating the teaching of Ukrainian is considered a Ukrainian nationalist and is, consequently, an object of harassment. The employers of parents are informed and discussions with their superiors and public criticism at meetings follow. The study of Russian is encouraged in Ukrainian schools; Ukrainian is taught in Russian schools only at the request of the students' parents.

As a result of this policy, in the Donbass and the Crimea there are no Ukrainian schools at all. In large cities, like Kharkov, Zaporozhye, Nikolayev, Kherson, Dnepropetrovsk, and Odessa, Ukrainian schools are few and usually limited to the suburbs. In Kiev the number of Ukrainian schools is constantly decreasing and those that remain conduct more and more classes in Russian. Such mixed schools gradually become completely Russified.

The National Resistance Movement

From 1939 to 1944, as a result of the additional secret protocols contained in the Soviet-Nazi pacts of August and September 1939, the western territories of the Ukraine that were formerly parts of Poland, Rumania, and Czechoslovakia were annexed to the Soviet Ukraine, boosting its population by almost 8 million and contributing greatly to the rebirth of the national movement. National Ukrainian traditions were and continue to be stronger in the western regions than in the original Soviet Ukraine.

Underground organizations fighting for national independence were active in the western Ukraine in 1939; the most well known and influential of these, OUN, the Organization of Ukrainian Nationalists, was active in the former Polish territory. When Soviet troops arrived in the western Ukraine that year, all those known to be active in the resistance were arrested. Immediately after the German attack in June 1941, the formation of the Ukrainian People's Republic was proclaimed unofficially in Lvov, and a few days later the Germans arrested those responsible and sent them to concentration camps, where they stayed until the end of the war. Those members of the OUN who remained at liberty began an armed fight against the German invaders; they formed the UPA, the Ukrainian Insurgent Army, in 1942 and fought against the Germans until 1944.

When Soviet troops arrived, the Insurrectional Army turned their weapons against the new enemy; the army's ranks were filled by Ukrainian peasants who opposed the collectivization that had begun with the arrival of the Soviet troops. The Insurgent Army fought until the beginning of the fifties. Thousands lost their lives, and hundreds of thousands of members and sympathizers were sent to Soviet camps with a standard sentence of twenty-five years. Entire villages, or about two million people, were exiled for aiding the Insurgent Army.

The total loss of population in the western Ukraine was enormous: in 1930–31 the number of Ukrainians living in districts later annexed to the USSR was 7,950,000, but by 1970 they numbered only 7,821,000; thus in forty years the population did not increase, but decreased. This indicates a loss of twenty million people, based on the average expected population growth.[9] Nevertheless, the national movement was concentrated in the western Ukraine for a long time after the war, as is apparent from the underground organizations which were exposed in the Ukraine in the fifties and sixties. These groups are listed below in the chronological order of their discovery.[10]

1. The United Party for the Liberation of the Ukraine (OPOU) was uncovered in Stanislav, now Ivano-Frankovsk, in the western Ukraine in 1958. Ten men, for the most part young workers, were tried and sentenced to labor camp terms ranging from seven to ten years.

2. The OUN-North was uncovered in 1960. This organization was founded by five members of the Organization of Ukrainian Nationalists from the western Ukraine who had spent time in Soviet camps: Yaroslav Gasyuk, Vladimir Leonyuk, Bogdan Khristinich, Vladimir

Zatvorsky, and Yaroslav Kobyletsky. (Some were forced to live in the areas where they had been imprisoned in the northern parts of the Soviet Union, hence the addition of "North" in the name of the organization) They received from five to twelve years in labor camps.

3. The Ukrainian Union of Peasants and Workers was uncovered in 1961 in Lvov (the western Ukraine). Its members included: lawyers Levko Lukyanenko, Ivan Kandyba, and Iosif Borovnitsky, a Party functioneer Birun, a militiaman Ivan Kipish, an engineer Aleksandr Libovich, and a club director Vasyl Lutskiv. Lukyanenko was sentenced to be shot, a sentence later commuted to fifteen years in labor camp; the others received from ten to fifteen years in camp.

4. The Ukrainian National Committee was uncovered in Lvov in 1961 and the names of eighteen of the defendants—all young workers—became known to the government, then to the public. Two of them—Bohdan Grytsyna and Ivan Koval—were shot; the rest received from ten to fifteen years in labor camp.

5. A group formed by a newspaper reporter, Grigory Gayev, was prosecuted in Donetsk in 1961. The number of members and their sentences remain unknown.

6. A trial of "the affair of the six" took place in 1962 in Lvov. Nikolay Protsiv was shot; Mikhail Protsiv, Kapitonenko, Iosif Nagrobny, Drop, and Khanas received from eight to fifteen years in labor camp.

7. A group of five was prosecuted in 1962 in Ternopol (the western Ukraine). Bogdan Goguys was condemned to be shot—a sentence later commuted to fifteen years in a camp; Grigory Kovalishin, Vladimir Kulikovsky, Palikhata, and Pavel Pundik were given labor camp sentences of ten, fifteen, four, and five years, respectively.

8. The group of Vasyl Romanyuk-Shust was brought to trial in Lutsk in the western Ukraine in 1962. The number of members and their sentences remain unknown.

9. The trial of another group took place in Zaporozhye in 1962. V. Savchenko, Yury Pokrasenko, Valery Rishkovenko, Aleksey Vorobyov, Vladimir Chernyshov, and Boris Nadtoka received from three to six years in camp.

10. The group of Bulbinsky-Rybich-Trasyuk was brought to trial in 1963 in Donetsk. Their sentences are unknown.

11. An organization calling itself the Democratic Union of Socialists was uncovered in the Odessa region in 1964. The director of a school for young workers, Nikolay Dragosh, was sentenced to seven years in camp; Nikolay Tarnavsky and Ivan Cherdyntsev, teachers in the

school, were sentenced to seven and six years in labor camp, respectively; a student Sergey Chemertan, was sentenced to five years in prison camp; students Nikolay Kucheryanu and Vasily Postalaki received six years.

12. The trial of the Ukrainian National Front took place in Ivano-Frankovsk (the western Ukraine) in 1967. Its nine members were the teachers Dmitry Kvetsko, Yaroslav Lesiv, and Grigory Prokopovich, lathe operator Vasily Kulynin, district militiaman Mikhail Dyak, engineer Ivan Gubka, writer Zinovy Krasivsky, choirmaster Miroslav Melin, and a miner, Nikolay Kachur. The sentences ranged from five to fifteen years in labor camp, plus five years of exile.

13. Nikolay Bogach, a student at the Nikolayev Agricultural-Technical School, was sentenced in 1969 to three years for attempting to create an underground organization called the Struggle for Social Justice.

14. Several persons who belonged to an organization called the Party for the Realization of Leninist Principles were sentenced in Voroshilovgrad in 1970. The names of only three are known: a construction worker, Aleksandr Chekhovskoy—six years of labor camp; Gennady Tolstousov—five years of labor camp; and Pototsky—sentence unknown.

15. A group of young people was prosecuted in 1973 in the Ivano-Frankovsk region of the western Ukraine for having created the Union of Ukrainian Youth of Galicia, including workers Dmitry Grinkiv, Mykola Motryuk, and Vasily Shovkovy; engineer Dmitry Demidov, and student Roman Chuprey. Grinkiv's sentence was seven years of labor camp, plus five years of exile. The others received four to five years in labor camp.[11]

16. A group of young people was arrested in 1973 in the Ternopol region (western Ukraine) for flying Ukrainian nationalist flags. Of those arrested, the brothers Vladimir and Nikolay Marmus, P. Vinnichuk, A. Kravets, Stepan Sapelyak, Vladimir Sinkiv, Nikolay Slobodyan, and Vladimir Marmus received the longest sentence—six years in camp, plus five years of exile.[12]

17. In 1973 in Lvov an underground youth organization of university and high school students called "The Ukrainian National Liberation Front" was exposed. Fifty of the organization's members became known to the KGB. Zoryan Popadyuk, a philology student at Lvov University was arrested and sentenced to seven years in labor camp and five years of exile, and Radomir Mikitko was arrested and sentenced to five years in labor camp.[13]

The population of the western Ukraine comprises only 16 percent of the entire Ukrainian population, but the majority of the underground organizations discovered from the 1950s to the 1970s, that is, ten out of seventeen, originated in the western Ukraine. We know the names of seven of these organizations and all include the word "Ukrainian." Nationalism was the leading, if not the sole, idea in the minds of these organizers. From the names of two of the earliest nationalist organizations, the United Party for the Liberation of the Ukraine and OUN-North, we surmise that they acted in the spirit of Organization of Ukrainian Nationalists (OUN) as did the Ukrainian National Front (Ivano-Frankovsk, 1967).

Of the six organizations uncovered in the eastern Ukraine, we know the names of three: the Democratic Union of Socialists (the Odessa region), the Struggle for Social Justice (Nikolayev), and the Party for the Realization of Leninist Principles (Voroshilovgrad). The names of these groups suggest that their orientation was not nationalistic, but that they resembled other organizations active at the same time in the Russian areas of the USSR. Nothing is known of the ideological trends of the other three organizations active in the eastern Ukraine. The group uncovered in Zaporozhye in 1962 was probably neutral on the national question, since both Russians and Ukrainians were among its members.

The connecting link between the nationalistic and the democratic orientation is represented by the Ukrainian Union of Workers and Peasants (Lvov, 1959–61). With the same separatist goals as other organizations, this group abandoned the traditional methods of OUN, which were suitable for the struggle against Polish rule, but ineffective under Soviet conditions.

Judging from the sentences, the leading role in the Union of Workers and Peasants belonged to Levko Lukyanenko, the only member of the group from the eastern Ukraine (Chernigov region). Lukyanenko received his degree from the law department of the University of Moscow and was a Party member. His broader experience of Soviet conditions may have influenced the ideas of the group, modern by comparison with those of other underground organizations in the western Ukraine.

The activities of the union were based on principles of law. It sought to obtain Ukrainian independence peacefully and legally, on the basis of the rights guaranteed under article 17 of the Soviet Constitution, which gives each republic the right to secede from the USSR. Lukyanenko reports that in 1960 he and his friends revised the union's 1959 program and "headed towards the creation of a legal organization, which set as its chief goal the protection of civil rights.[14] They had planned to change their name from the Ukrainian Union of Workers and Peasants to the Union for the Struggle for Democracy in accordance with the evolution of their goals. In the process the struggle for democratic rights took precedence over the idea of an independent Ukraine.

The Marxist orientation of the group, clear from reference to workers and peasants in their name, is confirmed in their platform. The members envisioned a socialist Ukraine as their major program; their purpose was to rid the country of the consequences of "Stalinist" oppression of nationalities and return to the "Leninist" way. Lukyanenko's group was close to the movement that appeared after the phase of nationalist underground groups and captured both the western and eastern Ukraine: the peaceful and open movement for national rights.

The Generation of the Sixties

The first stage of the nationalist movement was called "the generation of the sixties," because it began and flourished during the sixties, and because of the reference to the Russian revolutionaries of the 1860s who also called themselves the generation of the sixties. Young Ukrainian poets, writers, artists, and publicists gave the first impetus to the movement. During the brief Khrushchev period, which was relatively favorable for the development of Ukrainian culture, the movement revived. A group of gifted poets, actors, and artists made their appearance, among them the young poets Vasyl Simonenko, Mikhail Vingranovsky, Ivan Drach, Lina Kostenko, Irina Stasiv, Igor Kalenets and the artists Alla Gorskaya, Lyudmila Semykina, Galina Sevruk, Stefaniya Shabatura, and Panas Zalivakha. They renewed Ukrainian cultural life, which had almost died out during the Stalin period, and brought to it a sincerity lacking in officially inspired art. A vital sense of national and civic pride united this generation of the sixties.

The most popular of the poets of the period was Vasyl Simonenko, who died in 1963 at the age of twenty-nine. Although he was not an innovator of poetic form, he felt the paradoxes of his age keenly and was able to describe them boldly. Among his well-known civic lyrics are: "The Thief," a poem about a *kolkhoz* worker who steals from the *kolkhoz* in order to feed his family, "An Obituary for the Corncob That Rotted in the Storehouse," "Chauvinist," and "The Prophecy of 1917," in which the poet claims that "in the cemetery of murdered illusions there is no more room for graves." But perhaps the most successful is the poem in which Simonenko addresses the Ukraine: "Let America and Russia be silent when I talk with you." For Russia to be put on the same footing as America as an entity foreign to the Ukraine was seen as daring and exciting, since the leitmotif of all official Ukrainian culture was the indissoluble tie between Russia and the Ukraine. Thus the poem was an extraordinarily bold statement.

A group of bold and talented publicists, historians and literary critics also made their appearance in the sixties. Among them were Ivan Dzyuba, Ivan Svitlychny, Valentin Moroz, Vyacheslav Chornovil, Svyatoslav Karavansky, Yevgeny Sverstyuk, Vasyl Stus, and Mikhail Braychevsky.

Assessing the contributions made by the sixties generation, Valentin Moroz wrote that their most important service was to renew the significance of lofty words and concepts, which had been depreciated by officialese and to provide an example of heroic civic action. To the public this was an open challenge to the official line, which supported Ukrainian culture verbally, while, in fact, weakening it.

The call of the sixties generation found a warm response among members of the intelligentsia, workers, and even among some of the Ukrainian establishment. Their poetry sold out immediately and was committed to memory by many. Their public performances filled the auditoriums; exhibitions of Ukrainian folk and modern art drew large crowds; so did concerts of Ukrainian music. Everything with a national flavor was accepted enthusiastically.

The studios of artists working in the national style, like the sculptor Ivan Gonchar and Alla Gorskaya, and others, and the apartments of aficionados of Ukrainian folk art, like the physician-collector of Easter eggs, Erast Binyashevsky, became popular meeting places. As Kiev mathematician Leonid Plyushch testified, the sixties generation's central meeting place was the Club of Creative Youth in Kiev. Young people from various social strata met there: students, young professionals, and workers. A few hundred people gathered there on a regular basis, with literary evenings attracting the largest audiences in the October Hall, the largest hall in Kiev, with a capacity of more than a thousand. The majority of the Kievan patriotic opposition came from that club.

Nadia Svitlychna remembers an evening party in honor of the dramatist, Mekola Kulish, who had been declared "an enemy of the people" in the 1930s and had not yet been rehabilitated by the beginning of the 1960s. Another evening was organized to commemorate the Ukrainian producer, Les Kurbas, who perished in the camp at Solovki. At a party honoring the poet Shevchenko in 1964, a montage of three of his works that were obligatory reading material in high schools was staged. In response to the bold mood of the audience, the performance contained inflammatory overtones.

The club had been organized under the aegis of the Kievian Komsomol committee. Komsomol officials had hoped to make official propaganda more effective by making use of the talents of these young enthusiasts. But official fears of possible "deviations" forced them to close the club in 1965 after three years. Les Tanyuk, a young producer who was president of the club, lost his job and had to leave Kiev. Wherever Tanyuk worked after that, in Dnepropetrovsk, Lvov, Odessa, and elsewhere, he organized clubs similar to the one he led in Kiev.

After the close of the Kiev club an attempt was made to create another club for public discussions, but after only two meetings, devoted to the topics "Morality and Progress" and "Morality and Science" and attended by several hundred people, the new club was disbanded.

Participants in the national movement used official meetings to make public statements in the sixties. Among the best known of these meetings were a party honoring Vasyl Simonenko in 1964 in Kiev and a meeting in Babi Yar at which Ivan Dzyuba spoke. Similar events occurred frequently during this period.

In his memoirs, Leonid Plyushch describes one such party honoring Anatoly Petritsky, an artist of the Ukrainian Renaissance, who died in 1933: "In May 1962, an evening in honor of Anatoly Petritsky, the most prominent artist of the Ukrainian renascence of the 1920s, was held in Kiev. The hall was jammed with young people who applauded at every hint of the abominations of Stalinism. I would have applauded, too, if I hadn't been sitting with a man who had taken part in the renascence and was able to comment on the speeches for me. Almost all the speakers, who now claimed to have been Petritsky's friends, had either helped his persecutors or watched indifferently as he was hounded."[15] The general mood in Kiev was such that even former informers were in favor of the new Ukrainian Renaissance.

The movement of the sixties spread over the entire Ukraine, eastern and western. It was centered in Kiev, the largest and ethnically most Ukrainian city in the eastern Ukraine, the capital of the Ukrainian SSR, where the most talented and best known representatives of the Ukrainian intelligentsia are concentrated. Most cultural institutions are located there. "A small group of people in Kiev scattered sparks over the Ukraine. Wherever they fell, the ice of indifference and nihilism began to thaw at once," V. Moroz wrote.[16]

The people of the sixties accepted the values of Soviet society, although in an idealized way. For them socialism was inseparable from internationalism, democracy, and humanism, and they defended these values from the dead hand of bureaucracy and officialdom. Their goals were the democratization of the Soviet system and an end to the policy of Russification. They believed it was possible to achieve these under Soviet conditions.

Their credo was expressed in a work by Ivan Dzyuba, *International-*

ism or Russification?,[17] completed in December 1965, a study of the nationality problem in the USSR, which is based chiefly on Ukrainian materials and written from a Marxist-internationalist point of view. The work is critical of the policy of Russification, which Dzyuba defines as a Stalinist deviation from Leninist national policy.

The movement of the sixties was essentially an affair of the intelligentsia. It was concerned with the preservation of national culture. However, in the Ukraine no gap exists between the intelligentsia and the people as exists among Russians. The Ukrainian patriotic intelligentsia considers itself an organic part of the people, perhaps because of the non-Ukrainian composition of most city populations and a significant part of the bureaucracy. Also, most members of the intelligentsia are first-generation intellectuals who have come directly from the countryside. The old Ukrainian intelligentsia was almost completely destroyed before the Second World War.

Until 1965, the Ukrainian movement was not grossly interfered with. Censorship prevented publication of literary works with civic tendencies, but, nonetheless, the works of many of the 1960s activists saw the light of day. The most critical works were distributed through *samizdat*, which appeared at this time. Most of the sixties generation managed to express their views openly and still continue their careers. Some, for example, the film director Sergey Paradzhanov (*Shadows of Forgotten Ancestors*) or the director Yury Ilenko (*St. John's Eve*), even achieved success precisely because they expressed such views.

Among the Party and government leadership of the Ukraine were those who sympathized with the sixties generation and who tried to keep the movement within acceptable limits, to ward off reprisals from Moscow. Such may have been the attitude of First Secretary of the Central Committee of the Communist Party of the Ukraine Pyotr Shelest. Shelest was unusually gentle with respect to "ideological deviations" from the official Party line. He seemed to try to limit his actions against those who opposed official policy to "ideological" measures. Ivan Dzyuba's book *Internationalism or Russification?* was written as an appendix to a statement on national policy sent to the Central Committee. According to one version, Andrey Skoba, then Secretary of Ideological Affairs of the Central Committee of the Communist Party of the Ukraine, suggested that Dzyuba write the book. It is known that the book was distributed in a very small edition among a few top-ranking Party officials on the level of regional secretaries. That edition was withdrawn very quickly and the book was distributed first in *samizdat* and then in *tamizdat* (i.e. published abroad, lit. "published over there"). A special commission was created in the

Ukrainian Communist Party to formulate an answer to Dzyuba, but it all ended with the appearance of an article under the pseudonym of B. Stenchuk, entitled "What Dzyuba Advocates." Intended for publication abroad, the article was circulated semisecretly in the Ukraine down to the level of Party and Komsomol propagandists, but it was never published abroad or in the USSR.

Serious repressions came first in 1965, when in August and September more than twenty intellectuals were arrested almost simultaneously in various parts of the Ukraine. Most were to some extent participants in the movement of the 1960s.

The journalist, Vyacheslav Chornovil, generalizing about those who were arrested, wrote that if it were possible to create a "typical" biography, it would be as follows:

The arrested was twenty-eight to thirty years of age, came from a peasant (or blue-collar) family, finished high school with honors, and entered an institute (some after army service), where he was a serious student. He received a good position after completing his studies; wrote, or defended his dissertation; was published in journals or published a book. If he received a technical education, he was interested in art and literature and took the Ukrainian language problem to heart. Until the time of his arrest, his career and creative potential were in full swing. He was not married, or was just recently married, with a young child.[18]

The arrests made in 1965 appeared to be unusual in comparison with similar arrests by the KGB in other places. For some time after the arrests, the names of those arrested were not excluded from official use. The newspaper the *Literary Ukraine* published an article by Yevgeny Masyutko after his arrest, and the journal *Art* printed reproductions of the paintings of the arrested Panas Zalivakha. A newsreel continued to be shown that contained footage about the work of the arrested psychologist Mikhail Goryn, who himself appeared on the screen.

It is likely that Moscow had sent the order for the arrests to be made immediately, a fact that would account for the unpreparedness and carelessness of the local KGB in fulfilling the order. Russian writers secretly published their works abroad under pseudonyms. Andrey Sinyavsky and Yuly Daniel were arrested in Moscow at about the same time—the beginning of September.

It is unclear what guidelines were used to determine who would be arrested in the Ukraine in 1965. The center of the 1960s movement was Kiev, but only seven of those arrested were natives of Kiev and only one of those (Ivan Svitlychny) was a leading figure in the movement.

After eight months he was released for "lack of evidence." He had done nothing illegal. Neither had the rest of those who were arrested, yet they were put on trial.

Nadia Svitlychna voiced the opinion that those who were arrested were selected not because of the nature of their activities, but because of their potential for repenting and thus discrediting a movement that enjoyed enormous moral authority. If this was the reason, then the plan failed.

It is true that some of those arrested repented during the investigation and even gave evidence against the others, psychologically unprepared as they were for the difficulties that suddenly overtook them. Even Valentin Moroz, a historian who later behaved heroically both under arrest and at liberty, admitted that during the first investigation he "did not conduct himself in the best manner." However, to the great dismay of the authorities, these arrests did not frighten the public or turn them away from the sixties generation. "The greatest surprise of the last decade was the fact that the arrests of 1965 did not slow down, but speeded up the Ukrainian renaissance," Moroz wrote later from the vantage point of 1970. "The era of the Great Terror had ended. The arrests did not terrify but awakened tremendous interest, not only throughout the Ukraine, but throughout the entire world. To use repression against anyone under present conditions meant to create an aureole for him" to make of him a martyr, regardless of whether he suffered or not."[19]

There were many expressions of sympathy for and solidarity with those who were arrested. Ivan Dzyuba used the occasion of his appearance at the premiere of *Shadows of Forgotten Ancestors* for this purpose. He was to have greeted the creators of the film on behalf of the residents of Kiev. Instead he mounted the rostrum in the overcrowded Ukraine movie-theatre and, after a few introductory words, said that the present holiday of national culture was overshadowed by numerous arrests. He began to list the names of those arrested. The movie theatre director rushed to drag Dzyuba from the stage and a siren was turned on to drown out his voice. Someone from the hall shouted, "All those against tyranny—stand." Although only a few people heard this cry in all the noise and confusion, some stood up. Two of these were later expelled from the Party and fired from their jobs.

The trials of the 1960s activists took place half a year after the arrests. Most of the trials were closed, no doubt to conceal the weakness of the accusations and their legal grounds. In spite of this official silence, the final speeches of some of the brave defendants were widely disseminated.

Mikhailo Osadchy, who stood trial in Lvov, described the scene around the courthouse: " 'Bravo, bravo, bravo,' shouted the crowd that filled all of Pekarskaya Street. (This kept up for five days.) They threw us flowers, which fell on the metal roofs of the transport cars and through cracks in the doors. When we walked into the courthouse, we walked over a carpet of living spring flowers. It seemed a pity to walk over those flowers, but we were held so tightly that we could not step aside. 'Mikhailo, hold still,' Ivan Dzyuba shouted to Goryn from the crowd. I just managed to catch a glimpse of his face and then I saw Lina Kostenko break through the guards and deftly slip a bar of chocolate to Miroslava Zvarichevskaya. The prison warden jumped on Miroslava like a crazy man and grabbed the chocolate."[20]

All of the defendants were tried on charges of "anti-Soviet agitation and propaganda." All were declared guilty. The sentences ranged from a few months to six years of strict-regimen labor camp. A few individuals were put on probation.

Public criticism of those who were close or sympathetic to the defendants was widespread in work places and institutes, but the enthusiasm of support did not dissipate. Funds were collected to help the families of the defendants and those who lost their jobs. The money came in small but regular donations from sympathizers who kept their jobs and in larger contributions from comfortably-off members of the intelligentsia who did not participate in the movement. Money also came from collections from carolling-groups and from public lotteries for traditional handcrafted objects and paintings by contemporary Ukrainian artists. While in prison, the defendants received mail not only from friends and relatives, but from those they barely knew and from strangers. They received books, postcards, and warm clothing.

Vyacheslav Chornovil, the journalist from Lvov, compiled data on those who were convicted—biographical information, publications, speeches in court, and excerpts from camp correspondence—and entitled the collection *Woe From Wit*, after the classic Russian play by the nineteenth century playwright Aleksandr Griboyedov. It was circulated in *samizdat* under the author's name.

In spirit, means of self-expression, justification of demands, and social background, the Ukrainian national-democratic movement was close to the human rights movement begun in Moscow in the mid-sixties. The mutual recognition of these two movements began in the political labor camps of Mordovia, where the Ukrainians arrested in 1965 met the convicted Moscow writers Sinyavsky and Daniel. Through letters sent from the camps and relatives who visited the prisoners, personal contact was established between prisoners of both movements within the camps and on the outside. Since the route from the Ukraine to Mordovia goes through Moscow, relatives on their way to visit prisoners and released prisoners passed through that city. They began to stop at the Moscow apartments of friends and relatives of the political prisoners.

In 1968 a large-scale human rights campaign was launched to defend the Moscow *samizdat* distributors Yury Galanskov and Aleksandr Ginzburg. Most of the signatories of the petitions were Muscovites. The Ukraine was the only republic that supported this campaign (18.8 percent of the signatories were Ukrainian).[21] The Ukrainian Appeal was known as "the letter of 139."

After 1967, persecution of "nationalism" was intensified. Public expressions of national sentiments, which were characteristic of the early 1960s, became rare, while anonymous actions began to occur with increasing frequency. In March of 1968 at the University of Kiev and the Agricultural Academy, leaflets calling for a struggle against Russification were distributed by hand and by mail. Employees of the Kiev hydroelectric station Aleksandr Nazarenko, Vasily Kondryukov, and V. Karpenko, all of them night school students, were arrested. They were sentenced to five, three, and two-and-a-half years, respectively, of strict regimen labor camps for "anti-Soviet propaganda." Some of their friends were expelled from the university.[22] During this time other instances of distribution of leaflets occurred in the Ukraine.

Because of a general disillusionment with the process of democratization in connection with the Soviet invasion of Czechoslovakia in August 1968, the deterioration of the Ukrainian internal situation gave rise to tragic forms of protest.

On November 5, 1968, Vasily Makukha, a fifty-year-old Ukrainian teacher from the Dnepropetrovsk region, a father of two and a former political prisoner in Stalin's time, arrived in Kiev, two days before the anniversary of the October Revolution. On the main street of the capital, Makukha set fire to himself and ran along the busy street, shouting "Long live a free Ukraine!" When the flames were extinguished, Makukha was taken to the hospital. He died after two hours.

This appears to have been the first self-immolation as a sign of protest against national oppression. Jan Palach of Czechoslovakia in January 1969; Ilya Rips of Riga in April 1969; Romas Kalanta and his followers in Lithuania in May 1972 and the Crimean Tartar Musa Mamut in 1978 immolated themselves later.

The self-immolation of Makukha, witnessed by hundreds of people, hardly caused a stir because of the prevailing atmosphere of exhaustion and depression. During the early to mid-1960s, events of lesser significance gained a much stronger public reaction. It is known that a leaflet about this self-immolation was distributed (for which S. Berdilo was prosecuted), although not very widely.

In March of 1969, Nikolay Breslavsky also tried to immolate himself, probably influenced by the example of Makukha and Jan Palach. A forty-five-year-old teacher from Berdyansk and a father of three, Breslavsky was a former political prisoner under Stalin, like Makukha. He carried with him posters protesting Russification. He was saved and then sentenced to two-and-a-half years in a strict regimen labor camp for "anti-Soviet agitation and propaganda."

Another tragic incident occurred at the end of 1970 when the Kiev artist, Alla Gorskaya, was killed. Gorskaya was well-loved by those who knew her and her studio had, during the preceding decade, become a meeting place for members of the sixties generation. After having gone to the city of Vasilkov, an hour away from Kiev, to pick up a sewing machine from her father-in-law, Gorskaya was later found in the basement of his home with a broken skull. Her father-in-law, a sick old man, was found dead twenty or thirty kilometers from his house.

The circumstances of Gorskaya's murder and especially the investigation that followed gave rise to a general belief that the KGB was implicated. The KGB was annoyed at the fearlessness of the artist under interrogation by authorities and upset by her role as a ringleader of the Kievan movement of the sixties. At the funeral her friends Ivan Gel, Yevgeny Sverstyuk, and Oles Sergiyenko spoke in her memory. They paid dearly for their bold speeches when they were arrested a little more than a year later.[23]

By the end of the 1960s there were fewer public statements in defense of national rights, but less visible forms of the national democratic movement intensified—primarily *samizdat* activity.

Ukrainian *Samizdat*

In the early sixties Ukrainian *samizdat* consisted, for the most part, of typed copies of verse by the poets of the sixties, which was either not published by the Soviet press or was published in hard-to-find small editions. In 1965 the *samizdat* "catch" from searches made at the apartments of those arrested was meager, testifying to the weak development of *samizdat* at this time. Only in a few rare cases was anything found—usually poetry or a few articles, most often the anonymous pamphlet, "On the Trial of Pogruzhalsky," concerning the fire in the Ukrainian section of the Kiev Library.[24] Soon after the arrests of 1965, however, Chornovil's work about those arrests and Dzyuba's book, *Internationalism or Russification?* appeared in *samizdat*—two of the most popular works of Ukrainian *samizdat*. Shortly after, both volumes were published abroad in Ukrainian and in other European languages.

To Ukrainians living abroad these works exposed a new form of opposition, one alien to the majority of emigrés because of their hostile attitude toward socialism and Marxism. Although these books and articles were not lacking in Soviet prejudices and were quite ignorant about the early stages of the political struggle, their authors expressed sincere love for the Ukraine and courageously defended its welfare, as they understood it.

The publicist writings of Svyatoslav Karavansky were widely disseminated. Written in the form of complaints to the appropriate Soviet departments, they contained detailed evidence of the Russification of the Ukraine, demonstrating the total discrepancy between the politics of Russification on the one hand and Party programs and Soviet law on the other.[25]

During the second half of the sixties Ukrainian *samizdat* was much more widely distributed. It was enriched by articles written by Y. Sverstyuk ("Cathedral in the Woods"), by V. Stus ("Place in the Battle" in defense of Dzyuba), by M. Braychevsky ("Annexation of Reunification?"), by L. Plyushch who wrote under the pseudonyms of Losa, Maloross, and others, and by Moroz. While still serving time in a Mordovian labor camp, Moroz sent out his article, "Report from the Beria Reserve," and after he was released he wrote several articles: "Amid the Snows," in which he called for an "apostolic" service to honor the Ukraine; and "Moses and Dathan"; and "A Chronicle of Resistance," about the process of Russification. Upon his release from camp, Mikhailo Osadchy published in *samizdat* his book, *The Cataract*, an autobiographical account of his arrest, trial, and confinement. Also circulated widely was a collective letter written by a group of young people from Dnepropetrovsk. I. Sokulsky, Kulchinsky and Savchenko received labor camp sentences for this letter.[26] Descriptions of the trials of the thirties, including that of the director L. Kurbas, were distributed through *samizdat*.

One of the first works to be translated into Russian was Dzyuba's *Internationalism or Russification?* This book opened up the Ukrainian movement to Muscovites, who by that time had lived through events similar to those in the Ukraine. The movement that would later be called the human rights movement was just beginning in Moscow.

Russian works also were available in Ukrainian *samizdat*: Abdurrakhman Avtorkhanov's *The Technology of Power*; Aleksandr Solzhenitsyn's works and a transcript of his expulsion from the Writers' Union; Andrey Sakharov's article "Thoughts on Progress, Peaceful Coexistence and Intellectual Freedom"; a transcript of the proceedings against Pasternak in the Writers' Union; and other works. The *Chronicle of Current Events* appeared regularly and, beginning with its early issues, the *Chronicle* reported systematically on events in the Ukraine.

The systematic exchange of information and *samizdat* between the Ukraine and Moscow was established. Leonid Plyushch was the first to make special trips to Moscow to collect new *samizdat* materials and arrange for their duplication in Kiev, and for the translation of the most important Ukrainian *samizdat* materials into Russian for distribution in Moscow.

Ukrainian *samizdat* became more political and highly professional: historians published articles on history, literary critics on literature, etc. The professionalism of Ukrainian *samizdat* encouraged the creation and stabilization of a social stratum called "stokers with a university education," made up of specialists dismissed from their jobs for "nationalism" and former political prisoners and their friends and relatives compelled to take menial jobs. Beginning in 1965, a significant part of the Ukrainian intelligentsia was transformed into blue-collar workers. This social stratum grew as every year more people lost their jobs and more prisoners returned from the camps. Few people were able to return to positions for which they were qualified.

These "stokers with a university education" were all potential *samizdat* authors because there was no other outlet for their creative abilities. Most yearned for serious work in their own fields and discussions with colleagues, if only during their free time.

On May 22, 1971, instead of going to the Shevchenko monument, some of these unemployed professionals gathered together at a private apartment, to hold a "Shevchenko seminar." They read works specially prepared for the occasion: Y. Sverstyuk on "Shevchenko—the Apostle of Christian Forgiveness"; I. Dzyuba on the relations between Shevchenko and Russian Slavophiles; L. Plyushch on Shevchenko's "Prayer"; M. Kotsyubinskaya on a paper on language and metaphor in Shevchenko's poetry. The idea of a regular Academy of Ukrainian Studies was born. It was buried with the arrests of 1972.[27]

The *Ukrainian Herald*, a news publication, was begun in *samizdat* in January 1970. As Plyushch testified, Ukrainians had no uncensored news bulletin of their own, so Kiev residents often learned about events in their city from the *Chronicle of Current Events*. Ukrainian materials made up only a minor part of the reported news in the *Chronicle*, however. Many significant events were not covered. The editorial staff of the *Ukrainian Herald*, therefore, declared that their purpose was to inform the public about such unreported events, as well as about news that had been hidden or falsified by the official press: news of violations of freedom of the press and other democratic rights that had been formally guaranteed by the constitution; of judicial and extrajudicial repression in the Ukraine; of violations of national sovereignty and incidents of Russian chauvinism and Ukrainophobia; news on the status of Ukrainian political prisoners; and of the consequences of protests against civil rights violations. The *Herald* included reviews or complete texts of articles, documents, and literary works distributed in *samizdat*. The staff explained that because their publication was not the organ of any one organization or group with a unified program, they would publish *samizdat* materials representing diverse points of view and would provide objective information on all events and aspects of Ukrainian life.

The first issue of the *Ukrainian Herald* carried reports about self-immolations; the campaign against Dzyuba; a trial of Kiev hydro-electric-station workers; extrajudicial repression in the Dnepropetrovsk region; political trials, searches and investigations at the end of 1969. It reported a list of fifty-eight persons who had been subjected to extrajudicial repressions in 1968–69; summaries of Ukrainians in jails and labor camps; and a list of Ukrainian political prisoners.

From 1970 to 1972 six issues of the *Ukrainian Herald* were published.[28] Like the staff of the *Chronicle of Current Events*, the editorial staff of the *Herald* was anonymous. The most we can say is that V. Chornovil (Lvov) was credited with participation in the publication of the *Herald* in the judicial proceedings against him and that the Kievans, Vasily Lisovoy, Mykola Plakhotnyuk, and Zinovy Antonyuk were accused of distributing the bulletin.

By this time *samizdat* was widespread in the Ukraine. During the searches made in 1970, more than three thousand copies of *samizdat* publications were confiscated in the Lvov region alone.[29]

On June 1, 1970, less than a year after his release, V. Moroz was arrested again and in November he was tried for "anti-Soviet agitation and propaganda." The severity of his sentence was an indication of a new phase of repression: nine years of prison and camp, plus five years of exile.[30]

Moroz's conviction occasioned many strong protests from participants in the Ukrainian national-democratic movement. The arrest in December 1971 of Nina Strokata, the wife of the "eternal prisoner" Svyatoslav Karavansky, caused an equally stormy protest. A committee for Strokata's defense was formed; its members included Moscow human rights activists, as well as Ukrainians. It prepared two news bulletins about Strokata and her trial. It was the first attempt to create an open human rights organization in the Ukraine. But, because of the massive arrests in January 1972, it never materialized.

Ukrainian National Movement

Leonid Plyushch, first *samizdat* liaison in the 1960s between Moscow and the Ukraine, before his arrest in 1970

Mykola Plakhotnyuk, physician, initiator of the 1967 Kiev demonstration, before his arrest in 1972

Ivan Svitlychny, philologist and 1960s activist, Kiev, 1968

Group of 1960s activists in Lvov, 1971: (L to R, rear) Irina Stasiv-Kalynets, Stefaniya Shabatura, (L to R, front) Igor Kalinets, Vyacheslav Chornovil

Yury Badzyo, whose *The Right to Live* was confiscated by the KGB, with his wife, Svetlana

Ivan Dzyuba, leading Ukrainian activist until his arrest in 1972

Levko Lukyanenko and Ivan Kandyba, 1976, after release from prison term, founding members of the Ukrainian Union of Workers and Peasants and Ukrainian Helsinki Watch Group and now political prisoners

Mykola Rudenko, leader of the Ukrainian Helsinki Watch Group, with his wife, Raisa, and Pyotr Grigorenko, founding member of Moscow and Ukrainian Helsinki Watch groups, with his wife, Zinaida, Moscow, 1976

Lithuanian National Movement

Petras Paulaitis, member of the underground Union for the Struggle for a Free Lithuania and political prisoner, 1946–56, 1957–82, on his last release from prison in March 1982

Viktoras Petkus (R), founding member of the Lithuanian Helsinki Watch Group, with Albertas Zilinskas

Founding members, Catholic Committee for the Defense of Believers' Rights, November 1978: (L to R) the Reverends J. Kauneckas, J. Zdebskis, A. Svarinskas, S. Tamkevicius, V. Velavicius

Nijole Sadunaite, activist for the *Chronicle of the Catholic Church in Lithuania,* 1977, in exile

Lithuanian Catholic procession, Siluva, 1975

Estonian and Latvian National Movements

Dr. Juri Kukk and family in Tartu, before arrest in March 1980 for signing protest against the invasion of Afghanistan; he died in camp, March 1981

Mart Niklus, veteran of Estonian National-Democratic Movement, a political prisoner, 1958–66, and since 1980; with Andrey Sakharov, Moscow, 1978

Gunars Rode, founding member of the underground Baltic Federation in 1962, Latvia

Juris Bumeisters (R), leader of the underground Latvian Social-Democratic Party and political prisoner since 1980, with his family

Georgian National Movement

Viktor Rtskheladze and Zviad Gamsakhurdia, founding members of the Georgian Initiative and Georgian Helsinki Watch groups

Merab Kostava, founding member, Georgian Initiative and Georgian Helsinki Watch groups, 1977

Armenian National Movement

Paruyr Ayrikyan, leader of the underground
National Unification Party, political prisoner,
1969–84, in 1974

Robert Nazaryan, founding member
of the Armenian Helsinki Watch
Group, before his arrest, Yerevan,
1978

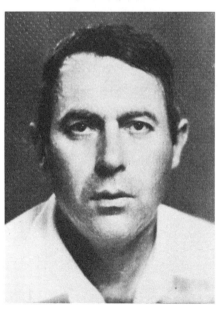

Eduard Arutyunyan, leader of the Armenian
Helsinki Watch Group, before his arrest in
1979, Yerevan, 1979

Crimean Tartars

Aleksey Kosterin, Russian writer involved in the Tartar movement, Moscow, 1968

Musa Mamut in Donskoye Village, three months before self-immolation in protest against national discrimination of Crimean Tartars, 1978

Rustem Nafiev's family, Grushevka Village in Crimea, 1976, evicted from their home

Activists Reshat Dzhemilev and Mustafa Dzhemilev, Tashkent, 1978

The arrests began simultaneously in Kiev and Lvov on January 12, 1972. By January 15, Ivan Svitlychny, Leonid Plyushch, Yevgeny Sverstyuk, Vasyl Stus, and other well-known members of the sixties generation had been arrested in Kiev, and shortly afterwards, Ivan Dzyuba was arrested. In Lvov, Vyacheslav Chornovil, Mikhailo Osadchy, Stefaniya Shabatura, Ivan Gel, Irina Stasiv, and later her husband, Igor Kalynets, and others were arrested.

Just as in 1965, these coordinated arrests doubtlessly proceeded on instructions from above. Almost simultaneously with the arrests in the Ukraine, arrests began in Moscow and Novosibirsk on January 14 in connection with the *Chronicle of Current Events* affair. But in this case, unlike the 1965 roundup, the Ukrainian KGB was prepared and carried out its part of the action according to accepted KGB practice.

On February 11, one month after the arrests began, an article in the *Soviet Ukraine* about the Belgian, Jaroslav Dobosch, who had visited leading dissidents in Kiev and Lvov at the end of 1971, reported that Dobosch made his visit "on instructions from the anti-Soviet center of Bandera followers abroad—OUN." Svitlychny, Sverstyuk, Chornovil, and others had been arrested, it said, in connection with the investigation of Dobosch. Dobosch himself was compelled to give evidence against others, then expelled from the country to the West. After several days of questioning, Zinoviya Franko, the granddaughter of Ivan Franko, the classic Ukrainian author and a close friend of many leading members of the sixties generation, wrote a penitent article for the *Soviet Ukraine*. She charged that Dobosh was an agent of "hostile nationalist organizations abroad that were closely tied to the intelligence operations of the imperialist powers."

Before the trial two of the people who were arrested, Leonid Seleznenko and Mykola Kholodny, were released. On the basis of their testimony charges were brought against most of the others arrested in 1972.[31]

Dobosch's own "confession" was not used during the trial, but it was used frequently during interrogations of those arrested and during "discussions" at universities or the workplaces of those who were either close to the arrested or known for their unfavorable opinions of the authorities. Expulsion from school or dismissal from work awaited all these people.

The scope of the 1972 arrests was much broader than the scope of the arrests of 1965. The *Ukrainian Herald* (no. 8) listed at least fifty people arrested but at that time in fact the number of arrests was even larger. As a result of the arrests, publication of the *Ukrainian Herald* ceased for two years. Communication with Moscow suffered. In November 1972 the *Chronicle of Current Events* halted publication for a year and a half. Information about events was, in consequence, harder to compile for the 1972–73 period than it had been either for earlier or later ones. My own file contains the names of 122 persons arrested in connection with the national-democratic movement in the Ukraine in 1972–74, but the number of those actually arrested was larger. Most of the names of those arrested for "anti-Soviet agitation and propaganda" are known. They served their terms in camps for political prisoners and news of them eventually reached Moscow. Others, tried either for "slander" or on the basis of fabricated criminal charges, received shorter sentences and were scattered throughout the camps for criminal prisoners. Data on such convictions is incomplete.

Just as in 1965, the majority arrested and sentenced were intellectuals. We have data on the background of 89 of those convicted. Seventy-two are intellectuals, including 10 priests, and 17 are workers. Distribution according to area is about equal: 48 are from eastern Ukraine (including 28 from Kiev), and 55 are from western Ukraine, including 13 from Lvov. As our figures show, Kiev holds first place. Practically all the leading figures and active members of the Ukrainian national-democratic movement were arrested, as well as some incidental people unconnected with the movement. Those arrested in 1972 were older than those arrested in 1965. Of the 85 persons on whom we have age data, only 29 were younger than thirty; 32 were from ages thirty to forty; 23 were older than forty.

During the trial, the smoke screen of the Dobosch affair and foreign intelligence networks was discarded and most of the accused were convicted of anti-Soviet agitation and propaganda. The charges stemmed from the samizdat activities of the accused: Sverstyuk, Dzyuba, Marchenko, Stus, Stasiv, Kalinets, and others were charged with the authorship of samizdat works; Plyushch, Serednyak, Plakhotnyuk, Lisovoy, Pronyuk, Semenyuk, and others, charged with distributing samizdat; Svitlychna, Plyushch, and Svitlychny, charged with storing samizdat materials.

Many of the actions the accused were charged with had occurred years before. Sverstyuk, for example, was accused of having made a speech at a meeting of teachers in 1963 in which he criticized the educational system. Almost all of the sentences meted out were the maximum allowed under anti-Soviet propaganda: seven years of labor camp plus five years of exile.[32]

Thorough searches were conducted when the arrests were made. In the Lvov region alone more than one thousand searches were made from January to March 1972, and countless people were interrogated.[33]

It is difficult to fix the number of those expelled from school or dismissed from jobs. Nobody recorded such incidents. The Ukrainian

Herald (no. 8) listed the names of sixty people dismissed from work, but this figure is limited to the residents of large cities who held prestigious positions. In the opinion of the *Ukrainian Herald* editorial staff, the total of those dismissed ran into the thousands. Dismissals took place all over the Ukraine, in large and small cities and in the country. The names of twenty-four students expelled from the University of Lvov were listed, with an acknowledgment that this number represented only a small portion of the total of those expelled, since expulsions had occurred in other universities, particularly Kiev University.[34]

Issue no. 8 of the *Herald* lists the names of fifty authors whose works were banned and about a hundred authors it was forbidden to mention in print.

In May 1971 came the first arrest for speaking at the Shevchenko monument, that of Anatoly Lupynos. Crippled during ten years of confinement as a political prisoner from 1956 to 1966, and on crutches, Lupynos read his own poetry, dedicated to the tragic and humiliating position of the Ukraine, which he compared to a violated woman. Lupynos was later convicted and confined to a psychiatric ward, where he remains to this day.

In 1973 the rector of the University of Lvov banned the traditional May celebration honoring Shevchenko. Students tried to hold the celebration on their own initiative, but the celebration was broken up. Protest leaflets appeared in the universities and the first issue of the satirical *samizdat* magazine, *Koryto* (The Trough) began to appear. Arrests of students began, and those arrested were beaten and taunted. The university carried out massive expulsions. The authorities tried to arrange public condemnations at Komsomol meetings of those expelled, but the students supported their fellow students and more students were expelled on the orders of the rector without benefit of public meetings.

At the University of Lvov, in 1974, the administrators organized an evening in honor of Shevchenko, but invited only student "activists." Songs about the Communist Party and the Komsomol were sung; few of the speeches referred to Shevchenko at all. Those who attended had been warned beforehand not to stand up, as was customary, when Shevchenko's poem "The Will" was read.

In the decade following 1974 secret instructions were issued to admit no more than 25 percent of the local, i.e., Ukrainian, youth to universities in the western Ukraine.[35]

Just as in 1965, in 1972–74 the Ukrainian intelligentsia suffered the brunt of the attack. The severity with which they were treated was out of all proportion to their direct connections to the movement. The arrests seemed to be part of a wide-ranging plan to eradicate Ukrainian national consciousness and to transform all Ukrainian intellectuals with nationalist sentiments into "stokers with a university education." The purge extended beyond the scientific and cultural institutions to rural intellectuals and to persons who were members of Party and state cadres.

In May 1972 Pyotr Shelest, the First Secretary of the Ukrainian Communist Party Central Committee, was dismissed from his post. According to the *Ukrainian Herald* (no. 8), he was accused of nationalism and of promoting the national movement in the Ukraine. He was replaced by V. V. Shcherbitsky. After that there was a large turnover of Party officials and 25 percent of the secretaries on ideology of territorial, city, and regional Party committees were dismissed, pensioned off, lowered in rank, or fired on charges of corruption or other misdeeds. Many workers with leadership positions in cultural and scientific institutions were dismissed, openly accused of "nationalism."[36]

Some were replaced, and the percentage of Russian officials in jobs was greatly increased. Eavesdropping on officials' private conversations, intercepting letters in the mail, and covert, as well as open, surveillance reached unheard of proportions. KGB staff was increased, particularly in the western Ukraine. All forms of public expression of nationalist sentiments were persecuted and the national movement was paralyzed. The atmosphere resembled in many respects that of the Stalinist terror: physical extermination was no longer used and there were far fewer arrests. Nonetheless, everyone fell under suspicion and the threat of reprisals for a careless word or expression of sympathy toward the wrong people hung over everybody. One old Kiev resident was deprived of his pension for visiting the family of a friend who had been arrested.

In 1973 Ivan Dzyuba, who had been sentenced in 1972 to five years in camp and five years of exile, was released after he agreed to write for the newspapers a condemnation of his old beliefs. This is the only case of recantation I know of among those who were "called-up" in 1972.[37] The rest behaved courageously during their interrogations and trials, although another recanted while in camp and was released. The other participants of the Ukrainian national movement joined the human rights movement of political prisoners while in the camps. The human rights movement that had begun in the latter half of 1965 was in full swing in the political camps during the seventies. Ukrainians, who formed a majority of the new camp arrivals, were a significant factor in this movement. By the end of 1976, thirteen of the twenty political prisoners in the special regimen camp were Ukrainian, and in a women's political camp one-quarter of the prisoners were Ukrainian.

After 1972 Ukrainian *samizdat* was filled primarily with the writings of political prisoners: petitions to official institutions containing reviews of the prisoners' cases and arguments demonstrating the legal groundlessness of the charges against them (by V. Chornovil, I. Gel, D. Shumuk, V. Romanyuk, N. Svitlychna, and many others); statements on behalf of the rights of political prisoners; and statements on the continuing struggle for national rights. Often Ukrainian political prisoners made these statements jointly with political prisoners of other nationalities, and in such documents the problem of national liberation is treated as a general problem of all the ethnic groups that make up the Soviet Union. Ukrainian prisoners became inevitable participants in collective appeals for democratic rights and particularly in the appeal to the Belgrade conference of countries that participated in the Helsinki agreements. Documents demanding democratic rights were signed by some members of Organization of Ukrainian Nationalists as well as by participants of the contemporary national movement.

Vyacheslav Chornovil, along with Eduard Kuznetsov, initiated the movement for political prisoner status that spread throughout the camps. Many Ukrainian prisoners participated in collective hunger strikes and in general camp strikes, and renounced their Soviet citizenship.

Appeals from relatives seeking the release of political prisoners made up a significant part of Ukrainian *samizdat* in 1972 and following years. Relatives sent complaints to the appropriate Soviet institutions and began to appeal to international organizations and societies—the letters of L. Plyushch's wife Tatyana Zhitnikova, Raisa Moroz, Oksana Meshko, the mother of O. Sergiyenko, and others.

Issues 7 and 8 of the *Ukrainian Herald* appeared during the period of 1973 to 1975 in Ukrainian *samizdat*. The compilers used the pseudonym of Maksim Sagaydak, rather than contributing anonymously, as earlier. Issues 7 and 8 were not, like previous issues, collections of news bulletins and *samizdat* documents, but articles addressing a particular subject. Maksim Sagaydak's article on secret diplomacy and his poetry, written from December 1972 to October 1973, appeared. So did an anonymous article, "Ethnocide of Ukrainians in the USSR," a well-documented statistical study of the physical extermination of the Ukrainian people from 1918 to 1950, of the Russification policy that continues to this day, of the repression of national consciousness, and the destruction of Ukrainian culture.

Not until 1980 were the real names of the authors of these issues of the *Ukrainian Herald* known. They were: Kievan journalists Vitaly Shevchenko and Aleksandr Shevchenko, and a dentist from the Lvov region, Stepan Khmara.[38] None had previously taken part in the national-democratic movement, a fact that had allowed them to remain unexposed for so long.

In the wake of the arrests of 1972 the desire to hide opinions and actions to which the authorities objected was a natural reaction. The publication of the last issues of the *Ukrainian Herald* under pseudonyms was not the only such incident. The historian, Mikhail Melnik, a watchman at a brick factory after 1972, worked on a manuscript on the history of the Ukraine for many years; it was a closely guarded secret. His entire archive was confiscated during a search on March 6, 1979, and he committed suicide soon afterward.[39] Yury Badzyo concealed his own historical-philosophical work on the fate of the Ukraine. Deprived of the right to work in his field of philology in 1972, he had worked since that time as loader at a bakery. His 1,400-page manuscript, "The Right to Live," was confiscated during a search before his arrest in April 1979.[40] These two works of Melnik and Badzyo could have become the most significant *samzidat* publications of the seventies, but they remain unknown to Ukrainian readers.

Human Rights Organizations in the Ukraine

In spite of the repression of all forms of unofficial public activity in the Ukraine, as well as in other republics of the USSR, the Ukrainian national-democratic movement developed in the direction of an openly organized movement. The first steps in this direction were made when Ukrainian activists were included in the Moscow human rights association. In May 1969, Leonid Plyushch from Kiev and Genrikh Altunyan, an engineer from Kharkov joined the Moscow Initiative Group for the Defense of Human Rights in the USSR, the first of such associations. Both were arrested and sentenced. (Plyushch was eventually sent in exile from the USSR to the West.)

When the Soviet chapter of Amnesty International was created in 1974 in Moscow,[41] the noted Ukrainian writer Mykola Rudenko, from Kiev, joined that group. In 1976, when the Moscow Helsinki Watch Group was formed, the Ukraine was the first republic to support that initiative. On November 9, 1976 the Ukrainian Helsinki Watch Group was created—the first open public association without official approval in the Ukraine. Mykola Rudenko was its founder and leader.

The formation of the Helsinki Watch Group in the Ukraine, an extremely significant event, gives some indication of the potential of the national movement in the Ukraine. Forced to conceal its presence, the movement was nevertheless ready to surface at the slightest of opportunities.

The Ukrainian Helsinki Watch Group was organized by the nine persons listed here, the majority of whom had been imprisoned earlier.

Name	Birth	City	Profession	Previous Terms of Political Imprison- ment
Mykola Rudenko (leader)	1920	Kiev	writer watchman, war invalid	—
Oles Berdnyk	1927	Kiev	writer, worker	1949–56
Ivan Kandyba	1930	Lvov region	lawyer, worker	1961–76
Levko Lukyanenko	1927	Chernigov	lawyer, electrician	1961–76
Miroslav Marynovich	1949	Kiev	engineer	—
Mykola Matusevych	1948	Kiev	historian, editor	—
Oksana Meshko	1905	Kiev	pensioner, former teacher	1947–56
Nina Strokata	1925	Tarusa	microbiologist, cashier	1972–76
Oleksa Tykhy	1927	Donetsk region	teacher, watchman	1957–74

In addition to these nine, Pyotr Grigorenko, who also belonged to the Moscow group, was included as a representative of the Ukrainian group in Moscow.[42]

With the exception of I. Kandyba, all the members of the Ukrainian Helsinki Watch Group were from the eastern Ukraine, and most of these, from Kiev. The median age was about fifty years old. As in the preceding stages of the national movement, the majority of the Helsinki group were intellectuals specializing in the humanities. At the moment of joining the group, none of the members were employed in their profession, a frequent circumstance among intellectuals in the humanities.

Representatives of all phases of the Ukrainian national movement participated in the Helsinki group: O. Meshko and O. Berdnyk who had served time under Stalin for "nationalism"; I. Kandyba and L. Lukyanenko, who had participated in the "underground" phase of the movement in the 1950s; O. Tykhy and N. Strokata, who helped initiate the movement of the 1960s generation. Marynovich and Matusevych were younger participants in this movement, the only two who had avoided imprisonment before joining the Helsinki group. This is also representative of the situation of the Ukraine as a whole where the repression of the national movement was harsher than in any other republic.

Mykola Rudenko is an unusual figure among the participants of the Ukrainian nationalist movement. His proletarian background and Party membership, in addition to his literary talents and his genuine Soviet patriotism, helped make possible a successful career. After finishing school, Rudenko served in the special NKVD (the former name of the KGB) forces during the 40s and during the Second World War served as an army political instructor near Leningrad, where he was seriously wounded in the spine and became an invalid. After the war he began to write professionally. From 1947 to 1971 he published eleven collections of poetry, two novels, and a collection of short stories. From 1947 to 1950 he was the editor-in-chief of the leading Ukrainian literary journal *Dnepro* and the secretary of Party organization of the Ukrainian Writers' Union. In 1949, he wrote in one of his articles that "the Ukrainian nationalists were and remain the most vicious of all the enemies of the Ukrainian people." His pro-Soviet attitude was delivered a fatal blow by Khrushchev's anti-Stalin speech at the Twentieth Party Congress in 1956. As one of the shapers of Party policy, Rudenko felt responsible for the crimes committed under Stalin. At the beginning of the 60s he began to write secretly, as a result of his new feelings of responsibility. At the same time he began writing letters to the Central Committee of the Ukrainian Communist Party, in which he criticized orthodox Marxism and the policies of the government. In 1972 he joined the Soviet chapter of Amnesty International. On April 18, 1975 he was detained for two days and afterwards expelled from the Party and the Writers' Union. He went to work as a watchman. Later in 1975 his critique of orthodox Marxism, "Monologues on Economics," appeared in *samizdat*.[43]

The biography of P. G. Grigorenko, a former Soviet general and a dedicated Communist, shows a similar unusual pattern of evolution. Grigorenko left the Ukraine as a young man and became completely Russified. Until he joined the group as its Moscow representative, he had not been concerned with the problems created by the Russification of the Ukraine. He became one of the most active members of the human rights movement, joined the Moscow Helsinki Group, and was distressed by all violations of civil rights in the USSR. His primary interest among nationality problems was the Crimean Tartars, whom he helped over the course of many years in their struggle to return to their native country and among whom he made many close friends.

Grigorenko's membership in the Ukrainian Helsinki Group was one measure of its close contacts with the Moscow human rights activists and especially with the Moscow Helsinki Group. The Ukrainian Helsinki Group was formed after the example of the Moscow group and made use of its experience. The first report on the Ukrainian Helsinki Group was issued by the Moscow Helsinki Group.[44] The members of the Moscow Helsinki Group noted that under the conditions existing in the Ukraine, the formation of a Helsinki Watch Group there was an act of great courage. Its activities were greatly hampered by the absence of Western correspondents or diplomatic representatives in Kiev, who could have been helpful in relaying information on violations of the humanitarian articles of the Final Act of the Helsinki Accords. As experience has shown, such information does not reach its destination through the mail. The members of the Moscow group announced that they would help the Ukrainian group send information to journalists and representatives of governments that had signed the Final Act.

The first words of the first memorandum of the Ukrainian Helsinki Group concerned the cultural genocide and ethnocide that began in the 1930s in the Ukraine and continues to this day. Memorandum no. 1, which set the program for the Ukrainian Helsinki Group, concentrated on the Ukrainian national problem, an emphasis expressed not only by the first memorandum, but also by all the later documents issued by the group. By the end of 1980, the Ukrainian Helsinki Group had issued a total of thirty declarations and appeals, including eighteen memorandums and ten news bulletins,[45] all devoted to aspects of the nationality problem.

In contrast to other Helsinki Watch groups, the Ukrainian group did not comment on religious persecution, although it is no less severe in the Ukraine than in other republics—as of August 1, 1980, 90 participants of the Ukrainian national movement had been imprisoned and 78 prisoners had been arrested in the Ukraine for their religious beliefs. These included 33 Baptists, 14 Uniates, 12 Pentecostalists, 11 Adventists, 6 Jehovah's Witnesses, and 2 Orthodox believers. There were also believers among the members of the Ukrainian Helsinki Group: the Orthodox Strokata, Lukyanenko who discovered his religious convictions while in camp, and the Baptist Pyotr Vins who joined the group in 1977. The group had a direct channel for receiving information on the situation of believers in the Ukraine, yet no document issued by the group mentions violations of religious rights nor the problems of the Jewish movement for emigration to Israel, even though tens of thousands of Jews living in the Ukraine have applied for permission to leave and many of them are subjected to discrimination in consequence.

The Ukrainian Helsinki Group also took no cognizance of attempts to defend social and economic rights in the Ukraine. News of the activities and the fate of the pioneers of the movement for workers' rights—Ivan Greshchuk (Kiev), Vladimir Klebanov, and Aleksey Nikitin (Donbass)—was carried instead by the Moscow *Chronicle of Current Events*,[46] and in documents of the Moscow Helsinki Group,[47] but not by the Ukrainian Helsinki Group.

The Ukrainian Helsinki Group, which had declared as its goal the implementation of the Declaration of Human Rights and the humanitarian provisions of the Final Act of the Helsinki Accords, narrowed its range of activities to the defense of only one right—the right of equality on the basis of nationality. It recorded only violations of that right and only if Ukrainians were involved. By restricting itself in this way, the Ukrainian Helsinki Group also restricted the basis of its support. It did not become a connecting link among various dissident movements in the Ukraine—for example, the religious movement, including Baptists, Pentecostalists, Adventists, Jehovah's Witnesses, Uniates, and Orthodox; the other national movements, including the struggle of the Crimean Tartars to return to their native land and the struggle of the Jews to emigrate; or the human rights movement in its pure form.

The human rights movement is stronger than the national movement in the major cities of the Ukraine, which have been strongly Russified—Kharkov, Odessa, and the Donbass area. To the extent that connections were made between these movements, they were made through the Moscow human rights activists, not by the Ukrainian Helsinki Group.

The Ukrainian group's concentration on one problem can be explained by many factors. Most important, the group was ethnically homogeneous; all of its founders were Ukrainian and the majority had been participants in the Ukrainian national movement long before the creation of the group. Only later did the Russians, Vladimir Malinkovich and Pyotr Vins, and Iosif Zisels, who was a Jew, join. The narrow range of the group's activities is due not only to the nature of the interests of its members, but also to the extremely difficult conditions under which they worked.

The formation of the Ukrainian Watch Group was announced on November 9, 1976 at a press conference given for foreign journalists in Moscow. When Rudenko returned to Kiev the next day, he learned that a few hours after the press conference bricks had been thrown through the windows of his house. One brick wounded his guest, Oksana Meshko, in the forehead. Rudenko turned to the militia for help, but it refused to investigate the matter; it even refused to prepare an official record of the incident.

The first step in the official attack on the Helsinki Watch Groups occurred on December 25, when searches were made at the apartments of several members of the Ukrainian group. During the search of Rudenko's house, dollars were "found" in his writing desk; a rifle was "found" in Tykhy's garden; pornographic postcards were "found" at Berdnyk's apartment. None of the materials seized were used during the trials, just as the Ukrainian dissidents' "criminal connections" with Jaroslav Dobosch were not used in 1972.

The first arrests of members of the Moscow and Ukrainian Helsinki groups occurred simultaneously. Aleksandr Ginzburg was arrested February 3, 1977 in Moscow and on February 4 and 5, M. Rudenko and O. Tykhy were arrested in the Ukraine.

In April 1977, M. Matusevych and M. Marynovich were arrested; in December, L. Lukyanenko. In November 1977 P. Grigorenko was permitted to visit his son in the United States and soon afterwards was deprived of Soviet citizenship. He was unable to return.

After the arrest of Rudenko and Tykhy, new members were accepted by the Ukrainian Helsinki Watch Group: Pyotr Vins, an electrician; Olga Heyko, the wife of M. Matusevych and a philologist by profession, employed as a kindergarten teacher; Vitaly Kalinnichenko, an engineer and former political prisoner; and Vasyl Streltsiv, an English-language teacher and former political prisoner. Both Kalinnichenko and Streltsiv had been refused permission to emigrate. In 1978 Petro Sichko, an engineer and former political prisoner, and his son Vasyl, a student of journalism at the University of Kiev, joined the group.

After 1978 the group began to issue news bulletins, instead of the memorandums that the early staff produced. Although not issued regularly, they accurately reflected the facts of the persecution of the Ukrainian national movement, including that of the Ukrainian Helsinki Group, and the conditions of Ukrainian political prisoners. *Samizdat* materials were included in these bulletins. For the most part, the *samizdat* concerned the repression of participants of the national movement and the fate of those arrested.

By 1979, repressions in the Ukraine had taken on clear Mafia-like overtones. A frequent method of reprisal was arranging for the victims to be beaten in the street by "persons unknown." Against women the threat of rape was used. In the spring of 1979 the young Ukrainian composer Vladimir Ivasyuk died under unexplained circumstances. He had written songs in the tradition of Ukrainian folk songs popular with young people. He was last seen at the end of April, leaving the conservatory, accompanied by an unknown man, as had happened when he was taken in for questioning earlier by the KGB, pressured to become an informer. He refused. On May 18, Ivasyuk's body was found hanging from a tree in the forest. Because of the organized violence in the Ukraine at the time, his relatives and friends did not believe the official version of suicide. They believe that the KGB was responsible for his death. Ivasyuk's funeral turned into a massive demonstration of about ten thousand people when on June 12, Whitsunday, the speeches of Petro and Vladimir Sichko, at Ivasyuk's grave were patriotic and the several hundred people gathered there chanted "Glory to the Ukraine."[48]

The political arrests of 1979–80 in the Ukraine as elsewhere were primarily directed against members of the Helsinki group. Criminal charges fabricated by the militia or secret KGB agents were widely used. Most often those articles of the criminal code that facilitated convictions on the basis of false testimony by the militia and their helpers were applied: "resisting the authorities," "hooliganism," "attempted rape," and "possession of narcotics" previously planted on the victim. Of the fourteen members of the Ukrainian Helsinki Watch Group, six were convicted on criminal charges, an apparent strategy to discredit the first open Ukrainian human rights organization, and possibly an attempt to disguise the crackdown on a group founded on the basis of the Final Act of the Helsinki Accords.

At the same time, those who were hitherto anonymously involved in Ukrainian *samizdat* and therefore not well known either abroad or in the Ukraine were tried for "anti-Soviet agitation and propaganda" and given maximum or close to the maximum sentence allowed by law, as were the members of the Ukrainian Helsinki Watch Group who were also tried under this article. Stepan Khmara, Vitaly Shevchenko, and Aleksandr Shevchenko, who compiled the *Ukrainian Herald* in 1973–75, were tried under the same article of the penal code forbidding "anti-Soviet agitation." So were other authors of *samizdat* materials like Yury Badzyo, Dmitry Mazur, Vasily Kurilo, Grigory Prikhodko, Pavel Cherny, and others.

Since it was clear by 1979 that membership in the Ukrainian Helsinki Watch Group almost automatically led to arrest, the last wave of volunteers who joined during the spring and summer of 1979 were virtual kamikazes. Most of the new members had just served out prison terms: S. Shabatura, V. Stus, M. Gorbal, Ya. Lesiv, I. Sokulsky, Yu. Litvin, and Z. Krasivsky. I. Senik and V. Chornovil were still living in exile, after having served prison terms.

Under conditions existing in the Ukraine at the time, public admission of having joined an independent group was a remarkable act of civic courage.

Ukrainian Helsinki Watch Group

During the 1970s, the Ukraine's role was established as the "testing ground" of punitive action. It has been carefully noted that new methods of persecution are first tested in the Ukraine, and then extended to other republics, as is apparent from this history of the persecution of the Ukrainian Helsinki Group.

The searches of Helsinki monitors began in the Ukraine, and the planting of incriminating objects was also tested there. Fabrication of criminal accusations was begun against the members of a Helsinki group; it was there that for the first time a woman, Olga Heyko, was sentenced to a labor camp term for participation in a Helsinki group. There, for the first time, a woman of retirement age was tried for "anti-Soviet agitation"—the 75-year-old Oksana Meshko. In the Ukraine, for the first time a sentence was passed on a woman who sought the release of her political prisoner husband (Raisa Rudenko). And it was with the Ukrainian Helsinki Group that repeat arrests were begun.

Several members of the Ukrainian Group, sentenced under criminal, rather than political, articles of the penal code for relatively short terms (two or three years), were not released from imprisonment upon serving these terms, but instead received new sentences while still in labor camp or immediately after release—some under political articles, others under newly fabricated criminal cases. But this time, they were sentenced to longer terms (V. Streltsiv; V. Ovsiyenko; V. Stus; Ya. Lesiv; P. Sichko, and others). The arrests of Ukrainian Helsinki Group members M. Gorbal and V. Chornovil were also "innovations": the two men were accused of rape. Such devious methods had not previously been used against dissenters.

Thus, in one way or another, by 1981, when Ivan Kandyba was arrested, the last member of the Ukrainian Helsinki Group still free, all the members of the Group were in prison. By the end of 1983, not a single one of them was yet released. Everyone who neared the end of a sentence was given a new term. By 1986, four Ukrainian political prisoners died in imprisonment: Valery Marchenko, Oleksi Tykhy, Yury Lytuyn, and Vasyl Stus, the latter three members of the Ukrainian Helsinki Group.[48]

Only in this way was it possible to put an end to the Ukrainian Helsinki Group. Only the foreign representatives of the group are active: P. G. Grigorenko and N. Strokata in the United States, and L. Plyushch in Europe. Of these Grigorenko and Plyushch had been exiled; Strokata emigrated. On the basis of information they receive from the Ukraine, they publish the *Herald on Repression in the Ukraine* in English and Ukrainian editions. That this information is sent out is an indication that the Ukrainian national democratic movement continues to exist, in spite of the 'fact that its participants were forced to refrain from public statements made in their own names. We know that not long before the last arrests occurred, new members joined the group, but their names were not revealed.

In Kharkov, Genrikh Altunyan was arrested, and in Lvov, Mikhail Goryn. There is much that is similar between these two arrests; both men are former political prisoners, and neither took active public positions after their releases. Nevertheless, friends gathered around them who were capable, in the opinion of the authorities, of "unauthorized" conversations, and even of the exchange of *samizdat* and this fact alone precipitated trials of these two men. Altunyan was sentenced to seven years of labor camp and five years of exile; Goryn was sentenced to ten years of labor camp and five years of exile. It is very possible that such trials will, in time, spread from the Ukraine to other republics. This has often been the experience with the Ukrainian KGB.[49]

After the Ukrainian Helsinki Watch Group was crushed, there were attempts to renew underground activities. In 1979 in the Ivano-Frankovsk province a group calling itself the Ukrainian National Front was uncovered (UNF). Only the names of three members are known: Nikolay Kraynik, a village teacher Ivan Mandrik, and Nikolay Zvarich, a machinist.

The first member of UNF to be arrested was Zvarich, in June 1979, and after him, Mandrik. On September 17 three men in plainclothes came for Mandrik at his place of work and took him away in a car. His wife was told that he had been sent away on an urgent business trip. Three days later they informed her that he had committed suicide by jumping from a hotel window. It was one more mysterious death in the Ukraine.

At Nikolay Kraynik's trial in August 1980, it was revealed that Kraynik was the leader of the National Front, that the membership of the group numbered forty people, and that the group's activities were educational. They tried to continue publication of the *Ukrainian Herald* (issues no. 10 and 11 appeared) and published two volumes of *Prozrenya* (The Enlightenment), a literary anthology.[50]

In sum, the Ukrainian National Front was an organization with many peaceful educational goals. It operated clandestinely simply because its members wanted to avoid the fate of the open Ukrainian Helsinki Group. After the Ukrainian National Front itself was eliminated, the Ukrainian Patriotic Movement made several appeals. The UPM also withheld the names of its members. Like the Ukrainian Helsinki Watch Group, the Patriotic Movement drew attention to the systematic strangulation of Ukrainian intellectuals and the earlier extermination of people under Soviet rule. The Ukrainian Patriotic Movement stated that the Soviet Union had become "a military police state with wide-ranging imperialistic goals." It held the Soviet Union responsible for the low standard of living in the Ukraine and believed that under these conditions the only way out was for the Ukraine to secede from the Soviet Union. The Patriotic Movement suggested that this could be done by referendum, under United Nations control. Calling on the West for support, the document of the UPM explained: "A free Ukraine might become a reliable defense for the West from Communist expansion, could improve the internal political situation in bordering countries and could help ethnic groups that are now a part of the Soviet Union achieve a genuine national existence. The decolonization of the USSR is the only guarantee of peace in the entire world."[51]

From the end of the 1970s until the beginning of the 1980s, the nationalist movement in the Ukraine went underground again. It is possible that it lost hope of resolving the Ukrainian national problems while the Ukraine was still a part of the Soviet Union—a hope that had inspired the participants of the movement during its early, open phase. The return to underground activities and the rebirth of the idea of separatism were the result of unrelenting Russification and the government's repression.

However, in spite of the fact that it could no longer act openly, the Ukrainian national movement preserved its democratic orientation, which was helpful, even when conditions worsened, in promoting the unification of the national movement with other movements in the Ukraine, and above all, with the human rights movement outside the Ukraine.

In the light of the greatly worsened political climate in the Soviet Union in the late seventies and early eighties, the non-Ukrainian population of the Ukraine who hold democratic inclinations can sympathize with the idea of secession in the hopes that a separate Ukraine would become a democratic country. Those that do, consider it only a remote possibility, although the rapprochement of non-Ukrainian human rights activists with members of the Ukrainian national movement is based on just such a platform.

In January 1981 in Kiev five young intellectuals were arrested in the "affair of the leaflets." On the anniversary of the mass arrests of January 12, 1972, they posted leaflets about the city that read: "Fellow countrymen! The 12th of January is the Day of the Ukrainian Political Prisoner. Support him!" Three of those detained for posting the leaflets were Ukrainians, and two were Jews. Natalya Parkhomenko, the mother of a young daughter, was released but expelled from the Komsomol and the university. Naboka, a journalism student at the University of Kiev; Leonid Milyavsky, a translator, Larisa Lokhvitskaya, a mathematician; and Ina Chernyavskaya, an endocrinologist, were all sentenced to three years of normal-regimen labor camp for "slandering the Soviet way of life."

The defendants were accused not only of posting the leaflets, but also of writing a joint manifesto about the internal political situation of the Soviet Union and a piece entitled "Prospects for Filling the Spiritual Vacuum of Soviet Society." They were accused similarly of writing and trying to distribute a leaflet calling for the boycott of the Moscow Olympic Games. Sergey Naboka was declared to be the author of "slanderous" poems and articles ("Pseudo-Socialism" and others). Larisa Lokhvitskaya was accused of writing the articles "The Future of Our Society," "Choose Freedom," and "Notes of a Radio-Listener," and of making statements supporting Polish Solidarity and condemning the invasion of Afghanistan.

During the trial, all those who were accused of "slander" refused to acknowledge their guilt, defending their positions vigorously.[52]

Efforts to continue open human rights activity still occur in the Ukraine.

Ukrainian Catholic Church

On September 9, 1982, five Ukrainian Catholics announced the formation of the Initiative Group for the Defense of the Rights of Religious Believers and the Church. Iosif Terelya, who had served 16 years of imprisonment, became the chairperson of this group. Three priests from the Ukrainian Catholic Church joined, along with Stefaniya Petrash, the mother of the political prisoners Vladimir and Vasyl Sichko, and the wife of political prisoner Petro Sichko, who herself had served a labor camp term under Stalin.

The Ukrainian Catholic church is one of the local churches of the Universal Roman Catholic church; the relation was established by a union documented at the Brest Synod in 1596. (That is why the Ukrainian Catholic church is frequently called the Uniate church.) At the end of the Second World War, there were fourteen million Ukrainians in the USSR for whom the Uniate church was a part of their traditions. On June 18, 1945, by order of P. Khodchenko, an official of the Council on Russian Orthodox Church Affairs in the Ukraine, the jurisdiction over the Ukrainian Catholic church was transferred, in a completely unlawful manner, to an initiative group of three priests whose assignment was to prepare for the transition of the Ukrainian Catholic church to the Russian Orthodox church. This decision was made at the Lvov Synod on March 10, 1946, after which the entire hierarchy of the Ukrainian church was sent into labor camps. Many died there. In recent years, there have been several trials of priests from the underground Ukrainian church. The majority of the priests were not in agreement with this reform, and although the official Ukrainian Catholic church has ceased to exist, it lives on in the catacombs. It is not known how many parishes have been preserved, but in the western Ukraine, quite a few villages are attempting—although unsuccessfully—to open churches and register their communities. The goal of the Initiative Group for the Defense of Religious Believers' Rights and the Church is to legalize the Ukrainian Catholic church.

On December 24, 1982, Iosif Terelya, the chairperson of the group, was arrested and then other members of the Group. In the 1980s, arrests were inevitable for any leader of an open human rights association; arrest was the fate of those who dared to speak out publicly, but also those whose "way of thinking" was disapproved.[53]

CHAPTER 2

The Lithuanian National Movement

Lithuania, Estonia, and Latvia were handed over to the Soviet Union on the basis of secret appendices to the Molotov-Ribbentrop pact, an agreement between the Soviet Union and Hitler's Germany in August 1939. The Lithuanian President Antanas Smetona, unlike the leaders of Estonia and Latvia, did not sign a formal renunciation of power and did not transfer his authority to the new government installed by the Soviet Union. It occupied the Baltic republics in June of 1940. The diplomatic representatives of the former Lithuanian government continue to be recognized by the United States, the Vatican, and those other countries that do not recognize the annexation of the Baltic countries by the Soviet Union.

Suppression and Decimation of Opposition

From its inception, the new regime in the Baltic began to crush all actual and potential opposition. On the night of July 11, 1940 just before the elections to the Seimas (the Lithuanian Parliament), approximately 2,000 Lithuanian intellectuals were arrested. The first massive deportation occurred in June 1941 and affected 36,000 of the most politically active Lithuanian citizens, for the most part, intellectuals.[1] During the German occupation from 1941 to 1944 Lithuania lost approximately 270,000 people.[2]

As Soviet troops approached the country in 1944, an additional 60,000 Lithuanians emigrated, among them the flower of the educated class, including about 3,000 professionals, 2,000 university students, and 3,300 high-school students.[3]

After the installation of the Soviet regime in 1944, resistance to occupation continued for more than ten years. Approximately 50,000 people were either killed in battle or executed during the guerrilla war against the Soviet government. The last partisans were seized in 1956. Another 50,000 were sent to forced-labor camps with twenty-five-year sentences.[4] According to one *samizdat* source, between 1945 and 1950 the overall loss of population was 270,000—equal to the loss during the years of German occupation.[5] All age groups and all levels of the population were decimated.

Young people formed the backbone of the partisan movement: high-school and university students, peasants from both poor and well-to-do families. Peasant youths made up the majority of those who died fighting, those who were executed, and those who were sent to the camps. In his memoirs Vladimir Bukovsky describes his general impression of the Lithuanians he met in camps: "Simple peasant lads, who had never been able to become the fathers of families."[6]

To those who either perished or were sent to camps must be added the 350,000 persons exiled without trial to eastern regions of the Soviet Union. Entire families were exiled: Lithuanians of all ages and social groups—peasants, workers, and intellectuals; everyone who was capable of resisting or who seemed to be capable of resisting the new regime. A significant number of the exiles perished in the alien land. Some have not to this day received permission to return to their native country. (A list of twenty-one persons are included in a statement of the Lithuanian Helsinki Group, dated June, 1977.[7])

Armed resistance was crushed by the midfifties, and occupation became a fact of existence for the Lithuanians. Peasants were forced to accept the collective-farm system; intellectuals went to work for the government. The Catholic church was unable to continue its active teaching. The way of life was Sovietized; people adapted to the "new life," which determined both personal goals and national aspirations. Radical changes took place during the quarter century after armed resistance was crushed. This is particularly evident if one compares the Lithuanians who served twenty-five-year labor-camp sentences and the great mass of present-day countrymen. Many of the former who participated in the struggle for national liberation had never lived under Soviet rule. They took up arms at the time of the Soviet invasion and have since spent most of their adult lives in prison camps. They preserved their old ideas, traditions, songs, and habits, and when they returned to their homeland, they were very much out of place. It was as if they had been returned from the distant past by a time machine. Bukovsky noted that the work ethic they had retained no longer existed on the outside. Even in the camps they worked diligently and showed a love for their work. Bukovsky writes that they were still living with the guerrilla psychology of the forties. For many of these people, contact of any sort with the authorities was unacceptable. They never recognized the legality of the present government.[8]

Among the Lithuanian long-termers, Petras Paulaitis is particularly noteworthy. Here is a short biography from the *Chronicle of Current Events:*

He studied in Rome and received his Doctor of Philosophy. During the German occupation of Lithuania, Paulaitis taught Latin in the eighth grade of a high school in Jurbarkas, where he directed the underground activities of his students. On February 16, 1942 (Lithuanian Independence Day), his students flew the Lithuanian flag atop the local gestapo headquarters. Everywhere in the city the students changed the new name, "Georgenburg," back to the old—Jurbarkas.

When Soviet troops arrived in Lithuania in 1944, 26 of Paulaitis's students joined the Union for the Struggle for a Free Lithuania. Paulaitis himself edited the union newspaper *Onwards to Freedom.*

In 1946 a military tribunal sentenced him to 25 years at hard labor. In 1956 he was released after his case was reviewed. He returned to Kaunas, where he worked as a stoker at a cannery.

On the condition that he condemn Lithuanian bourgeois nationalism, he was promised permission to teach once again. He refused. In 1957 he was arrested again and accused of subversive work with students of the Kaunas Polytechnic Institute . . . and of planning to revive the Union for the Struggle for a Free Lithuania. . . . On April 12, 1958 the Lithuanian Supreme Court sentenced seven students to various terms in prison camp from 1 to 10 years and sentenced Paulaitis once again to 25 years.[9]

The date for his release was October 10, 1982. At that time he was seventy-eight years old, of which six years were spent underground and thirty-six years in prison camp.

The Contemporary National Movement

The losses Lithuania suffered paralyzed its underground resistance for fifteen years—until the end of the sixties. For many Lithuanians this period of suspended animation was a period of intense reflection, during which their values were reconsidered and new methods of resistance were sought, since the old methods had proved ineffective under Soviet conditions. Contemporary forms of resistance in Lithuania are not a continuation of the partisan tradition, but a new struggle waged by different people under different conditions.

Lithuanian *samizdat* offers some interesting insights into the present mood of the most Sovietized strata of the population: the Soviet bureaucracy, the educated class, and the urban middle class; particularly helpful are two articles by T. Zenklys[10] and one by Eitan Finkelshtein.[11]

From all indications, Zenklys is a pseudonym for the well-educated bureaucracy. "Zenklys," claims that the conception of national goals

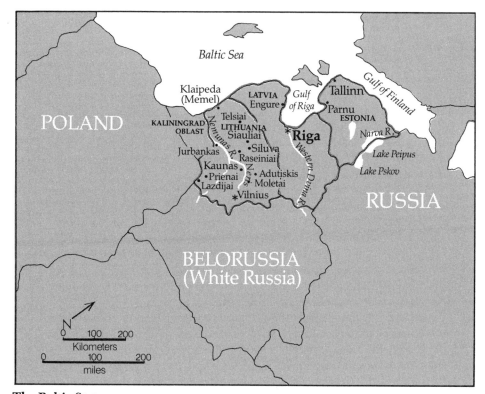

The Baltic States

widely held by his class is this: "The primary role of the people in an occupied country is a conservative one. Above all else . . . we must concern ourselves with physical survival and as far as possible we must preserve our solidarity and our health." Zenklys considers the First Secretary of the Central Committee of the Lithuanian Communist Party, Antanas Snechkus, an example of the kind of statesman who attempts to preserve a sense of nationhood under the conditions of occupation. He led Lithuania without interruption from the beginning of the occupation until his death in January 1974.

Zenklys writes that from the end of the forties until the beginning of the fifties, Snechkus conducted an increasingly nationalistic policy by strengthening and making use of his close ties with Moscow, especially with Mikhail Suslov; by influencing the second secretaries of the Lithuanian Communist Party Central Committee sent from Moscow; by skillful selection of personnel, based on personal loyalty and unquestioning willingness to carry out directives; by sabotage of many directives sent from Moscow under the guise of implementing them to the letter (examples are the campaign for introducing corn and the extension of planted acreage at the expense of pasture land); and by obtaining additional privileges and influence for Lithuania (one of the most important arguments used here was the necessity of proving to the large Lithuanian emigré population that Soviet Lithuania was indeed flourishing).

In Zenklys's opinion, Snechkus's greatest services were: preservation of the national integrity of the population; implementation of industrial development without irreparable environmental damage; provision of a level of goods and services for his people higher than available in other Soviet republics; and retention in the school curriculum of classic Lithuanian authors who fought for national independence. All this, Zenklys said, helped Lithuania preserve her own traditions to a greater extent than other republics and to become comparatively more modernized.

It is difficult to decide if the present leader of Lithuania, Petras Griskevicius, is continuing in Snechkus's tradition because some of the successes of Snechkus's policies have been sustained even after his death. According to E. Finkelshtein, the replacement of Moscow officials by Lithuanians that Snechkus began still continues. The use of Lithuanian as the official language has noticeably increased in government institutions, social organizations, in the Lithuanian Academy of Science, in institutions of higher education, and in many service and industrial enterprises.

Zhenklys describes the attitude toward the future of nondissident Sovietized Lithuanians in the following manner:

By our own efforts, we cannot rid ourselves of Soviet totalitarianism. Neither could the Eastern Germans, the Hungarians, the Poles, the Czechs and the Slovaks, no matter how heroic their efforts. The West will not help us, just as they did not help these other peoples, since their goal is to strengthen the political status quo. In such a situation, the fate of all peoples enslaved by the Communists, including the Russians, is the same and will be decided in Moscow. The Soviet regime is doomed to destruction by the internal laws of its own development. That time is not far away. The Russian dissident movement, most visibly represented by such spiritual giants as Sakharov and Solzhenitsyn, is the symbol and the guarantee of the imminent end of Communism.

When Moscow finally ceases to be a Soviet, Communist citadel, Lithuania will also be liberated. That will happen even if the Lithuanians do nothing to bring that day closer by violent or underground resistance. Therefore, in order to preserve the nation it is undesirable to widely encourage such activities.

This inevitable liberation will not by itself create idyllic social or political conditions. Emotions that have so long been held in check by severe repression will emerge and be destructive. The conflicts they give rise to may well entail much bloodshed. The primary task of the Lithuanians is to avert such a turn of events. It is essential that preparations for this period begin now, so that the people are organized as much as possible and the bloodshed is kept at a minimum. This goal inspires the work of those Sovietized Lithuanian officials and intellectuals who have retained a vital sense of their nationality.[12]

This social stratum, however, should not be idealized. The majority of its members do not have strong national sentiments, but are unprincipled careerists, who, having enjoyed the fruits of power, are ready to do anything to preserve that power and unquestioningly carry out orders from Moscow. This is, conceivably, the reason that they have begun to replace Russian officials with Lithuanians.

The point of view expressed by Zenklys was prevalent for a long time in Lithuania and is now widespread. The position of the majority of Lithuanians is one of stubborn, but passive resistance to the occupation in expectation of eventual liberation, an attitude that proved conducive to the development of an active dissident movement once the country began to recover from its enormous losses. After many years of suspended animation, such a movement made its appearance openly at the beginning of the seventies in the form of national, religious, and civic opposition.

The national movement has inherited the goal of the national liberation movement of the forties and fifties: the liberation of Lithuania from Soviet occupation. But its methods are different. In any case, as far as is known, there have been no attempts at armed resistance, and reversions to partisan ideology are rare.

The national movement has its heroes and martyrs, but it lacks leadership and a clear organizational structure. It was, in the beginning, organized in underground cells, which had arisen at the time of the massive liberation movement, but the last underground cell, called the Movement for the Liberation of Lithuania, did not survive into the sixties.

The national movement began to organize at the beginning of the seventies. Those who were prepared to take an active part naturally concentrated into historical, literary, and local folklore circles and were called the "folklorists." This was a widely based movement. Unlike the national liberation movement of the forties and fifties, the folklorists did not set for themselves the goal of an immediate end to the occupation. Most of their practical efforts went into the preservation and study of national culture. The peaceful nature of this movement did not, however, protect it from destruction. Movement activists were put on trial in March 1974 in Kaunas. Four (Sarūnas Zukauskas, and his codefendants) were sentenced to prison-camp terms of from two to six years.[13] The folklore and other circles are still in existence, but they are now under watchful control by the authorities and are extremely restricted in their activities. There are also unpublicized study circles that concentrate on historical events, especially on the liberation movement of the forties and fifties, the study of which is officially prohibited. Now, however, the most active elements of the national movement have begun to group themselves around *samizdat* journals, whose editorial boards and authors are anonymous.

The first such journal to appear and the most popular is the literary and public-issue-oriented journal, *The Dawn* (*Ausra*), which began publication in November 1975. In 1976 *God and the Homeland* appeared, a conservative Catholic journal. The nationalistic *Messenger of Freedom* appeared the same year and after eight issues ceased publication in 1977 as a result of repressions against its staff. In 1977 appeared *The Way of Truth*, which was devoted to advice to priests on preparation of sermons and discussions of theological and church matters. In the same year the public-affairs-oriented journal *The Champion* appeared, as well as *The Bell*, first published by a group calling itself the Revolutionary Front for the Liberation of Lithuania (later it concentrated on questions of national culture).

The Dawn and *The Bell* borrowed their titles from uncensored journals published at the end of the nineteenth century. They began the numeration of the issues after the last numbered issue of their namesake journals. *The Dawn*, originally nationalistic in orientation, devoted a great deal of attention to Lithuanian history. The original *Bell* was a patriotic liberal journal that had in turn taken its name from a journal published from 1857 to 1867 in London by the Russian revolutionary, Aleksander Herzen. The contemporary journals continue these same traditions.

In 1978 the liberal *Perspectives* was published, its motto, "Respect the opinions of others, even if you do not share them." The religious-philosophical journal *The Shelter*, aimed at a younger audience, was issued that same year. In addition to these, there is the *Sorrowing Christ*, a journal devoted to religious and cultural problems and aimed at a wide circle of believers, and *Alma Mater*, founded in 1979, in commemoration of the four-hundred-year anniversary of Vilnius University (at least four issues were published). In 1980 several other periodicals appeared, among them: *The Future*, a Catholic and nationalist journal; *The Path of the Nation; The Voice of Lithuania; Down with Slavery;* and *Strength in Sobriety*, a magazine whose aim is to combat alcoholism. The *Lithuanian Archive* for many years has published a multi-volume collection of documents and memoirs on Lithuanian history, for the most part devoted to the national liberation struggle of the forties and fifties.

These *samizdat* periodicals reflect the entire spectrum of opinions and orientations that make up the present-day Lithuanian national movement. The range of opinion is extremely broad: from liberal to conservative (*God and the Homeland*); from strictly Catholic to religiously indifferent; irreconcilably anti-Marxist to the one neo-Marxist (*Perspectives*). It is worth repeating that not one of these journals advocates violence in order to put an end to the occupation of Lithuania.

The national movement also includes isolated individuals and small groups (united more by ties of friendship than by a formal structure), who put up slogans at night on the streets and in public buildings. The most frequently used slogans are "Freedom for Lithuania" and "Russians, Go Home." A common form of expressing nationalist sentiments on All Souls' Day and on other historically significant days is visiting the graves of political figures active during the period of Lithuania's independence and during the struggle for liberation. Flags are also flown on Independence Day (February 16).

The majority of political prisoners who participated in the national liberation movement were freed during the seventies. Some joined the present-day national movement. Balys Gajauskas belongs to this group. In 1948, at the age of twenty-two, he was sentenced to twenty-five years in camp and served the entire term. He learned several languages while in prison camp. Upon his release in 1977, he found work as an electrician. He was again arrested in 1977 on charges of gathering materials for the *Lithuanian Archive;* of translating Solzhenitsyn's *The Gulag Archipelago* into Lithuanian; of transmitting information about Lithuanian political prisoners to the *Chronicle of Current Events* and to the West; and of working with the Russian Fund to Aid Political Prisoners. His sentence was ten years in a special-regimen camp and five years of internal exile. His fiancée, Irena Dumbryte, was present at his trial. Their wedding took place in camp, and a daughter was born to Dumbryte in March 1980.

The most accurate indicators of the depth of nationalist sentiments and their explosive potential are spontaneous demonstrations, some of which are accompanied by violence. The first such demonstrations occurred in Vilnius and Kaunas on November 2, 1956, the Day of Commemoration for the Dead, at the same time as the Hungarian uprising. Most of the participants were students. There were some arrests and some expulsions from school, but this was still just a reverberation from the forties and fifties.

The demonstration in Kaunas on May 18–19, 1972 is directly related to the present-day Lithuanian national movement. It was initiated by a tragic event—the self-immolation of an eighteen-year-old Kaunas schoolboy, Romas Kalanta, in the square in front of the municipal theatre. A huge crowd gathered for the funeral, but the authorities prohibited the mourners from participating in the service. The crowd then made its way to the center of the city where the immolation had occurred. More people joined the procession, chanting, "Freedom! Lithuania!" and singing folk songs. An unfounded rumor spread that Kalanta's parents had been arrested, and the crowd went to the Kaunas Party Committee to demand that the parents be released. Attempts of the militia to disperse the crowd led to skirmishes. One militiaman was wounded by a rock (according to one account, he was killed).

On the next day, May 19, the demonstration was renewed, and troops were called into the city. Local authorities, together with Kalanta's parents, pleaded with the crowd to disperse, and it did so. About four hundred people were arrested, most of whom were questioned and released within a few hours. Some were held for a few days, and others received sentences of fifteen days. Eight were tried on charges of public disorder; all were between the ages of eighteen and twenty-five, all either workers or technical-institute students, apparently, typical in age and class of the majority of the participants in the Kaunas affair.[14]

Romas Kalanta was from a Sovietized, educated family. Indifferent to religion, he was inspired by the idea of national liberation. He became a national hero of Lithuania. Fearing an outbreak of national feeling, the authorities now increase police protection in all Lithuanian cities on the anniversary of Kalanta's immolation. On that day in 1976 posters demanding the liberation of Lithuania appeared on the streets and the sides of houses in Klaipeda. Under them was the name of Kalanta. On the anniversary of Kalanta's self-immolation, the placing of flowers at the site became a tradition.[15]

All other demonstrations in Lithuania took place during sports events, when the passions of large "unorganized" crowds were already aroused. Such demonstrations occurred in 1960 in Kaunas during the boxing championship timed to coincide with the twentieth anniversary of the Soviet regime in Lithuania. A pitched battle between spectators and the militia cost the lives of ten young people, according to *The Bell.* In June 1972, just a few days after Kalanta's death, many spectators refused to stand when the Soviet national anthem was played at an international volleyball match in Vilnius.[16] In November 1975, after the Lithuanian soccer team Zalgiris won a match in Vilnius, about 2,000 spectators who marched through the city shouting political slogans were dispersed by the militia and army troops.[17] The largest demonstration of this nature (from 10,000 to 15,000, according to eyewitness accounts) took place in Vilnius on October 10, 1977.[18]

These demonstrations are of particular interest because they tend to recur. The demonstration in Kaunas in 1972 was set off by an event tragic enough to stimulate a mass outburst of feeling. The age and the slogans ("Lithuania! Freedom!") of the Kaunas demonstrators may have been determined by Kalanta's own age and political activities. In contrast, demonstrations that occur during sports events are set off by such insignificant events that they doubtless reflect the ordinary everyday mood of the people. In the demonstrations of October 7 and 10, 1977, following the victory of the Zalgiris team over the second-rate White Russian Dvina team from Vitebsk and the Russian Iskra team from Smolensk, the intensity of feeling aroused could not be attributed to the sporting event itself, especially as the victory had no effect on the Zalgiris's chances for winning the cup.

The social composition of the demonstrators can be readily determined. About half of all the soccer spectators participated in the demonstration on October 10. The seating capacity of the Vilnius stadium is 25,000, and it was full at that time; thus we may conclude that the social composition of the demonstrators is the same as that of the soccer fans. Soccer fans range from young to middle age, are mostly men, and include industrial and office workers and technicians, and other workers typical of an urban population. This conclusion is supported by information on the demonstrators published in the Vilnius paper the *Evening News* (October 12, 1977). Those arrested included: V. Kiznis, a worker; Sofronov, an employee at a radio manufacturing plant; R. Augustinavicus, a student at the Vilnius Institute of Engineering and Construction; and a technical-school student A. Karcinskas.

Since the participants of this demonstration are a spontaneous sampling, an analysis of their slogans and behavior is of particular interest. The "disorders" began after the soccer match on October 7, 1977. Several hundred spectators, mostly young people, marched along the streets, shouting, "Down with the constitution of the invaders," "Freedom to Lithuania," and "Russians, go home." The demonstrators ripped up posters commemorating the sixtieth anniversary of the October Revolution and smashed shop windows displaying such posters.

At the next soccer match, the spectators began shouting anti-Soviet comments before the match was over. Forewarned by the events of October 7, the authorities had increased security at the stadium, bringing in troops made up mostly of central Asian soldiers. The crowd left the stadium flanked by two columns of soldiers. Once they were past the soldiers, they made their way to the center of the city. At the Zaljasis Bridge an additional five hundred people joined the crowd. After this, new slogans were added to the usual anti-Russian ones: "Freedom to political prisoners," "Let's go to the KGB," and "Free Petkus." In response to the next anti-Russian shout, someone yelled, "There are Russians here with you, too" and "For your freedom and for our freedom." The demonstrators broke through a barricade formed by the militia and KGB troops with interlocked arms and went on to Lenin Avenue. Only then were they stopped by a second detachment. A few militiamen were hospitalized. Windows of the Central Committee building of the Lithuanian Communist Party and other windows displaying posters of the sixtieth anniversary of the October Revolution were broken.

On October 7, seventeen people were detained, and on October 10, forty-four. There were expulsions from colleges and universities. Expulsions were especially high at the Institute of Engineering and Construction. Other students were expelled only from the Komsomol. Punitive measures were taken at some industrial plants. This data confirms our contention that the social composition of the demonstrators coincides with that of ordinary soccer fans.

Two points are of particular importance. Our source mentions only anti-Russian slogans at the stadium (the most common form of expressing national sentiments in Lithuania), but after the five hundred "outsiders" joined the crowd, the slogans took on a more specifically political character: "Down with the constitution," "Freedom to political prisoners," "Free Petkus," and the appeal, "Let's go to the KGB." This allows us to separate the demonstrators into the vanguard—those whose national sentiments were possibly fostered and developed by Lithuanian *samizdat*—and everyone else. The Russian demonstrators belonged to the vanguard (the slogan "For your freedom and for our freedom" suggests a familiarity with the history of the Russian and Polish liberation movements). I do not share Thomas Remeikis's skeptical attitude to the participation of Russians in such a demonstration, especially since people with Russian names were among those arrested, as Remeikis points out.[19]

The point is that in Lithuanian the word *laisve* (like the Russian *svoboda*) includes the meaning both of "independence" and "freedom." If the majority of Lithuanians are inspired by the dream of independence, freedom also is important to many of them. Russians living in Lithuania no doubt find freedom attractive, whether under Soviet rule or as a consequence of Lithuanian independence. It is possible for Russians to feel genuinely sympathetic to the aspirations for national independence of peoples comprising the Soviet Union, as has been demonstrated convincingly by Moscow civil rights activists. Here, I have in mind the position expressed by the *Chronicle of Current Events* and the Moscow Helsinki Watch Group. In addition, we know that of the five arrested for participating in the Estonian Democratic Movement, three were Estonian, but the leaders were a Russian, Sergey Soldatov, and a Ukrainian, Artyom Yuskevich. The reaction of the Lithuanian demonstrators to Russian participation in the demonstration is of great interest. However, we have no information on whether or not the anti-Russian slogans ceased once it was known that there were Russians among the demonstrators. At any rate, those who were near the Russians did not react as if they were offended that Russians had "wormed" their way into the demonstration. Here we probably can see the influence of those Russians who set the liberal tone for Lithuanian *samizdat* and for the Catholic movement; Lithuanians distinguish between Russians who are colonizers and Russians who are civil rights activists.

Certain witnesses of this demonstration, such as Mina and Mikhaelis Kublanovas, expressed the opinion that it was led by some organized conspiratorial force.[20] There is, however, no evidence for such a force in Lithuanian affairs either before or after the demonstration.

In 1976 Genrikas Jaskunas and his friend Jvozas Daujotas were arrested for distributing a manifesto of the Union of the Organization of Free Peoples;[21] in 1978 the creation of the League for a Free Lithuania was announced in *The Dawn* (*Ausra*, vol. 12). In 1979 three organizations were announced in *Perspectives*, nos. 5–7: the Union of Lithuanian Communists for the Secession of Lithuania from the USSR, the Initiative Group for the Protection of the Lithuanian Language, and the Movement for the Secession of Lithuania from the USSR. However, all these announcements look more like unrealized attempts to create such organizations rather than evidence of their activity. They indicate only that activists in the national movement feel the need to organize. The difficulty in finding a solution to this problem appears to lie in the heterogeneity of the movement, which makes unification feasible only in the form of small groups. The forces at the disposal of such groups suffice only to publish their own journal. Each such journal disseminates its own ideas on how to liberate Lithuania.

The Role of the Catholic Movement

In addition to the anonymous editorial boards of *samizdat* journals, there are two open social organizations in Lithuania: the Catholic Committee for the Defense of the Rights of Religious Believers and the Lithuanian Helsinki Group. Both are civil rights rather than nationalistic organizations.

The Catholic Committee for the Defense of the Rights of Religious Believers, the voice of the Catholic movement, is the best organized and the largest organization in Lithuania. Rural areas and small villages provide most of the Catholic Committee's support, although with the recent increase in Catholic influence, the movement has gained ground in large cities. The priests and active believers of the Lithuanian Catholic church play the leading role in this movement.

The oppression of the Catholic church began the moment Soviet troops entered Lithuania. On July 2, 1940, diplomatic relations with the Vatican were broken and the Concordat was annulled. Soon after this, all Catholic organizations were prohibited, Catholic schools were nationalized, and the Catholic press was shut down. Monasteries were looted. Of four Catholic seminaries, only one, the Kaunas seminary, continued to function, although its buildings were confiscated. The number of students there decreased from three hundred to one hundred fifty by 1946 and was further reduced to only twenty-five. In 1979 there were seventy-five students. In 1946–47, all bishops but one were arrested. The bishop of Vilnius, Mecislovas Reinys, perished in Vladimir Prison in 1953; the bishop of Telsiai Borisevičius was executed in 1947. During the forties and fifties approximately six hundred Lithuanian Catholic priests (more than a third) spent time in prison. Many churches were closed. As the *Chronicle of the Catholic Church in Lithuania* stated, "for many years the Catholic Church in the Soviet Union was moribund."[22]

The efforts of church officials were spent in preserving the church from complete destruction. Prevented from openly fulfilling all its religious functions, the church divided its activities into open and secret (catacomb) areas. This allowed the monasteries to continue their existence; the church to prepare young people for the priesthood, thus ensuring that the holy sacraments were given to those who could not openly visit the churches because of their position (teachers, high-ranking government officials, and Party members); and, most important, to prepare children for communion and the sacraments. The last point was the most sensitive one in the conflict between the church and the government. The church stresses the teaching of catechism, considered basic to preserving its function as a spiritual force in the life of the nation. Realizing the crucial nature of religious instruction, the authorities concentrated their efforts on interfering in precisely this area of church activities.

As the repression decreased, the secret catacomb activities of the church and the religious instruction of children increased. In 1970 the authorities tried to stop this activity in their usual way—by intensifying repressions against priests found guilty of teaching catechism. This created a reaction never seen before.

In September 1970, the priest Antanas Seskevicius was sentenced to one year in a strict-regimen camp for teaching catechism to grade-school and middle-school children at the request of their parents—a circumstance that makes the teaching perfectly legal. As a result of the sentence, a petition signed by more than a hundred priests from different dioceses was sent to the Central Committees of both the Lithuanian Communist Party and the Communist Party of the Soviet Union.[23]

In the summer of 1971 a protest was raised for similar reasons, not by priests this time, but by parishioners. On July 18, 1969 members of the Prienai parish sent a complaint to the Control Commission of the Central Committee of the Communist Party of the Soviet Union because local authorities prevented their priest, Jvozas Zdebskis, from testing children on their preparation to receive the eucharist. Zdebskis was arrested within a few days. A protest against his arrest sent to the prosecutor was signed by 450 believers. Another protest, dispatched to the Central Committee of the Communist Party of Lithuania and the chief prosecutor of Lithuania, was signed by 350 more. The trial took place in November. Six hundred of Zdebskis's sympathizers gathered around the courthouse. The militia beat and dispersed the crowd. Zdebskis was sentenced to one year in a general-regimen camp.

P. Bubnys, a village vicar, was tried along with Zdebskis for teaching catechism. He also received one year in a general-regimen camp. In

December of 1971, 1,344 Catholics of the Raseiniai parish in which Bubnys served sent a request to the Presidium of the Supreme Soviet of the USSR for Bubnys's release.[24]

In January 1972, 17,054 Lithuanian Catholics sent a memorandum to Brezhnev in which they listed the facts relating to violations of the rights of religious believers. They demanded that the freedom of conscience guaranteed by the Soviet Constitution be recognized for religious believers. The authors of the memorandum pointed to the obstacles they had experienced in collecting signatures for their petition and declared that if their complaints were not properly considered, they would appeal abroad, to the pope and to the United Nations. This they did in February 1972.[25]

Until May 1973 the memorandum to Brezhnev was a record for the greatest number of signatures on a protest petition. Preceding petitions had been signed almost exclusively by peasants pleading for "their" priest. The 1972 memorandum had signatures from peasants and city dwellers all over Lithuania, although there were more signatures from peasants.

Neither Brezhnev nor the United Nations answered the petition. Perhaps for this reason no new attempts in this direction were made for some time. At the beginning of 1980 another petition was sent to Brezhnev demanding that the cathedral in Klaipeda, which had been built at the expense of the believers and taken away from them in 1961 for use as an orchestra hall, be returned to them. The signatures on this petition came from throughout Lithuania, and the total number was 148,149—eight times as many as on the memorandum of 1972.[26]

It is impossible to assert on the basis of these figures that the strength of the Catholic movement in Lithuania has grown by the same proportion. However, this increase is very significant inasmuch as it is supported by increased activity for church rights by the main body of Lithuanian priests. For example, 31 out of 100 priests in the Vilnius diocese decided to sign the petition for the return from exile of Julijonas Steponavicius in 1970. In 1975, 61 priests from this diocese signed a petition in defense of arrested Catholics.[27] In 1978, out of a total of 708 Lithuanian priests, 552 or 78 percent, supported the much more "criminal" document no. 5 of the Catholic Committee, demanding the repeal of the Statute on Religious Associations issued by the Presidium of the Supreme Soviet of Lithuania in July 1976. Catholic priests announced that they could not and would not observe this statute because it contradicted the canons of the Catholic church. The statute is a slightly weaker version of the regulations with which the Russian Orthodox church has lived almost without protest since 1961.[28]

Publication of the *Chronicle of the Catholic Church in Lithuania,* an information bulletin that records violations of the rights of religious believers and related protest actions, began in March 1972. A large portion of the material in the Catholic *Chronicle* concerns students who are forced to renounce their faith and who, if they resist, are harassed to the point of expulsion from school. This material is presented in a special section of the publication, "In Soviet Schools." The *Chronicle of the Catholic Church in Lithuania* includes appeals and speeches by priests in defense of the rights of religious believers, as well as petitions and protests concerning restrictions on freedom of conscience in Lithuania.

The Catholic *Chronicle* has a significant circulation. Beginning in 1973 the authorities periodically conducted searches to uncover the publishers and confiscate issues. They confiscated not only typewriters, but a copy machine, rotary presses, hundreds of kilograms of printing type, a homemade printing press, a binder, stocks of paper, and so on.

The *Chronicle of the Catholic Church in Lithuania* became a notable factor in Lithuanian society and influenced public opinion. Sinkevicius, an employee of the Central Committee of the Lithuanian Communist Party, warned his audience at a teachers' conference in Siauliai, August 1975: "Any tactless blunder made by a teacher in conversation with a student who is a religious believer or his parents will appear in detail and without exaggeration, together with the name of the teacher, the school and the date, in that journal. It will be distributed not only at home, but abroad as well."[29]

The authorities have still not managed to identify the editorship of the *Chronicle of the Catholic Church in Lithuania*, although more than ten persons have been arrested for printing and distributing it. Among them was the thirty-two-year-old Nijole Sadunaite, who in 1974 was sentenced to three years of labor camp and three years of internal exile. Sadunaite became a national heroine after giving a bold speech at her own trial: "This is the most happy day in my life, for I am being tried for participating in the *Chronicle of the Catholic Church in Lithuania*, which is struggling against physical and spiritual tyranny. That means that I am on trial for truth and love for my people! I joyously enter slavery for the freedom of others, and I am willing to die that others might live."[30]

In November 1978 a special civil rights organization, the Catholic Committee for the Defense of the Rights of Religious Believers, was formed. Unlike the Catholic *Chronicle*, the committee announced the names of its members. It was founded by five priests, and three more priests joined in November 1980. On December 22, 1980 Vytautas Skuodis, a professor of geology at the University of Vilnius, was accepted into the organization. That same day he was tried for writing *Spiritual Genocide in Lithuania,* for working with *Perspectives* and *Alma Mater,* and for writing open letters to the heads of governments that signed the Helsinki Accords and to President Carter.

The Catholic Committee releases documents and appeals that contain information of actual violations of the rights of believers, and it interprets the illegality of persecutions on the basis of the Soviet Constitution and international agreements approved by the Soviet Union. The committee initiated the refusal of priests to observe the Statute on Religous Associations in view of its illegality and unconstitutionality. As mentioned above, about 78 percent of all Lithuanian Catholic priests supported the appeal of the Catholic Committee and warned the authorities that they would not observe the new regulations. In consequence, as a practical matter the new regulations are not in effect. In November 1980, the committee directed an appeal to the Madrid Conference of Signatories to the Helsinki Accords in which it described the situation of Catholics in Lithuania and noted actual cases of infringements of religious freedom and the rights of believers.

In contrast to the national movement in Lithuania, the Catholic movement is well organized. Its natural leaders are at the top of the Lithuanian Catholic church hierarchy—bishops Ju. Steponavicius and V. Sladkevicius. Both men had been exiled without trial from their dioceses to small villages in the north of Lithuania: Steponavicius in 1961 and Sladkevicius in 1959. They have since remained in internal exile for daring to disagree with the chairman of the Lithuanian Council on Religious Affairs and Cults. The Vatican has not deprived them of their rank and has not appointed other bishops to replace them. In 1968, Sladkevicius was allowed to return to his diocese. The majority of Lithuanian priests still consider both bishops their spiritual leaders and visit them regularly in exile for advice and to receive their blessing.

Priests make up much of the active body of the Catholic movement, which has become centered around the parish churches. There were 628 functioning churches as of 1980, served by 708 priests.[31] Since the population of Lithuania has preserved its homogeneity and the majority of ethnic Lithuanians are Catholic, the Lithuanian Catholic movement rests on a solid and massive mobile base, accounting for its success.

As Bishop Steponavicius said in a private conversation in October 1976, the Lithuanian Catholic church considers the attraction of young people its most important goal. The church has had undeniable success in this regard. According to the *Chronicle of the Catholic Church of Lithuania,* approximately 70 percent of all children take catechism lessons.[32] Official sources claim that only 30 percent of the graduates of Lithuanian schools are believers, but the Catholic *Chronicle* thinks these figures are understated. Although the Catholic *Chronicle* does not have the resources to gather comprehensive data for all of Lithuania, the official figures are contradicted by examples like the following: In January 1974, when government questionnaires were given to school graduates in the regional center of Lazdijai about their attitudes toward religion, sixteen of the twenty Komsomol students surveyed said that they were believers.[33]

Although traditionally strong in rural areas, the influence of the Catholic church in urban areas has been sharply reduced under Soviet rule, especially among the educated classes. Now the church is once again winning converts here. According to the Catholic *Chronicle*, "hundreds of thousands of young people, students, and intellectuals, disillusioned with atheism, are putting their hopes in the Gospels."[34] Instances of religious fidelity are not infrequent among Lithuanian officials, even top-ranking officials and Party members. They try to keep their ties with the church strictly secret, but they request in their wills that they be buried according to the rites of the church. Of late, some people such as V. Skuodis have begun to return openly to the church.

Even according to official data (most likely underestimated) taken from a report the Commissioner of Religious Affairs in Lithuania Kazimieras Tumenas delivered at the Kaunas Politechnical Institute in the autumn of 1974, 45 percent of all Lithuanian infants are baptized, 25 percent of all marriages are performed in church, and 51 percent of the population is buried according to religious rites.

The mass support of the church has compelled the authorities to make certain concessions. In January 1977, the chairman of the Council on Church Affairs, R. Makartsev, admonished Party officials to treat priests "more politely." He said that government policy toward the church is softening.[35] Some churches were permitted to ring their bells on holidays. Persecutions for the organization of religious processions occurred less frequently. The yearly quota of students permitted to enter seminaries was increased, and so forth. In recent years, the official policy toward the church has vacillated from "softer" to "harsher" and back again, but the position of the church in Lithuania is much better than that of other churches in the Soviet Union.

The Lithuanian Catholic movement has clear nationalist overtones, yet from its inception it has considered Russian dissidents to be friends and supporters. Because of its influence, the Catholic movement has made this attitude popular in Lithuania, particularly evident in *samizdat* publications.

From the first appearance of the *Chronicle of the Catholic Church in Lithuania,* its publishers had contacts with Moscow human rights activists and received their support in distributing the journal. Muscovites helped in getting the Catholic *Chronicle* to the West. When, in 1975 Sergey Kovalyov, a leading human rights activist, stood trial in Vilnius, the charges against him included possession of the Catholic *Chronicle* and using material from it to compile corresponding issues of the *Chronicle of Current Events.* The authorities had taken advantage of this circumstance to move the trial away from Moscow, with all its foreign correspondents, but this was a miscalculation. A trial in Vilnius of Russians accused of helping Lithuanian Catholics caught the attention of people normally uninterested in politics. It made a great impression on Lithuanians and widened their sympathy toward Moscow human rights activists. Andrey Sakharov and his fellow dissidents went to Vilnius to attend the trial of their friend. They were not allowed into the courtroom and so waited outside the courthouse. Informed of the trial by foreign radio broadcasts, many Lithuanians converged on the courthouse. In spite of the government's attempts to prevent sympathizers from reaching the courthouse, about fifty Lithuanians, most of them active in the Catholic movement, spent time with the visitors from Moscow. They invited the Muscovites to stay in their homes, and they celebrated together the granting of the Nobel Prize to Sakharov. They shivered together in front of the courthouse.[36] Personal contacts were made that strengthened friendly ties between both movements and helped promote the joint documents of the Moscow and Lithuanian Helsinki groups and the Christian and Catholic Committees for the Defense of the Rights of Religious Believers, as well as a constant exchange of materials and of yearly greetings between the *Chronicle of Current Events* and the *Chronicle of the Catholic Church in Lithuania.*

Surfacing at the beginning of the seventies, the Lithuanian Catholic movement is by no means the successor to the liberation movement of the forties and fifties. These movements differ from each other both in form and content. The goal of the liberation movement was the independence of Lithuania, to which end weapons were used. The Catholic movement is trying to achieve religious freedom by insisting that the Soviet Constitution and international agreements made by the Soviet Union on human rights be observed. The movement does not infringe on the prerogatives of the governmental system and uses only peaceful and legal means in its struggle. According to an anonymous report entitled "Problems of Religious Life in Lithuania and the Soviet Union," "the church has no intention of revolting or fighting against the Soviet system with force. It does not prohibit Catholics from serving in the army, from taking an active role in social affairs, or from working in government institutions and factories. Many Catholics are exemplary and trustworthy workers."[37]

By its nature, the Lithuanian Catholic movement is oriented towards human rights. Although it emphasizes religious freedom, it does not ignore other civil rights. The methods of the Catholic movement in Lithuania coincide entirely with those of the human rights movement. The Catholic movement in Lithuania is evolving through the same stages and in the same order as the human rights movement in the USSR. The time lag is growing shorter between the beginning of new phases of the human rights movement and the entry of the Catholic movement into those phases. Thus, the peak of the petition campaign in the human rights movement was reached at the beginning of 1968 and in Lithuania at the beginning of 1972. The *Chronicle of Current Events* appeared in April 1968, the *Chronicle of the Catholic Church in Lithuania* in March 1972. The Catholic Committee for the Defense of the Rights of Religious Believers appeared fewer than two years after the Christian Committee for the Defense of the Rights of Religious Believers in the USSR (in December 1976 and November 1978, respectively). A Lithuanian priest who is alleged to have worked with the *Chronicle* and is a member of the Catholic Committee, told me that the *Chronicle of the Catholic Church in Lithuania* was modelled after the Moscow *Chronicle* and that the similarity in their names was not accidental, but was meant to emphasize their interrelationship. The similarity between the names of the Lithuanian Helsinki Group, the Catholic Committee for the Defense of the Rights of Religious Believers, and the corresponding associations in Moscow (the Moscow Helsinki Group and the Christian Committee for the Defense of the Rights of Religious Believers in the USSR) probably has the same explanation. But this does not mean that the Lithuanian Catholic movement is a product or an imitation of the human rights movement. The close similarities between the activities of both groups follow from similarities between the aims and strategies of movements that arose and developed independently of one another. Since their goals are identical, it is natural that the later Catholic movement would borrow from the experience of the human rights movement and, in particular, from its organizational structure. The *Chronicle of the Catholic Church in Lithuania,* as well as the Catholic Committee, has more than once expressed its gratitude to the human rights activists and especially to academician Andrey Sakharov and Sergey Kovalyov for their support of the right to religious freedom. Every issue of the *Chronicle of the Catholic Church in Lithuania* ends with an appeal to the reader, asking him to pray for those who "wear prison chains so that you might be able to live and believe in freedom." Among Lithuanian Catholics, Kovalyov's name is frequently mentioned, and the Catholic Committee for the Defense of the Rights of Religious Believers has taken up the cause of Russian human rights activists—not only that of Sakharov, but those of Tatyana Velikanova and the Orthodox priest Gleb Yakunin as well.[38]

The Lithuanian Helsinki Watch Group

It is possible that a human rights movement in the purest sense is not well developed in Lithuania because of the influence, popular support, and other strengths—mentioned above—of the Lithuanian Catholic movement.

The initiator of the human rights movement was the Lithuanian Helsinki Watch Group, organized in connection with the Moscow Helsinki Watch Group a half-year after that group was organized. On December 1, 1976 its formation was announced at a press conference in Moscow called by the Moscow Helsinki Watch Group, and its first document was issued together with the Moscow Group.

The founders of the Lithuanian Helsinki Watch Group were Karolis Garuckas, a Catholic priest, Tomas Venclova and Ona Lukauskaite-Poskiene, representatives of the Lithuanian intelligentsia, and the physicist, Eitan Finkelshtein, a Jewish refusenik. The central figure in the organization is Viktoras Petkus, a long-time activist in the Catholic movement.[39] He has already spent sixteen years in prison camp. Devoted to the liberation of Lithuania, Petkus is knowledgeable about Lithuanian history and culture and has the best collection of Lithuanian poetry in the country.

The Lithuanian Helsinki Watch Group began with the support of the Catholic movement. Its first document was devoted to the internal exile of bishops Steponavicius and Sladkevicius, and its second to the Statute of Religious Associations approved by the Presidium of the Lithuanian Supreme Soviet in July 1976. The group noted the discrepancy between this statute and the Final Act of the Helsinki Accords. Afterwards, the group dealt with problems that went beyond the interests of the Catholic and national movements. Later documents discussed discrimination against ethnic Germans living in Lithuania, violations of the right to emigrate (including non-Lithuanians), and the situation of former political prisoners not only in Lithuania, but in Latvia and Estonia as well.[40]

In the winter of 1977 Tomas Venclova was granted permission to travel to the United States to give some lectures. In an agreement with the Lithuanian Helsinki Group, he announced that he represented the group abroad, whereupon he was stripped of his Soviet citizenship. In August Viktoras Petkus was arrested, and in the spring of 1979 Karolis Garuckas died of cancer (before his death, Pope John Paul II sent his blessing). Garuckas was replaced by Bronis Laurinavicius, a priest from the village of Adutiskis. Activists of the Catholic movement, Mecislovas Jurevicius and Vytautas Vaiciunas, and activists of the national movement, Algirdas Statkevicius and Vytautas Skuodis, joined the Lithuanian Helsinki Watch Group.

After the arrest of Petkus, the group ceased to be the center of opposition, as were its counterparts in the Russian and Ukrainian republics. However, its purely human rights position made it a focal point for the forces of opposition in the neighboring republics of Latvia and Estonia.

For a number of reasons, dissent in these two republics was weaker than in Lithuania. Their common fate could serve as the basis for mutual actions (all the Baltic countries were occupied at the same time in accordance with the Molotov-Ribbentrop Pact), but the strong overtones of Catholic and nationalist tendencies of Lithuanian dissent have not been favorable to joint actions with neighboring non-Lithuanian and non-Catholic countries. The idea of joint opposition to the occupation gave rise to the formation of the underground organization, the Baltic Federation, in 1962 in Latvia. However, the name of the organization reflected only its intentions: in fact, all its members were Latvian.

Before his arrest, Petkus had begun to work on the creation of the Head Committee of the National Movements of Estonia, Latvia, and Lithuania. Former political prisoners questioned about this committee in connection with charges brought against Petkus included Lithuanians, Latvians, and Estonians.[41]

In the autumn of 1979, the idea of cooperative effort was realized in the so-called Appeal of the Forty-five, timed to coincide with the fortieth anniversary of the Molotov-Ribbentrop Pact. The authors of the Appeal disavowed the Pact and called upon the Soviet government to renounce the gains resulting from it. Most of the signatories were Lithuanians, but there were four Estonian and four Latvian signatures.[42] The Lithuanian Helsinki Watch Group devoted document no. 18 to the Appeal of the Forty-five and argued the demands of the Appeal on legal grounds.[43]

The authorities reacted with a wave of searches and interrogations. Three Lithuanians and two Estonians who had signed the appeal were arrested, sentenced, and imprisoned.[44]

Close in spirit to the Appeal of the Forty-five was an open letter on the Soviet invasion of Afghanistan, signed by twenty-one people: three

Estonians, one Latvian, and seventeen Lithuanians. The authors of the letter supported the resolution of the United Nations General Assembly on the immediate withdrawal of foreign troops from Afghanistan. They mentioned the fact that the Baltic countries, like Afghanistan, had had agreements of friendship and mutual aid with the Soviet Union and that, in 1940, Soviet troops had been sent into these countries, as they were recently sent into Afghanistan, all after these agreements. "So, the Estonian, Latvian, and Lithuanian peoples understand both the aims and the future results of such actions," the open letter said.[45]

Like its Ukrainian counterpart, the Lithuanian Helsinki Watch Group was destroyed by arrests. In the spring of 1981 Skuodis, Statkevicius, Vaiciunas, and Jurevicius were arrested. The priest Laurinavicius was called to Vilnius after a harsh article appeared about him in the newspaper *Tiesa;* he was hit by a truck while crossing the street.[46]

Attacks on Priests: Covert State Action?

The killing of Laurinavicius was the third instance of a suspicious death of a priest in 1980–81. Leonas Sapoka, a priest of the Telsiai diocese, was killed in his home on the night of November 10–11, 1980. A few days before his death, he was attacked in print in *Tiesa*. The priest Leonas Mazeika, who signed the appeal of the Catholic Committee that new restrictive church regulations not be carried out, was killed on August 8, 1981, also in his home. He was not robbed. These murders took place against a general background of attacks on priests, something that previously had been quite rare. On March 10, 1980 the dean of a church in Siluva was wounded with a knife; on April 28 the priest in Karmelava was beaten; on September 12, the chancellor of the Kaunas diocese was beaten; on October 12 an attempt was made to break into the home of Rev. Vladislav Zavalnyuk and, the following night, into his mother's apartment; and on October 18, a priest in Griskabudis received several knife wounds. Several churches were robbed and burned, and Catholic relics were defiled during the same period. In none of these instances were the culprits found.[47]

It was rumored that KGB agents and criminals acting on KGB instructions were responsible for these acts.

The punitive arm of the state has not dared openly to undertake any actions against priests. From 1971–1983, there was no case of an arrest of a priest, even though the church has been much more active in Lithuania than in any other republic of the Soviet Union. Reluctant to arrest Catholic priests and realizing that the weakening of the repression was unleashing an initiative by the priests, the KGB may have resorted to Mafioso methods. These methods would allow the KGB to avoid any direct links to the reprisals, but at the same time to frighten every priest.

The reaction to these attacks was swift and harsh. The Council of Priests of the Telsiai diocese, a group of twelve men to which Sapoka belonged before his death, sent a complaint to the general prosecutor of the USSR. The Catholic Committee sent one to the prosecutor of Lithuania. Both documents openly pointed out the participation of the authorities in crimes against the church and its members. The Catholic Committee stated that "all these crimes . . . are somehow intrinsically linked together" and that believers see them as "conscious, calculated acts aimed at the increased authority and influence of the Church in Lithuania." They said that connivance in these crimes "was compromising the Soviet government," which supports atheists and enemies of the church. The members of the Catholic Committee pleaded with the prosecutor of Lithuania: "We beg you to take serious measures to restrain this Soviet mafia and to institute criminal proceedings against these criminals."[48]

Sapoka's murderers were found within a year. (Father Bronis Laurinavicius was killed a few days before the trial.) Theirs was an open trial, and persuasive evidence was given that the motive was robbery. However, the personalities and biographies of the killers suggest that they expected to be able to rob priests without being punished for the crime. The progress of the investigation substantiated their hopes, until the government changed its plan, possibly under the influence of public opinion.

An article that appeared about the trial in the newspaper *Soviet Lithuania* (December 16, 1981) stressed the mercenary motive of the crime; it was explained that this incident was used to implicate the authorities in reprisals against priests. The newspaper cited a statement made by the priests of the Telsiai diocese: "There is reason to suppose that in this case employees of the Ministry of Internal Affairs either did not want to reveal who the sadistic murderers were or had not found a statute in the criminal code under which to prosecute them. What is more, the investigators did not ask about the crimes committed, but about the shortcomings of the priests." The citation was taken from Radio Vatican, which broadcast the statement.

If the murder of Father Laurinavicius was committed on instructions from the KGB, as the *Chronicle of the Catholic Church of Lithuania* (no. 50) asserts, then by putting Sapoka's murderers on trial the murder was timed to squelch accusations that the authorities were allowing killers of priests to go unpunished. Many people were convinced of the KGB's involvement in Laurinavicius's murder by an

event that occurred soon afterwards. On December 20, Richard Cerniauskas, twenty-eight-year-old priest of the St. Nicholas Church in
Vilnius, announced after Sunday mass that he had been warned by a
KGB agent that he might "unexpectedly die." Father Cerniauskas was
known for his protests against religious persecutions in Lithuania. In
the summer of 1981 during the rite of recollection, which was performed near the town of Moletai, fifty young parishioners belonging to
his cathedral were driven away by the militia, while Cerniauskas was
beaten up. He spent a few days under arrest, but even after this incident he did not moderate his participation in the Catholic movement.[49]

Other Trials, 1980–1984

From 1972 to 1983 the authorities did not dare arrest priests. Instead
they tried to hold back the development of the Catholic movement in
Lithuania by arresting laypersons on charges of organizing religious processions—rather than the priests who actually organized the events. In
1980 Jadvyga Stanelyte was sentenced to three years in camp for organizing the largest procession in Lithuania, the yearly procession to
Siluva. She had stood with a flag at a crossroad by which the procession passed. The car that transported her from the courthouse was
strewn with flowers.[50]

In 1981, Mecislovas Jurevicius and Vytautas Vaiciunas, members of
the Lithuanian Helsinki Watch Group, were charged with the same
crime and given the same sentence. While admitting their participation
in the procession, both men denied playing any role in its organization.
Jurevicius, a house painter and deeply religious man, declared in court
that he was being judged by a minority that feared the majority (since
religious believers make up 70 percent of the population, according
to official statistics). It was a great honor, he said, for him to sit in
the same defendant's chair in which church-rights activists Stanelyte,
Sadunaite, Kovalyov, and Skuodis had sat before him.[51]

There were several other trials of Lithuanian samizdat activists in
1980–81. The authors and compilers of Perspectives, Alma Mater, and
the nationalistic Champion, as well as those who were involved in
reproducing the Chronicle of the Catholic Church of Lithuania, sat in
the defendant's chair.[52] All together, twenty persons were tried on
political charges during 1980–81. In proportion to the number of participants in the movement, this number is considerably fewer than,
say, in the Ukraine. The sentences also were much lighter. In 1978,
two persons, V. Petkus and B. Gajauskas, received the maximum sentence for "anti-Soviet propaganda" and in 1981, only one, V. Skuodis.[53]
Twenty altogether were sentenced for political reasons.

It is entirely possible that the comparatively mild nature of political oppression in Lithuania is a result of Lithuania's proximity to Poland. Events in Poland are reflected in two ways in Lithuania: the major role of the Catholic church in Polish resistance inspires and activates the Lithuanian Catholic church and her adherents. At the same time, Lithuanian nationalist *samizdat* has become much more harsh, and at times an anti-Polish note can be detected, no doubt due to past Polish attempts to subjugate Lithuania. Nationalist passions have been roused to such a pitch that they can even be felt by Catholics who were formerly restrained in expressing them.

The first arrest of a priest in Lithuania after a twelve-year hiatus came in January 1983 when Fr. Alfonsas Svarinskas, a member of the Catholic Committee, was arrested. His sentence was harsh: seven years of strict-regimen labor camp and three years of exile. On the day of Svarinskas' trial, another member of the Catholic Committee, Fr. Sigitas Tamkevicius, was arrested and sentenced to six years' strict-regimen labor camp and four years of internal exile. These arrests were part of the sharp increase in persecution of dissenters throughout the Soviet Union that coincided with the Soviet invasion of Afghanistan and the end of detente in late 1979. By the time that Lithuanian priests were being arrested, all open human rights associations in other republics had been repressed by arrests, and the Catholic Committee was the only such association that had thus far been untouched by the KGB.

We have treated the three movements of Lithuanian dissent here—national, Catholic, and human rights—as three separate entities. In fact, it is not always possible to separate them. They are tightly interrelated by ideology and through their participants, not only in the sense that participants of different movements have close contacts with each other and often undertake joint actions, but also in the sense that many persons active in Lithuanian dissent, such as V. Petkus and V. Skuodis, can with equal justification be considered members of two or even of all three movements.

CHAPTER 3

The Estonian
National-Democratic Movement

Estonia was occupied by Soviet forces in the summer of 1940, at the same time as Latvia and Lithuania. In Estonia, as in the other two Baltic countries, immediately after the occupation persecution of actual and potential opponents of the new authorities began. At the beginning of 1941, 10,000 Estonians were caught up in a wave of arrests and deportations. The nation had already suffered great casualties during the Second World War and in 1944 the return of the Soviet Army to Estonia provoked a massive emigration the extent of which is not known. According to an Estonian *samizdat* document of 1982,[1] "tens of thousands" of Estonians left their homeland. From 1944 to 1953, there were constant arrests. Arrests and deportations reached an apex in 1949 when 40,000 Estonians were arrested or deported. By 1956, as a result of these losses, of 995,000 Estonians who had lived in their homeland in 1939 (the end of the period of Estonia's independence) every fifth person had either died or left the country. In 1982 in Estonia there were 948,000 Estonians, that is, 4.7 percent fewer than before the war.[2]

In Estonia, as in most of the non-Russian Soviet republics, a planned "dilution" of the native population has been brought about through in-migration of Russians. As a result of this policy, Estonians, who made up 88.2 percent of the population in independent Estonia, make up only 64.7 percent of the population of Soviet Estonia. From 1959 to 1979 the Estonian population of the republic increased by 50,000 and the Slavic population (Russians, Ukrainians, and Byelorussians) increased by 201,000 (from 267,000 in 1959 to 468,000 in 1979).[3] The immigrant population grew most rapidly in key areas—Tallinn, the capital of Estonia, the other large cities, new industrial centers, mining regions, and seaports. There are large military contingents located on the territory of Estonia; these are also non-Estonian. The soldiers, together with their families, make up a significant part of the growing immigrant population.

A *samizdat* document prepared by fifteen Estonian intellectuals in 1982 describes the development of relations between the central authorities and the Estonians in the post-Stalin era:

In the era of Khrushchev's reforms (the second half of the 1950s and beginning of the 1960s), Estonians began to hope for a future for their people and their national culture. These hopes were maintained by the rehabilitation of Stalin's victims, a welfare program adopted by the Communist Party in 1961, promises of greater autonomy in the national republics, an orientation towards a more cultivated and modern economy (along with an increase in the manufacturing of consumer goods) and some awakening of Estonian national culture after the Stalinist repression. Many hoped to direct the development along the lines of socialism with a human face, replacing the clique of Russian bureaucrats and Russified Estonians who had grown up in the Soviet Union with national leading cadres who would manage the economy more intelligently with a consideration of local interests.

A reduction in the development of heavy industry was promised, as was an increase in production limited to the increase in the productivity of labor. It was also promised that no new large factories would be built in Tallinn. All of this was supposed to limit the flow of Russian immigrants into Estonia. The explosive growth of Tallinn should have been stopped. And in conclusion, a hope appeared that along with the successful resolution of the problems of disarmament, the degree of Estonia's militarization would decrease, part of the Russian garrison would be withdrawn and the opportunity for a closer relationship with Western countries would increase. Therefore, the future did not seem so gloomy. Sometimes it seemed that for the existence and development of the people, a kind of living space was beginning to form.[4]

The first secretary of the Central Committee of the Communist Party of Estonia, Ivan Kebin, obtained for Estonia the special unwritten status of "testing ground" for the nationalities policy of the central government, with the "regime of most favor." Thus at first, Estonia's output was used to satisfy the needs of Estonia itself and only the excess was exported. Specialists who obtained their education in Estonia remained to work in the republic. The preservation of national cadres promoted the teaching of the Estonian language, not only in schools but in institutes of higher learning, sharply reducing the flow of students from other parts of the USSR.[5]

Apparently, it was precisely because of this special status for Estonia that there was, up until the mid-1960s no trace of underground or open citizens' movement opposing the authorities. With the development of national consciousness and democratic aspirations, the energy of the Estonians was directed toward utilizing the possibilities for national development offered to them by the authorities. These opportunities were available not only in the economy but in culture.

An Estonian friend of mine, a director of a research institute and a Party member, explained in 1961, "The Moscow Party bosses do not speak Estonian." That fact has given the Estonians a great deal of freedom in their educational system and has made it easier to "smuggle" forbidden materials and opinions into books and journals. For example, the Estonian-Soviet encyclopedia, which appeared in the sixties, carried relatively objective articles on Trotsky, Bukharin, and others. This would be unthinkable in a comparable Russian publication Estonian intellectuals valued this contact, however limited, with a wide audience. Nor did they wish to risk it by participating in *samizdat* publications, where they could be totally sincere since its readership was much more limited and less accessible; the danger of arrest was quite real. Perhaps this is why the *samizdat* in Estonia was scant until the middle of the 1970s. Only a few articles and appeals were circulated, and, as a rule, written anonymously or under pseudonyms. Their political and moral influence was greatly reduced as a consequence.

With the change of leaders in the Kremlin in October 1964, policy in regard to Estonia changed:

> By the end of the 1960s, a sharp turn backwards had already taken place in the direction of a strict and harsh Moscow centralism, based on the principle that the interests of the empire were higher than all others. The autonomy of the national regions, already not very significant, began to be restricted even further. All the most important branches of the economy of the national republics were subjected to the All-Union Ministers. Since nothing came of stimulating the growth of labor productivity, stress was once again placed on an extensive development of manufacturing, i.e. on the construction of large new factories and the importing of non-Estonian labor. . . .
>
> The change in the circumstances were politically symbolized in the expulsion in 1978 of Ivan Kebin, who had been first secretary of the Estonian Communist Party for many years. The efforts of communists in Estonia to promote an Estonian to the head of the party suffered complete disaster when, with direct interference from Moscow, a new head of the party was assigned who had been born in Siberia, spoke Estonian very poorly, and who did not have the support of even the ruling circles in Estonia. This was the Russophile Karl Vaino. Vaino's rise to power was virtually a slap in the face to the local Estonian communists who had been trying for a long time to promote their own people to the leading posts in the party. Vaino dem-

onstrated as well Moscow's deep distrust in the loyalty of the nomenklatura of the national regions.[6]

The change in the relations with Moscow also changed the public climate in Estonia. The *samizdat* document summarizes it: "The first half of the 1970s paralyzed the hope of the Estonian people for a future . . . during the second half in the national circles a mood of subjection, hopelessness, and fear began to reign."[7]

During the second half of the 1970s the economic situation in the Baltic states, where the standard of living is higher than in most areas of the USSR, deteriorated sharply. The overall worsening of the food supply stimulated the "Moscow bosses" to ship out of the Baltic states most of the foodstuffs produced there. At the same time, the policy on language was tightened up. Efforts to introduce Russian into the educational system, as well as into all other spheres of life, were intensified in all the non-Russian republics, including Estonia. All of this aggravated the awareness of the fact that Estonia was an occupied country, and increased the hostility toward the occupiers. These feelings are reflected in a letter by Estonian intellectuals to a Finnish newspaper:

Foreign tourists are first struck by the oversaturation of Tallinn with military personnel and policemen which inevitably creates the impression of an occupied city. In the center of town, it is rare not to see persons in uniform. The mood of Estonians about this "internationalization" of their home town is truly depressed. In the center of town one can still communicate and carry out business in the native tongue but in the new residential areas of the town this is usually impossible. Thousands of Estonians suffer numerous psychological traumas day in and day out when in a store or an office they stumble on the fact that the Russian personnel do not understand the Estonian language, nor do they want to understand it, and thus force them to communicate in Russian. In such cases Estonians keep asking themselves fearfully, where am I anyway? Is this really my home town? And is this really my native country?[8]

The Beginning of the Dissident Movement

In 1970 three separate political trials took place in Estonia: that of Villi Saarte; of four Estonians (Raivo Lapp, Andres Vosu, Enn Paulus and Kiiv) for attempting to create an underground Estonian national party; and the Baltic fleet officers Gennady Gavrilov, Georgy Paramonov, and Aleksey Kosyrev for their participation in the underground Union for the Struggle for Democratic Rights.[9] In 1975 members of the underground organization, the Estonian Democratic Movement, were put on trial. Of the five members of the Estonian Democratic Movement, the two most prominent were not Estonian—Sergey Soldatov, a Russian, and Artyom Yuskevich, a Ukrainian. Although the organization was called the Estonian Democratic Movement, the emphasis was probably not nationalistic, but rather democratic.

The Estonian Democratic Movement made the first attempts to create a *samizdat* publication in Estonia. The members of the organization published two journals in Russian, *The Democrat* and *The Ray of Freedom,* and a few issues of two magazines in Estonian, *The Estonian Democrat* and *The Voice of the Estonian People.*[10] When the Estonian Democratic Movement was broken up by the authorities, these journals ceased publication.

In the second half of the 1970s Estonian *samizdat* grew rapidly. By 1978 a bibliographic index, *The Most Important Samizdat Works,* had already been published; and the collection *Supplementary Materials on the Free Dissemination of Ideas and Information in Estonia,* the Estonian equivalent of the Moscow *Chronicle of Current Events,* and *The Saturday Gazette* were appearing twice monthly in the university town of Tartu.[11] No other *samizdat* periodical has appeared as regularly, as far as is known.

One indication of the wide dissemination of Estonian *samizdat* at the end of the 1970s is the large amount of materials confiscated during searches, not only in cities, but also in fishing villages and on farms. It is possible that *samizdat* was prepared primarily on farms, since it is more difficult to uncover such activity there.

The authorities tried to combat the spread of Estonian *samizdat* by the only means possible—arrests. From 1978 to 1980 three arrests are known to have been made in connection with the authorship or dissemination of *samizdat* materials: the architect Viktor Niitsoo, the worker Tiit Madisson and the engineer Veljo Kalep.[12] In 1983 four more *samizdat* arrests followed: in Tallinn, Johannes Hint, physicist and mathematician and *samizdat* author; Heiki Ahonen, chimney sweep and *samizdat* distributor; and in Tartu, Lagle Parek, woman architect and Arvo Pesti, who had been expelled from the university and was working as a fireman. These arrests were accompanied by numerous searches in Tallinn, Tartu and other Estonian towns, and everywhere *samizdat* was found.[13]

On the basis of its goals, the Estonian movement may be defined as national-democratic in orientation. The participation of young people is characteristic of this movement. It is perhaps the only dissident movement in the USSR in which the majority are primarily high-school students, rather than university students.

One of the most widespread ways in which Estonian youth demonstrates its nationalistic sentiments is by flying the national flag, particularly on Estonian Independence Day, February 24. In 1980, five young Estonians were tried and convicted of "hooliganism" for doing this. During 1981–1983 twenty-two people were convicted of ripping up or burning Soviet flags.[14]

However, the most frequent form of mass participation in the nationalist-democratic movement became the demonstration. The first such demonstration took place in Tartu on September 22, 1978. Approximately 150 high-school students gathered in front of the headquarters of the City Party Committee and the Komsomol. Shouting slogans like "Slavs, get out," "Long live the Estonian Republic," and "More education, less politics," they tore down signs on the buildings and were dispersed by the militia. "Discussions" were held with the organizers, but no one was arrested.[15]

On Christmas Eve, 1979 in Tartu a large crowd made its way to the cemetery to place candles on the graves of relatives and countrymen who had perished during the war in 1918–20. Afterwards many went to the city square to listen to speeches about freedom and national independence. The militia detained several persons, but they were soon released. On New Year's Eve the meeting at the cemetery was repeated. Among the participants were secondary students and university students.[16]

Nationalist Demonstrations

In 1980 there were several demonstrations in Tallinn. The first, on September 22, was caused by the cancellation of a rock concert by the Propellers, who were scheduled to appear after a soccer match. The concert was cancelled because its organizers discovered "nationalistic themes" in the texts of the songs to be performed. At least a thousand people participated in the demonstration, and there were some conflicts with the militia who dispersed the crowd. Some senior-high-school students were expelled for their participation in the demonstration. These expulsions caused new demonstrations in Tallinn on October 1 and 2 in front of City Hall, at the Baltic train station, at the monument of the Estonian writer, A. H. Tamsaare, and on Harju Hill. About five thousand people took part in these. The demonstrators waved flags of an independent Estonia and shouted, "Freedom to Estonia," "Russians—out of Estonia," "Truth and justice," and other slogans. They also demanded improvements in school conditions. The demonstration was broken up by the militia, who beat up many demonstrators. About 150 were detained and released after being identified. Ten people remained under arrest, but the names of only two are known: Alan Sepp, a technical school student, and Boris Serdyuk. They were both tried for "hooliganism."

Local newspapers in both Russian and Estonian (*Sovietskaya Estonia* and *Rahva Hääl*) and Tallinn radio reported "disorders" and the filing of criminal charges against some of the participants. Official sources put the number of demonstrators at a thousand. More expulsions from school followed these demonstrations. On October 7 and 8 there were further demonstrations protesting these expulsions, but they were much smaller—a few hundred people. Russian secondary-school students participated in these demonstrations.[17]

But there were also demonstrations by Russian teenagers against their rivals, the Estonians. After the October 5 demonstration, Russian schoolchildren wrote on walls: "Fascists out of Estonia!" The *samizdat* document written by fifteen Estonian intellectuals states:

During . . . the demonstrations of the Estonian youth in 1980, solidarity grew between the older and younger generations among the Russians. There was even collaboration and mutual help. During the day, shock troops made up of Russian policemen beat 13 sixteen-year-old schoolboys, and at night this same "activity" was continued "volunteer fashion" by Russian teenagers armed with weapons. There were incidents when high party functionaries justified this kind of "activity" by Russian adolescents. For example Zoya Shishkina, a well-known party figure, said at a meeting in a Tallinn institution at the time: "In our Russian schools teenagers are readying brass knuckles and knives now. This is only natural—we must defend *ourselves!*"[18]

While these demonstrations were taking place in Tallinn, about one thousand workers at the agricultural machinery plant in Tartu Katseremonditehas went on strike (October 1 and 2). They demanded that a recent increase in output quotas be rescinded, that delayed work bonuses be paid, and that improvements be made in the supply of goods and food in Tartu. A special commission was sent from Moscow and the workers' demands were partially met: the previous production quotas were reinstated and the bonuses were paid.[19] I doubt that these events had a direct connection with the demonstrations in Tallinn, but they were a reflection of the general state of agitation existing in a small republic.

The demonstrations of young people in Tartu, Parnu and other Estonian cities on October 10 were in direct response to the demonstration in Tallinn. In Tartu, besides a show of nationalist posters, the demonstrators demanded the dismissal of the Minister of Education of Estonia, Elza Grechkina, the first Russian to hold that post in Soviet Estonia. She was appointed in July, 1980.

On October 11, the Minister of Internal Affairs, Marko Tibar, made a radio speech calling for an end to the demonstrations. At the school meetings with parents were held and they were threatened with dismissal from their jobs in retaliation for their children's participation in demonstrations. Later in the month Yury Andropov, the head of the KGB, visited Estonia. About one hundred students were expelled, and the number of arrests grew to 20.[20]

On September 17, 1982, a student demonstration took place in Tartu, with about five thousand young people. At the celebrations on the occasion of the 350th anniversary of Tartu University the demonstrators demanded that the statue of the university's founder, the Swedish king Gustav Adolph II, which had been removed after the imposition of Soviet power in Estonia, be restored to its place near a university building. The demonstrators sang patriotic Estonian songs and shouted out slogans against Russification. On September 19, before a building for foreign guests who had arrived for the anniversary celebration, a red Soviet flag was replaced by the national Estonian flag. When the police noticed it, they took it down.[21]

In the Estonian youth movement an extremist tendency appeared together with democratic tendencies. At the end of the seventies an armed underground resistance group was formed in Tallinn. Imre Arakas was the leader. In order to procure arms for the group, Arakas organized the robbery of the storehouse of an amateur sports group, Dinamo. He was arrested early in 1979 and charged with "banditry." During the trial, armed supporters forced their way into the courtroom and released their leader. In mid-1979 Arakas fired at the car of the First Secretary of the Estonian Communist Party, Karl Vaino. Vaino escaped injury, but at the end of the year Arakas was arrested and sentenced to 12 years of imprisonment. He is presently serving his sentence at the Vilnius prison, Lukishki.[22] Arakas' group is the only known case of an armed underground organization in the Baltic republics (or in the USSR, for that matter) in the seventies. With this exception, the youth movement in Estonia has been peaceful and open.

The national-democratic movement in Estonia attracted not only "raw" youth, but mature people as well, although only a handful until the beginning of the 1980s. Three have come forth publicly: Mart Niklus, Enn Tarto, and Erik Udam. All three have already served out sentences on political charges. While in prison they met Lithuanian dissidents, among whom they made personal friends. From time to time all three had signed statements, composed by Lithuanians, on the fate of the Baltic republics. But no one else in Estonia supported Lithuanian dissent, since there was no sympathy for the Catholic or for the Lithuanian nationalist overtone of that dissent. Although Niklus, Tarto, and Udam are admired by their compatriots, they are still considered outsiders.

On August 23, 1979, the fortieth anniversary of the so-called Ribben-tropp-Molotov Pact, the citizens of the Baltic republics issued a public appeal demanding publication of the full text of the pact and, in particular, the secret addenda on which basis Soviet troops invaded the Baltic countries. The citizens included demands that the governments of the USSR, East, and West Germany declare the pact invalid and that the Atlantic Charter countries condemn the Stalin-Hitler agreement and all its consequences. The authors asked Kurt Wald-heim, General Secretary of the United Nations, to bring up this question before the United Nations General Assembly. There were forty-eight signatures to the appeal, and, as usual, they were mostly Lithuanian. Three Estonians signed it: Niklus, Udam, and Tarto.[23]

A change in the situation in the Baltic states can be dated from the beginning of 1980. In January 1980, a protest against the Soviet invasion of Afghanistan was signed by Mart Niklus and Juri Kukk, who belonged to the scientific establishment in Estonia, and who personally gave the protest letter to foreign correspondents in Moscow.[24]

Juri Kukk was a research assistant at Tartu University and had a Ph.D. in chemistry. A Party member since 1966 and even a Party Bureau member, he resigned from the Party in 1978; and in August 1979, he was fired from his job. He later applied for emigration, but was arrested on March 13, 1980, shortly after signing the letter protesting the Soviet invasion of Afghanistan. In protest against his arrest, a letter with twenty-one signatures (both Russian and Estonian) was sent to the Presidium of the Supreme Soviet of the ESSR. A letter protesting police cruelty during the demonstration of young people in October 1980, was signed by 40 Estonian intellectuals, including some very prominent persons.[25]

In October 1981, second-year history student Runno Vissak was expelled from Tartu University for demonstrating nationalist sentiments. Seventy-five students addressed a letter to the ministry of higher education in his defense.[26]

There was yet another manifestation of civil resistance by Estonians, together with Lithuanians and Latvians, in October 1981. A demand was issued to include the Baltic republics in a nuclear-free zone proposed for the Scandinavian countries. Sixteen Estonians were among the 38 Baltic activists who signed the appeal.[27]

There are indications that well-off Estonian citizens had begun to support their dissident compatriots. The authorities intended to declare Juri Kukk insane in order to avoid a risky public trial, but three commissions of Estonian experts in psychiatry certified that Kukk was sane. After this, even the Serbsky Institute in Moscow could not come up with a diagnosis more in keeping with the government's wishes. By

Soviet standards, Kukk received an unusually light sentence—two years in a standard-regimen camp—a demonstration of the authorities' desire to avoid a quarrel with the Estonian establishment.[28] However, on March 26, 1981, shortly after his trial, Kukk died in camp as a result of forced-feeding during a hunger strike carried out in violation of the most elementary rules for feeding hunger-strikers. This situation could hardly have occurred without the knowledge of camp officials.[29] It is possible that they acted on unofficial recommendations from higher-ups. Against the background of events in Poland and the continuing tense situation in Estonia itself someone could have decided that it would be useful to intimidate potential followers of Kukk.

In the summer of 1981 leaflets of the Democratic National Front of the Soviet Union appeared in Tallinn and other Estonian cities. Without disclosing the names of its members, this organization called for a demonstration of silence from 10:00 to 10:30 A.M. on December 1, 1981 to support the following demands: the withdrawal of Soviet troops from Afghanistan; Soviet noninterference in the affairs of Poland; an end to the export of foodstuffs from the USSR; an end to special secret provisions for high Party officials; the release of political prisoners; a reduction in the length of military service by one-half year; and observance of the universal Declaration of Human Rights and the Helsinki accords.

The authors of the leaflet suggested that demonstrators cease all activity and movement at work, at home, and on the streets. They warned against any violations of the public order and against manifestations of nationalism. They made the suggestion that revolutionary songs, such as "The Internationale," be played on tape recorders during the demonstration. They further suggested that the demonstration be repeated at the same time on the first working day of every month thereafter.

Long before December 1, news of the leaflet aroused much interest in the West. Many Western correspondents tried to arrange to be in Tallinn by that date but only the correspondent for the Swedish newspaper *Dagens Nyheter* managed to do so. On January 3, 1982 he reported an obvious increase in the presence of militia, as well as plainclothes agents across the city. Beginning in the morning, deficit items were put on sale so that the public would rush to line up for them. The correspondent saw workers quietly standing around in a factory yard, but it was difficult to tell whether this was part of the demonstration or merely the usual idleness so common in Soviet enterprises. He witnessed only one incident that was unmistakably part of the demonstration: construction workers stopped work exactly at the set time and did not respond to questions until the half hour was up.

When asked why they were wasting time, they responded by saying, "We are Estonians." It was later learned that workers declared the half-hour work stoppage at many factories and small businesses as their regular morning "break." Almost 150 people were detained on suspicion of participating in the demonstration and then released. Four persons were arrested, including Siim Säde, a worker, and Endel Roze, a doctor at a medical clinic who had been fired from his job in November 1981 for distributing leaflets of the Democratic National Front. He was sentenced to one year of labor camp.[30]

During the 1980s, to the previous forms of "everyday" nationalism (refusal to answer in Russian, signs on the doors of restaurants and cafes in Russian saying "no vacancies," etc.) were added others. In June 1982 three Estonians from the *nomenklatura* who used Brezhnev's portrait for target practice with a hunting rifle were sentenced to labor camp terms. They were managers of a meat plant in the city of Vija.[31]

In Estonia the church did not respond in any way to the revival of the national-democratic movement. The majority of Estonians belong to the Lutheran church (about 250,000). After the Second World War this church experienced bitter repressions because it was considered a "German" church. Now it belongs to the World Council of Churches and maintains close ties with its fellow believers in Finland. In contrast to the Baptist, the Pentecostal, and some other Protestant churches, the Lutheran church has no officially unregistered religious communities whose independent conduct would ease the pressure from the authorities. Therefore, the Lutheran church finds itself in a state of almost total subservience. Its leadership is helpless in the face of the state dictatorship, and Lutheran ministers, like Russian Orthodox priests, are forced to submit to authorized representatives of the Council on Religious Affairs and Cults.

The only known instance of a Lutheran minister openly defying government interference in church affairs is that of the minister Vello Sallum. In his sermons and his article "The Church and the Nation," which appeared in 1981, Sallum held that the aims of Christianity and communism are one and the same: the happiness and freedom of the people. However, Estonian communists have usurped the advocacy of and the struggle to realize these ideals by illegally depriving the church of the opportunity to do the same in its own way. They have deprived believers of the opportunity to participate in national affairs by treating them as second-class citizens. Sallum's sermons were cut short by his confinement to a psychiatric ward for a few months. He was released after he admitted that his ideas were the result of a sick mind. In 1985, pastor Harry Mytsnik was arrested; several other clergymen and active Lutherans were subjected to searches and other harassments.[32]

CHAPTER 4

The Latvian National-Democratic Movement

In Latvia, as in Estonia and Lithuania, immediately after the invasion by Soviet troops in 1940, came a mass deportation of politically active citizens. After the return of the Soviet Army in 1944, the repressions were renewed, and, after 1947, intensified during collectivization. Then, according to the official formula, the Party shifted "from a policy of limiting the kulaks to their liquidation as a class."[1] The course of collectivization in Latvia can be judged by the restrained acknowledgment of the authors of the official *History of Latvian SSR*, published in 1958.

The authors of this collective work write that "there were no attempts to use already existing forms of agricultural cooperation . . . as a point of departure"; that this cooperation which included 75 percent of the peasant farms in Latvia was destroyed, and "collectivization of the overwhelming mass of peasantry occurred in the spring of 1949 at a forced rate, which in some cases violated principles of voluntarism."[2] "Some of these instances" were on such a massive scale that they evoked the armed resistance of Latvian peasants and massive repressions against them: "The Soviet authorities were forced to isolate some of the kulaks and other hostile elements."[3]

The Latvians, although a small nation, represented a significant percentage of prisoners in Soviet prison camps after the Second World War. In the early 1950s, however, the armed resistance in Latvia died down—the balance of forces was too unequal. From then until the 1980s no open nationalist movement existed. In the 1980s, it reemerged but in a peaceful form and less widespread than in Lithuania and Estonia.

The Latvians, however, have made a unique contribution to the development of dissent in the USSR. In the early 1960s in Latvia there were at least two underground organizations: one was discovered by the authorities in 1961 and the other in 1962. The name of the latter,

"The Baltic Federation," indicates the concept of a joint effort with Lithuanians and Estonians to restore the national sovereignty of these peoples, although arrested members of the Federation were Latvians.[4]

During the 1960s and 1970s in Latvia occasional arrests on political charges and certain other events of protest occurred. But reports on these events are so brief and scattered that it is difficult to form a general picture about independent social life in Latvia during these years. The scarcity of these reports probably indicates that events were limited to episodic actions of small groups and isolated individuals. Such actions, nevertheless, expressed a prevalent mood among Latvians that did not find an outlet in practical activity. For example, in the eleventh issue of *Chronicle for Current Events* (December 1969) it was reported that November 18, "Memorial Day," is "an almost official date" in Latvia. In 1969, as had obviously happened before, on that day in the Latvian cemetery in Riga, a meeting was held and speeches were made (their exact content is unknown to *Chronicle for Current Events*) at the grave of the first president of Latvia, Janis Cakste, and the red-white-red flag of independent Latvia was raised. The surrounding graves were decorated with white and red flowers forming the pattern of the national flag. Red and white candles were lit. The militia detained ten people who had been at the cemetery but released them eight days later.[5] Fishermen at a collective farm in Engure, on August 21, 1968— the day of the Soviet invasion of Czechoslovakia—went to sea wearing black armbands of mourning. In this modest way, one small nation expressed its empathy for another.[6]

And, of course, in Latvia—as in all of the other Baltic states—slogans appear on walls both inside and outside official buildings: "Russians, get out of Latvia!" "Russians, go home!" In the mid-1970s, in my annual visits to Latvia I saw such slogans many times—they are written in Russian so that occupiers can read them. The desire for independence is manifest also by flying the national flag, particularly on November 18, Memorial Day. For doing this, even school children pay the price of a camp sentence,[7] and yet almost every year the red-white-red flag is raised somewhere.

From time to time there were reports of underground organizations or of secret unofficial groups of friends. Thus, three young workers, Gunar Berzins, Laimonis Markants, and Valery Akk, on the night of November 7, 1969, scattered about 8,000 leaflets in three regions, criticizing Soviet domestic and international policies, the Soviet invasion of Czechoslovakia, the state of Sino-Soviet relations, and the national problems. Investigation located about 3,000 leaflets and those who had circulated them. Berzins was sentenced to three years in camp; his two comrades received one-and-one-half-year terms.[8]

Several appeals in Latvian dated 1975 reached the West which were signed "Movement for Independence of Latvia,"[9] "The Committee of Democratic Youth of Latvia" and Janis Briedis (a pseudonym?) as "Head of the Committee,"[10] "The Latvian Christian-Democratic Association"[11] and joint declarations of these associations.[12] Some of these anti-Russian slogans and leaflets were obviously the result of the activities of these organizations. In early 1976, leaflets were distributed in Latvia by "The Democratic Union of Latvian Youth." Leaflets written in Latvian were appeals to struggle for democratic rights guaranteed by the Soviet constitution, their texts composed of letters cut out from newspapers and glued to sheets of paper reproduced by the *Era* copying machine. In the spring of 1976, leaflets appeared signed by the same organization and written in Russian and Latvian, with a call for Russians to leave Latvia. In the spring and summer of 1976, anonymously typed leaflets were distributed, demanding freedom for Soviet political prisoners. Other typed leaflets condemned the Helsinki accords because "they serve as the legal recognition of the territorial gains of the USSR during World War II." In May–June 1976, handwritten printed leaflets appeared in Latvian schools declaring "Freedom for Latvia." (After this event, schools conducted written exercises that had to be printed by hand in order to identify the culprits.) In the summer of 1976, on the long wall which blocks the view of the Central Prison of Riga from the railroad, a sign was written in big letters: "Release Soviet Political Prisoners!"[13]

The most widespread form of expression of Latvian national feeling is *samizdat*, judging from confiscations during searches, rather substantial already in the 1970s.[14] Among the earliest cases concerned with the distribution of uncensored literature had been the cases of Erik Danne and Lidiya Doronina. Danne was convicted in early 1969 and sent to camp for bringing books to Riga from abroad—he worked for an international airline.[15] Lidiya Doronina (her Latvian maiden name is Lasmane) was an employee of the Latvian Ministry of Culture. In August 1970, during a house search, Russian-language *samizdat*, an open letter by Solzhenitsyn and works by Andrei Amalrik, were confiscated from her. Numerous witnesses summoned to Doronina's trial were Latvian, not Russian, intellectuals. The investigation concluded that these Latvians were the readers of this *samizdat*.[16] According to the 1970 census, Latvia has a high percentage of Russians (29.8 percent[17]), and intellectual circles were not pure Latvian. All Latvians who read know Russian well enough to appreciate the wealth of Russian *samizdat,* and, therefore, Russian *samizdat* is circulated in Latvia along with Latvian. In the early stages (during the 1960s and early 1970s), *samizdat* appears to have been brought in primarily from Russia.

The next evidence of the distribution of *samizdat* in Latvia is also about Russian *samizdat*. Riga residents, Lev Ladyzhensky, candidate for a degree in physical-mathematical sciences, and an engineer, Fyodor Korovin, were arrested in December 1973 for possession and distribution of *samizdat* from 1966 until the time of their arrests. More than fifty titles were confiscated—about the same selection as in Moscow and Leningrad at this time, including the *Chronicle of Current Events*. Not a single Latvian was among the participants in this case. All the searches—about ten—were among the circle of occupiers. Searches were also conducted in Moscow and Leningrad, since Ladyzhensky and Korovin had admitted that they had received *samizdat* from those cities.[18]

Sometimes, Latvian and Russian *samizdat* currents intersected—in some searches both were found—for example, in the Riga apartment of Viktor Kalnins, a Latvian former political prisoner.[19] But to a significant degree these currents were separate because Russians living in Latvia seldom know Latvian, and few are interested enough in the problems of Latvians to subject themselves to the risk of participation in their uncensored literature. Although Ladyzhensky and Korovin lived in Riga among Latvians, they had better connections to Moscow and Leningrad *samizdat* than to Latvian.

It is difficult to see a strong link not only between Russians and Latvians in Latvia, but also between Latvians and Lithuanians and between Latvians and Estonians. The first joint written protest came in 1975,[20] the first attempt to form a joint organization (not including the failed attempt at unification in the 1962 Baltic Federation), the Main Committee of the National Movement of Latvia, Estonia, and Lithuania. Viktoras Petkus, a member of the Lithuanian Helsinki Group, worked to create the committee in the summer of 1977.[21] This attempt was intercepted in its initial stages. Several Estonian and Latvian former political prisoners were interrogated in this case. All knew each other well, and all had been in camp together. I think that this experiment, even if it had not been stopped by the arrest of Petkus, would hardly have gone beyond the bonds of friendship of former political prisoners. Yet this tendency toward unification, although it has grown only slightly, has not disappeared. It appeared again in August 1979, on the fortieth anniversary of the Molotov-Ribbentrop Pact, according to whose secret protocols Fascist Germany recognized the Baltic states as part of the Soviet sphere of influence, leading to their occupation by the Soviet Union. The anniversary of this event, equally tragic for Estonians, Latvians, and Lithuanians, was commemorated by a joint memorandum with forty-five signatures. Among those who signed were four Estonians and four Latvians; the others were Lithuanians.[22] In the next joint appeal, protesting the Soviet invasion of Afghanistan, only one Latvian name appeared among the twenty-one signatories,[23] but Latvians were, however, the initiators of the joint declaration in October 1981: an open letter to the leaders of the Soviet and Northern European governments.[24] The authors of this appeal, supporting an officially approved Soviet initiative to declare a Scandinavian nuclear free zone, proposed extending this zone to the Baltic republics and removing Soviet missiles from their territories. If the memorandum on the Molotov-Ribbentrop Pact grew out of the common elements in the historical fate of the Baltic peoples, then the 1981 memorandum—as well as the protest of the invasion of Afghanistan—reflected their present common concern not to become the testing ground for the nuclear weapons of the two superpowers. The thirty-eight signatories were equally divided among Lithuanians, Estonians, and Latvians.

The increase in the number of Latvians among the signatories of this memorandum compared to those of 1979 and 1980 shows that new people ready for public action had appeared among Latvians. It also demonstrates the increased strength of Latvian dissent, in particular, by the statement of Maigonis Ravins, which he sent to the Soviet leadership in March 1982.[25] Ravins, who was born in 1955 and served a camp term in 1976–1981 for participation in the Latvian national movement, demanded official recognition of the right of a Latvian secessionist movement to exist, based on the inability of the Soviet Union to guarantee the security of small Latvia in future imperial wars of the USSR.

In this statement, as in the 1981 memorandum, there is a close connection between national and pacifist motives, which in the 1980s became a typical characteristic of the Latvian national movement. Maigonis Ravins became the leading figure of this phase of Latvian dissent, whose proclaimed aim was the secession of Latvia from the USSR. Ravins, however, does not hold anti-Russian views. His experience in camp had helped him distinguish between the Soviet leaders and Russian dissidents, and he had friends in Moscow with whom he maintained close ties. His desire to save Latvia from participation in the imperial undertakings of the USSR was shared by other activists in the Latvian national movement of the 1980s, for example, in the distribution of leaflets in early 1982 in Latvia protesting the war in Afghanistan. One of these leaflets proclaimed: "Our sons should not kill Afghan sons and daughters. Freedom for Afghans and Latvians!"[26]

Among Latvians at large, however, an anti-Russian mood prevailed, as can be seen in this widely disseminated slogan: "Russians, go home!" In early 1982, the slogan "For Russians in Latvia" appeared on street signs indicating one-way traffic in the direction of Moscow.[27]

Latvian Social Democratic Workers' Party

The unique aspects of the Latvian national movement are apparent not only in its pacifist coloration, but also in its foreign Latvian Social Democratic Workers' Party (LSDRP), one of the most powerful parties, with a significant number of seats in the parliament of independent Latvia (1918–1940). For a time, the LSDRP and the liberals had ruled the country, but in 1934, after the Ulmanis *coup d'etat,* all parties except the ruling one were forbidden, including the Social Democrats. Some of the LSDRP leaders emigrated, while others were imprisoned. Mass repressions accompanied the invasion by Soviet troops in 1940 and their return in 1944. The Social Democrats were included in these repressions, although the "left" wing of the party cooperated with Moscow because they believed that the USSR was better than Hitler. In Soviet Latvia, the LSDRP leaders were so thoroughly extirpated that the party completely halted its activities; only a few LSDRP members who had stayed in Latvia survived imprisonment. Those members who emigrated formed an LSDRP committee in exile, which still continues. The Latvian Social Democrats managed to arrange for an influx of new members into the party. The LSDRP issues two newspapers in Latvian, one for party members and another for youth. The principal LSDRP committee in exile is in Stockholm, with sections in other countries. The proclaimed LSDRP aim is to regain independence for Latvia and to reestablish democracy there.[28]

In the early 1970s, LSDRP activity in Latvia started up again. Juris Bumeisters, an electrical engineer and a leading specialist in Latvia in the use of electronics in the fish industry, and Dainis Lismanis played important roles in this. Both were not young (Bumeisters was born in 1918), but they belonged to the new generation of Social Democrats, who joined party activities in the Soviet time. Both were arrested in November 1980 on charges of "treason" and went on trial in May and June 1981, in Riga. Their trial was closed to the public, and no details are known.[29] Evidently, their "treason" was deemed to be their contacts with foreign Latvian Social Democrats, which greatly aided the dissemination of Social Democratic ideas in Latvia. It was precisely these contacts that worried the authorities more than anything else. It is possible that these contacts directed the KGB to Bumeisters and Lismanis. In any case, these connections made reprisal easy and more cruel. A month before the trial, in April 1981, Martin Zandberg, director of the West German LSDRP office, was detained in Riga, forced to give testimony that was used against Bumeisters and Lismanis although he retracted his statements when he returned to West Germany.[30] Bumeisters was sentenced to fifteen years of strict regimen camp; Lismanis received a twelve-year sentence.[31]

On March 25, 1981, Valdis Vinkelis, a 70-year-old resident of Riga, was arrested. He had relatives among the leaders of the Latvian Social Democrats in Sweden and had maintained contact with them. Shortly after his arrest, Vinkelis died in prison. On May 11, his son, Juris Vinkelis,[32] was also arrested and later sentenced on charges of distribution of Latvian *tamizdat*.[33] Apparently, the LSDRP committee in exile played an important role in the publication of Latvian *samizdat* abroad and in the establishment of contacts for distribution inside Latvia. The arrests of three participants in social-democratic activities in Latvia and the death of a fourth couldn't paralyze this activity, even if those who suffered repression were its leading figures. In any case, the influx of *tamizdat* into Latvia has not stopped. During the 1980s *tamizdat* represented the basic type of uncensored literature distributed among Latvians. In Latvia, the LSDRP newspaper, *Briviba* (Freedom), published in Sweden, and other party literature has been distributed. A book written in Latvia by Pavils Bruvers, *Thus Dissidents Begin* (about KGB repressions against the author in 1974[34]), was published abroad as was *The Terrible Year* (about repressions in 1940). Other books circulated earlier in Latvia include books of the Latvian emigré writer, A. Egantis, *Five Days* (about the post-War repressions in Latvia) and *The Lucky Ones* (on the fate of Latvian deportees in the eastern areas of the USSR), and A. Barodis's *The Baltic Republics on the Eve of the Patriotic War*, and George Orwell's *1984*, earlier translated from English.[35] *Tamizdat* was brought into Latvia in ways such as the following: In April 1982, an 18-year-old Latvian, Martin Simanis (a US citizen) and Harald Ozols (a Canadian citizen) were detained at a border station as they were entering Latvia for vacation. They were searched and printed materials and personal letters were confiscated.[36] Many such trips were undertaken by citizens of Latvian origin from various countries. It is reasonable to assume that more succeeded than failed to bring such literature into Latvia.

The struggle against uncensored literature is not limited to searches of tourist luggage. In February 1981 four young Latvians were arrested in Riga for distributing *The Terrible Year*. One received a six-month camp term and was killed in camp shortly before his term was due to end.[37] The Latvian poets, Alfred Zarins and G. Freimanis, were arrested in 1981 and 1983, respectively. Both were charged with possession of *samizdat* and with publication of their poetry abroad.[38] On January 6, 1983, Lidiya Doronina, who had already served a camp term for *samizdat* distribution, was re-arrested, and a variety of *samizdat* and *tamizdat* materials were confiscated, including, as in her earlier case, documents from Moscow—the documents of the Moscow pacifist group. The basic charge against her, as against Bumeisters, was "foreign contacts."[39] On the day of Doronina's arrest, two Swedish tourists of Latvian descent, Vitolins and her 17-year-old daughter, were detained in Riga where they had gone to spend Christmas. They were imprisoned in separate cells for three days and interrogated about their involvement with the Latvian press in Sweden and about their contacts with Doronina. They were expelled from the USSR.[40] Fifty house searches were conducted in connection with the Doronina case—among Baptists (she is a Baptist) and among participants in the Latvian national pacifist movement. During the search of the home of Alfred Levalds, Levalds died of a heart attack, but the house search continued even after he had died. Levalds's widow was taken for several hours of interrogation immediately after the search.[41] Two of Doronina's friends, the rowing champion, Janis Veveris (a Baptist), and a metal worker, Gedert Melngailis (a Lutheran), were also arrested as part of the same case. Both were accused of "foreign contacts," particularly Melngailis for his contacts with Gunars Rode, a participant in "The Baltic Federation" who had emigrated to Sweden after a fifteen-year term of imprisonment. (*Tamizdat* and *samizdat* were confiscated from Veveris and Melngailis.[42])

During 1983 other people were arrested, including former political prisoners Gunars Astra, who had been warned not to maintain contacts with American journalists and diplomats,[43] and Janis Roskalns, accused of membership in the underground organization, "The Movement for an Independent Latvia," of distribution of leaflets and open letters and appeals, and of contacts with the Swedish Bible Society.[44] Those who were arrested, including Maigonis Ravins, who was forcibly hospitalized in a psychiatric hospital in October 1983,[45] were accused of participation in *samizdat* and in the national pacifist movement.

In small Latvia, the various adherents of the many strands of dissent are connected so closely that it is difficult—and sometimes impossible—to define to which "category" an activist belongs. Indeed, some dissidents are active in all the different "categories" of dissent. In 1982, some activists of the national pacifist movement were detained at the Freedom Monument in Riga. They had been present during a public Bible reading by high school student, Rikhard Usans—although not all of these dissidents were believers, let alone Baptists.[46]

The searches in 1981–1983 confirmed the impression of a significant increase in the circulation of uncensored literature in Latvia. Latvian dissidents had been active not only in distributing *samizdat* and pacifist appeals, but also in the organization of contacts with Latvians abroad and with Moscow human rights and peace activists and with the work of the Baptist humanitarian organization "Action of Light" (which is something like a Baptists' fund for the aid of political prisoners). Participation in "Action of Light" was one of the charges against Doronina and Melngailis;[47] since Melngailis is a Lutheran, one can suppose that "Action of Light" was not limited to assisting Baptists but it also helped other victims of repression in Latvia.

The arrests of those years had a noticeable negative impact on Latvian dissent. These arrests removed the leading activists of the Social Democratic underground as well as most who were willing to engage in public activity. But these small circles of activists had close connections and represented the tip of the iceberg of the independent social life of a small nation. Latvia, which feels it belongs to the Western world, does not want to acquiesce in its forcible isolation from it. The loss of this "upper crust" will probably retard—but it will not halt—the development of Latvian dissent and will not obliterate that which gave rise to dissent. Evidence of this persistence can be seen in the continuation of pilgrimages to the grave of Janis Cakste, president of independent Latvia; the demonstrations at the Freedom Monument in Riga; the raising of the flag of independent Latvia; and the impossibility of curtailing the distribution of leaflets and slogans, and, particularly, the equal impossibility of halting *samizdat*.

CHAPTER 5

The Georgian National Movement

The Soviets have been firmly entrenched in Georgia since 1924, but national pride, colored by anti-Russian and anti-Armenian feelings, remains alive. Under Stalin, separatist hopes were not manifested because of the periodic bloodlettings from which Georgia, contrary to popular opinion in the Soviet Union, suffered no less than other republics.

Because of the systematic falsification of Georgian history, from ancient times until the present, found in all official literature, and because of the physical extermination of separatists and anti-Bolsheviks, the generation of Georgians who grew up under Stalin lost the spirit of anti-Bolshevism, although they preserved the traditional distaste for the Russian presence. On March 9, 1956, a mass political demonstration of several thousand students took place in Tblisi, but the demonstrators' slogans were mainly pro-Stalinist. National pride was expressed by protests against the unmasking of Stalin at the Twentieth Party Congress as "anti-Georgian," one of the first open political dissents in the Soviet Union during the post-Stalinist era. The protest ended tragically: tanks were used against the demonstrators, and there were many casualties.[1]

After this incident, no more mass actions occurred for more than twenty years, but national sentiment did not disappear. Anti-Russian, anti-Armenian, and nationalist sentiments are common in all Georgian social groups. Among the lowest urban classes there are still strong pro-Stalinist elements, although Stalin is unpopular with the intelligentsia. However, all social groups are united in refusing to accept Moscow domination.

Georgia was the only Christian country in the Caucasus to preserve its national independence after the tenth century, and after the fall of Constantinople in 1453 Georgia remained the only Christian state free from Moslem dominion. When the Russian principalities began to free themselves from the Tartar yoke, Georgia naturally gravitated toward them because of religious similarities. Reliance on the Russians, however, was dissatisfying on several occasions when the Georgians did not receive the help promised to them in time—once during the reign of Peter I, when Georgia was at war with Persia, and again in the reign of Catherine II, at the time of the war with Turkey.

In 1783 the Georgian King Erekle II, realizing the impossibility of further resistance to Moslem expansion, placed Georgia under the protection of Russia. Taking advantage of Georgia's desperate situation, Russian emperors violated the agreement under which supreme authority in Georgia was to be invested in the Georgian dynasty and Georgia was to remain autonomous in its internal affairs. Georgia was soon turned into the "Tiflis province," where Russification was carried out. Georgians were extremely irritated when 30,000 Armenians immigrated into the southern areas of Georgia on the orders of the Russian governor, Count Paskevich. Later, the dominance of Armenians in this area gave rise to Armenian nationalist claims on the grounds that it lay within the "historical borders" of Armenia.

After the Revolution of 1917, Georgia gained its independence for a short time. The Mensheviks, the most influential among the opposition parties during the prerevolutionary period, assumed power. The Bolsheviks themselves were few in number and lacked support in Georgia. But in 1921 the Menshevik government was overthrown by Soviet troops headed by Sergo Ordzhonikidze, which were called in by the Georgian Bolsheviks. The Georgian Bolsheviks who came to power failed to gain popular support, partly because of their "internationalism," manifested by giving the northeastern part of the country to Azerbaidzhan. (This area called Saingilo is still part of the Azerbaidzhan republic, and the Georgians who live there are still discriminated against by the government and hated by the general population.) In 1922 the patriarch of the Georgian Orthodox church, Oleksandr Ambrosius, complained in a letter of the enslavement of Georgia by Soviet Russia. In 1924 a revolt aimed at the separation of Georgia from the Soviet Union was brutally suppressed.

Contemporary Nationalism of Georgian Youth

Nationalist sentiment today is strongest in Tblisi, the only Georgian city with a large number of institutions of higher learning, and is centered at the University of Tblisi. The strength of the contemporary national movement in Georgia, as in Estonia, lies in the participation of young people, but in Georgia the majority are university, not highschool, students.

Beginning in the midsixties, discontent expressed itself most commonly among university students and educated people through church attendance. Especially during Easter holidays, the churches were crowded; many young people attended the patriarch's sermons. All this enthusiasm did not come from a sense of Christianity but rather from patriotism. New converts worshiped all that was Georgian. Most of them considered the church a cultural more than a religious institution. In the fifties, when the Georgian Orthodox church had more freedom than the Russian Orthodox, the patriarchs were more independent both in their sermons and in administrative affairs. Patriarch Yefrem II, who headed the church from 1960 until 1972, frequently appealed to the patriotism of believers in his sermons. The growing popularity of the church naturally led to heightened control by the authorities. Sermons of the highest church officials and priests, in consequence, became more cautious and less individualized, to the displeasure of church members. In 1972 Patriarch Efrem II died and David V succeeded him. He constantly glorified Communism and Soviet power in his sermons. Most people took this as a sign of servility to Moscow,[2] and he became widely unpopular.

Patriotic and anti-Russian attitudes are considered good form by all social groups, even by high Party and administrative officials. Even those who, in fact, are loyal servants of Moscow observe this form of etiquette. Eduard Shevardnadze, First Secretary of the Georgian Communist Party, tries to create the impression among the intelligentsia that his zeal in carrying out orders from Moscow is only a mask behind which he hides his patriotism in order to serve Georgia better.

The prime concern of the patriotic intelligentsia is the preservation of Georgian culture. Efforts are directed against the falsification of Georgian history. In official versions of that history, no mention is made of events that show the independence of Georgians during any historical period, or of any Menshevik or anti-Bolshevik tendencies during recent times. Anything reflecting the former power of Georgia, its ancient culture, and the independent character of Georgians is extremely popular. In spite of censorship, an attempt is made to publish books and articles containing this sort of testimony.

The strongest resistance in Georgia is to the forceful imposition of the Russian language. Here, as in other republics, the policy of Russification intensified in the seventies. The number of hours spent studying Russian in grade schools was increased at the expense of time spent studying Georgian. Russian is gradually replacing Georgian as the language of instruction in other subjects; it is more and more widely used in the sciences and in the cultural life of the country.

The most famous acts in defense of the use of the Georgian language were a speech by the writer Nodar Tsuleykiris at a meeting of writers with the First Secretary of the Central Committee of the Georgian Communist Party, E. Shevardnadze; and a speech of the writer Revaz Dzhaparidze at the Eighth Congress of Georgian Writers.[3]

National passions erupted in Tblisi in the spring of 1978; the cause was the forceful imposition of Russian. Once again, most of the protestors were college students. The protest was triggered by a proposal to change article 75 in the draft of a new constitution for Georgia. The corresponding former article proclaimed Georgian the official language of the republic. The proposed article contained the following provision:

The Georgian SSR provides for the use of the Georgian language in state and public organizations, in cultural and in other bodies, and takes all necessary measures to insure its development. Under the principle of equality, the use of Russian, as well as of other languages spoken by the people, is also provided for in all organizations and institutions in Georgia. No privileges or limitations in the use of these or of any other language is permitted.

On March 24, the republic newspaper *Dawn of the East* published the proposal for article 75.

The session of the Supreme Soviet of the Georgian SSR for the approval of the new constitution was scheduled for April 14. "Public discussions" of the proposal preceded the session. The newspapers were filled with propositions to leave article 75 unchanged. Among those who proposed this was an eighty-year-old academician and linguist Akaky G. Shanidze. Students began collecting signatures at the University of Tblisi and at other institutes in support of his proposition. A few days before the session opened, leaflets appeared at the university, as well as in other places, calling for a demonstration on April 14 to demand that the original article making Georgian the official government language be retained.

On the evening of April 13, First Secretary E. Shevardnadze, in a speech at a meeting of deans of the university, called upon the deans to dissuade students from demonstrating; he reminded them of the demonstrators who were shot in Tblisi in 1956: "Spare our youth, our golden resource." It was common knowledge that the Eighth Regiment of the security forces was put on alert.

The demonstrators gathered at the university, nonetheless, and marched through the center of the city to Government Hall. They carried banners reading "Our Native Language" and chanted classic Georgian verse praising the Georgian language. Soldiers and militiamen were posted every ten meters along their route. In Tblisi, most militiamen are Ossets, but on this occasion they were replaced by

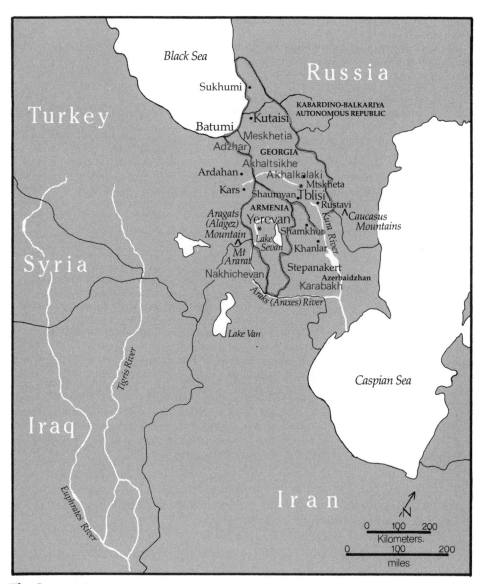

The Caucasus

Georgians from the countryside, evidently an attempt to avoid a clash between the demonstrators and the militia on the grounds of nationalism. The unarmed militia several times tried to block the path of the demonstrators by standing with interlocked arms. Young men at the head of the demonstrators broke through these blockades with their bodies. Close to their goal they found bread trucks blocking the street. The demonstrators removed one truck by pushing it to the side. The most determined of the demonstrators—about 10,000—managed to reach Government Hall. The rest were cut off by the militia, but they stayed at the university. Those who got through stopped in front of Government Hall: someone had warned the organizers that behind the last chain of unarmed militiamen were soldiers with machine guns, instructed to fire if the demonstrators tried to enter the building. An emergency session of the Supreme Soviet of Georgia was in progress at the time. Above the crowd strange banners appeared: medical students had ripped up their white coats and printed in lipstick demands that Georgian be retained as the official state language. Thousands of voices chanted the same demand. Leaflets were distributed by government officials offering a compromise on article 75: they suggested that Georgian be named the language of the republic. The demonstrators began to burn the leaflets and chanted: "The official language." Loudspeakers transmitting the session of the Supreme Soviet were turned on. E. Shevardnadze began his speech by saying that the government was seriously considering the text of article 75 and had consulted with Moscow. This was greeted with jeers.

At last the news was carried over the loudspeakers that the Supreme Soviet of Georgia had voted to keep article 75 without any changes. General rejoicing from the crowd and a fifteen-minute ovation from the delegates to the Supreme Soviet greeted this announcement. At about three o'clock in the afternoon a militia car drove up to those demonstrators who were gathered at the university, and an announcement came over a megaphone: "Your proposal has been accepted! This decision is now being announced on the television!" The Minister of Internal Affairs made the same announcement. He asked the demonstrators to disperse, but they continued to wait. "Believe me, at least this one time!" Finally Shevardnadze appeared and read the text of the approved version of article 75. It began with the declaration: "The official state language of the GSSR is Georgian." After this, the demonstrators began to break up.[4]

It is clear that the demonstration was not spontaneous. Leaflets had been distributed suggesting the time, the place, the route, and the slogans of the demonstration. However, it was not planned by an organized group, but by a group of friends at the university. One of them stands out: Tamriko Chkheidze, a twenty-two-year-old history student and the daughter of a well-known film director and head of Film-Georgia. At her father's request ("Save my daughter or she will be ruined"), the KGB searched her residence on the eve of the demonstration and confiscated some of the leaflets that called for the demonstration. Nevertheless, neither she nor anyone else was held responsible for the demonstration. No one was even expelled from the university. Evidently, a general feeling of sympathy and, possibly, the high positions of their parents saved the youthful demonstrators. The only person arrested in connection with the April 14th demonstration was a cameraman, Avtandil Imnadze, who filmed the events of that day.

Human Rights Groups in the 1970s

Two citizens' human rights organizations existed openly in Georgia: the Initiative Group for the Defense of Human Rights (1974) and the Georgian Helsinki Watch Group (1977). They had no direct connection with the student movement, and it is not likely that they had wide support. They seem to have resulted from the efforts of a mere handful of energetic and like-minded people.

The Initiative Group in Georgia was evidently modeled after the Moscow Group (as the similarity of their names suggests) and through personal contacts with Moscow human rights activists. The *Chronicle of Current Events*, no. 32, carried the news that one of the group (Yury Gastev) was detained for possessing *samizdat* materials in Tblisi on June 5, 1974. Only after this news did the existence of the group become known. It was formed by several intellectuals, including literary scholar Zviad Gamsakhurdia, music scholar Merab Kostava, and choirmaster Valentina Paylodze. There were apparently more participants, but a complete list of the members is not available, nor are any of the group's documents.

Zviad Gamsakhurdia played the leading role in the Initiative Group. Born in 1939, he is a member of the Georgian Writers' Union and the son of the "living classic" of Georgian literature, Konstantin Gamsakhurdia, who—after serving a prison term in the Solovki Islands in the twenties—enjoyed all sorts of special favors from the authorities. Thanks to his father's connections, Zviad had access to the highest officials in the Georgian Communist Party and in the government apparatus. He was one of the first to convert to the Georgian Orthodox church, and since 1965 he has been active in church life; he became a member of the church council of the Zion church in Tblisi. Since 1974 he has been in contact with the Moscow human rights activists. Thanks to this connection information on Georgia regularly appears in the *Chronicle of Current Events*. He was also the author of the overwhelming majority of human rights documents that appeared in Georgian *samizdat* and that subsequently became known in Moscow and the West.

After the death of Patriarch Yefrem II, whom Gamsakhurdia had known personally, he became deeply involved in the patriarchy. Within church circles there were rumors that David V obtained his position as patriarch unlawfully and that he destroyed the dying patriarch's will, according to which another bishop was to have succeeded him, and paid a half-million-ruble bribe to the wife of the then First Secretary of the Georgian Communist Party, Vasily Mzhavanadze, for the position of patriarch. David V was said to have shared his salary with an official on church affairs in the Georgian Council of Ministers for quite some time.[5]

In Georgia corruption riddles society from top to bottom. In 1972, just after the death of Efrem II and the appointment of David V, Mzhavanadze was removed from office because his bribe taking exceeded the limits tolerated by Moscow. E. Shevardnadze, who replaced him, declared a war on corruption, on the underground economy, and on other forms of illegal profits. Information from a closed letter of the Central Committee read at Party meetings was circulated in *samizdat*, according to which from 1972 to 1974, 25,000 people were arrested in the course of that battle against corruption. Of that number, 9,500 were Party members, approximately 7,000 were Komsomol members, and 70 were militia and KGB employees.[6]

The patriarchy was robbed just before these mass arrests. Many valuable objects disappeared, including some of artistic and historical value. A watchman and a few other witnesses indicated that a secretary of the patriarchy, Bishop Keratishvili (Gayoz), was involved in the robbery. The prosecutor conducted an investigation, which supported the claims, but in spite of the efforts of the man who headed the investigation, David Koridze, the case was hushed up. Apparently, part of the loot went to high KGB officers, or perhaps even to a high-ranking Moscow boss. A memorandum written by Koridze was circulated in Tblisi, summarized in the *Chronicle of Current Events*,[7] and later published in an emigré Georgian newspaper in Paris, the *Tribune of Freedom* (no. 6, 1974) and in summary in English publications (*London Times* and *Religion in Communist Lands* in 1975). Western radio stations broadcasting to the Soviet Union carried the news as well. Valentina Paylodze, a choirmaster in the church who assisted in unmasking the culprits, was arrested in March 1974, before any "noise" had been made in the West. She was accused of writing anonymous letters to various official organizations in Georgia that contained threats and "slander on the Soviet system." Paylodze denied the charge and insisted that her arrest was a reprisal by highly placed members of the Georgian church because she was a dangerous witness to their crimes. On June 24 she was sentenced to one-and-a-half years in a general-regimen camp.[8] A group of intellectuals, including some famous Georgians, gathered around the courthouse in sympathy. Yet, the case did not receive wide public support; interest in it was limited to a narrow circle of people close to the patriarchy.

The same story can be told of another problem that was raised in several *samizdat* documents written by Gamsakhurdia: the destruction of ancient relics of Georgia's past.[9] In 1975 Gamsakhurdia published a report on the trials of people who were tortured in Georgian prisons while under investigation for economic crimes. As early as 1974 the *Chronicle of Current Events* learned of a complaint from Karlo Tsulaya who was tried for bribery, that his testimony and that of his codefendant was obtained by means of blackmail and torture by Yury Tsirikidze, a prisoner who acted on orders from prison officials. The things Tsulaya described in his complaint were so shocking that they went beyond the bounds of credibility, and the *Chronicle* decided against publishing them. In April 1975, however, the prisoners Tsirikidze and Valiko Usupyan stood trial in Tblisi for beating to death N. V. Ismaylov, a man held in prison under investigation. The judge allowed Zviad Gamsakhurdia to examine the trial materials closely, and from them it became clear that torture in investigative confinement was a reality in Georgia.

Tsirikidze and Usupyan, accused of various criminal acts, were kept in investigative confinement in Tblisi for years instead of being sent to camp because of the assistance they rendered in obtaining confessions for the investigators. There were ten special cells in building no. 2 of the Tblisi prison, where these agents were confined together with their victims. The executioners were paid in drugs and vodka for their services. Because of the scandal the case created, the head of the Tblisi prison and several employees were later brought to trial. It is obvious from the reports of their trial that the court tried to hide the extent of their crimes by concentrating on three or four beatings, even though Tsirikidze admitted that he had "cracked" more than two hundred cases with the help of such methods.[10] But even this problem, brought to the attention of the public by Gamsakhurdia, did not give rise to any social outcry in Georgia.

The public was much more responsive to the Viktor Rtskhladze affair. Rtskheladze was an employee of the Georgian Ministry of Culture interested in the problem of the Meskhi, an ethnic group living in the South of Georgia that had converted to Islam under Turkish rule. In 1944 the Meskhi were among those peoples deported by Stalin. In the midfifties they began an active struggle to return to their homeland.

In June of 1976 Rtskheladze visited the Kabardino-Balkaria region, where a portion of the deported Meskhi had settled. He spoke at a meeting and, in the name of the Georgian intellectuals, promised the Meskhi help. He wrote an article called "The Tragedy of the Meskhi," which was circulated in *samizdat*. At his suggestion, the Meskhi collected signatures on a petition demanding that they be allowed to return to their homeland. This document was delivered to the Moscow Helsinki Watch Group. As a result MHG document No. 18 was issued.[11]

In January 1977 the Georgian Helsinki Watch Group was created, like the Initiative Group, modeled after the Moscow Helsinki Group. Four others, plus Gamsakhurdia, Kostava, and Rtskheladze joined the group, including the brothers Isay and Grigory Goldshteyn, Jewish refuseniks from Tblisi. The group published only one document—a protest against Rtskhladze's dismissal from his job for his work with the Meskhi.[12]

Gamsakhurdia and Kostava were arrested on April 7, 1977, and a short while later Rtskhladze and Grigory Goldshteyn were arrested. A noisy press compaign smearing them and their sympathizers coincided with their arrests.[13] In May, leaflets in defense of the arrested appeared on the grounds of the University of Tblisi and the Polytechnical Institute. The leaflets mentioned only the Georgian members, and not Goldshteyn. During a demonstration in Tblisi in the spring of 1978 calls to free Gamsakhurdia could be heard. Yet, all this appears to have been an expression of nationalist sentiment rather than solidarity with the platform of the Helsinki Group.

The trials of the Georgian Helsinki Group began in the summer of 1978. Gamsakhurdia and Rtskhladze publicly repented of their activities, considerably lowering them in the eyes of their compatriots. Their sentences were comparatively light: two years of internal exile not far from Georgia. Gamsakhurdia returned to Tblisi in the summer of 1979 and obtained a position as senior research assistant at the Georgian Language Institute.[14]

Nonofficial thought was reflected in Georgian *samizdat*, as well as in independent public organizations. The first *samizdat* document distributed in Georgia was the memorandum written by Koridze, the investigator of the patriarchy robbery. It was dated March 19, 1973. By 1974, before Georgia had its own *samizdat, samizdat* and *tamizdat* materials in Russian were circulated: the *Chronicle of Current Events,* the works of Sakharov and Solzhenitsyn, and other materials, some of which were circulated in typeset copies.

The literary and public affairs journal, *The Golden Fleece* (*Okros Satsmisi*) began to appear in Tblisi in 1975. It was written in Georgian, and the editor was Gamsakhurdia, whose name appeared on the cover. The journal published fiction rejected elsewhere on ideological grounds. On the public affairs side, the journal's main themes were the constraints placed on Georgian culture and, above all, on the Georgian language. The four issues of *The Golden Fleece* contained articles by Georgian historians, philologists, and others on the richness of Georgian culture, on its present state of neglect, and on the official obstacles preventing its preservation and development.[15]

In 1976 another *samizdat* journal written in Georgian appeared: the *Herald of Georgia* (*Sakartvelos moambe*). Gamsakhurdia and Kostava were the editors. Its aim was to publish information about "urgent national and social problems, as well as on the general situation in the USSR."[16] Reports of fires and explosions, numerous in Georgia from 1975–76, accounted for much of the material on internal Georgian affairs. Officials trying to conceal their own embezzlements were responsible for most of the explosions, but three had political overtones: one in Sukhumi in front of the regional Party Committee building, one in the city square of Kutaisi, and one in the square facing Government Hall in Tblisi. They were the result of one person working alone— Vladimir Zhvaniya. He was executed by firing squad shortly after his trial in January 1977. He had no followers.[17]

But the public human-rights movement enlisted no followers either. Evidently, the narrow range of topics, as well as the weakness displayed by Gamsakhurdia and Rtskheladze during their trial, detracted from the movement. In any case, there were no further attempts to create any public organizations. An underground organization discovered in 1980 was the only one in Georgia during the entire fifteen-year period under consideration.

Demonstrations and Trials of the 1980s

On September 29, 1980, three young Georgians from the city of Rustavi were put on trial by the Georgian Supreme Court: Vazha Zhgenti (instructor of the Znaniye (knowledge) Society at a metallurgical factory), Zurab Gogiya (chief of the letter section of a city newspaper), and Vakhtang Chitanava (deputy director of a technical and professional training school). They were charged with distributing leaflets in Rustavi, Tblisi, Gori and other Georgian cities. The leaflets called for the liberation of Georgia.[18]

Thus, Georgia differs from other republics in that open, public organizations preceded underground organizations. However, the Georgian national movement took the form of public, collective actions in defense of the native language directed neither by public, nor by underground organizations. The participants were not limited to young students. In 1980, 364 Georgian intellectuals, including a few academy members, signed a protest against the regulations requiring doctoral dissertations to be written and defended in Russian.[19] The authorities continued to open the way for the use of Russian in elementary schools and institutes, if not on the basis of the constitution, then through the back door, disarming the opponents of Russification from time to time.

On October 23, 1980, Nikolay Samkharadze was arrested. He was known for his protest against the elimination of Georgian history from the elementary-school curriculum for Georgia, as well as for accusing Moscow of chauvinistic policies. He was confined in a psychiatric ward for one year and was unable to find work for a long time afterwards. Soon after his arrest, leaflets appeared in Tblisi, reading: "Freedom to the fighters for Georgian independence—Kostava, Imnadze, and Samkharadze!"[20]

At the beginning of 1981, Akaky Bakhradze, an instructor of Georgian literature at the University of Tblisi who was popular because of his patriotic views, was dismissed. On March 23, about one thousand students marched in a demonstration protesting his dismissal; he was later reinstated.[21] A week later a demonstration of a few hundred people took place before the building housing the Georgian Supreme Soviet in Tblisi where a congress of the Georgian Writers' Union was in session. The demonstrators carried placards demanding that Georgian history courses in elementary schools and institutes be augmented and that the native language be preserved. Shevardnadze tried to convince the demonstrators of his sympathy for their demands. They gave him petitions addressed to himself and to Leonid Brezhnev. Then he talked to the demonstrators' spokesmen, promising to meet with them outside of Government Hall on April 14, the anniversary of the famous demonstration. Afterwards, the demonstrators went home.

Shevardnadze only partially fulfilled his promise: he met with the spokesmen at the university, but later than the date agreed upon and in an auditorium filled not with demonstrators, but with Komsomol activists. The spokesmen were admitted to the meeting after strong protests from the demonstrators. On May 18, people gathered in the university courtyard to hand over written "Demands of the Georgian

People" to Shevardnaze, but Tamara Chkheidze, Marine Koshkadze, Nana Kakabadze and Marine Bagdavadze, who were carrying the text of the "Demands" to the university, were detained on the way. They were taken to Telavi and detained for six days in the Intourist Hotel. The people who had assembled in the university courtyard were dispersed. On May 20, the "Demands of the Georgian People" were handed to Shevardnaze. They consisted of five parts, including one section on the Georgian language and on the plight of Georgians in Saingilo and Abkhazia.[22]

In the beginning of April 1981 another demonstration occurred in Tblisi. The participants were several hundred students from Abkhasia who had travelled to the capital especially for the demonstration. They protested restrictions of the rights of Georgians in Abkhasia (which is an autonomous republic within the republic of Georgia). In Sukhumi, the capital of Abkhasia, a university had been opened with both a department of Russian language and culture and a department of Abkhasian language and culture, but no corresponding department of Georgian culture.[23]

In the meantime, Tblisi activists moved their demonstration from Tblisi to the ancient city of Mtskheta, separated from Tblisi by the Kura River. The first demonstration there occurred on Palm Sunday, April 1, 1981. In order to obstruct the demonstration, traffic from Tblisi to Mtskheta was interrupted. Militia patrols were stationed along the road. Nevertheless, about two hundred people made their way to Mtskheta, some by a detour on foot and others crossing the Kura on rafts. The demonstrators gathered at the church and, kneeling with candles in their hands, prayed for Georgia. They swore that they would continue their struggle until all their demands were met.

Two priests addressed the demonstrators. One called on them to end their struggle and submit to the authorities; the other reminded them of the glorious past and the wonderful traditions of the Georgian people. After leaving the church, the demonstrators composed a petition to the patriarch of the Georgian Orthodox church demanding that he relieve the first priest of his duties. They then set out for the Zion cathedral in Tblisi, where the patriarch was conducting services that day.[24] It was decided to gather annually on April 14 to pray for Georgia to mark the anniversary of the 1978 demonstration, when demonstrators had succeeded in retaining the Georgian language as the official language.[25]

On October 12, 1981, about 2,000 people gathered at the Mtskheta church in order to protest once again curtailments in the use of the Georgian language in schools. Zviad Gamsakhurdia, Tamriko Chkheidze, and a few others were detained. Although they were released the same day, an investigation of charges of "hooliganism" was begun, and late in January 1982 Chkheidze, her friends Marine Koshkadze, Nana Kakabadze, Marine Bagdavadze, and another student, Irakly Tsereteli, were brought to trial. They were all at liberty until the trial. They were found guilty and sentenced to five years of prison each, but conditionally, that is, they were at liberty until their next violation of the law.[26]

In May 1982, Merab Bagdavadze, the father of Marine, was arrested on a crudely-fabricated charge of "Attacking a representative of authority." The investigators openly said that the affair was instigated by orders "from above," to bring pressure on Marine and her friends. After the judge sentenced Merab Bagdavadze to three years of deprivation of freedom, Marine announced she would conduct a hunger strike until her father was conditionally released.[27] He was released by decision of an appeals judge. Not long before this, Avtandil Imnadze, convicted for the filming of a demonstration on April 14, 1978, was pardoned and returned to Tblisi.[28] However, Merab Kostava, located in exile, was arrested in November 1981 for the fabricated reason similar to that under which Merab Bagdavadze had been sentenced, "attacking a representative of authority," and sentenced to five years in labor camp.[29] A written protest from 200 Georgian intellectuals protested this violence. Two researchers at the History Institute of the Academy of Sciences of the Georgian SSR who signed this protest were immediately arrested and sentenced to fifteen days. Their conviction provoked such a storm of resentment that they were released early. Kostava, however, remained in prison.[30] In 1983, Valentina Paylodze was again arrested, this time sentenced to eight years.[31] In 1986, Kostava was released, suffering from a terminal illness.

In 1983, preparations for the festival on the occasion of the 200th anniversary of the Georgian-Russian agreement of 1783, in which Georgia gave herself up to be under the patronage of Russia, provoked great passions. The Soviet press lauded the ceding as a display of the greatest governmental wisdom that had assured the happiness of the Georgian people. Georgian patriots, on the other hand, considered the agreement a tragic event in their history that brought the annexation of Georgia by Russia. A special issue of the magazine, Sakartvelo was published in samizdat,[32] with excerpts from historical works by Georgian historians at the beginning of the century from other samizdat documents. In Tblisi and in other cities leaflets were distributed with an appeal for boycott of the celebration of this jubilee. Irakly Tsereteli and Paata Sagaradze were arrested on June 15 for distributing these leaflets.[33] In the beginning of July history student David Berdzenishvili was arrested on accusations of editing the magazine Samreklo, an organ of the "Republican Party of Georgia.[34] This reference has been the first and only mention of such a party. On July 11 occurred a demonstration of about 100 participants with the demand to release all those arrested. Close to twenty demonstrators were arrested, but, soon after, most were released. Five remained under arrest (Tamriko Chkheidze, Zurab Tsintsinadze, Nana Kakabadze, Giya Chanturiya, Marine Bagdavadze), were each sentenced to three years of labor camp as was L. Shakishvili.

Thus the first blow was dealt to the "new generation" of activists of the Georgian national movement.

A comparison of events in Georgia, Lithuania, Estonia, the Ukraine, and other republics shows that prosecution for one and the same offense differs considerably from one republic to the next. It appears that everywhere the harshness of repression is in inverse proportion to the size of the movement in its open forms.

CHAPTER 6

The Armenian National Movement

The Armenians have an ancient cultural heritage that dates back three thousand years and a written language dating from the fourth century. Yet, it is five hundred years since that country lost its national independence. Situated between Russia and Turkey, Christian Armenia always gravitated toward Russia, which Armenians considered their only protection from Turkish enslavement. Since 1915, when the Turks drove the Armenians out of western Armenia and massacred 1.5 million people in the process, Armenians have reconciled themselves to alliance with Russia as the only possible way out of their predicament. Under tsarist Russia, Armenia found itself in the position of the "Yerevan district," but it was forced to choose between that evil and the total annihilation of its people.

During the October Revolution, Armenia was separated from Russia, and on May 28, 1918 was declared an independent republic. The National Dashnak Party, which was in power at the time, had a program similar to that of the Russian Social Revolutionaries. The Soviet Russian Republic recognized the independent Armenian government, but the Armenians were immediately faced with the Turkish threat: according to the terms of the Brest-Litovsk Peace Treaty signed by Soviet Russia and Germany, Turkey, which had been a German ally, received the Armenian cities of Kars and Ardagan. The first act of the Dashnak government was to sign the Batum Agreement with Turkey, which allowed Armenia to continue as an independent state for two more years. In November 1920, regular Red Army troops moved into Armenia. On November 29, Armenia was declared a Soviet republic, and the Dashnak government was forced to resign. Thus Armenia became part of the Soviet state.

Armenian Grievances

In the sixty years since becoming a part of the USSR, Armenians have collected a long list of grievances and claims toward Moscow. After World War I, the central Soviet government energetically opposed a proposal advanced by President Woodrow Wilson for the creation of an independent Armenian state between its historical boundaries of Lake Van and Mt. Ararat. Dispersed all over the world, descendants of the Armenians who survived the 1915 massacre would then have been returned to their homeland. This action was to be a part of the partition of the Ottoman Empire, which did result in the creation of the present states of Libya, Syria, and other countries in the Near East.

Armenia, however, remained part of the Soviet Union. From that time on the Soviet Union often neglected the interests and feelings of the Armenians while making advances to Turkey. The Armenians are particularly chagrined that the Soviet Union has taken no steps toward resolving the problem of western Armenia (now under Turkish rule), Kars, and Ardagan. Besides this, the neighboring Mt. Karabakh and Nakhichevan areas, given to Armenia when it became part of the Soviet Union on November 30, 1920 and with a population that is 80 percent Armenian, were later included within the area of Azerbaidzhan. Armenians living in these areas are oppressed by an administration of foreign nationality.

Relations between Armenia and Azerbaidzhan are always strained. At times the tension erupts into internecine skirmishes. For instance, when in Stepanakert in the Karabakh area, an Azerbaidzhani school director killed an Armenian pupil and was brought to trial, an Azerbaidzhani judge gave him a light sentence. A crowd of Armenians near the courthouse, incensed by this official act of connivance with the murderer, took the law into their own hands: the car in which the murderer, the judge, and a few others were sitting was burned. Patriotically inclined Armenians are working for the transfer of Karabakh and Nakhichevan. From time to time leaflets calling for union with Armenia are distributed in the schools of these areas. Agitators visit the villages and approach the peasants with the same call for union with Armenia.[1]

For the Soviet Armenians living outside the boundaries of Armenia, who constitute more than 40 percent of all Soviet Armenians, the border question is a sore point. They cannot return to their tiny homeland, which has a population of more than 3 million, because there is no "living space" for them. About 1 million Armenians live outside the USSR, for the most part in the Middle East.

Patriotically minded Armenians are sensitive about the dispersal of other Armenians, about the dismemberment of Armenia, and about its dependent status, which is often made apparent in a very humiliating manner. This sensitivity is experienced on all social levels, including the present Party establishment of Armenia. However, the national-patriotic movement, with its demand for a "just solution of the Armenian problem," has been driven underground and is now isolated from the majority of Armenians.

Underground Organizations

The earliest evidence of the underground movement was the announcement that an underground group had been formed—the Union of Armenian Youth, which appeared in 1963 and continued until 1966.[2] In 1965 the participants of this group made active preparations for the fiftieth anniversary of the death of 1.5 million Armenians at the hands of the Turks. It was celebrated on April 24, and in Yerevan moderate and restrained official gatherings took place—as well as an unplanned funeral procession of 100,000 people, most of them young.

Students gathered in the morning at the universities, but instead of going to classes, they took to the streets. On their way to Lenin Square, in the center of the city, they stopped along the way at libraries and businesses to urge others to join them. They carried posters, one of which read: "A Just Solution to the Armenian Question." From midday meetings began on Lenin Square. By evening the crowd had surrounded the opera house, where an official meeting of "representatives of the community" in honor of the anniversary was in progress. Stones were thrown through the windows. Firemen standing by directed their hoses on the crowd, and broke up the demonstration. Groups of volunteer police in the city stopped pedestrians wearing symbols of mourning and beat them savagely.[3]

Just how the Armenians wished to solve their national problems and the arguments they used are illustrated in a letter by E. G. Ovannisyan to the Central Committee of the Communist Party of the Soviet Union, written early in 1965. He appealed to the Central Committee with the suggestion that a monument be raised to the memory of Armenians who fell victim to the Turkish genocide of 1915 and formulated the Armenians' demands of the Soviet government:

> The Armenian nation is scattered across the world, while Armenian land remains empty, its cities and villages in ruins within the territory of Turkey (western Armenia).
>
> Sooner or later those who were driven from their native land must return. This should not be done through bloodshed. All imperialists must relinquish

control over the territories they have seized, although not without regrets. The Turks are no exception. This question would have been resolved long ago if the Party and the government had been interested in a solution, but for some reason, the sufferings of the Armenian people do not interest them. Of the 767,000 sq. kilometers (comprising Turkish territory), 200,000 belong to Armenia and should be annexed to the Armenian Republic. They include Mush, Van and Trebizond. More than 3.5 million Armenians live in the USSR. Our government should defend the rights of these people.

Ovannisyan also demanded "the annulment of the Batum Agreement, signed by the Dashnak government and Turkey," under which Kars and Ardagan went to Turkey.

In 1948, Arutyunov, then secretary of the Armenian Communist Party, raised similar demands in a speech at the U.N. Like Ovannisyan, he based his demands on the impossibility of otherwise resolving the problem of the Armenians who had been forced to leave western Armenia: the present Armenian republic is too small to accommodate all of those who were expatriated.[4]

In the meantime, a large portion of the expatriots who arrived in the USSR were sent directly from the port of Batum to the Altay Mountains and to Siberia. Armenians from the Armenian Republic were also sent there en masse, and their places were filled by inhabitants from war-ravaged Russian regions. Only after 1956 were those exiles who were still alive allowed to return to Armenia.[5]

Ovannisyan has made the following statement about the border areas settled by Armenians, but given to Azerbaidzhan in 1924: "The Crimea was given to the Ukrainian republic. Golodnaya Steppe, which is one and a half times larger than Armenia, was given to Uzbekistan, and so on. Why aren't the Armenians allowed to reunite with their own people within the borders of the republic? . . . The Armenian regions of Shalmkhor, Dashekesan, Khanlar, Shaumyan, and Mt. Karabakh should be annexed to the Armenian republic."[6]

In 1966 the underground organization, the National Unification Party (NUP), was founded in Yerevan on approximately the same platform as that outlined by Ovannisyan, organized by the artist Aykanuz Khachatryan, and the students Stepan Zatikyan and Shagen Arutyunyan. Khachatryan wrote the party program and the text of its membership oath. Together with Arutyunyan and Zatikyan, he published the first issue of the party newspaper, the *Beacon* (*Paros*). Other National Unification Party members wrote articles calling for the formation of an independent Armenia, distributed the leaflet "We Can No Longer Keep Silent," and prepared for the publication of a journal, *In the Name of the Homeland* (343 copies).[7]

In 1968 the founders of NUP were arrested and nineteen-year-old

Paruyr Ayrikyan, a student of the Yerevan Polytechnical Institute and author of patriotic songs, became the actual head of the party. He was arrested in 1969 and appeared in court with five other young persons, in what was called "the trial of the twenty-year-olds." Like all National Unification Party members before and after, they were charged with "anti-Soviet agitation and propaganda" and with participating in an "anti-Soviet organization." Ayrikyan was accused of leading the underground organization and of reading and giving others the *Beacon,* the program, and the rules of the NUP. He and the rest of the accused, on April 24, 1969, organized a radio broadcast from the monument erected in honor of the victims of the 1915 massacre. At private gatherings the young people read articles on the fate of the Armenian people and on Soviet national policy ("Not by Bread Alone," "Again on the Altar of Victims of Russo-Turkish Diplomacy," and others). The young people prepared and distributed leaflets protesting "Russian chauvinism," demanding the return of Mt. Karabakh and Nakhichevan to Armenia and calling for Armenian independence.[8]

After four years in a strict-regimen labor camp, Ayrikyan returned to Armenia in 1973 and was put under administrative parole. In February 1974 he was again arrested for "violating the rules of parole." While already under arrest he was charged with two counts of "anti-Soviet agitation" and sentenced to seven years in a strict-regimen camp. In 1980, at the end of this term, new charges were brought against him and he received three more years in camp.[9]

In 1974, while still in camp, Ayrikyan and another National Unification Party member, Azat Arshakyan, edited the program and the regulations of the NUP. They have not been changed.[10] The revised program rejects the anticommunism and anti-Marxism found in the original program and excludes the use of extremist measures and the use of force. Although the question of Armenia's "historical borders" is taken up, those borders are not specified, but treated as a remote rather than a concrete goal. The greatest emphasis is placed on achieving independence for present-day Armenia by secession from the Soviet Union, in accordance with rights found in the Soviet Constitution. Because the constitution does not specify what form the desire for secession should take, the National Unification Party suggests working toward an all-Armenian referendum on that issue. They suggest that all Armenians, not just those living in the territory of Soviet Armenia, participate in the referendum. They suggest that the referendum take place under international control, by which they mean through the United Nations. As a preliminary condition to the referendum, they demand freedom of thought for everyone and, as a manifestation of this freedom, the legalization of the National Unification Party. The program emphatically states that NUP is not an anti-Soviet organization, inasmuch as a free Armenia is conceived of as friendly to the Soviet Union. As for Armenia's future social structure, this question is not brought up by the National Unification Party but is to be decided by the people of a free Armenia.

The program defines the National Unification Party as a "national-democratic party," a pan-Armenian organization that any Armenian may join, regardless of political or religious beliefs and even of Communist Party membership. The only requirement is that one be ready to place "the general interests of the nation above personal gain and interest." NUP is closer to a national front than a party, since its goal is an independent Armenia and not the assumption of power. There is also the expectation that after Armenian independence is achieved, the National Unification Party itself will disintegrate into different parties in accordance with the political beliefs of its individual members.

At the head of the National Unification Party is a party council, consisting of the leaders of groups within NUP. The party leaders are chosen by members of the council. All decisions are to be reached by voting, and the party leader has two votes. All members must abide by the decisions of the council. NUP allows other groups and individuals with no previous contact with NUP to speak in the name of the party, as long as they act in accordance with the basic slogan: "Long live independent Armenia! We demand a referendum!" National Unification Party members distribute this message by leafletting, by hanging posters, by clarifying their goals through articles in *samizdat* periodicals organized specifically for this purpose, and by engaging in research and organizational work designed to raise the national consciousness of Armenians.

In their appeals to Armenians living abroad, the National Unification Party asks for support for their basic principle by demonstrations in front of Soviet embassies, by petitions and appeals, and by publishing and distributing NUP documents.[11]

Although Paruyr Ayrikyan denied his leadership role in court, in camp he openly declared himself secretary of the National Unification Party. Other members, mostly prisoners, followed his example and began to speak publicly in the name of the party and voice party demands. On August 5, 1974, Ayrikyan and five fellow NUP members conducted a three-day hunger strike in support of his appeal to Kurt Waldheim of the United Nations for creation of an international commission to investigate Soviet crimes against the people of Armenia.

On December 5, 1976, Soviet Constitution Day, Razmik Markosyan, a political prisoner and National Unification Party member, also staged a hunger strike. He sent a statement to the president of the Supreme

Soviets of the USSR and the ASSR, insisting on the absolute legality of the NUP, since it had "set itself the goal of Armenian independence within historical borders and by peaceful means, including a referendum in the Soviet portion of Armenia."

On the same day, the political prisoners Ayrikyan, Markosyan, and Arshakyan issued a statement calling for the legalization of the National Unification Party and a referendum in Armenia. Fifteen political prisoners (among them Russians, Jews, Ukrainians, and Lithuanians) sent a supporting statement to the Presidium of the Supreme Soviet of the Armenian SSR.[12]

Hunger strikes of political prisoners were accompanied by petition campaigns on NUP demands in 1974–75. Armenians wrote to Soviet agencies and to the United Nations, asking the legalization of the National Unification Party and freedom for NUP members arrested on political grounds. (By this time, approximately eighty members had been tried.)

The Beginning and End
of the Armenian Helsinki Watch Group

On April 1, 1977 a human rights organization, the Armenian Helsinki Watch Group (AHWG), was announced. Its members included: the economist Eduard Arutyunyan, who became the leader of the group; Samvel Osyan, a student of a polytechnical institute; and Robert Nazaryan, a physicist and deacon in the Armenian Orthodox church. Shagen Arutyunyan, one of the founders of the National Unification Party, and Ambartsum Khlgatian, both workers, joined the group later. In a public declaration, the group enunciated the goals of the Helsinki accords and added one more: to strive for Armenian membership in the United Nations. The purpose of this goal was to "resolve the common nationality problem of Armenians scattered over the world"; to pursue "the annexation of Mt. Karabakh and Nakhichevan, now autonomous regions of Azerbaidzhan"; and "to demand the use of the Armenian language in all spheres of life in Armenia." About half of all schools in Armenia now are Russian, and young Armenians frequently do not know their native language as they should.

The Armenian Helsinki Watch Group issued several reports on violations of civil and human rights in Soviet Armenia. The report of April 1, 1977 sent to the Belgrade Conference is a summary of incidents involving the oppression of Armenian national culture and discrimination against the use of the Armenian language. It enumerates violations of the human rights of political prisoners and provides lists of individuals who have been dismissed from work on ideological grounds; of others who have been denied the right to emigrate; of books removed from libraries and destroyed because their authors emigrated from the Soviet Union.[13]

Robert Nazaryan, who swore not to speak Armenian until Karabakh was returned to Armenia, appealed to Soviet Armenians and to Armenians living abroad to give material aid to Armenian political prisoners and their families. He was arrested on December 22, 1977, tried and sentenced to five years of labor camp and two years of exile. On the same day another member of the Armenian Helsinki Watch Group, Shagen Arutyunyan, was arrested, tried on fabricated charges of "malicious hooliganism" for beating militia workers, and received three years in camp.

After these arrests, the leader of the Watch Group, Eduard Arutyunyan, in a public statement to Armenians living abroad, reported that the Armenian Helsinki Watch Group had been destroyed.[14] Soon afterwards, S. Osyan left the group, convinced, as he said, that human rights work was senseless under Soviet conditions. No new members joined and activities ceased.

However, another form of human rights work—less unusual than an open public association—became widespread and influential.

In Armenia, as in Georgia, the discussion in the spring of 1978 of the draft for a new constitution of Armenia focused on retaining the native language as the official government language. There was no large demonstration as in Tblisi, but instead numerous letters to newspapers were sent and speeches were delivered at meetings in offices, plants, and institutes. The authorities, in consequence, decided not to risk a recurrence of events like those in Georgia, and the provision on the official language in article 72 of the Armenian Constitution remained unchanged.

The authorities conducted numerous interrogations of individuals during the period of the public discussions on the new constitution. Stepan Zatikyan and two young workers who lived near him—Akop Stepanyan and Zaven Bagdasaryan—had been arrested on November 3, 1977. By spring 1978, it was evident that all three were accused of setting off an explosion in the Moscow subway on January 8, 1977, which, *Izvestiya* reported on February 8, 1979,[15] had resulted in seven deaths and forty-four wounded. From the many interrogations of persons in connection with their pending trial, one can conclude that the investigation tried to link the National Unification Party and the Armenian Helsinki Watch Group with the metro explosion.

Stepan Zatikyan, one of the founders of the National Unification Party, had served a four-year sentence for his NUP activities. After his release in 1972, with no opportunity to continue an education interrupted by the arrest during his third year at the Yerevan Poly-technical Institute, he found work as a transformer assembler at the Yerevan Electromechanical Plant. Because he thought them hopeless, he did not resume his National Unification Party activities again. In 1975 Zatikyan renounced his citizenship and applied for emigration. (About Stepanyan and Bagdasaryan we know only that they are re-lated. There is no evidence that they participated in the Armenian national movement.)

The trial of the three took place in Moscow, but with such secrecy that it is not known when it began. None of the relatives of the accused were informed of the trial and so none attended.

All three were sentenced on January 24, 1979 to be shot. It is known that the accused did not admit any guilt, although *Izvestyia* reported otherwise. The relatives learned of the sentence only at a meeting after the trial. "They convicted us in ten minutes before an empty courtroom," said Stepanyan. "I didn't say one word to them the entire fifteen months," said Zatikyan. When his brother asked him if he actually did take part in the crime, he replied: "I am guilty only of leaving behind two children in this world. I am guilty of nothing else."

The sentence was carried out on January 31, before the period for filing an appeal had expired.[16]

Andrey Sakharov and the Moscow Helsinki Watch Group protested: "It is impossible to understand," the members of the group wrote, "why it was necessary to conduct a trial on such serious grounds in absolute secrecy. . . . After all, the explosion was greeted with public indignation, and if the prosecution had really convincing evidence that the accused were guilty, that would have contributed to the general condemnation of the criminals. The closed nature of the trial and the atmosphere of total secrecy gives reason to doubt the validity of the charges, the objectivity, and the impartiality of the court."[17]

Indeed, immediately after the 1977 subway explosion, Sakharov had suggested that it might have been a KGB provocation with political intent, considering, for example, the haste with which the authorities informed Western correspondents of the tragedy. Such matters are usually hidden from the Western press, and if reported, it is only after a long process of "agreement." If this incident was not a KGB provocation, either the real criminals had not been found, or they were found and their identity proved to be politically embarrassing. In Moscow, rumor had it that the investigation led to the city of Aleksandrov and that the criminals were Russian workers at a radio plant who had acted in protest against food shortages. If so, high officials could well have decided to conceal their identity in order to cover up worker dissatisfaction with economic conditions and to use the event to discredit selected "internal enemies." To accuse Moscow human rights activists was unpersuasive; they were well known in the West as men of peaceful activities.

Still, the numerous interrogations in Armenia connected with the Zatikyan case had led to a heated debate among NUP supporters on whether or not Zatikyan did take part in the metro explosion. Most of those who knew him personally reject this possibility, but the broad investigation nevertheless convinced some people of the guilt of the accused. Because Zatikyan himself had left the National Unification Party, and none of the NUP members were familiar with the others, even persons who believed the three guilty were certain that NUP was in no way involved. In these debates only the question of Zatikyan and his codefendants' involvement in the explosion came up.

It seemed easy to discredit the Armenian national movement both inside and outside of the Soviet Union by attributing to it terrorist methods. Armenia is the only republic in which a political party exists that sets as its goal secession from the USSR. During the fifteen years of the National Unification Party's existence, after each series of arrests, fresh adherents were found. Yet even the Moscow human rights activists were only vaguely aware of the NUP's goals and methods. In the *Chronicle of Current Events,* the section called "Events in Armenia" appeared only in issues 56 and 57 for April and August 1980. Until then, information on Armenia had been very sketchy and brief. The politically unorganized Armenian diaspora abroad provides no effective help for the National Unification Party and is poorly informed about the political situation.

In December 1978 and again in February 1979, leaflets critical of Brezhnev and the Soviet authorities were distributed in Yerevan, scattered in public places, and placed in mailboxes of private apartments. On December 27, KGB agents, in the presence of the tenants, confiscated some of these leaflets from the mailboxes of an apartment house for writers. According to rumors possibly originating from those responsible, about 30,000 leaflets had been distributed, but this is doubtful.[18]

On July 13, 1979 the leader of the Armenian Helsinki Watch Group, Eduard Arutyunyan, was arrested.[19] He was tried for slander in March 1980, and contrary to the usual practice, some of his friends were allowed in the court. His lawyer, Yu. Mkrtchyan, asked that the defendant be acquitted. Arutyunyan's father was permitted to speak in the capacity of public defender—an event unheard of in the history of Soviet political trials. Arutyunyan defended himself very boldly. His closing words were that he refused to ask anything of the court since he considered that beneath his dignity. He condemned Brezhnev and the government, demanded the release of all prisoners of conscience. He was happy, he said, to be a defender of human rights and be sent to prison because he struggled against the dirty deeds of the Soviet leaders. His sentence was two and one-half years in a general-regimen camp.[20] After that term, Arutyunyan was sentenced to a new three-year term.[21] He died in 1984 before completing that sentence.

The destruction of the Armenian Helsinki Watch Group, which had established contact with Moscow human rights activists, did not cut off information from Armenia. News appeared in the *Chronicle* even after the group had ceased to exist.

Trials of the 1980s

Underground activities continue along lines laid out by the Nationalist Unification Party.

On May 14, 1980 Aleksandr Manachuryan was arrested on charges of participating in an underground organization. Unlike the majority of National Unification Party activists, he was not a young man. He was fifty-one years old. His father, the Minister of Communications in Armenia, had been arrested in 1937 and had died in a forced-labor camp. Aleksandr was a senior research worker of the Armenian Academy of Science and a specialist in medieval Armenian epitaphs. His articles were published at home and abroad, and he had taken trips abroad—a sure sign that he was both trusted by the authorities and successful in his field.

In March 1981, the court convicted him and the village school teachers Smbat Melkonyan and Ashot Apokyan, not only of participating in an underground organization but also of writing "anti-Soviet" articles, "All About the National Question" and "Imperialism."[22] It is not known if any of the accused were members of the National Unification Party or if they created a separate organization.

Almost simultaneously, a similar trial was held in Yerevan. The defendants were five members of the "underground" Union of Armenian Youth: Mrzpet Arutyunyan, Vartan Arutyunyan, Ishkhan Mkrtchyan, Samvel Egiazaryan, and Oganes Agababyan. The union members wrote and disseminated poetry in which "the idea of a free and independent Armenia was glorified." The indictment named Mrzpet Arutyunyan the guiding spirit and ideologue of the organization (he was the brother of Shagen Arutyunyan, the founder of the National Unification Party and later a member of the Armenian Helsinki Watch Group). Ishkhan Mkrtchyan was named the actual leader.

Mrzpet Arutyunyan declared in court that the goal of the Union of Armenian Youth was to spread propaganda about the idea of Armenia's secession from the Soviet Union. In contrast to the neutral politics of NUP, the union took its own orientation from the Dashnak Party. Arutyunyan declared that the Communist Party would be outlawed in the future independent state of Armenia. On the last day of the trial, the defendants asked to send a letter to President Reagan with wishes for his rapid recovery from wounds suffered from the attempted assassination and the hope that "he would be true to his promises."[23]

It is possible the Manachuryan group was somehow linked to the Union of Armenian Youth. In any case, the investigation tried to demonstrate such a link. Arrests and political trials continued in Armenia in 1982 and 1983. In 1982, Ashot Navasardyan and Azat Arshakyan, members of NUP, were arrested. In 1983, three others were arrested: Georgy Khomizuri, a geologist and researcher at the Academy of Sciences, charged for writing the samizdat work A History of the Politburo of the CPSU; philologist Rafael Papayan, a professor at Yerevan University, and linguist Edmund Avetyan. These three were not accused of belonging to the NUP, but of promoting in their samizdat activities the same ideas that inspire the members of the NUP.[24] One can see that in the 80s, the social status and growth of activism and of the Armenian nationalist movement have risen. Armenian independence still remains the fundamental demand of patriots. It is not likely that these goals can be reached in the near future. Repression against those who support this goal has been harsh, and has doomed the movement to be small in number. Nevertheless, suppression did not succeed. New individuals replaced activists arrested. The idea of independence is deeply rooted in the Armenian people.

PART TWO

THE MOVEMENTS OF
DEPORTED NATIONS

CHAPTER 7

The Crimean Tartar
National Movement

Crimea is the historic homeland of the Crimean Tartars. They have lived there since the thirteenth century, right up to 1944. On May 18, 1944, soon after the Crimea was liberated from Hitler's troops, all of the Crimean Tartars were charged with "betraying their country" and were moved out of the Crimea.

This was the culmination of the persecution of the Crimean Tartars; it had begun as soon as the Crimea was annexed to Russia in 1783. Before the Crimean Tartars had numbered four million. Many perished before 1902, but still more—entire villages—resettled across the sea in Moslem Turkey and in the Balkins, reducing the population to roughly 120,000.[1]

Under the Soviets, in 1921 the Crimean Autonomous Republic was created, contributing to the economic and cultural development of the Crimean Tartars. By the beginning of the Second World War, the population was 560,000. The Soviet Army had 137,000 mobilized and 57,000 died at the front. More than half of the 200,000 children in the Crimean were orphaned when their fathers were killed. Half of all the partisans in the Crimea were Crimean Tartars.

"Special Settlers" 1944–1956

Without warning, in 1944 all the Crimean Tartars were driven from their homes in the middle of the night by NKVD soldiers (predecessor of the KGB). The Tartars were loaded into sealed freight cars and shipped to the eastern regions of the USSR—the Urals, Uzbekistan, Kazakhstan, Turkmenia, and Kirgizia—where they were located on reservations as "special settlers," and not permitted to leave. As a result of the harsh conditions during transport, the unfamiliar climate, and hunger and crowding in the settlements, 195,471 or 46.2 percent perished in the first eighteen months. After the war, Crimean Tartar soldiers who fought in the Soviet Army were also exiled (the figures are based on an unofficial census taken by activists of the Crimean Tartar movement through mass questionnaires in 1966–74).[2]

Until the war the majority of Crimean Tartars were peasants, but the special settlements were attached to factories and plants. All the Crimean Tartars, regardless of their former occupation, were required to work in factories located near their settlements. Even qualified specialists and educated persons were prohibited from occupying managerial positions. The Crimean Tartars were turned into a nation of factory workers, their legal status and living conditions were similar to those of the serfs who worked in factories in the Urals at the beginning of the nineteenth century.

The Crimean Tartars were housed in barracks, sheds, and huts. Like the serf workers, they were settled without regard for family relationships. Parents and grown children often found themselves in separate settlements, forbidden to see one another, prohibited even from attending a funeral if one of them died; to leave the boundaries of a settlement was punishable by long prison-camp sentences. Their children were deprived of schooling in their native tongue. There were no cultural institutions at the settlements, and no publications in their language. Over everyone hung the sweeping accusation of treason—the families of Crimean Tartar soldiers killed at the front as well as children born after the war.

After the native residents of the Crimea had been deported, all evidence of their cultural and material heritage they left behind was destroyed. All newspapers, magazines, and books in their langauge were burned, including the "classics of Marxism." Mosques were destroyed; Muslim cemeteries were razed to the ground and the tombstones used to construct new buildings. Tartar place names were changed to Russian names. Historical works were rewritten and new ones added in which the history of the Crimean Tartars was falsified from ancient times until the present. Everything possible was done to erase from memory the long history of the Crimea, which was inseparable from the history of the Crimean Tartars, and to discredit their people.

The Crimean Tartars lived under "special settlement" conditions for twelve years, until 1956. Some who could not reconcile themselves to the deportations escaped to the Crimea and later died in the camps. Authors of songs and poems about the Crimean Tartar tragedy were sent to camps.

Soon after the Twentieth Party Congress, on April 28, 1956, an edict issued by the Presidium of the Supreme Soviet of the USSR and labeled "not for publication," freed the deported peoples from the "special settlement" order. But the edict did not remove the charge of treason, and the prohibition on return to the Crimea remained in effect. In order to receive passports, they had to sign a statement surrendering all claims to material possessions left behind when they were deported.[3]

The Twentieth Party Congress at which the "mistakes of the period of the personality cult" were denounced and at which there was talk of "restoring Leninist principles of democracy," and the Edicts of 1956, was criticized for having failed to remedy the illegalities imposed on the Crimean Tartars, served as the impetus of the Crimean Tartar movement to return to the Crimean.

Birth of the Crimean Tartar Movement

The founders of the Crimean Tartar movement were former Party and government figures, war veterans, and persons who had received the title "heroes of labor," in short, the former Crimean Tartar elite, which the special settlements had reduced to one common level. Believing sincerely in the decisions of the Twentieth Party Congress on the democratization of Soviet life, they "went to the people," voluntarily spreading the word of the congress's decisions in the hope that the overall democratization of the country would lead to remedy of the injustices suffered by the Crimean Tartars. They called for courage from their compatriots and urged them to appeal to Party and Soviet leaders to resolve the Crimean Tartar problem promptly.

During this initial period the movement developed almost exclusively in Uzbekistan, and manifested itself only in loyal and pleading collective and individual petitions to high levels of government. Their long preamble usually included a list of the benefits the Crimean Tartars received from the Soviet authorities until 1944, followed by assurances of the Crimean Tartars' loyalty to the Soviet system, the Party, and the government. They expressed certainty that the authorities would correct the "mistakes of the period of the personality cult" and deviations from "the Leninist policy on nationalities" which the former leaders had committed against the Crimean Tartars. The emphasis was on getting the greatest number of petitions and signatures possible in order to demonstrate loyalty and the desire of all Crimean Tartars to return to their homeland.

After 1956 the majority of the Crimean Tartars continued to live on their reservations for a long time. In the process of organizing the petition campaign, they created a spontaneous organizational structure well suited to serve as a network of initiative groups with no common center, no leaders, and no claims to being a nationwide political organization, which the authorities, of course, would not have tolerated.

Within the boundaries of individual streets, villages, regions, cities, and areas, each initiative group formed the nucleus of a movement. Any Crimean Tartar who wished could join. Within a city, street groups informed the city group of their activities; the city group in turn informed the area group; the area group informed the republic group. Each group informed all the inhabitants of its area as well. The membership of these groups reached approximately 5,000.[4] Lists were sent to local authorities and to the Central Committee of the Communist Party of the USSR.

The initiative groups called meetings to read the text of each petition and to collect signatures. Representatives were chosen to take the petitions to Moscow and give them to the authorities. Money for the trip was collected. Twice a month the representatives were to give a report of their activities to the appropriate group and to the Central Committee, and on their return, to account for their activities.

The petition campaigns of the Crimean Tartars were truly national in scope. Some petitions had more than 100,000 signatures. Yet this expression of the will of an entire people met with no positive response from above Instead, from about 1961, repressions against the activists of the Crimean Tartar campaign began.

One of the first trials took place in Tashkent in 1962, involving the case of the members of the Union of Crimean Tartar Youth. In fact, there was no such organization, but only conversations about the possibility of creating one at a few meetings of young Crimean Tartars. Most were students, although there were some white- and blue-collar workers among them. They read poetry and discussed a variety of political questions, mostly those of their own people. In April 1962, four participants of these discussion groups were arrested: two were released soon afterwards and two were tried in closed court for "participating in an anti-Soviet organization": Marat Omerov, a factory foreman, and Seyt-Amza Umerov, a law student. Their sentences were three and four years in a strict-regimen camp. Others were expelled from their institutes, and a few were dismissed from work.[5]

In 1961–62, the authorities let the petition organizers know that their activities were looked on with disfavor and could have unfortunate repercussions. Some of the original founders left the movement, and by 1964 the petition campaign had begun to decline. People lost faith in the possibility that humble pleading would persuade high government organizations to resolve the Crimean Tartar question favorably.

The change in political leadership of the USSR gave a new impulse to the movement. The initiators regained their courage and again "went to the people," calling for faith in the new leadership. They again collected signatures for petitions to the new leaders. But after 1964, petitions represented just one part of the movement. The younger generation of Crimean Tartars, mostly students and members of a new educated class, began to join initiative groups. The ordeals of their people and the falsification of their history in official sources had led them to thirst for knowledge of their own history, culture, and traditions. Many began to study their own history, as well as the history of Russia and the Soviet Union, in order to understand the causes of the Crimean Tartar tragedy. They understood this tragedy as a result of Soviet national policy and not as some kind of sad "mistake." They discovered similarities between Soviet national policies and the colonial policies of tsarist Russia. This approach was widely disseminated by Crimean Tartar *samizdat* and met with full understanding from its readership. The new approach of movement activists to the Crimean Tartar problem was no longer based on hopes for a quick solution "from above." The people prepared themselves for a long and difficult struggle for the restoration of their national rights. The petition campaign continued, but its tone changed. No longer supplicant, from 1964 on such documents were critical of government policies toward the Crimean Tartars. Illegal acts against the Crimean Tartars began to be called by their accurate name: genocide.

Protests were not limited to petitions. Crimean Tartar youths (but not only youths) in Uzbek cities began to hold May Day celebrations, and meetings and demonstrations supporting the demands of their petitions, usually timed to coincide with some nationally significant date. A traditional day for such meetings was Lenin's birthday—Crimean Tartars set Lenin apart because he had signed a decree on the formation of the Crimean republic in 1921. Crimean Tartars began to lay birthday wreaths with appropriate inscriptions on monuments to Lenin, which can be found in any Soviet city. In national or holiday dress, Crimean Tartars marched in columns to the monuments, headed by Young Pioneer children who carried the wreaths. At the monuments, they sang national songs, performed national dances, and sometimes gave speeches on Lenin's benevolent role in their history and on the misfortunes they had suffered as a result of departures from Lenin's policy on nationalities.

They observed May 18, the anniversary of the deportations from the Crimea. On that day, they usually gathered at Muslim cemeteries, many wearing black armbands, to pay respect to the memory of compatriots who had died either in transit or in the first years of exile.

At night, some of the braver hoisted flags of mourning on public buildings.

The established custom of observing these important dates by meetings and demonstrations prompted the authorities to summon the Crimean Tartars to Party committees at their place of work or to the militia. This was done after the autumn of 1966, when new articles were added to the criminal code ("slander of the Soviet way of life," "defaming the flag or the official government insignia," and "mass public disorders"). The Crimean Tartars had to listen to the text of the new articles; they were required to sign a statement acknowledging that they understood and were familiar with them. Indeed many activists are convinced that these articles were enacted into law because of the Crimean Tartar movement.

These preventive measures did not stop the movement. On the contrary, it spread from Uzbekistan to all the areas of the Crimean Tartar diaspora. Petitions were collected and meetings held not only in Uzbekistan, but also in Kazakhistan, Tadzhikistan, Kirgizia, Turkmenia, and in the northern Caucasus. There was evidence of the movement in Moscow as well, where representatives of the movement, sent to deliver communications to high government organizations, were constantly presenting massive amounts of supporting documents. From the very beginning of the movement until June 1969, there had been a total of 5,000 representatives in Moscow.[6]

In 1966, movement activists, in order to conduct a national survey, made use of the network established by the initiative groups. The survey's purpose was to determine the number of victims of the deportation and the years in exile, as well as the population of the Crimean Tartars. The data obtained was sent to the Twenty-third Party Congress (March 1966) in an appeal signed by more than 130,000 Crimean Tartars—almost the entire adult population.[7]

In October 1966, in Bekabad, Angren, Fergana, Kuvasay, Tashkent, Chirchik, Samarkand, and other cities inhabited by Crimean Tartars, the Tartars celebrated the forty-fifth anniversary of the Crimean republic with mass meetings that were broken up by soldiers and the militia.[8] Participants were beaten. Many people were tried under article 190-3 for "mass public disorders," although—like all other events organized by Crimean Tartars—the meetings proceeded quietly and peacefully. Moscow was inundated with protests. Hundreds of representatives of the Crimean Tartars besieged the reception rooms of high Party and government officials.

In June 1967, a delegation of Crimean Tartars (20 of the 415 representatives then in Moscow) was received by the Secretary of the Presidium of the Supreme Soviet Georgadze, the Minister of Internal

Affairs Shchelokov, President of the KGB Andropov, and the Procurator General of the USSR Rudenko. Andropov promised the delegates that a decree on the rehabilitation of their people would be issued soon and that measures would be taken to return the Crimean Tartars to the Crimea. He told the representatives that they could inform their people of this discussion.[9] Nevertheless, a meeting of the delegates with thousands of people scheduled for August 27 in Tashkent was broken up. On September 2, thousands joined in a demonstration to protest this action, but this demonstration also was broken up, and 160 people were arrested.[10] On September 9, 1967, decree no. 493 of the Presidium of the Supreme Soviet of the USSR, "On the Citizens of Tartar Nationality Who Formerly Resided in the Crimea," finally appeared in the local press. The wording seemed to negate the very existence of the Crimean Tartars as a people. Without any censure of the brutal injustices inflicted on the Crimean Tartars and with little or no enthusiasm, decree no. 493 nonetheless annulled the blanket charge of high treason against them. What the movement had not been able to obtain in eight years of humble appeal was wrested from the authorities in three years of energetic national protest.

Decree no. 494 appeared, "On Procedures for the Application of Part 2 of the Decree of the Presidium of the Supreme Soviet on April 28, 1956." (This decree released the Crimean Tartars from the "special settlement" law, and the second part reaffirmed the prohibition on their return to the Crimea.)

The decree affirmed the right of "Tartars who had previously lived in the Crimea" to settle in any territory of the USSR, that is, in the Crimea as well. This was accompanied by the condition that it be done "in compliance with existing legislation on labor and passport policies" and by the assertion that the "citizens of Tartar nationality" who had been forcefully deported from the Crimea had established roots in their new areas, where they "enjoyed all the rights of any Soviet citizens."[11] Both these assertions were false. Those who drafted the decree must have known that the entire Crimean Tartar population wished to return to its homeland. The endless petitions with huge numbers of signatures presented to the Supreme Soviet over the previous ten years eloquently testified to this.

Document 10 of the Moscow Helsinki Group offers the following evidence on the rights of the Crimean Tartars in the areas of their forced settlement:

The majority of Crimean Tartars, who were forcibly and unjustly evicted from their land in 1944, live in central Asia. They were in fact removed from the list of Soviet nationalities. They do not have one native language school, although there were several hundred in the autonomous Crimean Soviet

Socialist republic before the deportation. They do not have one national magazine. The institution conducting research on the Crimean Tartar language and literature was liquidated in 1944. From 1944 to 1973 two textbooks on the Crimean Tartar language were published (as opposed to 58 in nine months of 1939). Out of seven newspapers published before the war, only one (a non-daily) is left.

It is obvious the authorities are counting on the assimilation of the Crimean Tartars into the population of the central Asian republics. But inasmuch as the policy of assimilation meets with the resistance of the Crimean Tartars, it is a violation "of human rights and fundamental freedoms, respect for which is an essential factor for the peace, justice and well-being."[12]

Limits of Resettlement

A number of Crimean Tartars relied on the letter of the decree and left for the Crimea. From the moment the decree was published until December 1967, about 1,200 families arrived in the Crimea—more than 4,000 Crimean Tartars—but only two families and three bachelors were able to meet all the formal conditions required to settle there on "a legal basis."[13]

When the decree was published proclaiming the right of "citizens of Tartar nationality" to settle, just like anyone else, in any part of the USSR, the authorities had made preparations to prevent the settlement of Crimean Tartars in the Crimea. Residence permits had been required only in cities and resorts in the Crimea. Most of the inhabitants of the Crimean steppe, as in rural areas elsewhere in the USSR, had no passports; no residence permits were required to settle there. Immediately after the publication of the decree, passports and residence permits for all inhabited areas were hastily issued for the entire Crimea during the course of the winter.

The Crimean Tartars who returned to their homeland knew very well that workers were being recruited from the Russian republic and the Ukraine to meet the shortage of workers in the Crimea. About 500,000 workers were needed—exactly the number of Crimean Tartars that would have resettled there, since the first to return were certain that they could find work easily in their native area. But a secret instruction had been given to the managers of all enterprises not to hire Crimean Tartars. Notary publics were instructed not to legalize the purchase of a home if the buyer was a Crimean Tartar.

Thousands of Crimean Tartar families wandered about the Crimea, searching for shelter. The majority failed and were forced to leave the Crimea. Those who were able to buy homes, settled down, but it is illegal to occupy a house without registration of the deed of sale. Many families were expelled from the Crimea even after they had purchased homes when the court ruled the purchase invalid. They had no deeds of sale because the notary publics had instructions not to confirm them. A description of one such expulsion is given by S. A. Smailova:

> On June 3 we were tried for illegally drawing up the papers on our house, when we desperately want to legally register it. A terrible knock on the door woke us . . . on the night of June 29, 1969. When we asked who was there, the window was broken and several men broke into the room. They were militia and volunteer police under the command of Novikov, the head of the militia in Belogorsk District. . . . They were all inebriated. After tying my hands, they dragged me through the window. When I began to call to my neighbors for help, they immediately stuffed a gag in my mouth. Then they dragged our sleepy children out. The children were frightened and began to cry. . . . They took us to the Ust-Labin station in the Krasnodar region, where they let us out into the open without a cent, with no food, and with our four children. We went hungry for three days.[14]

Because families that are expelled try to return to their homes, the authorities saw that their homes had been destroyed after their expulsion. Sometimes bulldozers or tractors are used. Returned owners would put up a tent next to the ruins or stay with neighbors. With the help of their compatriots, and sometimes even of Russian and Ukrainian settlers, they rebuilt their houses. The few who managed to have the purchase of their homes registered had to obtain a pass to live there. Many families spent years trying to break out of the vicious circle: without a deed of sale, they could not get a residence permit; without a residence permit, they could not work. Without a permit their children were not accepted into schools and newborns were not given birth certificates, even if only one of the parents was a Crimean Tartar. Living without a residence permit was treated as "a violation of the passport rules"; that, under Soviet law, could be punished in a number of ways, including labor-camp sentences. All Crimean Tartars who left for their homeland under the decree of 1967 had to endure these carefully planned and organized ordeals. Only the solidarity of their people sustained them. Those still living in the former settlement areas sent money or other material aid to compatriots who returned.

In the spring of 1968 the authorities declared that resettlement in the Crimea could occur only after official recruitment. One had to obtain a work contract approved by the appropriate officials from the Crimea, who were required to travel to the applicant's residence. Thus, in 1968, only 148 families were resettled in this way; in 1969, 33 families; and in 1970, 16 families. The selection process took place on the recommendation of the KGB. Contracts were signed only with those who had never participated in the Crimean Tartar movement, who had never signed statements, who had never gone to meetings, or who had never donated money for the support of people's representatives in Moscow.[15] Because of these harsh conditions, people continued to enter the Crimea without official approval. Among those who entered "independently" in 1967–68 were the most active participants in the struggle to return to the homeland. A new form of Crimean Tartar resistance began: returning to the Crimea on the basis of the law, but without prior permission and against the will of the government. The results in 1968 were similar to those in 1967: of the 12,000 Crimean Tartars who independently entered the Crimea, only eighteen families and thirteen bachelors obtained a pass and were registered; seventeen persons were sentenced to prison terms for "violations of the passport rules."[16]

Links to the Human Rights Movement

The year 1968 also marked a rapprochement between the Crimean Tartar movement and the human rights movement, a circumstance that played an important part in the development of both. The Crimean Tartars had a long-standing friend in Moscow—the Russian writer Aleksey Kosterin, a sincere Communist and long-time Party member who had lived in the Crimea and the Caucasus for many years. After the deportation of some ethnic groups of the Caucasus and the Crimean Tartars, he helped their representatives in Moscow in communications with government bureaucrats. On March 17, 1968, Kosterin's seventy-second birthday, the representatives organized a party in his honor. There they made the acquaintance of Kosterin's friend, Pyotr Grigorenko, one of the leading human rights activists. From that day on until he emigrated in 1977, Grigorenko defended the cause of the Crimean Tartars as if he were one of them. Kosterin died soon afterward, but before his death, he returned his Party card to the Central Committee as a sign of protest against illegal practices in the USSR. After Kosterin's death, the Crimean Tartars were still in communication with the Muscovites, thanks to their friendship with Grigorenko, and through him they met other human rights workers. This ended their isolation and informed people in the Soviet Union of their plight, arousing public condemnation of the injustice they suffered.

No documents exist on the Crimean Tartar movement for 1954–66 in either the *Samizdat Archives* nor in any Western sources. The earliest documents that have surfaced in the West relate to 1967; they began to be sent here only through Moscow human rights activists.

The Crimean Tartars themselves had no opportunity to establish contact with the West.

In the letter to the Budapest Conference of Communist Parties (February 1968), the first collective document of the Moscow human rights workers addressed to the West, the prohibition of the Crimean Tartars from returning to their native land is listed among the most intolerable violations of human rights in the USSR.[17] Since then, the Crimean Tartar problem has always figured as one of the most pressing concerns of the human rights movement. All leading human rights associations concerned themselves with this problem: the Initiative Group for the Defense of Civil Rights founded in 1969, the Committee for Human Rights in the USSR (1970–72), and the Moscow Helsinki Group. From its first issue (April 1968) the *Chronicle of Current Events* has continuously dealt with the struggle of the Crimean Tartars to return to the Crimea. With the help of friends in Moscow, the Crimean Tartars were able to find lawyers who courageously defended their activists in a series of court trials from 1967 to 1970. They included: Dina Kaminskaya, Sofya Kallistratova, Mikhail Romm, Leonid Popov, and Yury Pozdeyev. Constantly persecuted by the authorities, the Crimean Tartar representatives found shelter in the homes of their new friends. Yet, relations between the Crimean Tartars and the Moscow human rights workers were not restricted to the one-sided help from the Muscovites. When the two groups made contact, the human rights movement was in its early phase and inexperienced. The Crimean Tartar movement had more than ten years' experience from which to teach others. Natalya Gorbanevskaya, the first editor of the *Chronicle of Current Events,* later wrote: "Perhaps it was the contact with the Crimean Tartar movement that stimulated the appearance of what was later called the *Chronicle of Current Events.*" The informational bulletins released by the Crimean Tartars from 1966 or 1967 "were a sort of early form of the future *Chronicle.*"[18]

It is certainly no accident that the first independent public association to appear in Moscow was called the Initiative Group for the Defense of Human Rights (May 1968). Like the initiative groups of the Crimean Tartars, it had neither a leader nor a well-articulated organizational structure. One of the founders of the Moscow Initiative Group was Mustafa Dzhemilev. A representative of the younger generation of Crimean Tartar activists, he later became a national hero of his people.

The attempts of the Crimean Tartars to resettle in the Crimea en masse after the 1967 decree and their rapprochement with the human rights activists resulted in an intensification of repressions against those Tartars still living in their former settlements and against the representatives in Moscow.

The rout of a celebration of the Crimean Tartars in Chirchik on April 21, 1968—Lenin's birthday—exemplified this intensified repression. The Tartars decided to celebrate this event with a traditional folk fest or *derviza* in the city park. Residents of Chirchik and families from other cities and villages came, dressed in holiday costumes, and prepared for a peaceful and happy celebration.

They were surrounded by a detail of militia and soldiers with fire engines, beaten with rubber clubs, hosed with chemicals, and packed in cars. More than three hundred were arrested; ten were sentenced to various prison terms.[19]

Outraged by this unjust and crude reprisal, the Crimean Tartars sent about eight hundred representatives from virtually all Crimean Tartar groups to Moscow with protests. From May 15 to May 17, 1968 these representatives were rounded up and treated just as roughly as the participants in the Chirchik celebration. Three hundred representatives were detained and sent under guard back to their homes. But many of them returned to Moscow and continued their mission. They visited prominent people in the arts, public figures, and old Bolsheviks to relate their problems. Appeals were sent to 2,300 people.[20] As a result, twelve representatives were arrested and convicted of "mass public disorders" (statute 190-3). Since that occurrence, representatives began to be rounded up and removed from Moscow regularly.

On April 21–22, 1969—Lenin's birthday—wreaths were laid once again on his monuments throughout the cities of central Asia. In Samarkand about 1,500 people gathered for the occasion; in Margilan, more than 1,000; in Fergana, about 600; and in Bekabad, about 200. Everywhere the participants were surrounded by a circle of militiamen, and everywhere the wreaths were removed immediately after the Crimean Tartars left.

On May 18, 1969, the twenty-fifth anniversary of the deportation, mass meetings took place in the cemeteries just as before, even though the authorities tried to prevent it. They blocked the road to the cemeteries by the militia or closed them under the pretense that they were "quarantined."[21]

In 1968–69 the best known activists of the Crimean Tartars and their aides in Moscow were arrested. In September 1968, ten leading activists in the initiative groups, who gathered data on the Crimean Tartars and wrote national appeals, were arrested. Their trial date was set for May 1969. Three thousand Crimean Tartars turned to Pyotr Grigorenko, requesting that he act as public defender at the trial.

But Grigorenko was not able to do so, because he was arrested in Tashkent on May 7, 1969. On May 17 another Muscovite who had done much to help the Crimean Tartars was arrested—Ilya Gabay—and on September 11, Mustafa Dzhemilev.[22] Grigorenko was declared mentally ill and spent more than five years in a psychiatric prison. M. Dzhemilev and I. Gabay were convicted of "slandering the Soviet system" at the same trial. They were each sentenced to three years in labor camp.[23]

This prison term was not Dzhemilev's first. Included as an infant in the mass deportation of May 18, 1944, he had never lived in the Crimea, but he had devoted his life to his people's struggle to return. The young Mustafa spent his free time in libraries. He studied the history of his people, unscrupulously distorted in Soviet publications. (The article on the Crimea, for example, in *The Great Soviet Encyclopedia*, does not mention the deportation of the Crimean Tartars.) Dzhemilev wrote a history of the Crimean Tartars that was disseminated in *samizdat*. In 1962 he was implicated in the trial of the Union of Crimean Tartar Youth and dismissed from his job. His attempts to obtain an education ended with expulsion during his third year of study at an institute on the grounds that he was "politically unreliable." Dzhemilev became a youth movement activist; he joined the initiative group and participated in the unofficial census of the Crimean Tartars before the Twenty-third Party Congress. He was first arrested on May 12, 1966, allegedly for evading military service, and was sentenced to one-and-a-half years of labor camp. Freed in 1968, he went to Moscow as a people's representative, became friends with Grigorenko's family and with Gabay and other human rights activists, participated in collecting data on the Crimean Tartars and appeals to government departments, and became one of the most popular activists of the Crimean Tartar movement. In 1969 he joined the Moscow Initiative Group for the Defense of Human Rights in the USSR. During his trial, from January 12 to 16, 1970, he refused legal counsel and delivered a brilliant speech in which he defended himself, the entire Crimean Tartar people, and the right to live in one's native land and enjoy one's own cultural heritage.[24]

Dzhemilev was at liberty only a short time after he served this last prison term. In 1974 he received a new sentence: one year in camp for "refusing to take part in military exercises." While he was in camp, a case was initiated against him for "slander of the Soviet system," and he was resentenced to two-and-a-half years more, despite the fact that the only witness against him, another prisoner Vladimir Dvoryansky, had renounced his earlier testimony, explaining that the prosecutor had coerced him into testifying against Dzhemilev by threatening to extend his own term. Dzhemilev went on a ten-month hunger strike in protest against the false charges.

Andrey Sakharov, his wife Yelena Bonner, and a group of Crimean Tartars, including friends and relatives of Dzhemilev, went to Omsk where the trial of Dzhemilev was held, but only his closest relatives were allowed in the court. Dzhemilev's sentence led to massive protests: a petition signed by more than 3,000 Crimean Tartars, protests by human rights activists, including Sakharov and Grigorenko, and document no. 1 of the Moscow Helsinki Watch Group. There was public condemnation the world over.

Dzhemilev was next arrested on February 8, 1979, on his way to the airport to catch a flight to Moscow—fourteen months after his release, and on the very day his parole came to an end. His new sentence was four years of internal exile for violating parole—it had been extended one day longer without his knowledge.[25] In 1984, soon after serving his sentence in exile, Dzhemilev was once again sentenced to three years of labor camp for "slandering the Soviet system."

The year 1970 was a critical one. In that year the most active and influential Crimean Tartar movement activists were sentenced. From then on the movement went into a gradual decline. Seeing little use in further appeals to the Soviet government, movement activists guided the people toward yet another attempt to return to the Crimea, in spite of the failure of the first wave of returnees. They themselves took part in this effort.

The Crimean Tartars have not yet succeeded in overcoming obstacles put in the way of their return despite enthusiasm and willingness for self-sacrifice. From the decree of 1967 until 1978, only about 15,000 Tartars have successfully registered to live in the Crimea—less than 2 percent of the entire Crimean Tartar population.[26] Those 15,000 who did resettle in their native land found neither a satisfying nor a traditional way of life. They were uprooted from their own people and dispersed in an alien environment of nationalities that speak different languages. In not one village in the Crimea do Crimean Tartars constitute a significant portion of the inhabitants. Each family settles wherever it can obtain the all-important residence permit, and the authorities do not permit them to settle densely. Hence they are scattered all over the Crimea. They must constantly overcome the hostility of the authorities; they are treated as second-class citizens even more than they were in their former places of exile. As for institutions of national culture, there simply are none.

Those who were unable to settle in the Crimea did not as a rule return to their former settlements in exile. Instead they settled as close to the Crimea as possible in the hope that they could once again try to relocate there. But even outside the borders of the Crimea they were not allowed to settle in dense concentrations. The approximately 100,000 Crimean Tartars who left central Asia are fragmented into separate families and small groups in the areas bordering the Crimea. In Novorossiysk and environs live a few tens of thousands; in the Krasnodar region, about 30,000. They have even settled on Taman Peninsula and other places in the northern Caucasus, in the southern Ukraine, in Novoalekseyevka and environs, in the Kherson and Nikolaev *oblasts* and elsewhere. The difficult conditions that await them in these new areas require that all their time and energy be spent on everyday concerns. This is true even among those who used to be the most active participants in the movement: the majority either give up the movement after resettlement or participate only sporadically. The fact that the most active participants were sent to the Crimea immediately after 1967 had an impact on the development of the movement in central Asia, where the largest portion of Crimean Tartars still live. The necessity of constantly rendering material aid to those who settled in the Crimea has exhausted their financial resources. They cannot simultaneously carry the burden of supporting their Moscow representatives, whose number has been reduced from several hundred to only a few. Dispersal and constant psychological harassment from the authorities have caused many enthusiastic supporters and sympathizers to abandon the movement.

The supplicant posture of petitions to the government once again gained ground at the expense of demands that the rights of the Crimean Tartars be observed. Opposition to union with the human rights movement, formerly limited to a small number of participants in the Crimean Tartar movement, became stronger. Even now, however, only an insignificant minority oppose cooperation with the human rights movement. This is borne out by the facts surrounding a KGB-inspired letter sent to Andrey Sakharov in February 1977 and signed by fifty-two Crimean Tartars: "Do not interfere in our affairs. Stop causing harm to our people. We will find a way to reach the Crimea without you and your friends." Several of the signatories wrote to Sakharov later and said that their signatures were obtained under false pretenses; they had signed a different text. Then, in June 1977, Sakharov received another letter signed by 549 Crimean Tartars, thanking him for "supporting the hopes and aspirations of the Crimean Tartars" and assuring him that the first letter was "unworthy and did not reflect the opinions of the Crimean Tartar people."[27]

Decline of the Movement from the 1970s to the 1980s

During the 1970s the authority of the initiative groups suffered from lack of agreement among the members and, to an even greater extent, from the ineffectiveness of all the tactical measures proposed in the course of the twenty-five-year-old struggle to return to the Crimea. Nation-wide letters of the kind once signed by tens of thousands were now signed by a few thousand people at best. The gradual decline of the movement may be charted according to the number of signatures collected on petitions to the regular congresses of the Communist Party, because these petitions usually had more signatures than any other kind of public appeal. The petitions reached their peak during the Twenty-third Party Congress in 1966 with more than 130,000 signatures. Sixty thousand signatures were collected for the petition to the Twenty-fourth Party Congress in 1971, and in 1975, 20,000 for the Twenty-fifth Party Congress. In 1979 the largest number of signatures ever was collected for the "National Protest"—4,000.[28]

Nonetheless, the initiative groups continued their work, although on a much smaller scale. After the data was published from the all-union census, in which the Crimean Tartars were not even listed as a nation (in spite of their protests, they were listed simply as Tartars), the initiative groups conducted their own census in 1971, using their own resources. They included all Crimean Tartars, in whatever region they lived, including central Asia, the Crimea, the southern Ukraine, and the northern Caucasus. They set the population at 833,000.[29] Also in 1971 the initiative groups in the Tashkent region conducted a sample survey on the attitudes of Crimean Tartars toward returning to the Crimea. Of the 18,000 adults queried, only nine had objections to returning, and eleven did not respond.[30]

Meetings and gatherings usually take place only on important occasions and considerably fewer people participate, reflecting not only the understandable weariness of the Crimean Tartars after so many years of intense struggle, but also a change in their social structure.

While the annulment of the special settlement law in 1956 failed to solve the basic problem of the Crimean Tartars, it widened the scope of social and economic opportunity for each individual. Involuntarily assigned on a mass scale to factory work in 1944, the Crimean Tartars now left these jobs on a mass scale. Many returned to the traditional occupation of their people—agriculture—and a significant portion became mechanics, drivers, and construction workers, using the skills acquired in the factories.

Educated Crimean Tartars (teachers, engineers, doctors, etc.), repressed in 1944, reappeared as a social class. The older generation returned to their professions, and the younger generation was able to obtain an education after the reservations were eliminated. Changes in the social composition of the Crimean Tartars were accompanied by changes in their settlement patterns: as they left the factory settlements and moved to the places of their new jobs, they were spread out more sparsely. The living conditions of the majority of Crimean Tartar families improved, as did their standard of living, but this meant that the work of the initiative groups was complicated, their effectiveness reduced, and their difficulties in coordinating efforts magnified.

Educated Crimean Tartars suffered through all the ordeals the others endured and considered themselves part of the people. Intellectuals make up a significant portion of the activists in the Crimean Tartar movement: they participate in initiative groups, are among the people's representatives in Moscow, and, of course, have written the documents of the movement.

In order to deprive the movement of the intellectual strength it needs, the authorities use social bribery. To those who are aggressive and demonstrate managerial talents they offer posts in Party, administrative, and economic-planning enterprises, rapidly advancing those who are successful. The "national aristocracy" thus created serves as an ideological bulwark for the authorities. They do not insist that such people refuse to participate in the movement, but instead use them as their own "fifth column" to discredit active members by spreading rumors about them; they use them to instill conformist attitudes in the initiative groups, to counteract the active tactics of the movement and its union with the human rights movement, and to discourage appeals to international organizations.

The policy of encouraging the conformist wing of the movement is combined with the systematic removal of those who support decisive and active tactics, the rapprochement with the human rights movement, and appeals to international public opinion. In short, they encourage the removal of people like Mustafa Dzhemilev. During the most active period of the Crimean Tartar movement there were more than fifty court trials, in which more than 200 activists were convicted.[31] We have information on the social background of 74 of these 200. Thirty-five were highly educated, a number disproportionately large when compared with the number of educated people active in the movement. Of the 36 people convicted of compiling documents for the movement, 22 were professionals and only 9 were workers (the backgrounds of 6 of the defendants are unknown to me). But the statistics for the mass demonstrations are the same: of the 37 persons tried on these charges, the backgrounds of 27 are known—14 were workers and 13 were professionals. Obviously, a disproportionate number of professionals could not have made up one-half of the many thousands of Crimean Tartars who gathered, for instance, at the Chirchik celebration on April 21, 1968. Of the 300 detained at the site of the celebration, those indicted were selected not only on the basis of their activities that day, but also according to their level of education.

Of those convicted in the Crimea (usually under the articles for passport violations and later for resisting the militia), all are agricultural workers. This is because the same screening process used to weed out intellectuals from among those who returned to the Crimea after 1967, had been used during and after the deportation (1944–56) as well. We do not know of one case of a Crimean Tartar teacher or engineer receiving work in line with his or her qualifications in the Crimea, but there are many cases of engineers working as drivers or tractor operators and of teachers working as storekeepers or unskilled agricultural workers.

Until the second half of the seventies this situation was unchanged. Every year Crimean Tartars arrived in the Crimea, although in smaller numbers than during the sixties. Few of them succeeded in settling there although some repeatedly tried to do so. The most favorable period was from February to November 1977. Although forty-six persons were convicted of passport violations in the course of 1976, in September 1976 deportations ceased altogether for an entire year. From February to November 1977 about two hundred families received residence permits.[32] By the spring of 1978 approximately seven hundred families in the Crimea were unable to receive residence permits to live in houses they had purchased. Beginning in September 1977 deportations began once again. One of those deportations had a tragic outcome: on June 23, 1978 a forty-six-year-old Crimean Tartar joiner, Musa Mamut, committed self-immolation.

Mamut's family (himself, his wife, and three children) had arrived in the Crimea in April 1975. They bought a home in the village of Besh-Terek, now called Donskoe, in the Simferopol region, but they could neither formalize the purchase of the home nor obtain a residence permit. In May 1976 Mamut was sentenced to two years in labor camp for "violating passport regulations." He was released early for diligent work and exemplary behavior, and returned to his family in March 1978. With Musa unable to find work for lack of a residence permit, they were soon on the verge of starvation. In June 1978 he was warned that a new case was being prepared against him for "violating passport regulations." He replied that he would never "give himself up alive" and prepared a can of gasoline. When the militiaman arrived to take him in for questioning, Musa went to the back of his yard, spilled gasoline over himself, and set fire to himself as he approached the militiaman. The militiaman ran off, and Mamut's neighbors extinguished the "living torch." His burns were so severe that he died in the hospital on June 28.

Approximately one hundred people gathered for the funeral procession, even though the roads to Donskoe were blocked. The procession carried posters reading: "To our dear father and husband, who gave his life for his homeland—the Crimea," "To Musa Mamut—a victim of injustice—from the Crimean Tartar nation," and "To Musa, from your outraged Russian brothers. Sleep in peace, justice will triumph."

Andrey Sakharov sent a telegram to Brezhnev and Nikolay Shchelokov, the Minister of Internal Affairs: "The true cause of Musa Mamut's self-immolation lies in the national tragedy of the Crimean Tartars, whatever the specific circumstances. . . . The tragic death of Musa Mamut must lead to the restoration of justice and of the legitimate rights of his people that have been violated."[33]

On November 19, 1978 another tragic event followed: the Crimean Tartar Izet Memedullayev hanged himself. He had arrived in the Crimea with his wife and three daughters in September 1977. Like Musa Mamut, he could not register the purchase of his house and lived under the threat of prosecution. A local KGB agent promised to straighten things out for him if he would agree to become an informer. Izet agreed to do so and signed a receipt to that effect, but he changed his mind after a few days and asked for the receipt back. The KGB agent refused to return the receipt and increased the pressure on Izet through the local office. Izet killed himself and left this note: "I have never been a scoundrel. I want to die with a clean conscience."[34]

Such expressions of total despair did not stop the implementation on October 15, 1978 of resolution 700 of the Council of Ministers, "On Additional Measures for Strengthening Passport Regulations in the Crimea." This resolution simplified the procedures for deportations and evictions. It was no longer necessary to obtain a court order; a decision of the local authorities was sufficient.[35]

In Simferopol a battalion of MVD (Ministry of Internal Affairs) troops was organized to carry out evictions and deportations, since local volunteer police often refused to help the militia in these "operations," and there were instances of other Crimean Tartars, Russians, and Ukrainians interfering with such operations. Even when these deportations were carried out as military operations, they sometimes encountered resistance from the local population. In the *Chronicle of Current Events* (no. 51, p. 110) there is a description of the eviction of the Gavdzhi family from the village of Abrikosovka in the Kirov region. Fifty militiamen led by the head of the militia conducted the family to the Novoalekseevka station in the southern Ukraine. More than two hundred local inhabitants—Crimean Tartars—gathered there to express their outrage. They wrote on the sides of the militia cars "We demand equal rights," "The disgrace of the Soviet militia," and "Stop this lawlessness!" The demonstrators prevented the militia from loading the family's possessions onto the train for central Asia. A colonel of the militia promised the crowd that the family would be returned to the Crimea, and the Gavdzhi family returned to their home; a short time later they were deported from the Crimea.

Beginning in October 1978, deportations became more frequent. While twenty families were deported from January to October 1978, from November 1978 to February 1979 the number of families deported increased to sixty. For the most part, the families deported had arrived in the Crimea after October 15, 1978, but an earlier arrival time was no safeguard against deportation. Repressions against persons without residence permits became harsher: the electricity and water (if water was piped in) to their homes was cut off. They were deprived of their personal garden plots on which they depended for most of their food. Twenty-two Crimean Tartar families lived in Kurskoye (the Belogorsk district), of which eleven were not registered. Measures against those eleven families outraged the local non–Crimean Tartar population. The Russian electrician A. Isayev refused to disconnect power to the homes of Crimean Tartars, for which he received a Party reprimand and was transferred to locksmith work. A Russian tractor operator refused to sow oats on land taken from the plots of Crimean Tartar families and was fired from his job. A tractor brigade refused to demolish a building from which Crimean Tartars had been evicted.[36]

By 1980 there were only sixty unregistered Crimean Tartar families left in the Crimea. No new families arrived. The danger of intensified repressions and the impossibility of overcoming a fresh obstacle, a new unpublished instruction from the Minister of Interior Affairs of Uzbekistan, stood in their way. The new edict went into effect on April 25, 1978. Instruction no. 221 prohibited the militia from releasing Crimean Tartars from Uzbekistan without a certificate stating that work and housing were available in the area to which they wished to move.[37] There is no comparable regulation in any other republic, and in Uzbekistan this regulation relates exclusively to Crimean Tartars.

This entire network of official measures froze the number of Crimean Tartars relocating in the Crimea to the 1979 level. These regulations are still in effect—a fact that caused increased protests from

1977 to 1979, particularly among the Crimean Tartars in the Crimea. From May to June, 896 signatures were collected on a petition to the United Nations, requesting that a commission be formed to investigate the situation of the Crimean Tartars in the Crimea.[38] On November 9, 1978 a delegation of Crimean Tartars arrived in Simferopol to deliver a protest of the deportations signed by seventy-five Crimean Tartars from various parts of the Crimea to the First Secretary of the Crimean Regional Party Committee. The delegation was not received.

At the end of November, more than 2,000 Crimean Tartars sent a statement to Soviet governmental departments and to the United Nations protesting the deportations.[39] Early in December a delegation of twenty-three went to Moscow to protest increased persecutions. Another delegation visited Moscow at the end of January with a "National Inquiry." They demanded an answer to the following inquiry: Did resolution no. 700 on the forced deportation of Crimean Tartars from the Crimea in fact exist? If it did, then they demanded that it be annulled as being unconstitutional. Later a number of other delegations, totalling 130 people, went to Moscow with additional signatures to this inquiry.

Initially, the Communist Party Central Committee answered by saying that there was no such resolution. Then on February 9, 1979 a subsequent delegation in Simferopol was received by the Crimean Party Committee. They were told that resolution no. 700 would in the future be implemented. No further delegations were received by the Communist Party Central Committee in Moscow. When the nationwide protest was taken to the Komsomol Central Committee, it was accepted only after the delegation members threatened to turn in their Komsomol membership cards.[40]

During their stay in Moscow, the delegates of Crimean Tartars were detained and taken to the militia for interrogations on several occasions. Once freed, they protested their detention by staging a two-day hunger strike in the reception room of the Presidium of the Supreme Soviet of the USSR.

In Uzbekistan in 1977 more than 4,000 signatures were collected for an appeal to Brezhnev requesting that all legislation passed from 1944 to 1976 that adversely affected the rights of the Crimean Tartars be annulled. According to the authors of this appeal, the Crimean Tartars are the only people in the USSR whose civil inequality is based on judicial decree.

In September 1977, a meeting of initiative-group representatives took place in Uzbekistan. They decided to plan all their future activities around legal appeals, a decision confirmed at another meeting of representatives in November 1979. Representatives were sent from

Uzbekistan to Moscow to obtain an answer to the appeal. They resumed publication of the Crimean Tartar informational bulletins, and three issues appeared, nos. 126, 127, 128.[41]

Reshat Dzhemilev, an active participant in the Crimean Tartar movement from Tashkent, wrote to the king of Saudi Arabia about the death of Musa Mamut and the Crimean Tartar problem, asking the king to help his fellow religious believers. Dzhemilev was sentenced to three years in a labor camp for writing the letter.[42] In April 1980 the Muscovite Aleksandr Lavut was arrested. He had helped the Crimean Tartars in their struggle for many years, and after Grigorenko emigrated in 1977, Lavut became their main support in Moscow.[43]

Several attempts undertaken to make the Crimean Tartars "take root" in Uzbekistan came to nothing. These attempts were based on alloting a separate territory to the Crimean Tartars, in which they could occupy the highest government positions. One such attempt occurred in 1974, when a Crimean Tartar, S. Tairov, was appointed to the post of First Secretary of the Dzhizkak Regional Party Committee. A few other high positions in the region were given to Crimean Tartars as well. Their compatriots expressed no desire to move into the region and continued efforts to relocate in the Crimea. Tairov was transferred to the post of Minister of Forestry of Uzbekistan. Hopes that the Crimean Tartars would establish themselves there had obviously been abandoned.[44] According to the Crimean Tartar *samizdat* magazine *Yemel* (Hope), "not one Crimean Tartar, even if he were an agent of the KGB or a provocateur, gave up the desire to return to his homeland."[45]

A dead-end situation had been created: the Crimean Tartars did not and obviously would not reconcile themselves to the prohibition on returning to the Crimea or to the destruction of their national culture. On the other hand, it is psychologically impossible for the present leadership of the Soviet Union to agree to settle a strategically important frontier area with a people who have ethnic and religious ties with nearby Turkey (a consideration that probably motivated the mass deportation of 1944). Yet the Crimean Tartars have demonstrated over a period of twenty-five years a truly national will to assert their rights and to present the government with a bill for the destruction of human life, the destruction of their national culture, and for its ongoing discrimination.

A solution to the Crimean Tartar problem may be possible only as a result of the democratization of the Soviet system.

Ayshe Seytmuratova, the foreign representative of the Crimean Tartars, has emigrated to the United States and given speeches at several conferences of Islamic countries which have attracted the attention of the Islamic press and some Islamic politicians. Perhaps as a result of this interest, as well as the interest of the American public, the United Nations has at last paid some attention to the documents they have received from the Crimean Tartar movement over a period of many years.

CHAPTER 8

The Meskhi Movement

The problem of the Meskhi is similar to that of the Crimean Tartars. Located in the south of Georgia, Meskhetia borders Turkey. The Meskhi are related ethnically to the Georgians. They were under Turkish rule during the sixteenth and seventeenth centuries, as a result of which they converted to Islam and adopted many Turkish characteristics. At the present time, some Meskhi consider themselves to be Georgians, while others consider themselves Turks. Most of them face at least some difficulty in determining their identity.

In November 1944, the entire population of 300,000 Meskhi were deported to the eastern regions of the Soviet Union under the pretext of evacuation as the Germans approached. Within a few months the Meskhi found themselves under the regime of special-settlements regulations, that is, the same regulations under which the Crimean Tartars and other peoples proclaimed "traitors" were included. Meskhi soldiers who returned from the front were sent to settlements of exile as well. The Meskhi were used as the principal labor force in constructing the irrigation system in the Golodnaya Steppe. Thanks to artificial irrigation, this dead land was transformed into the flourishing region of Gulistan. Tens of thousands of Meskhi, exhausted by the labor, denied medical attention, paid for this with their lives.[1]

In 1956 the Meskhi were released from special-settlement regulations, but the ban on returning to their homeland was not lifted, in spite of the fact that all the Meskhi, regardless of the degree of national identity, wanted to return. At the end of 1956, the Meskhi sent representatives to Moscow to deliver a collective request that they be allowed to return to Meskhetia. In response, the Meskhi were declared to be Azerbaidzhanis; they were given permission to return to the Caucasus, but not to Meskhetia, nor even to Georgia. They were permitted to go either to Azerbaidzhan, where a work force was needed to irrigate the Mugab Steppe (an area with a poor climate and no water) or to the Kabardino-Balkaria autonomous republic. A considerable number of Meskhi moved to these areas in order to be closer to the homeland to which someday they hoped to return.

For a number of years the Meskhi representatives, having formed an ad hoc Committee to Return to the Homeland, travelled to Moscow and Tblisi to persuade Party and high administrative officials to hear them out. They were put off with ambiguous answers or else the authorities simply refused, sometimes in a very crude manner, to consider their problems. The Meskhi appealed to Georgian writers, journalists, and cultural figures, but received only moral support. The Meskhi who did attempt to return to Meskhetia were immediately turned back.

On February 15, 1964 the first general meeting of the Meskhi took place on the collective farm of Lenin Yuli in the Tashkent district of Uzbekistan. Representatives from local Party and administrative centers were invited to attend, but only unidentified plainclothesmen showed up and tried to interfere with the meeting. Nevertheless, six hundred Meskhi delegates elected at local meetings in the settlement areas of central Asia, Kazakhstan, and Azerbaidzhan gathered to hear lectures on the history of the Meskhi, their current condition, and the consolidation of their efforts to return to Meskhetia. The delegates elected new members of the ad hoc Committee to Return to the Homeland, headed by Enver Odabashev, a veteran and war invalid who was a history teacher. One hundred twenty-five new representatives were elected; they were to go to Moscow and again appeal to the authorities to allow them to return to their homeland. Since then, such meetings have been held regularly.

The representatives made a series of trips to Moscow, where they were told that the problem could best be solved in Tblisi. The Tblisi authorities kept insisting that the question could only be decided by the Soviet government. In the meantime, local authorities used threats and material temptations to stop the movement.

In April 1968, the twenty-second meeting of the Meskhi was held in Yangiyul (in Uzbekistan). Six thousand people attended. The area was surrounded by soldiers and militia armed with clubs and fire trucks. The meeting proceeded without incident, but on their way home, many delegates were detained and taken to Tashkent; thirty were held there for periods ranging from two weeks to six months.

In May 1968, a resolution of the Presidium of the Supreme Soviet of the USSR was issued. It stated that "citizens of Turkish, Kurdish, and Azerbaidzhan nationality, who had been deported from the Akhaltsik, Aspind, Akhalkal, and Adigen regions and from the Adzhar ASSR enjoyed the same rights as all other citizens of the USSR." But since these citizens had established roots in the republics where they presently resided, it was necessary to create conditions that would take their national characteristics into account. Seven thousand Meskhi representatives went to Tblisi and on July 24, 1968 gathered in front of Government Hall to demand a hearing. They were surrounded by soldiers and the militia, who beat them. But they neither allowed themselves to be provoked, not did they leave the square. After two days, they were received by First Secretary of the Central Committee of the Georgian Communist Party Vasily Mzhavanadze. He promised that the Meskhi would be allowed to settle in the various regions of Georgia in small groups of one hundred families per year. His promise was deceptive. The Meskhi who arrived in Georgia were at first accepted and even given jobs, but after a short time they were fired and turned back to their former places of residence or to the Mugab Steppe.[2]

On April 19, 1969, Enver Odabashev, who had already been detained several times, was arrested again. When they learned of his arrest on April 21, the Meskhi in various Azerbaidzhan settlements stopped work and gathered at the District Party Committee in the village of Saatly, where Odabashev was being held, and demanded his release. When this was denied, they sent an express telegram with the same demand to Brezhnev and to the First Secretary of the Azerbaidzhan Communist Party V. Akhundov. The crowd stood in front of the District Party headquarters until early morning, when the secretary of the District Party Committee appeared and ordered Odabashev's release, although he was scheduled to be sent to prison that morning. When he appeared, the Meskhi greeted him with joyful cries: "Freedom! Equality! Our homeland or death! Our teacher is alive!"[3]

In August 1969, the thirty-third delegation of one hundred twenty representatives went to Moscow to the Central Committee of the Communist Party. This time they were received by a certain Moralyov, who refused their demands in an insulting manner. In protest, the delegates threw down their passports in the reception area and renounced their citizenship. The next day, the authorities conducted a city-wide search for the delegates and deported them under guard.

In despair, the representatives of the Meskhi who considered themselves Turks appealed to the Turkish embassy in April 1970, requesting Turkish citizenship and permission to enter Turkey. The sixth meeting of the Turkish Meskhi, held on March 15, 1971 in the Saatly region of Azerbaidzhan, approved this decision. A list of Meskhi who were prepared to emigrate was submitted to the Turkish embassy, and the Meskhi sent to Soviet officials a protest concerning the unlawful ban against returning to their homeland. In addition, they sent documents expressing their demands to international organizations, including the United Nations.[4]

After this action, repressions against both the Turkish and Georgian Meskhi were intensified. On August 7, 1971 Enver Odabashev was again arrested and sentenced to two years in a general-regimen camp for "illegally seizing collective-farm land." While in camp, he was convicted of "slandering the Soviet system" and sentenced to one more year in camp. His deputies were also jailed on fabricated charges. M. Niyazov was arrested on October 3, 1971 for "hooliganism." (He gave a speech at a meeting of front-ranking workers at the express wish of 2,500 Meskhi, but without permission to speak from the chairman.) He was sentenced to three-and-a-half years in camp. Islam Karimov was charged with "passport violations" and sentenced to eight months in camp.[5]

The attempts of Turkish-oriented Meskhi to emigrate to Turkey aggravated existing disagreements between their representatives and those of the Georgian-oriented Meskhi, and have culminated in a split.

In 1976, Viktor Rtskheladze, a member of the Initiative Group for the Defense of Human Rights in Georgia, took up the cause of the Meskhi. He went to Kabardino-Balkaria and, at a Meskhi settlement, gave a talk promising help from the Georgian intelligentsia at a meeting held especially for the purpose. Rtskhladze advised the Meskhi to write to the Moscow Helsinki Group. In the spring of 1976, delegates of the Georgian Meskhi, L. Abashidze and A. Abasturmaneli, travelled to Tblisi where they were met with great respect by Georgian intellectuals who organized a dinner for them at the apartment of V. Rtskhladze. They tried to meet with the First Secretary of the Georgian Communist Party, Eduard Shevardnadze, but were received by his deputy instead. In their statement the representatives asked that their children be accepted in Georgian boarding schools until the question of the return of the Meskhi to their homeland could be resolved. They also asked that ten to fifteen Meskhi freshmen be admitted to Georgian institutions of higher education, and that specialists be sent to Meskhi settlements to lecture and show documentary films on the history and culture of Georgia.[6] Their request was denied.

The Georgian Meskhi who resided in central Asia, Azerbaidzhan, and Kabardino-Balkaria sent a letter to the Moscow Helsinki Group, signed by 1,100 family heads (representing about 7,500 individuals). They asked for support and cooperation in their struggle to return to Meskhetia or at least to Georgia. The Turkish-oriented Meskhi did not appeal to the Moscow Helsinki Group, but instead provided documents concerning resolutions passed at their sixth and eighth meetings, the last in the summer of 1976. There they demanded resettlement in Meskhetia or permission to emigrate to Turkey; the most radical among them declared that if the repatriation problem were not settled, they would demand that Meskhetia be separated from the USSR and be annexed to Turkey. They asked the Moscow Helsinki Group for support on this demand. Yury Orlov, the chairman of the group, explained that their demand contradicted the Final Act of the Helsinki Accords, and therefore could not be supported.

The Moscow Helsinki Group devoted a special document to this matter (no. 18): "We assert that in relation to the Georgian and Turkish Meskhetians, the Soviet government is grossly violating its obligations to national minorities as stated in the Final Act: 'The participating States on whose territory national minorities exist will respect the right of persons belonging to such minorities to equality before the law.' "[7]

PART THREE

THE MOVEMENTS
FOR EMIGRATION

CHAPTER 9

The Soviet German Emigration Movement

In 1938 Friedrich Ruppel's father, his twenty-five-year-old brother, his uncle, both of his uncle's sons, and four other cousins were all arrested. Six of them died in camp, and Ruppel's father returned home blind. In September 1941, Friedrich, then eighteen years old, was arrested and so were his mother, who was sentenced to be shot, and his cousin Andrey Ruppel. Three other cousins received, like Friedrich, ten-year sentences in camp, and one cousin died in camp. The authorities admitted the innocence of all those who survived.[1] The Ruppels' story appeared in the Soviet German *samizdat* publication, *Re Patria,* written by Friedrich Ruppel, one of the compilers.

This was a typical history for Soviet German families. For Soviet Germans, the terror of the thirties was only a prelude to the tragedy that began during the war with Nazi Germany.

The ancestors of the Soviet Germans, whose population was 1,937,000 in the 1979 census, moved to Russia from Germany, Austria, and Switzerland, beginning in 1764 under Catherine the Great and continuing during the Napoleonic Wars. The first wave settled mainly in the Volga area and the second wave in the southern Ukraine and the Caucasus. Settlers received virgin land and cultivated it under very difficult conditions. The colonists had self-government, schools taught in their native language, and their own press. But their situation was unstable, depending to a large extent on relations between Germany and Russia. Germans born in Russia considered Russia their native country, but the authorities distrusted them. Under the terms of the imperial decree of December 13, 1915, the German colonies were to be liquidated and the colonists forcefully resettled in Siberia after April 1917. The February Revolution hampered these plans. In 1921 the German autonomous republic was established in the Volga region; in the Ukraine, the Caucasus, and the Altai Mountains, German national districts were formed. Before World War II, there were about 170 German schools, 11 technical colleges, 5 institutions of higher education in the autonomous German republic; 21 German newspapers, German national theatres, clubs, and cultural institutions. It was the first republic in the USSR with virtually total literacy, and it possessed a national intelligentsia.[2]

Under the Soviet regime the German population was increased by immigrants from the United States and Germany—Communists who moved their families to "the first government of workers and peasants" in the world in order to participate in the building of socialism. With rare exceptions, all these immigrants were arrested in the thirties, and most died in prison.

Persecution during World War II

On August 28, 1941, a decree of the Presidium of the Supreme Soviet of the USSR was issued: "On the Resettlement of Germans Living in the Volga Region." It stated that "according to information received by military organizations, there are thousands upon thousands of spies and saboteurs among the Volga Germans. They are prepared to set off explosions in this area at a signal given from Germany. Not a single German in the Volga region has informed Soviet security of the presence of these numerous spies and saboteurs. Therefore, the German population of the Volga region is hiding the presence of enemies of the Soviet people and the Soviet state." In order to "avert undesirable eventualities and avoid unnecessary bloodshed," all Soviet Germans (not only from the Volga area, where one-third of the German population lived, but from the entire country) were forcefully exiled to Siberia and central Asia. The republic of the Volga Germans was abolished.[3]

In 1942, Germans—men and women over fourteen years old—were mobilized into an army of laborers to work on construction projects under the control of the NKVD (as the KGB was then called). They were treated more like prisoners than like construction workers. They were housed in camp barracks behind barbed wire and under guard; they were taken to work in convoys; the men and women were separated; families were split up; children under fourteen years old were taken from their mothers and placed with unfamiliar families or sent to children's homes. Here is an account by Konstantin Wuckert:

All the able-bodied members of our family were mobilized into the work battalions: my father, my 15-year-old brother, and my stepmother. Only one member of our family stayed home, that is to say, in Siberia, where we were compulsorily settled: my 7-year old sister. She was placed with a family. In 1944 my father was able to have her sent to him, in the work battalion. She was exhausted from the hunger and humiliations she had suffered at the hands of the strangers who took her in."[4]

When the war was over, the work battalions were disbanded. The Germans were sent to the same kind of special settlements in which the Crimean Tartars, the Meskhi, and other exiled peoples lived. The decree of the Presidium of the Supreme Soviet of the USSR of November 26, 1948, under the terms of which the Germans were transferred from the work battalions to the special settlements, declared that they were to be sent there "for all time."

Special settlements for Germans were annulled on December 13, 1955. As the decree of the Presidium of the Supreme Soviet put it, this action was based on "the consideration that existing legal restrictions placed on those in special settlements . . . will not be necessary in the future." However, the second point of the directive stated that: "the removal of the restriction to special settlements does not entail the return of property confiscated from the Germans during their deportation, nor does it give them the right to return to their former residences."[5] Thus the Germans were no longer required to report to the commandant's office every month, and they were permitted to move beyond the limits of the settlements. Still, the accusation of treason hung over their heads until August 29, 1964, when it was formally removed by the next decree of the Presidium of the Supreme Soviet. This decree recognized that "the groundless accusation" of "actively helping and collaborating with the Fascist German invaders," brought against them in the directive of August 28, 1941, was without basis in fact. The 1964 directive recognized that "during the years of the Great Patriotic War the overwhelming majority of Soviet Germans actually contributed to the victory of the Soviet Union over Fascist Germany by working with the rest of the Soviet people, and in the postwar years they actively participated in the building of communism."[6] But this recognition of the injustice done to the Soviet Germans did not mean that they were permitted to return to their former areas of residence. As in the case of the Crimean Tartars and the Meskhi, it was decided that the Germans had "put down roots" in their new areas of residence and that they ought to remain there.

The first delegation of exiled Germans—thirteen members of the Initiative Group of Communists, Komsomol Members, and NonParty People—went to Moscow on January 2, 1965. They brought letters for the President of the Presidium of the Supreme Soviet Anastas I. Mikoyan, signed by a total of 660 Germans. The letters expressed gratitude toward the Party and the government for removing "baseless accusations" from the "Soviet German people" and declared that they were not a part of the German, Swiss, or Austrian people, but were a separate nation whose homeland was Russia.[7] They insisted not only on permission to return to their native areas, but also on the restoration of the German autonomous republic as well.

The question of restoring autonomy to the Germans was the more substantial one. It would signal their complete rehabilitation and create the necessary conditions for the preservation and development of their national culture. And it offered them their only opportunity for an island of peace in a country still alive with hatred that had arisen toward all Germans during the war.

The terrible war losses and the cruel treatment of prisoners of war and the civilian populations of occupied territories by the Nazis provided fertile soil for wartime propaganda. To this day, Soviet schools present history so as to make Germany appear the age-old enemy of Russia. There is no mention of the history of the Volga Germans. The peculiar features of their history, their role in the Revolution, in the civil war, in peacetime construction, and the injustices they suffered during the war are unknown to most Soviet citizens. Konstantin Wukkert recalls that during their tragedy, the Soviet Germans were denied any sympathy from those around them: "I heard more than once . . . the refrain, 'What did you expect? Just as many of our people died during the siege of Leningrad!' In other words, we were put in the same category as those Germans who surrounded Leningrad and strangled the city by starvation; we were expected to die in exchange for those who died in Leningrad. As the saying goes, 'an eye for an eye, a tooth for a tooth.' "[8]

Wukkert describes how in 1967 he stopped in to visit a Russian neighbor in the village of Novotroitskoye, Kazakhstan. Among the guests he met a brother of his neighbor who had lost both legs at the front. When he learned that Wukkert was German, he attacked him, yelling " 'I'll get you now, you rat!' His family managed to drag him off with great difficulty."[9] German children in particular suffer from the hatred of those around them. They do not want to speak their native tongue, embarrassed that they are Germans.

The next delegation of Germans went to Moscow on June 7, 1965 and was received by Mikoyan. After hearing the wishes and complaints of the delegation, Mikoyan warmly praised the German contribution to the cultivation of the virgin lands. Although he commended the Germans on their love of work, he refused their request. "Not everything created in the course of history can be undone," he said, and went on to explain why the government refused to restore the autonomous German republic: "At the present time it is impossible to carry

Soviet-German Emigration Movement

Soviet-German activist Friedrich Ruppel (R) and his family, before emigration, with Andrey Sakharov and his daughter, Tatyana (L), Moscow train station, 1974

Soviet-German participants in Red Square demonstration, 1980: (L to R, rear) Gotfried Oblinder, Viktor Fritsler, Viktor Ebel, (L to R, front) Lidiya Ebel, Alvina Fritsler

Jewish Emigration Movement

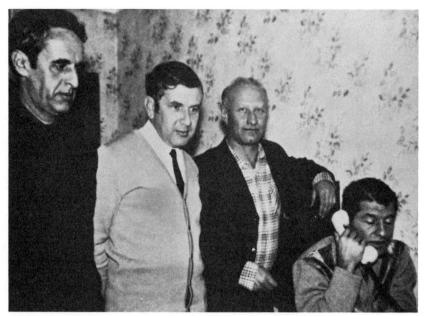

Members of the Jewish refuseniks' scientific seminar, Moscow, 1973: (L to R) Aleksandr Lunts, Viktor Brailovsky, Mark Azbel, Aleksandr Voronel

Jewish refusenik Aleksandr Paritsky, founder of the independent university for young refuseniks, with his family before his arrest, Kharkov, 1981

Memorial Day, Minsk, 1975: former Soviet Army colonels Lev Ovsishcher and
Yefim Davidovich, in front

Evangelical Christian Baptists

Council of Relatives of Evangelical Christian Baptist Prisoners, 1980: (L to R, front) Nina Skornyakova, Aleksandra Melashchenko, Aleksandra Kozorezova, Galina Rytikova, Lyubov Rumachik, (L to R, rear) Antonnia Senkevich, Zinaida Velchinskaya, Rita Prutyanu, unknown, Serafima Yudintseva, Lidiya Bondar

Ivan I. Leven, manager of Baptists' underground printing press in the Leningrad area, with his family; Leven was arrested in 1977

Georgy Vins (R), founding member of the Initiative
Group and Council Secretary, Independent Baptist
Church, with his son Pyotr, member of the Ukrainian
Helsinki Watch Group, who visited his father in a
Yakutsk camp, 1977

Yakov Skornyakov, Baptist minister, in camp flanked by his two prisoner converts, ca. 1980

Pentecostalists

Vasily F. Patrushev, initiator of 1965 Pentecostal exodus, with his family

Pentecostal exodus leaders: Fyodor Sydenko (R) with Bishop Nikolay Goretoy and his wife, Varvara

Trial of Boris Perchatkin, 1980, leader of the Pentecostalist Emigration Committee in Nakhodka

Bishop Ivan Fedotov preaching at a Pentecostal service

True and Free Seventh-Day Adventists

Vladimir Shelkov, in camp near Yakutsk, 1979, leader of the Independent Adventist church since 1949; he died in camp in 1980

The Reverend Rostislav Galetsky, baptizing an Adventist who is masked to conceal his identity

on agriculture in the virgin lands without the Germans," and "the restoration of the republic would entail enormous economic losses."[10] The members of the delegation who were especially active were invited to live in Moscow, where they were given good positions, and eventually gave up their Soviet German agitation.

The Germans are spread out all over the country, with the areas of densest German population their former places of exile: Kazakhstan, Kirgizia, and Tadzhikstan. The majority live in rural areas, because they were for many years forbidden to live in large cities. More than half the entire German population is involved in agriculture. During the past ten years, a considerable number of Germans have moved to the Volgograd region, Moldavia, the Caucasus, and the Baltic republics. But as before, conditions are not conducive to normal cultural life anywhere. There are practically no schools and only occasional classes taught in German. The German press consists of two newspapers—one in Moscow and the other in Tselinograd, Kazakhstan. Their circulation is small, and the topics they cover are far from being specifically national in scope. There are no German cultural institutions, theatres, or publishing houses. A large number of younger Germans have lost the ability to speak or to read and write in German. Assimilation has progressed rapidly. In 1959, 75 percent of the Soviet Germans considered German their native tongue; in 1970, only 66.8 percent thought so; and by 1979, only 57 percent.[11]

Germans still experience veiled discrimination in job promotions and admissions to college. As a result, they have been almost totally deprived of the opportunity to create an educated class. But the most difficult obstacle is the alien environment. The spontaneous hostility of the population is encouraged by higher authorities and the local press. For example, on April 2, 1980 the *Chelyabinsky Rabochy* published an article that depicted Aleksandr Bous, a German resident of Chelyabinsk, as follows: "a high forehead, thin reddish hair and bright blue eyes. . . . All of a sudden my war days came back. . . . I can still remember those dark, venomously green helmets . . . with swastikas. . . . And the eyes under the helmets. . . . Cold blue eyes as if touched with ice went particularly well with those helmets. . . . Nordic eyes—the sign of belonging to the higher race.' "

Postwar Emigration Movement

Many German families began to apply for exit visas to join relatives in West Germany in the fifties. Some did so as early as the twenties. However, a mass emigration movement began only in the midsixties, after all hope for the restoration of the Volga German

Republic had vanished. Of course, German emigration, like its Jewish counterpart, has its roots not only in national problems, but also in repression. Soviet Germans could have sought to emigrate to East Germany, which has a social structure analogous to the Soviet Union's. But most Germans have a preference in the choice between East or West Germany; the overwhelming majority wish to solve their national and social problems simultaneously by choosing the West.

Only in 1974, after years of efforts to emigrate by Soviet Germans, did the West German government try to obtain permission for Soviet Germans with relatives in West Germany to do so. According to the *Chronicle of Current Events,* by 1974 approximately 40,000 Germans had applied to emigrate.[12] They organized special emigration committees in Estonia, Latvia, Kazakhstan, and other places. In January 1974, activists of the German emigration movement published a collection of articles in *samizdat—Re Patria,* devoted to problems of the German emigration movement. Although the collection was published as volume one, presumably the first in a series, no further collections were published after the editors—Vytautas Grigas, Friedrich Ruppel, and Lidiya Bauer—were allowed to emigrate to West Germany.

On February 11, 1974, a demonstration of Germans seeking permission to emigrate occurred in front of the Communist Party Central Committee building in Moscow. Lyudmila Oldenburg and her two underage sons chained themselves to a stoplight post. A similar demonstration took place on February 17 in Tallinn, Estonia.[13] Since then, demonstrations have been widely used in the German struggle to emigrate. The demonstrations most often occurred in Moscow, and usually in Red Square, although sometimes outside the city, as in Dushanbe in front of the Tadzhikstan Communist Party Central Committee. Most of these demonstrations are small, the largest no more than twenty to forty people. The norm is less than ten, often members of a single family. The following is a description of a demonstration that took place on March 31, 1980 in Red Square; it is typical.

Thirty people were supposed to participate, but just before the demonstration was to begin, the Germans who had arrived from the city of Narkal (in the Kabardino-Balkar autonomous republic) were detained by the militia. Only five people from the city of Kotovo in the Volgograd region were able to come. They carried posters reading: 'We want to live in our homeland—West Germany.' All five were immediately seized by the militia and taken to a militia station near Red Square. They were: Viktor (born 1952) and Lidiya (born 1957) Ebel, Viktor (born 1953) and Alvina (born 1955) Fritsler, and Gotfried Oblinder (born 1953). The Ebel and Fritsler families had been denied permission to emigrate five times.[14]

A favorite form of protest peculiar to the Soviet Germans was the renouncing of their Soviet citizenship by turning in their passports. Three hundred Germans from Kazakhstan and Kirgizia first used this tactic at the end of 1976, and wrote of their plight to international human rights organizations and the Moscow Helsinki Group. A number of such activists were arrested later for "violations of passport regulations" and sentenced to prison terms ranging from a few months to one-and-a-half years. After serving their terms, some received permission to emigrate, but many still have not.[15] In 1976 the Germans began to appeal to the Moscow and Lithuanian Helsinki Watch Groups, which issued special documents on this problem. Appeals to official Soviet organizations, the West German government, and various international organizations continue.[16]

The organizers of the collective German protests suffered repressions, such as some labor-camp sentences on various fabricated charges for "slandering the Soviet system," a common response to Soviet German complaints of official discrimination.

Since 1980 the pressure against Germans seeking to emigrate has been intensified. The Moscow Helsinki Group devoted four of their documents to the problems of the German refuseniks, three of them issued in 1980–81.[17] A statement by 246 German refuseniks from Kabardino-Balkaria, sent in 1980 to the president of the Presidium of the Supreme Soviet, to the German Bundestag, and the Madrid conference of countries that signed the Helsinki accords, complained of the arbitrary and rude treatment received at the hands of local officials to whom they are obliged to apply for permission to emigrate.

The Deputy Director of the Regional Office of the Ministry of Internal Affairs in the city of Maysky, D. M. Timofeyev, explained that we were needed here as a labor resource, and, in his own words, before letting us go, they would first squeeze us dry. The head of the local KGB department Prokhladny expressed the desire to send us all to BAM [the Baikal-Amur Railroad, the most recent "great construction project"—L.A.]. Deputy Director Timofeyev blamed the death of 20 million Soviet citizens during the Great Patriotic War on us. The head of the passport desk of the Ministry of Internal Affairs of Azerbaidzhan, Khuranov, said on one occasion that if he had his way, we would all be shot.[18]

Compelled to lodge their complaints against local authorities, German refuseniks met with lawlessness from higher government departments. A letter signed by 246 Germans reported that on November 10, 1980, fifteen Germans had been detained and sent back home under guard merely for visiting OVIR (Office of Visas and Registration) in Moscow. Two were thrown by KGB agents from the platform onto the train tracks. Georgy Miller (whose return address had been supplied in the letter), was arrested. In 1981 several other Germans were arrested for actively pursuing permission to emigrate.[19] In 1971, 1,145 people emigrated; in 1972, 3,423; in 1973, 4,494; in 1975, 5,985; in 1976, 9,704; in 1977, 9,274; in 1978, 8,445; in 1979, 7,226; in 1980, 6,650; in 1981, 3,723; and in 1982, 2,069; in 1983, 1,447; in 1984, 913; in 1985, 460.[20] In all, about 50,000 Germans have left the Soviet Union during the past six years. But the number of people refused has been increasing, and the number of emigrants has been decreasing. According to the International Red Cross in 1985, 832 ethnic Germans applied to emigrate to West Germany from the USSR.[20]

CHAPTER 10

The Jewish Emigration Movement

Even before the movement for emigration to Israel surfaced in cities that had witnessed mass killings of Jews during World War II, the custom of honoring the dead with funeral prayers and wreaths on the anniversary of the massacres had been established. Baby Yar in Kiev is the most famous of such mass graves. For many years friends and relatives of the victims would gather there on September 29, and, after the emigration movement began, many refuseniks from Kiev and other cities, who were denied the right to emigrate, began to attend the memorial ceremonies at Baby Yar. As the movement grew, more and more began to attend: in 1968, 50 to 70 people gathered there; in 1969, 300 to 400 people; and in 1970, 700 to 800. In 1971 about 1,000 people gathered at Baby Yar, among them refuseniks from Moscow, Leningrad, Sverdlovsk, and Tblisi. They laid wreaths with appropriate inscriptions at the site of the mass grave.[1]

The authorities tried to prevent the gatherings by organizing competitive official meetings on the same day. Prepared speeches on Israeli "aggression" were delivered, but the fact that Jews were buried there in mass graves and had been killed because they were Jews was never mentioned.

In Riga a gathering of protesters took place every November 29 in the Rumbola cemetery. A funeral prayer or kaddish was read near the monument to World War II victims. In 1970, about two thousand people gathered to demand the release of those arrested in connection with this trial. The authorities closed the cemetery on November 29.[2]

In Minsk it was customary to gather on May 9, Victory Day, at the site of the former Jewish ghetto, where five thousand Jews had been shot. Here the authorities also began to hold official meetings. In 1975 Yefim Davidovich, a refusenik and retired colonel with eighteen orders and medals, pushed aside the official chairman at such a meeting and began to speak, calling on his audience to fight anti-Semitism in all its forms and under whatever government it appears. In 1976, Lev Ovsishcher, a friend of Davidovich and retired colonel and refusenik, made a similar speech.[3] In 1977, two hundred people attended the anniversary meeting. This tradition has continued almost every year since then.

Since the early seventies, participants in the Jewish movement have gathered every year in Moscow and in other cities near synagogues on Saturdays. Here they learn who received permission to emigrate, who was denied, who was harassed and how. The activists collect signatures protesting violations of the right to emigrate and petitions in defense of those persecuted. People ask for material help from abroad and agree on joint protest actions. Here also they meet with foreign tourists who are interested in the problems of Soviet Jews.

After 1970 the crowds around the Moscow synagogue were large on Jewish holidays. Not only refuseniks, but many others, young and old, gather there. The entire street in front of the synagogue is packed with people who dance and sing Jewish songs. Often the militia tries to disperse the crowds, sometimes with force. On September 5, 1975—Jewish New Year's Eve—the militia directed traffic through the crowd by closing the other streets in the neighborhood. The people did not run away. Instead, they began to sit and lie down in front of the traffic so that the militia had to close the street.[4]

Demonstration of Refuseniks

In 1971 the first demonstration of Jewish refuseniks occurred in front of the press center for an international film festival. Later demonstrations took place in front of the office of the Presidium of the Supreme Soviet, in front of the TASS News Agency building, and in front of the Lebanese embassy. Gesya Penson, an old woman and mother of refusenik and imprisoned highjacker Boris Penson, conducted several lone demonstrations. She stood near the Communist Party Central Committee building with a placard reading "Free my son!" On one occasion Gesya Penson was imprisoned for ten days. She reappeared with another placard near the Central Committee building. Although her son was not released, she herself received permission to emigrate to Israel.[5]

The first demonstration in defense of the "prisoners of Zion" was on December 24, 1975, the fifth anniversary of the death sentences given to the highjackers. These demonstrations have occurred every year up to the present time at the same place—on the steps to the Lenin Library in Moscow, just across from the office of the Supreme Soviet of the USSR. The demonstrators carry slogans reading "Freedom for the Prisoners of Zion," and "Visas Instead of Prisons." After the first demonstration, two of the nine participants were sentenced to internal exile, yet the next demonstration attracted thirty-seven people.[6]

On September 19, 1976, twelve Moscow refuseniks made a collective appeal to OVIR (Office of Visas and Registration under the Ministry of Internal Affairs), demanding that refusals of their applications be issued in writing together with the reasons for the refusal and the period of its effectiveness. They received no answer for about a month; then the authors of the application went to the office of the Presidium of the Supreme Soviet, demanded an answer, and refused to leave the office until their request was granted. In the evening volunteer police forcefully removed them from the office, threw them into a bus, and drove them to the suburbs, where they were deposited. The next day the same process was repeated, only this time the refuseniks refused to get out of the bus in a remote, deserted area far from Moscow. They were then thrown out and beaten with fists. After this incident, not twelve, but forty-four people showed up at the office of the Supreme Soviet. They repeated the demands of the original twelve, and demanded that those who were responsible for the beatings be punished. The delegation was met by the Minister of Internal Affairs Nikolay Shchelokov, but he did not answer their questions; whereupon the forty-four marched through downtown Moscow wearing yellow stars of David to the Central Committee of the Communist Party of the Soviet Union. This pattern was repeated for a month, until the authorities began to detain the marchers at their apartments or on their way to the government offices. They would then be fined and jailed for fifteen-day periods.

Two of the refuseniks who were beaten on the bus, Iosif Ass and Boris Chernobylsky, were arrested and charged with striking the volunteer police. On October 30 it was learned that the investigation of the case had been completed. None of the refuseniks who witnessed the beatings on the bus were questioned. It became quite clear that the defendants would be convicted on the basis of false testimony by the volunteer police, a tactic used more than once during trials of dissidents.

On November 1, 1976 the Group for a Public Investigation into the Reasons and Circumstances of the Arrests of Ass and Chernobylsky was formed. The group included activists of the Jewish movement, an observer from the Moscow Helsinki Group, and a consultant on legal affairs, the lawyer Sofya V. Kallistratova. It began an active investigation of the case and sent several letters to both Soviet and international organizations, describing the circumstances of the arrests and indicating that none of the numerous witnesses had been questioned nor had steps been taken to punish the volunteer police responsible for beating the refuseniks. On November 15, both Ass and Chernobylsky were unexpectedly released. Their release document stated that their "actions were no longer dangerous to the public."[7]

In this case as in many others it is difficult to determine which factor was responsible for the success of the dissidents: international pressure or the efforts of the participants themselves. In regard to the Jewish movement, it is impossible to make this determination in any concrete instance because external pressures are frequently not applied publicly. Even if pressure is not exerted in a specific instance or is very weak, it can nevertheless have had a decisive effect on the outcome.

The peak of the Jewish demonstrations came in 1978. Since October 1977, twelve long-time female refuseniks have unsuccessfully demanded a meeting with Brezhnev to reconsider their cases. One of them—Dina Beylina—was allowed to emigrate. The rest decided to intensify their demands. They planned to gather on International Women's Day (March 8) at the traditional place for Jewish demonstrations in Moscow—the Lenin Library across from the Presidium of the Supreme Soviet. However, the majority of the demonstrators were detained on their way to the Lenin Library. Only two of the women reached the library and unfolded placards written in Hebrew. They were detained by the militia and held until the evening.

On March 12 there was another Jewish demonstration. About twenty-five to thirty people, including Andrey Sakharov protested an attack by Arab terrorists on Israeli civilians. They unfolded placards reading "Shame on the Murderers of Children!" People surrounding the demonstrators pulled the placards from their hands and tore them up. On May 23 a second demonstration of female refuseniks occurred, this time near the Kremlin wall. Six women stood holding a placard reading "Visas to Israel!" The demonstration lasted seven minutes.

On May 25, twenty-four female refuseniks informed the Presidium of the Supreme Soviet of the USSR that they were going to demonstrate with their children on Children's Day (June 1). They asked that security be provided. On the eve of June 1 they gathered at the apartments of Rozenshteyn and Tsirlin with their children. That night militiamen were posted at the doors to both apartments. The following day the streets in front of the buildings were closed to cars and pedestrians. The militia checked documents of people in the vicinity. Unable to leave the apartments, the women demonstrated inside; they hung placards expressing their demands in the windows and chanted "Visas to Israel." The demonstration lasted for twenty minutes, during which the militia tried to break down the apartment doors. On the morning of June 3, the sidewalk in front of the Rozenshteyn's apartment was inscribed in indelible paint with the words "Jews—into Coffins." Standing at the sides of the inscription, the Rozenshteyns, joined by several refuseniks who lived nearby, read psalms and passages from the Torah. The militia immediately appeared. They did not interrupt the prayers, and after the refuseniks left they painted over the inscription.

On June 1 demonstrations were conducted in the apartments of other refuseniks, including those of Ida Nudel and the Slepaks. Ida Nudel and Vladimir Slepak were sentenced to internal exile on charges of "hooliganism" because of their demonstrations.[8]

Emigration As Escape

Anti-Semitism has always been a feature of everyday life in the Soviet Union. After the second World War it was intensified by a state-sponsored anti-Semitism, which before Stalin's death threatened to take on the dimensions of a pogrom. It was somewhat subdued after his death, but subsequently developed quickly.

During the entire Soviet period Jews have been almost completely deprived of their national culture: Yiddish schools, press, movies, theatres, and synagogues are limited. The move to exclude them from all forms of cultural life has recently become quite noticeable: it is extremely difficult for a Jew to make a career in any field and no other group suffers such restricted access to higher education. It is important to recognize that Jewishness in the USSR is considered a nationality and is so stated on identification documents. The activists of the Jewish movement and the Moscow Helsinki Group conducted a survey of the nationality of students accepted to the department of mathematics and engineering at Moscow University during the past few years and found that there exists a secret quota for the admission of Jews—a quota set at about half the number of the officially observed tsarist quota.[9] Restricted access to higher education is the most effective form of discrimination against Jews, since the desire to give one's children an education is one of the strongest traditions preserved in Jewish families. The desire for emigration is a consequence. Nevertheless, ethnic discrimination is not the only reason for the phenomenon commonly called "the Jewish movement for emigration to Israel." This general formulation does not completely describe its nature.

What percentage of the applicants for emigration to Israel are not Jewish cannot here be stated with accuracy: perhaps 5 percent to 15 percent or more, if we take into account the members of mixed families. According to information available in 1977, only one-third of all requests filed in Rome for invitations to Israel came from people with

Jewish surnames. Non-Jews are among the most active members of the movement. Of the eleven persons convicted in the highjacking case of 1970, two were non-Jews. Of the movement participants arrested in Kiev in 1979–80, at least three were non-Jews (Valery Pilnikov, Ivan Oleynik, and Viktor Yanenko). The informational bulletin of the Movement for Emigration to Israel, *Exodus*, was begun by a Russian, Viktor Fedoseyev. Russians Lidiya Voronina and Oleg Popov were represented at the demonstrations in support of the Zionist Prisoners.

If the prerequisite for obtaining permission to emigrate were not being Jewish, but included any other people—even Russians—the percentage of others applying for emigration would be no less than the percentage of Jews now applying. If such were the case, the movement would deserve to be called the Movement for Emigration Anywhere Outside of the USSR. However, since Jews do at present constitute a majority in the movement, and the proclaimed goal of the movement is the return of the Jews to their historic homeland, I will use the commonly accepted term, the "Jewish Movement for Emigration to Israel."

The real goal of the majority of the movement participants is not immigration to Israel, but emigration from the Soviet Union. Of those who emigrate on Israeli visas, most go elsewhere than to Israel, and the number going to Israel is growing smaller every year.

Under Stalin some permits for emigration were issued to those with relatives in Israel. Four thousand people left between 1960 and 1970.[10] Jews from Riga were the first to receive permission to go; they were genuine Zionists, and so they went to Israel. This first crack in the Iron Curtain was a major achievement, made possible by the sacrifices and enthusiasm of Soviet Zionists and the enormous efforts of international Jewish organizations. As soon as the crack appeared, however, other groups joined the Zionists in trying to leave.

The roots of the Jewish Movement for Emigration to Israel lie not merely in nationalism, but in the socio-economic and political spheres of Soviet life. Scientists, artists, and professionals leave because they suffer from a lack of creative freedom in the USSR, a lack of freedom in general, and poor monetary compensation. Workers leave because of low pay and the impossibility of a legal struggle to improve their lot. Those who want to engage in business—an activity considered normal in the free world, but subject to prosecution in socialist countries—also leave.

From the moment the first emigration visas were issued, the number of applications quickly grew during the 1970s, as did the number of refuseniks. One becomes a refusenik for an indefinite period of time which may last for years. Becoming a refusenik usually results in a lowering of one's social status (engineers become repairmen, scientific researchers become guards or load trucks), or the complete loss of a job and other harassments.

Refuseniks are united by their common goal of leaving the Soviet Union and their common status as outcasts. Although the goal of each is his or her own emigration, they all need each other, if only to discuss the possible means of achieving their cherished goal. Thus it is natural that they cooperate with each other in the Jewish movement.

The Jewish Movement and Early Activism

The earliest form of joint action was the writing of petitions and open letters, individual as well as collective complaints about personal plight and violations of the right to emigrate, discrimination against Jews as a group, and anti-Semitic campaigns in the Soviet press.

The Six Day War in the summer of 1967 gave marked impetus to the Jewish movement. The Israeli military victory gave Soviet Jews, in particular, occasion to rejoice. It served to heighten their low self-esteem by demonstrating the military prowess of their people, previously denigrated. In the USSR there was a widespread notion that the Jews "sat out" World War II behind front lines and that they were generally poor soldiers. This opinion was a standard feature in the arsenal of anti-Semitism before the Six Day War, but not since. Unlike previous campaigns, the anti-Semitic press campaign was intensified during this period, eliciting strong protests in the form of open letters to newspapers, nonconformist speeches at meetings convened to denounce "Israeli aggression," and similar actions. This rising nationalist spirit promoted unity among the Jews, and the number of people who wanted to emigrate increased. Protests over application denials were addressed not only to Soviet authorities, but also to newspapers, international Jewish organizations, and to the United Nations.

Interest in Jewish history and culture rose among all Jews, not only among those wanting to leave. Due to an almost total lack of relevant Jewish literature, this interest gave rise to Jewish *samizdat*. As early as the fifties, a few Jewish intellectuals (E. Margulis, S. Dolnik, and others) began to copy and pass on articles and even books about Jews which were published before the Revolution, to compile summaries of Israeli radio broadcasts, and to translate from European languages into Russian books on Jewish issues. Original works based on pre-revolutionary and Western literature, and on personal experience, also made their appearance. Jewish *samizdat* and *tamizdat* (books written in the USSR and published in the West that make their way to the USSR—Trans.) were widely distributed. An underground organization called The Committee was created in Leningrad by Gilel Butman and others to print Jewish *samizdat* on a large scale. In Kishinev David Rabinovich, Aleksandr Galperin, and others managed to find a mimeograph machine for the same purpose.

The so-called highjacking trial was an important landmark in the development of the Jewish movement. In the summer of 1970, twelve people who planned to highjack an airplane en route from Leningrad to Priozersk were arrested. Most of the highjackers had unsuccessfully applied for permission to emigrate to Israel. Soviet authorities used this case to destroy the increasingly active Jewish movement. Soon after the arrest of the highjackers, twenty-two activists with no connection to the highjackers were arrested in Leningrad, Kishinev, and Riga. A wave of searches spread throughout many cities. In Leningrad alone more than forty searches were carried out. The authorities were looking for Jewish *samizdat, tamizdat,* and Hebrew textbooks.

The trial of the highjackers was scheduled for December 1970. All insisted that they had no intention of harming the pilot, but rather planned to tie him up and leave them in Priozersk. The single pistol the highjackers possessed did not work. They were aware of this and meant to use it only to frighten people. Among the highjackers was a pilot, Mark Dymshits, who was to have flown the plane outside the country. The highjackers disavowed any anti-Soviet intent. They said that their only desire was to reach Israel.

The sentences were harsh: M. Dymshits and Eduard Kuznetsov were to be executed by firing squad; the rest were to be given sentences from eight to fifteen years. The cruelty of the punishment and particularly the death sentences shook the world. The Soviet Union was in good company. At the same time, death sentences for Basque guerrillas were announced by General Franco's government in Spain, but on December 30, 1970, Franco commuted the death sentences for the Basques. In the face of denouncements from all sides, the Soviet Union had no choice but to commute the death sentences of the highjackers. An appeals court reduced them to fifteen-year prison terms and lessened prison terms for several of the other defendants.[11]

The so-called highjack-related trials took place in Riga, Leningrad, and Kishinev in the summer of 1971. The actual charges were for distributing Jewish *samizdat* and participating in Jewish self-education groups. The sentences ranged from one to five years of labor camp. Two defendants in the Leningrad trial were charged with treason: one received ten years and another seven years in a labor camp for connections with the organizers of the highjacking attempt.[12]

During the same period of 1970–71, Reyza Palatnik was tried in Odessa; Valery Kukuy, in Sverdlovsk; and Igor Golts, in Lutsk. In all instances there was insufficient evidence for opening a case, even by

Soviet standards. These trials appeared to be the result of overeagerness on the part of local authorities who did not want to "fall behind" Leningrad, Kishinev, and Riga. The cases of Emiliya Trakhtenberg in Samarkand (1971) and Yakov Khantsis in Kishinev (1972) were similar: both were charged with "slander of the Soviet system."[13]

After this, open convictions for "Zionism" ceased, although anti-Jewish trials continued. Isaak Shkolnik, a locksmith, was tried in Vinnitsa in 1973 for espionage.[14] After this followed a series of trials of Jewish-movement activists in different cities and on a variety of fabricated criminal charges. The first such trial we know of took place in December 1970—simultaneously with the highjacking trial. Igor Borisov, who openly claimed that Israel was his homeland and that he wanted to emigrate, was convicted of "malicious hooliganism" in the village of Toskovo (the Leningrad district).[15] Later, similar charges became the norm for dealing with Jewish activists. Aleksandr Feldman was tried in Kiev in 1973 for "hooliganism"; Mikhail Shtern, in Vinnitsa in 1974 for bribery taking; Aleksandr Gilyutin, in Leningrad in 1975 for smuggling silver; Lev Roytburt, in Odessa in 1975 for resisting the authorities; Amner Zavurov, in Dushanbe in 1976 for hooliganism and violating passport laws.[16] Several people who wanted to emigrate were tried for refusing to serve in the military. Their situation was tragic, since their military service would be used as a reason for denying them permission to emigrate over a period of many years. This kind of trial began in 1972. Four of them took place in 1975: Aleksandr Silnitsky in Krasnodar, Yakov Vinarov in Kiev, Aleksandr Slinin in Kharkov, and Natan Malkin in Moscow.[17]

If, by organizing these trials, the authorities meant to frighten Jewish-movement activists and to weaken the movement, they miscalculated. The effect was just the opposite. After the highjacking trial, the movement became more active and support from the West grew. This increased activity was, first of all, manifested by a qualitative and quantitative rise in *samizdat* materials. Periodicals appeared. In 1970 the Jewish *samizdat* magazine *Summing Up* began publication in Riga: two issues appeared; a third was confiscated during a search; and afterwards publication ceased. In 1970 the informational bulletin *Exodus*, published by Viktor Fedoseyev, began publication. *Exodus* (*Iskhod*) consisted of open letters, appeals, and official documents related to the Jewish movement. These materials gave the first complete picture of the movement and allowed estimates of the number of participants to be made. In the summer of 1971, *Exodus* was replaced by the *Exodus Herald*, published by Boris Orlov, Vadim Meniker, and Yury Breytbart. In 1972 two issues of the *White Book of Exodus* appeared. Roman Rutman, one of the editors, pointed out that all of these publications continued the tradition begun by the *Chronicle of Current Events* and the *White Book* on the Sinyavsky-Daniel trial.[18] A literary and public affairs journal, *Jews in the USSR*, came out in October 1972. Unlike the informational bulletins, this journal published the names of its editors. Aleksandr Voronel and Viktor Yakhot were the first editors. In May 1975 the first searches occurred relating to charges against the publication of this journal.[19]

The Jewish refuseniks worked out their own specific means for achieving the right to emigrate. In the first hunger strike, in Moscow's Central Telegraph Building on June 22, 1971, thirty refuseniks from the Baltic republics participated. They sent telegrams to Soviet leaders saying that they would not leave the building until they received permission to emigrate. They remained in the building for three days. A month later forty-four refuseniks from Tblisi conducted another hunger strike in the same building, and afterwards Moscow refuseniks did the same. In August 1971, three hundred Jewish refuseniks went to the Central Committee of the Georgian Communist Party in Tblisi. About one hundred made their way inside the building and were received by the Minister of Internal Affairs. They were given assurances that emigration permits would be issued every week. This practice continued for several months.[20]

The participants of the Jewish movement created a network of seminars on Jewish history, culture, and various scientific disciplines for unemployed refuseniks in those fields. They also created study groups for learning Hebrew and studying the principles of Judaism. In 1972 a physics seminar was organized in Moscow with meetings at the home of A. Voronel and later at the homes of Aleksandr Lerner and Mark Azbel. For scientists who could not work in their own fields because of their desire to leave the Soviet Union or because of their dissident activities, these seminars provided an opportunity to keep in touch with their colleagues on work in their fields.

At the seminars in Voronel's home, the first suggestion made was that an unofficial international scientific conference be held, the proposed topic of which was the application of mathematics and physics to other scientific fields. The conference was planned for July 1–5, 1974. Participants in the seminars set up an organizing committee that invited the international scientific community to take part in the conference. More than thirty papers were received from scientists living in the Soviet Union. Among them were papers by academician Sakharov and associate academy member Yury Orlov. More than 120 papers were received from the United States, England, France, Israel, and other countries. Among those who expressed a desire to take part in the international conference were famous scientists and Nobel Prize recipients. Beginning in May, the authorities began to move against the preparations for the conference. The telephones of some of the seminar organizers were disconnected, their foreign mail was intercepted, and telephone calls from foreign colleagues were interrupted. In the middle of May members of the organizational committee were arrested and taken to prisons in and around Moscow. They were held until July 5, the day on which the planned seminar was to have ended. No charges were brought against them. Wives of the participants were put under house arrest during the period for which the conference was planned. Militiamen stood at the doors of their apartments and would not let anyone in or out. The conference could not be held.[21]

Next, an attempt was made to organize an international session on the theme "Jewish Culture in the USSR: Its Present State and Future Prospects." The date was set for December 21–23, 1976. Thirty Jewish activists from ten cities joined the organizing committee. Reports from the USSR, England, Switzerland, Israel, and the United States were received for the session. One of the most eagerly awaited participants was Judge Telford Taylor from the United States who had served as chief prosecutor at the Nuremberg Trials. The authorities used the same tactics they had used against the organizers of the international seminar on physics: they did not allow foreign participants into the USSR. Nonetheless, the session did take place, even though it lasted only one day instead of the planned three due to the absence of many people invited to give papers. A total of fifty people participated, including the academician Sakharov and foreign correspondents.[22]

Jews and the Human Rights Movement

The founding of the Group for a Public Investigation into the Reasons and Circumstances of the Arrests of Ass and Chernobylsky is of interest precisely because it was the open public association. Besides this group, only the committees for international scientific seminars are known. Like the group for the investigation of the Ass and Chernobylsky case, these committees were not intended to be permanent organizations, but to meet concrete, short-term goals. Nevertheless, both the active and the rank-and-file participants of the Jewish movement readily appealed to other independent, human rights associations. There were numerous appeals to the Committee on Human Rights in the USSR (1970–72) and later to the Moscow Helsinki Watch Group.

The Helsinki Watch groups were the first human rights associations to include both human rights activists and Jewish activists. The attitude of the Jewish movement to human rights is of interest in this regard.

In seeking permission to emigrate, the refuseniks use the methods of the human rights movement. The Jewish Movement for Emigration to Israel is in fact a collective human rights struggle that has united lone refuseniks into a single social force. It became apparent early in the struggle that the refuseniks who were able to leave the soonest were not those who quietly waited, but those who created a stir and insisted on their right to emigrate.

In June 1969 three people who had been refused permission to emigrate, Yu. Kleyzmer, Boris Borukhovich, and Boris Shlaen, issued a public statement. They demanded permission to leave not on the basis of their desire to be reunited with relatives (the only reason officially recognized by the government), but because they are Jews and want to raise their children as Jews—an impossibility in the Soviet Union, due to the absence of conditions necessary for the development of Jewish culture. By 1970 all three had received permission to emigrate.[23] Evidently the government wanted to rid itself of these troublesome citizens. Of course, in any given situation it is risky to make public demands because one cannot count on immediately receiving permission to emigrate. One could just as well be sent to a camp first. (Those who end up in camps for their activities in the Jewish movement are, as a rule, allowed to emigrate after they have served out their terms.) In spite of this risk, many refuseniks choose to wage an open fight.

Once engaged in the struggle for emigration, the overwhelming majority of refuseniks built a wall between themselves and the human rights activists, even though activists warmly sympathized with the plight of a people whose indisputable right to emigrate was violated. Human rights activists spoke up against the forceful detainment of Jews in the USSR, but the majority of refuseniks reasoned: "I do not want to have anything to do with this country. I want to leave, and to achieve this I must avoid quarrels with the authorities. After all, permission to leave depends on them, not on the dissidents. So the further away one is from the dissidents, the better."

In 1969 Yulius Telesin, one of the first human rights activists, applied to emigrate to Israel. Immediately afterwards, a refusenik approached him and insisted that he cease his human rights activities. They feared that such activities would compromise the Jewish movement in the eyes of the authorities and bring the wrath of the government down on their heads. The refuseniks were shocked when Telesin quickly received permission to leave; his farewell party was the first joint event including participants of both the Jewish and the human rights movement. Since then a rapprochement has developed slowly between the two groups.

The case of Telesin was the first in a series of human rights defenders, both Jewish and non-Jewish, who emigrated on Israeli visas. It became clear that the government was inclined to rid itself of those human rights activists whose arrests would be an embarrassment to them. Jewish activists helped people in this situation obtain invitations from Israel. Since then, participants in the Jewish movement ceased being so cautious about their communications with human rights activists and even went as far as to support them from time to time. Jewish refuseniks began to sign protests against persecutions of human rights activists. Although it was rare, involvement in human rights activities sometimes preceded the actual application for emigration.

The signing of the Helsinki accords noticeably furthered cooperation between the Jewish and human rights movements. Soviet law does not prohibit emigration, but neither does it establish a right to emigrate. It simply does not mention the topic. The Final Act, however, contains a special section devoted to the reunification of families. This section was one of the most precisely defined of all those devoted to humanitarian questions, and the Soviet government pledged to consider such requests in a favorable light. The refuseniks cited this document. The goal of the Moscow Helsinki Watch Group was the implementation of the humanitarian articles of the Helsinki accords. When this group was formed, refuseniks joined it. Among the founding members were the refuseniks Vitaly Rubin and Anatoly Shcharansky. Later Vladimir Slepak and Naum Meyman joined. Refuseniks also took part in the activities of the Lithuanian and Georgian Helsinki groups (Eitan Finkelshtein in Lithuania and the brothers Grigory and Isay Goldshteyn in Georgia). Anatoly Shcharansky became one of the leading activists in the Moscow Helsinki Group.

These activities brought the Jewish movement closer to other dissident movements—religious and nationalist, as well as the German and Pentecostal emigration movements. It was through the Moscow Helsinki Group that Jewish-movement participants Lidiya Voronina and Arkady Polishchuk became acquainted with the problems of the Pentecostalists and began to help them actively. They continued to help after they emigrated. Polishchuk became an official representative of the Pentecostalists abroad. Refusenik Viktor Yelistratov began to help the Pentecostalists from within the Soviet Union. Anatoly Shcharansky spent a great deal of time working on German emigration. He helped English film makers, who had come to Moscow without official permission, to make a film about Soviet emigration policies, about Soviet

Germans and Jews. Shcharansky introduced the German refuseniks to Western correspondents at a press conference organized for this purpose. Vladimir Slepak went to Leningrad at the behest of the Moscow Helsinki Group when Emiliya Ilina, a Russian trying to emigrate, declared a hunger strike there.[24]

The authorities try to prevent cooperation between dissident movements. Their choice of setting-up Shcharansky for the role of "spy" was largely determined by the fact that he had become a symbol of the increasing tendency toward a unification of the Jewish movement with the human rights movement on the one hand, and with Jewish organizations in the West on the other. A list of the Jewish refuseniks who were the object of repression during the high point of rapprochement between the Jewish and the human rights movements from 1977–78 confirms the thesis of an effort to prevent the incipient unification of these groups. The list includes Shcharansky, Slepak, Ida Nudel, and Iosif Begun—all activists in both the Jewish and human rights movements. After their arrests, the human rights activities of Jewish activists in Moscow became more subdued. Up to this time Moscow had been the center of the Jewish movement; the nucleus of long-time refuseniks was formed there. It included A. Lerner, V. Rubin, V. Slepak and others known for their scientific work, and people who spoke English—a capability that furthered communication with the numerous emissaries of Jewish organizations in Moscow and, with interested tourists. This nucleus was made up of people determined to succeed in their own struggle to emigrate, and also to have some effect on the resolution of the Jewish problem in the USSR. Around them gathered successive groups of Moscow refuseniks, to whom people from other cities came for advice and help. They became the central figures in the Jewish movement and served as a link with the West. They were the ones who in 1976 entered into close relationships with the leading Moscow human rights defenders. At the end of the 1970s a withdrawal of Jewish activists from the human rights movement was observed, influenced partially by the obvious personal danger such an alliance created.

The overwhelming majority of emigrés from the Soviet Union are Jews, and Jewish groups abroad are often reluctant even to provide lip service to other dissident movements. When it was suggested to one Chicago rabbi that he change the sign outside his synagogue from "Free Soviet Jews" to "Free People from the USSR," he replied that this would be "absurd universalism."

The fact that the Jewish emigration movement, which took its methods from the human rights movement, is made up of people whose goal is not to improve life in the USSR but to leave it was the decisive factor in the disunity between both groups. The majority of those who apply to emigrate were less concerned with civic problems than with their own lives and those of their families. They genuinely wanted to avoid conflict with the government. Once they became refuseniks, they had to face a dilemma: whether or not to commit themselves to a conflict with the government. The majority could not resolve on such a course of action. Thus, civic concerns are foreign to the mass of Jewish-movement participants, even to the bolder activists. In any case, they are not preoccupied with civic concerns to the detriment of their personal goals. Participants in the Jewish movement are not dissidents in the specific sense that term has acquired in the Soviet experience. In its accepted sense, the term can be applied only to a small portion of the Jewish-movement activists.

Cultural Revival and Emigration

Two separate tendencies in the Jewish movement emerged: the "cultural revival proponents" and the "emigration proponents."

The idea of the cultural revivalists lay in a rebirth of the national consciousness of Jews by making Jewish culture accessible. Their basic task was to spread knowledge of their own history and religion among Jews and to create a rebirth of national traditions and social life. Their line of reasoning went approximately as follows: Our concern is the rebirth among Jews in the USSR of the consciousness of belonging to the Jewish people. Once this is done, let each decide whether to remain in the USSR or to emigrate. Whether in Israel or in the Soviet Union, a Jew ought to be a Jew.

The cultural-revival proponents were grouped around the journal *Jews in the USSR*, and in 1975 they created the journal *Tarbut* (Culture). Among the well-known refuseniks, Viktor Brailovsky, Veniamin Fayn, Vladimir Prestin, Feliks Dektor, Mark Azbel, and others belonged to this faction. Due to its energetic efforts, seminars on Jewish culture, Judaism, and Hebrew study circles became widespread in Moscow, Leningrad, and other cities. They introduced the custom of gathering in the countryside to celebrate national Jewish holidays. They learned and sang Jewish songs in a spirit of national unity. They organized groups of Jewish children—unofficial Jewish kindergartens—that encouraged a Jewish upbringing: Hebrew lessons, stories from Jewish history, etc. Not only refuseniks, but also Jews who had not applied for emigration but were conscious of belonging to the Jewish people, enjoyed the fruits of their efforts.

The cultural revival proponents thought that a rebirth of national consciousness, by stopping or reversing the process of assimilation, would have beneficial effects on those who were to remain in the USSR and, at the same time, on those who were to emigrate. Emigrés who were conscious of being Jews would go to Israel, rather than to the United States or some other country. The cultural revivalists placed the blame for the rise in visas to the United States on the inactivity of those members of the Jewish movement who did not make the necessary contributions toward a Jewish nationalist education.

The emigration proponents were not in principle opposed to efforts to revive a Jewish culture, but they took a skeptical attitude toward the success of such a project under conditions in the Soviet Union. They claimed that not one single group within the Soviet Union had a full life and that Jews were even less likely to attain one. The only viable option for Soviet Jews was an exodus.

The emigration proponents, including A. Lunts, A. Shcharansky, V. Slepak, A. Lerner, V. Rubin, M. Agursky, and others formed a larger and more influential faction than the cultural-revival proponents. They directed their efforts toward furthering connections between the Jewish movement, international Jewish organizations, and political forces who supported them. They collected a great deal of information on refuseniks all over the Soviet Union: their numbers, status, family and marital situation; the reasons their applications were turned down (both official and factual); the length of time each refusenik waited; and so on. Their emphasis was not only on collecting comprehensive data, but also on the efficient use of this information: they tried to relay the data to the West as it was collected.

The emigration proponents began to compile detailed accounts on a monthly, quarterly, and yearly basis on the Jewish movement and analyzed its potential. Their efforts met with a hearty response from Jews abroad, especially American Jews. Both existing and new Jewish organizations, created with this specific purpose in mind, began to help. Their emissaries constantly travelled to the USSR both as tourists and as members of delegations. Some material aid had been given earlier, but it flowed into the country in greatly increased amounts in the midseventies. Large demonstrations in support of Soviet Jews and individual refuseniks were organized abroad. Lobbyists supporting Soviet-Jewish emigration intensified their efforts. The United States government undertook specific actions on behalf of the Jewish movement, especially in passing the Jackson-Vanik Amendment.

Jews in the USSR printed many articles by emigration proponents who took part and read papers in some of the seminars organized by the cultural revivalists and supported Hebrew study groups. Both cultural revivalists and emigration proponents celebrated Israeli Independence Day together and made joint preparations for the International Seminar on Jewish Culture in December 1976. Nevertheless, when a delegation of American congressmen and senators visited Moscow in 1975, they had to speak with emigration and cultural-revival proponents separately because of the groups' incompatible positions on a very important question—emigration to the United States. The emigration proponents insisted on the freedom of Jews to choose the country to which they wished to emigrate, convinced that it would be easier for Jews to acquire Jewish consciousness and have access to Jewish culture in any country than it was in the Soviet Union. The cultural-revival proponents held that emigration to Israel was essential; some of them even demanded that help be denied to Jews who did not emigrate to Israel and that administrative measures be taken against them. It is common knowledge that the Israeli government supported the cultural revivalists on this issue, but the emigration proponents had closer ties with interested Jewish organizations.

Soviet Offensive and Jewish Hunger Strikes

The Soviet offensive against the Jewish movement was intensified in 1977, beginning with the arrests of the most active emigration proponents. Their close contacts with both international Jewish organizations and human rights defenders within the country were unacceptable to the authorities.

On March 15, 1977 Shcharansky was arrested. His arrest was accompanied by a mudslinging anti-Semitic campaign in the press. The arrests of the Slepaks, Ida Nudel, and Iosif Begun followed in the summer of 1978.[25] After suppressing the active emigration proponents, the authorities went after the cultural-revival proponents. They arrested the editors of *Jews in the USSR*, Igor Guberman (August 1979) and Viktor Brailovsky (November 1980), although the journal ceased publication even before their arrests. Arrests of the leading activists of both parts of the Jewish movement reduced its activity significantly.

At the reduced level of activity, differences between the emigration and cultural-revival proponents were erased. Jewish-movement activists continued to gather and send information on the emigration situation to the West, but their channels of communications were curtailed. Their data was not as comprehensive nor as efficiently used as it had been at the height of the movement, despite the fact that information on the Jewish movement in the West is to this day more complete than that of any other movement because of the active interest in the movement on the part of Jewish organizations in the West.

Refuseniks staged demonstrations more rarely. The only demonstration known to have occurred in 1979 was staged by nine female refuseniks on April 19 in front of the Ministry of Foreign Affairs in Moscow, precipitated by the refusal of the Communist Party Central Committee to receive fifty female refuseniks. The demonstrators held placards reading "Visas to Israel!" They were detained for several hours by the militia; some of them were fined; and Batsheva Yelistratova was put under arrest for fifteen days.[26]

In 1979 only forty-four people gathered at Baby Yar, where official meetings in memory of the Jews massacred on that spot had not been held since 1977. Muscovites had been detained and could not reach Kiev. In 1981, on the fortieth anniversary of the massacre, Jews from various cities headed toward Kiev. However, only four people from Odessa reached Baby Yar. They read a prayer for the dead. But on Memorial Day in 1981 an unheard-of number of people gathered in Minsk—30,000 to 40,000. The refusenik Gorelik was given permission to speak, but when his speech displeased the organizers of the meeting the loudspeakers were turned on to drown out his voice.[27]

Demonstrations of solidarity of those called "the prisoners of Zion" had been an annual occurrence since 1975, but demonstrators were prevented from holding them in 1980 and in 1981. Only two or three people managed to get to the steps of the Lenin Library. In 1980, fourteen people who tried to hold a demonstration there were detained. In 1981, sixty Jewish activists from various cities staged a hunger strike rather than a demonstration on that day. In the same manner Jewish refuseniks observed the opening of the Madrid conference of countries that had signed the Helsinki Accords in November 1980. More than two hundred people participated in that hunger strike.[28]

After 1979 individual and family hunger strikes were used more frequently as a means of protesting denials of emigration applications. Some of those who staged hunger strikes were: Mariya Fleyshgakker and Natalya Khrakovskaya from Moscow, the Ocheretyansky family from Kiev, Frida Breslav from Riga who fasted for forty-five days, and others.

In 1981 Moscow refuseniks observed Israeli Independence Day with an outing to the country, although not without some delay. On May 3 they arrived at the meeting place in a wood outside of Moscow only to be greeted by the militia, who informed them that a "clean-up day" was in progress. The refuseniks decided to meet elsewhere a week later. They were discovered again, but only after about two-and-a-half hours; when the militia arrived, they were forced to leave. Boris Chernobylsky was accused of assaulting a militiaman, even though numerous witnesses insisted that Chernobylsky had not come near him. He was sentenced to one year in a forced-labor camp. Thus, five years after the unsuccessful attempt to imprison Chernobylsky for "resisting the militia," sentencing was finally carried out.[29]

The refuseniks continued to write petitions. In 1980 the largest number of collected signatures (143) was on an appeal to the Madrid Conference. The signatories themselves took the appeal to the reception room of the Supreme Soviet. The most representative petition written in 1981 was the petition to the Twenty-sixth Party Congress. It contained a detailed account of discrimination against Jews in the USSR in all areas of life and culture and concluded that the only alternative for Soviet Jews was emigration, sharply curtailed by the authorities in 1980.[30]

Since mid-1978, seminars and various kinds of study groups became the major form of activity for Jewish refuseniks. From 1977 on, the seminar in physics met in the Brailovsky apartment. On April 12, 1980 the organizers of the seminar held an international session that was more successful than any of the three earlier attempts. On April 10 the militia broke the door of the Brailovsky apartment and conducted a search. Brailovsky was taken to the militia station, where he was informed that he was under arrest and was taken to a predetention room. But after five hours no charge was lodged, although he was prohibited from leaving town. After being "advised" to stop conducting the seminars, he was released. The homes of other people who helped in the preparations for the international seminar on collective phenomena in physics were searched, and scientific materials were confiscated.

Nonetheless, the international session took place. Twenty Soviet scientists and twenty-six of their colleagues from abroad participated. Some of the foreigners who indicated in their visa applications their intention of attending the seminar were issued visas. Among the papers delivered was one by Yury Orlov, sent from his labor camp in Perm, and another from Andrey Dmitrievich Sakharov from his exile in Gorky. After the international session, weekly seminar meetings continued until the arrest of Brailovsky on November 23, 1980. Soon afterwards, the seminar was squelched: uniformed militiamen and plainclothes officers prevented the participants from entering the Brailovsky apartment. The participants met instead at the apartment of Aleksandr Ioffe. The next day Ioffe was called into the KGB and warned of the "serious consequences" if he continued to offer his apartment for the seminar sessions. He ignored the warning. On the night of November 9, his apartment door was doused with gas and set on fire. On November 10, Ioffe was again refused permission to emigrate. Similar obstacles beset the scientific seminar conducted by

Aleksandr Lerner. Ninety-five refuseniks signed a protest against inter-ference with the activities of these scientific seminars.[31]

Seminars on Jewish culture and one on the legal problems associated with emigration were held in Moscow. In 1979 the latter seminar began to issue a bulletin, *Immigration to Israel: the Law and Common Practice*. It was published by the refusenik Mikhail Berenshteyn. There were many more Hebrew study groups than seminars, and those who attended were not all refuseniks. Since the end of 1980, Hebrew teachers were under constant pressure from the KGB. One of them, Leonid Volvovsky, had his permit to reside in Moscow revoked and was sent to Gorky, where he had formerly resided. In November 1981, about eighty Moscow Hebrew teachers were warned that the same fate awaited them if they did not stop taking part in the study groups.[32]

Seminars and Hebrew study groups also spread to other cities. A seminar was formed in Kishinev in 1977, and there were others in Kharkov, Riga, and Kiev. In Leningrad at least two seminars on Jew-ish culture met in 1980–81. Refusenik Leonid Kelbert, a film director, organized an unofficial theatrical group there. The participants pre-sented plays on Jewish themes. A similar group appeared in Moscow.[33] In Kiev, a battle was waged for several years for a permanent home for the Jewish amateur theatre. A professional Jewish theatre troupe was authorized in Moscow.[34]

After the arrests of 1977–78, the central unifying role of the Moscow refuseniks was diminished, and independent activities were under-taken by refuseniks in Leningrad, Kharkov, Kishinev, and especially Kiev. Moscow ceased to be the indisputable center of the Jewish movement. Refusenik channels to the West do not now necessarily pass through Moscow, but may go directly from these other cities. Channels are established through tourists and by telephone. Musco-vites conducted the largest number of hunger strikes before the Madrid Conference; activists in provincial cities now began to outdo Muscovites in other activism.

In Kharkov, where there were only twenty refusenik families in 1977, a seminar on Jewish culture was held. The number of refuseniks there has increased to four hundred since the end of 1979. An engi-neer, Aleksandr Paritsky, organized an unofficial university for the children of refuseniks who were deprived of studying in state-run educational facilities. In this floating university the teachers were also refuseniks, unable to work in their own fields. Courses in both the sciences and the humanities were given.[35] In 1979, three activists in Novosibirsk founded the Society for Friendship with Israel, modelled on official societies of friendship with other countries. In spite of the fact that the founders were dismissed from their jobs, the society continued to function.[36]

In the same city of Novosibirsk, four refuseniks provoked panic among city officials when they appealed to the city Party committee with an application to hold a demonstration, planned for April 25, 1981 in the center of the city (the route was marked exactly). They planned to carry placards with the slogans "All Power to the Soviets!", "Long Live Democracy," and a quotation from Brezhnev's speech at the XXVI Party Congress about the necessity of observing all Soviet laws. The authors of the letter wrote that the purpose of their demonstration was to draw the public's attention to the fact that Soviet laws were ignored in Novosibirsk, in particular with regard to city residents who sought exit visas from the USSR. The letter was sent to 55 government offices in Novosibirsk and to the central authorities. On the day of the demonstration, rumors circulated around town about a demonstration planned for thousands of people. The police not only cordoned off the apartments of the authors of the letter, but also the neighborhoods where they lived and the streets marked for the route of the demonstration. Two of the four who had signed the letter soon received permission to leave the country.[37]

Refuseniks in Kiev were the most resolute in their public activities until the beginning of the 1980s. They numbered about two thousand by the end of 1979. By April 1980, their numbers had increased as a consequence of strict regulations on emigration procedures. The authorities began giving permission to emigrate only on the basis of invitations from the parents or children of the applicant. According to information supplied by the Kiev refuseniks in March 1980, in the preceding six months seventy permissions and three thousand denials of emigration applications had been issued.[38] The Kievans answered these mass denials with collective protests. They began to meet at the Kiev OVIR office on Saturdays. On Thursdays they met at the Ministry of Internal Affairs, where they conducted silent demonstrations.

The first collective complaint is dated February 7, 1980. It was signed by ninety-seven persons. On February 18 a delegation of one hundred two refuseniks took the complaint to Moscow. On March 18, a delegation of forty people went to Moscow with another appeal containing one hundred seventeen signatures. Beginning at the end of April, about a hundred of the most active members of the Jewish movement had been summoned to the KGB, the militia, or elsewhere. They were warned that if they did not stop their activities, they would be severely prosecuted. On April 23, four representatives of the Kievan refuseniks signed an appeal to the international Jewish community asking for help in the face of the anticipated mass repressions. In May and in following months delegations that went to Moscow from Kiev were removed from trains, subjected to house arrest, individually arrested for fifteen-day periods on charges of "hooliganism," or beaten by "unknown persons" in the street.[39]

The number of ten- and fifteen-day arrests in the Jewish movement increased drastically after 1979. In accordance with the level of movement activity, convictions that carried labor-camp sentences were distributed among Kiev, Moscow, Tashkent, Kishinyov, Odessa, and Kharkov. Kiev had the largest number of convictions given to members of the Jewish movement from 1979 to 1983: here, ten refuseniks were sentenced. The overwhelming majority of defendants were convicted on fabricated criminal charges, usually for "hooliganism" or "parasitism," although the Kievan Stanislav Zubko received a labor-camp sentence for possessing a weapon and narcotics planted in his apartment.[40] After 1980 the practice of convicting Jewish-movement activists on political charges was renewed; however, convictions were not for "Zionism," the charge used in the early stages of the movement, but for "slandering the Soviet system." Among those convicted on this charge were: Boris Tsukerman and Yakov Lokshin in Kishinyov, Aleksandr Magidovich in Tula, Aleksandr Paritsky in Kharkov, and Viktor Brailovsky in Moscow.[41] In November 1982, Muscovite Iosif Begun was arrested a second time charged with "anti-Soviet agitation and propaganda and sentenced to seven years labor camp and five years exile."[42]

During the decade 1970–80, more than seventy activists were sentenced to forced-labor camps or internal exile. During the same period, 250,000 people emigrated on Israeli visas. In the midseventies, the number of emigres gradually increased each year: in 1975, 13,000; in 1976, 14,000; in 1977, 17,000; in 1978, 36,000; and in 1979, 51,300. Then the number began to decrease sharply: in 1980, 21,470; in 1981, only 9,460; in 1982, 2,629; in 1983, 1,315.[43]

The number of those emigrating directly to other countries gradually increased. In 1979, 17,550 emigrated to Israel, or 34.2 percent of all those emigrating on Israeli visas; in 1980, 7,220, or 33.6 percent; in 1981, 1,790, or 18.9 percent. In 1982, 733, or 27.2 percent.[44] The majority of Jews leaving the Soviet Union chose to decide their future as did Jews who left Russia from the last century: they went to the United States of America.

The more restrictive regulations for granting permission to emigrate in 1980 took the form of limiting acceptable invitations to immediate family. The number of refusals on the basis of "classified work" increased. The total number of refuseniks by the beginning of 1981 approximated 40,000.[45] Among these, highly qualified specialists in the natural sciences (about five hundred holders of "candidate degrees" and forty Doctors of Science) found themselves in a particularly difficult situation. The authorities had virtually stopped granting such people permission to emigrate in order to stop the "brain drain." Approximately half had been dismissed from their jobs when they submitted their applications and were not employed in their areas of specialization; they were generally stripped of their professional titles and their degrees.[46]

By 1982 it became apparent that the authorities, who through some miraculous concurrence of circumstances, had advanced to increasing the emigration in the 1970s, were retreating to their usual "locked borders" policy. Tens of thousands of people remained who had already applied to emigrate; they were forced into tragic situations. The fact that they had applied to emigrate not only deprived them of their previous social status, but it relegated them to the ranks of the "disloyal," in the view of the authorities. With the curtailing of emigration, these people became doomed to banishment from society for an indefinitely long period—perhaps for life.

In cities with significantly large Jewish populations, these desperate refuseniks had formed close-knit communities. Gradually, their joint efforts to emigrate died down. Those who were able to do so returned to their former lives, but not everyone was able to do so, either in the practical or in the psychological sense. Refuseniks, as well as those who had not applied to emigrate, saw an ominous sign in the end of emigration. The solidarity of Jews (both refuseniks and non-refuseniks) grew stronger with the increase in open anti-Semitism, both in everyday life and at the official level. With the impossibility of an exodus, Jews redirected their awakened national energy toward the creation of something like a life in the Soviet Union itself. Thus the "cultural revivalists" won over the "emigrationists."

Yet there were some refuseniks for whom the loss of their hope to emigrate did not lead them to cultivate their Jewishness, but rather redirected them toward more general domestic and international problems. They grew closer to human rights activists, even though the human rights movement at the beginning of the 1980s was greatly weakened by arrests and, hence, in crisis. This convergence of activists of the Jewish movement with human rights activists can be traced from 1980, by comparing the participants in the traditional annual demonstration of human rights activists (December 10, Human Rights Day) and the demonstration in defense of prisoners of Zion (December 24). During 1980–1983, a significant number of those who took part in the Jewish demonstration also took part in the human rights demonstration. A particularly clear indication of Jewish refuseniks' movement toward civic activity outside the Jewish movement can be seen in the founding of a new citizens' group—the Group to Establish Trust Between the USSR and the USA, announced on June 4, 1982, in Moscow. Six of the Group's 11 founders were refuseniks.

Following the creation of the Moscow Trust Group, similar groups arose in Leningrad, Odessa, and Novosibirsk, and refuseniks also joined these groups.[47] The new citizens' movement to preserve peace was born in the same environment as the human rights movement—among the Moscow intelligentsia. But this overall democratic initiative, at a time when the human rights movement was in decline, was made by people forced into a desperate situation with the reduction of emigration from the USSR. This declaration of a new citizens' group was in part conceived as a last chance to break away to freedom, but this unusual initiative should not be attributed only to personal motives. Refuseniks are by definition people who have psychologically broken with Soviet society, and who have a critical attitude toward it. In such an environment, with the lack of opportunity to separate themselves from the Soviet system, it is inevitable that fearless opponents to the system will appear.

PART FOUR

THE MOVEMENTS FOR RELIGIOUS LIBERTY

CHAPTER 11

The Evangelical Christian Baptists

With a resolution of April 8, 1929 "On Religious Cults," the Soviet government embarked on a policy of eradication of religion in the Soviet Union. It revised, and in the process virtually abolished, the constitutional statute on freedom of conscience that had been established by the Constitution of 1917 and by a decree of January 22, 1918 on "The Separation of Church and State." In reformulations of May 1929 and 1936, freedom of religious conscience was reduced to nil.

From the beginning the Soviet regime was aggressively atheistic. But before 1929 persecution focused on the Russian Orthodox church and Moslems and barely touched the Protestants.

From 1918 to 1929 Baptist prayer meetings were held without interference and religious literature was published in the USSR without restriction and imported from abroad. Beginning in 1929 and continuing until the Second World War, Baptist ministers and many active believers were arrested, charged with "anti-Soviet propaganda" and sentenced in closed sessions of *troikas* to concentration camp terms of twenty-five years each. Approximately 50,000 Baptists, including most Baptist ministers, were sent to the camps during this period; around 22,000 perished.[1] Baptist churches were closed across the country. Only four in Moscow and other large cities survived.

Change of Government Strategy to Internal Control

During the Second World War governmental policy on religion was modified to exert internal control over the churches. In 1942–43, a governmental Council on the Affairs of Religious Cults (CARC) was formed under the Council of Ministers of the USSR. The members of the council began to "tame" the churches and undermine them from within. Baptist ministers who were inclined toward collaboration were released from the camps and from exile before the completion of their sentences. They formed the All-Union Council of Evangelical Christian Baptists (ACECB) during this period.

After the war approximately 5,000 Baptist communities were revived, and from 1945 to 1948 the authorities registered one-third (1,696) of these communities.[2] The communities were compelled to submit to registration; in those that refused, the churches were closed. Registration was granted at the price of serious curtailments in the religious lives of these communities. One of the conditions of registration was recognition of the supremacy of the All-Union Council of Evangelical Christian Baptists and of government-appointed senior church officials, who, assigned by territory, virtually controlled the Baptist communities. The All-Union Council's chief task was to ensure that its own people filled all church posts. Then they would agree to guarantee that all restrictions of religious life imposed by the government were observed.

This Baptist brotherhood of registered communities, artificially reduced to one-third its original size and controlled by the All-Union Council, was exhibited by the government to the outside world as a showcase of religious freedom of conscience. In 1947, members of the All-Union Council and hand-picked members of the religious communities began to travel abroad to meet with their fellow believers and began to receive visits from them in the USSR. They created an impression of the well-being of religious believers. The existence of religious prisoners in the Soviet Union and the lack of religious freedom is not recognized abroad.

In 1960 the All-Union Council published two documents on the regulation of church life: "New Regulations of the All-Union Council of Evangelical Christian Baptists" and the secret "Instructive Letter to Senior Church Officials."[3] Both documents were based on the government's position on religion and both conflicted with the basic principles of Baptist doctrine.

Although Baptists consider the primary task and fundamental mission of the church to be the teaching and promulgation of the Gospel, the "Instructive Letter" stated that "at the present time, the primary task of religious worship lies in the fulfillment of the basic needs of the believer, rather than in attracting new members." The letter charged senior church officials with the duty of "restraining unhealthy missionary tendencies" and with "overcoming the unhealthy pursuit of new members." The new regulations placed limitations on religious services: certain musical instruments, such as guitars, were prohibited; choirs from neighboring communities could not be invited to sing; no part of a service could be performed outside of the church building. Church attendance by children under eighteen years was forbidden;

those over eighteen could be baptized only after a strict probationary period of two to three years. All preaching was limited to the confines of each individual religious community and within the confines of the church. In violation of the characteristic Baptist practice of frequent and extensive communication between church members, attendance at religious services outside one's own community was forbidden. The traditional forms of these exchanges were also prohibited, including children's meetings and Sunday school outings attended by members of different communities, and the performance of religious services within the home. The rules against mutual help between members of communities created hardships for families of members who had been arrested or fined for holding religious services.

The result was a sharp reduction in baptisms and the dissolution of some religious communities. From 1944 to 1965 more than 800 communities in the Ukraine alone were closed, and the total number of Baptists in the Ukraine decreased from 180,000 to 120,000. In Estonia and Latvia, where 1,246 persons had been baptized from 1957 to 1959, only 195 were baptized from 1960 to 1962, and fourteen Baptist communities were closed.[4] The situation was similar elsewhere. In consequence the Evangelical Baptist church experienced a deep spiritual crisis; nevertheless, these early attempts to use the "New Regulations" and the "Instructive Letter" as regulatory documents were to prove a miscalculation of the powers of the All-Union Council.

The "Instructive Letter" was issued secretly, intended only for senior church officials, they did not manage to prevent ordinary members of the communities from learning of it. It aroused general indignation and provided the spark that led masses of Baptists to oppose a church leadership that had become entirely submissive to the government. Thus began the rebirth of the Evangelical Christian Baptist church.

Rise of Church Resistance

The goal of the rebirth of the Evangelical Baptist church was to purify religious services from all the distortions imposed by the government, the All-Union Council, and its supporters. It was an internal struggle not concerned with dogma, but rather with civil matters: it touched only on the question of the interrelationship between church and secular authorities. The advocates of church independence struggled with both church and secular authorities, basing their arguments on the Gospels and on the constitutional right of religious freedom.

A few influential Baptists, A. F. Prokofyev, Gennady K. Kryuchkov, and others, all of whom had managed to obtain access to the "Instructive Letter," saw this document as evidence of a betrayal of faith by the All-Union Council. They decided they could keep silent no longer. In May 1960 they formed an initiative group. In a letter to the All-Union Council they accused that organization of violating the most important principle of Christianity: do not render unto Caesar the things that belong to God. The initiative group called on All-Union Council members to repent before their fellow believers. The council did not answer the letter.[5] Whereupon the initiative group dispatched copies of the "Instructive Letter," and their own explanation of the significance of the letter and of the "New Regulations," to all Baptist communities whether registered or not. The initiative group called on all Baptists to write to the government for permission to convene a congress (none had occurred since 1926) for the purpose of revoking the "New Regulations" and the "Instructive Letter" and resolving the question of church leadership. They thought a reelection of All-Union Council members was essential and proposed that the congress represent all the Baptist communities in the USSR, both registered and unregistered.[6]

The founders of the initiative group admitted later that they thought they would be arrested within a month after announcing the formation of the group, and that their efforts would fail.[7] However, their appeal for a purification of the church aroused many communities from years of apathy. Their strong support inhibited the government from immediate arrest of the initiative group members (only A. F. Prokofyev was arrested, in 1962; some Baptists who were not members of the group, but supporters of the group were also arrested). Initiative group members and ordinary Baptists, individuals as well as entire communities, began to write to the Council on the Affairs of Religious Cults, demanding permission to convene a congress. The All-Union Council responded by excommunicating active supporters of a congress and assisted in new arrests. They insisted that opposition to the "New Regulations" and the "Instructive Letter" could be equated with opposition to the government.

From 1960 until 1963, the period of the most intense agitation for the congress, about two hundred supporters of the initiative group were arrested. Their arrests did not weaken, but rather strengthened the movement. The All-Union Council's authority was eroded. One after the other, religious communities refused to recognize its supremacy; they excommunicated its members from the church; they no longer wished to participate in the ritual of communion with All-Union Council members. They demanded a congress even more persistently. On February 25, 1962 the initiative group was reorganized into the Organizational Committee for an All-Union Congress of Evangelical Christian Baptists.[8] The members of the Organizational Committee held negotiations with the All-Union Council and the government's Council on the Affairs of Religious Cults. They appealed to the government in open letters, copies of which they then distributed to the communities. The Organizational Committee began to publish the *Fraternal Pamphlet*, in which the legality and the fairness of the Organizational Committee's demands were explained, from the dogmatic point of view.

The government understood that to continue to resist the demand for a congress would make the split between the believers and the All-Union Council irreversible. In the interests of preserving its loyal collaborators, they agreed to sacrifice the "New Regulations" but kept silent about the "Instructive Letter." The Council on Religious Affairs and Cults gave its permission, not for a "congress," but for a "conference" of the All-Union Council.

The conference met on October 15, 1963 and renamed itself a congress. The congress annulled the "New Regulations" and replaced them with the rules of the All-Union Council, which were much less explicit in their anti-evangelical bias. The Organizational Committee and its supporters did not recognize the self-proclaimed congress, since not all religious communities, only those that supported the All-Union Council, were represented there. The Organizational Committee was convinced that the Council on the Affairs of Religious Cults was completely on the side of the All-Union Council.

At a closed meeting in August 1965, the president of the Council on the Affairs of Religious Cults, Puzin, explained the council's strategy: "As you know, local agents have already tried to arrest the dissident Baptists, but that has not produced the desired results. . . . Persecutions have only succeeded in strengthening the authority of the Organizational Committee and helping it . . . attract new members. It must be openly said that some time ago there was a very real threat that the Organizational Committee would succeed in capturing the leadership of the entire church. . . . Even now that threat has not been entirely eliminated."[9]

Establishment of an Independent Baptist Church and Official Repression

Organizational Committee members began to seek meetings with government leaders to voice their complaints about the actions of the council. On September 2, 1965 a delegation of five Baptists was received by Anastas I. Mikoyan, then president of the Presidium of the Supreme Soviet of the USSR.[10] It achieved nothing. In two years of fruitless attempts to have the decisions of the "false congress," as they called it, annulled, they saw that there was no hope of convening a true congress. Their religious communities, refusing to recognize the All-Union Council, created a separate church, and in September 1965, it elected a permanent governing body, the Council of Churches of the Evangelical Christian Baptists (CCECB). In the first Council of Churches were eleven individuals, most of them former members of the Organizational Committee; later the council grew to fifteen to seventeen members. Gennady Kryuchkov became president of this independent Baptist Church, Georgy Vins, its secretary.[11]

The independent Baptist church has engaged in missionary work, unintimidated by the ban on such activity. Russian Orthodox church members point to the success of the independent church in attracting new converts as a model to be followed.[12] The Baptists' missionary work has been conducted on a large scale particularly in eastern Siberia and in the Far East: in Kolyma, Kamchatka, Chukotka, and Sakhalin, where most of the inhabitants are Russians whose traditional religion is Russian Orthodoxy. But the Russian Orthodox church, in a state of complete abjection toward the government, had not dared to take a stand against the closure of churches. Its officials obeyed the "New Regulations" without a murmur. As a result, in many parts of the country there are today no functioning Orthodox churches or priests over regions of hundreds or even thousands of kilometers. Protestant missionaries rushed to places abandoned by the Orthodox hierarchy. According to the Orthodox priest Gleb Yakunin, their efforts have been extremely effective.[13]

The independent Baptists proselytize not only in remote, sparsely populated areas, but also in the center of Russia. Ignoring government prohibitions, they have organized prayer meetings on religious holidays in the major cities of Rostov and Odessa. Thousands of believers come from all over the country to attend. At these meetings new converts are baptized, filling up Baptist communities faster than they are emptied by arrests. The Evangelical Christian Baptists as a whole now have the largest following of all Protestant religions in the USSR. According to the figures of the Baptist World Alliance, in 1975 there were 535,000 Baptists in the Soviet Union, and their number is constantly growing.[14]

The Orthodox priest Gleb Yakunin explains the success of the missionary work of the Baptists and other Protestants by the fact that, side by side with the registered communities united under the leadership of the All-Union Council, there exists a semilegal independent Baptist church. Although these independent communities do not hide from the government, they do refuse to register or to participate in other forms of governmental control. The official and unofficial churches are thus interdependent, in the manner of interconnecting vessels: when the official church is under increasing pressure, members of a registered community oppose registration and transfer to the unofficial independent church. The government hesitates, therefore, to apply excessive pressure to registered communities. Yakunin considers this structure of "interconnecting vessels" an "ideal form of existence for churches" under Soviet rule. It enables them to sustain the heavy repressions inflicted by an aggressively atheistic government.[15]

Baptist communities that obey the All-Union Council, in consequence, enjoy more freedom than the Orthodox parishes do. The authorities accept the election of the leaders of the communities and permit them to hold conferences more or less regularly. At these conferences the All-Union Council gives an accounting of its activities. Restrictions on children participating in services and other religious functions are much less severe than in the Orthodox Church for example.

This relative freedom of registered Baptists is possible only at the expense of the Council of Churches of the Evangelical Christian Baptists. Persecution of the independent church has continued for twenty years, particularly harsh from 1980 on.

The leaders of the independent Council of Churches, G. Kryuchkov Nikolay Baturin and G. Vins, had been arrested in May 1966. They had received three-year terms in labor camps.[16] Since that time all the members of the Council of Churches have been in hiding to avoid arrest. Most have served out several prison terms and constantly hide lest they be arrested again. Since 1971, the president of the Council of Churches, G. Kryuchkov, has lived successfully in hiding, despite a country-wide search for him. In May 1974, a listening device (with the label "Made in USA") was discovered in the electricity meter of his wife's apartment.[17]

As of 1981 almost all of the members of the Council of Churches, with the exception of Kryuchkov, had been imprisoned: Nikolay Baturin, who has served out five terms for a total of sixteen years; Pyotr Rumachik, the secretary of the council has spent twelve years in camps; Nikolay Khrapov spent twenty-six years in prison and died in a labor camp in 1984. The members of the Council of Churches are charged with articles 142 and 227 of the criminal code of the RSFSR: "violation of the law on the separation of church and state" and "the performance of rites injurious to church members," and sometimes with article 190-1, "slander of the Soviet system." The sentences go as high as five years in a strict-regimen camp, sometimes with internal exile afterwards.[18]

As formerly, Baptist communities that refuse to register cannot have their own church buildings. Services in private homes are prohibited by the regulations of the All-Union Council but not by Soviet law itself. Yet such meetings are broken up by the militia and volunteer police, often in a rough manner, with insults and beatings. Ministers and community leaders, subject to arrest for holding prayer meetings outside of church, have been tried for violations of articles 142 and 227 of the criminal code. If a minister does not work in a secular job, but is provided for by the community, he is often charged with "parasitism," with the usual sentence of up to three years in camp. Many ministers have served several terms.

The host in whose home the service has taken place is also often arrested. The standard charge is "hooliganism" or "resisting the police," based on false testimony from the militia or volunteer police. The sentences run from one to two years in a standard-regimen camp. Baptists have also been charged with giving religious instruction to the children of their fellow believers, accused of violating the law on the separation of church and state. In 1980 Pavel Rytikov, his son Vladimir, and Galina Vilchinskaya were charged with organizing a summer camp for the children of Baptists who had been arrested or were in hiding.[19] Ordinary members of the unregistered communities experience persecution; they are systematically fined for participating in religious meetings outside of the churches. Often these fines exceed their monthly salary.

Baptists are severely hindered in performing rites prohibited by the authorities. Baptist weddings, traditionally large because of the custom of inviting the entire religious community and often neighboring communities, spill out into the garden or the yard. In the larger communities, the guests run into the hundreds and a private home cannot contain them. Yet, according to the instructions of the government's Council on the Affairs of Religious Cults, "ritual assemblies" may not be held in the open air. It is not a rare occurrence for Baptist weddings to be forcibly dispersed.

On 15 May 1977 at the home of dissenting Baptist M. A. Boyev (Latnaya station, Semiluki district, Voronezh region), a daughter's wedding was being celebrated. On the day of the wedding the local authorities hung a sign by the approach to the house: "Quarantine. Passage prohibited for pedestrians and vehicles." Then the electricity supply to the house was shut off, and as a result the orchestra that had been invited to the wedding was unable to play. Near the house there gathered officials of the KGB, the district soviet executive committee, and the police—altogether several dozen people. When, to the ritual singing, bride and groom came out into the garden, chairman of the village soviet Ivanenko began to make out an order about the violation of public order and went about having all those present noted down. The believers and the Boyevs' neighbors tried to explain to him that this was out of place. Police officials asked the people who had gathered in the garden and at the fence around the Boyevs' house to disperse, and began to talk and laugh deliberately loudly. Then a bulldozer drove up to the house and stopped with its engine still going, drowning the sermon. They began to photograph the believers. The latter in their turn began to photograph the bulldozer. It was removed. The officials tried to avoid being photographed.[20]

It is common for Baptists to try to establish frequent and various forms of communication with their sisters and brothers in Christ, yet the customary youth outings beyond city limits, and harvest festivities, usually celebrated by several communities together, are prohibited. Here is a description of the disruption of one youth outing:

Young Baptists in the Omsk, Kokchetav and Tselinograd Regions decided to hold a united open-air service on Sunday, 4 June, in a forest in Isilkul district. The day before, the traffic police had already blocked all approaches to the place where the service was to be held and were stopping and turning back cars, checking the documents of all drivers, taking their numbers and fining them. Those who managed to reach the place held a service for about two hours in relative peace, but then the clearing in the forest was surrounded and tractors were brought up, which began to tear up the ground, trying to run people over and drowning the prayers with their powerful engines. In the end police and vigilantes began to provoke a fight. Despite the fact that the believers did not physically resist, the police filled Black Marias with those arrested and drove them to a police station, where they were detained until the evening. The rest were dispersed with insults and violence: rough wrestling methods were used—they were dragged along by the hair, beaten with sticks, threatened with firearms. The food, dishes and other things which had been prepared for supper were confiscated and taken away. The tractors broke down shrubs and saplings while chasing through the wood after the Baptists. Many of the vigilantes were drunk.[21]

The necessity of constant defense of their freedom of conscience and the conduct of their religious life has fostered among the Baptists the development of legal consciousness. Although, since access to education is closed to believers in the Soviet Union and since the Baptist faith forbids the concealment of one's church membership, most Baptists have no more than a secondary education and earn their living by physical labor. According to pastor Georgy Vins, most Baptists of the older and middle generations are blue-collar workers and the only Baptists with a technical education are younger people. The level of legal competence among Baptists is higher than that of the educated segment of Soviet society. The logic of the struggle for religious freedom has turned the supporters of the Council of Churches into civil rights activists. Many years of collective resistance for the sake of spiritual independence has developed a strong sense of civil rights, of solidarity and of dignity. In their understanding of civil and moral responsibilities, they are much closer to Westerners than is the general Soviet population.

In February 1964 Baptists who supported the Initiative Group founded a civil rights association: the Council of Relatives of Evangelical Christian Baptist Prisoners. This elected council was formed as a temporary organization during the period of repression that coincided with the internal struggles of the church, but it became a permanent organization as a result of the constant persecutions of Baptist communities. The Council of Relatives took upon itself responsibility for collecting and disseminating information on: arrests and sentences of fellow Baptists; names of families deprived of their children for providing a religious upbringing; forced dispersals of religious services; fines; confiscation of homes in which services were performed; dismissals from work; persecution of school children for their religious beliefs. It appealed to the authorities for the release of prisoners, for the return of children to their homes, and for an end to other repression; it also helped prisoners and their families.[22]

The first president of the Council of Relatives was Lidiya Vins, the widow of the Baptist minister Pyotr Vins who had perished in the Stalin camps, and the mother of minister Georgy Vins. She was the head of the organization for thirteen consecutive years, excluding 1970–73, when she was in a forced labor camp.[23]

Baptist *Samizdat*

The legal and moral education of the Baptists was reinforced by their own *samizdat*—dissemination of ideas and information by means of typewriters or hectographs. Baptist *samizdat* dates from 1961, when the initiative group began to distribute appeals to the religious communities in the only way possible. From time to time the initiative group published their *Fraternal Pamphlet*, with news of their activities and appeals to fellow believers on religious and social matters. In 1965 it began to appear on a regular monthly basis. The Council of Churches continued this publication. In 1963 the *Herald of Salvation*, a journal of spiritual instruction, was released by the initiative-group Baptists. In 1976 the name was changed to the *Herald of Truth*, and it continues to be published under that name.[24] In 1964 the Council of Relatives of Evangelical Christian Baptist Prisoners had begun to release "extraordinary reports" on current repression. In 1971 the *Bulletin of the*

Council of Relatives of ECB Prisoners, began to appear every two months, and later became a monthly publication.

Baptist communities were in need of religious literature such as Bibles and hymnals. The All-Union Council occasionally printed such literature, subject to government approval, in extremely small quantities and only for "their" communities. For many years all unofficial Baptist literature was printed on hectographs, and it was impossible to print a sufficient quantity to meet the needs of Baptist communities. In 1966 the Council of Churches of Evangelical Christian Baptists requested official permission to print 10,000 copies of the Bible and 5,000 copies of hymnals. When the authorities failed to respond to this request,[25] Baptists created their own typography and publishing house.

The Christian Publishing House printing press was designed and built by the believers themselves. They learned the printing trade and set their own type. The publishing house keeps the names of its workers and the location of its presses secret. In June 1971 in an assertion of their right to publish, the newly formed Christian Publishing House notified the president of the Council of Ministers of the USSR, Aleksey Kosygin, of the inception of its hitherto secret publishing activities. The notice read: "The Christian Publishing House is a voluntary association of Evangelical Christian Baptists for the purpose of publishing and distributing religious literature. The publishing house is supported by voluntary donations from believers and therefore distributes literature without charge."[26] By 1983 it had published half a million Bibles and hymnals in Russian, Ukrainian, Moldavian, Georgian, Osset, German, and other languages.[27] They began to print the *Fraternal Pamphlet* and the *Herald of Truth* on their presses, although the Bulletin of the Council of Relatives of ECB Prisoners continued to be printed on a hectograph until after 1980, when it also was printed typographically.

Over a ten-year period the Christian Baptists' printing shops were discovered four times by the authorities, but it took three years of investigation to locate the first shop, when in October 1974 a helicopter spotted the printing press on the Ligukalns Latvian farm. Seven workers were arrested and the press confiscated along with nine tons of paper and 15,000 Bibles.[28] Presses were discovered in 1977 in Ivangorod of the Leningrad region, in January 1980 in the village of Starye Kodaki in the Ukraine, in June 1980 in the village of Glivenki in the Novorossiysk region, and in 1982 in the city of Tokmak (Kirghizia).

Those who work in the underground presses are tried, as a rule, under Article 190-1, "slander of the Soviet system," and for "engaging in a forbidden business." The standard sentence for these typesetters is three years in an ordinary regimen labor camp.[29]

In its struggle for independence and freedom of conscience, the

Council of Churches of the Evangelical Christian Baptists and the
Council of Relatives appealed to their fellow believers not only in
the Soviet Union, but abroad as well. The All-Union Council was no
longer the only source of information on the situation of Baptists in
the USSR. In May 1970 the president of the Baptist World Alliance,
William R. Tolbert, visited the Soviet Union. In his own words, he
was "received like a king" by the All-Union Council. Although he was
unaware of it, while he was visiting a registered community in the
Leningrad region, a prayer meeting in a nearby nonregistered community was broken up; the believers, forbidden to enter their prayer
building, were encircled by the militia so that none would be seen by
the honored guest. The information Tolbert gathered during his visit
was, as a consequence, favorable toward the government and All-
Union Council.[30] Later, through appeals to international public opinion, the Council of Churches and the Council of Relatives succeeded
in penetrating the wall of official disinformation, and in August 1970
Ulf Oldenberg, a Danish missionary Baptist who visited the Soviet
Union as a tourist, came to the oppressed communities of Baptists in
central Asia. He was expelled from the country, but at home described
what he had seen that Tolbert had not seen.[31]

The leadership of the Baptist World Alliance continues to maintain official relations with the All-Union Council, and official visits of
Baptist religious figures from abroad continue. Tourists also visit the
supporters of the opposing Council of Churches, and approximately
eight hundred Baptists per year now visit the Soviet Union.[32] A significant number of Western Baptists now support the oppressed Baptists, collecting funds for the Council of Relatives, to be distributed
among the families of prisoners. Appeals for the release of Georgy
Vins, who had been arrested again in 1974, were signed by tens of
thousands of American Baptists; he was among the political prisoners
exchanged with the Soviet Union for Soviet spies in the spring of
1979.[33] President Jimmy Carter met with Georgy Vins at that time.

Links with Civil Rights Groups

Vins organized in Indiana the U.S. office of the Council of Churches,
and Lidea Vins was foreign representative of the Council of Relatives
of Evangelical Christian Baptist Prisoners until her death in 1985.
Their joint effort is intended to inform Western public opinion and the
signatories of the Helsinki Accords of the status of Baptists in the USSR
and to organize help for oppressed believers and communities there.

Years of civil rights activities have enabled the Baptists to come out of their isolation within the USSR and to establish contacts with civil rights activists in a feat perhaps no less difficult than overcoming official disinformation abroad.

The first mention of Baptists in the bulletin of the civil rights activists, the *Chronicle of Current Events*, appeared in December 1968 (no. 5) in the form of a letter from a Kiev Baptist community in defense of G. Vins. The next reference to the Baptists in the *Chronicle of Current Events* appeared in 1970, concerning the 1969–70 arrests of Baptists in the south of the USSR. One can see how incomplete the *Chronicle's* information on the Baptists was by comparing it with information provided by the Council of Relatives: from 1968 to 1975 the *Chronicle of Current Events* lists a total of 21 arrests, but according to information collected by the Council of Relatives, from 1961 to 1970, 524 of their fellow believers had been arrested; (from 1961 to 1963 about 200 occurred in the period of the struggle to hold a congress; in 1971, 61; in 1972, 62; in 1973–75, 116).[34]

Information on the Baptists appeared regularly only after 1974, when the *Chronicle of Current Events* began regularly to receive the *Bulletin of the Council of Relatives*. The first statement by Moscow civil rights activists on behalf of the persecuted Baptists also appeared in 1974 when the Initiative Group for the Defense of Human Rights in the USSR and Andrey Sakharov appealed to international public opinion on behalf of G. Vins.[35] In 1976, immediately after the formation of the Moscow Helsinki Group, Baptists appealed to the group with complaints about the abrogation of their parental rights, and the Moscow Helsinki Group issued a statement on this topic in their document no. 5, "On the Persecution of Religious Families."[36]

On December 5, 1976 Pyotr Vins, the son of Georgy Vins, participated with other young Baptists in a traditional demonstration of human rights activists in Pushkin Square in Moscow. They threw a bouquet of red carnations to Andrey Sakharov, over the heads of a ring of KGB agents and volunteer police. In 1977 Pyotr Vins joined the Ukrainian Helsinki Group.[37]

Repressions against the Baptists were intensified toward the end of 1979 and have continued to increase until the present time. As of January 1, 1980 there were 49 Baptists in prison. As of May, 1982 there were 150, half the total number of those imprisoned for their faith.[38] By 1984 there were more than 200. The increase in repression is evidenced not only by the greater frequency of arrests, but also by an increase in the number of women among those arrested and by harsher sentences.[39]

Constant repressions have decreased the number of adherents of the independent Baptist church. In the second half of the sixties, right after the break within the church, at least half of all Baptists joined the Council of Churches. Now only 2,000 communities, containing about 70,000 adult members, remain faithful.[40] The rest have reluctantly agreed to registration: heroism is always the lot of the minority. Yet, it is only thanks to the heroism of the independent religious communities that the Baptist church has preserved a certain measure of independence.

CHAPTER 12

The Pentecostalists

The Pentecostalists' emphasis on proselytizing is the primary cause of the constant persecution they have suffered in the USSR. When in 1929 the Soviet government changed its policy on religion, Pentecostalists were sentenced en masse to labor-camp terms of twenty to twenty-five years. Some were executed. A portion of those sentenced to long camp terms were released after Stalin's death, but others served full terms. Many did not return at all but died in the camps. Among these was Ivan Voronayev, an American of Russian descent. He had come to the Soviet Union in 1921 and arrived in Odessa where he was to play an important role in the spread of Pentecostalism. One day because of severe fatigue Voronayev lagged behind a column of prisoners returning from work. The guards released the guard dogs and Voronayev was so severely mutilated that he died within a few hours. A few years after his death, his wife and two minor children were allowed to go to the United States.[1]

Trying to avoid persecution, Pentecostal communities often moved from place to place. At the present time there are communities in the western-most regions of the USSR (the Baltic republics), in the Far East (Nakhodka and Vladivostock), and along the path of their movements to the east and west in the Rovno, Zhitomir, and Kaluga regions, in the Ukraine, Stavropol, and Krasnodar regions, and in Azerbaidzhan, Georgia, Siberia, and central Asia.

In August 1945, after another change in government policy on religion, the Pentecostalists were directed to register their communities with the Council on the Affairs of Religious Cults. Registered communities were formally included under the All-Union Council of Evangelical Christian Baptists; they were not allowed their own central religious organization. Unlike the Baptist communities, which the authorities allowed the option of registering or not, all Pentecostalists were encouraged and even forced to register.

However, the conditions imposed were such that important areas of their religious life were prohibited: the religious education of their children, gatherings of women and children, proselytizing, missionary and philanthropic activities, and some religious ceremonies. As a result, approximately one-half of all Pentecostalists have to this day refused to register.[2]

In the words of the Pentecostalist Vasily Patrushev: "We have no choice here: either we become criminals in the eyes of the government by refusing to submit to the Regulations on Registration and thereby observe the teaching of Christ, or we become criminals in the sight of God by submitting to the demands of the government. For us, believers living according to our conscience, the higher law is the law of God. We cannot become criminals before God.[3]

In its present form, the Pentecostal doctrine has existed in Russia since the turn of the century. Pentecostalism grew rapidly during the postrevolutionary period, when followers of this religious doctrine were not persecuted as a sect. By 1928 there were, according to official figures, 200,000 Pentecostalists in the USSR.[4] Pentecostals preach salvation not only through faith, but through good works; for them the highest form of virtue is honest labor and family life. The name "Pentecostal" comes from the special attention they give to the events that occurred on the fiftieth day after Christ's resurrection, the day of Pentecost, when the Holy Ghost descended upon the disciples and caused them to speak in foreign tongues not known to them. This miracle was taken as a sign that Christianity should be preached to foreign peoples.

The incompatibility of the Pentecostalists' religious instruction with official Soviet orders determines their lives from childhood. As early as grade school, the children must accept the enmity they encounter as members of a "sect." When they receive a religious upbringing, Pentecostal children refuse to join the Soviet youth organizations: the Octobrists, Pioneers, and the Komsomol. As a consequence their grades are lowered; they suffer public criticism at school meetings; they are beaten by other children, sometimes at the instigation of their teachers. Teachers subject Pentecostal children to hostile questionings in an attempt to make them accuse their parents of forcing them to take part in religious ceremonies, and prayer meetings. If the children admit to these things, criminal proceedings may be instituted against their parents or the parents may be deprived of their parental rights. Trials on such grounds involving Pentecostalists, Baptists, Seventh-Day Adventists, and others are known to have occurred.

For young Pentecostalists, obligatory military service is a difficult trial because church doctrine forbids them to enlist, to bear weapons, or to kill. The *Chronicle of Current Events* reports that in May 1977, 160 Pentecostal recruits in the Rovno region refused to serve in any but construction or medical units.[5] Refusal to take the oath of military service carries a five-year camp sentence. Such refusals are occasioned not only by religious considerations, but also by intolerable conditions in the army. Pentecostal soldiers have frequently been beaten, sometimes to the point of being crippled.[6]

Because of the difficult conditions they face in school, the majority of Pentecostal youth limit their education to the compulsory eight years. If some do complete the tenth grade, they receive recommendations that virtually exclude the possibility of their being accepted into any institution of higher education. For such children the customary formula is that they "persist in active anti-Soviet opinions." Thus, higher education is rare among Pentecostalists. As a rule they do not even receive positions commensurate with their limited qualifications; most are hired as common laborers. Pentecostalists usually work in the lowest paying, least desirable positions, for which there exists considerable demand: construction workers, watchmen, etc. They are frequently fired by order of the Party leadership, which is watching out for "ideological unity." No matter how hard they work, Pentecostalists do not advance on the job. As the head of Corrective Labor Camp Colony 27 in the Primorsky territory explained to the Pentecostalist Yevgeny Bresenden: "A foreman or an engineer is primarily an educator. Educators with religious convictions, educators who are Pentecostalists, are of no use to us.[7]

Pattern of Official Persecution

Unregistered Pentecostal communities are now most often subjected to persecutions in the form of fines for conducting religious services. Residential homes in which the Pentecostalists gather for prayers are often confiscated or even destroyed by the authorities. In Chernogorsk (in the Krasnoyarsk region) in 1971, the authorities dispersed Pentecostal prayer meetings with fire hoses and bulldozed the homes in which they were held. No. 47 of the *Chronicle of Current Events* reported the breaking up of a Pentecostal wedding; no. 49 reported the dispersal of a funeral service.[8]

Pentecostalists are not now threatened with arrest simply because they belong to the church, as was the case from 1929 to 1945. Nonetheless, imprisonment is not an uncommon measure against the leaders and elders of Pentecostal communities. Those tried are most commonly charged with the article on religious propaganda, or sometimes with articles 190 or 70 (slandering the Soviet system and anti-Soviet propa-

ganda). Occasionally, clergy are accused of causing psychic disturbances in religious believers by performing savage religious rites or
even by sacrificial murder. In 1960 Ivan Fedotov, a Pentecostal elder,
was sentenced to ten years for allegedly attempting to influence a
woman in his community to murder her daughter. Trials like these are
accompanied by attacks in the press. This kind of antireligious propaganda creates an atmosphere of general wariness and even hatred toward members of "sects." The wife of Nikolay Goretoy, a Pentecostal
bishop, relates that in the children's hospital where she worked as a
cleaning woman a doctor told her, "We need someone to work in the
kitchen badly, but I cannot send you there. Everyone knows you are a
sect member, and people will think you are poisoning the children's
food." This was said to a woman who had borne and raised fourteen
children in unbelievably difficult circumstances.[9]

In November 1980 a young woman, Zolotova, and her son were
killed in Yaroslav when their gas stove exploded. Knowing that Zolotova was a Pentecostalist, the officials offered two versions of the
event: that Zolotova killed her son and then herself because she was
a religious fanatic, or that her husband killed her and their son, again
because of religious fanaticism. The night after this tragedy, militiamen broke into the home of Zolotova's parents and took away her two
remaining children. They were held until morning at the militia station for fear that they too would be killed.[10]

The Soviet newspapers and antireligious organizations spread rumors that sect members use religion to cover base motives, that they
"are at the service of the West" for payment in dollars and hide American spies. The "dollar" version is readily acceptable to the public,
since it explains in understandable terms a way of life that is strange
to them: the Pentecostalists' Protestant ethic, which elevates love of
work and honesty to two of the highest virtues; their total sobriety;
their practice of living in communities founded on a sense of brotherly
cooperation; and, therefore, in spite of the fact that they often have
ten or more children they are materially better off than their neighbors. In films, Pentecostalists are shown praying on a desolate beach
(where they go to avoid harassment from the authorities), and it is
explained that they are waiting for an ark filled with American dollars.

In Maloyaroslavets after the Pentecostal bishop Ivan Fedotov received packages of clothing and gifts from fellow believers abroad on
several occasions, an article entitled "Fedotov Gets Paid for Everything" appeared in the local paper. It stated that "the packages are
nothing more than payment for the libel against his country that
Fedotov sent abroad or an advance for which he must work up some
new slander of our Soviet way of life."[11]

Newspapers often accuse sect members of shielding their children from life by forbidding them to go to movies, dances, and such. In fact, young Pentecostalists are doomed to a life of seclusion not because of religious prohibitions, but because of the prejudices of those around them. When they go to social functions, they are often subjected to abuse and sometimes beaten.

In spite of the difficult trials in store for anyone who becomes a sect member, Pentecostal communities, like those of the Baptists and other Protestants, are constantly growing. Children of Pentecostal families, with rare exceptions, remain in the fold. There are many new converts. In one survey, Catholic activists in Lithuania singled out the Jehovah's Witnesses, the Seventh-Day Adventists, and the Pentecostalists as the most successful proselytizers: "They have found methods suitable for the Soviet Union"; they have "created a stable organization," and nurtured within themselves "the apostolic spirit, which fears neither suffering or death."[12]

In their missionary zeal, the Pentecostalists have always found other people who are hungering for a righteous and spiritual life. They attract such individuals to their communities, where the moral climate is in sharp contrast to ordinary Soviet life with its alcoholism and pervasive sense of alienation.

Constant persecution, the prejudices of Soviet society, and the sharply contrasting moral values of the general populace have contributed to the development of a remarkable solidarity among the Pentecostalists. They refer to each other as brothers and sisters, not only because of a long-standing tradition, but because they indeed feel themselves to be one large family surrounded by a hostile world. Their life is based on cooperation, both within and between their communities. Such ties take the place of all others, even national ties. It is no accident, for instance, that there is no contact between the numerous Protestant communities in the Ukraine and members of the nationalist movement. Among such Protestants in the USSR it is common for their sense of religiosity to transcend their national feelings. A brother to them may be of any nationality, provided he accepts their religious teachings.

Official statistics that show the same number of Pentecostalists now as in 1928 reflect an actual increase in the population of Pentecostalists. The losses suffered from repression, from 1929 on, costing the lives of a large number of sect members, have been made up for by new recruits. Moreover, official statistics always underestimate figures the government considers undesirable. Only registered Pentecostalists are included in their enumeration. The Pentecostalists themselves put the number of registered communities at only half their actual number.

The representative of the unregistered Soviet Pentecostalists in the West, Arkady Polishchuk, estimates their own population to be one million.[13]

Origin of Efforts for Exodus

Perhaps it was the constant discrimination in civil and private life that contributed to the formulation soon after the Second World War of a new idea in the Pentecostal doctrine: the necessity of an exodus from the Soviet Union. They believe that the Lord's cup of wrath must some day spill over on that godless country and that before that happens, God will lead the Jews, the chosen people (whose emigration had already begun), and the righteous from the sinful land. But because God's will is not fulfilled of itself, it is the duty of true Christians actively to seek to emigrate.

In 1965 the Pentecostalist Vasily Patrushev compiled a list of fellow believers who wanted to emigrate. The Pentecostalist Fyodor Sidenko, a plumber in the hotel Vostok in Vladivostok, entrusted this list to a Japanese trade representative to transmit it to the United Nations. Patrushev and Sidenko were convicted and served out their camp terms, but there was no reaction from the United Nations.

In the spring of 1973 the Pentecostal movement for emigration began. Members of two communities—Nakhodka in the Far East and Chernogorsk in the Krasnoyarsk region—who asked for permission to emigrate were told to submit invitations from relatives or from the governments of the countries to which they wished to emigrate. In the absence of such documents their applications were not accepted.

The Pentecostalist Yevgeny Bresenden went to Moscow to seek out human rights activist Pavel Litvinov, whose name he knew from foreign radio broadcasts, to which Pentecostalists constantly listen. In February 1974 Moscow human rights activists gave a letter from Bresenden and the minister Georgy Vashchenko to foreign correspondents. The letter contained an appeal to the United Nations on behalf of twenty fellow believers for help in emigrating to Israel or to Australia. They appealed to the president of the United States and to the Christian world as a whole for assistance in helping Soviet Pentecostalists obtain permission to emigrate.

In May 1974 human rights activists introduced Bresenden and Vashchenko to foreign correspondents. They told of the persecution of Pentecostalists and of their struggle to emigrate. Afterwards, Bresenden's family was given permission to emigrate, and later a few other families received permission. All the others were either refused permission or received no answer from the authorities.[14]

Bresenden's visit marked the beginning of contacts between the Pentecostalists and the Moscow human rights activists. Having lived in total isolation for a decade, the Pentecostalists were glad of the opportunity to relate their grief to sympathetic listeners. At this point they began to release, at first irregularly, reports on persecutions of their communities and their struggle for emigration. These reports were initially called the *Informational Service of Pentecostal Christians of the Evangelical Faith,* and later *Facts and Only Facts.* From 1976 on these reports appeared approximately once every other month, thanks to which information on the Pentecostalists appeared regularly in the *Chronicle of Current Events.* These reports appeared in every issue under two headings: "Persecutions of Believers" and "The Right to Emigrate." The first report, in connection with the public statement of Bresenden and Vashchenko, appeared in issue no. 32 (1974).

In 1975 another community joined those that had declared their intention of emigrating—Starotitarovskaya in the Krasnodar region. The elder of this community, Nikolay Goretoy, became the leading figure in the Pentecostal emigration movement.

Nikolay Goretoy had been critically wounded on the front lines during the war. He worked as a grade-school art and mechanical-drawing teacher until elected elder of an unregistered community in 1947. He then had to leave his teaching job and earn his living as a laborer (painter, plasterer). In an effort to save himself and the members of his community from arrest and deprivation of their parental rights, Goretoy and his flock moved east several times until they reached Nakhodka, on the Pacific Ocean. There Goretoy was arrested in 1961, and spent three-and-a-half years in camp and five years in internal exile. When he was released in the early seventies, he settled in Starotitarovskaya,[15] in the Krasnodar Region.

The Starotitarovskaya community numbers about a hundred adults, larger if one includes the children—Goretoy alone has eleven children and twenty-nine grandchildren. In the communities of Starotitarovskaya, Nakhodka, Chernogorsk, and a few others that are pursuing emigration, emigration councils were founded in 1975. Their function was to coordinate the efforts of all these communities. In the summer of 1976 the members of the emigration councils of Nakhodka and Starotitarovskaya appealed to the Moscow Helsinki Watch Group for help in focusing world attention on the situation created by the Pentecostalists' decision to emigrate. The members of the Moscow Helsinki Group helped the Pentecostalists compile a collection of more than five hundred typewritten pages entitled *My People, Let Us Leave This Country.* The collection included notes on the history of the Pentecostal families trying to emigrate, along with documentation (complaints sent to government departments, court decisions, newspaper articles on the Pentecostalists, and photographs.)[16]

On December 1, 1976, the Moscow Helsinki Group presented the members of the Pentecostal emigration councils to Western correspondents. They gave this collection to the correspondents, together with an appeal to the signatories of the Helsinki Accords requesting assistance for the Pentecostalists in emigrating to their countries, in accordance with the obligations of the USSR under the Final Act of the Helsinki Accords. The Moscow Helsinki Group pointed out that "religious dissidents fleeing government persecution have made a considerable contribution to the development of states participating in the Helsinki Conference, such as the United States and Canada."[17]

On behalf of the Moscow Helsinki Group, Lidiya Voronina, a Muscovite, visited the communities in Nakhodka and Starotitarovskaya to get a complete picture of the Pentecostalists' situation. She spent several days in both communities, talking with members from practically every family in Starotitarovskaya and with more than forty Pentecostalists in Nakhodka. She attended their meetings, listened, and herself answered numerous questions. Her visit made a strong impression on the Pentecostalists. After a decade of isolation they had met with sympathetic concern from, of all places, Moscow—a window on the rest of the world in closed Soviet society. The support of the Moscow human rights activists and contacts with journalists from the free world were seen as a long-awaited turn for the better. In contrast to the average Soviet, who views the unknown West with suspicion, the Pentecostalists and Protestants in general see the West as part of the Christian world, a world of fellow believers. They were convinced that only the isolation imposed by Soviet authorities prevented their free and powerful fellow believers from coming to their aid as selflessly as their own communities help each other. They were just as convinced that the Soviet government would be forced to back down and allow them to emigrate. These convictions were reinforced by the reaction of the authorities to their contacts with the Moscow human rights activists.

Voronina was followed by several KGB agents during her visits to the Pentecostal communities. During her visit to Starotitarovskaya, Nikolay Goretoy and another Pentecostalist were called into the village Soviet to explain the purpose of her visit. When Voronina was leaving Nakhodka, a rock was thrown at her car. The window was broken, but no one was injured. Immediately following her return to Moscow, her apartment was searched and all the notes she had taken during the trip were confiscated. After her departure from Nakhodka, official Pentecostal officers arrived in town and attacked all those who were actively trying to emigrate or communicate with the Moscow Helsinki Group. "We must seek help from God, and not from some leftist forces," they declared at a meeting.[18]

A KGB agent visited Anatoly Vlasov, a Moscow Pentecostalist who was in communication with the Moscow Helsinki Group, and advised him to confine his activities to religious affairs and not support human rights activists.[19]

The authorities were clearly worried that the Pentecostalists would break out of their isolation. Using both the carrot and the stick, they put pressure on those who had already applied to emigrate to withdraw their applications. Olga Krasun, a Pentecostalist from Rovno, was promised, in exchange for giving up her attempts to emigrate, help in moving closer to her job, a raise, and no interference if she applied to an institute. In the Primorsk region the authorities organized a Committee for the Defense of the Rights of Religious Believers, in imitation of independent organizations. The committee was composed of an officer on the government Council on the Affairs of Religious Cults, teachers, and others who refused to explain who they were. The committee members made the rounds of Pentecostalists attempting to emigrate and tried to persuade them to withdraw their applications. To some they promised help, apartments, access to education, and good jobs; others they threatened and showed letters from emigré Pentecostalists, describing the difficulties of life abroad.[20]

The authorities refused to accept emigration applications without invitations from abroad and then did not deliver invitations when these had been mailed. In Nakhodka invitations from the United States for forty-seven Pentecostal families were held up at the post office. The families finally were given the invitations only after staging a ten-day hunger strike that coincided with the Belgrade Conference, when authorities promised Bishop Nikolay Goretoy that, if he submitted his documents separately, they would allow his own family to emigrate, but not the other members of his community. He refused.[21]

The fortitude of the Pentecostalists in their attempts to gain emigration for whole groups and even communities has deep spiritual, historical, and psychological roots. The majority of Pentecostalists belong to the indigenous population—Russians and Ukrainians—and therefore, unlike the Jews and Germans, their request to emigrate cannot be explained as a desire to join family or to return to a "historic homeland." The reason for their desire to emigrate is to escape from religious persecution. The authorities have, indeed, declared that they do not and never will acknowledge emigration on religious grounds.

In order, apparently, to avert the spread of the Pentecostal emigration movement, extreme measures of repression against the Pentecostalists have ceased. In 1976 there were no arrests, and no Pentecostalists were deprived of parental rights for giving their children a religious up-bringing. The repression of unregistered communities for conducting prayer meetings has been sharply reduced. For the first time in forty-five years, the authorities stopped imposing fines, and no one was called in "to talk matters over" with the militia or KGB. The campaign for registration of religious communities was promoted under the slogan of creating "a union of autonomous Pentecostalists." Until this time, registered communities of Pentecostalists came under the authority of the All-Union Council of Evangelical Christian Baptists. The matter at hand concerned the convening of a constituent congress of "autonomous communities" in October 1978. Once the Pentecostal-ists were registered, the authorities promised to lift many of the more burdensome restrictions.[22] To back up this promise a registered com-munity outside of Moscow was given a prayer house in a new con-struction site without the onus of paying taxes on it.[23]

However, these promises attracted few people, since, according to Boris Perchatkin, a member of the emigration council in Nakhodka: "the Pentecostalists were drawn to emigration not by any particular event in recent years, but by their entire history since the inception of the Soviet regime." A temporary lifting of repression could not make them forget how incompatible their religious doctrine was with Soviet ideology, "If it is written in the Party platform that Communism and religion are mutually incompatible, and that the goal of this country is the construction of Communism, then naturally we have nothing to hope for. Considering the long experience of our grandfathers and our fathers, as well as our own, we do not believe there will be any im-provement in our situation, even if such promises are now made. The only solution for us is emigration."[24]

The Pentecostalists' hopes for emigration were greatly encouraged when Jimmy Carter, a Baptist, was elected president of the United States. Convinced of the influence of their fellow Christians in the strongest country in the free world, they hoped that under a Baptist president they would receive the kind of support from the United States that the Jewish emigration movement had received for many years. Evidently, this belief contributed to the spread of the Pente-costal movement for emigration. In February 1977, approximately 1,000 Pentecostalists announced their wish to leave; by May, 1,700 believers were trying to emigrate. (The Pentecostalists were joined by the Baptists, although the Pentecostalists were always in the majority in the movement to emigrate on religious grounds.) Within a month the number of applicants had grown to 3,500 and by September, to

10,000. By December 1977, 20,000 had applied to emigrate. In 1979 this number had increased to 30,000.[25]

Pentecostalists from the Rovno and Brest regions, from the Caucasus and the Rostov regions, from the Ukraine and from Estonia, from near Leningrad and from Chernogorsk, wrote to "their" President Carter to ask him to request the Soviet government to allow them to emigrate to the United States and to intercede on their behalf with Brezhnev.[26]

In June 1977, 3,500 Pentecostalists and Baptists trying to emigrate appealed to Brezhnev with a statement of their demands: that procedures for emigration be simplified; that groups and communities be given permission, rather than just individuals and families; that those who have declared their intention of emigrating not be called up into the army and then demobilized early; that emigration fees be lowered for poor families; and that Pentecostalists be allowed to use the financial aid donated by Pentecostalists abroad.[27]

Participation in the Human Rights Movement

The struggle for religious liberty and for the right to emigrate led the Pentecostalists to participate in the general human rights movement. Signatures of active Pentecostalists can be found on the collective appeals of the Christian Committee for the Defense of the Rights of Religious Believers in the USSR and on the Moscow Helsinki Watch Group's appeals concerning the need to create an international Helsinki Commission.[28] There are also Pentecostalist signatures on letters in defense of arrested members of the Moscow Helsinki Group: Orlov, Ginzburg, and Shcharansky. In a separate letter signed by five hundred Pentecostalists, Bishop Nikolay Goretoy called upon Christians the world over to pray for the arrested members of the Helsinki Group:

"Greater love hath no man than to lay down his life for his friend." Alexander Ginzburg, Yury Orlov and Anatoly Shcharansky have fulfilled this precept of Christ to the end. . . .

In the 1960s there were in the Soviet Union hundreds of trials of our brother Pentecostalists. We were sent to labor camps, to psychiatric hospitals, and into exile, our children were taken away from us. . . . When in 1975 we refused to register our communities officially . . . despite pressure from the authorities and the direct threat of sending us to camps, these threats would most probably have been carried out if we had not appealed to the Moscow Group for the Observance of the Helsinki Agreements. And when this group, in particular, Yu. Orlov, A. Ginzburg and A. Shcharansky, raised their noble voices in our defense, the local authorities drew back from us. If now we do not raise our voice in their defense, then by this we will commit a crime before God and before our conscience. . . . On 27 March 1977 thousands of our brothers and sisters in the USSR . . . will be fasting and will bow their heads in prayer for Yury Orlov, Aleksandr Ginzburg and Anatoly Shcharansky.[29]

The Pentecostalists made contact with world public opinion not only through the Helsinki Group, but also through their own direct efforts.

Since church is separated from state according to the Soviet Constitution, Pentecostalists consider that they have the right to make contacts independent of the state. They have suggested that Christian organizations, governments, and human rights organizations in other countries contact them on religious and legal issues. Pentecostal communities have invited Queen Elizabeth, Kurt Waldheim, and President Carter to visit them.[30]

The *Chronicle of Current Events* (no. 48) reported an appeal of the Pentecostalists to the United Nations Human Rights Committee and the Belgrade Conference. The senior presbyter Nikolay Goretoy, speaking at a press conference for foreign correspondents in March 1977 in Moscow, said: "We are free people; we are neither captives nor slaves. We appeal to President Carter as to a brother in Christ to help believers exercise the right to emigrate on the basis of the Universal Declaration of Human Rights Covenants signed by the Soviet government."[31]

Pentecostalists seeking emigration have selected as their representatives in the West Yevgeny Bresenden, now living in the United States, and Arkady Polishchuk, who represented the Pentecostalists in Moscow after Lidiya Voronina emigrated. Polishchuk was forced to emigrate because of his activities, and in the fall of 1977 left the Soviet Union and settled in the United States. Here he helps organize aid to the Pentecostalists from fellow believers in the United States and Europe, from international organizations, and from governments that are signatories of the Helsinki Accords.

In January 1978 President Carter received the representative of the senior Pentecostal presbyter and member of the All-Union Council of Evangelical Christian Baptists, P. Shatrov. In response to his question about the Pentecostalists' emigration, Shatrov said that only the unregistered wished to leave, that is, those who recognize no governmental authority, and that they were few in number.

In the spring of 1978, two Pentecostal families trying to emigrate, the Vashchenkos and the Chmykalovs, forced their way into the American embassy in Moscow. They hoped their direct testimony to American diplomats would go directly to President Carter, and that he would help them as well as the rest of their fellow believers. They could not be persuaded to leave the embassy. They were not thrown out on the street into the arms of waiting KGB agents, as had happened to other "visitors" to the embassy, but instead, were led to a basement room, where they took up residence for five years.[32]

In 1979 Polishchuk attended the Twelfth World Conference of Pentecostalists in Canada, and to draw attention to the position of the Pentecostalists in the USSR, he stood for a week in front of the conference building. He fasted and distributed letters from Soviet Pentecostalists, describing the persecutions to which they are subjected. In 1980 he went also to the Madrid conference on Helsinki accords to win sympathy for Soviet Pentecostalists from the official delegates and made an attempt to bring their situation before the conference.

In this way, the governments and Western public opinion, formerly dependent on the leadership of the All-Union Council of Evangelical Christian Baptists for information about their fellow believers in the USSR, first learned about unregistered communities. Although the leaders of the International Union of Pentecostalists now, as before, acknowledge only this official leadership, there are Pentecostalists and even communities in the West ready to help their persecuted brethren. They have initiated correspondence with Pentecostal families and send needed packages of clothing to Pentecostal families. Pentecostal tourists sometimes succeed in bringing in religious material. To receive Bibles and children's versions of the gospels is a great joy for Soviet believers. Such books are so rare that they are sometimes copied by hand. With the aid of their coreligionists from the West, the Pentecostals organized the printing of religious literature in the USSR on duplicating machines and by photocopying. Tourists brought in this equipment, as well as religious films and projectors for home viewing.

In the summer of 1977, the Swedish Pentecostalists Bengt-Gunnar Sareld and Nils-Erik Engstroem travelled by car to the USSR as tourists. They went on behalf of the Slavic Mission. They brought in a large number of Bibles and returned with several hundred letters requesting invitations to emigrate as well as documents on the Pentecostal emigration movement, in particular the collection *My People, Let Us Leave This Place.* The two Swedes were arrested at the border, and soon after publicly denounced the Slavic Mission as an "anti-Soviet organization" and their own activities in the Soviet Union as "criminal." They gave extensive testimony about the believers whom they visited. They were released in November 1977, but numerous searches and investigations were continued until 1980 on the basis of their testimony.[33]

Contact with the West enabled several hundred Pentecostal families to receive invitations from abroad, but tens of thousands were needed.

No single West European government exhibited a persistent interest in the fate of Soviet Pentecostalists. The mass enthusiasm of the Pentecostalists did not find sufficient support in the West, although such support represented their only chance of success.

In the meantime, the Soviet government changed its tactics from carrot to stick. From approximately mid-1977, fines, militia summonses, and forced dispersals of weddings and other Pentecostal functions began to occur.[34] Public attacks on communities that had expressed a desire to emigrate radically increased. Special meetings about the Pentecostalists in the villages of Starotitarovskaya and Leningradskaya were organized in July and September 1977. Komsomol members and volunteer police from other villages and cities were invited, along with local authorities from Krasnodar. Pentecostalists who had applied to emigrate were asked to come and promised a hearing of their opinions on emigration. However, only orators coached beforehand were allowed to speak at the gathering; they called those wanting to emigrate traitors and renegades, and accused them of acting in concert with Sakharov, Orlov, and Ginzburg as "enemies of the Soviet system." People from the crowd shouted that the emigration applicants ought to be sent to prison or even shot or hanged. The gathering at Starotitarovskaya was filmed and taped, but when the believers turned on their own tape recorder, it was taken away from them.[35] After these gatherings, Goretoy found himself under virtual house arrest, and the Nakhodka emigration council became the leading force in the emigration movement.

The situation of the Pentecostalists in Nakhodka and Vladivostok is described in a letter to the Belgrade Conference of signatories to the Helsinki accords:

Several times a week from the platforms of clubs, houses of culture and lecture-halls of institutions and hostels, lectures are read out informing the population that believers are enemies, fanatics, traitors, CIA agents, spies. Notices are printed in local newspapers presenting us as monsters and traitors. . . . This officially conducted campaign incites the population to beat up believers.

Thus it was, for example, with the beating-up of a group of believers which occurred on New Year's night. As a result there were many injured, and one of them, Ivan Durov, will be a cripple for the rest of his life. His skull was broken and his kidneys were crushed. In the hospital he was intimidated with threats that if he did not leave the hospital he would be killed. The court rejected his complaint, the bandits went unpunished.

The atmosphere in the town is tense, our women cannot go out on the street: they are threatened, beaten up. L. I. Vasileva was beaten up on the street. Bandits cried out: "Baptist, you work for the CIA, take this." In the middle of the day they punched Nina Mironenko, who is pregnant, and dragged her into a swamp, crying out, "You wanted to go to America? We'll show you America!" The hooligans enjoy the silent approval of the authorities, throw stones and glass into our courtyards, and sprinkle our gardens with broken glass.

On 19 May an attack was carried out by bandits on the house of widow Chuprina, in which our prayer meetings are held. The house was burgled, the children were severely frightened, and the glass in the windows and on the verandah was knocked out by blows of an axe. . . . The police authorities tried to force Chuprina to sign a statement that she had no complaints against the attackers.[36]

In addition to informing world opinion of their plight, the Pentecostalists undertake efforts to organize themselves so as to more effectively protect their civil rights and to coordinate the activities of communities scattered across the country. Representatives of unregistered communities met in Moscow on June 16, 1979 and elected a governing body, the Fraternal Council of Christians of the Evangelical Pentecostal Faith, organized along the lines of the Council of Churches of Evangelical Christian Baptists. This congress took place in spite of the fact that the authorities did everything in their power to prevent it. On their way to the congress, Pentecostalists were removed from trains, caught in train stations and airports, and sent home under guard.[37] In the summer of 1979 representatives of the Fraternal Council, Boris Perchatkin and Timofey Prokopchik, met with a delegation of American congressmen, including Senator Robert Dornen, in Moscow. They asked the congressmen to intercede on their behalf with the Soviet government.[38]

In the winter of 1979 arrests of Pentecostal-movement activists began. Fyodor Sidenko, Nikolay Goretoy, and then Nikolay Bobarykin (all from Starotitarovskaya) were arrested.[39] But the struggle for emigration continued. On May 17, 1980 a human rights group of Pentecostalists was formed. In view of the increased repressions, only the number, but not the names, of the members was announced: there were seven. In July 1980, the group published an almanac called *The Red and the Black*, with documents on Pentecostalists trying to emigrate and on persecution of their church.[40] After this, the group systematically relayed information to Moscow human rights activists, with particular attention to the continuing arrests of Pentecostalists. On August 18, 1980, Boris Perchatkin was arrested. Other members of the Fraternal Council appealed to Brezhnev in a letter asking that he meet with them before the Madrid Conference. The letter consisted of thirteen questions, among which were the following:

1. Would the Pentecostalists be allowed to have their own Council of Churches?

2. Would present legislation on religious cults be annulled?

3. Would private printing presses be permitted?

4. Would the teaching of atheism in the schools be stopped?

5. Would religious and other prisoners of conscience be released from prison with admission of their innocence?

6. Would freedom to emigrate be instituted?[41]

Expecting no response from Brezhnev, the Pentecostalists sent a collective letter with 1,310 signatures to President Carter. Again, they asked him to appeal personally to Brezhnev, since he is "our President and will not receive us." They asked Carter to publicize their plight as widely as possible among their fellow believers in the West whose assistance they did not perceive as substantial: "Either we do not hear them or they believe the slander and attacks on us."[42]

The lack of strong support from the West made it easy to terrorize the Pentecostalists. During the investigation of the Perchatkin case, a KGB investigator, Lieutenant Colonel Kuzmin, told the Pentecostalists in Nakhodka: "Don't compare yourselves to the Jews. They cost a lot, but we won't get much for you."[43]

A large number of letters from Pentecostalists were sent to the Madrid conference, both individually and collectively. Beginning on November 11, 1980, the day the Madrid conference opened, 1,300 Pentecostalists held a five-day hunger strike in hopes of attracting attention to their plight. However, the strain of four years of fruitless efforts has weakened their resolve. In Nakhodka, where the Pentecostal community consists of approximately five hundred adults, about three hundred families applied to emigrate. But by 1980, only one hundred continued to pursue emigration.[44] The situation was roughly the same in other communities. In a letter to President Reagan written in the beginning of 1981, a note of despair is sounded:

The government of the Soviet Union responds to all our lawful requests either with silence or with the curt response: "You are not going anywhere and you are needed by no one." Our appeals to international organizations have only succeeded in bringing the wrath of our own government down on our heads. . . . They promise to settle the score with us once and for all as soon as the Madrid conference has ended. We have no one we can rely on. May God inspire you to act on our behalf, Mr. President! Accept us into your country! As long as we remain in the Soviet Union, please advise your representatives in the Soviet Union, diplomats, and correspondents, not to avoid contacts with us, Mr. President. After all, we lack the necessary connections, means, and freedom to communicate with foreigners either verbally or by letter. . . . We are suffering and cannot tell the world about it. We beg of you, Mr. President, to make a public statement on our behalf and to appeal to Brezhnev to allow us to leave. . . . Please, Mr. President, answer us.[45]

Again no answer followed.

Even the Pentecostal families in the American embassy were denied permission to emigrate. During the negotiations about the Pentecostals' fate, the Soviet representatives demanded that the Pentecostals leave the embassy, return to Chernogorsk and submit their emigration applications in the usual manner. But the Pentecostals refused to do this because they did not believe that such a tactic would work. During the winter of 1981–1982, Avgustina and Lidiya Vashchenko began an open-ended hunger strike, demanding that their family be granted permission to emigrate. In their statements to the press they expressed the bitter realization that had evidently become common among Pentecostalists: the West is indifferent to the fate of Protestants persecuted in the USSR. Meanwhile, in the U.S., a fairly active citizens' movement was launched in support of the Vashchenkos and the Chmykalovs. But not until June 1983 did American diplomats manage to obtain a firm promise that if these families submitted their documents in Chernogorsk, they would receive permission to emigrate to the West. This was one of the unwritten conditions for signing the Concluding Document of the Madrid conference. But this concession was only a partial victory, since it only concerned the fates of two Pentecostal families. The rest remain prisoners in the USSR to this day.

After the first wave of arrests from 1979 to 1981, there was a second wave. Activists in the emigration movement who had gathered for a conference in Rovno were arrested, as were several other people.

Pentecostalists continued to be arrested in the following years as well. Activists of the Pentecostal emigration movement bore the brunt of the arrests. Again persons who refused to serve in the army were arrested, as well as the most active ministers (I. Fedotov, V. Murashkin, and others).[46]

In spite of these conditions and in spite of giving up all hope of an exodus, Pentecostalists continue to refuse to register; they preserve an independent civic position; they do not permit the authorities to interfere in internal church affairs; and they continue their missionary work.

CHAPTER 13

The True and Free
Seventh-Day Adventists

The very name of the religion of the Seventh-Day Adventists suggests its fundamental tenet: the expectation of an imminent Second Coming and Final Judgment Day. The Adventists' plan of salvation consists of a rigid observance of the moral law contained in the Ten Commandments. They treat all the commandments as equally important and do not permit the transgression of a single one.

The church was founded in 1844 in the United States, and its adherents appeared in Russia in the last century. An internal split occurred within the Russian Seventh-Day Adventist Church in 1914 over the sixth commandment, "Thou shalt not kill"—a commandment the Adventists follow to the point of not eating animal flesh. The entry of Russia into the First World War and the subsequent general mobilization created a dilemma for the group: either the Adventists had to transgress the sixth commandment and join the army, or they had to disobey the mobilization order. After the October Revolution, arguments over this point ceased for a few years, because the decree of January 4, 1919, signed by Lenin, released from military service any people whose religious beliefs forbade them to bear arms. This decree gradually ceased to be observed. At the Fifth Congress of Seventh-Day Adventists in 1924, the church suspended the categorical ban on carrying arms; it was resolved that every church member should individually decide whether or not to serve in the military. The Fifth Congress also modified adherence to the fourth commandment on observing the Sabbath in the same way—a decision that complicated the lives of those Adventists who refused to work on Saturday, a workday in the Soviet Union at that time.

At the Sixth Congress of the Seventh-Day Adventists in 1928, the church leadership, under pressure from government authorities, passed a resolution that forced members to renounce both the fourth and sixth commandments. The new resolution required that every member, under the threat of excommunication, "carry out state and military service of all kinds, just like any other citizen." Orthodox Adventists refused to recognize this resolution, and an internal schism resulted. Adventists who held to the conviction that moral law obliged them to observe all Ten Commandments without exception (even under conditions in the Soviet Union where this obligation inevitably leads to conflict with the authorities) called themselves the All-Union Church of True and Free Seventh-Day Adventists.

From its inception, the True and Free Adventist church was not recognized by the authorities, and so was subjected to persecutions. Gregory Ostvald, the first leader of the church, died in a labor camp in 1937. His successor, Pyotr Manzhura, died in camp in 1949. Vladimir Shelkov, the third church leader, was arrested several times and in 1945 was sentenced to be shot. The sentence was, after fifty-five days, reduced to ten years in a labor camp; Shelkov spent a total of twenty-six years in camps and in internal exile. Between prison sentences he lived "illegally," that is, with a country-wide search warrant out for his arrest.[1] Like his predecessors, Shelkov died in camp, in January 1980 at the age of eighty-four.[2]

Commitment to Spiritual and Civil Freedom

Like other religious groups in the USSR, the True and Free Seventh-Day Adventists formulated their civic position vis-à-vis an atheist government that imposes its will on them. The position adopted by the independent Baptists and the Pentecostalists was a direct result of their religious doctrine. They considered it a sacred duty of the church and its members to stand up for an independent religious life and freedom of conscience in the face of government pressure. The civic position of present-day True and Free Seventh-Day Adventists does not follow from their religious teachings, but rather is an organic part of those teachings. In the words of Shelkov, this consists of "a struggle, without bloodshed, for the basic rights and liberties of every citizen."[3] The church of True and Free Seventh-Day Adventists is founded on the conviction that man is created in the image of God and retains his divine likeness as long as he observes the Ten Commandments with a free conscience and conviction, a process that ensures the development of a harmonious and whole personality. One's duty before God is to preserve one's freedom and moral principles under any circumstances and at any sacrifice. If one relinquishes one's freedom, one ceases to be a human being in the full sense of the word. The most important human rights concern civil, rather than economic freedoms, since the soul is more important to believers than the body.

The cultivation of this moral principle by present-day True Adventists seems to have resulted in part from the influence of Vladimir Shelkov, a gifted and prolific religious writer of sermons, essays on Biblical themes, and the history of the Adventist church. His works, which would fill a library, are embued with civic concerns. He also wrote many articles on legal issues: "The Interrelationship of Church and State," "Legislation on Cults," "The Foundations of a Genuine Free Conscience and Equal Rights," a series of brochures entitled "The Struggle for Freedom of Conscience," and "The Legal Struggle with the Dictatorship of Government Atheism for Freedom of Conscience."[4]

Shelkov's major interest was in the interrelationship between church and state, and the attitudes of believers to state authority in general, and to the Soviet state in particular. This conflict was an area of passionate interest in all of Shelkov's writings. He maintained that religious believers ought to recognize and submit to the authority of the state as an institution established by God for the preservation of social order. It is in this sense of "pure statehood" that government is understood. But "pure statehood" ought to be neutral in regard to all religions and ideologies: " 'Pure statehood' ought to be objective. Government should not intrude in the sphere of religion. . . . To believe or not to believe—that is a question of individual conscience. The materialism of atheism is also a kind of belief or religion. For this reason, it should not be a state religion that imposes its materialistic world view through schools and other government agencies. It should be considered a personal ideology among other ideologies. The principle of separation of church, state, and school also applies to the separation of government atheism from the state and the education system."

Shelkov strongly denounced both the Soviet state, which had made atheism the state ideology, and "bureaucratic," "restricted" churches, which have agreed to recognize the regulations on religious cults imposed on them by an atheistic government: "The government-sanctioned registration of religious organizations facilitates the process of unification of church and state and the interference of government in internal church matters."[5] In the process the government exploits the state-sanctioned churches for its own purposes. "Honest" governmental support of any church is, according to Shelkov, no better than government atheism. In either case, persecution, administrative and criminal prosecution, and even the annihilation of dissident believers and thinkers are inevitable. This is amply demonstrated by past experiences of the Russian Orthodox church, the Catholic, and the Protestant state-sanctioned churches: "Believers who are free and true to their religious ideals," he said, "ought to resist any pressure whatsoever from the government and refuse all government support; they ought to struggle "for equal rights by peaceful means, for the independent spirit of the individual, and for freedom of conscience and of faith."

Shelkov insisted on government neutrality not only in the relationship to religion, but also to nationality. In this regard, he wrote:

The present supremacy of government atheism has created ideological confusion and moral decay in the land. Appeals to recreate a national consciousness in the Russian people and a Russian Orthodox church in the spirit of the past are heard: it is said that only a national rebirth and a national church will save the country from spiritual bankruptcy. But Russian Orthodoxy prevailed in the past as the official religion, and it stained its hands with blood by crushing freedom of conscience and of faith in dissident believers and thinkers. A Russian Inquisition took place, which destroyed 12 million Old Believers and hundreds of thousands of Evangelical Christians and sect members. How does this historical violation of freedom of conscience differ from the Catholic Inquisition, which killed 52 million Christians over a period of twelve-and-a-half centuries? . . . [In the light of this experience] legal guarantees of freedom of conscience and of religious faith are essential, so that they will not be restricted either by the reigning state religion of atheism-materialism-evolutionism, or by the tyranny of any religion that favors unification with the state on the basis of nationalism. . . . [On the basis of these considerations] the equal rights of all men, given by God at birth and enunciated by the Constitution, which have not been guaranteed, but ignored like orphans, ought to be observed by all citizens as a law of God and of pure statehood. Such international and universal laws should be observed in the same way as the laws of one's country.[6]

Connections with Human Rights Groups

During the trial of Shelkov and his associates in 1979, it was noted that the human rights activities of the True and Free Seventh-Day Adventist church had begun in the late sixties, when the human rights movement was gaining influence, and that their human rights activities were intensified in the midseventies when they made personal contact with the Moscow human rights workers.[7]

The first mention of Seventh-Day Adventists in the *Chronicle of Current Events* was in June 1970, but this was not based on personal contacts. Issue no. 14 contained a report on the trial of Mikhail Sych, a Seventh-Day Adventist minister, on whom a regional Vitebsk newspaper reported.[8] The next information on the Adventists appeared five years later in issue no. 38 (1975)—a report of police searches of homes of Seventh-Day Adventists in Samarkand, during which religious literature as well as the United Nations' Declaration of Human Rights and the International Covenants on Human Rights were confiscated. The *Chronicle* reported that believers demanded the return of the confiscated materials; they managed to get back the confiscated Bibles.[9] In the section of no. 38, entitled "Statements by Church Officials and Believers," an article of Shelkov's, "A Unified Ideal," was cited,[10] indicating some contacts between the Seventh-Day Adventists and human rights activists. However, after issue no. 38, no further information on the Adventists appeared for two more years. From issue no. 44 (March 1977) on, reports on the persecution of the Adventists and their legal battles appeared regularly. This indicates that contacts between the Adventists and human rights activists had become regular. These contacts seem to have been established at the end of 1976: in document no. 5 July 1976 of the Moscow Helsinki Group, "Repression Against Families of Believers," among instances of children being taken away from parents was the case of Seventh-Day Adventist Mariya Vlasyuk in the village of Ilyatka in the Ukraine. The affair was reported in detail and supported by the relevant documents.[11]

In 1977 Shelkov wrote an open letter on behalf of arrested Moscow Helsinki Group members Yury Orlov, Aleksandr Ginzburg, and Anatoly Shcharansky to President Carter and the Belgrade conference of countries that had signed the Helsinki Accords. He described the persecutions of Seventh-Day Adventists in the Soviet Union—searches and the break-up of prayer meetings, the persecution of Adventist parents for giving their children a religious upbringing, and prison terms for refusal to bear arms in the military.[12] He and an associate, a minister of the True Adventist Church, Rostislav Galetsky, also in hiding, both signed an appeal to the Belgrade Conference as representatives of the All-Union Church of True and Free Seventh-Day Adventists (document no. 26 of the Moscow Helsinki Group).[13] This document appealed to the conference delegates to look into violations of religious freedom in the USSR. It referred also to violations of the right to choose the country of one's residence and of the rights of national minorities, and on the use of forced prison labor and on the existence of political prisoners in the USSR—prisoners of conscience—and the difficult conditions in camps for political prisoners.

In February 1978, Rostislav Galetsky participated in a press conference of the Moscow Helsinki Group on the anniversary of the arrests of Orlov and Ginzburg.[14] Galetsky popularized the religious and legal views of the True Adventists in the articles "The Situation of Religion and the Believers in the USSR" and "On Our Attitude to the Government." Following Shelkov's lead in justifying the active human rights position of the True Adventists, Galetsky writes: "Biblical history is replete with examples of faithful believers engaging in lawful protests and waging decisive (exclusively nonviolent) and just battles. They upheld the principles of freedom of thought, conscience, and of religion—a God-given birthright of every human being and an integral part of the personality."[15] He considers such a position even more essential at the present time: "Our epoch is one of a specific and decisive battle for human rights. . . . The year 1977 was declared a year of religious freedom, yet freedom is not the fruit of inactivity and joyful expectation; it never comes to us of itself."[16] Galetsky appealed to the West for support, not only to Seventh-Day Adventists, but to all Christians, all religious believers, and, in general, "to all people of good will . . . who value human rights and liberty." He asked them to disregard mendacious information released by official Soviet organizations and to avail themselves of newspapers and radio broadcasts to discover the true situation of dissidents in the Soviet Union. He requested support for religious believers, and also for independent human rights associations and for human rights activists in the Soviet Union. He asked that they "make good use of the up-coming Belgrade Conference . . . to condemn inhuman and illegal acts of violence and oppression in the USSR and support those who are deprived of their rights."[17]

During discussions of proposals for the new Soviet Constitution, many True Adventists wrote to the Commission on the Constitution in 1977, criticizing the proposed formulations, in particular those concerning religion and freedom of conscience. Galetsky signed the "letter of the twelve" sent to the Politburo of the Central Committee of the Communist Party of the Soviet Union, criticizing the proposed constitution. The letter was also signed by the Russian Orthodox priest Gleb Yakunin, Tatyana Velikhanova, and other Moscow human rights activists. The letter claimed that the new constitution would reduce and limit democracy in the Soviet Union at a time when the country needed to democratize itself in every possible way.[18]

Persecution and the Search for an Underground Printing Press

Beginning in the midseventies, the Adventists' underground publishing house, True Witness, raised the level of its activity. It acquired a printing press and published religious literature and works on human rights. It also published the works of Shelkov.

As soon as the KGB became aware of its existence, steps were taken to liquidate the True Witness; an investigation was conducted to discover the identity of its contributors and workers, as well as the location of the press. Numerous attempts to recruit informers among the members of the True and Faithful Seventh-Day Adventists are known to have been made. During the KGB's recruiting attempts several persons were prosecuted on the basis of fabricated evidence because they refused to help the KGB in its efforts to discover the publishers. Nina Ruzhechko and Semyon Bakholdin were arrested. In good health before their arrest, both died in imprisonment—Ruzhechko within a month and Bakholdin within two-and-a-half years—of unexplained illnesses.[19] Just what some of those religious believers whom the KGB counted on to find True Witness had to endure is clear from the report of a nineteen-year-old Adventist, Yakov Dolgoter. He was stopped at the marketplace in Pyatigorsk in February 1978, and brochures printed by the True Witness were found on his person. He was detained for a month, supposedly to ascertain his identity, while the investigators demanded that he reveal the source of the literature. Two KGB agents were assigned to the investigation:

They beat me by turns, first one, then the other. They beat me on the head, the face, and the jaws; they beat me on the neck, being careful to raise the collar of my shirt each time so that there would be no marks. . . . They beat me under the ribs and near my kidneys, each time cursing and repeating, "Tell us where you got it and who gave it to you, or else we'll show you what Soviet power is!" They suspended me by the neck with a scarf and beat me under the ribs. They stood on either side of me; one of them beat me from one side and the other from the opposite side, so that I bounced like a ball between them. They stood me against the wall and beat my face so hard my head was smashed against the wall. . . . Several times they beat me unconscious and then revived me with cold water. They made me squat down as many as 500 times. They used a kind of chemical preparation, which they made me smell and then sprinkled on my left arm. It turned red immediately and began to swell.

After three-day "investigations" like these, Yakov said, they threw him into a cold room full of bedbugs, and the next morning they took him to a psychiatric hospital where the doctor repeated the same questions: Where did he get the brochures? Who gave them to him? Later the investigators frightened him by saying that the doctor had declared him insane and that now they would send him to a psychiatric hospital. They threatened him with the arrest of his father, with the electric chair, with castration, and with a long sentence for "distributing anti-Soviet literature." Having learned nothing from the youth after a month, they released him. On March 20, 1978 he reported to foreign correspondents in Moscow what had happened, after which he was re-arrested.[20] Along with Rikhard Spalin and Anatoly Ryskal, he was convicted of organizing an underground press. Ryskal and Dolgoter received a four-year term in camp and Spalin, a seven-year term.[21]

In March 1978 Vladimir Shelkov and his closest aids Ilya Lepshin, Arnold Spalin, Sofya Furlet, and Sergey Maslov were arrested. During the search conducted at the time of the arrest, the walls of their home were destroyed and the floors taken up in a vain effort to find the printing press.[22]

At one of his press conferences in Moscow during May 1978, Galetsky announced the formation of a human rights group of seven Seventh-Day Adventists who had worked for two years under his direction. Galetsky gave the journalists the names of the members, as well as copies of five documents, issued by the group, that were concerned with various incidents of illegal persecution of Seventh-Day Adventists and with the status of the investigations of their leaders.[23] This group, with the Moscow Helsinki Group and academician Sakharov, came to the defense of Shelkov.[24]

The trial of the Seventh-Day Adventist leaders took place in Tashkent in March 1979. As is almost always the case, the trial was for all practical purposes a closed one. Only the immediate families of the accused were admitted to the courtroom. The defendants were accused of writing works printed by True Witness. Shelkov and Lepshin received five years each in a strict-regimen labor camp and their houses were confiscated; Spalin and Furlet received five and three years respectively in a standard-regimen camp; Maslov received two years probation and his home was confiscated also.[25]

In spite of many protests against the cruel sentence given to eighty-four-year-old Shelkov, he was sent to a camp in Yakutia, which has one of the harshest climates in the USSR. After a few months, he died. His children tried for several days to get permission to receive his body so that they could bury him according to his last wish, but permission was refused on the grounds that his sentence would not be completed for three more years, and even though he was dead, his body had to remain in the camp. After his term was up, his children could again request permission to take his ashes home. From all over the country supporters of Shelkov's church came to the funeral in the Yakut village of Tabaga. Evidently, this unorganized demonstration of support had an effect, since the authorities took the unusual step of giving permission for a religious burial and for a cross bearing the name of the deceased to be placed on the grave. Other graves in the camp were simply marked by boards with the number by which the prisoner was known in camp.[26]

After Shelkov's death, Leonid Murkin, his deputy, became head of the True and Free Seventh-Day Adventists. Immediately after Murkin's election to this post, he went underground, and a country-wide search warrant was put out for his arrest.

The death of the leader of the True and Free Seventh-Day Adventists and the incarceration of its leading advocates did not interrupt the work of the True Witness. After Shelkov's arrest, the press began to publish open letters from the Council of Churches of True and Free Seventh-Day Adventists, in addition to the usual religious literature. Each letter described some concrete example of persecution with explanations of unlawfulness of these occurrences. Each letter ended with the same demands. The demand "to free the unlawfully sentenced religious leader and champion of legal equality between believers and atheists, Vladimir Shelkov, President of the All-Union Church of True and Free Seventh-Day Adventists" was later changed to a demand to "posthumously rehabilitate" him. Further demands were:

1. To free all arrested and convicted ministers and members of the True and Free Seventh-Day Adventist church, with compensation for any moral, physical, or material damage they may have suffered.

2. To return all materials confiscated during searches or at the time of arrest.

3. To restore the reputation of the church president Vladimir Shelkov and of other church members slandered and defamed in the eyes of the world by government atheists because of the members' purely religious way of life and their lawful struggle for freedom of conscience and equal rights.

4. To condemn the repression and violations of the rights of believers by government atheists as an illegal consequence of the state-sanctioned religion of atheism-materialism-evolutionism; and also to condemn all those who violate the rights of others.

5. To put an end to all forms of religious oppression in the USSR: surveillance, eavesdropping, intercepting the mail, and discrimination in the workplace and in educational institutions.

6 To revoke the antireligious legislation on cults, enacted from 1929 to 1975, because it is a contradiction of: Lenin's teachings and his directive of January 23, 1918, "On the Separation of Church and State and Church and School," article 13 of the constitution enacted under Lenin in 1918, articles 34, 39, 50 and 52 of the present constitution of the USSR, the Universal Declaration of Human Rights, the Declaration of the Rights of Children, the Convention Against Discrimination in Education, the International Covenants on Human Rights, and the Final Act of the Helsinki Accords.

7. To separate atheism, as a private world view, from the state and from schools; to make the Society of Atheists a private organization supported not at government expense, but at the expense of individual atheists, just like any other religious society in the USSR.

8. To declare and enforce a fundamental law of complete equality among believers and atheists.

9. To enforce complete freedom of the religious press, religious meetings, and other religious rights and freedoms on an equal basis with the rights and freedoms of atheists.

10. To guarantee and enforce complete freedom in educating children in a manner compatible with their parents' views, conscience, and convictions.[27]

Since 1978 the KGB has not stopped trying to locate the printing press and the publishers of True Witness. Over a three-year period, they conducted more than 350 searches, during which they confiscated literature printed by the True Witness and arrested more than seventy people.[28] Most of those arrested had publicly spoken out in support of Shelkov and his helpers; all were charged with "slandering the Soviet system" on the basis of article 190-1 of the RSFSR criminal code. They were specifically charged with disseminating letters of the Council of Churches of the True and Free Seventh-Day Adventists, as well as other Adventist literature on human rights. The standard sentence was three years in a general-regimen labor camp. Rostislav Galetsky was among those arrested. He was arrested on July 1, 1980, during one of his usual visits to Moscow and sentenced to five years in camp on the basis of articles on religious activities and of article 190-1.[29]

In spite of the searches and arrests, both True Witness and the human rights struggle of the True Adventists continued. The Council of Churches of the True and Free Seventh-Day Adventists published the voluminous report of the conference between the countries that had signed the Helsinki accords in Madrid in 1980. The report described in detail the situation of the church since the 1977 conference in Belgrade and the Madrid conferences.[30] In addition, True Witness published at least fifteen open letters from the Council of Churches up to 1982. All this material was typographically reproduced.

In March 1981, three Adventists accused of outfitting an underground press were put on trial in Kalinin. On April 19, the *Kalinin Pravda* published a long article on the trial entitled "The Secrets Revealed," stating that in June 1979 Vera Kaduk purchased a house in Kalinin for 18,000 rubles (with money from "the sect"). It said that with the help of Vladimir Fokanov, a twenty-five-year-old Muscovite, and Vasily Kovalchuk, a twenty-three-year-old resident of Dnepropetrovsk, she began to build in the basement of the house a printing shop. Although it never went into operation, it was modelled after functioning publishing operations:

A camouflaged hatchway led from the veranda of the house to a tunnel one-and-a-half by two meters and considerably higher than the average person's height. A trapdoor connected the tunnel to an entryway made of concrete, from which one entered the room. The room was equipped with a water heating system run by two batteries and a boiler that heated the water by an electric heater. The "bunker" received current by circumventing the meter. The cabin contained four typewriters, a hectograph, a rotary press, a large supply of rotary ink, stationery, and printing paper, thirty-five rolls of rotary film, and other printing equipment. In addition, 16,433 rubles was found in a total of three hiding places. A large quantity of illegal literature of the Reformist-Adventist Sect—more than twenty different titles—was stored there.

The article claimed that Fokanov was responsible for obtaining the necessary building materials, copy equipment, paper, and such for the press, while Kovalchuk collected the necessary funds from believers. This fund allegedly came from tithes levied on church members. Shelkov was supposed to have raised the tithe to one-fifth of the members' earnings.

Vera Kaduk received a two-year prison term; Fokanov and Kovalchuk each received three-year prison-camp terms.[31]

The legal educational activities of the True Adventist Church yielded unquestionable results. Church members accepted the civil rights position of Shelkov and Galetsky and courageously upheld them. On October 15, 1979, a twenty-five-year-old Adventist, Nina Ovcharenko, a floor polisher from Pyatigorsk, defended herself during her trial for disseminating open letters of the Council of Churches. Her defense speech would have done honor to any lawyer: her arguments were persuasive; her ability to deal with complex legal issues was impressive; and her political courage went beyond what is permissible for a Soviet lawyer:

Throughout the centuries, people with different views on life and different religious beliefs have lived on the earth. Everyone has the right, as a complete individual endowed with all rights and liberties from birth, to his own convictions. This right is enforced by Article 19 of the Declaration of Human Rights and international pacts on human rights ratified by our government in 1957 and 1973. . . .

All laws, both international and state, guarantee freedom of conscience for all. This is the most fundamental and most important right of all; it makes every citizen a free and complete human being. The lack of freedom of conscience deprives man of dignity and reduces him to the status of an animal, having only the right to work and to rest. . . . Even if atheists were in the majority and believers in the minority in our state the government is nonetheless obligated to consider the interests of believers. Truth and justice are not always on the side of the majority, especially in the sensitive area of freedom of conscience. . . . I consider myself a happy person because I am a part of the struggle for truth. . . . Truth requires sacrifices; for the sake of truth, one must stand firm or even hang from the cross. A just cause is worth the devotion of one's entire life.[32]

Nina Ovcharenko's defense speech was distributed in one of the regular letters of the Council of Churches.

The ability to hide leaders wanted by the authorities for many years, to keep the whereabouts of a printing press secret, and to keep the press in operation while under constant surveillance testify to a flexible and functional organizational structure within the True Adventist church. This is confirmed in a report on religious life in the USSR (published in the *Chronicle of the Catholic Church in Lithuania*). Catholic priests have recognized the success of Jehovah's Witnesses, Pentecostalists, and Seventh-Day Adventists in the dissemination of religious teachings. This they attribute not only to missionary zeal, but also to "the creation of a strong organization, with leadership at every level: community, club, village, city, province (*oblast*), republic, etc."[33]

For obvious reasons, the church does not report on the number of its membership, although it sometimes refers to itself as "many thousands of God's people." Estimates of church membership may be made by comparing data of recent arrests of members of the Evangelical Baptist church and Seventh-Day Adventists. From 1978 to 1981, 152 members of the Council of Churches of Evangelical Christian Baptists were arrested, and 87 members of the True and Free Adventist Church. Total membership in the independent Baptist Church is 100,000, according to G. Vins, their representative abroad, but if the level of repression is similar for both churches, the membership of the True Adventist church would be approximately 50,000.[34]

CHAPTER 14

The Russian Orthodox Church

According to official sources, approximately 25 percent of the adult population of the USSR are religious believers;[1] applied to the total number of Russians, that would mean roughly 30 million. According to the Russian Orthodox writer Anatoly Levitin-Krasnov, the Russian Orthodox church has now approximately 40 million members, the largest of all Christian churches in the USSR. At the same time, it is the most submissive to the dictates of the government.

The Catholic church of Lithuania displays considerable opposition to government interference in the internal affairs of the church; priests are the leading force in its opposition. The Protestant churches of the USSR have been split by schisms over the permissible degree of church subservience to government dictates. The number of Seventh-Day Adventists and Pentecostalists resisting government control is about equal to the number of those who accept such control. A significant proportion of Baptists does not agree to government control. The authorities are forced to take into consideration the fact that increased pressures on the official Protestant churches can have the effect of driving religious believers into unofficial churches. As a result, while the government constantly persecutes those who resist control, at the same time, it makes advances to members of the official church. Thus the Protestant churches have much more independence than the Orthodox church, where opposition to government pressures is barely noticeable. The reasons for the weak resistance of the Russian Orthodox church and its present humiliating position are above all historical.

The Orthodox church, created in Byzantium sixteen centuries ago, was from the beginning under the protection of government authorities and submissive to it. Orthodoxy was introduced in Russia at the will of the ruling Russian princes and was accepted as the government religion, and remained such until 1917. Since the rule of Peter the Great, the church was officially subordinate to the Holy Synod, which was headed by a tsarist official, the chief procurator.

At the beginning of this century, Orthodox believers, as all of Russian society, experienced a period of intense quest. The educated clergy and secular social groups worked to revive the church by freeing it from the compromising and corrupting influence of the government. In 1905, during the period of the first Russian revolution, the majority of the Orthodox hierarchy spoke out in favor of abolishing the synod and restoring the patriarchate. The head of the church was to be elected by the All-Russian *Sobor*—an idea that was appealing as a gesture of unity (*sobornost*) both to the mass of believers and to the clergy. The restoration of the patriarchy and regularly convened councils operating as the highest church authority was a logical path toward the spiritual rebirth of the church and the renewal of its authority among disillusioned segments of Russian society. It is a tragedy of the Russian Orthodox Church that the council that reinstated the patriarchy (lost for more than two centuries), proclaimed the long-awaited *sobornost*, and determined that church rule would be based on independence, took place in 1917, coinciding with the coming to power of the Bolsheviks—irreconcilable atheists. Thus, the first independent steps in the long history of the church took place under extremely unfavorable conditions. Neither the church hierarchy nor the lower clergy had the opportunity to experience independence from the government or to form the habit of independent thinking. The old tradition of dependence on government and the complete lack of any experience of resistance had rendered the Orthodox church defenseless against the new authorities, which hardly offered the church its accustomed protection. The new government had set itself the task of destroying the church and exterminating religion.

Government Pressure against the Church

Government pressure on the Orthodox church began earlier than pressures on sect members, who did not experience persecution until 1929. Arrests of Orthodox priests took place from the very first days of Bolshevik rule. Neither the new authorities nor the Orthodox clergy could always separate a purely church position from political support for the deposed system. Many priests actually spoke out as political enemies of the Bolsheviks, who dealt with them more cruelly than warranted by their opposition, which was usually only verbal. It was not rare for mere membership in the clergy to be punished by imprisonment or even death. In the eyes of apologists for the new system, every Orthodox church priest personified the "cursed past," and was "for the Tsar."

In the atmosphere of the early revolutionary years, masses of believers left the Orthodox church. Those who were Orthodox by tradition or only for the sake of conforming to the official government religion not only lost all ties with the church, but reacted to the Bolsheviks' destruction of the church with indifference. Arrests of priests, closures of churches, and even the destruction of churches took place throughout the country. Only in a few instances did such actions meet with opposition. Of the 8,000 people listed as martyrs of the Orthodox church during the beginning of the Soviet period, only an insignificant portion actively opposed the destruction or the desecration of the church. The majority of the martyrs meekly accepted their martyrdom.

Against the general background of government attacks on the Orthodox church during the twenties, the beginnings of a movement to renew the church became evident. The idea of modernizing the decrepit traditions of the church, which had resulted from its submission to governments and the theological backwardness of the Russian clergy, was at the heart of this movement. To this movement's misfortune, the new authorities exploited it to tame and destroy the Orthodox church. The leaders of the movement were either terrorized or corrupted by government support. Those who did not compromise were arrested and thus isolated. But the government went too far: these "Red priests" were compromised by participating in reprisals against the clergy of the traditional church, and the churches of the movement for renewal stood empty. The traditional church strengthened its authority through the firmness and even the martyrdom of its adherents. Those who remained followers of the church were true to it.

When the authorities saw that the renewal movement had failed, they ceased supporting it and began to subdue the traditional church, which by that time had been weakened by the persecutions. The results of several years of seeking out clergy ready to compromise, as well as the physical elimination of those unwilling to compromise, produced results by 1927. In that year Metropolitan Sergy announced a program of conciliation with the new government, hoping to save the church from further persecutions. He issued a statement on the church's complete loyalty to the atheist government and its ideology: "We wish to be Orthodox and at the same time to recognize the Soviet Union as our native country, whose joys and successes are our joys and successes and whose failures are our failures." In the name of the Church, Sergy agreed to the government's major demand, which the church had until then opposed: government registration of all church officials. A significant portion of the clergy followed Metropolitan

Sergy, although not immediately and not without strong pressure from the government, which herded unsubmissive church officials and priests mercilessly into the camps, where many of them died.

Only a minuscule number of clergy publicly refused to participate in the policy of "accommodation," as Sergy's policy was called at the time. The schismatics formed several groups, which were not united. The name of one such group, the True Orthodox church, became the general term for all of them; sometimes they were referred to as the "Tikhonovites," after Patriarch Tikhon, who died in 1925; or as "those who do not commemorate," since all of these groups were related by their refusal to mention the government during their prayers or to enter into any kind of relationship with the government, including official registration. The extreme right wing of the Orthodox clergy was predominant among the schismatics. There were also those without any political position, but who were firm on questions of faith and prepared to be martyred for them. It is difficult to say how many people belonged to these groups in 1928, or how many belong to such groups now. After the Second World War, the majority of "those who refuse to commemorate" returned to the church of Sergy. The True Orthodox church, which has been banned from the moment of its inception until the present time, is now a sect without any official hierarchy, whose influence is practically unnoticed. Frequently the ideology of present-day members of the underground church is of an apocalyptic nature.

The policy of adaptation did not save the Orthodox church from oppression and mass arrests of priests during the thirties. By 1938, three of the eight members of the patriarchal synod had been shot; only four bishops were free. No more than a hundred parishes were under the patriarchy in the entire country.[2]

During the war, government policy on religion was reversed; for the Orthodox church that reversal dates from September 4, 1944, when Stalin received three of the conciliatory Metropolitans: Sergy, Aleksy, and Nikolay. On September 8, eighteen bishops quickly rounded up from the camps chose Metropolitan Sergy as the patriarch. Since then, election to this, as well as to all higher church positions, depends completely on the government.

"Concordat"

After the death of Sergy, the *Sobor* (council) convened in 1945 chose Aleksy as patriarch; he headed the Russian Orthodox church until 1971. The restoration of the patriarchy in 1944 meant that a kind of "concordat" had been reached between the atheist government and the Orthodox church. This unwritten concordat was observed until Stalin's death. The Moscow patriarchy fulfilled its part of the agreement by remaining silent about the humiliations and the submission of the church, and by direct collaboration in international policies of the USSR to the point of publicly lying about government oppression of the church and claiming that there were no Christian prisoners in the USSR; in exchange the government opened 22,000 Orthodox churches it had earlier closed, two theological academies, eight seminaries, and a certain number of monasteries. Nevertheless, many Orthodox priests remained in prison camps until the general amnesty following Stalin's death Khrushchev violated this concordat, and from 1960 until 1964, more than half of the recently reopened churches were again closed, as were the majority of seminaries and monasteries. Of the 30,000 Orthodox priests who had their own parishes in 1959, only 14,500 had parishes by 1962.[3] By 1975 only 7,500 Orthodox churches remained open.[4]

By far the most destructive effects were not the result of direct government intervention, but of the actions of high church authorities carrying out government orders. In July 1961 the Council of Bishops adopted changes in the parish regulations,[5] subordinating the priests to the parish councils of twenty lay persons, selected chiefly by local authorities and the Council on the Affairs of Religious Cults. As a result, Orthodox priests were no longer able to control their parishes, and they found themselves in the position of mere employees. Since that time, without the permission of the local authorities or government agents, a priest is not permitted to visit his parishioners, even if they are dying, whether at home or in a hospital, and he may not perform last rites at home. He cannot allow children into the church, give them the Eucharist, or hear their confessions. He is required to demand identification from parents who bring their children to be christened and from young couples who want to be married. Upon request, he is required to provide appropriate officials with a list of those who have been christened, married, or for whom last rites have been performed. He is forced to inform on his parishioners, since this information is often used to persecute such persons on their jobs and in the institutions where they study.

The registration certificates of priests who in any way violate these harsh measures are immediately cancelled, leading to the loss of their parishes. The patriarchate is not inclined to defend the rights of such priests, nor to assign them to new parishes. Instructions concerning registration certificates, in fact, give the authorities the opportunity to censor sermons. Once again, the patriarchy does not insist on the right of the priest to speak freely to his flock, even within the church. As a result, sermons in the Orthodox church have become rare occurrences, and as a rule, those that are delivered are devoted to themes unrelated to the social interests of believers. Nor does the low level of instruction in religious educational institutions facilitate the preparation of competent preachers or develop a taste for preaching, so most priests limit their activities to rituals.

In 1961, the Council of Bishops accepted the new regulations on a temporary basis—until the following council meeting. This gave the Council on the Affairs of Religious Cults, which had imposed this document on the bishops, and the bishops themselves who accepted it, the option of easily rejecting the regulations, if they were met with strong opposition. Once the council had been convened, it would have been easy either to weaken or even to repeal the regulations, as had been done in 1963 at the congress of the All-Union Council of Evangelical Christian Baptists, which revoked the new regulations of the All-Union Council of Evangelical Baptists introduced in 1960.

Changes in the parish regulations caused general discontent in the Orthodox church, both on the part of the clergy, against whom the regulations were directed, and on the part of the parishioners, who were totally isolated from parish life under the new regulations. Even more to the point, the parish as such simply ceased to exist, leaving only the twenty-member parish council. Nonetheless, this dissatisfaction was given only very weak expression, especially in comparison to the reactions of Baptist communities and of the Catholic church in Lithuania to analogous regulations. In Lithuania the majority of priests and believers simply refused to fulfill the regulations imposed on them as incompatible with the canons of the church.

Four years after the introduction of the parish regulations, eight hierarchs, headed by Archbishop Germogen, the bishop of Kaluga, sent a letter to the patriarchate. Although not an open letter, it became well known in church circles. The bishops asked the patriarchate to reconsider the regulations of 1961, inasmuch as the regulations had had a destructive effect on church life. The patriarchy did not respond—that is, if one does not consider Germogen's dismissal from his diocese and transfer to a monastery a response to the letter. After this occurred, most of the other bishops who had signed the letter renounced their signatures.[6]

In December 1965 two young priests, Nikolay Eshliman and Gleb Yakunin, also issued statements on this topic. They sent open letters to the patriarchate, all bishops, and the President of the Presidium of the Supreme Council of the USSR Nikolay Podgorny.[7] In their letter to Podgorny, they demanded that the Council on the Affairs of Religious Cults and their agents cease interfering in internal church affairs, citing the law on separation of church and state and constitutional guarantees of religious freedom. In their letters to the patriarchy and the bishops, they asked for repeal of the regulations of 1961, since they violated canonical law and were threatening to destroy the church. They tried to convince the hierarchy to convene a general council to repeal the regulations and resolve the question of membership in the ruling body of the church. In this way, Nikolay Eshliman and Gleb Yakunin fulfilled the same function as did the initiative group of the Evangelical Baptist Church in 1961, but none of the parish priests supported them. Eshliman and Yakunin were dismissed from the priesthood,[8] and with this, efforts to repeal the 1961 parish regulations from within ended.

Eshliman and Yakunin were supported by a few letters from outside the church. The best known was the letter of twelve believers from the Kirov region, composed by one of the signatories, Boris Talantov.[9] A sixty-five-year-old mathematics teacher at the time, he was the son of a priest who had died in forced-labor camp under Stalin. Talantov had written several articles on illegal actions taken toward the Orthodox church and on its disastrous situation, as well as articles on general political themes.[10] The letter of the twelve believers was sent abroad and transmitted back to the Soviet Union over the BBC. The journal L'Humanité asked Metropolitan Nikodim, in charge of the patriarchy external affairs, several questions about this letter. Nikodim said that the letter was anonymous and that information on government pressures contained in the letter did not correspond to reality. Local KGB organs sought to obtain confirmations of Metropolitan Nikodim's statements from signatories of the letter. The pressure was so intense that three of the elderly authors of the letter died during the period of interrogation. These were elderly people; the stress and worry was too much for them. The seminary student Nikodim Kamenskikh was dismissed from the seminary, but not a single signatory renounced his signature. Moreover, in a public statement Talantov confirmed the facts contained in the letter.[11] He was arrested in 1969, sentenced to three years of imprisonment for "slander," and died in a prison hospital.[12]

Neither the dismissal of Archbishop Germogen, nor the deprivation of Yakunin and Eshliman from their parishes, nor the tragic fate of the authors of the letter from Perm (that had made the direct cooperation of the higher Church hierarchy with the government quite clear) evoked from the clergy or church members even the slightest attempt to oppose the authorities or the submissive patriarchate. Reaction was limited to a few letters in *samizdat*, for the most part anonymous, and to gossip in circles close to the church.

The next council met in 1971, after Patriarch Aleksy died, to choose his successor. Only Eshliman and Yakunin, deprived of their positions, resolved to appeal to the council to repeal the parish regulations.[13] Also Priest Nikolay Gaynov and three laymen requested the dismissal of Metropolitan Nikodim, who had compromised himself on many occasions by lying to fellow believers abroad on the actual position of the church.[14] Gaynov, like both of his unsubmissive colleagues, was deprived of his parish. The council confirmed the detested regulations and thus set the course of the Orthodox church until the present time. The only public protest against all of this was a letter by Aleksandr Solzhenitsyn to the new patriarch: "We are losing the last semblance of a Christian people. Is it really possible that this is not the major concern of the Russian patriarchy? What kinds of rationalization must one resort to in order to convince oneself that the calculated destruction of the body and soul of the Church under a government of atheists is the best way to preserve the Church."[15]

There was some response to this letter in *samizdat*. Some people supported Solzhenitsyn; others reproached him for calling on the patriarch to sacrifice himself because of a religious prohibition, or injunction, against calling on others to sacrifice themselves.[16] Soon discussion of the letter ceased, and once again everything was quiet.

A seemingly intolerable situation was being tolerated. Priests who tried to fulfill their duties to their flock under these conditions risked losing their parishes by violations of the regulations. On the whole, however, the church submitted. In an article called "The Split Between the Church and the Outside World," Orthodox believer Yevgeny Barabanov explains the amazing "submissiveness" of thousands of priests and millions of Orthodox church members by "an unhappy paradox": "External limitations on church life answer a secret wish on the part of many priests. This wish results from the premise that worship in church constitutes Christianity, and that nothing else is necessary for a Christian. Everything else is only a distraction. Many new converts try to adopt this ideology as the fundamental Church position. Once they have adopted it, they make it into a fetish and an essential church canon."[17]

A Lone Example of Dissidence

The only attempt to violate openly this unwritten but nonetheless harsh ban were the teachings of Father Dmitry Dudko from 1973 until

1979. He began this work in the St. Nicholas Church in Moscow, where he had served for many years, enjoying the love and respect of a large parish for his sermons and penchant for moral instruction.

On December 8, 1973, during his usual worship service, Father Dudko asked his congregation to jot down questions they would like him to address the following Saturday, without signing their names, of course. Dudko was able to conduct eleven such discussions, and transcriptions were published in the collection *Of Our Hope.*[18] For the most part, the subjects were moral and religious. Dudko called on his flock to give up drinking and swearing and to shun luxuries; he insisted that the family be preserved. Dudko's discussions were full of transgressions of church canons, his language was poor and spiced with vulgarisms, yet the success of his discussions was astounding. During the second discussion, which had been announced the week before, the church was filled to overflowing. With each successive discussion, his audience grew larger. Those who wanted to attend had to arrive early, stand in the stuffy church, and wait. But that did not stop those hungry for spiritual nourishment.

After his tenth discussion, Father Dudko was dismissed from the St. Nicholas Church, and he conducted his next discussion in a private home. A petition from hundreds of his parishioners begging the patriarchy to allow their favorite priest to remain had no effect. He was transferred to a parish outside of Moscow—a great improvement over the way in which Eshliman and Yakunin were dealt with. Perhaps the patriarchy's "lenient" treatment of Dudko can be explained by his extreme popularity with members of the Orthodox church abroad; the emigré Russian press gave Dudko high praise and transcripts of his discussions ran into several printings.

The long trip from Moscow to his new parish did not stop Dudko's numerous followers, and his new church was also full. In 1978 Father Dudko began publishing a weekly church newspaper in *samizdat*—*In the Light of the Transfiguration.* He publicly expressed his opinions on not only religious questions—including censuring the murder of the tsar's family by the Bolsheviks. On several occasions he openly expressed solidarity with civil rights activists on questions that went beyond the bounds of purely religious matters.

On December 10, 1975—Human Rights Day—Father Dudko signed a collective statement by human rights advocates on the situation of human rights in the USSR.[19] In January 1976, he signed a letter in defense of Sergey Kovalyov, convicted of participating in the publication of the *Chronicle of Current Events* and the *Chronicle of the Catholic Church in Lithuania.*[20] For a period of six years, Father Dudko's teaching and civic activities continued almost without interference. He was once more transferred to another church outside of Moscow.[21] He was the only priest to undertake such activities on his own initiative. No one followed his lead—a circumstance that possibly determined and doubtless facilitated his arrest on January 15, 1980.[22]

Father Dudko's experiment in religious teaching demonstrated that there indeed was a rebirth of interest in religion within Soviet society. Dudko himself, as well as many Orthodox believers, tended to attribute the appearance of this interest in religion to a rebirth of the Orthodox church. However, I think it is more accurate to call this phenomenon a possibility for such a rebirth, rather than a genuine rebirth.

This hunger for religion was not a result of the efforts of the church, but rather of the decay and corruption of official ideology. It spread over the entire country and affected all social groups. Enormous numbers of people tried to fill the resulting spiritual and intellectual vacuum with alcohol; others tried to fill it with the most diverse kinds of activities, from gardening to philosophy. The overwhelming tendency, naturally, was toward the displacement of official ideology with traditional forms of consciousness, both nationalist and religious. However, renewed interest in religion did not lead to a rebirth of the Orthodox church itself. The appearance of new members (most noticeable in Moscow and Leningrad, less so in the provinces) did not change the dead atmosphere of church life, which was limited to rituals. A large number of new church members accepted the Orthodox religion in the conservative form then predominant in the church (in Barabanov's words, "the old women's church").[23]

Orthodox believers are obliged to conduct their spiritual and philosophic quests outside since the church hierarchy in no way supports such a search. (Even Father Dudko advised his flock not to look elsewhere for spiritual truth.)

Orthodox *Samizdat*

Several *samizdat* authors exemplify the general outlines of this common quest. The most active and popular response is not a purely religious one, but a national-religious one. The most common motif of this tendency is the Russianness of its participants, a necessary and important element of which is orthodoxy. Some representatives include A. Solzhenitsyn, I. Shafarevich, V. Borisov, as well as participants of the underground organization, the All-Russian Social Christian Union for the People's Liberation, and the publishers of the uncensored journal *Veche* (Public assembly).

Those few writers whose Christian consciousness expressed itself in "a pure form" performed an essential service, without which the understanding of the church and its present problems would not be possible. (This chapter is based on materials written by them.)

The most prolific of these religious publicists was Anatoly Levitin-Krasnov, who emigrated in 1974 and now lives in Switzerland. In several books and many articles, he wrote a detailed history of the Orthodox church after the Revolution, its rout before World War II, and its strangulation in the postwar period.[24] Lev Regelson published *The Tragedy of the Russian Church*, a collection of documents and review of church arguments during the twenties and thirties.[25]

In their well-known letters of 1965, N. Eshliman and G. Yakunin provided an analysis of Soviet legislation on religion and a comprehensive description of the present sad state of the Orthodox church. In 1979 Yakunin issued a report, "On the Present Position of the Russian Orthodox Church and Prospects for the Religious Revival of Russia."[26] This report is, in effect, a continuation of his analysis of the situation of the church, and corresponds with the views of I. Shafarevich, who wrote a report on Soviet legislation on religious matters for the Committee for Human Rights in 1972.[27]

Father Aleksandr Men published an entire series of books, first under the pseudonyms Svetlov and Bogolyubov, and then, under his own name. Together, these works make up a broad introduction to the history of religion and the fundamentals of the Russian Orthodox service, written in a popular form. The books of Aleksandr Men serve an educational function and are aimed at believers as well as non-believers.[28]

The defense of the rights of the Orthodox church and of its believers occurred outside of the church. Neither the patriarchate nor the bishops became involved, either openly or by the use of "secret diplomacy." After the appearance of Archbishop Germogen's letter (referred to above), there is only one known public statement in defense of the Orthodox church by the higher Orthodox hierarchy—a letter to Brezhnev from Feodosy, the bishop of Poltava and Kremenchug, written in 1977. This letter describes the oppression Feodosy and his flock suffered at the hands of officials in charge of religious affairs.[29] Not a single bishop or priest signed any of the letters written by Orthodox believers to local authorities complaining of church closures, or requesting that a closed church be opened, or complaining of oppression by local authorities. The existence of Orthodox prisoners of conscience, tried for their defense of the church, is not revealed through public statements from church officials, as is the case among Catholics and Protestants, but through the *Chronicle of Current Events* or independent human rights associations. At the beginning of the seventies, the

Committee for Human Rights in the USSR made such announcements, and in the midseventies the Moscow Helsinki Group did so.

The Christian Committee for the Defense
of the Rights of Religious Believers

On December 30, 1976 the Christian Committee for the Defense of the Rights of Religious Believers in the USSR was formed.[30] Its founder was Father Gleb Yakunin. In addition, Hierodeacon Varsonofy Khaybullin, who had no parish, and an Orthodox layman Viktor Kapitanchuk were on the committee. In their declaration of the creation of the committee, its founders announced that the realization of freedom of conscience enunciated in the Soviet Constitution met with a significant hindrance in the government's relationship toward religion—a government intent on creating a nonreligious society. This was evident not only in legislation, but also in government violations of even those few rights granted to religious believers by law. In view of the fact that believers constituted a significant portion of the population, the normalization of their position was necessary for the entire society. Since the bishopric of the Russian Orthodox church and leaders of other religious organizations did not defend the rights of believers for a number of reasons, it was felt that the believers' legal defense ought to become the concern of Christian society. It was for this purpose that the Christian Committee for the Defense of the Rights of Religious Believers in the USSR was organized.

The committee set itself the task of collecting, studying, and disseminating information on the situation of believers in the USSR; to render counselling to believers when their civil rights were violated; to apply to governmental departments concerning questions of believers' rights; and to assist in the improvement of Soviet laws on religion. Committee members declared that although they themselves were Orthodox, they intended to take the initiative in defending religious freedoms of all believers in the Soviet Union, regardless of faith. The creation of such a committee was a practical step toward unifying the efforts of all Christian churches in the Soviet Union in order to jointly insist on religious freedom and protest discrimination against believers. This trend first found expression in the June 1975 collective appeal to the Soviet government by members of Christian churches on the situation of religion in the USSR, signed by Evangelical Christian Pentecostalists, the president of the All-Union Church of True and Free Seventh-Day Adventists, members of the Church of Christ, the Catholic church of Lithuania, and the Russian Orthodox church.[31]

Religious believers turned to the committee with the most diverse complaints: for more than ten years the militia had closed access to the New Athos on the name day of Apostle Simon Kanonit, one of the most deeply revered of the Orthodox saints, whose remains were located there; the monks in the Pochayevo-Uspensky Monastery were placed in difficult straits by the local authorities when their garden, which provided them with food, and their hotel, where visiting worshippers stayed, were taken away from them, and the building that formerly housed the monastery was used for a club and a psychiatric hospital; in Georgia a firing range was built next to the ancient monastery complex David-Garezhd, and artillery fire was destroying this Christian shrine; in the city of Gorky, with a population of one-and-a-half million, Orthodox believers had for ten years been unable to effect the opening of at least one church, in addition to three small open churches, even though the request to open the church was signed by more than two thousand people (by law a request by twenty believers was sufficient); in the Ternopol region, the authorities closed a church in 1961 built with donations from believers, and a fifteen-year-old struggle to repeal this illegal closure had yielded no results; in the Chkalov district of the Gorky region, since 1952, more than three thousand believers had been petitioning to open a church, but had not received a positive answer.[32]

Some documents of the Christian Committee devoted to problems of the Pentecostalists included: searches made of the Moscow Pentecostal community; the arrest of Mikhail Yurkiv, a Pentecostal believer from the Trans-Carpathian area; and difficulties placed in the way of emigration. The committee responded to the trial of the Evangelical Christian Baptists who had been deprived of their children for raising them in a religious spirit, as well as to the destruction of Baptist prayer houses and to the detainment of Baptists for participating in communal prayer. The committee appealed to the Pope about the situation of 15,000 Moldavian Catholics deprived of the opportunity of hearing mass or going to confession because the authorities constantly hindered the only Roman Catholic priest in Moldavia from visiting believers.[33]

In May 1977, members of the Christian Committee for the Defense of the Rights of Religious Believers appealed to the World Conference of Religious Movements for a Durable Peace, Disarmament, and Just Relations Among People, which took place in Moscow. After describing the persecutions to which all religions in the Soviet Union had been subjected for sixty years, as well as legal discrimination against religious believers, members of the committee called on the conference participants to speak out in defense of religion in the USSR and in particular in defense of prisoners of conscience languishing in camps.

They called for support of the Baptist minister Georgy Vins, Orthodox priest Vasyl Romanyuk, and the Jewish believer Iosef Begun whose trial coincided with the conference.[34]

More than once, members of the Christian Committee protested the arrest of human rights advocates. On the anniversary of the arrest of the head of the Moscow Helsinki Group, Yury Orlov, committee members wrote:

The appearance of an international movement for the defense of human rights is one of the outstanding events of the twentieth century and an indication of a deep understanding by society of the value of every individual, created in the likeness of God. It is becoming more apparent with time how important and valuable is the creation of public groups assisting in the observance of the Helsinki Accords. Everyone to whom the freedom and worth of every individual is important cannot but feel thankful toward the initiator of these groups, Yury Fedorovich Orlov. . . . We, the members of the Christian Committee for the Defense of the Rights of Religious Believers in the USSR, express our profound gratitude to Yury Fedorovich Orlov for his self-sacrifice and his efforts to defend the rights of the individual. We ask all religious believers to pray for him and to take part in the movement for his release.[35]

In November 1977, an appeal was made to the Belgrade Conference by the committee, together with the Moscow Helsinki Group, the Working Commission to Investigate the Use of Psychiatry for Political Purposes, and representatives of the True and Free Seventh-Day Adventists. They asked the conference participants to evaluate the human rights situation in the Soviet Union, to make use of the massive information on violations of human rights in the USSR, and to speak out in defense of prisoners of conscience languishing in Soviet prisons and camps, those who were seriously ill, and the members of the Helsinki Group arrested for collecting information on human rights violations.[36]

Committee members took an active part in discussions of the proposal for the new Soviet Constitution. They were particularly disturbed by the proposal which, for the first time in Soviet history, proclaimed the goal of the Communist Party to be identical with that of the government: the goal of Marxism-Lenism was translated as the creation of Communism and the education of man in a communist, that is, an atheist society. Thus, every believer in the Soviet Union, by virtue of being a citizen, was by law obliged to perform what had formerly only been the obligation of Party members. This responsibility contradicted religious conscience. Members of the committee objected to such a statement in the constitution of a country with a large number of religious believers.[37]

On November 1, 1979 Father Gelb Yakunin was arrested;[38] then followed the arrests of Father Dmitry Dudko, V. Kapitanchuk, and L. Regelson, who had, with Yakunin, on several occasions protested violations of the rights of the Orthodox church.[39] Dmitry Dudko gave in before his trial: he appeared on Moscow television and condemned his former activities as harmful and "anti-Soviet." He was forgiven, released from prison, and assigned to one of the best parishes in Moscow.[40] Similar confessions led to freedom for Kapitanchuk and Regelson; they received probationary sentences.[41] Father Gleb Yakunin, who firmly defended the legality of his activities during his investigation and trial, was sentenced under article 70 for "anti-Soviet propaganda" to five years in a strict-regimen camp and five years of internal exile.[42]

Founded by Yakunin, the Christian Committee for the Defense of the Rights of Religious Believers in the USSR was filled with new members shortly after his arrest. Two priests joined: Nikolay Gaynov, who was not attached to a parish, and Vasily Fonchenkov, who taught at a theological academy. Gaynov stated that the committee had received ten new members, but considered it impossible under existing conditions to announce their names.[43] Since then, the committee has issued only one statement—an appeal to the VI Assembly of the World Council of Churches in Vancouver, dated July 1983, with a protest about persecution of believers of various faiths in the USSR.[44] Since that time, documents signed by the Christian Committee have no longer appeared; however, the custom the Committee had introduced of informing the public about the violation of the rights of churches and believers had taken root. This information continued to come out regularly, although anonymously, from Russian Orthodox sources. And the selflessness of Fathers Yakunin and Dudko did not remain unnoticed; they found followers and successors among Russian Orthodox priests. Preaching began to be renewed, albeit slowly, in Russian Orthodox cathedrals, particularly in remote areas. The situation of the Russian Orthodox Church is such that priests do this almost in secret; at any rate they try not to call attention to their initiatives. Sometimes these sermons even take on the ring of civic statements. Such was the sermon by Deacon Vladimir Rusak of Minsk on the situation of the Russian Orthodox Church, in the spirit of Fr. Yakunin. Deacon Rusak was immediately relieved of his church duties.[45]

The courageous action by Fr. Kirill Chernetsky has also become known. During the trial of Fr. Yakunin, Fr. Chernetsky led a prayer service for his well-being. For this, Fr. Chernetsky was transferred from the Cathedral of the Kazan Mother of God in Moscow to a remote parish in the Moscow Region.[46] But apparently, Fr. Chernetsky is not alone in his position regarding Fr. Yakunin and the hierarchy of the Russian Orthodox Church had to reckon with this. On the eve of the VI Assembly of the World Council of Churches in Vancouver, Archmandrite Grigory, a representative of the Moscow Patriarchy, went to visit Fr. Yakunin in his labor camp. He heard his confession and gave him communion and a copy of the Bible—Fr. Yakunin had staged several hunger strikes to obtain one.[47] Of course this visit could be seen primarily as a gesture toward the Christian community in the West before the important meeting in Vancouver.

On January 30, 1984, Fr. Sergy Zheludkov passed away. He had been an active member of the human rights movement and had consequently fallen into disfavor with the Church hierarchy and had been forced into retirement. Nevertheless, a funeral service was held for him in the Patriarchy Cathedral. This was undoubtedly out of deference to the civically active Russian Orthodox inside the USSR. Such signs—rare for the time being—indicate the existence of latent forces within the Russian Orthodox Church working for the hastening of its spiritual renewal. One educated lay person makes a case for such a renewal in the near future in an anonymous *samizdat* work "Seven Questions and Answers About the Russian Orthodox Church."[48]

Seminars and Study Groups

The necessity of providing one's own religious education coupled with an interest in religion gave rise to unofficial seminar and study circles. The Christian Seminar, founded in 1976, is widely known because of frequent appeals to the West by one of its founders, Aleksandr Ogorodnikov. Born in 1950, he had studied at the Institute of Filmmaking in Moscow and was subsequently employed as a watchman. The other founder was an assistant at the library of the Academy of Sciences in Leningrad, Vladimir Poresh.

The seminar consisted of about thirty participants, most of them young people from various cities: Moscow, Leningrad, Ufa, Smolensk, Minsk, Grodno, and Lvov. Seminars members emphasized their continuity with the religious societies of Moscow and Leningrad that had been forcibly disbanded in the twenties. The seminar was limited to discussions of religious and philosophical problems and avoided political discussions. Nonetheless, its participants were subjected to constant harassment. KGB agents rounded them up every time they tried to meet. Two issues of the journal *The Community*, begun by a few seminar members, were confiscated before their appearance in *samizdat*.[49]

In 1978 A. Ogorodnikov was arrested and sentenced to a year in camp for "parasitism." While still in camp, new charges were pressed against him. Then followed the arrests of Poresh, Tatyana Shchipkova, and several other seminar participants. The founders, Ogorodnikov and Poresh, were sentenced under article 70 to close to the maximum allowable terms: six years of strict-regimen camp with five years internal exile and five years of strict-regimen labor camp with three years of internal exile, respectively. The others were sentenced to shorter terms under fabricated criminal articles.[50]

Religious self-education and the study of religion and Christian philosophy are fairly widespread in Moscow and Leningrad. (Similar circles no doubt exist in other cities, but they can hardly be as widespread: the necessary literature is lacking and it is difficult to find members.) Usually such groups are small, made up of people who have known each other for a long time. In Leningrad a special social group has arisen, consisting of humanists unemployed in their areas of specialization and working as unskilled laborers. The majority of them prefer low-paying jobs that give them leisure time: lift operators, watchmen, and stokers. Many compensate for a low professional status by engaging in "forbidden" studies. Sometimes several such groups hold joint sessions during which they give papers;[51] these materials are published in the numerous Leningrad *samizdat* journals.

In Moscow there also exists a group of unemployed people educated in the humanities, and many of them are also attracted by the study groups, but Moscow lacks the corresponding *samizdat* publications. With "amateur" groups in Moscow (and perhaps in Leningrad also), there are study groups of highly qualified professionals and nonprofessionals: philosophers, historians, etc. Their work is published both in *samizdat* and in *tamizdat* (usually in the *Herald of the Russian Christian Movement* and usually under pseudonyms).

Herald of the Russian Christian Movement is fairly widely distributed in the Russian Orthodox circles, particularly within the large cities. In Moscow in the midseventies, *Hope: Christian Reading*, a *samizdat* periodical, also began to appear, edited by Zoya Krakhmalnikova, with the blessing of the Russian Orthodox church hierarchy. Krakhmalnikova, a talented philologist and a professional literary person, published the journal openly; her name appeared on the cover of the magazine, and articles under her name were published there.

Hope continued the tradition of the prerevolutionary church journal *Christian Reading*. *Hope* was essentially the only religious digest for contemporary Russian Orthodox readers, a means of communication for their community, a way of preaching the gospel, and the spiritual experience and traditions of the Russian Orthodox church. The journal, in effect, resurrected the church's memory; it was universal, intended for people of the most diverse levels of education and spiritual life—new converts and those already deeply rooted in orthodoxy. The style of *Hope* is restrained, traditional, and apolitical on principle. Krakhmalnikova collected for *Hope* texts unique in the USSR, those of the Holy Fathers, the pastoral missives, the teachings of Russian Orthodox ascetics, the testimonies of Russian Orthodox martyrs, letters from priests and bishops in exile, and contemporary works on the Russian Orthodox service.

Hope immediately attracted a wide circle of readers and was circulated far beyond Moscow, retyped and recopied by hand. In time, the journal began to come out in *tamizdat* and was returned to Russia in printed form. In August 1983, Zoya Krakhmalnikova was arrested and tried for "anti-Soviet agitation and propaganda." Several open letters in defense of Krakhmalnikova appeared, among the signatories, Vladimir Shibayev, a priest of the Russian Orthodox church. *Hope* did not end with the arrest of Krakhmalnikova; her friends took on the responsibility for its continuation.

Work on religious themes, both published in the Soviet Union and smuggled in from abroad, in Russian and in other European languages, enjoys a wide readership. The demand for religious literature and the impossibility of obtaining it legally has stimulated the reproduction of such materials, not only by those interested in it, but also by people interested in making money. Such materials, therefore, occupy a special section of the black market. In April 1982 there were several arrests in Moscow and environs for the sale and reproduction of religious literature.[52]

Before the arrests, 600 gospels were confiscated from an apartment in Moscow, all of them printed on a duplicating machine. A duplicator was found during searches of Russian Orthodox *samizdat* activists; so were book-binding materials and religious literature. For the most part, the duplicated material consisted of prerevolutionary publications of the lives of the Russian saints. Religious and philosophical *tamizdat* books were also found, apparently used only for personal reading. This group of *samizdat* workers appears to have been aiming to meet a demand for reading materials not only from the Russian Orthodox intelligentsia, but even more from the mass of Russian Orthodox parishioners, a fact confirmed by lists of religious believers from various regions (Vladimir, Gorky, and others) discovered during the searches. Apparently these were individuals who had placed orders for the literature.[53] The Russian Orthodox *samizdat* activists were tried for "engaging in prohibited manufacturing." One of those tried, A. Sidorov-Rozanov, testified that he had duplicated religious literature in order to make a profit, but the others indignantly denied the mercenary motives ascribed to them by the court.[54]

The religious *samizdat* case was closely connected to the case of a

Russian Orthodox archpriest, Aleksandr Pivovarov, who was secretary of the Novosibirsk bishop. Pivovarov was one of the people who received the religious literature duplicated by the Moscow *samizdat* workers. Later, it was learned that he himself had duplicated such literature and supplied it to religious believers. He was arrested in April 1983 and sentenced to three-and-a-half years of strict-regimen labor camp for "prohibited manufacturing" and for "speculation," although the court offered no evidence of any commercial motives for the *samizdat* activity.[55]

In February 1982 in the city of Tomsk, four persons were arrested for distributing *samizdat*, chiefly duplicated by photocopying, including religious and philosophical books. Similar books were confiscated in Kaluga, where a *samizdat* circle was uncovered.[56]

The religious activity of Russian Orthodox believers is demonstrated not only in an intellectual search, but in a striving to live a Christian way of life. Outside Moscow, and a few other places, Russian Orthodox have settled together in small colonies to embody Christian values, in the manner of Protestant communes—to help one another. They refrain from smoking or drinking, observe fast-days and church holidays, raise their children in the religious traditions, and, of course, refrain from "ideological duties." These Russian Orthodox communities, unlike Protestant groups, are secluded and virtually cut off from one another. The Russian Orthodox church does not play the role of a unifying center; its function consists of nourishing each community separately.

Several such communities sprang up outside Moscow through the pastoral activity of Fr. Men. On principle, he avoids all types of secular activity, not merely political but also human rights activity. He is concerned simply that his parishioners, including the newly converted, fulfill the law and also live as Christians.

The burgeoning interest in religion during a period of profound crisis and conformism within the Orthodox church intensified the age-old question of the relationship between the church and the world. No thinking member of the Orthodox church can avoid taking a stand on this issue. Father Sergy Zheludkov, a "retired" Pskov priest, devoted a book to the subject; A. Levitin-Krasnov, M. Meerson-Aksyonov, and Y. Barabanov wrote several articles on it. Barabanov has summed up the common elements of their position: "Christian actions must lead . . . to the transformation of Christian consciousness and life and thus to a transfiguration of the world."[57]

Contemporary Orthodox thinkers who share this position participate to some degree in the human rights movement. A. Levitin-Krasnov was among those who spoke up in defense of Yury Galanskov and

Aleksandr Ginzburg in 1968 and demanded civil liberties in the Soviet Union in an appeal to the Budapest session of the Communist Party in 1968.[58] In 1969 Levitin-Krasnov joined the Initiative Group for the Defense of Human Rights in the USSR—one of the first human rights associations. In 1971 he was sentenced to three years in camp for his polemical writings and human rights activities. In his final words to the court he said: "I am a believing Christian, and the duty of a Christian is not just to attend church. It consists of fulfilling the precepts of Christ in one's life. Christ called on us to defend the oppressed. Therefore, I have defended the rights of people, be they Pochaev monks, Baptists, or Crimean Tartars."[59]

Father Sergy Zheludkov spoke up in defense of the rights of both believers and nonbelievers on many occasions. His first statement was an open letter on the situation of Soviet political prisoners to the president of the Worldwide Christian Conference in 1968. In 1974 he became a member of the Soviet chapter of Amnesty International, and in 1980 signed a letter in defense of Andrey Sakharov.[60]

In 1973 Yevgeny Barabanov lost his job and was threatened with arrest for sending *samizdat* materials abroad on several occasions, including issues of the *Chronicle of Current Events*. Tatayana Goricheva, founder of a religious and philosophic seminar, participated in a demonstration in memory of the Decembrists in Leningrad in 1975.[61] Orthodox believers were among the earliest participants of the human rights movement and have made a significant contribution to the movement until the present time. They include: Yury Galanskov, Aleksandr Ginzburg, Natalya Gorbanevskaya, Tatyana Khodorovich, Andrey Tverdokhlebov, and others. Some came to the movement as believers, and others joined the church afterwards. However, the mass of Orthodox churchgoers and even the Orthodox intelligentsia do not oppose government infringements on their right to freedom of conscience, and even censure such opposition as "un-Christian." The letter of Eshliman and Yakunin was received negatively by many of those close to church circles: the two were reproached for interfering where they did not belong out of a sense of "spiritual pride," instead of placing their faith in prayer.

The majority of the converts take a position of "comfortable Christianity," which is quite compatible with a concern for one's own salvation and separated from a world "mired in evil and sin." This rejection of the Christian concept of responsibility for the world's fate is a popular form of conformism to Soviet life. Being christened, attending church, and participating in religious discussion groups provide the illusion of freedom from government dictates in one's free time. During work hours such people complacently render to Caesar his due, as do their colleagues, even if this means teaching Marxism or writing officious philosophical tracts.

Fr. Sergy Zheludkov was the first of the Russian Orthodox writers to analyze the religous meaning of life and the experience of human rights activists (in his terminology—"people of good will"). Fr. Sergy thought that although most human rights activists were separate from the church, the sources of their moral inspiration were Christian. He called them "anonymous Christians," who had founded a "Church of good will" open to people at all levels of spiritual and intellectual consciousness, from any religion, or even without a religion.[62]

But among the Russian Orthodox intelligentsia, there was a widespread attitude of derision, contempt, and suspicion toward human rights activity, and it grew stronger in the 1980s. It was deemed "secular heroism," a "vanity fair" and even "Satanic good." Thus the present-day Russian Orthodox Church is little concerned with the improvement of civil society.

PART FIVE

THE MOVEMENT FOR HUMAN RIGHTS

CHAPTER 15

Emergence of the
Human Rights Movement

This movement, previously known as the "democratic movement," the "liberal movement," and the "civic protest movement" before it became known as the "movement for human rights," or "the human rights movement," was formed by the midsixties. At that time events were taking place on another continent, in the United States of America, that were similar in conception and spirit: the civil rights movement. It is striking that in societies as different as the Soviet Union and the United States similar social impulses independently arose at the same time. In both countries citizens began to demand that the provisions of their laws be observed. Many sacrificed their personal welfare in protesting civil rights violations that had gone unnoticed by the majority. In both countries a handful of activists acting out of moral, not political considerations, inspired large numbers of people. In the United States, these demands resulted, after suffering and resistance, in the introduction of certain major correctives in government practice and social custom which did not change the basic foundations of these institutions. In the Soviet Union the observance of these demands would have radically changed the entire way of life, since the Soviet system is not based on law, but on Party rule, that is, the ideology of the ruling party prevails over the legal system. In addition, there is no tradition of respect for the law or for the rights of the individual in the Soviet Union.

Human rights activists did not borrow ideas from the international human rights movement because they were poorly informed about it at the time the movement emerged in the USSR. By the same token, they were not a direct continuation of the Russian democratic tradition. Rather, they came out of a tradition of sympathy for "the little man," on which the Russian classics are based. Nevertheless, the "legalistic" context of the human rights movement was original. This was not because it had never appeared in Russian history before; the Constitutional Democrats (the Cadets) were the predecessors of the human rights movement. They did not come out of nowhere, but arose from a certain tradition. But since this tradition was so thoroughly rooted out during the Soviet period, one can safely say that the initiators of the human rights movement knew little about it and were not inspired by it.

The human rights movement was born out of the experience of people who lived their lives under conditions of lawlessness, cruelty, and assault on the personality "in the interests of the collective" or for the sake of "the bright future of all humankind." Refusing to take this "collective" approach meant negating the foundations of official ideology, defended by all the might of the Soviet government. A demand to observe the constitution and human rights under Soviet conditions was revolutionary since it was essentially a demand that the Soviet state stop being totalitarian and start being democratic. The implementation of this demand would mean a change in the nature of power, changes in the entire way of life. Moreover, human rights activists renounce on principle and condemn the use of force no matter what the aim, and will never resort to violence. Then in what way do they act?

In the words of the human rights activist Andrey Amalrik, "the dissidents accomplished something that was simple to the point of genius: in an unfree country they behaved like free men, thereby changing the moral atmosphere and the nation's governing traditions." He added that "inevitably this revolution of minds could not be rapid."[1]

Human rights activists insist on the "definitive significance of civil and political rights for the future of mankind."[2] This point of view substantially differs from the Marxist view, as well as from the technocratic view, both of which are based on the primacy of material interests, economic and social rights. Human rights activists also proceed from the assumption that only in a country where there are political freedoms will citizens be able to effectively defend their material interests. On their own initiative human rights workers exercised the civil rights guaranteed by the Soviet Constitution: freedom of speech and of the press, the right to public demonstration and to free association, and other rights. They gathered and distributed information on the situation of human rights in the Soviet Union and gave moral as well as material support to those who were persecuted for their beliefs. By preparing social consciousness for a democratic transformation of society, they help strengthen an awareness of individual worth and respect for law.

Their persecution at the hands of the authorities complicate an already difficult task. From the outside, the history of the human rights movement presents an unbroken chain of trials, confinements to psychiatric hospitals, forced emigration, dismissal from work, and other sorts of persecution.

The First Steps of the Human Rights Movement

December 5, 1965 may be considered the birthday of the human rights movement. On that day the first demonstration using human rights slogans took place in Moscow's Pushkin Square. This demonstration, of course, had a long incubation period that lasted, under Soviet conditions, for an entire decade.

Absolute terror ceased after the death of Stalin. Masses of prisoners convicted on political charges began to return from the camps. But the country remained in a state of shock while attempts to comprehend what had occurred went on behind the scenes, only rarely making a faint splash in the official literature and the press. *Samizdat* played an immense role in the spiritual emancipation of Soviet society.

It made possible a change in the life-style of Muscovites and others in the late fifties. Under Stalin, when informing had become the norm, unofficial contacts between people had been reduced to a bare minimum. As a rule, two or three families would associate only among themselves, and there were very few homes where many people gathered. After the fear of mass arrests had passed, people threw themselves at each other, deriving satisfaction from merely being together. A normal Moscow circle numbered forty to fifty "close friends." Although divided into smaller subgroups, the entire group regularly gathered for parties that were held on the slightest excuse, and everyone knew everything about everybody else. All these circles were connected with other similar circles and the links led to Leningrad, Novosibirsk and other cities. Everyone gathered around the table and imbibed tea and more than tea. Affairs were begun; families formed and broken up. Together everyone sang, danced, and listened to music. Tape recorders had gone on sale, and they were not prohibitively expensive. They facilitated the distribution of songs by Bulat Okudzhava, Vladimir Vysotsky, and a little later Aleksandr Galich that took the country by storm. Many circles had their own bard who performed these songs, as well as his own and the camp songs that spread over the entire country after the mass return of prisoners from the camps. These songs were a form of contemporary folklore, like the anecdotes, inspired by almost every important event. Exchanging anecdotes is a favorite pastime for Soviets from all walks of life because they allow one to formulate and express political judgments and observations on life.

Here is an example of an anecdote from 1980: "Do you know how Hungarians, Czechs, and Afghans interpret a dream about army tanks? It means, expect friends to visit." But most of all, people in these circles simply "chewed the fat."

Yuly Daniel, who published under the pseudonym of Nikolay Arzhak, accurately described a typical Moscow circle in his stories "This Is Moscow Speaking" and "Atonement."[3] His descriptions of the ideas and judgments typical of Moscow intellectuals during this period were labelled anti-Soviet in order to incriminate him, even though people such as he described were loyal Soviet citizens without any intention of subverting the system. The problem was that the shortcomings of the system were so obvious that people talked on about them, sometimes seriously and sometimes joking about the absurdities of Soviet life and the general submissiveness of the people. These conversations gave people the opportunity to understand their society: how to live within the society; what one could accept and reject; how to withstand official interference in one's personal and professional life. Not only young people, but mature and even old people needed to engage in such discussions, and they all took their first steps along this path.

Large groups that fostered mutual trust created ideal conditions for the spread of *samizdat*. *Samizdat* was probably first circulated within such groups and then spread to various others. Although everyone knew it was necessary to be very careful, few, in fact, were. Most people confined their efforts to awkward attempts at camouflage, which were often the object of humor. At the time an anecdote made the rounds in Moscow about two friends arranging, over a telephone that everyone knew could have been tapped by the KGB, to exchange *samizdat* materials.

"Have you finished the pie my wife gave you yesterday?"

"Yes."

"And has your wife finished it?"

"She has."

"Then pass it on to Misha: he wants to try it, too."

The fifties were marked by the appearance of some people who did not hide themselves or their activities at all.

The official position enunciated at the Twentieth Party Congress was clearly illogical: once having voiced (a) censure of Stalinism, it was possible to (b) ensure that the system would be changed to exclude a return to Stalinism. The official position implied that once the "personality cult" was verbally condemned, the entire problem was solved. The obvious desire of the authorities to confine themselves to the minimum of change at all levels aroused general anxiety. The suppression of the Hungarian Revolution occurred in 1956, soon after the Twentieth Party Congress.

Proof of this resistance to change was encountered everywhere in the internal life of the country. Nonetheless, the majority believed that since the unstable position could not endure for long and since the past was too horrible to contemplate, the government would, even against its own will, follow the path toward liberalization. Mihajlo Mihajlov noted after his 1964 visit to Moscow that "there is general dissatisfaction with the half-hearted liquidation of Stalinism, but all are firmly convinced that the struggle against Stalinism has just begun and that the outcome will be positive."[4] His observations were based primarily on his contacts with students and writers in Moscow, but this mood also prevailed in factories, scientific institutions, and among Party members, including high-ranking managerial workers. Most often, the mood was displayed in critical speeches at party and Komsomol meetings.

In March 1956 at an open meeting in the Academy of Sciences Institute of Physics, the young scientist and future founder of the Moscow Helsinki Watch Group Yury Orlov spoke. He talked about the general decline in honesty and morality and the necessity for a democratic reorganization of the country. He was supported by three members of the Party organization, and his speech was greeted with general applause, but later all those who spoke were expelled from the Party and dismissed from their jobs. Their colleagues could not help them, except by collecting money for their support. Orlov was forced to leave Moscow for a period of fifteen years; he could find work only in Armenia.[5] General Pyotr Grigorenko, a department head in the Academy of the General Staff, is also known to have made a similar speech at a regional Party conference in Moscow in September 1961;[6] the writer Valentin Ovechkin spoke in Kursk at the same time.[7] They were both expelled from the Party, and their careers ruined.

The passion for poetry, which was a distinctive feature of social life at the end of the 1950s and the beginning of the 1960s, gave rise to the first unofficial outdoor gatherings to occur in the capital of the Soviet Union. On July 29, 1958 a monument to Vladimir Mayakovsky was unveiled in the city square named after him. Officially recognized poets read their works at the official ceremony, and when they were finished, volunteers from the crowd read their own poetry. This spontaneous reading pleased a great many people, who agreed to meet there again. There were readings almost every evening, most by students from Moscow universities and institutes. They read from the works of approved poets, from repressed or forgotten poets, as well as from their own work. Occasionally there were literary discussions.

At first the authorities did not interfere. The *Moskovsky Komsomolets* (August 13, 1958) even carried an approving article about the meetings and printed the time and place of the readings. Such a "Hyde Park" could not exist for long in Moscow, and soon the meetings were stopped. Two years later, in September 1960, a group of students that included the Moscow University student Vladimir Bukovsky began holding readings once again. Once word was out, the old participants began gathering at the monument on Saturday and Sunday evenings. Usually a few hundred people gathered. Some were genuinely interested only in art and heatedly insisted on the right of art to remain "free from politics" a position that paradoxically led them into the thick of the current social struggle. But many of the participants were drawn to the readings because of the social implications.

The authorities quickly began to interfere. Volunteer police detained the readers, took down their names, and informed their institutes. The usual punitive measures were expulsion and blacklisting from other institutes. The active participants were periodically subject to searches, during which typed manuscripts and other *samizdat* materials were taken from them. Fights were provoked in Mayakovsky Square, and sometimes the monument was cordoned off during the usual meeting times.

The meetings continued until the fall of 1961, when "order" was restored in Moscow in preparation for the Twenty-second Party Congress. That summer several regular participants were arrested. Vladimir Osipov, Eduard Kuznetsov, and Ilya Bokshteyn were convicted under article 70 ("anti-Soviet agitation and propaganda"), allegedly for attempting to create an underground organization; Osipov and Kuznetsov received seven-year camp terms and Bokshteyn five years.[8]

A few articles appeared in Moscow papers reviling those who attended for "lack of principles" and for being idlers without jobs. The latter accusation had some merit: students who had been expelled for attending the readings were not hired anywhere. In such an environment, drinking, swearing, and moral attitudes unfamiliar to the general population were common. In the midsixties the first unofficial literary society, SMOG, grew out of this youth subculture; SMOG can be decoded as "Bravery, Thought, Image, Profundity," or as was most frequently the case, "The Youngest Society of Geniuses." [In the Russian, the initial letters correspond to the acronym.] Closest to this movement in Russian literature and art were the avant-garde at the turn of the century, whose experiments were curtailed by force at the end of the twenties.

In February 1966 the SMOGists issued a manifesto that read: "We poets and artists, writers and sculptors, are renewing the tradition of our immortal art. . . . At the present we are engaged in a desperate struggle with everyone and everything, from the Komsomolists to Philistines, from the secret police to the bourgeoisie, from the untalented to the ignorant. Everyone is against us."[9]

These young people combined an aversion to the forms of socialist realism with an aversion to the established way of life and Party propaganda. Theirs was not a conscious political protest against the system, but rather an aversion to banality. Although they lacked experience and, for the most part, talent, they burned with a need to say something of their own. Its members were inclined to outrage in order to shock the public. In April 1965 they organized a demonstration in front of the Central Writers' Club, perhaps the first unofficial demonstration to take place in Moscow in the post-Stalin era. The demonstrators carried signs that demanded creative freedom, including one that read, "Deprive Socialist Realism of its virginity."[10]

It is difficult to determine just how large SMOG was because there was no strict membership. Individuals were supposed to decide for themselves if they were members and were not obliged to inform anybody else. About two hundred people took part in the demonstration, but it is hard to say how many considered themselves members and how many just happened to take part.

The SMOGists published a *samizdat* journal, *Sphinxes*, which was primarily distributed among students. They also issued a few collections of short stories and poetry. Their writings were not widely circulated, and in order to invest the necessary time on reproduction and to run the risk of expulsion or dismissal from one's job or even a prison-camp term one had to be very enthusiastic about their literary work.

There were political arrests at this time: in 1956 a group of young Leningraders (Revolt Pimenov and his friends).[11] In 1957 a group of Muscovites (Lev Krasnopevtsev and others) were arrested for participating in underground groups and distributing leaflets critical of the regime; in 1958 the members of Sergey Pirogov's group in Moscow suffered the same fate.[12] In 1960 Aleksandr Ginzburg, who openly compiled the *samizdat* journal *Syntax*, was arrested; in 1961 three activists in the meetings at Mayakovsky Square (V. Osipov, E. Kuznetsov, and I. Bokshteyn)[13] and in 1962 members of Moscow underground groups Yury Mashkov and Viktor Balashov shared the same fate.[14] In 1964 Grigorenko was confined to a psychiatric hospital.[15] Because *samizdat* infor-

national bulletins did not exist at this time, no one knew about these events except the friends of the victims; only vague rumors circulated beyond the confines of their own groups. Most people believed Khrushchev, who had many times publicly stated that there were no political prisoners in the USSR.

The First Human Rights Actions

In the autumn of 1965 the Moscow writers Andrey Sinyavsky and Yuly Daniel were arrested. Like Pasternak, they attempted to publish their writings abroad, because they could be distributed only in *samizdat* under Soviet conditions. They learned from the experience of Pasternak, who was subjected to bitter persecution, and published their works under pseudonyms (Abram Terts and Nikolay Arzhak).[16] Their arrest occurred less than a year after the "palace revolution" that ousted Khrushchev and was interpreted by their friends as a prologue to ominous changes. It was clear that their arrest had been calculated as a declaration of war on *samizdat:* on its contributors, distributors, and readers. Theirs were the first arrests reported by foreign radio stations broadcasting to the Soviet Union. They referred to Daniel as Danielo and from time to time reported on the indignation of the West: Terts and Arzhak had been translated into several European languages and their books were successful.

These foreign radio reports made everyone aware of the arrests and caused consternation among all those connected with *samizdat*. Everyone, not just friends and family of the arrested, argued hotly over how the incident would turn out: would the authorities quietly dispose of the arrested or would they put on a "show trial" in the Stalinist tradition in which, somehow, defendants were induced to slander themselves monstrously and even ask to be tried without leniency. Afterwards, would new arrests begin? What would the sentences be? Speculation included death by firing squad. (Experience during the Stalinist period taught that the word "enemy" in the newspaper meant just that.)

In this uncertain and anxious environment the first demonstration in the history of the Soviet regime that was accompanied by human rights slogans took place in Moscow's Pushkin Square on December 5, 1965. A few days prior to December 5, which was celebrated as Constitution Day, typed leaflets containing a "civic plea" appeared around Moscow University and other liberal-arts institutes:

A few months ago KGB agents arrested two citizens: the writers A. Sinyavsky and Yu. Daniel. Under the circumstances there is reason to fear violations of the law with regard to the public nature of court proceedings.

As is well known, all sorts of illegalities may take place behind closed doors, and a closed trial is itself an illegal act (article 3 of the constitution and article 18 of the RSFSR criminal code). It is unlikely that the works of writers constitute a crime against the state.

In the past illegal acts of the government cost the lives and freedom of millions of Soviet citizens. It is easier to sacrifice one day of peace than to suffer the consequences of unchecked arbitrary authority for years to come.

Citizens have the means to struggle against judicial arbitrariness: public meetings, during which one well-known slogan is chanted—"We demand an open trial for (insert the names of the defendants)," or is displayed on placards. Any shouts or placards going beyond the limits of a strict observance of legality are definitely dangerous and may possibly serve as a provocation. They must be stopped by the participants in the meeting themselves.

It is essential that everything be orderly during the meeting. At the first official request to disperse, it is necessary to disperse after having informed the authorities of the purpose of the meeting.

You are invited to a public meeting on December 5 at six o'clock in the evening at Pushkin Square near the statue of the poet. Invite two more citizens using the text of this plea.[17]

The author of this leaflet and a remarkable man in many respects was Aleksandr Yesenin-Volpin, the son of the popular folk poet Sergey Yesenin, a mathematician and poet, who was twice confined to a psychiatric hospital: in 1949 at the age of twenty-five for "anti-Soviet poems" and in 1959, after the death of Stalin, for sending a collection of his poems and his *Free Philosophical Treatise* abroad.[18] Aleksandr Volpin had been a pioneer in judicial education. He would explain to anyone who cared to listen a simple, but unfamiliar idea to Soviets: all laws ought to be understood in exactly the way they are written and not as they are interpreted by the government, and the government ought to fulfill those laws to the letter. One of Volpin's most cherished ideas was the necessity of publicizing judicial proceedings, and this is reflected in his appeal.

Those who belonged to the same age and social group as Volpin, did not support the idea of a demonstration, and many tried to dissuade him from it. Young outsiders from the SMOGists and their friends helped distribute the leaflets. Three of them were detained: the sixteen-year-old school girl Yuliya Vishnevskaya, twenty-four-year-old Vladimir Bukovsky, and nineteen-year-old Leonid Gubanov. They were all hidden away in a psychiatric ward. Vishnevskaya and Gubanov were released after a month, but Bukovsky was held for about eight months.

Based on reports from his friends, Bukovsky estimates that about two hundred people gathered at the appointed time,[19] but I was there and it seemed to be a much smaller number of demonstrators. However, KGB agents in plainclothes and volunteer militia had been sent, so it was difficult to tell who was who. In addition, the majority, like myself, only watched from the sidelines. Volpin and a few people with him unfurled some small placards, but they were grabbed so quickly by well-trained hands that people standing beside them did not succeed in reading the signs. Later it was learned that the placards read: "We demand an open trial for Sinyavsky and Daniel" and "Respect the Soviet Constitution." Twenty people were pushed into automobiles and detained. They were easy to see because of the flash bulbs from Western correspondents, who also heard of the affair, and who came to see the unusual event in the Soviet capital. Fortunately, the detainees, most of them students, were released after a few hours. Together with others who had been noticed on the square that night, about forty in all, they were expelled from their institutes.

The trial of Sinyavsky and Daniel was declared open, possibly owing to the publicity abroad and to this demonstration. But the trial was "open" in a peculiar fashion. Entry into the courthouse was guarded by militia, who allowed only people given special passes approved by the KGB into the building. (To this very day trials with political implications are called "open," but with few exceptions they are no different.) Of those close to the defendants, only the wives of Sinyavsky and Daniel were allowed into the courtroom. Cold weather lasted all four days of the trial. Friends of the defendants, foreign correspondents, and KGB agents in plainclothes all gathered together in a rather small courtyard, stamping their feet and jumping about so as to warm themselves. None of the three groups mixed. Until this time only three or four Muscovites, not including government officials, maintained even irregular contacts with Western correspondents. Strict silence was maintained by the defendants' friends when any of the reporters came near, partly from fear that the KGB would notice the "association with foreigners," a basic Soviet taboo, but even more the result of an ingrained consciousness that the West was different from us and that only idle curiosity had sent these representatives of a strange world to us. The correspondents also kept their distance, possibly because they had difficulty distinguishing the informers from the friends of the defendants, or possibly because they felt the same cautious estrangement from "those Soviets."

However, when people left the courthouse, either for a lunch break or at the end of a session, everyone rushed up to the wives of the defendants, who told their friends what was going on inside. Both the correspondents and the KGB could hear them. And every evening reports on the trial and commentary were carried by foreign radio broadcasts. Thanks to this procedure, the West learned about the trial and, especially important, so did people all over the Soviet Union. Thus, future human rights activists discovered the only means available to them to spread ideas and information under Soviet conditions.

The trial ended with harsh sentences: Sinyavsky was given seven years in a strict-regimen labor camp and Daniel, five years. Yet the defendants and their supporters considered themselves the victors. The defendants did not repent and renounce their "criminal activities," but instead insisted on their right to act as they did. The defendants questioned the competence of the courts from a position previously unheard of in Soviet society. They demanded that their constitutional rights, creative freedom, and individual integrity be respected. Their public, but loyal criticism of their society was a valuable example for the Soviet people.

The Sinyavsky-Daniel trial helped bring to light another important matter: the authorities refrained from extrajudicial repressions, from torture or beatings during the investigation, from ascribing terrorist intentions to those they accused of "anti-Soviet agitation," and, consequently, from capital punishment for verbal "anti-Sovietism." In comparison with practices under Stalin, this restraint was a considerable improvement. However, the authorities still interpreted the law as meaning "he who is not with us is against us." Still, the actual realization of the freedom of speech guaranteed by the constitution was, as before, treated as "anti-Soviet agitation and propaganda for the purpose of undermining Soviet society and its government," as formulated in statute 70 of the criminal code, under which Sinyavsky and Daniel were tried. This trial appeared to set the current price for dissent. The maximum sentence under statute 70 was set at seven years of strict-regimen labor camp with five years of exile. Subsequent events showed that there were more than a few who were not deterred by this cost from their desire to speak the truth aloud. The sentences given to Sinyavsky and Daniel neither stopped the spread of *samizdat* nor the practice of publishing abroad.

There was yet another important consequence: the appearance of *The White Book* in *samizdat*, which included a transcript of the trial, newspaper coverage, and protest letters written in behalf of the defendants.

The letter-writing campaign was initiated by the wives of the imprisoned. In December 1965 Daniel's wife, Larisa Bogoraz, wrote a letter to the procurator general protesting the arrest of the writers on the basis of their literary works and the illegal methods employed during the investigation:

The senior investigator, Lieutenant Colonel Gregory P. Kantov, asserted in conversation with me that my husband was guilty and would be punished. . . . This prejudicial attitude during the process of investigation forces me to doubt the objectivity of the means used to conduct the trial. . . . The investigator made indirect threats: If I did not behave myself ("You understand what I mean," he said, although I had no idea what he was talking about), there would be unpleasant consequences for me at my job "after everybody finds out." Finds out what? That my husband is under investigation? But he has not admitted his guilt. And if he had, what kind of consequences would I suffer and why? Is it possible that we are returning to the repressions applied against the families of people accused, convicted, or merely suspected of wrongdoing? The very fact that such threats are still possible is an outrage. I demand that standards of legality and humanity be observed.[20]

Although countless letters like this have been written since, at that time both the tone and the arguments used were innovative.

Larisa Bogoraz had a great influence on the course of events during this early period. The defendants' supporters gathered around her; her natural sense of justice and her calm fearlessness created a fine example for others. Of the twenty-two letters written in their defense, twenty were from Muscovites.[21] There was a total of eighty signatures to these letters, sixty of which were members of the Writers' Union.

The concern of writers was naturally founded to a great extent on the fact that the question of creative freedom was at stake and that their colleagues were on trial. In Russian literature there has always been a traditional antagonism between writers and the government: Russian writers have always supported respect for the individual. People who signed the letter in defense of Sinyavsky and Daniel were all about the same age as the defendants or a little older; all held higher degrees, including some doctoral degrees; all held positions commensurate with their educational background. They represented the Soviet "middle class" and were very different from the initiators of the Mayakovsky Square meetings and the SMOGists, who began their confrontations with the government while still very young and never entered into official society.

To voice their complaints, the new public group chose the epistolary form rather than demonstrations. This choice gave them greater opportunity for individual expression. With the exception of Yesenin-Volpin, none had participated in the December 5 demonstration, although a few witnessed the event. Letters in defense of persons unjustly repressed had been written earlier, even during the Stalinist terror. To write such a letter then was either the result of colossal naïveté or great courage, since it could have resulted in the arrest of the author. These earlier letters were, however, not human rights documents but protestations that the accused was loyal to the Soviet government and had been arrested "by mistake." While Boris Pasternak was being persecuted in 1958 for having *Dr. Zhivago* published in Italy, a stenographic record of the Writers' Union meeting at which Pasternak's colleagues "condemned" him was circulated in *samizdat*.[22] It is quite possible that some expressed their outrage at the persecution of Pasternak, but such letters were only read by the officials to whom they were addressed. Thus, any efforts made to defend Pasternak went unreported. This is also true of letters protesting Brodsky's 1964 trial in Leningrad, after which he was sentenced to five years of internal exile for alleged parasitism. None of these letters circulated in *samizdat*.

Those who wrote in defense of Sinyavsky and Daniel did not expect the government to consider their arguments seriously or to change their plans to prosecute. The aim of these letters was to express their objections to the official view of the trial and the general issue of relations between the individual and the government. Letters were directed not only to officials to whom they were addressed, but also to *samizdat* readers. Like *The White Book*, these letters played an enormous role in the formation of an emerging and independent public opinion, as well as a growing awareness of human rights.

The trial was not the only event that signaled the re-Stalinization of the new regime. Some works were published that sought to justify or glorify Stalin; anti-Stalin opinions were censored; and censorship, noticeably more permissive after the Twentieth Party Congress, was intensified. These alarming symptoms gave rise to many individual and collective protests. Ordinary citizens, well-known writers, scientists, and many others took part in them. Each individual protest became an event in itself: the letters of Lidiya Chukovskaya (April 1966 and February 1968); Solzhenitsyn's appeal to the Fourth Congress of Writers (May 1967), to which more than eighty writers responded, including Pavel Antokolsky, Georgy Vladimov; Lev Kopelev (letter of December 1967), and Grigory Svirsky (letter of January 1968); the letter to the Central Committee from forty-three children of Communists who were repressed by Stalin without any basis in fact (September 1967); the letter of Roy Medvedev and Pyotr Yakir to the journal *Kommunist* with a list of the crimes of Stalin; and the letter of Roy Medvedev, Andrey Sakharov, and Valentin Turchin to Brezhnev on the necessity of democratizing the Soviet system.[23]

The most representative letters were an appeal to the deputies of the Supreme Council on the decree which extended the punishment under statute 190 to three years for "slander of the Soviet system and society" and "organizing group actions that interfere with public transportation," and a letter to Brezhnev on the new tendency toward the rehabilitation of Stalin.[24] Among the signatories were thirteen academicians, the composer Dmitry Shostakovich, the ballerina Maya Pliset-skaya, well-known directors, actors, artists, writers (including Valentin Katayev, known for his extreme caution and cynicism), and old Bolsheviks (who joined the Party before the Revolution). The reasons given for their objections to re-Stalinization were carefully chosen with a view toward influencing the Soviet leaders: re-Stalinization would cause disorder in the Soviet consciousness and society, and it would worsen relations with the Communist parties of Western Europe, but the protest itself was energetically expressed.

Early in 1968 letters protesting re-Stalinization were added to the protests of the judicial repression of young *sami*-*dat* participants Yury Galanskov, Aleksandr Ginzburg, Aleksey Dobrovolsky, and Vera Lashkova. All four were part-time students who supported themselves by working in unskilled positions; except for Lashkova, all had been expelled from their institutes; Ginzburg and Dobrovolsky had even spent time in prison camp as political prisoners. These were the defendants in "the trial of the four," which was intimately connected with the Sinyavsky-Daniel trial. Ginzburg and Galanskov were accused of compiling and sending *The White Book* to the West. Galanskov was accused also of compiling the literary-publicist journal *Phoenix-66;* Lashkova and Dobrovolsky were accused of assisting Galanskov and Ginzburg.[25]

The protests of 1968 formally repeated the protests of two years earlier, but on a larger scale. A demonstration of the "half-educated" was held in which about thirty people participated and for which Vladimir Bukovsky and his friend Viktor Khaustov were sentenced to three years under the new statute 190.[26] During the trial the crowd gathered around the court. But this time it was not a small group of friends of the defendants (as had been the case earlier), but people of various ages and social position. When sentence was passed about two hundred people crowded around the building.[27] The letter-writing campaign was also conducted on a larger scale. The "signers," as those who took part in such campaigns came to be called, numbered more than seven hundred.[28] In his study "Will the Soviet Union Survive until 1984?" Andrey Amalrik analyzed the range of participants. The majority were intellectuals: scholars and scientists, 45 percent; creative artists, 25 percent; publishing-house employees, teachers, doctors, and lawyers, 9 percent. A significant number belonged to the "technical intelligentsia," 13 percent; workers outnumbered students—6 percent and 5 percent, respectively.[29] Admittedly, these workers were atypical—for the most part, young people who had been expelled from universities.

Thus, the most prevalent form of protest in 1968 were letters to Soviet officials. Andrey Amalrik observed that appeal by means of petition is characteristic of authoritarian societies; the French Revolution began with a petition to the king in 1830, as did the movement that toppled the Ethiopian monarchy in 1975.[30] Petitions were also circulated during the last few decades of the tsarist regime in Russia. The appearance of petition-writing campaigns seems to confirm that after Stalin's death, the Soviet government began to change from a totalitarian form to an authoritarian one. It seems that these petitions and appeals slowed down the appearance of re-Stalinization. Without them this process would have been more rapid and extreme. However, the petition campaign of 1968 was not immediately successful: Ginzburg was sentenced to five years in camp and Galanskov to seven years, where he died after an unsuccessful operation for a stomach ulcer in 1972. "Signers" were subjected to mass retaliations. With rare exceptions, those who had been Party members were expelled from the Party, and this automatically led to dismissal from their jobs. Many non-Party "signers" were also dismissed or transferred to less important positions; students were expelled from their institutes; artists and writers were expelled from their unions, and their works were no longer exhibited or published; scientists ready to defend their dissertations were not allowed to do so. Previously prospering, all these people were banished from official Soviet society.[31]

Directing protests to the authorities was an exceedingly important factor during the petition campaigns. This was a revolutionary step in comparison with the last several decades, when the people who criticized the government in private duly repeated the standard formulas of submission and praise of the regime in public. The simultaneous release in *samizdat* of critical letters addressed to official bodies served as an example, and this created independent public opinion. This practice constituted an appeal to the newly created independent public opinion. Of all the letters written in connection with the "trial of the four," the appeal of Larisa Bogoraz and Pavel Litvinov to world opinion stands out. It departed from the accepted tradition of addressing appeals to Soviet officials, which was often only a subterfuge for giving such appeals to *samizdat*. In case of an inquiry, the author could shrug his shoulders and say he did not know how his letters ended up in *samizdat* or in the West—he had addressed them to the proper officials. But direct appeals to the authorities carried implications of servility to the government. The appeal of Bogoraz and Litvinov was even more unusual in that it was addressed to not only Soviet citizens, but the West as well. In the letter they compared the "trial of the four" to medieval witch trials and listed the more important violations of legal procedure; they asked the public to demand that the prisoners be released from custody and that the trial be repeated in the presence of international observers.[32] Their letter evoked a response in the West, where it was carried by many newspapers, including an editorial in the London *Times*.[33] Radio stations broadcasting to the Soviet Union repeatedly transmitted the entire text of the letter. As a result the authors were flooded with letters from Soviet citizens, both sympathetic and abusive.[34]

The circle of human rights activists was formed as a result of the events of 1966–68. The "selection process" was not primarily based on sympathy toward liberal ideals (such sympathies were, at least in Moscow, too widespread), but on one's readiness to openly stand up for such ideals in the face of attempts from above to restore Stalinism. The first round of the selection process consisted of participation in the letter-writing campaigns. Under Soviet conditions such participation was a serious test of one's civic-mindedness. In 1968 a significant number of signers acted in hopes that the government would take public opinion into account. The government responded by repression. To the credit of the signers, only a very few agreed to "admit their errors" and publicly "censure such actions," even though they were threatened with the loss of their livelihoods and professional standing. The repression that began in the spring of 1968 and the invasion of Czechoslovakia a few months later made clear both the dangers and the futility of public appeals demanding that civic rights be observed. It became quite obvious that the Soviet system was not becoming an authoritarian one, but would remain essentially totalitarian, and that opposition would not bring quick results. Having realized this, most signers did not openly defend their views, but returned to passive criticism. Almost all the prominent participants whose names lent a special significance to the 1968 campaign ceased trying to influence the authorities.

Only a few were reluctant to give up the inner freedom they found in their civic activities and return to the double-think that is such an essential part of official Soviet life. These few maintained open opposition to current policies. The price they paid was isolation and very often labor-camp sentences. But the events of 1966–68 helped those prepared for such risks to find each other. Their civic feelings, sense of morality, and their banishment from official society united them. This comradeship initially constituted the human rights movement; as the movement grew it served as its core.

CHAPTER 16

The Communication Network
of Dissent and the Pattern
# of Suppression

There is no formal structure in the human rights movement in the USSR. There are neither leaders, nor subordinates; no one assigns tasks to others; instead each is prepared to do what is necessary if other volunteers cannot be found. No one has obligations other than those of conscience. But because of the voluntary and fraternal nature of this association, people work with a selflessness not encountered under orders or compulsion.

At least in the early stages of the movement, this informal structure demonstrated its effectiveness. Someone was found for every job, or rather, everyone found jobs that needed to be done that were in accord with their own inclinations. Tasks were coordinated between friends, and this ensured mutual trust without which organized activities would be impossible under conditions of constant surveillance. This system made it possible to fill vacancies frequently created by arrests: someone close to the arrested would take over his responsibilities. Ties of friendship also made penetration by provocateurs difficult. Over the past twenty years a few activists have been pressured into giving evidence against their friends while under arrest, but there is not one known instance of a KGB agent successfully infiltrating human rights groups.

Samizdat: The Core of the Movement

The backbone of the Soviet human rights movement is *samizdat,* which facilitates the dissemination of human rights ideas. The channels of communication used by *samizdat* provide the connecting links essential for organizational work. These channels spread out silently and invisibly; like mushroom spores, they emerge here and there in the form of public statements.

Most of the activists' energies are spent on the entire process of *samizdat.* Because of the lack of sophisticated technology and the necessity of working in secret, the reproduction of *samizdat* materials requires an enormous amount of labor. Human rights activists have dramatically increased the scope of *samizdat* distribution by making major changes in this process. They have transformed isolated instances of transmitting manuscripts to the West into an entire system of *samizdat-tamizdat-samizdat.*

The first regular contacts with the West were established by Andrey Amalrik. Until 1969 he was practically the only "specialist" in this area. Through him passed most of the human rights documents—transcripts of trials, as well as political and artistic literature.[1] Amalrik considered his outstanding success as "contact officer" to be the transfer of Sakharov's *Thoughts on Progress, Peaceful Coexistence, and Intellectual Freedom* (1968) to the West.[2] Amalrik himself enriched the body of *samizdat* with his "Will the Soviet Union Survive until 1984?" and other essays. In addition to works already mentioned by Sakharov and Amalrik, before 1972 the following works went through the *samizdat-tamizdat* process: Vasily Grossman's *Forever Flowing,* Lidiya Chukovskaya's novellas, Venedikt Yerofeyev's *Moscow to the End of the Line,* Aleksandr Solzhenitsyn's *Cancer Ward* and *The First Circle,* Vladimir Maksimov's *Seven Days of Creation,* poems by Joseph Brodsky, Natalya Gorbanevskaya, and Naum Korzhavin. These works as a whole represent the best of Russian literature at the time.[3]

The limited quantities of these books returned home from the West by complicated routes could not possibly satisfy the colossal demand. So *tamizdat* books were not only read, but used to make copies, usually photographically—a less time-consuming process, but one that requires access to a print shop. Because of the poor quality of Soviet paper, typing ribbons, and carbon paper, the use of typed originals for this process is impossible. The use of copy machines began in the midseventies when people capable of designing and building them could be found. Technical know-how is not enough; the ability and determination to organize the theft of parts not available to the public is also essential. Changes in the method of retyping *samizdat* manuscripts were also made. Side by side with the familiar "cottage industry," typists could be hired because the sale of *samizdat* works in demand had become common. People who devoted all their time and effort to reproducing and distributing *samizdat* made their appearance—for example, Yulius Telesin (now in Israel), who earned the nickname "Prince of Samizdat," and Ernst Rudenko (now dead). As a rule, price was determined by the cost of typing and materials. Neither the time nor risk involved in distribution were calculated into the price; these were considered a contribution to society. Usually the paid typists were friends of the activists; certain efforts to enlarge the pool of typists met with disaster. Some new typists, once they realized the nature of what they were typing, turned the manuscripts over to the KGB.[4] After years of painstaking and dangerous work, *samizdat* channels, and thus links between human rights activists, were consolidated and greatly enlarged.

The *Chronicle of Current Events*, which ten years later Sakharov called the greatest achievement of the movement,[5] was born in 1968, a fruitful and important year for the human rights movement. The first issue appeared on April 30, amid the heat of repression against the signers. Its prototype was the informational bulletin of the Crimean Tartars about which the Moscow activists learned. By the summer of 1983 sixty-four issues of the *Chronicle* had reached the West.[6] A reliable source of information on the situation of human rights in the USSR, the *Chronicle of Current Events* is, as its name implies, intended to report violations of human rights in the USSR, human rights statements, and facts relating to the implementation of human rights "without prior official permission." The factual nature of the *Chronicle* determines its approach to material: in principle it refrains from giving commentary. However, the *Chronicle* is not only a register for human rights violations in the USSR or a chronicle of the human rights movement, but also, since it provided the first link between geographically isolated segments of that emerging movement, as well as between human rights activists and members of other dissident movements, it aided in the dissemination of the ideas and influence.

The editors of the *Chronicle* are anonymous, and no postal address is printed in any issue. As the *Chronicle* itself has explained, this policy is the result of "the peculiar notions about law and freedom of information which, in the course of long years, have become established in certain Soviet organizations."[7] The first editor was Natalya Gorbanevskaya;[8] after her arrest in December 1969 Anatoly Yakobson filled the job until 1972;[9] since then editors have replaced each other every two to three years, usually due to arrests. Changes in editorship are not noticeable to the reader since the personal views of the editor are not reflected in the journal; during the almost 15 years of the *Chronicle's* existence neither the format, the style, nor the approach toward selection and presentation of material have changed.

The mechanism whereby information reaches the editors and is disseminated is explained in issue no. 5: "Anybody who is interested in seeing that the Soviet public is informed about what goes on in the country, may easily pass on information to the editors of the *Chronicle.* Simply tell it to the person from whom you received the *Chronicle,* and he will tell the person from whom *he* received the *Chronicle,* and so on. But do not try to trace back the whole chain of communication yourself, or else you will be taken for a police informer."[10]

In the very first issue there is an indication of what facets of Soviet life would be illuminated by the *Chronicle.* Like almost all subsequent issues, the first begins with a report on a political trial. Considerable space has been devoted to events that occurred in Moscow, not only because the *Chronicle* is published by Muscovites, but because Moscow is the center of the human rights movement. The movement was born in Moscow, and it was here that the circle of activists and sympathizers of the movement was the widest. It is primarily through Moscow that contact with the West is made; to this day this is the most effective means of distributing information outside of government control—via Western radio stations that broadcast to the USSR, and through *tamizdat.*

Five of the seven sections in the first issue were devoted to events occurring in Moscow and two to events in Leningrad. With each succeeding issue the geographical parameters of information reported were widened. The specific conditions under which the editors work explain the occasional drying up of a network of information, yet the geographical areas included increased during the first year: issue no. 7 (April 1969) reports on events in 34 different places; no. 11 (December 1969), on events in 32 places; no. 12 (February 1970), in 18 (no doubt some correspondents were lost in connection with the arrest of Gorbanevskaya); and no. 27 (October 1972), in 35 places.

There was practically no information on the national republics in the first issues. Reports on the Ukraine have been in every issue, and information on the Crimean Tartar movement has been available from the very beginning. Information on the Meskhi movement, which began in the midfifties (like the Crimean Tartar movement), first appeared in 1969.[11] Reports on events in Lithuania began to appear periodically from August 1970, and from September 1971 (issue no. 21) they have appeared regularly.[12] Reports on religious movements during the early years of the *Chronicle* appeared only occasionally; they concerned the Russian Orthodox and, less frequently, the Baptist movement.[13] Contacts with other dissident movements began with a mutual desire to include complete and reliable information in the *Chronicle*: activists from these various movements learned of the publication from foreign radio broadcasts and sought it out. Personal contacts with human rights activists ensured mutual understanding, knowledge, and help.

Each issue has included information originating in the places of confinement of political prisoners. Data on changes in prisoners' places of confinement and on new arrivals and releases are regularly published. A section called "Previous Trials" was initiated with issue no. 16. The *Chronicle* reported on more than five hundred individuals sentenced on political grounds and approximately fifty confinements to psychiatric hospitals up to 1968. Data is published on illnesses of political prisoners, their punishments, curtailments of correspondence and visiting rights, food rations, living and work conditions, as well as prisoners' protests against oppression by the camp administration and open letters written by prisoners. In spite of all attempts to stop the flow of information from the camps and in spite of punishments for transmitting information to the outside, *samizdat* sources continue to operate from the camps. Soviet political prisoners have for the first time the opportunity to appeal to world opinion.

Help for Political Prisoners

Material help for political prisoners was organized by human rights workers on the same principles used in the distribution of *samizdat*, except that in this case the mechanism worked in reverse—from the donors to the collectors. The first parcels and letters arrived in the camps in the spring of 1966, immediately after the existence of political prisoners in the USSR became known. The first information was from Sinyavsky and Daniel, who had discovered thousands of political prisoners in the Mordovian camps, where they were confined. This information was very scant because of the censorship of correspondence. Anatoly Marchenko made the picture of political prisoners' background and conditions more complete. A worker from Siberia, he ended up in a camp for politicals after an unsuccessful attempt to cross the border. He was released from Mordovia in November 1966, and in 1967 his book, *My Testimony*, a comprehensive description of his six years in camp, appeared in *samizdat*.[14]

The inhabitants of political camps were divided into the following groups: participants of nationalist movements (primarily from the Ukraine and the Baltic republics), those convicted on the basis of their faith (primarily Protestants), those who attempted to flee across the border, members of underground groups, and those sentenced for criticizing the Soviet system in leaflets and anonymous letters to newspapers and various Soviet institutions. Those who wanted to help political prisoners at first contributed money to the wives of Sinyavsky and Daniel, either for them or for their fellow prisoners. No distinctions were made on the basis of the prisoners' convictions, a factor that distinguished this aid from previous forms of aid (members of the Ukrainian movement helped their fellow members, Baptists helped their fellow believers, etc.).

By 1968 help for political prisoners had been systematized and expanded. The fund was made up of small individual monthly dues (from one to five rubles) collected among groups of friends and coworkers and supplemented with large irregular contributions from writers, scholars, actors, and others. These monies were either directly or through a chain passed on to a few people who gradually became collectors in writers' circles, research institutes, universities, etc. There were even instances of people making bequests to the fund, although not officially, but through a third party to whom they had entrusted the matter.

These monthly collections were used to send food, warm clothing, writing materials, books, and even money (by secret route), by means of which the prisoners could improve the quality of their food by paying civilian workers three times the normal price to buy and bring it into the camps. The simplest and least dangerous aspects of demonstrating sympathy for dissenters was, of course, buying the food and other items to be sent and obtaining the needed books. Large numbers of people helped the prisoners in this way, especially on an irregular basis. Those more involved took on the task of sending off the parcels—a time-consuming job under the conditions of Soviet postal service. Each person usually had one (or more) pen pal; this correspondence sometimes resulted in marriage after the prisoner was released. Money from the fund was also used for subscriptions to newspapers and journals for each camp, to pay legal fees, and to cover travel expenses for the relatives of prisoners.

In 1970 regulations on sending parcels to the camps became much more restrictive, and political prisoners were almost totally deprived of foodstuffs from the outside. (Up to the present time they are only allowed one five-kilogram parcel per year after half of their sentence has been served, and each time permission must be given by the camp head, who often refuses.) The only remaining possibility was to send money to buy food, but controls had been made so strict that this practice has also ceased. In 1970 books from friends and relatives were forbidden. Since then prisoners have been allowed to order books from shops, where there are almost no books available. Human rights activists became unable to improve the living conditions of political prisoners. The camp regimen became stricter in an attempt to stop aid to political prisoners from concerned people on the outside. But the prisoners no longer felt forgotten.

Beginning in 1968 some homes were purchased for those sentenced to internal exile. Later, in 1969, a separate fund was created by contributions collected at concerts held in private homes for helping the children of political prisoners. Both the fund for the prisoners and for their children continued up to 1976. At that time the Russian Fund to Aid Political Prisoners founded by Aleksandr Solzhenitsyn to aid political prisoners began, and funds started to come primarily from abroad.

Open Protests

The Soviet invasion of Czechoslovakia prompted a large number of protests, most commonly a refusal to support this action by vote at meetings and special gatherings. As a rule, dismissal from one's job was the result of this modest form of protest. The most famous appeal in defense of Czechoslovakia was the demonstration in Red Square on August 25, 1968. Seven Soviet citizens—Larisa Bogoraz, Pavel Litvinov, Konstantin Babitsky, Natalya Gorbanevskaya, Viktor Faynberg, Vadim Delone, and Vladimir Dremlyuga—sat on the parapet of the old place of execution in Red Square and unfurled placards. Written in Czech was "Long live a Free and Independent Czechoslovakia," and in Russian, "Shame on the Invaders," "Keep Your Hands off Czechoslovakia," "For Our Freedom and Your Freedom." KGB agents in plainclothes, who were waiting for a Czech delegation to emerge from the Kremlin, surrounded the demonstrators and tore up their placards. The demonstrators were beaten and dragged into nearby cars.[15] They were tried in October: two received camp sentences, three were exiled, and one was confined to a psychiatric hospital. Natalya Gorbanevskaya, who was nursing her child, was released. News of the demonstration spread outside the Soviet Union, and, of course, the people of Czechoslovakia learned of it.[16]

Although many think that this was the only protest against the occupation of Czechoslovakia in the USSR, there were other protests: in Moscow, Leningrad, the provinces, and in the non-Russian republics. On July 26, 1968, before the occupation, Anatoly Marchenko sent open letters to *Pravda* and the Prague newspaper *Rude Pravo* criticizing the press campaign against Czechoslovakia then in progress.[17] On July 29 he was arrested and shortly afterwards sentenced to a year in prison camp on a fabricated charge of "violating passport regulations."[18] On July 29, five Soviet Communists—Pyotr Grigorenko, Aleksey Kosterin, Valery Pavlinchuk, Sergey Pisarev, and Ivan Yakhimovich—called on the Czech embassy and gave the ambassador a letter approving the new course of the Czech Communist Party and criticizing Soviet pressure on Czechoslovakia.[19] On the night of August 21 leaflets protesting the invasion of Czechoslovakia were scattered in parts of Moscow.[20]

A few days after the invasion a graduating student in the physics department at the University of Moscow, Vladimir Karasev, hung a poster condemning the occupation in a university vestibule and collected signatures supporting the condemnation. Only four people succeeded in signing before university guards beat Karasev and dragged him to the militia. He was sent to a psychiatric hospital and released after three months, but by then he had already been expelled from the university and deprived of his permit to live in Moscow, so he had to settle for a job as a stoker in a factory outside of Moscow.[21]

On August 24 an unidentified man shouted a slogan condemning the invasion. He was beaten up by unknown persons in plainclothes, tossed into a waiting car, and driven off.[22] On the day the young Czech Jan Palach's self-immolation—January 25, 1969—two women students carried posters onto Mayakovsky Square which read: "To the Eternal Memory of Jan Palach" and "Freedom to Czechoslovakia." They stood there for twelve minutes while a crowd gathered around them. A group of young people approached without arm bands and said they were volunteer militia. They ripped the posters up and after discussing it among themselves, they let the girls go.[23] In the spring of 1969 twenty-three-year-old Valery Lukanin from the Moscow suburb Roshal placed a poster protesting the presence of Soviet troops in Czechoslovakia in his apartment window. He was taken to a psychiatric hospital and released—after ten years (1978).[24]

Demonstrations were held also by participants of various national movements: the Jewish, German, Crimean Tartar, and other movements. In 1971 Nadezhda Yemelkina staged a lone demonstration in Moscow demanding the release of political prisoners.[25] There were no other human rights demonstrations, except the annual Constitution Day (December 5) demonstrations in Pushkin Square, which began in 1965. By 1966 demonstrators no longer used posters or chanted their demands at December 5th gatherings; they simply removed their hats and stood in one minute of silence to express their solidarity with victims of lawlessness. From 1966 on Sakharov and close associates in the human rights movement took part in the December 5th demonstration, in which some twenty to fifty people joined. Every year KGB agents in plainclothes looked on, but they did not disperse the demonstrators until 1976.

The Initiative Group and the Committee on Human Rights

In the early phase of the human rights movement the majority of the activists were opposed to the creation of an organization, perhaps because of a general weariness with forced membership in all kinds of Soviet organizations and an aversion to the "democratic centralism" that directed the Party and the Soviet cult of "the collective." All who joined the fraternal association of activists treasured the voluntary and independent status of each to choose one's own place and associates. A general expectation that an experiment in creating an organization would lead to arrests at first prevented even its supporters from implementing the idea. The first human rights association was formed in 1969, the direct result of the most widespread form of joint action: collective letters.

On May 28, fifteen active signers sent out a letter complaining of violations of civil rights in the USSR. The addressee was the United Nations. The authors of the letter explained: "We are appealing to the U.N. because we have received no answer to the many protests and appeals which we have sent over the course of several years to high government and court institutions. Our hopes of being heard and our hopes that the authorities would desist from the lawlessness that we have persistently pointed out have been disappointed." They asked the United Nations to "protect the human rights that are being trampled underfoot in the USSR." An even more important difference between this letter and previous testimonies was that the signers called themselves a group—the Initiative Group for the Defense of Human Rights in the USSR. Most of them were from Moscow: Tatyana Velikhanova, Natalya Gorbanevskaya, Sergey Kovalyov, Viktor Krasin, Aleksandr Lavut, Anatoly Levitin-Krasnov, Yury Maltsev, Grigory Podyapolsky, Tatyana Khodorovich, Pyotr Yakir, and Anatoly Yakobson. A few were from other cities: Vladimir Borisov (Leningrad), Mustafa Dzhemilev (Tashkent), Henrikh Altunyan (Kharkov), and Leonid Plyushch (Kiev).[26] The Initiative Group wrote about violations of "one of the most basic human rights: the right to hold independent convictions and to disseminate them by any legal means." The letter listed political trials of human rights activists, beginning with the Sinyavsky-Daniel trial, and pointed out "an especially inhuman form of persecution: the confinement of normal people to psychiatric hospitals on the basis of their political beliefs."[27]

Less than a month after the first letter, further convictions called for a supplementary letter. The affair involved the author of *My Testimony*, Anatoly Marchenko, who was sentenced to a second term while still in prison camp.[28] The supplementary letter was signed "The Initiative Group," with no names of the members because it was sent without the approval of the majority. This somewhat accidental occurrence determined the continued existence of the group. There was no answer from the United Nations to either letter. A third letter, addressed to U Thant, Secretary-General of the United Nations, reported persecutions of Initiative Group members: Vladimir Borisov had been confined to a psychiatric hospital; Mustafa Dzhemilev and Anatoly Levitin-Krasnov were arrested. "The silence of an organization of international law unties the hands of those who will be inspired to further persecutions," wrote the members who were still free.[29] There was no answer to this appeal either nor to a statement signed in 1969 with a list of sixty-three prisoners of conscience who were confined in camps and psychiatric hospitals.[30]

On the first anniversary of the formation of the Initiative Group, the members explained in an open letter that the group had no program, no staff, and no organizational structure, yet the members,

believers and nonbelievers, optimists and skeptics, those with and those without Communist views, are united by a sense of personal responsibility for everything that is taking place in our country and by the conviction that the basis for any normal life of society lies in the recognition of the unconditional value of the individual. . . . Our attempts to defend human rights spring from this belief. We understand social progress to mean, above all, an increase in freedom. We are also united in our desire to act openly and in the spirit of the law, whatever our personal attitude to particular laws. We are not absolutely certain that our appeal to the U.N. is the most correct action to take nor that it is the only possible one. We are trying to achieve something under conditions that, from our point of view, make it immoral to do nothing.[31]

When their fifth appeal to the United Nations went unanswered, the Initiative Group looked elsewhere. In January 1972 they appealed on behalf of prisoners of conscience and those confined to psychiatric hospitals to the Fifth International Congress of Psychiatrists held in Mexico City, to the International League of Human Rights, and one more appeal to the United Nations—to the new Secretary-General Kurt Waldheim.[32] None of the letters were answered. Depleted by the arrests of eight members, the Initiative Group stopped sending appeals to the West.

Its experience confirmed that the personal danger to its members was greater than to authors and coauthors of open letters. Arrests were not immediate (the group was protected by its very openness) and statements by people who were united by declared goals created a greater effect than a packet of statements on the same issues written individually or signed by all as coauthors. Yet another important discovery resulted from the open declaration of the group. The names of its members were carried by foreign broadcasts into the Soviet Union, and people who viewed them as authorized representatives of the human rights movement began to communicate with the group.

People who had announced themselves as group members, but who did not claim to be its representatives, nevertheless came to personify the movement for other people and ended up as spokespeople for the movement. Outside observers knew only them (which explains why it was thought that the movement had ended with the periodic arrests of its "speakers"). The experience of the Initiative Group convinced activists of the value of integrating open associations into the structure of the human rights movement.

The Committee for Human Rights in the USSR was formed in Moscow in November 1970; its initiator was Valery Chalidze, and other founding members were Andrey Tverdokhlebov and academician Andrey Sakharov. All three were physicists. Later Igor Shafarevich, a mathematician and corresponding member of the Academy of Sciences, joined them. Aleksandr Yesenin-Volpin and Boris Tsukerman became legal experts for the group; Aleksandr Solzhenitsyn and Aleksandr Galich became honorary members.[33] It was thought that the scientific and literary renown of some members and the experience of others in legal matters would serve as protection from repression. The goals of the committee were stated in their founding statement: joint consultations with government organizations in the creation and application of human rights guarantees; studying the theoretical aspects of this issue and its specific manifestations in Soviet society; legal education of the public, including the publication of international and Sovet documents on human rights. Government organizations, alas, did not consult with the committee members, whose activities were reduced to studying human rights in Soviet legal practice and the theoretical implications of human rights in the context of Soviet law. Neither Soviet legal scholars nor human rights activists had previously studied the theoretical aspects of these problems. The educational activities of the committee were also needed, in particular by participants of the human rights movement who, for all their inspired ideas, usually had neither experience nor much knowledge in these areas.

This was the first independent association with parliamentary procedures and rules of membership. Membership in the committee was open only to persons who were not members of any political party or other social organization claiming to participate in governing the country.[34] This experiment confirmed the right to independent associations without prior approval by providing an example of such an association formed on strictly legal grounds. The Committee for Human Rights was founded as an association of authors, which, in accordance with Soviet law, requires neither permission from the authorities nor even official registration.[35]

The committee was the first independent association in the Soviet Union to receive membership in an international organization. In June 1971 it became an affiliate of the International League of Human Rights, a nongovernmental organization with consultative status under the United Nations, and International Institute of Human Rights; it also became a member of the International Institute of Law, headed by René Kassen (Strasbourg). Members of the committee maintained regular relations with international organizations by telephone and exchanged documents with them.

Some of the problems the committee studied included: (1) a comparative analysis of the obligations of the USSR under international human rights agreements and Soviet law; (2) the right to defense in Soviet courts; (3) the rights of persons declared mentally ill; (4) a definition of what is meant by "political prisoner" and "parasite" (*tuneyadets*): (5) persecutions for "parasitism" in the Soviet Union; (6) the problem of the so-called resettled peoples, like the Crimean Tartars.[36] Although the committee was founded as a research and consultative organization, many individuals turned to its members not only for legal advice, but for concrete help. Valery Chalidze, in particular, frequently interceded in individuals' legal battles, not as a committee member, but as a private person. He represented cases involving permission to emigrate from the USSR, appeals to the Supreme Court for reviews of incorrect sentencing (once he was able to obtain a review and a positive ruling on the emigration of Dora Kolyaditskaya, whose husband was in Israel), a lawsuit on the registration of a religious community in Naro-Fominsk, as well as many others.[37]

Several things determined the central, coordinating role of the Moscow nucleus of the human rights movement in relation to participants in other cities and non-Russian republics: the activities of open human rights associations, aid to political prisoners and their families, and the dissemination of information on human rights in the USSR. These same factors also broadened the activists' awareness of independent social efforts beyond the confines of Moscow, an awareness that can be easily traced in the *Chronicle of Current Events*.

Leningrad

The distance between Leningrad and Moscow is quite short: the express train Red Arrow covers it in one night. There are close ties of family and friendship between inhabitants of both cities. Trips between both cities are a common occurrence not only on holidays, but on weekends as well. Nonetheless, the atmosphere of each city is quite different. Before the Revolution, St. Petersburg (Petrograd) was Russia's "window onto Europe" and the city most subject to foreign influence, while Moscow was the incarnation of a patriarchal attitude and lived according to the old customs. At the present time, however, all official and almost all unofficial contacts between the USSR and the West are made in Moscow. For all its considerable cultural strengths, Leningrad is more provincial.

During the late fifties underground circles appeared in both cities, provocative public statements were heard in official forums, and heated discussions were common at friendly gatherings. In Moscow the era of underground circles did not last long; they sprang up in the late fifties and quickly collapsed without being replaced. After the arrests of Telnikov and Khaybullin, the Krasnopevtsev and Mashkov groups in the fifties,[38] and P. Grigorenko's group,[39] there were no known underground organizations from 1964 until 1982. Independent civic activities were open.

In Leningrad underground activities continued longer. In 1957, even after the arrests of members of underground groups, Pimenov-Vayl, Trofimov, Molostvov, and others,[40] the underground tradition continued. In the summer of 1965 members of the groups that published the *samizdat* journal *Kolokol* were arrested;[41] in 1967–68 members of the All-Russian Social Christian Union for the People's Liberation were brought to trial.[42] The last underground group (Ushakov and Sarkisian) was uncovered in Leningrad in 1976.[43] Before this the Sergey Malchevsky and Nikolay Braun groups were uncovered in 1969; the group of Vyacheslav Dzibalov and the Purtov brothers went on trial at the beginning of 1972;[44] other groups existed about which only the names of some members are known, but not the time of discovery or the particulars of their cases. (The case of the Malchevsky group was a criminal matter: the group was accused of "searching" the home of a wealthy elderly woman, using false documents and "confiscating valuable items." There were fascist and anti-Semitic overtones to both the Malchevsky and Braun groups.)

With varying degrees of organization, other underground group members in Leningrad were occupied with an undertaking that occurred on a much larger scale in Moscow: *samizdat*. The only exception is the distribution of leaflets by the *Kolokol* group, the most unorganized and most active of all underground groups in Leningrad. Up to the moment of their arrest, the "Kolokolchiki," who were all friends and graduates of the Leningrad Institute of Technology, had only held discussions about the formal organization of the group (membership, program, and so forth). They can be credited with the relatively wide distribution of a book by members of the group, Valery Ronkin and Sergey Khakhayev *From the Dictatorship of Bureaucracy to the Dictatorship of the Proletariat*,[45] three leaflettings (using a hectograph), and the publication of the informational-political journal *Kolokol*. (Two issues came out and a third was prepared when the group members were arrested.)

The most highly structured and conspiratorial of the Leningrad groups was the All-Russian Social Christian Union for the People's Liberation, yet it was the least productive. Over a period of three years its members managed only to write out their program and exchange a few books among themselves (by Berdyaev and others).

Thus, underground activity lasted longer in Leningrad and involved a greater number of people. In connection with the *Kolokol* case about two hundred people were questioned and about one hundred in connection with the Social Christian Union case. There were some weak relations between members of the Leningrad underground and those of other cities in the provinces (Kursk, Petrozavodsk, Saratov), but these links did not reach Moscow, where the underground groups found no effective support. The only known connection with Moscow was between Leningraders and the Moscow group of Telnikov and Khaybullin.

On the other hand, the open public activities of the Leningraders were, for the most part, conducted jointly with Muscovites. Open protests in Leningrad were almost identical in form to those that took place in Moscow, but they found fewer and less active participants. The poetry "boom" of the late fifties and early sixties was about equal in both cities. Leningrader Natalya Rubinshteyn writes about this period: "Wherever you looked people were writing and reading poetry. . . . The very air seemed to be clouded with poetry."[46] Typed poems were passed from person to person, but there were no collections of poems. The unofficial Leningrad poets were printed in one of the three issues of *Syntax*, published by the Muscovite A. Ginzburg. All three issues circulated both in Moscow and Leningrad. The meetings on Mayakovsky Square in Moscow that began in 1958 had their analogue in discussions on contemporary painting in the Square of the Arts and the Artists' Union in Leningrad in 1957.[47] Because of energetic and immediate dispersals by Leningrad officials, there were only two discussions. The next attempt to gather on Mars Field in 1961 was also broken up.[48]

Political trials of the post-Khrushchev era began earlier in Leningrad. On November 23, 1964 a month after Khrushchev's fall, an article appeared in the *Evening Leningrad* by Yakov Lerner, entitled "Quasi-literary Drone," about the talented young poet Iosif Brodsky, whom Anna Akhmatova had called "our Premier." Brodsky's poems were widely circulated in *samizdat* and were often sung to guitar accompaniment. In the article, Brodsky was accused of leading "the life of a parasite" because he was not regularly employed in any Soviet organization. Soon afterwards he was arrested.

The flower of Soviet culture rose to the defense of Brodsky. Anna Akhmatova, Dmitry Shostakovich, Korney Chukovsky, Konstantin Paustovsky, Samuil Marshak, and others wrote or asked high-ranking officials to intercede on his behalf. More than twenty writers came from Moscow to attend his trial, including Lidiya Chukovskaya, Lev Kopelev, and even Aleksey Surkov, who was hardly inclined toward liberalism. The witnesses for the defense included Leningrad professors Yefim Etkind and Vladimir Admoni, as well as the poet Natalya Grudinina.[49] The Moscow journalist Frida Vigdorova contributed most to Brodsky's defense. She compiled a transcript of the trial—the first such document in *samizdat* to describe a political trial.[50] Brodsky's trial was shocking in that no facts were produced to support the charges. The judge was distinguished by his rudeness and stupidity. Suitably briefed construction workers were trucked in to serve as the public. They hooted and hollered at the accused and his parents. Besides them, only Vigdorova and two or three of Brodsky's friends were admitted into the courtroom; the rest gathered outside. The sentence given Brodsky was the maximum provided for under the article on "parasitism": five years of internal exile. Immediately after the trial the defense witnesses were called to a meeting with the secretariat of the Leningrad Writers' Union, where Chairman A. Prokofyev shouted and stamped his feet. All three were reprimanded.

All this occurred early in 1965, before the "thaw" had come to an end. At the next elective session of the Leningrad writers, Prokofyev lost his post by secret ballot, and all three defense witnesses were elected members of the board of the Leningrad Writers' Union. Dmitry Granin, the only member of the former secretariat to defend Brodsky, became president of the board. The new secretariat annulled the reprimands given to the defense witnesses. But the most important event was Joseph Brodsky's rehabilitation—in September 1965 he was allowed to return to Leningrad.[51]

The trial of the *Kolokol* group took place in November 1965. The accused conducted themselves gallantly by disputing the authorship of the incriminating articles. In an attempt to corroborate their wrongdoing, the prosecutor exclaimed that " they send people to jail for this even in the West." Friends of the accused stood by the courthouse throughout the trial, and a respectable amount of money was collected for the defense lawyers. The sentence was: seven years of camp and three years internal exile for V. Ronkin and S. Khakhayev; from two to four years in camp for the others. After the trial a large group of graduates of the Institute of Technology, friends and acquaintances of the accused, were subject to "group criticism" and dismissed from their jobs.[52]

The trial of the leaders of the All-Russian Social Christian Union was closed, and access to the trial of the other members was limited to a select public to whom passes had been issued, just as in the *Kolokol* and subsequent political trials. Because they were underground groups, the *Kolokol* group and the Social Christian Union did not attract like-minded people who learned of their existence only after their arrests. In Leningrad there were no circle formed on the basis of an activist civic stand, as was true of the human rights workers in Moscow. Such like-minded Leningraders were drawn to Moscow; in Leningrad itself only isolated individuals or groups consisting of a few people existed.

The 1968 petition campaign that swept over Moscow was joined by Leningraders who wrote "the letter of the ten" and a few individual letters, which mentioned the lawlessness of "the trial of the four," and also the Leningrad trials of the *Kolokol* group and the Socialist Christian Union.[53] The Leningrad director Georgy Tovstonogov and actor Innokenty Smoktunovsky signed a letter against re-Stalinization with twenty-five other cultural figures.[54] In April 1968 a fifth-year student at the Leningrad Electrotechnical Institute, Boris Shilkrot, circulated his own petition among fellow students in support of democracy, against re-Stalinization, and in protest of the trial of the four. A large number of *samizdat* materials were confiscated from Shilkrot, including Solzhenitsyn's novels and stories by Daniel. He was sentenced to three years in a strict-regimen camp.[55]

Leningrader Viktor Faynberg was among the 7 demonstrators protesting the invasion of Czechoslovakia in Red Square on August 25. In 1969 Leningrader Vladimir Borisov joined the Initiative Group for the Defense of Human Rights in the USSR. The invasion of Czechoslovakia prompted the first separate attempt by Leningraders at a collective public protest. Twelve Leningraders (including Lev Kvachevsky, Yury Gendler, Anatoly Studenkov, Nikolay Danilov, and Yevgeny Shashenkov) were accused of having *samizdat* connections with the

Russian Orthodox Church

Boris Talantov in 1968, Orthodox layman
who died in a labor camp in 1970

Father Gleb Yakunin, initiator of the defense of Orthodox church rights, and founder of the
Christian Committee for the Defense of Human Rights of Believers, with his family, Moscow,
1978

Father Sergy Zheludkov, active in
Orthodox and human rights movements
who died in 1984

Father Dmitry Dudko, popular Moscow preacher in the
1970s

Zoya Krakhmalnikova, Moscow, editor of the religious magazine *Hope*, before her arrest in 1983

Movement for Social and Economic Rights in the Soviet Union

Vladimir Skvirsky, founding member of SMOT (Free Interprofessional Association of Workers), Moscow, 1978

Lev Volokhonsky, founding member of SMOT, Leningrad, 1978

Arkady Tsurkov, activist in group of young Social-Democrats in Leningrad, 1976

Aleksey Nikitin, fighter for independent trade unions, Dovetsk, 1980; died in a psychiatric hospital in 1984

Yury Kiselyov, Moscow artist and founding member of Initiative Group for the Defense of the Rights of Invalids in the USSR, 1980

Russian National Movement

Igor Ogurtsov, leader of the All-Russian Social Christian Union for the People's Liberation, sentenced to fifteen years imprisonment and to five years in exile, Leningrad, 1967

Gennady Shimanov, Russian national-Bolskevik and *samizdat* writer, with his family in Moscow, 1973

Vladimir Osipov, editor of the Russian National
Movement *samizdat* magazine *Veche*

Moscow human rights activists. Danilov and Shashenkov were put away in a psychiatric hospital, and their friends were sentenced to prison camp.[56] Aleksandr Gusev, a biologist and World War II veteran, in a letter to Brezhnev expressed his disagreement with "the decision of the Central Committee on the Czech question" and suggested that the invasion of Czechoslovakia would lower the international prestige of the Soviet Union. Although Gusev did not circulate his letter in *samizdat*, it became known after Brezhnev's office forwarded it to the Party organization of the Academy of Sciences Institute of Zoology where Gusev worked. He was expelled from the Party (forty Party members voted for his expulsion, eleven voted against, and one abstained) and was subjected to persecution on the job.[57] Other protests against the invasion, of which a total of sixteen were recorded in Leningrad, were anonymous.

On the night of the invasion a graffito appeared on the horse statues on Anichkov Bridge: "Brezhnev, Out of Czechoslovakia!" The twenty-year-old Leningrader who had written the graffito, Boguslavsky, was caught and beaten at the scene and afterwards received a three-year camp sentence.[58] The name of the organizers of other protests are unknown. On another occasion, an automobile drove through the Winter Palace Square and dropped a bundle of leaflets. The next day Leningrad radio asked its listeners if anyone had noticed the license plate number of the car.[59]

In 1970, Revolt Pimenov and Boris Vayl were again arrested, this time for distributing *samizdat*. The trial was not in Leningrad, but in Kaluga. Academician Sakharov attended the trial, although others who came from Leningrad and Moscow were not admitted into the courtroom. After the trial there were the usual dismissals and expulsions of friends and relatives of the accused who refused to give incriminating testimony or to make accusations. This also occurred after the Lev Kvachevsky and other trials.[60]

The lack of open public life in Leningrad is explained by the fact that it was more difficult to publicize such events there than in Moscow, where the presence of foreign correspondents ensured that such events would be carried by foreign broadcasts. Leningrad authorities were much quicker to nip in the bud the first sign of any unorthodox activities. In this respect, the affair of Vladimir Chernyshov, who became a prisoner in a Leningrad psychiatric hospital, is very enlightening. Chernyshov was graduated from the department of applied mathematics at Leningrad University and taught mathematics at the Leningrad Institute of Technology. He was an avid collector of books and records and privately wrote poetry, stories, and philosophical essays, some of which were anticommunist. He typed out his manuscripts, bound them in three notebooks, and showed them to two friends over a five-year period. Both he and his friends were arrested. One repented and asked for pardon; Chernyshov and the artist Vladimir Popov ended up in a mental hospital, where they were diagnosed as "chronic schizophrenics." They were kept there for several years and subjected to a treatment of strong neuroleptics.[61]

In Leningrad there were more than a few trials for distributing leaflets and writing anonymous letters critical of the Soviet system. Sent to newspapers and various Soviet institutions, these letters were a tragic testimony to the plight of people who suffered spiritual isolation and were forced to remain silent.[62]

The Russian Provinces

The atmosphere in large provincial cities in the Russian areas of the USSR is similar to that of Leningrad, although the smaller number of inhabitants and cultural circles meant there were fewer people with civic goals. However, the limited cultural circles made it easier for civic-minded people to seek each other out. From the late fifties on, many Russian cities with developed industries, institutions of higher education, and research institutes had their own circles of dissidents. They exchanged samizdat materials, which were usually brought in from Moscow. It was sufficient to obtain one copy through a friend or a group in Moscow; copies were then made on the spot.

In the provinces public expressions of dissidence invariably led to arrest. In some places young people who formed undeclared organizations, distributed leaflets, or wrote slogans on walls often went undiscovered. Older people usually went no further than organizing samizdat distribution or even writing samizdat (usually anonymously), but they neither joined secret organizations nor made statements in public.

Dissidence invariably exists, but because of the danger involved in revealing dissident ideas we know only those who have been arrested or those whom prisoners (or informers) have exposed. In any case, the Chronicle of Current Events carries only information of such cases and does not endanger activists known to them but unknown to the KGB.

In the Chronicle of Current Events approximately fifty cities in the Russian provinces are mentioned in connection with cases of public dissent. Each of the cities has produced one or two news items: samizdat was discovered in the possession of a certain person, someone was arrested or dismissed from work because of opinions unacceptable to the authorities. From 1968 until 1973 there are a few items on each of the following Russian cities: Vladimir, Gorky, Ryazan, Saratov, Sverdlovsk, Kirov, Rostov, Novosibirsk, and Obninsk.

Vladimir

In December 1968 two issues of a typed informational bulletin called *Youth* appeared here; it announced that in the city a Union of Independent Youth had been organized as a legal organization. Vladimir Borisov, a laborer educated as a philologist, was the leader, and he submitted a statement of registration with the city executive committee.

According to their regulations, the Union of Independent Youth was an organization in which young people themselves directed their own activities within the framework of Soviet law. "The basic goal of the Union is to facilitate by all means the development of socialistic democracy and social progress in our country." The union demanded "that truly democratic elections be held, that freedom of speech, publishing, public meetings, demonstrations, and unions be observed, that persecutions on the basis of beliefs cease, that illegal and unconstitutional censorship be abolished, and that the fight against crime be intensified." In addition to an announcement on the formation of the union, there was current information about the country and the city of Vladimir, with harsh criticism of the highest city and regional authorities.[63]

On May 31, 1969 Vladimir Borisov was duped into entering a psychiatric hospital. He was told that he was to be given a physical examination by the military; instead he was injected with potent drugs and brought to a state of physical shock. In response, his friends distributed leaflets about the union and its leader. The publicity was effective: Borisov was soon pronounced mentally competent and released from the hospital.[64] But after a month he was arrested, subjected to another examination, and declared mentally unsound. The union was broken up,[65] and Vladimir Borisov hanged himself a year later in the hospital ward of Butyrka Prison.[66] This is the tragic end of the only legal youth organization in the provinces reported in the *Chronicle.*

Gorky

In contrast to the unusual Vladimir experiment, events in Gorky paint a picture of the "normal" life of dissidents in the provinces.

Gorky is the center of automobile manufacturing; there are various institutes of higher education, a university, and technical institutes in the city. From the early sixties certain circles of friends began to exchange *samizdat* materials. There were both circles of older people (teachers, engineers, and their families) and student circles. The most politicized of these circles was the group connected with the university's department of history and philology; its members, future historians who thought along neo-Marxist lines, included: Mikhail Kapranov, twice dismissed from the university for his independent views, and two others who had been previously dismissed for "freethinking." More "respectable" students were also interested in *samizdat*, like Vladimir Zhiltsov, one of the best students in the history department, and the children of some of Gorky's ruling elite. In the midsixties *samizdat* was read almost openly in the universities. Students sometimes took new materials to classes and passed around pages among themselves; in the course of the day they were able to read entire articles or even books. *Samizdat* was also exchanged between students and interested teachers—political *samizdat* among history students, literary *samizdat* among students of literature. But, most often, poetry was read and sung to guitar accompaniment.

The attack against the signers in Moscow, which began in 1968, coincided with an attempt by dissidents in Gorky to coordinate their activities with Moscow dissidents. Two anonymous letters protesting the "trial of the four" were hand printed. (Rumor had it that the authorities had more difficulty identifying printing than handwriting.)[67] In the same month of April leaflets appeared across the city: near the university, the Polytechnical Institute, medical and teaching institutes, and were even posted near the KGB headquarters. They called for democratic freedoms, the rehabilitation of the victims of the political trials of the thirties, and improvements in the present living conditions of political prisoners. People were asked to "follow the example of Czechoslovakia." The distributors of the leaflets were not found, but a few students were expelled from their institutes for distributing or reading *samizdat;* a few were expelled for refusing to give evidence; some teachers were dismissed.[68]

Sometime after this five students in the history department arranged for a discussion of a work they had written, "Socialism and the State." It was based on available Soviet sources and expressed in a Marxist spirit, but the conclusions departed from the official point of view. All five were members of the Komsomol, and their case was discussed at a Komsomol meeting. The five were by no means censured unanimously; many were sympathetic to the heretics. When they were expelled, Klara Geldman, a student, left the Komsomol out of solidarity with the five; she was expelled from the university just before she was to complete her undergraduate thesis. The authors of the paper were driven from the university and immediately drafted into the army. One of the five, Vitaly Pomazov, was sentenced to one-and-a-half years in camp, after he had completed his military service, for his part in coauthoring this Marxist paper.[69]

In connection with the "case of the five," a new wave of arrests and searches began. In the summer of 1969 Mikhail Kapranov, Sergey Ponomaryov, and Vladimir Zhiltsov were arrested. They admitted that they had distributed leaflets the previous spring. Their friend and teacher of political economy at the technical school, Vladlen Pavlenkov, was arrested at the same time for possession of *samizdat*. The investigators accused him of being a "corrupter of young minds."

The month-long trial was closed to the public. The prosecution demanded that the accused admit that they constituted an organization and that Pavlenkov was their leader, but the three denied Pavlenkov's participation in distributing the leaflets as well as the existence of any kind of formal organization. Pavlenkov and Kapranov received seven years each in a strict-regimen camp; Ponomarev received five years; Zhiltsov received four years.[70]

Even before the trial was over, relatives and friends of the accused were caught up in a whirlwind of repression. The wives of the accused were dismissed from their jobs and deprived of the right to work in their professions. Pavlenkov's wife, who had taught German at the university, was reduced to working as a furnace stoker. The other wives experienced similar fates. Zhiltsov's woman companion was expelled from the university two weeks before graduation. All were accused of failing to report that the defendants had read *samizdat*. For testimony in defense of the accused and even for knowing them dozens of people lost their jobs and many others were expelled from the university and various institutes.[71] After this incident, student groups disintegrated, but the next generation of students formed similar groups, although they were more careful about distributing *samizdat*. Some of the older participants dropped out in order to avoid unpleasantness, but persecution united even more closely those who remained. The arrests failed to put an end to the receipt of *samizdat* from Moscow or its duplication and circulation in Gorky.[72]

Similar events happened in other Russian cities, and young people took the most active role.

Saratov

In 1968, an underground student group called the Party of True Communists was formed in Saratov. Their program was liberal-democratic and their aim was creative research into Marxism based on original sources, including official and *samizdat* publications.

Arrests disrupted the group in August 1969. During their trial the accused emphasized that they were not involved in agitation ("doing a little for many") but in propaganda ("doing much for a few"), and that newcomers were enlisted only after they had familiarized themselves with the literature of propaganda and then only if their views coincided with those of the group. About fifty witnesses were called during the trial, students or recent graduates of Saratov institutions of higher education. Only relatives and a hand-picked public were admitted into the courtroom, while 100 to 150 students gathered outside the courthouse. All seven accused admitted their guilt and recanted. Despite this, the head of the organization, law student Oleg Senin, received seven years in camp; the rest received from three to six years. After the trial more than sixty friends and relatives suffered extrajudicial repression—dismissals from their jobs and institutes.[73] After the trial was reported in the *Chronicle*, there was no news from Saratov for a long time. However, irregular communications have confirmed that this was not due to the absence of independent civic activity, but to a break in contact with the *Chronicle*.

On February 4, 1971 an article in the Saratov newspaper *Kommunist*, titled "At the Pillory," named twenty people who frequented the black market in books. The author accused six of trafficking in *samizdat*: director of a children's toy factory Viktor Strelnikov, film actor V. Yampolsky, employee of the local children's library Yury Boldyrev, musicians A. Kattse and M. Belokrysa, and teacher V. Nulman. They listened to radio broadcasts regularly, taped some of the broadcasts, and bought works by Solzhenitsyn, A. Kuznetsov, and others on the local black market, and travelled to various other cities in order to obtain *samizdat* and *tamizdat* works. They typed these works on an old typewriter at night: "one copy they hid away for themselves and the rest for distribution." The article stated that dozens of *samizdat* works were found in various hiding places. The article did not mention the sale of *samizdat* materials, so one can assume that this was an ordinary case of exchange.[74]

One more brief item about Saratov: on March 17, 1971 Nina Kakhtsadzova, a doctor-radiologist, was taken from her place of employment to be questioned by the KGB after a search revealed *samizdat* materials and leaflets that had been distributed by foreigners in Moscow's GUM department store. She fainted twice under questioning; a few of her friends were also called in for questioning that same day; the next morning Kakhtsadzova hanged herself.[75]

Ryazan

In the latter half of 1968 students at an electronics institute formed an illegal organization called the New Brand of Marxism. A part-time student and lathe operator at the Ryazan farm-machinery factory,

Yury Vudka wrote a brochure, "The Decline of Capital," that set the program for the Ryazan group. This group clearly had contacts with groups in other cities, because the Saratov group also used Vudka's work as their program. The Ryazan organization was uncovered after a confession of members Yevgeny Martimonov and Semyon Zaslavsky, given to the KGB. At the trial in Ryazan witnesses were called in not only from Saratov, but from the greater Moscow region, Leningrad, Kiev, and other cities. Sentences of from seven to three years in labor camp were given out; the informers were paroled.[76]

Sverdlovsk

In 1969 the youth organization Free Russia made its appearance in Sverdlovsk, with the brothers Valery and Viktor Pestov (sons of a military doctor, they both worked as factory repairmen after military service), candy-factory technican Nikolay Shaburov, railway dispatcher Vladislav Uzlov, and repairman Vladimir Bersenev. While trying to decide on a course of action, some in the group suggested shooting at the "city fathers" during a holiday celebration. But they soon gave up their terrorist ideas and obtained a typewriter, which they used to type a leaflet entitled "The Rising Sun." In November 1969 about a hundred copies were thrown from a bridge onto the Ural machinery factory and distributed among students of the railway technical institute. By spring the organization held another meeting, changed its name to the Russian Workers' Party, selected officers, and adopted a program advocating freedom of the press, an end to censorship, a raise in wages and student stipends, better living conditions, and independent labor unions. They also collected membership dues. They dreamed of establishing contacts with Moscow, where, in their conception, a "center" existed. Its members did not hide their participation from their friends. By May 1970 they had written a new leaflet, "The Sword Is Heavy: We Need to Join Forces," and distributed it in Serov, Tagil, and Sverdlovsk. Shaburov left for Moscow, Leningrad, and the Baltic states to distribute some leaflets and find the "center," but a relative in Liepaya convinced him to go to the KGB and confess. Shaburov sent a telegram to his friends informing them of his confession. Five members of the organization were arrested on May 19 and 20, 1969, by which time members numbered about fifty. The trial took place in November 1970, and sentences ranged from three to five years of prison camp.[77]

Precisely a year later seven young workers were tried in Sverdlovsk—all members of another organization called the Revolutionary Party of Soviet Intellectuals. The leader was a twenty-seven-year-old machinist from Lower Tagil and former Party member Georgy Davidenko, who called himself a social democrat. The organization had existed since

1970; it held regular meetings, possessed certain printing equipment, and distributed literature, primarily the works of its twenty-five-year-old ideologue Vasily Spinenko, a graduate of the philosophy department of Donetsk University. According to Spinenko, only a technocratic intelligentsia is capable of producing a just society, and only it should be allowed to participate in the government of that society. One of his articles is called "The Birth of New Classes and the Struggle under Socialism." After completing military service, group member Viktor Semiletov entered a training school of the Ministry of Internal Affairs to study conspiracies.

The investigation of this case was conducted in Sverdlovsk, in Krasnoyarsk, Gorky, Khabarovsk, and possibly in other cities. Davidenko and his associates each received four-year prison-camp terms. Spinenko was sent to a psychiatric hospital, where he remained as late as 1983.[78]

Kharkov

Kharkov is located in the Ukraine, but it is a Russified city. The public dissent that sprang up there in 1969 did not follow the pattern of the Ukrainian national movement, but of democratic movements in general. The small circle of Kharkov dissidents was closer in spirit to the Muscovites than to the Kievans. Primarily employed as engineers, people of all nationalities joined this group. The group evidently consisted of ten to fifteen families united by ties of friendship; decency, mutual support, and steadfastness prevailed. Like the majority of dissidents during the period of the Prague Spring, most Kharkov dissidents were Marxists who hoped to see "socialism with a human face" and hung portraits of Lenin in their homes. The most active member was a military engineer, Genrikh Altunyan. He and his friends in visits to Moscow had met pro-Marxist Moscow activists Pyotr Yakir, Pyotr Grigorenko, and others. Altunyan joined the Initiative Group for the Defense of Human Rights in the USSR; seven of his friends had signed the Initiative Group's appeal to the United Nations. Altunyan was one of the first Initiative Group members to be arrested—in June 1969.[79] By that time he had already been expelled from the Party, demobilized, and dismissed from his job. Then his friends were arrested one after the other: Vladislav Nedobora, Vladimir Ponomaryov. Arkady Levin.[80] The idealism and belief in people that had contributed to the unique social virtues of this group was turned against them during the investigation of their case. They could not believe that it was impossible to convince the investigators of their pure motives and the irreproachableness of their civic position, and so they were very open with their investigators. The brutality and injustice they encountered were especially intolerable to these trusting people. But all four of the accused, as well as their wives and friends who were criticized during "public discussions" at their places of work, conducted themselves bravely.

The accused were not allowed to explain their conduct, nor were the contents of the letter they signed taken into account. Nonetheless their co-workers attacked them ruthlessly for having turned to the United Nations, that is, to foreigners. They were called traitors and pawns in the hands of the imperialists and the United Nations was labelled an American spy organization. At all such meetings it was decided to dismiss the guilty parties; they were all denied the opportunity to work in their own professions and forced to work for years in unskilled positions.[81]

Research Towns: Akademgorodok in Novosibirsk, Obninsk, Pushchino on the Oka River, Chernogolovka and Others

In designing research towns, the authorities wanted, above all else, to isolate scientists from the general population because of the scientists' habit of independent thought. But within the towns themselves conditions were ideal for the creation of a special microclimate, where independent thought was not limited to scientific questions.

The philosopher Boris Shragin compared the reactions he encountered while lecturing in small research towns near Moscow to those of the free world: listeners were not afraid to ask genuine questions and express their own opinions on the most controversial political questions.[82]

Research towns provided an ideal environment for *samizdat* activities, and there *samizdat* and *tamizdat* circulated almost publicly. It is well known that the majority of those who protested re-Stalinization and the "trial of four" in 1968 were scientists; they accounted for 45 percent of the signatures on letters protesting the trial.[83] Among these letters was a separate one from Akademgorodok with forty-six signatures.[84] Research towns near Moscow did not write separate letters, since they were close enough to join the Muscovites in their appeals.

The signers were subjected to "public criticism" in their own communities. In the Novosibirsk town of Akademgorodok, corresponding member of the Siberian Section of the Academy of Sciences Roald Sagdeyev suggested that "they all be expelled from Akademgorodok; let them go load lead pigs onto trucks."[85] According to an analysis Shragin made of these "public criticisms" on the basis of reports appearing in the *Chronicle*, the majority supported the signers. Party authorities, in order to fulfill their orders on "public criticism," were forced to make a trade-off: in exchange for verbal condemnations they agreed to a significant reduction in punishment for the signers. Of the five

Party members who signed petitions from Akademgorodok, three were
not expelled from the Party, but received strict reprimands. In Moscow
and Kiev this could only have been obtained at the expense of recantation. This trade-off is of considerable importance since expulsion from
the Party automatically entails dismissal from one's job. Those who
were only reprimanded were able to keep their jobs and, in addition,
after about two years the reprimand was removed from their records.
Shragin is right in his conclusion that a "strict reprimand represents a
peculiar compromise between Party members who are colleagues of
those subjected to repression and official representatives of regional or
city Party committees, who had to insist on their exemplary punishment."[86]

Other forms of compromise were reductions in rank, instead of dismissal, and "voluntary" resignations, which made it easier to obtain
new positions. Two signers were offered work and apartments in Novosibirsk if only they would leave "of their own volition." Evidently, it
was not easy to "organize" dismissals.[87]

Workers at the Institute of Biophysics in Pushchino-on-the-Oka reacted similarly when two of their colleagues were denounced for "anti-
Soviet" conversations during a vacation. Although their conversation
was not extraordinary for such intellectual circles, it upset outsiders
who overheard the intellectuals and demanded "appropriate measures"
from the authorities. The participants in the Party core group, where
discussions about the accused took place in their absence, did not
recommend any punitive measures. Extreme pressure was required
from representatives of the District Party Committee before a recommendation to dismiss the accused was adopted.[88]

The same atmosphere apparently prevailed in student circles at the
University of Novosibirsk. Although students did not participate in the
letter-writing campaign surrounding the "trial of four," several of them
wrote slogans at night in indelible ink on buildings in Akademgorodok:
"Their Crime was Honesty," "Stop Closed Trials—We Want to Know
the Truth," and so forth. Authors of anonymous signs are frequently
encountered in camps for political prisoners. However, in Akademgorodok, once the KGB authorities discovered those responsible for the
signs, they only insisted on expulsion from the Komsomol and Komsomol efforts to effect their expulsion from the university. It is clear that
the sympathetic attitude of the majority of students was known to the
authorities, since they negotiated with the students. The students
agreed to expel from the Komsomol those who painted the signs only
if they were permitted to remain in the university. Finally, the authorities proposed a compromise with some advantage on their side: the
culprits were to be expelled from the Komsomol and forced to leave

the university for a period of two years. But less than the two-thirds required by Komsomol regulations for expulsion voted for this proposal.[89]

On August 25, 1968 more signs appeared on buildings in Akademgorodok, but this time in connection with events in Czechoslovakia: "Out of Czechoslovakia, Barbarians!" This time the culprits were not found.[90]

Refusals to approve of the Soviet Union's "brotherly aid" to Czechoslovakia occurred most frequently in the Party collectives of research institutes, at least until the end of the sixties. According to physicist Yury Mnyukh, more than half of the employees of the design office in Pushchino-on-the-Oka abstained from voting for such approval.[91] In the seventies, open statements by scientists in defense of democracy and the observance of legality became rare. Although they belong to the social stratum that is most devoted to these values, they are also most vunerable to the simplest forms of repression: dismissal from work or, in the case of students, denial of work in the area of specialization. For them this is a more tangible loss than for those who are not engaged in creative work and can more easily find substitute employment. However, scientists have constituted a significant and very influential portion of human rights activists and supporters in recent years. Private forms of independent social interaction, including *samizdat* activities and aid to political prisoners and other victims of political repression, continue to be most deep-rooted in the scientific community.

The Baltic Fleet

In 1969 an underground organization formed by officers of the Baltic fleet, the Union for the Struggle for Democratic Rights, was uncovered. Approximately thirty people in Tallinn, Leningrad, and Kaliningrad and two Soviet officers in Poland were arrested.[92] The leader of the organization was naval officer Gennady Gavrilov, who wrote for *samizdat* under the pseudonym of Alekseyev (we know of an article by him on the Czech invasion).[93] Gavrilov had gone to Moscow and met Pyotr Yakir, who gave him the phone number of an engineer in Tallinn. The engineer, Sergey Soldatov, was a leading figure in the Tallinn underground organization, Democratic Movement of the Soviet Union. The officers' Union for the Struggle for Democratic Rights published a *samizdat* journal called *Democrat* in both Russian and Estonian. The organization needed printing type, and Soldatov helped in obtaining it. The members of the union were military personnel and so were tried in closed proceedings. Georgy Paramonov was declared mentally unfit; G. Gavrilov received six years in prison camp; Aleksey

Kosyrev, who recanted during the trial and provided a great deal of evidence against the others, received two years in camp; the sentences of the others are unknown.[94]

Repression of the Human Rights Activists

Each issue of the *Chronicle of Current Events* begins with reports on political trials. In early issues these were usually trials of Muscovites.

In 1967 Vladimir Bukovsky and Viktor Khaustov were each sentenced to three years in camp for demonstrations against political arrests;[95] in 1968 came the "trial of four" and the sentencing of Anatoly Marchenko and participants in the Red Square demonstration;[96] in 1969–70 Pyotr Grigorenko, Ilya Gabay, Natalya Gorbanevskaya, Vladimir Gershuni, and Andrey Amalrik were arrested.[97] Up to the end of 1972, thirty-four such trials, in which fifty-one defendants were sentenced, were reported.

In 1969–70 the use of psychiatric repression was increased. Beginning with the trial of Sinyavsky and Daniel, the government, aware that political repression was harmful to the Soviet Union's reputation as a democratic country, sought a way out by declaring mentally unsound those human rights activitists they were unable to put on trial for fear of scandal. Of the 106 persons tried for political reasons, as reported by the *Chronicle* for 1970, 20 were sent to psychiatric hopsitals. Eleven Muscovites were sentenced at the end of 1969; in 1970, eight of them were declared mentally unsound, including Pyotr Grigorenko and Natalya Gorbanevskaya. Of the eighty-five persons sentenced for political crimes in 1971, twenty-four were declared mentally unsound, that is, almost every third person.

The struggle against psychiatric repression was begun by Sergey Pisarev, a dedicated Communist and old-time Party member, who was confined to the Leningrad Special Psychiatric Hospital in 1953 after the report to Stalin in which he maintained that the affair of the recently arrested Kremlin doctors, who supposedly undermined the health of their patients, was a fabrication. After Stalin's death, both Pisarev and the Kremlin doctors were released, and Pisarev's diagnosis was declared false. In 1956, after three years, Pisarev's efforts resulted in the appointment of a special commission by the Communist Party Central Committee to investigate the Serbsky Institute of Forensic Medicine where, according to Pisarev, healthy people were not infrequently diagnosed in such a way as to be indefinitely isolated in special psychiatric hospitals, which were a special kind of prison. The commission supported Pisarev's allegations, and hundreds of healthy people were released from psychiatric hospitals, while those responsible for their false diagnoses were relieved of their duties. Among those demoted was Daniel Lunts, the head psychiatrist at the Serbsky Institute. Like other special psychiatric hospitals, the Serbsky Institute was not under the jurisdiction of public health organs, but of the investigation agencies, a factor that contributed to the misuse of psychiatry. The commission recommended that the jurisdiction of the Serbsky Institute and other special psychiatric hospitals be changed. However, the material collected by the commission was not considered at any official level and after two years was placed in archives. Under various pretexts, all the members of the commission were removed from the staff of the Central Committee, the doctors and administrators removed from their posts by the commission were reinstated, and new psychiatric prisons were added to the system.[98]

The *Chronicle* constantly addressed the problem of psychiatric repressions,[99] as did the Initiative Group[100] and the Committee for Human Rights.[101] A significant contribution in this area was made by Vladimir Bukovsky, who himself has twice experienced the horrors of confinement in psychiatric hospitals (in 1963 and in 1965 he was confined for a total of three years).[102] Bukovsky was able to obtain medical documentation on six inmates of psychiatric hospitals: himself, Pyotr Grigorenko, Natalya Gorbanevskaya, and other dissidents. In 1971 he transmitted this documention to the International Congress of Psychiatrists that convened in Mexico City. Bukovsky requested that they examine the documents and determine whether or not they provided sufficient grounds for confinement in a psychiatric hospital. But the congress leadership did not think it appropriate to do so: the scientists of the free world did not want to "become involved in politics."[103] For his efforts, Bukovsky was arrested and sentenced to seven years in camp and five years of internal exile for "anti-Soviet propaganda." His trial took place in January 1972 and heralded a general attack on the human rights movement.[104]

The *Chronicle of Current Events* received the brunt of the attack. The arrest of its founder, Natalya Gorbanevskaya, on December 24, 1969[105] did not halt publication: issue no. 11 appeared a week after her arrest. On the last page of that issue appeared this announcement: "The year of Human Rights in the Soviet Union continues. The *Chronicle* will appear in 1970."[106] As before, subsequent issues regularly appeared every two months and departed from previous issues neither in style, content, nor volume. The only difference was that contact was lost with some informants for a period of time. It was clear that the KGB did not know who the editors or the informants for the *Chronicle* were, and they continued to work. Anatoly Yakobson became the new editor, and the appearance of the twenty-third issue in January 1972 marked the fifth year of publication.

Rumors circulated in Moscow that the Central Committee of the Communist Party of the Soviet Union had adopted a special resolution in December 1971 to stop the publication of *Chronicle* and of *samizdat* in general, both within the Soviet Union and across its borders. On January 14 eight house searches took place in Moscow, including searches of Pyotr Yakir and his daughter Irina Yakir. Searches were conducted in connection with various cases, but Case no. 24 was the one most often cited.

Searches were simultaneously made in Vilnius, Leningrad, Novosibirsk, Uman, and Kiev.[107] In Kiev Leonid Plyushch was arrested in connection with Case no. 24; in Vilnius, Vaclav Sevruck was arrested; in Leningrad, Yury Melnik.[108] Throughout the rest of January and all of February there were mass questionings in all the cities affected by searches and arrests. Not only those subjected to searches were questioned, but their relatives, friends, and co-workers were as well. In Vilnius alone more than a hundred people were questioned.[109]

From the questionings it became clear that all the arrests and searches were made in connection with *samizdat*. Most of those summoned in connection with Case no. 24 were questioned about the distribution and preparation of the *Chronicle*. Subsequent events confirmed that Case no. 24 was the case of the *Chronicle*. On May 6 in Moscow, fifteen more searches were made, including a repeat search of Pyotr Yakir's apartment. He was arrested on June 12, 1972. The first news item in issue no. 26 of the *Chronicle* (July 5) was the arrest of Yakir.[110] Son of Iona Yakir, the executed Red Army commander, from the age of fourteen Pyotr had spent a total of seventeen years in camps and prisons under Stalin.[111] He played an active role in the struggle against re-Stalinization and was well known not only in the Soviet Union, but in the West as well. On the day of his arrest foreign correspondents in Moscow were officially notified that he was charged under article 70 (anti-Soviet agitation and propaganda).

By September the following were arrested in connection with the Moscow *samizdat* case: Aleksandr Rybakov in Novosibirsk (a collotype press was found in his possession),[112] Georgy Davydov and Valentin Petrov in Leningrad (a mimeograph machine was found),[113] Vladimir Shaklein, Yu. Yukhnovets, Aleksandr Bolonkin, and Valery Balakirev in Moscow (homemade copying equipment was found in their possession),[114] and Pyotr Starchik, arrested for leaflets, although forty-one copies of the *Chronicle* were found during a search of his apartment.[115] Vladimir Popov was arrested in connection with the case of Cronid Lubarsky, an astronomer from the research town of Chernogolovka near Moscow, who was implicated in the distribution of *samizdat* and, in particular, of the *Chronicle* and who had been in prison since January 1972.[116] Muscovite Yury Shikhanovich (connected with the *Chronicle*),[117] Roald Mukhamedyarov (for *samizdat*),[118] and a friend of Pyotr Yakir, Viktor Krasin (in connection with Case no. 24),[119] were arrested.

Despite these arrests, on October 15 the twenty-seventh issue came out, late by a month and a half. It contained information on arrests, searches, and questionings associated with Case no. 24 and other cases involving *samizdat*. It also carried news about repression in the Ukraine, events in Lithuania, the persecution of the Crimean Tartars, news from political camps, prisons, and psychiatric hospitals, additional information on the 1970 highjacking trial in Leningrad, new *samizdat* works, and other items.

On November 4 Irina Yakir was allowed to meet with her father Pyotr Yakir in Lefortovo Prison in the presence of two investigators. Yakir stated that his relationship to the democratic movement and its activities had changed. In his own words, material shown to him during his investigation convinced him of the tendentious character and the objectively harmful effects of the *Chronicle*. He explained that each new issue of the journal would lengthen the sentences to be given to him and Viktor Krasin and asked that publication be stopped. He added that every new issue would cause new arrests, not necessarily of those immediately responsible for the *Chronicle*'s continued publication. It was clear that Yakir was actively collaborating with the investigation.[120]

Nine days after this meeting Yakir's apartment was again searched and the recent twenty-seventh issue was confiscated. On January 3, 1973 Irina Belogorodskaya was arrested. The chief investigator told her husband that she had been arrested in connection with that issue, even though the KGB was aware that Belogorodskaya, previously involved with the *Chronicle*, had not taken part in its preparation. Thus, the government security workers kept the promise that Yakir had transmitted.[121] These developments forced the editors of the *Chronicle* to make a decision that would affect others. This difficult moral predicament delayed publication of the subsequent issue. In the meantime, the investigation of both Yakir's case and that of Krasin, who also provided his investigators with evidence, continued. The investigation included many forced confrontations between Yakir and Krasin and those who refused to confirm their accusations.[122]

Neither Yakir nor Krasin had been editors of the *Chronicle*, although they had actively gathered information for the journal. Both were well known for human rights statements circulated in *samizdat*. Because of his impressive biography, much attention was given to Yakir's activities in foreign radio broadcasts to the Soviet Union. People not directly connected with the *Chronicle*, but who wished to obtain copies or who wished to pass on information to its editors tried to meet Yakir, thinking that he knew how to get in touch with the *Chronicle*. This was particularly true of those who were from areas outside Moscow or were from non-Russian republics. Yakir and Krasin knew the second echelon of *Chronicle* correspondents, without direct contact with the editors. Yakir and Krasin could only offer suppositions or incomplete testimony about people with connections to the editors and editors themselves.

Thus, despite the abundance of testimony the investigators received from Yakir and Krasin, who gave evidence about more than two hundred people,[123] many of those who participated in the publication of the *Chronicle* remained unknown or their participation could not be confirmed. The investigators tried to obtain testimony from those who were named by Yakir and Krasin. Testimony extracted during investigation undermines the self-respect and trust of all those concerned. The investigators tried as much as possible to create this effect.

Although they were few, some dissidents did cooperate with the investigation. Those inclined to cooperate either were given light sentences or avoided punishment altogether. I know of no instance in which such people returned to their former dissident activities. They themselves either made the decision or were forced to do so by the impossibility of renewing former contacts or making new ones. Each such instance lowers the moral prestige of the dissident movement, especially among those who know of it secondhand, say from foreign radio broadcasts. In this sense the case of Yakir and Krasin was without precedent, since neither before nor after had there been an example of such unstable behavior by the leading dissidents.

All those who had been named by Yakir and Krasin were compelled to give testimony not only through the use of fear and assurances that everything was already known to the investigation team, but also by appealing to their sense of morality. The investigators would say, "You yourself are free (for the time being), but if you refuse to confirm testimony given by the arrested, you will make it more difficult for them." This is a common-enough ruse, but Yakir and Krasin contributed to the efforts of the investigators by making the same statement during confrontations with witnesses, accusing those who refused to cooperate of egoism and telling them that by concealing their own participation in the *Chronicle* they were placing all responsibility for publication onto Yakir and Krasin. Under such pressure, Yakir's daughter Irina began to give testimony, but only about her own activities. She stated that she had assumed editorial responsibilities beginning with issue no. 12, that is, after the arrest of Natalya Gorbanevskaya, until the most recent issue no. 27.[124]

An extraordinary ruse was employed to force confessions from others: letters from Yakir and Krasin were obtained while they were in Lefortovo Prison. Yakir's letter to Sakharov was delivered to his door by a KGB officer. After expressing his deep respect for Sakharov, Yakir asked him to stop all public statements because they were harmful in their effects on others and were used as anti-Soviet propaganda. Krasin sent a letter to "his friends at liberty" through an investigator. He wrote that the "democratic movement" had recently embarked on a course dangerous for the government, and that the government was forced to protect itself. The attack of the government on the movement had led to its rout; now it was essential to think of saving the people. To stop repression it was not enough to desist from oppositional activity; the government required guarantees that the opposition would not be renewed, and such a guarantee could be provided only by cooperating with the investigation. Krasin called upon all those still at large to overcome the psychological barriers preventing them from giving honest testimony, not only about their own activities, but about the activities of all others known to them.[125] These letters did not yield any tangible results. A few people confirmed the testimony of Yakir and Krasin concerning the *Chronicle* under questioning, and this aggravated the already despondent mood of those whose friends had been arrested and heightened the sense of personal danger of *Chronicle* workers still free.

In July 1973 there were new arrests in connection with Case no. 24: Gabriel Superfin in Moscow, Viktor Nekipelov in the Vladimir region, and Sergey Pirogov in Arkhangelsk.[126] In August Yakir and Krasin were brought to trial. Both acknowledged their guilt and repented of what they had done. Both admitted that they had wanted to undermine the Soviet system and recognized the slanderous nature of their earlier human rights position, including their membership in the Initiative Group and the slanderous and seditious character of the *Chronicle*. A great deal of attention was paid to the problem of psychiatric repression. A prominent Soviet psychiatrist, Academician Andrey V. Snezhnevsky, was brought in as a witness and stated that there had never been and there were not at the time any healthy people in Soviet psychiatric hospitals. Yakir called statements by the human rights movement on the use of psychiatry for political purposes slanderous.

The court delivered its verdict on September 1: three years of camp and three years of exile for both Yakir and Krasin. On September 5 at

the House of Journalists Yakir and Krasin appeared at a press conference in the presence of foreign correspondents, and parts of the press
conference were carried by Soviet television. They reaffirmed statements they made during their trial.[127] On September 28 the Supreme
Court lowered their terms to the time they had already served in
prison and allowed the term of internal exile to stand. The location
was determined: large cities not far from Moscow (Kalinin for Krasin
and Ryazan for Yakir).[128]

Four members of the Initiative Group still at liberty (Tatyana Velikhanova, Grigory Podyapolsky, Sergey Kovalyov, and Tatyana Khodorovich) publicly announced that the group did not share the position
taken by its members Yakir and Krasin; they did not consider their
documents slanderous; they denied the accusation that their statements were of a seditious, or even a political nature. They repeated
the claim that psychiatry was used in the Soviet Union as a form of
political punishment. In connection with the trial and press conference of Yakir and Krasin, the group wrote: "We protest such methods
of coercion, which violate the integrity of the individual and force one
to slander one's own actions and those of one's friends." This was the
only statement made by the Initiative Group between January 1972
and January 1974.[129]

The sense of moral defeat inflicted by the unprecedented testimony
given at the trial was aggravated by the unbridled press campaign
against Sakharov and the fact that his colleagues took part in this
campaign (the letter of forty academicians, some of whom had been
his personal friends).[130]

The most extreme expression of the despondency experienced by
Moscow human rights activists at this time was the suicide of Ilya
Gabay on October 20, 1973. A close friend of Yakir, Gabay was the
father of two children, a poet and a grade-school teacher, and among
the most active and most respected members of the human rights
movement. As the *Chronicle* wrote after his death: "One can only con-
jecture about the cause of his death. But explanations such as the
effects of prison, interrogations, searches, or the enforced idleness of a
talented individual do not accord with one's conception of Gabay. To
all those who knew him Ilya Gabay—an exceptionally compassionate
man with an unrelenting sense of personal responsibility—was the em-
bodiment of a moral presence. And even his last desperate act contains, probably, a message which it is incumbent upon his friends to
understand.[131]

From the end of 1972, at about the same time that the *Chronicle*
stopped publication, the Committee for Human Rights also fell silent.
In September 1972 Valery Chalidze left the committee. In November

he received permission to travel to the United States to lecture and almost immediately after his departure was deprived of Soviet citizenship—one of the first times this method of getting rid of unwanted citizens was used.[132] In December Andrey Tverdokhlebov left the committee,[133] and Grigory Podyapolsky joined the committee.[134] In January 1973 the members of the committee heard a report by Igor Shafarevich on religious legislation in the USSR, and in October the Committee published three more documents. With this its activities came to an end.[135]

Once again public statements were limited to individual or collective letters, just as in the very beginning of the movement, although they were rare and signatures were few. From 1973 to 1974 both enemies and well-wishers spoke of the movement in the past tense. But there is an old superstition: whoever is prematurely buried will live a long life.

CHAPTER 17

The Human Rights Movement
During Détente

In the 1972–73 attack on the human rights movement, the visible parts of the movement were almost wholly destroyed. Most of the leading figures of the movement were removed. Of the twelve persons who signed the appeal to the conference of Communist parties in Budapest early in 1969, only two remained in Moscow; of the fifteen members of the Initiative Group, only four remained. The work of human rights organizations was interrupted. The *Chronicle of Current Events* ceased publication.

The relocation of the movement activists had an effect on the atmosphere in political prison camps; the activists demanded the observance of legality and protested against brutality and tyranny by camp officials. Members of the various national movements and other prisoners began to join the protests together with the activists of human rights movements. Paradoxically, at the time of crisis in the human rights movement in the civilian world, the movement in the political prison camps was growing stronger.

A stream of complaints to various official institutions on living conditions, medical services, and brutality and arbitrariness issued from the prison camps to the officials to whom they were addressed; they were published in *samizdat* as well, and from there, communicated to the West. Bukovsky, who at that time was serving a sentence in camp, said that both the prison guards and their superiors listened to foreign radio broadcasts; if injustice in the camps became known in the West they could expect an inspection and all sorts of unpleasantness from above. Prisoners often learned about their own situation from guards or prison personnel who regularly listened to Western radio stations.[1] This gave the prisoners strength. Statements by prisoners on prison and even political matters, once rare, now became a common occurrence. Statements on nationality problems in the Soviet Union were made jointly by activists of various non-Russian nationalist groups and by Russians.[2] In the Mordovian camps in 1974 a report on the status of political prisoners included the following demands: separation of political prisoners from criminal and military offenders; an end to forced labor and required work norms; an end to restrictions on correspondence, including restrictions on correspondence with foreigners; improvements in medical care; provisions to permit writers, artists, and scientists to engage in creative work; permission to speak in one's native language in camp and during visits with relatives.[3]

From 1969 on, December 10—Human Rights Day—was observed by hunger strikes, and every year more political prisoners with different convictions took part.[4] As a memorial to the victims of the Red Terror, September 5 began to be observed as the day in 1918 when the directive was signed under whose terms prison camps were built, where millions of people subsequently perished. On that day each year candles were lit to their memory.[5] In 1974 October 30 was declared the Day of the Soviet Political Prisoner on the initiative of inmates of the Mordovian and Perm camps.[6] This day is observed by hunger strikes of political prisoners to the present time.

Human rights activists who remained at liberty concentrated all their efforts on helping the political prisoners, who now included their friends. The system of aid to political prisoners continued to function and to be improved. At the initiative of Andrey Tverdokhlebov, Group 73 was announced as a philanthropic organization to aid the children of political prisoners,[7] a symbolic gesture since in practice, help did not reach the prisoners through this group. Those who did help the prisoners were not formally connected; they were not an organization; and they did not publicize their names. Those who contributed aid to the prisoners also shunned publicity. A rare exception was the public donation to aid children of political prisoners made by Yelena Bonner, the wife of Sakharov, in 1975. She created a fund by contributing the prize, Cino del Ducca, won by her husband.[8]

Samizdat of the Early 1970s

Intense work continued in another "invisible" area—*samizdat*. Many seizures during the searches from 1972 to 1974 did not greatly affect the volume of circulating literature. Confiscated material was reduplicated and new works continued to appear. The book that aroused the greatest interest in the entire history of *samizdat* was Solzhenitsyn's *Gulag Archipelago,* which appeared during the heat of the KGB's assault on *samizdat.*

The KGB learned of the existence of *Gulag Archipelago* and set itself the goal of seizing the manuscript. In August 1973 Leningrad KGB agents questioned seventy-year-old Elizaveta Voronyanskaya about it for five days. She could not stand up under the pressure and told them where the manuscript was. Then she went home and took her own life.[9] The copy given to Voronyanskaya was not, of course, the only one in existence: a second copy had already been sent to the West, where it was held awaiting the author's further instructions. Since the existence of the manuscript had ceased to be a secret from the KGB, the author decided to delay publication no longer. In December 1973 the book was published by YMCA Press in Paris; excerpts were broadcast by foreign radio stations into the Soviet Union. Not only dissidents, but common laborers crowded around radios to listen to the terrible truth about their recent past. When the radio station Deutsche Welle announced in August 1973 that it would air some chapters of *Gulag Archipelago*, which had not yet been published, the USSR began to jam the air waves. In September the jamming stopped, evidently by mutual agreement between the respective governments, since it was accompanied by the station's self-imposed restriction on themes unacceptable to the Soviet government. Until 1980 these restrictions preserved a state of "détente."

In evaluating the effects of *Gulag Archipelago*, Soviet historian Roy Medvedev wrote: "I think there are very few people who have not been deeply changed by reading the book. In this connection, I can think of no other book, either in Soviet or world literature, with which to compare it."[10] *Gulag Archipelago* played an enormous role in drawing international attention to political repression in the Soviet Union and to the living conditions of political prisoners.

Fifteen years earlier Pasternak had been the first Soviet writer to receive the Nobel Prize in Literature by publishing through channels not subject to government and Party control: *samizdat* and *tamizdat*. The press that had labelled the author of *Doctor Zhivago* a traitor attacked another Nobel laureate of *samizdat*, the author of *Gulag Archipelago*, yet neither writer was sent to prison camp for publishing his works, as were Sinyavsky and Daniel, although this is not only explained by the protection that the Nobel Prize afforded them, but by a softening of the authorities' approach toward publishing abroad. Solzhenitsyn was arrested, deprived of Soviet citizenship, and on February 13, 1974, expelled from the Soviet Union.

The campaign against Solzhenitsyn was accompanied by persecution of a number or writers whose works had appeared in *samizdat* and *tamizdat,* and they too preserved their freedom. For the majority, punishment was limited to expulsion from the Writers' Union, as were

Vladimir Maksimov, Lev Kopelev, Aleksandr Galich, Lidiya Chukov-skaya, and Vladimir Voynovich in 1973 and 1974.[11]

Naturally, writers who published their works unofficially were not entirely immune from prison camp terms during the seventies. Andrey Amalrik was arrested in May 1969 and in 1970 was sentenced for writing open letters and the essay "Will the Soviet Union Survive until 1984?" After he had served out his term, he received three years of internal exile.[12] In April 1974 the Leningrad writer Mikhail Kheyfets was arrested for writing the introduction to an unpublished collection of poems by Iosif Brodsky (the manuscript had been seized during a search), and sentenced to four years of labor camp.[13] But this form of reprisal became the exception during the seventies. The political scandal of the Sinyavsky-Daniel trial forced the authorities to look for other methods of combating *samizdat*. Although expulsion meant the loss of opportunity to publish openly at home, the writer was no longer threatened with hopeless silence but merely pushed into the arms of *samizdat*. "What will those who are expelled do?" asked Lidiya Chukovskaya in a letter to the secretariat of the Russian Writers' Union: "They will write books. For even prisoners have written and do write books."[14]

The notion of preventing the transformation of *samizdat* into *tamizdat* prompted the Soviet Union to become a party to international copyright conventions, but this method also proved to be ineffective. In 1973 the All-Union Agency for the Protection of Authors' Rights (which supposedly spoke for and acted to protect the interests of Soviet writers) was organized.[15] The intention was that all publications of works by Soviet writers abroad would have to be cleared through this agency. The creation of the agency was to have been supplemented by a resolution that would have enlarged the scope of the government's monopoly on foreign trade to include manuscripts of literary works. But an increasing amount of contemporary Russian literature continued to be published abroad circumventing the copyright agency.

Another method of getting rid of *samizdat* authors by forcing them to emigrate was employed against Joseph Brodsky and Andrey Sinyavsky in 1973, and in 1974 Vladimir Maksimov emigrated from the USSR.

Once the KGB realized the difficulty of pursuing the writers, it tried to stop the *samizdat-tamizdat* process by pursuing those responsible for transmitting the manuscripts. In the summer of 1973 these efforts were concentrated on the transmission to the West of the diaries of Eduard Kuznetsov, an inmate in a special-regimen camp.[16] In connection with this case Gabriel Superfin and Viktor Khaustov were arrested,[17] and a search was conducted at the apartment of the

Moscow art historian Yevgeny Barabanov, who had never shown the slightest tendency toward dissidence publicly. Many books of a religious nature that had been published abroad were found. The search took place on the night of August 24, 1973, at the same time that Voronyanskaya was being interrogated in Leningrad about the *Gulag Archipelago* manuscript. Barabanov's interrogation began on August 27 and continued for about three weeks. The investigator felt that he was in full possession of all the facts: over a period of several months Barabanov's apartment had been bugged and the investigation had evidence that Barabanov had systematically transmitted to the Paris journal, *Herald of the Russian Christian Movement,* unpublished works by Anna Akhmatova, Marina Tsvetayeva, Osip Mandelshtam, Boris Pasternak, Nikolay Berdyaev, Pavel Florensky, and Lev Karsavin, as well as the *Chronicle,* poetry by prisoners Daniel Andreyev and Anatoly Radygin, and the diaries of Kuznetsov. He had received books published abroad. The investigator repeated verbatim confidential conversations Barabanov had had with various people in his own apartment. He told Barabanov's wife: "Your husband's guilt has been proven. A sincere admission would lighten his punishment."

Instead of an admission of guilt, Barabanov gave an open letter to foreign correspondents:

Soviet legislation . . . does not forbid the actions they're trying to charge me with. On the contrary, confiscation of manuscripts and persecution of authors, arbitrary bans on publication, measures taken to stop the publication of certain works not only here, but also abroad—these are clearly illegal actions which must be brought to an end. . . . Thus I have believed, and continue to believe, that the materials I transmitted are an important contribution to the heritage of Russian culture, of Russian thought and self-awareness. . . . I would consider my arrest an act of crude despotism. But the issue concerns not only me; the issue is also whether Russian culture is to exist independently of its approval or non-approval by the official ideology and the censors. . . . .The world would not know the whole truth about our country, all the complexities of its life, the problems of its spirit, the tragic nature of its historical experience. Our century would be deprived of some of its purpose and profundity if it did not absorb this experience.[18]

After the publication and transmission of this letter to the West, the interrogation of Barabanov ceased, and he was not arrested. When the Moscow economist Vladimir Dolgy was implicated in the transmission of Kuznetsov's diaries to the West, he also answered with an open letter to his friends: "I believe that man's duty is to oppose intimidation and treachery with human dignity."[19] The authorities backed down in this case, too.

Then in September 1973 Yelena Bonner came forth with a public statement in which she said that she also had sent various materials abroad and that she was the one who had sent Kuznetsov's diaries out.[20] People who barely knew each other or who did not know each other at all disputed about who was responsible for this act and simultaneously subjected themselves to the threat of many years of imprisonment. Among the possible victims, the KGB decided to limit its reprisals to Superfin and Khaustov, already in custody, in order to prevent a political scandal like that caused by the Sinyavsky-Daniel case and to avoid attracting attention to the *Diaries,* which had in any case already been published.

Samizdat not only performed the service of preserving Russian literature for Russia and for world literature, but it also contributed to the self-knowledge of Soviet society and the formation of the historical perception of its present and future. Years of exchanging ideas through *samizdat* helped both author and reader (and through them, ever wider circles of Soviet society) in forming ideas about possible and desirable changes in the Soviet system.

In the 1950s and 1960s the initial search for an alternative to official propaganda was conducted almost exclusively within a Marxist framework, the only school of thought available for almost half a century. Critics saw official Marxism as having sterilized and distorted the teachings of both Marx and Lenin, and their own task as restoring "true Marxism" and "true Leninism." Many were engaged in studying basic works of Marxism that had been ignored in official programs of education. Especially popular were remarks by Marx and Lenin that the society they envisioned rising out of the ruins of capitalism would be a "kingdom of freedom."

The majority of the critics of the Soviet system at that time were adherents of "true socialism," which, in their perception, differed from bureaucratic Soviet socialism, in that it was a democratic socialism. The degree of democratization necessary was defined variously by critics, and on this difference depended the types of reforms they proposed, all of them variations of "socialism with a human face," in the Czechoslovak manner. The "Prague Spring" was met with warm sympathy; hopes for improving the Soviet system hinged on the success of the Czechoslovak experiment. The best known representative of this reformist position was Roy Medvedev. Both Sakharov and Solzhenitsyn were influenced by his ideas and had close personal contact with him. Not until the early seventies did dissidents, united in their censure of the evils of Soviet society, begin to differ in their explanations of the nature of that society and, particularly, in methods for the country's recovery.

The Soviet invasion of Czechoslovakia dealt a heavy blow to the moral attractiveness of socialism. It destroyed the hope in a possibility of the Soviet leadership moving in the direction of democratization. At the same time as the invasion of Czechoslovakia, a tendency of Soviet leaders to embrace re-Stalinization grew more sharply defined. The economic reform which was about to be started was rejected once and for all, crushed by the Soviet bureaucracy's reluctance to cede, even in part, its omnipotence. For many, the destruction of the hope for democratization sparked a mistrust in any possibility for the "humanization" of socialism, and consideration of other social systems, first and foremost those of the Western free world, although at the beginning thinking was biased against "capitalism" as a stage through which the Soviet Union had already passed.

The first "Westernizer" in *samizdat* was Andrey Sakharov. In June 1968, Sakharov's *Thoughts on Progress, Peaceful Coexistence and Intellectual Freedom* appeared.

Sakharov, an outstanding physicist, participated in the creation of the Soviet hydrogen bomb; he was a member of the Academy of Sciences, recipient of government prizes, and was three times awarded the highly regarded title of Hero of Socialist Labor. He belonged to the highest Soviet scientific elite and enjoyed close relations with high government and military circles. His humanitarian activity had begun with the struggle against nuclear-weapons tests which contaminated the environment and presented an extreme danger to human health. His appeals to Soviet leaders and high-ranking military authorities yielded tangible results: in 1963 the Soviet Union and the United States agreed to conduct all nuclear tests underground, a much less dangerous procedure than the above-ground tests.

In 1966, Sakharov, in his first public appearance, signed a collective protest against re-Stalinization and in Pushkin Square on December 5 joined in a silent demonstration of solidarity with the victims of lawlessness.[21] For the next ten years he participated in these annual demonstrations.

However, most readers learned of Sakharov through his *Thoughts*. Sakharov went beyond the usual topics discussed by dissenters. He did not think only in terms of the country, as they did; he thought on a scale of the whole world. The "progress" and "peaceful coexistence" of his title were global problems. As a "citizen of the world," he viewed the problem of intellectual freedom as applicable not only to the USSR. *Thoughts* are permeated with the conviction that in this century, not a single country can solve its problems in isolation from the rest of humanity; rather, the universal problems of the preservation of peace and the flourishing of humankind on our planet can only be resolved through the common efforts of all countries. Intellectual freedom is a necessary condition for healthy development and is also necessary on a world-wide scale.

Sakharov finished his *Thoughts* at the end of June 1968. He wrote them in the atmosphere of the "Prague Spring," sharing the hopes of his fellow citizens in the possibility of democratic transformations in the USSR in the coming years, and characterizing his view as "deeply socialist." However, Sakharov did not consider the desired direction for world development to be "the victory of communism throughout the whole world" as it was supposed in the official version. He declared himself to be an advocate of convergence, that is, of the world-wide rapprochement of socialism and capitalism, the blending of the two systems in one, open, pluralistic society with a mixed economy.

The Soviet scientific elite to which Sakharov belonged, with access to Western literature and the press, was familiar with the theory of convergence and supported it. However, most of Sakharov's democratically inclined fellow citizens became acquainted with this theory only through his *Thoughts*. The fact that many had been dissuaded from the belief in the ability of socialism leading toward democratization created a fertile soil for a mass acceptance of the theory of convergence. But this did not come about at once. The lack of knowledge about the Western world had taken its toll as had the unaccustomed thinking in "global terms" and the novelty of that approach. Most readers of Sakharov's *Thoughts* acknowledged the desired direction of world development through progress toward peaceful co-existence and intellectual freedom, but perceived his global approach as something too general, too abstract, without any practical application. They did not perceive any way for them to become part of and foster this worldwide process. The discussion focussed on the problems of intellectual freedom not at the international level, but again, in their own country.

Subsequently, Sakharov's own views underwent some changes, primarily his evaluation of the Soviet system. In 1973, in an interview with Ole Stenholm, a Swedish correspondent, Sakharov described the Soviet system as "state capitalism"; in later years he called it "totalitarian socialism" and "party-state totalitarianism."[22] Nevertheless, the main features of Sakharov's worldview as outlined in *Thoughts* did not change. He refined and developed them in the works of later years. A consciousness took root among human rights activists of the unity of the rights of an individual person, the rights of nations, and the rights of humankind. This gradually became for them the chief ideology of the human rights movement.

At the beginning of the 1970s, yet another trend in people's thinking appeared—"neo-Slavophilism."

In September 1973 Solzhenitsyn wrote his "Letter to the Soviet Leaders,"[23] and confidentially mailed it to the addressees. The letter appeared in *samizdat* in March 1974, in accordance with his wishes, immediately after his exile from the Soviet Union. The "Letter to the Leaders" was immediately adopted as the program for the emerging Russian national-religious movement. During discussions centered around this letter, lines of demarcation developed between those who supported his position and those who adhered to the idea of the transformation of the Soviet Union into a just and democratic society. However, human rights activity does not require ideological unanimity among its participants: it is politically neutral. The refusal of Solzhenitsyn and his supporters to cooperate with human rights activists occurred only after 1978, prompted by the purely political aspects of their later position that the Russian government should be authoritarian, not legalist.

Major divergencies of opinion with Solzhenitsyn and his followers were formulated, once again, by Sakharov, in his answer to *Letter to the Soviet Leaders* (published in English in *Kontinent*, Anchor Press/Doubleday, Garden City, New York, 1976):

Solzhenitsyn argues that our country may not yet be ready for a democratic system, and that an authoritarian system combined with legality and Orthodoxy cannot be all that bad if Russia managed to conserve its national vitality under such a system right into the twentieth century. These assertions of Solzhenitsyn's are alien to my way of thinking. I consider a democratic mode of development the only satisfactory one for any country.

In response to Solzhenitsyn's call for isolationism, Sakharov writes:

I object to the notion that our country should be fenced off from the supposedly corrupting influence of the West . . . I am quite convinced . . . that there is no really important problem in the world today which can be solved at the national level. . . . [A] strategy for the development of human society on earth, if it is to be compatible with the continuation of the human species, can only be worked out and put into practice on a global scale. Our country cannot live in economic, scientific, and technical isolation.

Sakharov maintains that:

the nationalist and isolationist tendencies of Solzhenitsyn's thought, and his own patriarchal religious romanticism, lead him into very serious errors. . . . Among the Russian people and the country's leaders are a good many who sympathize with Great Russian nationalism, who are afraid of democratic reforms and of becoming dependent on the West. If they fall on such well-prepared soil, Solzhenitsyn's misconceptions could become dangerous.[24]

❋   ❋   ❋   ❋   ❋   ❋

In the early seventies, the most popular *samizdat* works, besides the works of Pasternak, Amalrik, Marchenko and Solzhenitsyn's *Gulag Archipelago*, were the works of Georgy Vladimov and Vladimir Voynovich; Roy Medvedev's historical investigation of the mass repressions under Stalin, *Let History Judge;* Zhores Medvedev's *Fruit of Meetings Between Scientists of the World,* and other works; Valentin Turchin's *The Inertia of Fear;* the memoirs of Yevgeny Ginzburg, Nadezhda Mandelshtam, and Yekaterina Olitskaya; the philosophical essays of Grigory Pomerants; articles by Boris Shragin (his pseudonyms were Ventsov and Yasny) and those written under the pseudonyms of Alekseyev and Komarov, and fifteen issues of *Social Problems* published by Valery Chalidze from 1969 to 1972. After the precedent set by Frida Vigdorova's transcript of Brodsky's trial and *The White Book* on the Sinyavsky-Daniel trial, it became routine to publish transcripts and related documents of political trials.[25] Collections of documents appeared on the major trials, such as the trial of Bukovsky and other demonstrators in 1967, and the "trial of four" (compiled by Pavel Litvinov). *Red Square at Noon* by N. Gorbanevskaya told of the August 25, 1968 Red Square demonstration. Yulius Telesin published a collection of the most striking statements made by defendants during political trials, *The Final Fourteen Pleas.*

Most important, the *Chronicle of Current Events* once again resumed regular publication. As subsequent events demonstrated, the editors of the *Chronicle* did not stop working after the publication of no. 27 on October 15, 1972. With staff replacements, they continued to collect material for their regular issues without publishing it. In early May 1974, after an interruption of a year and a half, no's. 28, 29, and 30 appeared simultaneously. On May 17, no. 31 appeared.

Members of the Initiative Group for the Defense of Human Rights in the USSR Tatyana Velikhanova, Tatyana Khodorovich, and Sergey Kovalyov gave the new issues to Western correspondents and announced that in the future the correspondents would assist in the distribution of the *Chronicle.* They pointed out that the editors of the *Chronicle* were working under conditions that made it extremely difficult to collect and verify information, but despite the obstacles over the past years the *Chronicle* had gained a reputation as an accurate source of information on violations of human rights.[26] The KGB unwittingly confirmed the irreproachability of the *Chronicle* as an informational source during the investigation of Case no. 24. Out of the first twenty-seven issues of the *Chronicle* the only false report they could find was the death of Baranov.[27]

Confined to one of the criminal camps in Mordovia Baranov had been placed in the psychiatric ward of a hospital next to the work zone for political prisoners. Still in his robe, he ran out of the hospital into the forbidden zone and threw himself at the barbed wire. He was fired upon and bystanders thought he had been killed. But his wounds were not fatal. The investigator in the Yakir-Krasin case used this unintentional error to accuse the *Chronicle* workers of "slander." In May 1973 the editors printed a correction to the earlier report. The correction was printed in *Chronicle of the Defense of Human Rights in the USSR*, which had begun publication in March 1973 in New York in both Russian and English.

The title page of the *Chronicle of the Defense of Human Rights* was designed to look like the typewritten copies of the *Chronicle of Current Events*. It contained the same running title, "The Movement for the Defense of Human Rights in the USSR Continues," and the same epigraph from article 19 of the Universal Declaration of Human Rights. Valery Chalidze, who had settled in New York after being deprived of Soviet citizenship, became the chief editor of the *Chronicle of Human Rights*.[28] The other editors of this magazine were well-known Amnesty International activists, Englishman Peter Reddaway and American Edward Kline. In 1974, Pavel Litvinov, who had emigrated by that time, joined the editorial board. The Chronicle Press (Khronika) became the publisher of the Soviet human rights movement in the West, and when the Chronicle of Current Events resumed publication, Khronika Press in New York printed its issues and sent them back to the USSR.

Issue no. 28 begins with a statement from the editors:

The reason for the interruption in the publication of the Chronicle lies in numerous and unambiguous threats made by the KGB that every issue would be answered with arrests of people suspected of publishing or distributing either old or new issues of the Chronicle. The kind of situation in which people are forced to make a decision affecting others as well as themselves does not require any explanation. However, continued silence would have supported, albeit passively and indirectly, the tactic of taking hostages—a practice incompatible with law, morality, and human dignity. Therefore the Chronicle will renew its publication, trying to adhere to the style and position of former issues.

Resumed publication meant that information channels of the human rights activists had begun working again. Connections between separate groups and with other dissident movements had revived. It meant that once again the human rights movement was in a highly visible position, which was important psychologically—it inspired hope and courage.

There were other indications that the crisis was over. In February 1974, even before the *Chronicle* resumed publication, leading human rights activists had come to the defense of Solzhenitsyn the day after his arrest. In the so-called Moscow appeal,[29] they demanded that the writer be released and that the circumstances surrounding the *Gulag Archipelago* be investigated. This statement was one of the first manifestations of the rebirth of human rights activism.

The Initiative Group for the Defense of Human Rights in the USSR revived after a silence of almost two years. Starting in January 1974 it began to issue new statements. On October 30, 1974 members of the Initiative Group held a press conference presided over by Sakharov,[30] a new mode of action for the Initiative Group and the first press conference held by an independent group concerned with social issues in the USSR. Earlier press conferences had been held by individuals and at very long intervals. (The first one had been held by Amalrik, Bukovsky, and Yakir in 1969. Several press conferences had been given by Sakharov and Solzhenitsyn.) The Initiative Group's press conference was devoted to the basic concern of the group: the defense of those persecuted because of their convictions.

October 30 was declared the Day of the Soviet Political Prisoner, on the initiative of the inmates of the Mordovian and Perm prison camps. Sakharov and the Initiative Group members announced that the press conference was an expression of their solidarity with the political prisoners. Mass hunger strikes of one and two days' duration were being conducted that day in the camps in support of demands that the status of political prisoners be recognized. They gave the correspondents a copy of the text of their demands, as well as an appeal and open letters from the prisoners, among them one addressed to the International Democratic Federation of Women on the position of female political prisoners and the Universal Postal Union on the systematic violation of its regulations in prisons and camps. Reporters received a transcript of an interview with eleven political prisoners from camp no. 35 in the Perm region on their legal status, the prison-camp regimen, relations with administrative personnel, and statements of political prisoners in defense of their own rights. In commemoration of this day, the *Chronicle* devoted an entire issue, no. 33, to the concerns of the prisoners.

The Initiative Group emphasized that political prisoners were "sentenced for actions, beliefs, and intentions that would not be cause for prosecution in a democratic country." They explained that political prisoners take a conscious risk when they appeal to those who are free: "It is their wish that these statements and letters be published; it is the duty of those of us who are free to try to protect them from cruel punishment; that is our responsibility, and yours."[31]

In 1974 another independent association concerned with social issues made its appearance, the Soviet chapter of Amnesty International, founded on the initiative of Valery Chalidze, who had carried on negotiations with the leaders of Amnesty International since 1971. The president was Valentin Turchin, a professor of mathematical physics, and the secretary was Andrey Tverdokhlebov.[32] The chapter consisted primarily of Muscovites, but included residents of other cities. The by-laws of Amnesty International required that members work on the cases of political prisoners from countries other than their own, and the Soviet chapter received the names of their wards from Amnesty International's central bureau through Yugoslavia, Uruguay, and Sri Lanka. Thus, the activities of the Soviet chapter of Amnesty International, while not directly connected to human rights activities in the Soviet Union, was a part of the international movement for human rights, and its appearance increased the contacts of Soviet human rights activists and provided human rights workers with an understanding of human rights in other countries. In addition, the experience gained by one more independent civic association totally legal within the context of Soviet law was in itself a valuable exercise. Both the founders and active members of this group were active in the human rights movement. Tverdokhlebov was one of the founders of the Committee for Human Rights in the USSR and initiated Group 73. Valentin Turchin had participated in the human rights movement since 1968; he was the author of *The Inertia of Fear,* as well as of many open letters. In 1970 he joined Sakharov and Medvedev in an appeal to Brezhnev, suggesting that the Soviet Union be democratized.[33] On October 30 Turchin attended the press conference held in connection with the Day of the Political Prisoner as an Amnesty International observer. Andrey Tverdokhlebov began to publish the *samizdat* journal *Amnesty International,* which familiarized Soviet social opinion with documents and norms of international law on the status of political prisoners and their living conditions.[34]

The renewed activities of open civic associations that had appeared to be defunct and of the *Chronicle of Current Events* elicited the usual reaction of the authorities: more arrests.

In December 1974 Initiative Group member Sergey Kovalyov was arrested, and in April 1975, Andrey Tverdokhlebov.[35] Kovalyov was charged with participating in the Initiative Group, signing several documents of the group, giving Western correspondents material on political prisoners during the October 30 press conference, announcing the resumed publication of the *Chronicle of Current Events,* aiding in the publication of seven issues beginning with no. 28, having in his possession three issues of the *Chronicle of the Catholic Church in Lithuania* and using material from them for the *Chronicle of Current*

Events. On the basis of the final charge, trial venue was set for Vilnius, the capital of Lithuania (December 9–12, 1975), evidently so that there would be fewer witnesses to the trial. The militia detained some of Kovalyov's friends, who wanted to attend the trial, before their train left. They were put under constant surveillance and prevented from travelling to Vilnius. But several . . . Muscovites (including Sakharov), and also Leningraders and Lithuanians who had learned of the trial from foreign radio broadcasts gathered around the court building. The latter were shocked to learn that a Russian had been accused of distributing material on the persecution of the Catholic church in Lithuania.

The most important charge against Kovalyov was assisting in the publication of the *Chronicle.* The issues in which Kovalyov assisted considered 694 cases. The prosecution had examined 172 of them, 89 of which it confirmed as accurate and 83 of which were termed "slanderous." Kovalyov insisted on the accuracy of 72 of those 83, although he did not exclude the possibility of error in the others. Of these 11 possibly erroneously presented cases, the 7 the prosecution considered the most obviously "slanderous" figured in the trial. Only in two minor details was any doubt raised about the *Chronicle*'s reliability. Thus the Kovalyov trial confirmed the high quality of the *Chronicle*'s reports.

Kovalyov was sentenced to seven years in a strict-regimen camp and three years of internal exile.[36] Kovalyov's trial coincided with the ceremony awarding the Nobel Peace Prize to Sakharov. Sakharov could not attend the ceremony but as soon as the news of his award became public, a press campaign was initiated against Sakharov. The high point of that two-month campaign was a letter of condemnation signed by seventy-two academicians and corresponding members of the academy.[37] Congratulations from various places in the USSR, including prison camps, appeared in *samizdat.*[38] The newspaper campaign publicized the fact that Sakharov was awarded the Peace Prize. The public reaction may be gauged from the following report from the *Chronicle:* "A Swedish correspondent walked through the Krasnaya Presnaya Square in Moscow and asked the first twelve passersby he came upon how they felt about the awarding of the Nobel Peace Prize to Sakharov. Ten expressed approval, and two were indignant."[39] Sakharov reacted to the award in his own way: "I hope that it will be good for the political prisoners in our country. I hope it will provide support for the human rights struggle, in which I participate. I consider the award to be not so much a recognition of my personal services as of the services of everyone who struggles for human rights."[40]

Sakharov was never a leader of the human rights movement (the movement does not have leaders), despite some assertions of this sort in the West. He was, however, generally considered to represent the spirit of the movement; he embodies the human rights movement in his own person: self-sacrifice, a willingness to help persons—whether or not they hold the same convictions—who are illegally prosecuted; intellectual tolerance, unwavering insistence on the rights and dignity of the individual, and an aversion to lies and to all forms of violence. He considers the development of "rapprochement between socialist and capitalist systems, accompanied by democratization, demilitarization, and social and technical progress the only alternative to the destruction of mankind."[41] His numerous statements on the human rights movement indicate that he sees moral opposition to illegality and brutality as the real cure, "corresponding to existing necessities and opportunities," for sick Soviet society. By infecting all of humankind with its disease and depriving its own citizens of freedom, the Soviet government poses the fundamental threat to peace.

The task of helping individual political prisoners has required an enormous amount of work every day for the past fifteen years. Sakharov has written in defense of at least two hundred politicals, repeatedly on behalf of many of these. He has spent time at trials, has visited those in exile, dispatched packages to political prisoners, spent time with a constant stream of visitors who turned to him with complaints and has answered many of the thousands of letters he has received. All of this created immense difficulties for Sakharov's scientific work, yet he himself chose this course. The award of the Nobel Peace Prize to Sakharov pointed out the high international prestige enjoyed by the human rights movement, and increased and broadened its influence within the country.

The unifying role of the human rights movement with respect to other dissident movements was indicated in the collection of signatures in defense of Sergey Kovalyov after his sentencing. The letter declared: "We demand a halt to persecution for exchanging ideas and information. We demand a halt to the persecution of people who champion human rights, who defend those who have fallen victim to political repression. We demand the revocation of Sergey Kovalyov's sentence!"[42] It was signed by 179 people—a remarkable fact in itself since that number of signatures had not been seen on human rights documents since 1968. But especially interesting was the fact that almost half the signers were not human rights activists but activists of other movements: Crimean Tartars, Lithuanians, Georgians, Ukrainians, Armenians, and Jews. This was the first instance of such a broadly based joint statement. It is significant that it was a statement in defense of Initiative Group members and the *Chronicle* workers, that is, members of associations representing the human rights movement. The rapid growth in contacts between the human rights and other movements can be traced through the *Chronicle*. no. 28, which appeared in May 1974 after a lengthy interruption, was devoted to events of late 1972 and contained reports collected from twenty-eight different locations; no. 34, which appeared in December 1974, offered reports from seventy-one different locations.

The Tverdokhlebov trial (April 1976) demonstrated that in Moscow the number of open sympathizers had also increased: a large crowd had gathered around the courthouse. An American embassy representative joined foreign correspondents for the first time. It is entirely possible that the interest of Westerners in the fate of the founder of the Soviet chapter of Amnesty International influenced the relatively lenient (by Soviet standards) sentence. Tverdokhlebov received five years of internal exile.[43]

At that time, during 1974–75, came the first organizational successes of non-conformist artists. Even during the darkest periods, individual artists did not work in the style of "socialist realism"; their work was known only to their close friends. The International Youth Festival, which took place in Moscow in the summer of 1957, helped these artists to find each other and to found something like an artists' society. During the Festival, a large exposition was organized of the works of both Soviet and foreign artists. Abstract works were exhibited, as were works in other styles not previously seen publicly in the Soviet Union. Not only was this the first contact between Soviet artists and their foreign colleagues, but they also became acquainted with one another. From that time on the center of creative life for unofficial artists became Lianozovo, a suburb of Moscow. The Lianozovo school was born there; its nucleus consisted of a family of artists: Yevgeny P. Kropivnitsky, his wife, Olga A. Potapova, their son, Lev E. Kropivnitsky, their daughter, Valentina E. Kropivnitskaya and her husband Oskar Rabin.

In 1962, at an official art exhibit at the Manezh Exhibition Hall, several paintings and sculptures shown were not in the style of socialist realism. Premier Khrushchev who visited the exhibit denounced the paintings in strong language, determining the authorities' attitude toward the artist's search beyond the limits of socialist realism until the end of the Khrushchev period. Nothing changed after the "palace revolution" in the Kremlin, particularly because the leadership of the Union of Artists fervently supported the official rejection of non-conformists, who challenged the socialist realists' artistic monopoly. Yet in the 1960s several exhibits were mounted abroad of the works of artists Anatoly Zveryev and Oskar Rabin, and sculptor Ernst Neizvestny. On January 22, 1967, the first public exhibit of artists not recognized in Moscow took place. It was organized in the district Friendship Club on Enthusiasts' Chausee by the engineer Aleksandr Glezer, the public affairs director of the club. Eleven artists participated in the show. Many visitors gathered to see it, but in two hours the exhibit was closed and the artist Oskar Rabin and Aleksandr Glezer were fired from their jobs.[44] Art officials increased their vigilance. Exhibits were only to be held with the permission of the district party committee and of the local cultural administration. Independent artists continued to organize exhibits but only in private apartments. By that time unofficial Soviet artists had become "fashionable" with foreign art lovers among diplomats, correspondents, and tourists and it became the custom to visit the studios of these artists along with the Tretyakov Gallery. Foreigners were happy to purchase paintings that took their fancy. Thus was created a society of artists independent from the authorities not only in spirit, but in the material sense. Unlike contemporary Western artists who had rejected tradition in search of something new, these artists saw that their mission was to preserve those articles of culture which still survived despite the efforts of the authorities to suppress them.

Nonconformist artists made repeated efforts to hold public exhibits, but without success—they were denied the use of public spaces. In September 1974, deciding to hold an open-air exhibition, they chose an empty lot in the southwest part of Moscow at the corner of Profsoyuznaya and Ostrovityanova Streets. They applied to the Moscow City Council with the proper forms but did not obtain permission for the show. They did not receive a rejection; the authorities were simply silent. The organizers of the exhibit sent out numerous invitations to this "first fall art show" to cultural institutions, Soviet newspapers, and foreign correspondents. On September 15, twenty-four artists began to set up the painting exhibition on the empty lot, but soon the show was broken up on the pretext that the lot was supposed to be seeded with grass that day. Bulldozers and street-cleaning machines arrived, with police and men in plainclothes—"representatives of the public." They moved against the artists and viewers, beating them and forcing their arms behind their backs. They took their paintings away, stamped them into the mud, and ran over them with bulldozers, which then headed straight at the crowd. Among those beaten were foreign correspondents: one had a tooth knocked out and another was hit over the head with his own camera. Five of the artists who had been beaten were arrested for "hooliganism."[45] The incident provoked a storm in the international press: "Art Surrounded by Thugs," was the headline in the story in the *Los Angeles Times* (September 17, 1974); "Art Under the Bulldozers" (*Christian Science Monitor*, September 17); "Russians Break Up Modern Art Exhibit With Bulldozers" (*New York Times*, September 16).

Apparently, this reaction explains why the artist's application was accepted to hold a "second show" of their works in two weeks in the open air. The exhibit opened in Izmaylovo, in a field beyond the park. Sixty-five artists took part, not only from Moscow, but from Leningrad, Vladimir, Sverdlovsk, and other cities; the majority of them were non-conformists although also members of the Union of Artists. About 15,000 people visited the exhibit. This time, the authorities simply observed it from the sidelines.

After such a success, the unofficial artists finally found a space for their shows. They received permission to hold a show in the Central Home of Art Workers. In the fall of 1975, a 10-day show took place in Leningrad and in Moscow at the National Economic Achievements Exhibition. Similar exhibits followed in subsequent years, although each time organizers had to fight for many of the paintings particularly disliked by officials of the cultural administration, and they did not win all of these struggles. A painters' section was founded within the City Committee of Graphic Artists, and all the non-conformists were accepted, thus providing them with membership in a union with official status, relieving them of the necessity of explaining to the police that they were not "parasites." They now had registered employment.

From time to time, exhibits were permitted at the end of the 1970s and the beginning of the 1980s. But when Muscovites and Leningraders conceived of an international festival—"Paris-Moscow"—with simultaneous shows in both of these cities, festival participants were taken to the police station under administrative arrest before the opening. A fire was started in the room of art collector Ludmila Kuznetsova, where the paintings for the exhibition were stored, and soon after, under threat of arrest, she was forced to emigrate. The festival did not open.[46]

The Moscow Helsinki Watch Group

On May 12, 1976 at a press conference called by Sakharov, Yury Orlov announced the creation of a group to promote compliance with the Helsinki accords in the USSR. It became known as the Moscow Helsinki Watch Group.[47] Its appearance and the wave of support it generated in the Soviet Union and in the West marked the entry of the human rights movement into a new period, the Helsinki period. This sudden strength was the result of ten years of work by human rights activists, in a time of repression when open statements by activists had been rare and had drawn little attention.

In the late sixties it had seemed, and the KGB leadership supposed, that the human rights movement was finished. It is otherwise impossible to explain why the government took the unusual step in August

1975, of publishing in newspapers the complete text of the Final Act of the Helsinki Accords, including the humanitarian articles. Up until then almost total silence had prevailed within the country on the international obligations of the Soviet Union with regard to human rights. The relevant documents had been published only in special editions with very limited circulation. It is possible that the Soviet leadership was in this instance overcome by a desire to boast to its own people of its success in Helsinki; for many years they had worked toward such an agreement. By the terms of the Final Act the Soviet Union received some substantial benefits; most important of these was recognition of the post–World War II boundaries in Europe in exchange for the promise to observe human rights. Neither the Soviet leaders nor their Western counterparts had counted on substantial changes in Soviet internal politics. The commonly held opinion was that the humanitarian articles of the Final Act were nothing more than a joint gesture by the signing governments in deference to public opinion in democratic countries.

But Soviet citizens, reading the text of the Final Act in the papers, were stunned by the humanitarian articles; it was the first they had heard of any kind of international obligations in the human rights field of their government. A spontaneous reaction was to refer to the Helsinki accords when appealing to Soviet officials in cases where they had refused to satisfy a vital need of the petitioner. In evaluating the Final Act, most human rights workers leaned more toward Western commentators than toward their own compatriots, who lacked experience in the issues involved. Human rights activists thought the Final Act was regressive in comparison with the Universal Declaration of Human Rights and the International Covenants on Human Rights. But there were some, above all Yury Orlov, who saw in this document a new idea.

Orlov had devoted years to searching for ways to create a dialogue between the government and the society. He considered such a dialogue the only means of liberalizing the regime and resolving the economic, political, and moral crisis confronting the Soviet Union. He twice attempted to appeal directly to the government, once in 1956, when he lost his job for it, and was forced to move out of Moscow to Armenia, and again in 1973. After working in Armenia for fifteen years, during which time he became a corresponding member of the Academy of Sciences, he returned to Moscow and, soon after, sent a letter to Brezhnev.[48] Orlov received no direct response, although he once again found himself without work. Similar unsuccessful appeals by Sakharov, Turchin, Medvedev, Chalidze, Solzhenitsyn, and others during 1970–74, convinced him of the necessity of finding intermediaries who would persuade Soviet leaders to listen to their own citizens.

The natural allies of the human rights movement were the publics of the countries of the free world, since their moral values coincided with the traditional values of Western democracies, and the organic pluralism and political neutrality of the human rights movement in the USSR placed it outside the struggle of political forces in the West, making it possible for the movement to be supported by both the left and right.

An attempt was made in 1968 to appeal directly to the public opinion of the West with the petition by Larisa Bogoraz and Pavel Litvinov in connection with the "trial of the four." The first public association founded by human rights activists—the Initiative Group for the Defense of Human Rights in the USSR—appealed to the West, to the UN, in its very first document. The members explained this measure by the absence of answers to direct appeals to Soviet authorities and the evident intention of the authorities to prosecute for such appeals. After this experience there were constant individual and collective letters to various public organizations and public figures in the West. All of these appeals contained information about the harassment of Soviet citizens for the independent public positions, and called on Westerners to help those persecuted.

The West was not indifferent to the fate of dissenters in the USSR. Starting with the trial of Sinyavsky and Daniel, and perhaps even earlier (the cases of Pasternak and Brodsky) the Soviet leaders experienced pressure from the Western public and made concessions at the time, since they were striving to preserve in the West the impression that the USSR was a democratic state. Sometimes there were obvious concessions by the authorities, for example the release of Brodsky and Sinyavsky before they had served their sentences, and the repeal of the death penalty for the hijackers. Less visible, but still a significant result of this pressure was a certain restraint in the harassment of dissenters. I believe that without the consideration of public opinion in the West, the harassment of both human rights activists and members of other movements would have been far more "efficient" and would have encompassed far wider circles and possibly would have been much harsher.

The help of citizens of the West was from the very beginning based chiefly on professional solidarity—writers helped writers, scientists aided scientists, nationalist organizations abroad helped people of their nationality, religious organizations supported their fellow believers; Amnesty International was concerned about all prisoners of conscience. But even this support was limited to protests about the fate of people who were suffering from persecution. No one in the

West appealed to the Soviet leaders with a demand that they observe human rights and the law, although the West was vitally interested in this for the sake of its own security. A firm guarantee of such security can only be expected from an open society where the authorities are under the constant, active control of the public. This is possible only under a real observation of civil rights by the authorities. But the governments of democratic countries did not demonstrate interest in the status of human rights in the USSR. The Soviet Union had ratified the Universal Declaration of Human Rights in the UN, the international covenants on political and economic rights. But not once did the appropriate international organizations try to verify if the Soviet Union was fulfilling its obligations and urge them to fulfill them. The Initiative Group in particular constantly appealed to the UN, but did not receive a single answer.

Orlov saw an opportunity to use the Final Act, despite its unwieldy formulations and purposely convoluted language, to spur the West on to a mediating role. The Final Act pointed out to the signatory countries the legitimacy of mediatory functions in the area of human rights by declaring them to be an indissoluble part of the major goal of the Helsinki accords: the preservation of peace. In this light the question of the degree of freedom given to citizens and the freedom of information available under different governments ceased to be a simple matter of internal affairs and became a general concern. In the case of violations of the humanitarian articles, just as of any other articles, it would be normal for the other partners to apply appropriate pressure. In Orlov's view, the rights of citizens enumerated in the humanitarian articles were to be treated as minimal international standards for countries who had signed the Helsinki accords. Orlov took the spontaneous response of his fellow citizens to the Helsinki accords as a guide to action, especially since the Final Act contains a direct appeal to the citizens of signatory countries to assist their governments in observing the Helsinki accords, because mere governmental efforts for the preservation of peace might well prove inadequate.

The original declaration of the Moscow Helsinki Watch Group read that the group would limit its activities to the humanitarian articles of the Final Act. The group announced that it would accept information on violations of these articles from citizens, compile documents, and familiarize the public and signatory governments of the Helsinki accords with their contents.[49] The eleven persons who signed the constituent document of the Moscow Helsinki Watch Group were: Ludmilla Alexeyeva (myself), Mikhail Bernshtam, Yelena Bonner, Aleksandr Ginzburg, Pyotr Grigorenko, Aleksandr Korchak, Malva Landa,

Anatoly Marchenko, Yury Orlov, Vitaly Rubin, and Anatoly Shcharansky. Most of the founders had been long-time participants in the human rights movement. Rubin and Shcharansky had been active in the Jewish Movement for Emigration to Israel. (The Moscow Helsinki Watch Group was the first independent public group to be joined by Jewish refuseniks.)

The Moscow Helsinki Group called on other countries to create similar groups, but the first response was from the Soviet non-Russian republics. On November 9, 1976 the Ukrainian Helsinki Group was announced; on November 5, the Lithuanian Helsinki Group; on January 14, 1977, the Georgian Helsinki Group; and on April 1, the Armenian Helsinki Group. All of these groups were composed primarily of members of the corresponding national movements. In the Ukraine, Lithuania, and Armenia the Helsinki groups were the first open social-action associations. Similar groups appeared outside of the Soviet Union. In September 1976, the Committee for the Defense of Workers, which became the Committee for Social Defense in the summer of 1977, was formed in Poland, and on January 1 the Charter 77 group appeared in Czechoslovakia. Although these associations did not call themselves Helsinki groups, they took positions on civil rights based on the constitutions of their own countries and on international agreements on human rights signed by their governments. In Hungary, Romania, and East Germany the same demands were made. In the United States the Commission for Security and Cooperation in Europe, or the Helsinki Commission, was formed, of six congressmen, six senators, and one representative each, with consultative authority, from the U.S. State Department, the Defense Department, and the Department of Commerce.[50]

After the Helsinki meeting at which the Final Act was signed, a delegation of American congressmen visited Moscow. Congresswoman Millicent Fenwick met with Yury Orlov, Valentin Turchin, and refusenik Veniamin Levich to hear their views on the Final Act. She was impressed by what they told her, and later introduced a measure for the creation of the Helsinki Commission, making direct use of the opinions of Moscow activists. The commission was to facilitate the fulfillment of the obligations of the signatory countries to the Helsinki accords.[51] Later, public Helsinki groups were formed in the United States and in Western European countries.

Thus, the Moscow Helsinki Group was the seed from which the international Helsinki movement grew. Its purpose was to bring the civil rights situation up to the standards defined in the Final Act in those countries where they fell short. The Moscow Helsinki Group not only initiated a whole era of similar associations, but it stimulated the appearance of several "specialized" human rights associations in the Soviet Union.

On January 5, 1977 the Working Commission to Investigate the Use of Psychiatry for Political Purposes, connected to the Moscow Helsinki Group, was announced.[52] On December 27, 1976 the first document of the Christian Committee for the Defense of the Rights of Religious Believers in the USSR was released. The Christian Committee in turn served as a model for the Catholic Committee for the Defense of the Rights of Religious Believers.

The appearance of these groups coincided with the initial operations of the Russian Fund to Aid Political Prisoners, founded by Solzhenitsyn in Switzerland in 1974, and with the organizational channels to transmit that aid. Funds came from abroad and were distributed in the USSR by Aleksandr Ginzburg, who was helped by those who previously collected funds within the USSR. They remained anonymous but their function changed: they received funds from the distributor and were accountable to him.

Thus, within a short period of time the human rights movement created a network of open associations. At the time, of course, they were few, and there were no more than a few dozen participants, but the human rights movement nevertheless now became visible, stimulating others to join. Western sources, primarily those stations broadcasting to the USSR, revealed the existence of the movement to Soviet citizens.

The contacts of the Moscow human rights activists noticeably broadened. Long-standing relations with Ukrainians, Crimean Tartars, and Lithuanians had, by 1974, been supplemented by contacts with Georgia, Armenia, and the German Movement for Emmigration to West Germany (news of which was regularly published from 1974 on).

The Helsinki groups in the non-Russian republics were not in any way branches of the Moscow Group, even though they had the same general goal: compliance with the humanitarian articles of the Final Act. This brought the national movements closer in ideology and organization to the human rights movement.

From 1974 the *Chronicle of Current Events'* section on the persecution of believers became a regular feature. It contained reports on the Russian Orthodox, Catholic, Baptist, Pentecostal, and Adventist churches. All such contacts went through the Moscow Helsinki Group and were strengthened due to efforts on its part. Baptists had their own long-standing human rights organization: the Council of Relatives of Evangelical Christian Baptist Prisoners, which regularly gave its informational *Bulletin of the Council of Relatives of ECB Prisoners* to the Moscow Group and the *Chronicle.* The Moscow Group made use of these materials in one of its first documents (no. 5),[53] thus conferring international publicity on the practice of taking children from Baptist and Seventh-Day Adventist families who gave them religious instruction. Millions of Soviet citizens learned of this practice through radio broadcasts. Believers of all faiths began bringing their problems to the Moscow Helsinki Group.

Representatives of the Pentecostalists regularly went to Moscow to meet with Moscow Helsinki Group members, and Moscow Group envoys visited Pentecostal communities on several occasions. Formerly rare and superficial, contacts between Moscow human rights activists and the independent Adventist Church groups became constant and friendly.[54] In time both the Pentecostalists and the Adventists arranged for the systematic collection of information on human rights violations within their communities and created their own human rights groups in 1978 and in 1980. Moscow Helsinki Group members helped publish and send to the West the first collection of Pentecostal documents, *My People, Let us Leave This Country.* Through the Moscow Group, human rights groups of Baptists, Pentecostalists, and Adventists were put in touch with the Christian Committee for the Defense of the Rights of Religious Believers in the USSR. For the first time joint human rights statements by Russian Orthodox and Catholics were made, as a result of contacts facilitated through the Moscow Helsinki Group.

Many "messengers" made their individual way to the Moscow Group, often from isolated areas a long distance from Moscow, from which there had previously been no news of independent civic activities and no means of contact. They came asking that illegal actions taken against themselves or those close to them be publicized. In this way, *kolkhoznik* Ivan Kareysha from the village of Vysokoe in the Vitebsk oblast came to the Moscow Helsinki Group. He had been expelled from his *kolkhoz* because of complaints he made about the local authorities and was seeking to be reinstated. Taking upon itself the function of collecting and producing information on human rights violations, the Moscow Group became the voice for civil demands from all strata of Soviet society, from citizens of various ethnic and religious groups, and members of different faiths. The group provided the connecting link between different dissident movements previously isolated from each other; they adopted the tactics of the Moscow Group to stimulate the mediation of the West between the Soviet government and its citizens. Participants in the national and religious movements also began to address appeals to the Belgrade Conference, to the governments that had signed the Helsinki accords, the Congress and President of the United States, world opinion, and "people of good will."

By 1976 the annual Constitution Day (December 5) demonstrations in Pushkin Square, begun in 1965, showed the effects of increased interest and sympathy toward the human rights movement. Formerly several dozen people, usually the same every year, participated. Volunteer police would circle the demonstrators and without a word observe the silent ceremony. At six in the evening the demonstrators would bare their heads for a few minutes as a sign of mourning for constitutional freedoms and the victims of lawlessness.[55] But in 1976 the crowd filled the public garden on Pushkin Square. Volunteer police tried to prevent Sakharov and those with him from reaching the Pushkin statue by encircling and forcing them to one side. But about fifteen regular participants reached the statue. I was among them. At six o'clock the people who had gathered around joined in removing their hats. Those who bared their heads far outnumbered those who did not. For the first time the demonstration was not conducted in silence. Pyotr Grigorenko gave a short speech: a few words mentioning the participation of Vladimir Bukovsky, then languishing in the Vladimir Prison, in the preparations for the first demonstration. He concluded, "I thank you all for coming here to pay your respects to the millions who perished. Thank you for your sympathy for prisoners of conscience!" In response the crowd cried, "We thank you." Bukovsky was released two weeks later: he was sent directly out of the country in exchange for Secretary of the Chilean Communist Party Luis Korvalan. Similar demonstrations occurred in 1976 for the first time in Leningrad and Odessa, also near Pushkin monuments in both cities.[56]

These events, although on a small scale, were an indication of social cohesion firm enough for coordinated statements on general themes. The almost simultaneous formation of Helsinki groups in four non-Russian republics and their joint work with Moscow human rights activists demonstrated the positive prospects for the resolution of the sensitive problem of mutual relations between Russian and non-Russian nationalities on a legal basis. The alliance with Protestant religious movements convinced those in the lower social strata (Baptists, Adventists, Pentecostalists—almost all blue-collar workers) of the feasibility of the human rights position.

The authorities reacted immediately to the creation of the Moscow Helsinki Group. Three days after the formation of the group was announced, leader Yury Orlov was warned that if it became active, he and those associated with him would feel "the full force of the law."[57] But there were no arrests until February 1977. The government doubtlessly understood that to persecute such a group would be a gross violation of the Helsinki accords, in which they placed a great deal of hope. The risk of open retaliation against the Helsinki groups was great.

On January 8, 1977 an explosion rocked the Moscow subway. Several persons were killed. Official Soviet informational sources usually observe a strict silence when natural disasters or plane accidents occur, but the subway explosion was reported by the government to foreign correspondents. An immediate search for the terrorists was begun among the Moscow human rights activists. At meetings held in institutions and industries, as well as through intermediaries in the West, it was reported that the explosion was the work of dissidents.

The Moscow Helsinki Group called a press conference and distributed an announcement to foreign correspondents, "On the Explosion in the Moscow Subway,"

In the Soviet Union, the word "dissident" has become firmly associated with participation in the human rights movement. Dissidents hold a variety of political, religious, and philosophic views; they are united by their efforts to realize fundamental human rights; they absolutely reject violence or calls for violence as a means to their goals. Dissidents are repulsed and disgusted by terrorist methods.[58]

This statement was signed by the Moscow and Ukrainian Helsinki Groups, the Working Commission on Psychiatry, the Christian Committee, the Initiative Group for the Defense of Human Rights in the USSR, the Georgian Initiative Group, and Jewish movement activists.

In a letter Sakharov listed instances of the KGB's criminal activities known to him: "I cannot rid myself of the notion that the Moscow subway explosion and the tragic loss of life it caused are the latest and most dangerous in a series of provocations perpetrated in recent years by the organs of repression." He speculated that whoever committed this crime did so in order to create a pretext for massive persecutions of dissidents and to influence the political climate in the country.[59] On January 25 the deputy general procurator of the USSR, S. I. Gusev, officially warned Sakharov that his statement on the subway explosion was considered "slanderous" and any repetition of this nature would lead to his arrest. On January 27 the U.S. State Department reacted with an expression of admiration for and full confidence in Sakharov,[60] which was greeted with joy by the Helsinki groups. Was this not the first step toward the long-awaited mediation by Western governments?

President Carter almost immediately said that the State Department had acted without conferring with him. Nonetheless, it was clear that this step made an impression on the Soviet government: they stopped referring to the subway explosion as having been instigated by human rights activists.

Open support by the West did not, however, stop repression against the Helsinki groups. During February 1977 the leaders of the Moscow and Ukrainian Helsinki groups, Yury Orlov and Mykola Rudenko, were arrested, as well as members Aleksandr Ginzburg and Oleksa Tykhy, and in March, Anatoly Shcharansky.[61] In Moscow many explained these arrests as a consequence of a lack of firmness on the part of President Carter. In the West certain people began to say that open sympathy for human rights activists created dangers for them. President Carter compensated in January with a personal letter to Sakharov; it was delivered on February 14, soon after the arrest of Orlov and the others.[62] In April Carter made a no less sensational gesture when he received the hero of the human rights movement, Vladimir Bukovsky.

In no. 44 (March 1977), the *Chronicle* reported that a special group in the APN publishing house (the Soviet news agency) was at work on a brochure entitled "The Exile of Sakharov," to be published primarily in foreign languages. The first proofs were ready. It was also reported that in a February-March 1977 meeting of newspaper and journal editors in the agitation and propaganda section of the Central Committee, an unnamed speaker (not from the Central Committee) said that "in order to show our strength without regard for the West it has been decided that fifty of the most active dissidents are to be jailed and all hangers-on to be dealt with harshly. It is time to show strength and not pay attention to the West."[63]

This plan waited until 1980, when Sakharov was, in fact, exiled and when mass arrests of dissidents had replaced earlier selective arrests. In 1977 repression was still concentrated on the Helsinki groups, whose members were arrested one after the other from 1977 until 1979.

On October 4, 1977 the Belgrade conference on verification of the Helsinki accords, to which the Helsinki groups most often addressed their appeals, opened. The democratic countries did not take a strong position; the European countries could not agree to support the American delegation, which accused the Soviet Union of violating the humanitarian articles, and so weakened its efforts. Nonetheless, this was the first international meeting on a governmental level in which the Soviet Union was accused of human rights violations. The form in which this question was raised was also unprecedented: materials from independent social-action associations (such as the Helsinki groups), containing complaints by Soviet citizens about their government were used. It was a great victory for human rights activists and the first step by Western democratic governments toward meeting halfway the forces for liberalization within the Soviet Union.

It appeared that the goal of the Helsinki groups had been reached:

the free world learned about demands that Soviet citizens had made of their government and openly supported those demands, but the anticipated result—a lessening of repression within the USSR—was not forthcoming. The arrests and harsh sentences of members of the Helsinki groups, during and after the Belgrade Conference, confirmed this bitter lesson.[64]

Even before the Belgrade Conference the dilemma facing the Soviet government had become quite obvious: either it lost prestige in the West or lost control over its own citizens. The government preferred to sacrifice its prestige. It would have been possible to attribute the continuing repression to weakness of opposition in the USSR and to insufficient support from the West, but the Polish experiment in 1980–81, despite a unified national movement and more decisive support from the West, had the same outcome.

The Helsinki groups have not, at least until the present, achieved the goal of moderating the repressiveness of government power with the help of Western mediation. For his "miscalculation" Yury Orlov received a sentence of seven years in a strict-regimen camp with five years of internal exile. His fate was shared by the majority of his comrades in the Helsinki groups.[65]

But there was another result no one had anticipated: unification of the human rights movement with religious and national movements working toward the goal of the Moscow Helsinki Group—civic liberties enumerated in the humanitarian articles of the Final Act. The national and religious movements that seemed to be based on a common ground, while not united among themselves, were united, in many respects, in the human rights movement. A kind of coalition was formed under the flag of Helsinki.

Beginning in 1977 the arrests of Moscow Helsinki Group members gave rise to protests comparable in size to the petition campaign of 1968.[66] But in 1968, 70 percent of the petition signers were Muscovites, and the overwhelming majority were liberal intellectuals for whom signing a protest was their first expression of independent civic-mindedness. Unambiguous threats to deprive them of their livelihood had been sufficient to put an end to their civic activities. Only a small number of pioneers refused to retreat in 1968. In 1977–78, on the other hand, only 27 percent of those who signed protests against the Moscow Helsinki Group arrests were Muscovites; most were human rights activists with a long record of service who were inured to adversities resulting from publicly advocating human rights. There were more than a few newcomers taking their first public stand, but, with rare exceptions, they were aware of the risks. The Muscovites who joined the human rights activists themselves became activists, and from then on their signatures regularly appeared under human rights documents.

But the majority of the signers (73 percent) were from outside Moscow, where it is much more dangerous to make public statements.[67] Most of these had long been activists in the human rights, national, or religious movements; the repression against the Moscow Helsinki Group did not diminish their support. Most likely, the signers from outside Moscow were people who directly put others in touch with Moscow activists. But those who sympathized with or even helped the Moscow Helsinki Group were not limited to protest signers.

During 1976–78 the organizational structure of opposition forces that had appeared earlier assumed its final form. Open civic associations became the backbone of the human rights movement and of the national and religious movements working in cooperation with it. This general scheme continued to function until 1980–82, when almost all of the participants of open social-action associations and many of their supporters had been arrested.

From 1977 until 1978 arrests in the Helsinki groups were: three from the Moscow Group (Shcharansky's arrest in March and the earlier arrests of Orlov and Ginzburg); six from the Ukrainian Helsinki Group; one from the Lithuanian Helsinki Group; three from the Georgian Helsinki Group; and two from the Armenian Group; two Moscow Group members, forced into emigration. One other Lithuanian Helsinki Group member left the USSR. The loss was significant even though it did not paralyze the movement. The Georgian Group was the only one effectively liquidated after the arrest of its leading participants; others found fresh members and continued to function.

In 1976 Vladimir Slepak joined the Moscow Helsinki Group, taking the place of Vitaly Rubin, who had received permission to emigrate; in 1977, Naum Meyman, Yury Mnyukh, Sofya Kallistratova, Tatyana Osipova, and Viktor Nekipelov joined; in 1978, Leonard Ternovsky, Feliks Serebrov, and Yury Yarym-Agayev; in 1979, Ivan Kovalyov.

The Moscow Helsinki Group prepared 26 documents for the Belgrade conference; for the Madrid conference in November 1980, 138 documents were prepared.[68] These documents can be divided by theme, corresponding to the provisions of the humanitarian articles of the Final Act:

1. Equal rights and the rights of ethnic groups to determine their own destinies
2. Freedom to choose one's place of residence
3. Freedom to leave and reenter one's country
4. Freedom of conscience

5. The right to know one's rights and to act in accordance with them

6. Inadmissibility of cruelty and degradation of the human dignity of political prisoners

7. Freedom of information and contacts between people

8. The right to a just trial

9. Socioeconomic rights affirmed by the Universal Declaration of Human Rights and by internal pacts on civic and political rights

10. The proposal of the Moscow Helsinki Group to the Belgrade and Madrid conferences on improving controls over compliance with the humanitarian articles

In addition to the Moscow Helsinki Group, also active and effective from 1977 to 1980 were the Christian Committee for the Defense of the Rights of Religious Believers and the Working Commission to Investigate the Use of Psychiatry for Political Purposes, the latter founded by Vyacheslav Bakhmin, Irina Kaplun, Feliks Serebrov, and Dzhemma Kvachevskaya. Pyotr Grigorenko from the Moscow Helsinki Group joined also. The lawyer Sofya Kallistratova acted as legal consultant; a psychiatrist of the Moscow region public hospital system, Aleksandr Voloshanovich, whose name was not revealed until later, served as psychiatric consultant.

The Working Commission operated for four years, until February 1981, when its last participant was arrested. Before that time this tiny group prepared twenty-four voluminous informational bulletins, issued at least once every two months.[69] Even from a cursory glance at these bulletins it is hard to understand how so few people managed to carry out such an enormous task, while carrying on their everyday jobs. With no access to official sources they compiled an index of political prisoners detained in psychiatric hospitals; collected information on dozens of previously unknown victims of psychiatric repression; and collected detailed data on those already known to have been so detained.

Its basic thesis was this: we do not assert that all who are confined to psychiatric hospitals for political reasons are healthy; there are some mentally unsound minds among them; yet it is also necessary to observe the law in the treatment of those who are mentally ill. They kept tabs on all cases of psychiatric prisoners and reported in their bulletin who was ill and what the nature of the illness was; who needed what; who was transferred where, and so forth. The Working Commission assisted in providing material aid to individuals and needy families. They compiled a list of psychiatrists, heads of special psychiatric hospitals, and psychiatric wards in regular hospitals where there were political prisoners. They wrote hundreds of letters to doctors and administrators in an attempt to abolish harmful methods of cure and cruel treatment. On numerous occasions members applied to appropriate Soviet institutions demanding the release of healthy persons and appealed to Western public opinion in hopes that people in the West would work toward the same end. Members often spent their short vacations traveling to remote areas to visit those most in need of help.

On more than one occasion participants in the Working Commission experienced a pleasure rare enough in the human rights movement: the chance to embrace those they had snatched from incarceration. The creation of the Working Commission was a direct response to an increase in the use of psychiatric repression at the end of 1976. Several former psychiatric-hospital inmates had been re-hospitalized simultaneously: Vladimir Borisov in Leningrad, Pyotr Starchik in Moscow, Eduard Fedotov and Aleksandr Argentov in the greater Moscow region. The newly formed Working Commission worked on those cases and within a short period of time obtained the release of all.[70] They also freed Mikhail Kopysov from a psychiatric hospital in the small town of Bobrov, Voronezh region, when the commission publicized the information they received on Kopysov, he thereupon obtained his freedom.[71] For the release of Yury Belov, who had spent seven years in a psychiatric hospital, they fought for two years.[72]

The unusual success of the Working Commission on Psychiatry can be explained above all by the fact that its activities were the continuation of efforts made by many people over a period of twenty years; it began with loners like Sergey Pisarev, but later it grew to include the entire human rights movement.

The self-sacrifice and accomplishment of Vladimir Bukovsky, who had smuggled out the histories of six dissidents confined in psychiatric hospitals, was not in vain. Even though the International Congress of Psychiatrists meeting in Mexico refused to examine these documents, others in the West did and were convinced that psychiatry was indeed used for political purposes in the USSR. Several dissidents who had been confined to psychiatric hospitals emigrated to the West, where they were examined by specialists and found to be mentally sound. In this way the West had learned of the abuse of psychiatry in the USSR by 1977, when the commission began its work, and when a few organizations were trying to stop the practice.[73] The International Congress of Psychiatrists, meeting in Honolulu in 1977, examined the evidence sent by the Working Commission with full confidence in its veracity and passed a resolution condemning the USSR.[74] The continued and active support of Western public opinion was instrumental in the success of the Working Commission on Psychiatry.

In May 1978 Aleksandr Podrabinek was arrested and tried for writing a book, *Punitive Medicine*, on abuses in Soviet psychiatric practice.[75] Shortly after his arrest, Leonard Ternovsky and Irina Grivnina joined the commission.[76] In August 1978 the name of psychiatric consultant Aleksandr Voloshanovich was revealed at a press conference for foreign correspondents. Voloshanovich stated that he had conducted twenty-seven examinations of people who had been placed in psychiatric hospitals for political reasons and had not found a single case for which there was any medical basis for hospitalization and treatment.[77]

In an obvious attempt to avoid an international scandal, in October 1978 the plenum of the All-Union Society of Neurologists and Psychiatrists created a commission to investigate the cases Voloshanovich presented. A few of the patients were released, but Voloshanovich himself began to be persecuted and was forced to emigrate.[78] (He settled in London, where he practices psychiatry.) After Voloshanovich's emigration in February 1980, psychiatrist Anatoly Koryagin took his place as consultant to the commission. In February 1980, V. Bakhmin was arrested, and in April, L. Ternovsky; in September, I. Grivnina; and in January 1981, F. Serebrov.[79] All of them were tried for "slander" under article 190-1 of the RSFSR criminal code, except for Serebrov who was tried under article 70.[80] In February 1981 Koryagin was arrested after examining Aleksey Nikitin, who fought for workers' rights in the Donbass, finding him to be of sound mind, and then reporting his findings to foreign correspondents. Koryagin was sentenced to seven years in a strict-regimen camp and five years of internal exile.[81] He had been the last member of the Working Commission at liberty.

Independent Social-Action Associations, 1978–1979

During 1978–79 a few other independent associations appeared in Moscow. Unlike the Moscow Helsinki Group which was concerned with the entire complex of human rights, their aim was to defend the rights of specific groups or individuals. In this they resembled the Christian Committee for the Defense of the Rights of Religious Believers and the Working Commission against psychiatric abuses. There was also the Initiative Group for the Defense of the Rights of Invalids in the USSR (announced in March 1978), the Free Trade Union (February 1978), and, after the almost instantaneous destruction of this group, the Free Interprofessional Association of Workers (SMOT). In mid-1979 a group called the Right to Emigrate was formed. After some reshuffling of staff the following people, all refuseniks, began to work within this group: Lyudmila Agapova, Ivan Lupachev, Mark Novikov,

Vyacheslav Repnikov, and Vladimir Shepelev. Later they were joined by Vasily Barats.[82] The group set itself the following goals: the regularization of emigration policies and conformity with general democratic norms, the adoption of emigration laws, the collection and publication of civil rights violations in connection with the emigration process.

In June 1979 the group sent to the president of the Supreme Soviet of the USSR a draft entitled "Regulation of Emigration Procedures in the USSR." By attempting to introduce legislation on emigration the group offered practical help in obtaining permission to emigrate. In 1979 it was involved in two cases: the Pentecostalists from Nakhodka and an Iranian community that entered the Soviet Union in 1949 and then was denied permission to return to Iran. Bebut Saman, a member of the Iranian group from Dushanbe, joined the Right to Emigrate.[83] The group also published an informational bulletin.[84]

The Elections 79 group appeared in February 1979. Its members planned to nominate candidates for election to the Supreme Soviet of the USSR in accordance with the constitutional right that the authorities had usurped from its citizenry. Formally, candidates were supposed to be nominated by workers at meetings held in various enterprises located within each electoral district. In fact, candidates are selected from above and then their names are introduced at the workers' meetings.

The next elections were to take place on March 4, 1979. A total of forty people, of which we know the names of Vladimir Sychov, Vadim Baranov, Lyudmila Agapova, and Vladimir Solovyov, united to form the group Elections 79 and approached Sakharov with the suggestion that he become their candidate to the Supreme Soviet. He refused. Roy Medvedev was nominated as candidate to the Supreme Soviet by the Sverdolvsk district of Moscow and engineer Lyudmila Agapova was nominated as candidate to the Soviet of Nationalities from a district in the Moscow suburbs. The group submitted registration papers for their candidates, but did not receive a response in time to meet the deadline stipulated by election regulations. On these grounds the appropriate election commission refused to register their candidates.[85]

The Initiative Group for the Defense of the Rights of Invalids was announced in the customary manner: at a Moscow Helsinki Group press conference. The other independent social-action groups formed during 1978–79 were created and worked outside of the Moscow human rights activists circle. With rare exceptions, they received no support from this circle. They were formed by newcomers whose appearance in the social arena was inspired by the earlier activities of human rights activists. Their heroic opposition had become an exciting example not only to like-minded people, but to those who only superficially grasped the concepts of the human rights movement. The principled rejection of all violent methods and the insistence on tolerance and quiet intellectual pursuits were often foreign ideas to Soviet citizens. Yet people of the most varied convictions were drawn to the leading human rights figures whose names were constantly repeated in foreign broadcasts. These citizens ranged from true fellow thinkers to ones who demanded money from the Fund to Aid Political Prisoners (or from the West's mythic "rain of gold" that the Soviet press constantly talked about) to build an underground radio set, or to supply weapons to underground organizations for the overthrow of the government, not to mention assorted self-interested demands. There were some proposals that either the petitioner himself or Sakharov, or one of his friends, should become leader. Those who visited the Moscow activists usually left disappointed. Even the slightest acquaintance with leading human rights figures revealed that they were neither suited nor interested in playing the role of Robin Hood. Some were offended by the refusal of activists to meet with them, a not uncommon occurrence considering the exhaustive demands on most active members of the human rights movement.

The human rights movement spread to new social levels and entered the international arena, yet its nucleus was still made up of the circle of friends who had founded the movement. They continued to rely on contacts between friends and preserved old work habits. Only those close in spirit to themselves were accepted as participants in the nuclear circle. Others were either not allowed in or were treated as alien, because they did not do things in the same way as the original members. This created ill will, and accusations of conceit and arrogance, and it created an enormous amount of work for a very few people.

Newcomers who received no help undertook independent actions similar to those they heard about over the radio. There were more than a few with reasonable and even innovative ideas, completely in keeping with human rights ideology, as, for example, the Free Trade Union, the Right to Emigrate, or Elections 79. But very often the newcomers' ideas and actions were inconsistent with the ideology and moral norms that had developed among the human rights activists, such as the persistent attempts by the initiator of an independent trade union, Vladimir Klebanov, to convince the KGB that his trade union posed no threat to the government; and the reshuffling of members within the Right to Emigrate because of mutual accusations of cooperation with the KGB. To transform this new layer of activists into effective human rights workers took a long period of patient work, just as it took time in Poland to develop a relationship of intellectuals with the workers. The majority of Moscow activists were ill suited to effect this education. Their pluralism and concept of free will did not allow them to propagandize their ideas; they were only disseminators. In 1977–78 the nucleus of Moscow activists consisted of the movement founders, who considered the movement a form of purely moral opposition without political goals. Their aim was not to widen the movement's scope by including members from other social strata, as had occurred in Poland. The history of relations between movement veterans and the reinforcements that their ceaseless activities spontaneously inspired showed that both sides were unprepared to find a common ground or a common language.

Samizdat of the Late 1970s

During the late 1970s more than one hundred Moscow Helsinki Group documents were added to human rights *samizdat*. They concerned a variety of themes and contained extensive information, surpassed in volume only by the *Chronicle of Current Events*. Data presented were analyzed and evaluated, a practice avoided in the *Chronicle*. There were analytical surveys like "An Evaluation of the Influence of the Conference for Security and Cooperation in Europe in Areas Concerning Human Rights in the USSR (August 1975–August 1976)"[86] and formulations of the Moscow Group's position on questions of principle, such as "A Summing-up of the Belgrade Conference."[87] The Moscow Group's documents, and those of other Helsinki groups, were a solid contribution toward elucidating the human rights problem in the USSR.

The Moscow Group did not issue collections of documents; individual documents were sent to the West as they were written; there they were published in the form of collections by the Khronika Press (New York) in Russian and by the Commission for Security and Cooperation in Europe (Washington) in English.[88] After the arrests of Moscow Helsinki Group members in 1977, four collections were published in an attempt to help with their defense.[89] At the end of 1979, after Tatyana Velikanova's arrest, two collections were compiled in her defense.[90] From 1977 to 1979 the following periodical informational bulletins of the following organizations began to appear regularly: *Working Commission to Investigate the Use of Psychiatry for Political Purposes*,[91] *Initiative Group for the Defense of the Rights of Invalids in the USSR*,[92] *SMOT* (Free Interprofessional Union of Workers),[93] and the *Right to Emigrate*.[94] With the exception of *SMOT*, all included the names and addresses of their compilers on the cover.

At this time foreign correspondents interviewed Sakharov more and more frequently. These interviews were annotated by the *Chronicle;* they appeared in *samizdat;* and they were published in the collection *Alarm and Hope* (before August 1977) by Khronika Press.[95] Three collections of materials critical of the draft for the new constitution of the USSR also appeared during this period.[96]

Publicist works in *samizdat* tended to be collections, often periodical in nature. The first such periodical is the historical *Memory (Pamyat)*, whose editorial board is anonymous. Every issue runs to about six hundred pages and appears about once a year or more. From 1976 to 1983, six collections were issued.[97] This explanation appeared in the editors' foreword:

The editors consider their chief goal to be the collection of historical testimony and its publication and other such material, to . . . introduce it into scientific and social circulation.

The editors stress the importance and enormity of this task in view of the fact that knowledge of the past is constantly being destroyed in the interest of the Soviet official ideology; it has been falsified from the most remote historical periods until the most recent. This is particularly true of the Soviet period, for which myth has been totally substituted for reality. Therefore, the editors of *Memory* give special attention to Soviet history in order to preserve what they can. After all, everyone who has attained the age of 70 must know something about the past that he cannot openly say. This journal was created to collect such testimony, both personal and documentary. This is a vital need of the Soviet society.

Wherever social memory is destroyed, the possibility for all kinds of misfortune and adversity exists. . . . Without the past the future is closed.[98]

In accordance with editorial intentions, *Memory* is a nonpartisan publication, without any political or ideological commitments. In the first issue, the "Memoirs" section contained reminiscences by an emigré with monarchist sympathies, a Petersburg teacher arrested because of her religion, a Communist, and a socialist. This universality was preserved in succeeding collections. Among *samizdat* publications, *Memory* is distinguished by its extensive and highly professional indexes.

In 1979 *Quest (Poiski)* appeared, a literary-publicist journal averaging two to three hundred pages per issue. *Quest* bears the legend "a free Moscow journal" and carries the names of its editors on the title page: Valery Abramkin, Pyotr Abovin-Yegides, Raisa Lert, and Pavel Pryzhov, a pseudonym later revealed to be that of Gleb Pavlovsky. In subsequent issues the names of other members of the editorial staff were published: Vladimir Gershuni, Yury Grimm, Viktor Sokirko, and Viktor Sorokin.[99] The first issue opened with an "invitation":

Our purpose is best contained in a title too long to be used: "The Quest for Mutual Understanding." . . . We invite everyone who stands for mutual understanding to participate in our journal. . . . Since 1953 we have gone through the entire range of hope and disillusionment and have rid ourselves of illusions both old and new. . . . This period, . . . which was cut in two in 1968, has come to an end. . . . Looking at our own dead ends, and placing a finger in our wounds, who would dare to say with complete conviction: "I know the cure; I see a way out"? Bitterness and enmity between those seeking different solutions have made the general impasse even deeper and more aggravating. The editors of *Quest* appeal for give-and-take and patience in the interests of looking for a way out of our general misfortune.[100]

Thus, in its conception, the journal offered a nonpartisan forum for all points of view and ideas. The editors planned to publish six issues per year.

One more serialized collection appeared early in 1978: *In Defense of Economic Freedom*. About two hundred pages in length, it was put out under the pseudonym of Konstantin Burzhuademov by Viktor Sokirko.[101] In 1979 the journal *Sum* (*Summa*) began to appear periodically. It contained papers about and annotations of *samizdat* works, journals, collections, and corresponding Western publications.[102]

At the end of 1978 a sensation was created by the emergence of the literary anthology *Metropol*. Among its editors and authors were both unknown and famous *samizdat* writers, as well as well known authors who had published officially, such as Vasily Aksyonov, Andrey Bitov, Fazil Iskander, Bella Akhmadullina, Vladimir Vysotsky, Semyon Lipkin, and Andrey Voznesensky.[103] This was perhaps the first instance of such a massive unofficial exercise in creative freedom and circumvention of censorship by professional writers. The editors and contributors were immediately subjected to harsh criticism in the Writers' Union and to material pressures, such as cancellations of existing publication contracts and refusals to sign new ones. Demands that the *Metropol* participants recant and renounce were made, but they all remained firm.[104]

While it is possible to limit the list of *samizdat* works released by the midseventies to those appearing in Moscow, by the second half of the seventies such a list would be incomplete without works published in Leningrad. In 1976, three periodicals appeared in that city. The first to come out was the literary almanac *Hours* (*Chasy*), approximately five hundred pages per issue; it was semiannual. The editors included Yuliya Voznesenskaya, Vyacheslav Dolinin and others. Novels, memoirs, plays, poetry, translations, and articles on art by Leningrad writers were included in the almanac.[105] The literary-religious and philosophical journal 37 derived its name from the apartment number of its editor, Viktor Krivulin. Other editors were: Lev Rudkevich, Natalya Kononova, and Tatyana Goricheva. Approximately 250 pages in length, it is issued once every two months.[106] The collection *Art Archives*, published by Vadim Nechayev and Marina Nedrobova, contained prose, poetry, essays, articles on art, as well as a chronicle of cultural events.[107] At the very end of 1979 the journal *Women and Russia* appeared; it was intended as a periodical that would reflect the appearance of a new independent movement in the USSR: the feminist movement.[108]

Leningrad

Beginning in the midseventies, independent social actions surfaced in the form of a "second," unofficial culture. This "second culture" was the work of Leningrad's traditionally large layer of professionals trained in the humanities who were not employed and had no prospects of ever being employed in their fields. There are no fewer than a dozen institutions for the humanities here, including the first-rate departments of literature and history at Leningrad State University, the Academy of Arts, the Herzen Institute, as well as film-making and theater institutes. At the same time, there are far fewer establishments in Leningrad than in Moscow that employ specialists in the humanities. In the fifties, when Leningrad was still devastated as a result of the blockade during the Second World War, the overabundance of professionals in the humanities was not especially noticeable; by the midsixties graduates of humanities institutions found it nearly impossible to find even the most modest position in their fields.

Gradually, as noted earlier, an entire social stratum was formed of graduates in the humanities who made their living as unskilled laborers. To a lesser extent, those specializing in the exact sciences also had difficulty finding suitable work. The presence of this stratum of "superfluous people" explains the deep conformism of even decent members of the Leningrad "civil service" intelligentsia. The slightest offense to one's superiors or, to an even greater extent, to the KGB threatened a loss of one's livelihood and status. Among the liberal intelligentsia this strict dependence gave rise to a general avoidance of the "vulgarities of life" and of involvement in vital problems by the tactic of becoming completely absorbed in one's profession. An entire cult grew up around one's profession. Not only did it provide a living, but it gave meaning to life and was used as a justification of one's actions: "I preserve and develop Russian culture; that in itself justifies any sacrifice."

There were few contacts between this "civil service" intelligentsia and their "superfluous" colleagues, who constituted a separate world. These superfluous people preferred low-paying jobs as elevator operators, watchmen, and stokers as long as they were assured of ample leisure time. Like the service intelligentsia, they distanced themselves from everyday life for the sake of "higher" interests. This way of life was inculcated by the best teachers, themselves from the service intelligentsia, during their student years, and was facilitated by the lack of independent social action and the narrow range of social contacts, usually formed during student years. The only forms of spiritual and intellectual life that remained were books and friends. This virtual isolation, combined with pride in the cultural tradition of Leningrad, strengthened the cult of "pure spirituality," "pure art," and an avoidance of the problems of life and society among the superfluous Leningrad intelligentsia.

Combined with a traditional rivalry with Moscow, these attitudes created hostility toward the independent Moscow activists, "bustling about on the surface of life," and gave rise to a slogan frequently encountered in Leningrad: Down with politics. Having divorced itself from life, the superfluous Leningrad intelligentsia occupied itself with the search for new art forms and new spheres of spiritual life, usually in forbidden areas like religious philosophy and art, at a time when Muscovites had barely considered these areas. The lack of contact with human rights activists can be explained not only by the lack of interest in human rights issues, but also by tactical considerations: such contact would have attracted the attention of the KGB more than did the unusual interests of the superfluous intelligentsia.

The process of consolidation was directly related to the growth of this superfluous stratum. In the sixties, the Café of Poets on Poltava Street became their unofficial meeting place. The KGB tolerated this gathering spot because it made the task of surveillance easier. Nonetheless, the café was later transformed into the Café of Komsomol Poets and finally closed down. From time to time readings were arranged at special gatherings at the House of Writers, but they were also forbidden, as were attempts to hold readings at Leningrad State University and the Polytechnic Institute. On one occasion a "tournament of poets" was planned at Tsarskoe Selo, but it was broken up.[109] These events did serve to bring together people with similar interests, and large groups of friends, similar to those in Moscow during the fifties, were formed. Access to like-minded people enlivened and strengthened these Leningraders.

The fundamental artistic and moral principles of participants in the second culture (as they themselves dubbed the movement) were creative freedom and free choice in questions of art and style. They considered themselves heirs and continuers of the 1920s of Russian culture. It was as if they were stepping over the intervening years of government interference that had perverted this tradition and the subsequent discrediting and abolition of all artistic and intellectual movements, except socialist realism and dialectical materialism, for the sake of uniformity. In the midseventies this second culture emerged openly after years of semivoluntary underground existence. Artists were the first to break through. By their own admission, their activity was prompted by an unofficial exhibit destroyed by bulldozers on September 15, 1974 and by the Izmaylovo exhibit, both in Moscow.[110] A few Leningrad artists participated in these and in later exhibits at the Agricultural Exhibition grounds in Moscow: Yury Zharkikh, Yevgeny Rukhin, Vladimir Ovchinnikov, and others. This experience contributed to a collective victory over inertia and fear of public exposure.

The first exhibit by second culture artists took place at the Gaas House of Culture in December 1974. A few exhibits in other houses of culture followed, and then exhibits were hung in apartments of Leningrad art collectors such as Natalya Kazarinova and Georgy Mikhaylov. In 1977 physicist Marina Nedrobova and her husband, writer Vadim Nechayev, created a museum of contemporary painting in their apartment that was open to all. Exhibits, discussions, and conferences were held there.[111]

In 1974, while Leningrad nonconformist artists were fighting for the right to exhibit, a literary group consisting of employed professionals conceived the idea of publishing a five-volume collection of works by Joseph Brodsky (in *samizdat*), who by this time had been forced to emigrate. Many people helped prepare the edition by bringing in typed copies of poems they had saved and writing down others they had committed to memory. Mikhail Kheyfets, a grade-school literature teacher and author of several books on the history of the Russian revolutionary movement, undertook to write the introduction, which Yefim Etkind, a well-known literary scholar at the Herzen Institute, read and commented upon. Kheyfets was soon arrested in connection with this unauthorized edition; so was the writer Vladimir Maramzin, a friend who had helped collect materials. After recanting in court, Maramzin was released; then Etkind emigrated. Kheyfets received four years in camp with two years of internal exile, after which he too emigrated from the USSR.[112]

These drastic reprisals against their "employed" colleagues did not prevent the first attempt to second culture writers and artists to end an intolerable isolation. Following the example of Leningrad artists, they also tried to obtain official recognition. In the summer of 1975, thirty-two unpublished Leningrad poets gathered together their best works from a ten-year period of forced underground writing in a collection called *Lepta* (Contribution). They took *Lepta* to the Leningrad Publishing House, where it was rejected with the insulting explanation that it was of low artistic value. However, the local KGB was interested in *Lepta*. Agents expressed a desire to meet with the editors and contributors, who, tempted by the KGB's promise to help them publish the journal, invited them for a discussion. Inexperienced in such matters, the writers agreed to try their luck. Yuliya Voznesenskaya, whom the editors singled out as their representative, met with the agents on several occasions. She tried to convince them that the authors were not conspirators or revolutionaries, but simply poets who yearned for an audience. As time went on, no progress was made toward publishing the collection. So the second culture activists took unauthorized steps to realize their right to an audience.[113]

A group of poets and artists sent the Leningrad Office of Park and Garden Management a notice that they planned to hold a reading of their poetry in commemoration of the Decembrists on December 14, 1975 at eleven o'clock in the morning on Senate Square where 150 years earlier the Decembrists had revolted. On December 14, Senate Square was surrounded and blocked off by militia and volunteer police. Streets leading onto the square were blocked by cars. Six people who had signed the application for the reading were detained on their way to the square. The artists Igor Sinyavin and Vadim Filimonov broke through to the square and were arrested. Filimonov managed to throw a poster into the Neva River; it floated text-side up: "The Decembrists Were the First Russian Dissidents." In March 1976 an application was sent to the Office of Culture. This time second culture activists asked that a place be provided to hold an evening commemorating the poet Nikolay Gumilyov on the ninetieth anniversary of his birth. (Gumilyov was shot in 1921 for his participation in a conspiracy against the new Bolshevik government.)[114]

After these maneuvers, discussions with the KGB on publication of *Lepta* were resumed, but the collection never saw the light of day. In 1976, three thick journals appeared in *samizdat: Hours, 37,* and *Art Archives.* In these journals unpublished Leningraders specializing in various areas of the humanities and artists of various schools found a haven. *Art Archives* provided a refuge for artists and art specialists; *37* appeared as a result of a series of seminars on literary, artistic, and philosophical-theological themes.

Once they began to struggle for their rights, second culture activists used methods similar to those of the human rights activists. Written during the night, expressions of sympathy and solidarity on the sides of streetcars were seen by Leningraders the morning of April 6, the first day of Andrey Tverdokhlebov's trial in Moscow. The signs read: "Freedom for Political Prisoners" and "Freedom for Tverdokhlebov."[115] At this time (spring 1976) Yuliya Voznesenskaya, artists Igor Sinyavin and Vadim Filimonov, and Poet Gennady Trifonov began preparations for an illustrated collection of poetry, *Mera vremeni* (Measure of Time). They also participated in preparations for the next event of independent artists: outdoor exhibits like the Belyaev exhibit in Moscow. They chose to hold the exhibit on the embankment near the Peter and Paul Fortress on June 1. It was broken up by the militia and the KGB; on June 12 attempts were made to repeat the exhibit, but they were also unsuccessful. Then artists anonymously expressed their in- dignation, without avoiding politics. On the night of August 3, an enormous sign was painted on the walls of the Peter and Paul Fortress: "You strangle freedom, but the soul of man recognizes no chains." Signs appeared in other places reading: "Down with the Party Bourgeoisie," "The Party is an Enemy of the People," "The USSR is a Prison," "Freedom for Political Prisoners," and "Listen to the Voice of America."[116] On September 13, artists Yuly Rybakov and Oleg Volkov, together with Natalya Lesnichenko and Yuliya Voznesenskaya, were arrested. The men were blackmailed by threats to the women. Rybakov and Volkov confessed to having painted the signs that appeared in the city in April and August.[117]

The first demonstration for human rights in Leningrad took place on December 5, 1976 at the same time as the traditional Pushkin Square demonstration in Moscow. As in the capital, Leningrad demonstrators, who numbered thirteen, bared their heads near the city's Pushkin monument as a sign of mourning for constitutional freedoms and of solidarity with victims. The demonstration was peaceful, and unsuspecting militia saw nothing criminal in the silent ceremony. But the authorities were prepared for a repetition of the reading to commemorate the Decembrists on December 13, 1976. Only seven of the fifty who planned to participate were able to reach the square, and they were immediately detained.[118]

On December 21 Yuliya Voznesenskaya was arrested, and on December 29 she was sentenced to five years of internal exile for *Measure of Time*, which never was published. The claim made in the editor's manifesto that there was no freedom of press or free expression in the USSR was considered slanderous.[119] The remaining members of the editorial board were also "neutralized": Trifonov and Filimonov were sentenced on criminal charges, and Sinyavin was allowed to emigrate.[120]

The trial of Rybakov and Volkov took place in March 1977. They agreed to a trial scenario in which the signs were referred to as "hooliganism" and "destruction of state property," without any mention of their content. Friends of the defendants and foreign correspondents were permitted in the courtroom, where the defendants obediently repeated what they were ordered to say. Rybakov was given six years in a harsh-regimen camp, and Volkov seven years in a strict-regimen camp.[121]

The trials did not prevent a rapprochement between the activists of the second culture and the human rights movement. Many independent Leningrad intellectuals began to realize that their former aloofness from social problems threatened the second culture with spiritual crisis, sterilization, and decline. Just as in Moscow, human rights demonstrations became annual occurrences in Leningrad. Since 1977 they have been held on Human Rights Day—December 10. When Leningrad nonconformist artists decided to hold an exhibit in honor of the Venetian Bienalle–77, they timed its opening to coincide with the first day of the Sakharov hearings in Rome, on November 15; seventeen Leningrad and seven Moscow artists participated in the exhibit.[122] Of all the independent social-action movements in Leningrad, second culture was the most widespread and most active.

In spite of favorable changes in relations with Moscow human rights activists, the Moscow variant of the human rights movement did not find followers in Leningrad. The only consistent and independent human rights worker in Leningrad to remain active over the years was Ernst Orlovsky.[123] Leningraders who were drawn to human rights activities usually cooperated with Muscovites, as they had in the past. Among the founders of SMOT (Free Interprofessional Union of Workers) created in Moscow were Leningraders Lev Volokhonsky, Nikolay Nikitin, Vladimir Borisov, and Aleksandr Ivanchenko.

The KGB suspected Leningraders of participating in the serial collection *Memory,* the journal *Quest,* and the *Chronicle of Current Events.* In any case, searches were conducted in Leningrad simultaneously with those conducted in Moscow during the spring of 1979. In connection with *Memory,* the homes of Arseny Roginsky, Sergey Dedyulin, and Valery Sazhin were searched. The investigation of the other publications was intensified, and many people were called in for questioning. In August 1981 Arseny Roginsky was arrested and sentenced to four years of camp on fabricated criminal charges.[124]

Although much weaker than second culture, socialist trends had persisted since the midfifties. To this trend belong the ineradicable distributors of leaflets, most often with criticism of the Soviet system from a "purely socialist" point of view. It is not always clear if these distributors act alone or in groups, since they are not always apprehended.

There were two more Leningrad trials. In May 1978, photographer Aleksandr Lyapin from near Leningrad tried to immolate himself in Moscow's Red Square in protest of Yury Orlov's sentence. Twenty-five percent of his body was covered with burns; he was charged with "hooliganism."[125] On January 6, 1979, brothers Vadim and Aleksey Arenberg, Vadim's wife Lyudmila Krylova, and her friend Lyudmila Listvina tried to highjack an airplane. They planned to exchange the plane for the release of arrested Moscow Helsinki Group members.[126] These events clearly indicate that admiration for human rights activists had been transformed into actions that were in no way advocated by them.

Odessa

In the petition campaign of 1968, in which 70 percent of the signers were Muscovites, some of the signers were members of the Ukrainian national movement and the Novosibirsk academic settlement. Two signers were from Odessa: Leonid Tymchuk and V. Kryukov.[127] They differed from other signers by their social position: one was a sailor, the other a lathe operator. (Workers made up only 6 percent of the total number of signers in 1968.)[128] They were not ordinary workers. In his open letter, Tymchuk quoted Cicero's "On the Commonwealth" and John Robinson Pierce's *Symbols, Signals, and Noise;* Kryukov quoted Graham Greene and John Donne. Their letters indicated that they had discussed problems of democracy and law with each other and possibly with others before they decided to undertake the unusual step of publicly standing up for democratic and legal values. Apparently they belonged to a circle of friends who shared their views.

Although Odessa is located in the Ukraine, it is, like Kharkov, a Russified city. Odessa dissidents, like Kharkov dissidents, were drawn to Moscow rather than to Kiev, despite close ties with Nina Strokata, a Ukrainian-national-movement activist living in Odessa, who named Tymchuk her power of attorney after her arrest in 1971.[129]

Until 1974 there were only a few short reports from Odessa, and they all concerned *samizdat.* In 1967 correspondent student David Naydis, author of a work on the likelihood of a rebirth of Stalinism (which was not discovered during the search of his home), was charged in connection with leaflets on the Jewish question.[130] In 1969 Yelena Krupko was fired from her position at Odessa University, after working there for eighteen years, for loaning *samizdat* works by Sinyavsky, Daniel, and Solzhenitsyn.[131] One trial in the series of trials of Jews in 1970–71 took place in Odessa: that of librarian Reyza Palatnik. She was given a three-year sentence because an appeal of a Jewish movement activist, *samizdat* copies of works by Akhmatova, Mandelshtam, Galich, Okudzhava, and open letters from Lidiya Chukovskaya were found during a search of her apartment. Chukovskaya, Sakharov, and Chalidze made public appeals in her behalf. During a search of Tymchuk's apartment in 1974 a copy of the "Moscow Appeal in Defense of Solzhenitsyn" was found. On the spot, Tymchuk added his own signature.[132] From that time on other Odessa residents—friends and fellow thinkers of Tymchuk—began to be mentioned in the *Chronicle of Current Events*. Teacher Anna Golumbiyevskaya was expelled from the Party and dismissed from her position for mentioning Solzhenitsyn favorably during a literature class.[133]

In the summer of 1974 a photocopy of *Gulag Archipelago* was confiscated from Alekseyev-Popov, a docent at Odessa University. He said he had obtained his copy from Gleb Pavlovsky, who in turn implicated a young electrician, Vyacheslav Igrunov, known to the KGB since 1968 because of his interest in *samizdat*. After Pavlovsky's testimony, a search made of Igrunov's apartment revealed *samizdat* materials, and thus began the Igrunov case.[134] Soon afterwards, a friend who came to visit Igrunov from Kalinin, physicist Oleg Kurs, was detained. He had brought with him a briefcase full of photocopies of *tamizdat* books, including *Gulag Archipelago*, Grossman's *Forever Flowing*, the two-volume collection of Mandelshtam's works, and a microfilm of A. Avtorkhanov's *The Technology of Power*. On the basis of Pavlovsky's testimony, a few of his and Igrunov's mutual friends were questioned, but nobody said anything about *samizdat*.

During political seminars at Odessa institutions of higher learning, speakers explained that after the arrest of Palatnik and Strokata, Igrunov became the leader of the Odessa group. On March 1, 1975, Igrunov was arrested after microfilms of works by Avtorkhanov, Solzhenitsyn, and others, as well as photographic equipment, were taken from Valery Rezak in a secluded meteorological station in the Crimea. Rezak testified that Igrunov had given him the film, which he had brought from Moscow. Rezak admitted that for several years he had been paid to make photocopies from film of *tamizdat* books for Igrunov. Igrunov himself refused to cooperate in the investigation in any way after announcing that he considered his activities neither anti-Soviet nor illegal.[135] He was declared mentally unsound and confined to a psychiatric hospital until 1976.[136]

About thirty people, whose participation in the Igrunov case varied

Movement for
Human Rights

Larisa Bogoraz and Pavel Litvinov,
authors of first open appeal of Soviet
dissidents to Western opinion, 1968

Yuly Daniel, after his release from a five-
year sentence for publishing his novels
abroad, Moscow, 1971

Yulius Telesin, distributor of *samizdat* in the late 1960s

Vyacheslav Igrunov, after his release from a 1976 sentence for possession of a *samizdat* library in Odessa

Anatoly Marchenko, author of *My Testimony* (1968), the first book about the post-Stalin political camps, Moscow, 1980, between arrests

Natalya Gorbanevskaya, first editor of *Chronicle of Current Events*, with her children, 1973

Anatoly Yakobson, editor of *CCE* in 1970–72, Moscow, 1972

Ivan Kovalyov and Aleksandr Lavut, sentenced for work with *CCE* and Moscow Helsinki Watch Group

Irina Yakir, daughter of Pyotr Yakir and assistant of *CCE,* 1969–72, Moscow, 1980

Valery Abramkin, Moscow, 1972, who was sentenced in 1979 for participating in the independent *samizdat* magazine *Quest*

Vladimir Gershuni, Moscow, 1980, who was sentenced in 1983 for participating in *Quest* and the information bulletin of SMOT

Sergey Pisarev, initiator
of struggle against psy-
chiatric persecution for
political reasons

Dr. Anatoly Koryagin (R, rear), consultant for the Working Commission to Investigate the Abuse of Psychiatry for Political Purposes, with
his family, in Kharkov, 1979, before his arrest

Aleksandr Podrabinek, Irina Kaplun, Vyacheslav Bakhmin, founding
members of the Psychiatric Commission

Ilya Rips, who tried self-immolation to protest invasion of Czechoslovakia and now lives in Israel

Dr. Valentin Turchin, first head of Soviet branch of Amnesty International

Members of Initiative Group for Defense of Human Rights in the USSR: (L to R) Sergey Kovalyov, Tatyana Khodorovich, Tatyana Velikanova, Grigory Podyapolsky, Anatoly Levitin-Krasnov

The Moscow Trust Group, September 1982: (L-R, rear) Gennady Krochik, Yury Medvedkov, Mariya Fleyshgakker, Mark Reitman, Natasha Batovrin. (L-R, front) Igor Sobkov, Viktor Blok, Vladimir Fleishakker, Olga Medvedkova, Vladimir Brodsky, Valery Godyaki

(L) Pyotr Yakir in 1979, active in human rights movement until his arrest in 1972; (L, below) Andrey Tverdokhlebov, founding member of the Human Rights Committee, Group-73 and Soviet branch of Amnesty International, Moscow, 1974; (R) Svetlana and Vladlen Pavlenkov, human rights activists, Gorky, 1974

Human rights activists of Kharkov, 1969: (L to R, rear) Semyen Podolsky, Arkady Levin, Genrikh Altunyan, Pyotr Grigorenko, Vladislav Nedobora; (L to R, front) Aleksandr Kalinovsky, Roman Kaplan (now in Israel), Vladimir Ponomaryov

Yuliya Voznesenskaya and Tatyana Goricheva,
activists of the "Second Culture" in Leningrad,
1980

Arseny Roginsky, sentenced in 1981 for participating in the underground publication *Memory*,
Leningrad, 1979, in front of billboard, "In unity, strength. Victory is in struggle."

Dr. Yury Orlov, leader of Moscow Helsinki Watch Group, in Moscow, just before being taken prisoner, February 1977

A typical gathering outside the Moscow trial of Dr. Yury Orlov—one of the few available means of expressing support. Andrey Sakharov, fourth from left

considerably, were questioned in Odessa, Kalinin, Moscow, Leningrad, and other cities. It became clear that the investigators were looking for the *"samizdat* library," presumably located in Odessa, and were especially interested in Igrunov's Moscow contacts. In order to find the library and its Moscow suppliers, a listening device was installed in Tymchuk's apartment. Tymchuk found and disconnected it, and hid it in his room. The KGB searched his place and confiscated his property. With the help of the militia they involved Tymchuk in a provocation. A militiaman stopped him in the street, put him in a militia car with several other people, including two women. When they arrived at the station, the women testified that Tymchuk had insulted and abused them. The other passengers appeared as "witnesses" and confirmed the women's testimony. Tymchuk was arrested and served fifteen days for "hooliganism."[137]

The KGB also tried to gather evidence about the library from Tymchuk's friend, Aleksey Tikhomolov. He was picked up on the street and taken to a hotel room, where two agents questioned him about Igrunov and his friends. They asked Tikhomolov to become an informer, but he agreed only to supply information on the activities of Zionists, after which they all sat down to supper. The next day Tikhomolov told his friends what had happened, and his deal with the KGB was over.[138]

The activities of the Odessa human rights activists did not end with the arrest of Igrunov and the associated persecution of others. At 6:00 P.M. on December 5, 1976 the first human rights demonstration took place in Odessa; thirteen people gathered at the Pushkin monument. Like their comrades in Moscow and Leningrad, they stood silently with bared heads.[139]

Contacts with Moscow were not broken, but on the contrary, strengthened. After the Moscow Helsinki Group arrests in 1977, residents of Odessa and Kharkov wrote a letter containing ten signatures in defense of those arrested,[140] indicating that the Odessa and Kharkov activists were acquainted with each other.

Samizdat did not disappear in Odessa. This we know from the arrest of Viktor Goncharov in the summer of 1976[141] and the case of Vasily Barladyanu, arrested in March 1977.[142] Goncharov distributed *samizdat* from Moscow and Barladyanu from both Moscow and Kiev (documents of the Ukrainian Helsinki Group). Their friends continued to be persecuted for writing letters in their defense and, as before, for distributing human rights, appeals, and religious literature, as well as for trying to broaden their knowledge through unofficial seminars on religion, art history, and other subjects.[143] In May 1978 material for a literary-publicist almanac that Igrunov and others planned to publish was confiscated during a search of Igrunov's apartment.[144] In 1980 librarian Anna Mikhaylenko was arrested, also for distributing *samizdat* and participating in seminars on Ukrainian culture.[145] In 1982 physicist Pyotr Butov was arrested. This arrest was preceded by searches, beginning in the summer of 1981, at the homes of both Butov and his acquaintances. Copies of the *Chronicle of Current Events* and of the *Chronicle of the Catholic Church in Lithuania* were confiscated, as well as photocopies of many *samizdat* and *tamizdat* works.[146] At the interrogations it became clear that the investigators were very familiar with the topics of conversations in the room where Butov worked. It would seem that a bugging device had been planted there. After Butov's arrest, his wife was told that the reason for his arrest was his refusal to hand over "the library and files of films with anti-Soviet literature," and name the person who had made the photocopies. Butov was tried and sentenced to five years of strict-regimen labor camp and two years of exile.[147] The library apparently continues to exist.

Kuybyshev

Beginning in 1973 a circle of "nihilisticly-inclined youth" in Kuybyshev fell under KGB surveillance.[148] It is unlikely that *samizdat* was widely circulated among members of this group; it is more likely that foreign broadcasts were their basic source of information and ideas. They taped foreign broadcasts of interest and then made written copies from the tapes. Some of the programs were then read aloud and discussed. Only tapes of broadcasts, handwritten transcriptions, and statements made outside the group on the lack of free speech in the USSR, figured in the indictment against Vladislav Bebko, one of their leaders who was arrested in 1978.[149] Bebko, from a working-class family and himself a worker, was twenty-five at the time of his arrest. His friends were either young workers or students at technical institutes. In 1976 they decided to "take to the streets," at first without any political overtones. On April 1, thirty to forty people set off from Samara Square, chanting humorous slogans. Within half an hour the militia blocked their path; twelve were detained and three were given ten- to fifteen-day sentences for "disturbing the peace."

The following year on April 1, Bebko and two friends, workers V. Solomko and Anatoly Sarbayev, held a demonstration, using placards calling for freedom of speech. This time there were no arrests: officials took the placards away and released the youths.[150]

In 1977 Bebko entered a polytechnical institute. In the winter of 1978 he and Sarbayev were warned to stop "engaging in anti-Soviet conversations, distributing anti-Soviet and Charter-77 materials, and to stop attempting to create an anti-Soviet group."[151] On the anniversary of the October Revolution, Bebko ripped up an official poster and was arrested for hooliganism and slander; he was sentenced to three years in camp. His trial was truly open: Bebko's friends were allowed into the courtroom. He promised not to voice any forbidden thoughts. After the sentence was read, he was showered with flowers his friends had smuggled into the courtroom.[152]

At the end of 1979 Bebko's comrade, Viktor Davydov was arrested, and in June 1980 Anatoly Sarbayev was arrested as well,[153] both accused of writing *samizdat* works—the next stage in the internal development of the group's activities. Articles by Sarbayev include "Soviet Society According to the 1977 Constitution" and "The Constitution of Society Beyond the Iron Curtain." In addition, he was accused of participating in the formation in Kuybyshev of the Mid-Volga Group for the Defense of Human Rights. Leaflets about the group, which never saw the light of day, were found in Sarbayev's possession. Davydov, who was educated as a lawyer, was accused of writing and reproducing *samizdat* works "The Phenomenon of Totalitarianism" and "The Second Coming Will Not Take Place" (on the possible rebirth of Stalinism in the USSR).[154]

Other Cities

There is some information on the creation of a human rights group of nine people in the town of Sovetsk in the Kaliningrad region in early 1978, but nothing is known of the group's activities. Evidently, the only significant event was the group's formation. In August 1978, a local photographer and designer for the town park, Romen Kosterin, was arrested. He had been named as the founder of the group.[155]

In Saratov there was a similarly unsuccessful attempt at the end of 1979. Physicist Aleksandr Komarov tried to form an affiliate of the Helsinki Group, but was forcefully confined to a psychiatric hospital.[156] In Pyatigorsk, Zheleznovodsk, and Kislovodsk on the eve of December 10, leaflets were posted that read: "If you are aware of general lawlessness or if you are a victim of illegal actions, come to the flower garden next to the store Kristal in Pyatigorsk at 6:00 P.M. on December 10, 1978 for a silent meeting. There is nothing illegal in such a meeting. On December 10, 1948 the Soviet Union signed the Universal Declaration of Human Rights." On December 9 KGB agents arrived at the home of the person responsible for posting the leaflets, Oleg Solovyov. A resident of Pyatigorsk and graduate of Tomsk University, he was a chemist by profession, but had worked as a stoker after undergoing a compulsory cure in a psychiatric hospital in connection with previous leaflets. In consequence of the KGB's visit, the demonstration was cancelled.[157] Cameraman Viktor Monblanov, who held a one-man demonstration on Kiev's main street, carrying a placard reading "Freedom to Prisoners of Conscience," was sentenced to four years in camp for hooliganism.[158]

In the latter half of the seventies, inhabitants of the Russian provinces began to contribute a larger share of works to *samizdat*. In addition to articles mentioned above by Davydov and Sarbayev, a valuable work was contributed by geophysicist Iosif Dyadkin from Kalinin, "Stage Extras," about the population losses in the USSR resulting from experiments in socialist construction (collectivization, ideological terror). Dyadkin and his friend Sergey Gorbachyov were arrested and sentenced as "slanderers."[159]

In September 1975 the trial of fifty-year-old engineer Mikhail Zverev was held in Pyatigorsk. He had written about twenty articles critical of the Soviet Union and sent them through the mail to the addresses of people he did not know. He was pronounced mentally incompetent,[160] a fate shared by Popov from the city of Oktyabrskoye in Bashkiriya. Popov was held in a psychiatric hospital for writing poems declared to be anti-Soviet.[161] In Togliatti *samizdat* materials, as well as the personal literary archives of self-taught artist Mikhail Zotov were confiscated.[162] In Bobruysk a worker and former political prisoner Mikhail Kukobaka was sentenced in July 1979 to three years in labor camp; he was implicated in transmitting his articles "International Détente and Human Rights Are Inseparable" and "The Stolen Homeland" to the West and for taping foreign broadcasts, like Bebko from Kuybyshev, and making them available to his friends.[163] On charges of taping and organizing collective listening sessions of foreign broadcasts, a worker at the combine factory in Taganrog, Eduard Kuleshov,[164] and worker Yevgeny Buzinnikov in Gomel were put on trial.[165] Apparently the number of people who listened to and were influenced by foreign broadcasts during this period increased, especially in the provinces.

Samizdat was also circulated more widely in the provinces. From 1975 to 1979, the *Chronicle of Current Events* is full of reports of confiscations of *samizdat*, dismissals from work, and penalties for reading *samizdat*. Sentences in labor camps were applied in cases involving the distribution of *samizdat* during this same period.

After Détente

In order to receive material and technical assistance from the West, it was necessary for the Soviet government to observe some restraint in international as well as internal affairs, about which the West was particularly sensitive. Policies on Jewish emigration and the treatment of dissidents who were known in the West, especially Solzhenitsyn, Sakharov and members of the Helsinki groups, were directly affected by such considerations. For nine months the authorities could not bring themselves to arrest members of groups that had violated the age-old Soviet taboo against taking internal problems outside and directly appealing to the West with complaints of illegal practices on the part of their own government.

The Soviet government recognized that arrests of Helsinki Group members would be even more revealing than the documents those groups released. Still, arrests of Helsinki Group members began and continued despite energetic protests from the West. The attack on the Helsinki groups reaffirmed the fundamental principle of Soviet internal policy: when the choice is between saving face in the West and losing control, even in insignificant ways, at home, the choice will be to preserve control at home. From 1977–79, twenty-three members of the Helsinki groups were arrested and seven were sent abroad. This left thirty-four, including new members, to carry on.

The beginning of the general attack may be dated from November 1, 1979, on the day when the KGB received the go-ahead to undertake a plan, worked out as early as 1977, of successive routs of independent social action.

On November 1, three people were arrested: Tatyana Velikanova and Gleb Yakunin in Moscow and in Vilnius, Antanas Terleckas.[166] All three were well-known activists, even though they had not joined any of the Helsinki groups. That they were arrested indicated that arrests had gone beyond the frail boundaries temporarily imposed by the peculiar international situation. It also indicated who would be next in line for repression after the Helsinki groups—other open associations. Gleb Yakunin was a key figure in the Christian Committee for the Defense of the Rights of Religious Believers in the USSR; Tatyana Velikanova represented the Initiative Group for the Defense of Human Rights; and Terleckas actively participated in production of samizdat Lithuanian periodical literature. Before the end of 1979, editors of the Moscow journal Quest (Poiski) Valery Abramkin and Viktor Sorokin were arrested, and beginning in January 1979, other editors of the journal were terrorized by searches, interrogations, and the threat of arrests, finally carried out in December.[167] Also arrested was the leading activist of the Pentecostal emigration movement, Bishop Nikolay Goretoy,[168] Yakunin's assistant Lev Regelson,[169] and Mikhail Solovov, member of Elections 79 and SMOT.[170] Arrests within the

Helsinki groups continued: Viktor Nekipelov of the Moscow Helsinki Group,[171] and Yaroslav Lesiv and Vitaly Kalinnichenko of the Ukrainian Helsinki Group.[172]

These arrests at first were considered minor repressions necessitated by the upcoming Moscow Olympic Games. However, the invasion of Afghanistan in December 1979 and the exile of Sakharov to Gorky in January 1980[173] left no doubt that this was a drastic change in the international and the internal policies of the Soviet Union away from détente.

The exile that had been planned as the means of putting an end to Sakharov's civic activities in 1977, was employed in January 1980. He was exiled without a trial or any official order other than an oral communication from an official of the procurator's office. The "leniency" of this measure was, from the very beginning, deceptive. His exile soon turned into de facto arrest (not even "house arrest," since his home was in Moscow, not Gorky). The conditions of his arrest became harsher, and with every year the conduct of his jailers became more and more brazenly abusive. The great isolation of the Sakharovs, and the constant slander campaign directed against him and his wife in the Soviet newspapers leads one to think that psychological preparations are being made to get rid of him once and for all. Retaliation against Sakharov in 1980 was a signal that the constraints had been abandoned. While prestige in the West had earlier offered some measure of protection, now it seemed to be a signal for the issuance of arrest orders.

The repressions begun in 1979 were distinguished from previous ones in that: several dissident movements were attacked simultaneously; open social-action groups were the primary target everywhere; the leading figures of all independent movements and people involved in the well-established network for uncensored distribution of information and ideas were swept up first. By this time, information was being received in Moscow from all directions; from Moscow it went to the West; and from the West it returned through radio broadcasts or *tamizdat* publications. Repression was strategically aimed at leading human rights activists, at the nucleus of the movement in Moscow, and at the network branching out to the rest of the country.

Moscow human rights activists fulfilled the requirements of those singled out for arrest in several different ways. Almost all open associations were concentrated in Moscow, and the leading activists either joined or worked closely with them. Information from all areas and on all movements was compiled by this nuclear circle and then sent to the West; Moscow dissidents were the primary receivers and distributors of *tamizdat*. By the end of 1980, twenty-three Muscovites had been imprisoned; by the end of 1981, so had another eleven of the most respected, experienced, and active members of the human rights movement.

After the arrest of Tatyana Velikanova and Aleksandr Lavut,[174] not one member of the oldest of the human rights associations was free—the Initiative Group for the Defense of Human Rights in the USSR. After Gleb Yakunin's arrest, the Christian Committee, the center of the human rights struggle of Russian Orthodox believers and the connecting link between believers of various faiths in their mutual struggle for their rights, almost completely ceased to function. The journal *Quest* closed down after four of its editors were arrested.[175] Early in 1981 the last free member of the Working Commission to Investigate the Use of Psychiatry for Political Purposes was arrested.[176]

Throughout 1980, leading activists of all the non-Russian national movements and of the unregistered churches were arrested, the only exception being the Lithuanian Catholic church. Although there were arrests among church activists, until 1983, no priest who belonged to the Catholic Committee for the Defense of the Rights of Religious Believers was affected. Instead, the attack was concentrated on the Lithuanian national movement and was directed primarily against its *samizdat* periodicals and on the Lithuanian Helsinki Group.

The increasing severity of repressive policies could be seen in an increase of arrests of women. In Moscow, from 1968 to 1978, only nine women had been arrested in connection with human rights activities. Only one of these had been sentenced to a labor camp (one year); the others were either given terms of internal exile, pronouncd mentally incompetent, or released before their scheduled trials.[177] The arrest of Tatyana Velikanova marked the beginning of a new phase. A grandmother, Velikanova was sentenced to four years in a strict-regimen labor camp and five years of internal exile.[178] Sixty-five-year-old Malva Landa, a Moscow Helsinki Group member, was sentenced to five years of internal exile.[179] In 1982, more than one hundred women were sentenced to camps on the basis of ideological considerations.

A particularly ill omen of the repressiveness of the early eighties was the re-arrest of political prisoners, either before release or just after they served out their terms. The practice of repeated arrests had been widely used under Stalin and had never been completely discontinued. Instances of repeated arrests were rare until 1980, when they became more frequent and just as under Stalin, systematic, especially in the Ukraine. After 1980 not a single participant in the Ukrainian Helsinki Group was released at the end of his prison term: all received second sentences either equal to or longer than the original sentence. Those released before 1981 were returned to the camps during 1981–82. From the Ukraine repeated convictions gradually spread throughout the country. The second arrests were not the result of fresh charges, but seemed to be additional punishment beyond the sentence set by the court: all who remained firm in their convictions were threatened. They were formally charged with blatant fabrications, ranging from "anti-Soviet propaganda" within the camps to "attempted rape" and and "resisting authorities."[180]

The increased number of arrests was combined with a sharp rise in the severity of the sentences. The terms applied to repeaters were astounding; many received the maximum allowed under article 70— ten years in a special-regimen camp with five years of internal exile added on to the previous sentence. This happened to Anatoly Marchenko, arrested in March 1981, who received a sentence of fifteen years, on top of the fifteen years he had already served.[181]

Judges began to flaunt violations of the most elementary rules of jurisprudence; it became commonplace to deprive the defendant of a final word before the court.[182] A new genre appeared in *samizdat*— active dissidents wrote statements in case of arrest. Such statements were made by Anatoly Koryagin, Viktor Nekipelov, Feliks Serebrov, Ivan Kovalyov, Vsevolod Kuvakin, and Valery Senderov.[183] Their statements were issued after their arrests. Like the defendants' final words these statements are remarkable human documents—unselfish, noble, and brave.

One other peculiarity of trials after 1980 was the impossibility of finding lawyers who would agree to defend persons charged with political offenses, since these cases had become a danger to the lawyers themselves. It became quite common for the defendant in a political trial to conduct his or her own defense[184] or to be defended by a court-appointed lawyer.[185] Unexpectedly, there were persons among them who were prepared to fulfill their professional obligations, and it was not uncommon for them to ask for acquittal.[186]

The attack of the KGB was also felt inside the camps and prisons, where the regimen became harsh. The *Chronicle* reports in no. 62 (April–July 1981) four attempted suicides in various camps for a variety of reasons—the first such figure in fourteen years.[187] Such was the result of introducing a system of punishment for the slightest infraction of very severe camp regulations and of the increasing degradations to which political prisoners were subjected. Control over prisoners' correspondence with their families became unbearable due to petty regulations carried to absurd extremes. Any information that concerned life in the camps or the mood of the addressee was deleted on suspicion of containing a secret message. Even complaints about one's health were forbidden. In an attempt to stop the flow of undesirable information on the difficulties of life in the camps, meetings between prisoners and their relatives were sharply curtailed. Regular visits were once a right; now they became a rare stroke of luck. stroke of luck.

Since the 1970s, in yet another sign of the return of Stalinist methods in suppressing dissent, the practice of beating has been reinstituted against political prisoners. In Stalin's day, cruel and systematic beating was employed during investigations of many political cases. From 1937 until the time of Stalin's death in 1953, such beatings occurred so frequently and openly that it was evident that investigators were acting under instructions or the equivalent.

After the death of Stalin, torture and beatings during political investigations were rarely used, the exceptions apparently explained by the ill will of individual investigators. But, in the 1970s, reports of such beatings increased in non-political cases, and later in political cases. Reports came first from the Ukraine in the 1970 beating of political prisoner Pavel Kampov,[188] and then from other republics and provinces; for example, the beating of Yakov Dolgoter and Aleksandr Bolonkin[189] in 1978; of Mark Morozov in 1980;[190] of Mikhail Kubobaka in 1981.[191] Other incidents of this type are known. In 1983 came the first reports of beatings during political investigations in Moscow prisons, as of Sergey Khodorovich, manager of the Fund to Aid Political Prisoners.[192] From the investigation prisons the practice migrated to the labor camps and prisons. In 1983, Yury Orlov was beaten in labor camp,[193] as were Anatoly Koryagin and Tatyana Osipova, and in 1984, Anatoly Marchenko.[194] Beatings in women's camps began in 1984, when Tatyana Osipova, Natalya Lazuriva and Irina Ratushiaskaya were beaten.[195]

The fact that beating of political prisoners known in the West had begun suggests that some form of permission for such procedure had been handed down from above. The authorities had obviously decided to ignore the prospect of publicity and indeed may have counted on such publicity as a means of intimidating active or potential dissidents.

In his final word before the court, Anatoly Marchenko characterized the situation resulting from the new punitive policies as a civil war waged by the government against its people.[196]

That the plan for suppression initiated at the end of 1979 appears to have been intended to operate for two years was indicated by an unusual article by the vice chairman of the KGB, Semyon Tsvigun, in the journal *Kommunist* (September 1981). As if he were rendering an account, Tsvigun reports that "anti-social elements masquerading as 'human-rights activists' and 'advocates of democracy' have now been exposed and rendered harmless."[197] It was, of course, unnecessary to "expose" those "elements," since they spoke out publicly. As for "rendering them harmless," in Tsvigun's vocabulary that meant arresting them. In this respect, the plan launched by the KGB was obviously fulfilled.

The 1977 plan assumed that the exile of Sakharov from Moscow and the arrest of fifty of the most active dissidents would be sufficient to end independent social action in the USSR. By 1982 almost this many Helsinki Group members were in confinement (forty-seven in all), and five had been forced to emigrate. Total arrests from 1979 to 1981 were ten times more than was thought necessary in 1977 for the total eradication of dissidence. These five hundred were the most respected and most active members: those who published informational and publicist *samizdat* periodicals, writers of outspoken *samizdat* works, those who relayed data on illegal actions by the authorities to the Moscow activists, and those who relayed that data to the West. Tsvigun affirmed in his article that such repression had produced the desired result: the human rights movement no longer existed. This can be accepted as true with one crucial correction: as a result of repressions, the human rights movement ceased to exist in the form it had taken from 1976 to 1979.

During this earlier period open associations provided the base from which the movement had operated. By 1982 the Moscow circle, which had founded the movement and functioned as its nucleus during the seventies, ceased to exist in its previous form. Arrests and forced emigrations had decimated this circle.

Until the early eighties this nucleus of leading activists, united by years of working together, had represented the human rights movement to Soviet citizens and to the rest of the world. They preserved its spirit and traditions, and assured the continuity of experience gained in movement work. The destruction of this circle was a painful loss not only for the movement, but for all dissident trends that expressed solidarity with it in the Soviet Union. By 1982 this circle had ceased to exist as a unit; only fragments remained. Yet the removal of leading activists from Moscow did not interrupt human rights work. Those members who had previously assisted arrested members now took over their functions. In a sense all members were leaders. Critics frequently pointed to the lack of an organizational framework and structural hierarchy as the major shortcoming of the human rights movement, yet it was this factor that made the movement indestructible when under attack. When the movement became less active this feature made possible the relatively smooth continuation of its fundamental activities.

The Moscow Helsinki Group continued its work until September 1982, even though only three members remained: Yelena Bonner, Sofya Kallistratova, and Naum Meyman. It was impossible to replenish the group with new members because of the certainty of their arrest.

Although it received unpublicized assistance, in 1982 the group's activities declined. Its documents began to appear less frequently and those that did appear were almost exclusively short reports on new trials and arrests. On September 6, when Sofya Kallistratova—the oldest member of the Moscow Group—was threatened with arrest, the three remaining members announced that they were ceasing their activities.[198]

The *Chronicle of Current Events* assumed their informational functions. In February 1981 the mock-up for no. 59 was confiscated during a search of the apartment of Leonid Vul, a graduate of the Department of Philology at Moscow State University who worked as a knife sharpener in a cafeteria. The discovery of the mock-up made it possible to identify the current editors on the basis of their handwriting. The editors then announced their forced resignation from further work on the *Chronicle,* and no. 59 never appeared.[199] But publication did not cease: a new group of editors prepared further issues.

In September 1982, Aleksey Smirnov, the grandson of Aleksey Kosterin, was arrested and sentenced to six years of labor camp and four years of exile for his part in the *Chronicle.* At the end of 1983, Yury Shikhanovich was arrested on the same charges.[200]

By the end of 1983, sixty-four issues of the *Chronicle* had been published but the efficiency of production had decreased even before the arrests of 1980. The editors had found it impossible to publish all of the increasing volume of information, given the conditions under which they worked. Two additional information networks appeared in consequence—*Bulletin V* (apparently "V" stands for the first letter of the Russian word *vesti,* news), prepared two or three times a month from the "raw" news available but typed in only a few copies. It was not intended for wide distribution, but rather as a source publication for those engaged in collecting and editing information on the human rights situation. Only beginning in January 1983, with issues no. 94/95 was *Bulletin V* openly distributed. Ivan Kovalyov took responsibility for *Bulletin V* at his trial; he announced that he was its founder.[201]

In February 1984 former political prisoner Sergey Grigoryants was arrested and sentenced to ten years of labor camp for issuing *Bulletin V.* The prosecutor remarked during the trial that the scope of events described in *Bulletin V* would have required a large staff. Grigoryants answered that the *Bulletin V* workers were all honest people. In May, in issue no. 105, the editorial board announced that *Bulletin V* was closing down. As with the *Chronicle,* the authorities had threatened arrests of those suspected of close contact with the editors if publication were not stopped.[202] In December 1983, the first issue of the *Herald of the Human Rights Movement* appeared in *samizdat,* the title page designed just as the *Chronicle* was designed, with the same quotation as a colophon: "The struggle for human rights continues."[203] At the beginning of 1984, Yelena Sannikova was also arrested for the *Herald. USSR News Brief* has been coming out since 1978, parallel to these publications. This information sheet, six to eight typed pages, appears twice a month and receives information from the same sources as the *Chronicle.* However, this publication is compiled and published not in Moscow, but in Munich by Cronid Lubarsky, a former political prisoner and human rights activist who emigrated from the USSR. Since the end of 1981, *USSR News Brief* has been coming out in English.

This method was not an original idea of the human rights activists. The first uncensored Russian newspaper was Herzen's famous *Bell* (*Kolokol*) published in London in 1857–1867, from where it made its way to Russia. Information from human rights activists became more manageable than it had ever been before because of the inclusion of *USSR News Brief* in the information network. The initial links in the chain—the collection and relay of information to Moscow and then to the West—had not been lost.

No. 60 of the *Chronicle* contained information from more than 90 different localities; no. 62 contained information from 142 places and names 756 individuals; no. 63 has information from 141 places and 1,141 names are mentioned. The collection, revision, and publication of all this information required the efforts of many people, all of whom entrusted their fates to their co-workers and all of whom ran the risk of ruin and imprisonment.

The expansion of the geographical area from which information reached the *Chronicle of Current Events* occurred in spite of the almost total removal of well-known activists from Moscow. Their absence slowed down the flow of new information from the provinces and non-Russian republics because people there did not know how to find the activists or to whom to turn for help. This was no simple task even in the best of times. The *Chronicle* no. 53 (August 1979), reported the efforts made by one resident of Severodvinsk, Aslan Rustamov. Having heard several names over the radio, he made trips to Moscow five years in a row, trying to find these people through the municipal information bureau and the militia. He was unsuccessful until 1979, when a visitor he met in the reception room of the Supreme Soviet of the USSR put him in touch with the Moscow Helsinki Group.[204] The almost total disappearance of the possible addressees complicated the already difficult task of contacting human rights activists.

Of the former informational publications, only the *Chronicle of Cur-*

rent Events (published from 1968), the informational bulletin of the Initiative Group for the Defense of the Rights of Invalids in the USSR (from 1978), and the informational bulletin of SMOT (from 1978) continued publication.

Of the thick Moscow journals, only the historical collection *Memory* remained. Due to the arrests of its editors, *Quest* ceased to exist in 1980 after eight issues. But that same year a thin journal, *Quest and Thought*, appeared. Like *Quest*, this new journal called itself a "free Moscow journal" and adopted a dual system of numbering issues. The first issue carried the number 9, together with the number 1 in parentheses. The editors said they considered their work a direct continuation of *Quest*—a nonpartisan, nongovernment journal and forum for all political, religious, and philosophical schools of thought. However, the editors of *Quest and Thought* declined the "heroically open" position of the editors of *Quest*, who printed the names and addresses of participants in the journal. "Such a position is, without doubt, noble, yet it is impractical," wrote the editors of *Quest and Thought*. From 1980 to 1981 eight issues appeared.[205]

In 1979 the journal *Duel* began publication. It published translations from the Western press of articles of interest to, but unobtainable by the Soviet reader.[206] The literary anthology *Our Contemporary* appeared in 1981.[207] The editors were anonymous, and the contributors used pseudonyms.

An outstanding event of *samizdat* in the early eighties was the appearance of the *Sakharov Collection,* issued in commemoration of the sixtieth birthday of Andrey Sakharov and later published by Khronika Press in New York.[208] A photograph of Sakharov that appeared on the cover was circulated in Moscow on his birthday (May 21) in the form of leaflets. In this way more than 5,000 photos were given out.[209] The editors wrote that the collection brought together authors of different generations, both creative writers and scientists, believers and atheists: the whole spectrum of the diverse period, which Vladimir Kornilov has called the "Sakharov period."[210] The collection contained congratulations—"expressions of love, voiced aloud"—from Georgy Vladimov, Lidiya Chukovskaya, Vladimir Voynovich, Grigory Pomerants, Sergy Zheludkov, and many others.[211] There were appraisals from Sakharov's contemporaries of his life's work, his contribution to spiritual emancipation, his insights into our society, and his ennobling influence on the world. Besides greetings and literary works dedicated to Sakharov, there were evaluations by specialists of Sakharov's scientific work, excerpts from his own works, and statistical studies of the response of the Soviet people to Sakharov's civic activities.

In 1981 *samizdat* was enriched by a few articles written by Sakharov, the most widely distributed, "The Responsibility of Scientists."[212] Addressing himself to his colleagues in the USSR and in the West, Sakharov called upon them to fulfill the obligation of all scientists: to speak out in defense of justice, of specific victims of violence, and for the higher interests of mankind. Another article by Sakharov, written in 1981, was "How to Preserve World Peace."[213] Here, Sakharov suggests that the "balance of terror," on which deterrence of a nuclear attack is now based, be replaced by a "redundant balance of sense," to be created by a general atmosphere of trust and openness based on the democratization of Soviet-bloc countries.

In Leningrad publication of 37 and *Hours,* which appeared in 1976, continued, as well as the journal of essays, *Sum,* which appeared in 1979. To these were added: *Northern Mail, Metrodar, Dialogues,* and the journal of the women's club *Maria* (two issues appeared).[214] Previously Moscow publicist *samizdat* had been primarily political, while in Leningrad it was primarily philosophical and religious. At this time a philosophical and religious current appeared in Moscow *samizdat,* while a political current made its appearance in Leningrad *samizdat.*

Not so long ago publicist *samizdat* was almost totally limited to human rights documents and liberal works. In recent years philosophic and religious literature, for the most part Russian Orthodox and, more generally, Christian, have been added. Other forms of *samizdat,* down to the teaching of mantras, have also spread. Of the politically oriented works in *samizdat,* Russian nationalism has become noticeable. All shades of this orientation are represented—from patriotism to nationalism to chauvinism. *Samizdat* reflects the enormous interest in the history of Russia and in history in general, which is seen in efforts to understand the present and future of the country.[215]

Practical subjects of interest to the reader, almost totally absent from *samizdat* before, began to appear, for example Igor Gerashchenko's instructions on how to find telephone listening devices and render them inoperative.[216] Also unusual is an article by S. Probatova on Soviet social-service organizations,[217] comments from "simple workers" about the general mood of the working class (the letter of Mikhail Zotov from Togliatti on a meeting held in a milk plant to discuss events in Poland); notes by Moscow worker Nikolay Alekseyev on rush work, worker initiative, and reactions to the Soviet Union's external expansion, as well as to events in Poland.[218]

Beginning in 1980, the number of searches rose dramatically in all areas of the country. After the almost total annihilation of open associations, these searches were aimed at *samizdat.* In April 1982 in Moscow alone more than fifty searches were conducted during the single day of April 6 and twelve arrests were made, all in connection with *samizdat*.[219] This number was unprecedented for the capital in the entire post-Stalinist period, in spite of the fact that over the twenty-five years of *samizdat*'s existence, the majority of political arrests were in some way connected either with the authorship or distribution of *samizdat*. But repressions are quite ineffective in this sphere, as the results of searches conducted in the eighties bore out. The amount of *samizdat* was much larger than in previous years.

The attack on *samizdat* was conducted not only in Moscow, but also in Leningrad, Kaluga, Obninsk, Sverdlovsk, Voronezh, Bobrov, Smolensk, Rostov, Sochi, Tomsk, Novosibirsk, Krasnoyarsk, Irkutsk, and other provincial cities,[220] and in the non-Russian republics as well. Even though the haul from these searches was enormous, it was, however, only a fraction of the total volume of *samizdat* in the USSR.

The stories of searches in Kaluga and Tomsk show something of the network of *samizdat* dissemination. In the summer of 1981, the KGB in Kaluga summoned for interrogation Tatyana Belova, a graduate of Kaluga Pedagogical Institute. Belova said that the KGB advised her to stop meeting with her friends Anatoly and Svetlana Verkhovsky, who were suspected of *samizdat* activities, but she continued to meet with them and with the KGB, as well. She acknowledged that she was not always discreet in her conversations with the KGB, although she always spoke the truth. She would justify her actions to her friends, saying "You yourselves say that you don't hide your views." On graduation Belova was assigned to a teaching job in one of Kaluga's best schools, and, on April 27, 1982, Anatoly Verkhovsky was arrested.

Anatoly Verkhovsky, a geologist, first came to KGB attention in 1978, when *samizdat* was confiscated from his home. Forced to resign from his job, he found work as a security guard. When he was arrested in 1982 and his home searched, *samizdat* and *tamizdat* were discovered among drafts of his own writings. He was sentenced to three years in a standard-regimen labor camp for "slandering the Soviet system." On the day Verkhovsky was arrested, acquaintances of his were also searched: two in Kaluga, four in Obninsk, three in Moscow, and one in Sverdlovsk.

Among Verkhovsky's friends in Kaluga was an archivist-historian, who worked part time as a security guard, and the supervisor of the security guards, who was a member of the Union of Writers. After Verkhovsky's arrest, this supervisor was advised to resign quietly. He applied for a job as a painter.

Another acquaintance in Kaluga, Dmitry Markov, an archivist and historian, who worked as a photographer, was searched. (He had already had some unpleasantness with the KGB in the beginning of the 1970s when Pyotr Yakir gave testimony against him, to the effect that

Markov was involved with the distribution of the *Chronicle*.) More than 200 rolls of film of *samizdat* and *tamizdat* were confiscated from his apartment, and in February 1983 he was arrested along with Sergey Grigoryants.

One of Verkhovsky's Moscow acquaintances was Mikhail Sereda, head of the radioelectronics department at the Institute of Scientific Research, who was fired from the Institute and then arrested for duplicating *samizdat* on the Institute's copying machine. Two other friends of Verkhovsky's, Yelena Frolova and Olesya Zapalskaya, suffered repeated interrogation. Manuscripts by Verkhovsky were found at Frolova's apartment, and *samizdat* and *tamizdat* in book form were found at the home of Zapalskaya, along with typewritten manuscripts, negatives, and photocopies. Altogether 277 items were mentioned in the protocol of the search.

The case of Verkhovsky was somehow linked to the case of *Bulletin V* and Sergey Grigoryants, and to the case of the photocopying of religious literature. Fr. Valery Suslov, who lives in Moscow but serves in Kaluga, was called in for questioning about the latter case, as he was at the time of Verkhovsky's arrest.[221]

In Tomsk on April 1, 1981, as *Chronicle* no. 63 reported the "Tomsk Affair," five KGB agents burst into a greenhouse and searched S. Bozhko, a security guard. They found several photocopies of *tamizdat* books and interrogated him and five of his acquaintances. *Samizdat* and *tamizdat* were found in their possession as well. Apparently the KGB found some clue and unravelled the case before the end of the year.

In December the KGB searched thirty-two homes of students and professors at the university and of employees of scientific research institutes in Tomsk, and found a large number of *samizdat* and *tamizdat*, most of them photocopies. In the course of the next two months, first one person, then another, was summoned for interrogation. On February 1, 1982, Valery Kendel and Anatoly Chernyshov were arrested. Kendel, who had a master's degree in philosophy from Tomsk University, worked as a scientist in the university laboratory of concrete sociological research. In 1980 he had been discovered to be engaged in *samizdat* activity and was fired from the laboratory; he had found work as a pipefitter. During the search in connection with the "greenhouse affair" in April 1981 the KGB found *samizdat* among his things, but he was not investigated at that time. On the day of his arrest, photocopies of religious and philosophical literature were seized at his home.

Anatoly Chernyshov was an employee of the Tomsk City Procurator's Office, where he ran a forensic laboratory. His home and workplace were searched, and a large number of film rolls and photocopies of *tamizdat* books on sociology, religion, philosophy, and even yoga and karate were located in a safe at his laboratory.

On the day Chernyshov and Kendel were arrested the homes of more than twenty of their friends were also searched. Among them was the home of Aleksandr Kovalyevsky, a mathematical physicist, head of a biology and biophysical laboratory at Tomsk University. Both originals and photocopies of *samizdat* and *tamizdat* were confiscated from Kovalyevsky's home—literature, information publications, cameras, and a typewriter. In a search of Nikolay Kartashov, a worker at a rubber footware factory, *samizdat* and *tamizdat* were confiscated—Kartashov explained during interrogations that Kovalyevsky was simply storing his own materials at his place (Kartashov's son worked in the same laboratory as Kovalyevsky), and on February 9, Kovalyevsky was arrested.

A month later, several additional searches were conducted and a fourth *samizdat* activist was arrested, historian Viktor Artsimovich, a translator in the Tomsk Institute of Geophysics. Seized in addition to a large number of *samizdat* were books on philosophy and history, volumes of the works of Marx and Engels in German, and a manuscript entitled "Contradiction upon Contradiction," a critical analysis of the works of Marx. Artsimovich was later charged with writing this article.

Searches and interrogations in connection with the case of the Tomsk *samizdat* activists were carried out in Moscow, Leningrad, Krasnoyarsk, Omsk, and Barnaul. During interrogations of Muscovites, the KGB expressed interest in their acquaintances in Tomsk, as well as in friends who had emigrated, evidently trying to find the route by which *tamizdat* had penetrated through to Moscow, and from Moscow, to Tomsk. Searches in connection with the "Tomsk Affair" can be traced through cities where members of an amateur geological expedition, and their friends, were living. The expedition had been running since 1958, out of Tomsk, to examine the Tungussk meteorite. Kovalyevsky had taken an active part in this expedition.

The trial of the several accused took place at the end of September. All were charged under Article 190-1, "Slander of the Soviet state and social system." Viktor Artsimovich was also charged with writing *samizdat* and pronounced unfit to stand trial; he was sent for compulsory treatment in a special psychiatric hospital. Anatoly Chernyshov was accused under Article 190-1 and Article 162, "Engaging in prohibited manufacturing," and sentenced to three and a half years of labor camp. Evidently it was he who was considered to be the photographer of the *samizdat* and *tamizdat* that had been distributed in Tomsk. Kovalyevsky and Kendel were only accused of being *samizdat* "customers," so to speak, of distributing *samizdat,* but not preparing it. Each received one and a half years of labor camp.[222]

The Russian Fund to Aid Political Prisoners continued to function, although its participants were under constant pressure. Since its creation, distributors of the fund have been replaced a number of times. The first was Aleksandr Ginzburg, who, before his arrest in February 1977, named his successors: Malva Landa, Tatyana Khodorovich, and Cronid Lubarsky. Before the year was out, Lubarsky and Khodorovich had emigrated, to be replaced by Ginzburg's wife, Irina Zholkovskaya. After she emigrated with her husband in February 1980 as one of five prisoners released and exchanged for two Soviet spies, Sergey Khodorovich became the only Russian Fund distributor. He had been dismissed from work, had been arrested for short periods and subjected to searches and then sentenced to three years in labor camp—a fate shared by any undeclared helpers discovered by the KGB.[223]

In December 1981 Leningrader Valery Repin, an undeclared participant in the Russian Fund, was arrested. He had handed over the archives of the Russian Fund and revealed the names of relatives of political prisoners who were receiving aid. During the course of interrogations in Moscow, Leningrad, the Baltic republics, and the Ukraine masses of wives and mothers of political prisoners were blackmailed. KGB agents presented the matter in such a way as to make it appear that money received from the fund was payment for information from the camps which was transmitted to Lubarsky for *USSR News Brief* and, of course, for foreign intelligence.[224]

Anonymity in civic activities became a hallmark of the eighties among open associations forced to take refuge in anonymity after arrests of their members. After the founders of the Christian Committee, Gleb Yakunin and Viktor Kapitanchuk, were arrested, committee members still at large announced they would not reveal names of new members, but only the number. They correctly assumed that these newcomers would be arrested, were their names revealed. The Moscow Helsinki Group and the Russian Fund to Aid Political Prisoners did not make similar announcements but simply refused to accept new members formally, although new people did enter these groups to take the place of members who were lost. Thus, these groups came to consist of both declared and anonymous workers. The human rights group of the Pentecostalists created in the summer of 1980 announced only the number, not the names of their members.

Thus, even after the destruction of its nucleus, the human rights movement was able to fulfill its basic functions, although its activities were reduced to pre-Helsinki levels. Essentially, the former "second echelon" people who had performed auxiliary tasks, now replaced those they used to work under, in turn now finding replacements to take over their old tasks. The names of these people appeared together with the customary signatures on human rights letters, which at this time appeared after every arrest. While the number of letters increased with the avalanche of arrests, the number of signatures decreased to lower than pre-Helsinki levels. One of the well-known open appeals in the early eighties was the protest against the Soviet invasion of Afghanistan (document no. 119 of the Moscow Helsinki Group). Open to all signers, it was signed by nine persons in addition to the Moscow Group members, and this included the signature of Sakharov. It was the last collective appeal he signed before his exile from Moscow.[225] Another protest was the one against Sakharov's exile, which included protests from the Moscow Helsinki Group, the Lithuanian Helsinki Group, the Initiative Group for the Defense of the Rights of Invalids, the Catholic Committee for the Defense of the Rights of Religious Believers, several individual letters, and two collective letters (a general appeal signed by fifty people and one from literary figures containing fifteen signatures).[226] Most of the signatures were by newcomers to the human rights movement.

It is impossible to approximate the number of newcomers or determine the dynamics of this movement, although it appears that by 1981 the depleted Moscow association had been noticeably supplemented by new people. The usual number of participants in the December 10 demonstrations had ranged from twenty to fifty, but in 1981 there were one hundred participants according to the cautious estimates of the Moscow Helsinki Group and about two hundred according to other sources.[227]

After the impressive demonstration in 1976, the authorities began to interfere with the demonstrations, varying their methods each year: they would fence up the monument and the square and post "under repair" signs or conduct preventive arrests of potential participants and detain them at their jobs with the cooperation of their superiors.[228] In 1981 preventive arrests were carried out on a large scale, and the entire area of Pushkin Square was filled with a mass of volunteer police and KGB agents in plainclothes. Only a few demonstrators were able to make their way to the monument and take off their hats. About fifty persons were detained on the steps leading to the square and taken to the nearest militia stations, where they did proceed with the demonstration by baring their heads at the appointed time.[229]

The demonstration on Human Rights Day occurred in all subsequent years. But by 1984, these demonstrations remained the only open expression of the human rights position. The human rights movement was deprived of its chief feature—publicity. This radically changed the situation.

*   *   *   *   *   *

During the Helsinki period the human rights movement advanced, within a complex conglomerate of opposition forces interested in the democratization of Soviet society, to a role of unifying these diverse forces. Although its leading activists made no claim to such a role, other movements spontaneously grouped themselves around human rights associations on the basis of common ideology proceeding from demands that human rights be observed. The most active period of the Helsinki groups also showed that the organizational structure spontaneously arising from the work of the human rights activists fostered the movement's survival during periods of intense repression. Such a structure was, however, not conducive to realizing the movement's role as the unifier of other groups during periods of increased activity. The primitive organizational structure of the human rights movement could well become a brake on the general success during a new period of intense activity.

Once again, the defenselessness of open organizations, which became apparent as soon as the government ceased to take into consideration the reaction of the West, could not help but cause disillusion with the human rights doctrine of the importance of open, independent civic action. At the same time, doubts about the feasibility of relying on the West for support could not be dismissed.

The aim of the unifying role of the human rights movement during periods favorable for dissidents will in the future demand some ideological correctives. They must widen their approach toward national problems, give more attention to the economic problems of Soviet society, etc. In this, the very formulation of the problem is new.

The founders of the human rights movement constantly emphasized that the movement was apolitical in nature and that their goal did not lie in some future result. Their silence would be broken every time human rights and human dignity were trampled, despite the hopelessness of overcoming the evil of each specific instance and without regard to the possibility of success. However, those who replaced the veterans' places reacted to this heritage in their own fashion.

In the early eighties not only the participants, but also the social composition of the movement changed. The overwhelming majority of the founders belonged to Moscow's creative and liberal-arts intelligentsia. Gradually, members of the technical intelligentsia and workers joined. During the Helsinki period the technical intelligentsia, white-

and blue-collar workers, contributed most to the influx of new participants. Representation from these strata increased noticeably, even among Moscow activists. In the provinces, activists had come from these strata from the beginning. The increase in the proportion of provincials among human rights activists in general had a corresponding effect on the social structure of the movement. The rapprochement between the human rights and other movements, as well as the transfer of some of their constituents to the human rights movement, contributed to this process, since the majority of the participants in the other movements belonged to these same social strata. Beginning in 1976, workers made up 40 percent of those arrested for political reasons, and together with the technical intelligentsia and white-collar workers, they constituted an impressive majority. Only the second culture in Leningrad preserved its social composition: the majority belonged to the creative and liberal-arts intelligentsia.

However, the movement's representatives continued to come from Moscow's creative intelligentsia, and they represented the movement both for their fellow citizens and for the West. The outstanding representatives were responsible for the prestige and distinction of the human rights movement, so that sometimes all Soviet dissidents were referred to as human rights activists and were considered to be of the same ilk as the representatives of that movement. Beginning in 1981, a new generation of human rights activists that almost entirely replaced the old, was not content with the moral opposition that had inspired the founders. They wanted to see practical, if not immediate results. This desire led to changes in the spirit, the original impulse, and the goals of the movement. Perhaps at some future time these changes will help overcome the movement's weaknesses and lead to practical results, but in the early eighties changes in the original composition of the movement were felt principally in a lowering of its moral and intellectual level.

These newcomers initiated a discussion in *samizdat* of the future of the human rights movement, its adaptability to the tasks that lay ahead, and remedies for shortcomings that arose during the Helsinki period. These problems troubled activists of other movements, as well as all thinking people concerned about the fate of their country. Among the participants in the discussion were those who sympathized with and those who were inimical to the human rights movement. The recognition that the human rights movement was the only force capable of uniting all the various democratically oriented opposition elements was not shared by everyone. To many the weakness of the movement and the unsuitability of its leaders for the roles in which they unexpectedly found themselves were more evident than the potential of the human rights ideology within the heterogeneous society of the Soviet Union.

An inevitable consequence of the reprisals against open associations were revived hopes for underground groups, especially among young people. In the early eighties underground groups apparently appeared in the provinces and even in Moscow, where they had not been seen for fifteen years. Leaflets and signs that appear from time to time indicate that underground groups exist at present. In September 1981 leaflets were distributed in Novocherkassk containing an appeal "to demand that our government not interfere in the internal affairs of other countries."[230] During the 1981 anniversary celebration of the October Revolution, a sign reading "Freedom to Poland and Afghanistan" and anti-Party slogans appeared on Zhukovsky Street in Moscow as well as slogans against the omnipotence of the Communist Party. Many such incidents are known to have occurred.[231]

Beginning in 1980 a few programmatic documents appeared in *samizdat*, the product of groups whose names include the words "democracy" and "democratic," although the groups revealed neither their names, the names of their members, nor the number of members. They only reported where the group had been formed: in the Ukraine,[232] the Baltic republics,[233] or Moscow.[234] Characteristically, in a declaration (July 1981) of the creation in Moscow of the Initiative Group for a People's Democracy, a short history was given of the independent social-action movement that began with the seventies and with open associations. The founders of the underground Initiative Group considered their refusal to go public and their replacement of the goals of the human rights movement with political goals (the establishment of a people's democracy) as the next and more advanced stage in the development of the dissident movement. They were unaware that underground groups had been fairly common from the midfifties to the midseventies, because the groups left virtually no trace of their existence. The founders did not realize that this stage was already over.

Along with the tendency to go underground and act anonymously, there existed an ineradicable yearning for open forms of social action, which once it emerged, collided with the KGB.

In November 1980, seven Moscow writers (Filip Berman, Yevgeny Klementovich, Yevgeny Kozlovsky, Vladimir Kormer, Yevgeny Popov, Dmitry Prigov, and Vladimir Kharitonov) applied to the Moscow city council for permission to found a club under the auspices of the city council for young unpublished writers; they also wanted to found an independent journal *Katalog*. They had already compiled the first collection for the journal for discussion at the club. They were subjected to searches, during which not only the journal, but their own works and *samizdat* literature were confiscated.[235] In December 1981 Yevgeny Kozlovsky was arrested after having two of his stories published in the Russian-language emigré journal issued in Paris, *Kontinent*.[236] He was released before his scheduled trial after writing a letter of repentence for the newspaper.[237] There was no further discussion of a club.

In Irkutsk there was a similar attempt to create an independent writers' club with similar results: the writer Boris Chernykh was arrested.[238] In Leningrad, on the other hand, developments were more successful. On December 7, 1980, second culture figures announced the creation of a union of workers engaged in creative labor; on December 20 they held a conference of *samizdat* journal authors and editors.[239] After a long period of bargaining with the KGB a compromise was reached: in exchange for abandoning the union, discussions were begun on the creation of a city committee of writers affiliated with the Leningrad Writers' Union. At the suggestion of KGB officials, a group of unofficial writers wrote a tentative charter for the committee.[240] The KGB considered the charter too unorthodox. After a long period of discussion, toward the end of 1981 Klub 81 was created in the Dostoyevsky Museum, which brought together *samizdat* journal writers and editors. Evidently the KGB considered this a convenient method of control.[241] It is possible that their experience with the independent women's club *Maria* influenced their decision.

This club had been created early in 1980, immediately after the journal *Women and Russia* was disbanded and its editors, Yuliya Voznesenskaya, Tatyana Goricheva, Natalya Malakhovskaya, and Tatyana Mamonova were forced to emigrate.[242] The club began to publish the journal *Maria*,[243] different from other Leningrad journals, which are traditionally far removed from "politics," in its critical stand and its dedication to the problems of women in Soviet society. Club members were tormented with searches and interrogations, and two of them (Natalya Lazareva and Natalya Maltseva) were arrested.[244]

In 1981 the only open independent association to be announced in Moscow was the Group of Separated Spouses, formed by the spouses of foreigners.[245] Only by means of a long hunger strike in the summer of 1982 did most of the group members receive permission to emigrate.

Early in 1981 an attempt was made in Moscow to create a human rights group, called Publicity, with the modest task of publicizing instances of violations of investigations of workers' complaints. Those who initiated the group, Vsevolod Kuvakin and Mikhail Ikonnikov, did not envision cooperation either with human rights activists or with "foreigners." They planned to send their bulletin only to official institutions. However, in April 1981 the confiscation of materials they had collected put an end to their plans, and the group did not materialize.[246]

Attempts to create unofficial associations apparently became a fairly widespread phenomenon in the USSR, since the previously mentioned article by Tsvigun cited attempts to create "various 'leagues,' 'societies,' 'clubs,' 'theaters,' and 'seminars' made up of antisocial elements to counter existing public associations and working people's organizations."[247]

All attempts to create open associations in the early eighties occurred outside the circle of human rights activists. Each such association had its own goals, but, without official approval, they all stood for the realization of civic rights and made use of the experience gained by human rights activists.

✿   ✿   ✿   ✿   ✿   ✿

In spite of the repressions of the eighties, unprecedented in the post-Stalinist period, the authorities were powerless to wipe out dissent and return the country to the predissident period of silence.

In his article "An Anxious Time" (written during his exile in July 1980) Sakharov assesses these possibilities:

> The slogan "The People and the Party Are One" which hangs from every fifth building, consists not entirely of empty words. But it was from the ranks of the people that the defenders of human rights emerged, standing up against deceit, hypocrisy, and silence, armed only with pens, ready to make sacrifices, yet lacking the stimulus one derives from the certainty of quick success. They had their say. They will not be forgotten. On their side, they have moral force and the logic of historical development. I am convinced that their activity will continue in one form or another, whatever the size of the movement. What is important is not the arithmetic but the qualitative fact of breaking through the psychological barrier of silence.[248]

The Independent Peace Movement

The most evident traditions of the human rights movement were continued in the activity of the Groups to Establish Trust Between the USSR and the USA. The first of several such groups was announced in Moscow on June 4, 1982.[249] Its founders called a press conference for foreign correspondents and released the founding documents of the group, signed by its participants and with their addresses indicated. The purpose of the Moscow Trust Group was to coordinate efforts to preserve peace among Soviet citizens and U.S. citizens and peoples in the West in general. The founders emphasized that they were not dissidents. Not one of them had participated in the dissident movement. Nevertheless the methods employed—a press conference of foreign reporters, the group's complete openness, and its appeal to the Western public—indicated a direct inheritance from the human rights movement itself and a utilization of that movement's experience.

The Moscow Trust Group's founders belong to the same strata of Soviet society as the pioneers of the human rights movement—the Moscow intelligentsia. But there were differences between the human rights activists and "peaceniks," as the Trust Group activists came to be known. For example, those who started the human rights movement were successful members of society who had sacrificed their social positions for the movement. In the 1980s, only among "outsiders" could individuals be found prepared to continue open and independent civic activity, the majority of peaceniks were refuseniks.

The "peaceniks" do not criticize the governments of the superpowers; rather they strive to attain a lessening in tensions between the two countries by establishing as wide as possible communication among citizens of the two nations. The peace activists repeatedly came forth with such proposals. The Moscow Trust Group proposed that Moscow be made a nuclear-free zone, and asked that demonstrations be held; it was their intent that simultaneous actions be conducted in the USSR and in the West under identical slogans. But the appropriate authorities never responded to the Group's requests for permission to hold the demonstrations. The Group was confined to organizing apartment exhibitions, readings, and seminars on the problems of preserving peace.[250]

The Moscow Trust Group, like the Moscow Helsinki Group, brought forth other analogous groups—in Odessa, Leningrad, and Novosibirsk—which also publicized the names of their members and their addresses. The Odessa Group proposed declaring the Black Sea a sea of peace and removing all military ships and coastal military installations. Vladimir Kornev, suspected of writing this document, was immediately arrested on trumped-up criminal charges. The activity of the Odessa, Novosibirsk, and Leningrad Trust Groups was limited to the release of several appeals.[251]

The Moscow Trust Group's initiative very much alarmed the Soviet government since it created an unwanted alternative to the long established "peace" movement, which was headed by the official Soviet Committee for the Defense of Peace and directed by officials selected by the party. The appearance of the Moscow Trust Group introduced an element of uncertainty in Soviet plans to launch in the West a movement against the proposed deployment of new types of American missiles in Europe. Just as the Helsinki Group before it, the Moscow Trust Group maintained the Western public's interest, but unlike the Helsinki Group, which arose in the USSR earlier than in the West, the Trust Groups relied on a widespread and well-organized movement for peace that had existed in the West for many decades. Activists of peace groups in West European countries and the US rushed to Moscow to assist the Group from the moment of its appearance, writing and demonstrating in its defense.[252] Under such circumstances, repression of the "peaceniks" threatened to undermine Soviet influence on the peace movement in the West.

The KGB, just as they had warned the Helsinki monitors six years previously, now warned the "peaceniks" that their activity was impermissible. Repression was at first limited to shutting off telephones, blocking apartments where exhibits and other peace activities were going on, and house arrests. Then came the temporary incarceration, in a psychiatric hospital, of an initiator of the Moscow Trust Group, Sergey Batovrin, and fifteen-day arrests of other members on charges of "hooliganism."[253] The artist Batovrin, who played a leading role in the group, and three of the group's active members were expelled to the West. For these long-time refuseniks this did not seem like a violent measure, but rather a show of official good will.

In October 1982, Moscow Trust Group member Oleg Radzinsky was arrested and charged with writing "anti-Soviet" *samizdat* essays. He "recanted" and received a relatively mild sentence: one year of labor camp and five years of exile.[254]

The constant pressure on the Moscow Trust Group included not only direct harassment and intimidation but also demoralization through a combination of threats and promises. To some degree this tactic was successful: by 1984, almost all of the Group's founders had left, and Radzinsky had even issued a public statement denouncing his former comrades.[255] But the Group's work was continued by new members. Its call received a response in Soviet society. Its appeal to the governments of the US and the USSR to cease confrontation was signed by about 1,000 persons.[256] The majority of those who signed were students but workers also joined in support of the peace initiative. Aleksandr Shatravka and Vladimir Mishchenko received prison sentences for collecting signatures to these appeals among workers at a sawmill in the Tyumen region of Siberia.[257]

By 1984, the Trust Groups remained the most visible public manifestation of an independent citizens' initiative—by that time public discussion was virtually smothered. But society did not return to its paralyzed predissident state.

Soviet Society After Détente

The overall image of dissent changed radically. In the 1970s, all dissident movements were politically amorphous. Liberal elements set the general tone. In the 1980s, dissent lost its liberal homogeneity and in all the movements spokespersons of extreme points of view grew stronger. Among Catholics and Russian Orthodox, nationalist sentiments developed, and in the non-Russian nationalist movements, the mood grew sharply anti-Russian. The Russian nationalist movement began to gather strength, including not only those concerned with preserving Russian culture but also people with imperialist ambitions. Alongside the former movements arose a wide spectrum of political tendencies—from democratic socialism, hardly noticeable in the 1970s, to fascism, which sprang up in the 1980s. But none of these trends, neither the extreme or the moderate, had the same influence on society as the human rights movement did in the 1970s.

Soviet society as a whole also changed greatly in comparison with the predissident period. Sergey Grigoryants wrote in 1982: "Now, albeit with caution, everybody curses the authorities, makes sarcastic remarks in lines and in street cars, and doormen and members of the Central Committee crack political jokes."[258]

This criticism became universal, and the authorities were forced to adjust to it—in the 1980s, no longer was anyone punished for candid criticism, as he would have been in Stalin's day. Harassment began at the next stage, for writing and distributing criticism, that is, for *samizdat*.

At all levels of society some people went beyond the usual gossip about the personal qualities of Lenin and Stalin, about the colorless Soviet leaders of the post-Stalin era, and extended their criticism to the faults of the Soviet system and the possible paths for its future development. Among circles of friends, there were discussions about Czechoslovak socialism "with a human face," about the Portuguese and Chinese variations, about Eurocommunism. In other circles, hopes focussed on Russian patriotism or on the strengthening of totalitarianism; there was a longing for a "strong boss" and dreams of a new Stalin. In these circles the cult of Stalin grew, among old bureaucrats and the military in particular, and also among unskilled workers. In the lower echelons of society, this cult was a peculiar protest against Stalin's heirs, against the corruption of the Soviet bureaucracy, economic ruin, and the decline of the standard of living.[259]

In the 1980s, admirers of the Third Reich appeared among young party, Komsomol and KGB functionaries. They praised Hitler's firmness and even more, that of Himmler and Bormann; they promoted Göring's speech at the Nuremberg trials, and discussed the merits of the structure and methods of work of the apparatus of the Nazi party and of the Minister of Propaganda.[260]

With the variety of searches for future paths for the USSR in the the 1980s, people ceased to talk about progress toward communism; the subject was not even mentioned in the newspapers. The Communist Party's program of the Khrushchev era, when the arrival of communism was promised for 1981, was pointedly hushed up. In 1981, two young workers, Ivan Khakhulin and Ivan Provotorov, received three-and-a-half years of labor camp for "anti-Soviet propaganda"[261] for reading this 1961 program aloud in a public place.

Youth Sub-Culture

The process of differentiation from official ideology went furthest among youth. The values of the new youth culture did not coincide with and sometimes even contradicted official values. Its outward appearance was a Western style of dress, jeans, and haircuts, a special slang containing anglicisms, and so on. The emergence of a special youth culture began in the post-war years and perhaps even during the war, when the relations with the Allies opened up a small crack to the Western world. In the 1960s, this process was reflected in *samestrada*, which were unofficial, amateur musical, theatrical, and choir-singing groups, made up principally of young people.

The most distinctive independent music was created by "bards," individuals who performed their own songs to the guitar. There were many thousands of such composers, but most were known only in the circle of their own friends. Bulat Okudzhava, Vladimir Vysotsky, Aleksandr Galich and Yuly Kim were, however, widely popular. Their songs, disseminated by tape recordings, became public property. Hundreds of thousands of Vysotsky's admirers flocked to his funeral in 1980. So large a crowd was unprecedented for an unofficial gathering in Moscow. It demonstrated a dislike of official mass culture, and a clash between the tastes of the man in the street and the standards worked out for him by officialdom. In the songs of the bards the words were usually more important than the music. This genre, which attained its greatest popularity in the Russian-language milieu, broke through to the foreign language audience only with difficulty. The very genre of guitar folk singing presupposes solo performances for a small group of listeners. Rock music, which knows no linguistic limitations, on the other hand, spread much further. Even the Soviet press recognized this.[262] Emigre music critic Solomon Volkov, who studied this phenomenon while still in the Soviet Union, estimates that millions of people are drawn into the orbit of rock music's influence. By this, he meant not listeners, but composers and performers.[263] Members of rock groups must overcome the most diverse obstacles—attacks in the press, dismissal from their jobs, not to mention difficulty in finding rehearsal spaces or in receiving permission to hold concerts.

Rock songs are often written with patriotic lyrics and rock music includes national folk elements—Russian, Ukrainian, Azerbaidzhan, Georgian, and so on. National instruments are often used. In Byelorussia, the rock opera "Song of Fate" (music by Vladimir Mulyavin, lyrics by Byelorussian poet Yanka Kupala) became popular. The first rock group to attain universal fame in the USSR was the Byelorussian group Pesnyari. Leading rock groups in Georgia, Azerbaidzhan, and the Baltic republics are also widely known. Some of them are fairly open about expressing nationalist sentiments. In Estonia a mass youth demonstration occurred in response to a prohibition against the amateur group Propeller's playing at a stadium after a soccer match.[264]

Rock music in the USSR, as in the West, is also used to express religious themes. One such rock opera is "Yunona and Avos" (music by Anatoly Rybnikov, lyrics by Andrey Voznesensky). The rock group Trumpet Call, organized by young Baptist members of a registered Leningrad Baptist community, wrote and performed a rock opera about Jesus Christ, that had become popular after excerpts were heard over the BBC. The leaders of the rock group, Valery Barinov and Vladimir Timokhin, tried unsuccessfully to obtain permission to hold concerts. In 1984, they were arrested.[265] Rock music festivals, held without permission, are constantly broken up by the authorities.[266]

One manifestation of youth culture was the hippie movement, which also emerged in the 1960s and was preserved throughout the 1970s and 1980s. The first documented report of the hippies concerned an episode on June 1, 1971, which is celebrated in the USSR as International Children's Defense Day. About 150 hippies gathered in the courtyard of a building at Moscow State University, intending to go to the nearby US consulate with anti-war posters. The demonstrators were surrounded by policemen and volunteers, and taken to the police station.[267] During the first few days of May each year, hippies organize gatherings in the Baltic republics. From time to time, police round up participants, cut their hair and send them back home; some are confined briefly in psychiatric hospitals.[268]

Hippies, who are an organic part of rock culture, are proponents of pacifist ideas. In 1982, in Moscow in the Lenin Hills, on the anniversary of John Lennon's death, a pacifist demonstration occurred with about three hundred participants of the hippie association known as Independent Initiative. Members of Independent Initiative have signed the documents of the Moscow Trust Group. In 1983, Independent Initiative held a similar demonstration with posters of Dutch pacifists.[269] Another group, known as Good Will, held a demonstration on June 1, 1983 in Tsaritsyno Park outside Moscow. The demonstrators passed out leaflets against the death penalty and against the war in Afghanistan. About two hundred were detained, and eight arrested. The name of only one of those arrested is known—that of Yury Popov.[270]

The development of a youth culture and the creation of spiritual independence by youth was retarded by the universal military draft. Most young men go into the army at eighteen or nineteen years of age, where, in the course of three or four years, they are subjected to intensive re-education. Those who enter an institute are exempt from the army because military preparation is included in the program of study and graduates receive the rank of officer. Yet the youth culture has developed among students, in particular. It was students who made up the majority of the members of the Amateur Song Club, the largest of the unofficial youth organizations, founded in Moscow in 1967 on the crest of the *samestrada* movement. By 1976 there were about two hundred branch members—song clubs at institutes, schools, factories, and housing offices. Their annual rallies and concerts, held in Moscow suburbs, drew thousands of participants.

In 1973, a KGB official reported to a plenary session of the Moscow City Committee of the Communist Party that the Song Club had escaped the ideological leadership of the party and Komsomol organizations. Whereupon, the Komsomol City Committee and the Trade Union City Council co-opted the Amateur Song Club and an arts council and club board were created. In 1975, dissatisfaction with the ideological pressure by the co-opted group led to a split in the board. Despite harassment of the critics of the official line, some of the sections of the Amateur Song Club, in addition to taking part in the club's principal factions, began to organize mini-factions. Some left the Club altogether and began to hold Sunday meetings during the spring months. On the first such Sunday, May 1, 1976, several dozen participated in the meeting. A composition of selections from Campanelli's "City of the Sun" was performed; speeches by Krylenko, the prosecutor at the political trials of the Stalin era, were read; and the songs of Aleksandr Galich were sung. The organizers of these "Sundays" were harassed (e.g., expelled from their institutes and fired from their jobs) but the Sunday meetings continued and the number of those who attended grew steadily. In June 1976, the number had reached two hundred, and by October, there were four hundred. The Sunday meetings were continued into the 1980s, and those who attended continued to be harassed.[271]

The only known proposal for the creation of a youth organization to counterbalance the Komsomol (Young Communist League) took place in December 1968 in the city of Vladimir, one of the first attempts to create an organization not under the control of the party. This experiment ended tragically: the Union of Independent Youth was broken up and its leader, Vladimir Borisov, was arrested; he was pronounced unfit to stand trial and committed suicide while in prison.[272]

Among Moscow university students ten years later, another association, known as the People's University of Mathematical Studies, was created, sparked by an anti-Semitic policy toward Jews who were seeking admission to institutes. In the course of several years, a practice developed, based on nationality, of differentiating the degree of difficulty of entrance examinations. From 1977 through 1979, an unofficial survey was made of the examinations for the mathematics department at Moscow State University, at the Moscow Physical Technical Institute and at the Moscow Engineering and Physics Institute. The survey established that the percentage of Jews admitted to these institutes never rose above .08%, including even those with only one-quarter Jewish ancestry. In 1979, the People's University of Mathematical Studies was created by a group of citizens for those who could not enter the state institutes because of the artificial obstacles at the examinations.[273] The curriculum for the People's University was drawn up by volunteers—young teachers and scientists. The program was planned for five years, with classes three times a week for six hours each time. Lectures and seminars were given by volunteer teachers and senior students at Moscow institutes. The People's University existed until 1982, when its two leading activists, Valery Senderov and Boris Kanevsky, were arrested.[274]

Unofficial associations more frequently arise not between universities and institutes, but within them, usually amateur theaters, film clubs, choirs, musical groups, and other clubs. Members of these associations try not to call attention to themselves from outside, in order not to alarm party and Komsomol authorities, who are reconciled to the existence of these groups. In *samizdat* information publications, reports about semi-official and unofficial student groups appear rarely, usually only if they are broken up by the authorities. This was the way that the Rockwell Kent Club at the Moscow Engineering and Physics Institute became known. The club had a music group called Aquarius; two youth music groups from other institutes, Zoo and Toadstools, also performed there. Starting in 1981, the *samizdat* journal *Mirror* began to appear in the Moscow Institute of Engineering and Physics. It was never distributed outside the institute, and perhaps its only readers were the club members.[275]

Clubs and student journals have long existed in universities and institutes in the provinces, too. In 1972, in Voronezh University, a journal in manuscript form was published, called *Sexual Democrat*, with an appendix called *Pacifist*. The journal advocated more serious and open discussion of sexual issues. Articles dealt with the special role of the intelligentsia in public life in the USSR, the issue of censorship, and the question of the necessity of democratic transformations.[276]

Student clubs and their journals are usually apolitical, to some degree reflecting the apolitical nature of most of their members, and to some degree dictated by caution. Students are very vulnerable. A student may pay for the slightest display of nonconformity with expulsion from an institute, which for young men means automatic drafting into the army, and, in the 1980s, the threat of being sent to Afghanistan. Nevertheless, in Georgia, it was students who made up the majority of participants in demonstrations with nationalist slogans, held at the end of the 1970s and the beginning of the 1980s.[277] In Estonia during the 1980s, both high school and university students took part in such demonstrations;[278] one was held in Tselinograd in 1979, led by Kazakh students who were provoked by rumors that an autonomous republic of Germans was to be created on the territory of Kazakhstan. The demand of the demonstrators was "Kazakhstan for the Kazakhs."[279] However, the majority of open student protests were directly connected with academic problems. Thus students at Tblisi University protested against the firing of their favorite teacher, Akaky Bakhradze, who had irritated the authorities with his Georgian patriotism. After about a thousand students demonstrated Bakhradze was restored to his position.[280] At the philology department of Moscow State University, Vyacheslav Ivanov was suspended for ideological reasons from reading lectures. On May 14, 1981, officials announced that from that day on, the students would have a different teacher. The students who had come to Ivanov's lecture that day (about a hundred) silently rose and left the auditorium. The next day, in the smoking room of the philology department, a sign appeared on the wall: "Down with the Party Committee! Give us Professor Ivanov's lectures!" At the department building, leaflets were scattered with the same text. The day after that a leaflet appeared on the bulletin board: "We protest the arbitrariness of the Party Committee! We protest against the dictatorship of the party in literature and language study." It was signed "Philology Department." The leaflet was removed and an order by the Party Committee and Administration was posted forbidding any announcements not approved by the Party Committee. As soon as this order appeared, the bulletin board was set on fire and burned down.[281]

Graffiti on the walls of smoking rooms are used for anonymous exchange of opinions on prohibited subjects. In December 1981, a discussion was held via these notices. On December 14, someone wrote: "Shame on the military dictatorship in Poland! Long live Solidarnosc!" The next day, an answer appeared: "We'll finish off the dissidents in the philology department! It's time to end the anarchy in Poland! Fools! We'll have to feed them!" On December 16 followed this sign: "To Messrs. Marxists and Anti-Dissidents: Read Engels! The less freedom in a state, the more it stifles the freedom of other nations . . . Freedom for Poland is our freedom." In the same way discussions were conducted on the walls of smoking rooms on human rights in the USSR, on Stalinism, and on pacifism. From time to time, these writings were painted over by order of the administration.[282]

During the entire post-Stalin period, student bodies were the chief milieu for the emergence of underground and semi-underground circles.[283] Students made up the majority of those who took part in the first open meetings during the Khrushchev "thaw"—the poetry readings at the Mayakovsky statue in Moscow and at Arts Square in Leningrad.[284] However, students and young people in general were not a noticeable part of the human rights movement—the majority of human rights activists were older people. Only in the late 1970s did youth participation in this movement begin to grow. When authorities exposed those who had written graffiti and distributed signs, it became clear that they were all young people;[285] but the underground and the semi-underground of the 1980s was not all democratic. The most diverse organizations began to increase, including fascist groups, also comprised of young people (high school and university students, students of technological and trade schools and young workers). The first known public demonstration of pro-Nazi youth occurred in Tallinn on September 22, 1980, after a concert in honor of the anniversary of the liberation of Estonia from German occupation. In a crowd leaving the concert a group of about two dozen people appeared carrying swastikas, and chanting "Heil Hitler."[286] On November 1, 1981, a fascist demonstration took place in Kurgan. About one hundred high school students wearing armbands with swastikas shouted slogans such as "Fascism will save Russia!" Demonstrations of neofascists also took place in Yuzhnouralsk, Sverdlovsk, and in Leningrad at the Kazan Cathedral.[287] In 1982 on April 20, Hitler's birthday, there was a fascist demonstration in Moscow at the traditional place for human rights demonstrations—Pushkin Square. At the Russia Movie Theater, which faces this square, pro-fascist leaflets were distributed. The demonstrators—nearly fifty young boys and girls, wore black shirts and black pants, short haircuts; one had a swastika on his cap. News of this demonstration spread widely before it was held: teachers in the higher grades of Moscow schools warned of such a demonstration and urged students not to go to the Square. Naturally, the entire square was packed with people who had come to catch a glimpse of the fascists. Among the onlookers were opponents of the fascists. The militia and the volunteers did not interfere until a fight broke out between the onlookers and the fascists. About ten were taken to the nearest hospital for treatment.[288]

In Leningrad, at the beginning of June 1982, a group of young people with swastikas knocked down statues in the Summer Garden.[289] In 1983, demonstrations on Hitler's birthday took place in Moscow, Sverdlovsk, Kuybyshev, Omsk, Rostov-on-the-Don, and in the Ukraine.[290] An anonymous *samizdat* document, dated August 1983, describes these fascist demonstrations:

In some towns, in neighborhoods, on streets or in courtyards, fascists marched in formation, chanting "Heil Hitler!" and "Sieg Heil!"; in other towns they were dressed in their uniforms, with armbands, and broke into young people's cafés and discothèques, shouting the same slogans; in still others there were night demonstrations. In many cases the fascists started fights, sometimes even beating up war veterans, who were wearing their medals. They used their fists as well as brass knuckles.

This document speaks of fascism as a "persistent tendency in the development of Soviet society in the 1980s."[291] It explains the credo of Soviet fascists: "strong authority, iron discipline, a mighty state, purification from the Jews, 'rotten intellectuals,' and in general all whiners, pacifists, and traitors. They welcome the creation of anti-Zionist committees, the imposition of martial law in Poland, and the invasion of Afghanistan."[292] In the document, attention is drawn to the mild measures, by Soviet standards, taken against fascist demonstrators. They are brought to the militia station to view a documentary film exposing fascism and neofascism and for instructive talks. Only rarely do they receive a brief labor camp sentence on charges of hooliganism. The student Pyotr Maslov, a former border guard, on the other hand, was recommended for expulsion from his institute when he said during classes that he had been among those who had been against the fascists on Pushkin Square.[293]

The opponents of the fascist demonstrations in Moscow in 1982 were the fans of the Spartak soccer team. It is not clear what provokes their animosity toward the fascists, perhaps competition between youth gangs, an apolitical motive. Hostility is also a phenomenon of the

1980s. The fans' associations are characterized in a *samizdat* document as "semi-organizations—semi-gangs of 'fans,'" who represent themselves as "a strong and unified movement." Such semi-organizations have sprung up in many large cities—in Moscow, Leningrad, Riga, Tallinn, Vilnius, Minsk, Kiev, Tblisi, and elsewhere. Each member pays monthly dues (five rubles). The organizational leadership is subdivided into organizational, housekeeping, finance, and other sections. The fans prepare posters, T-shirts, buttons with sports slogans and the emblems of their teams, often inscribed in public places with indelible ink. As a rule, they do not display political slogans.[294]

Other forms of semi-legal and illegal youth associations in the USSR exist; for example, one demonstration by veterans of the Afghanistan war occurred on August 1, 1982 in Moscow, once again on Pushkin Square. About three dozen men appeared, some in sailors' striped shirts and blue berets, and others in ordinary clothing. They lined up in columns of three or five and marched from the Pushkin monument to the Russia Movie Theater and back. They formed a circle, and, in the center, a demonstrator sang. Once again, they formed ranks and moved across Gorky Street, shouting "Down with fascists! Long live the military dictatorship!" The militiamen tried to block the demonstration, but drew back in the face of the clear intention of the demonstrators to use force. The traffic stopped on Gorky Street while the demonstration passed by.[295]

In the 1980s "punks" appeared in the USSR. So did associations of yoga, Hari Krishna, spiritualists, and others who communicated with the dead and with extraplanetary civilizations. The closed nature of all manifestations of public life makes it exceptionally difficult to study them. The more visible trends of public life which developed in the 1980s along with former movements were the struggle for socio-economic rights, the advocates of true socialism, and the Russian nationalists.

PART SIX

THE MOVEMENT FOR SOCIAL AND ECONOMIC JUSTICE

CHAPTER 18

The Movement for Social and Economic Rights in the Soviet Union

The movement for social and economic rights appeared in the Soviet Union much later than the national, religious, and human rights movements. It began in 1978 and is still in an embryonic stage. Solidarity in Poland has demonstrated the potential of a workers' movement in a country with a Soviet-style socioeconomic system and has heightened interest in similar developments within the Soviet Union.

Sometimes this movement is referred to as a "workers' movement," an inaccurate definition if taken to mean a blue-collar workers' movement. Workers are not the only participants in the movement for social and economic rights; in fact, they do not even constitute a majority in the movement as they do in Poland. Nevertheless, it is also inaccurate to say that workers in the Soviet Union are politically passive and that the dissident movement consists exclusively of intellectuals. Of all the dissident movements, only the human rights movement in its earliest stages was made up almost entirely of intellectuals.

Workers in Dissident Movements

From as early as 1976 more than 40 percent of those sentenced for human rights activities were workers. The membership of national and religious movements had always included a large number of workers, and in some movements the workers even formed a majority.[1] This is especially true of the Crimean Tartar movement, the movement of Soviet Germans to emigrate to West Germany, the Baptist, Seventh-Day Adventist, and Pentecostal movements. But in no dissident movement was the class membership of the participants evident in their demands: all of these movements concentrated on obtaining civil, and not socioeconomic, rights. Even those movements in which workers formed the majority never formulated specific workers' demands. Nor did the human rights movement make such demands as long as no one group advocated them.

A. D. Sakharov, V. N. Chalidze, A. Marchenko, and Yu. Orlov—the participants in the human rights movement—wrote about shortcomings in the area of social conditions.[2] The Moscow Helsinki Watch Group touched on this problem in its documents. But until recently, statements made by human rights activists on social rights were based only on their personal evaluations of general conditions in the Soviet Union and were not reactions to protests defending social rights. For a long time there was no connection between the human rights movement and those who demanded their social rights, and human rights activists did not possess sufficient information on the topic.

Disturbances that occurred in the USSR were put down with force by the authorities. The best known of these disturbances was in Novocherkassk in 1962.[3] There were disturbances in other areas, but there were no accurate data or eyewitnesses of these. Most of the disturbances occurred in the beginning of the sixties, when there was still no human rights movement to create regular channels for informing Soviet society and world opinion of events not carried by official sources. But strikes and other worker actions occurred in the latter half of the sixties and during the seventies, when these channels were already open. Information about religious or nationalist claims, for instance, was systematically relayed by the activists of each corresponding movement, but not information relating to socioeconomic problems.

The *Chronicle of Current Events* reported all verifiable cases in which social and economic claims were made. Over a period of twelve years there were only a few such cases. The first, reported in no. 8, concerned the settlement of Bereyozka near Kiev where workers at the hydroelectric power station lived in wooden barracks.[4] In May 1969 a newly elected tenant committee headed by Ivan Greshchuk, a retired major, organized a workers' meeting that formulated a decision to write a complaint to the Communist Party Central Committee about the administration of the hydroelectric power station. They complained that the administration did not spend the resources designated for repairing the barracks and that newly constructed buildings were occupied by members of administrative staff and their friends. Six hundred villagers signed the letter. Ivan Greshchuk headed a delegation of representatives that went to Moscow to deliver the letter personally. He was arrested there in July. The workers wrote another letter demanding Greshchuk's release, but Greshchuk was declared mentally insane and sent to a mental hospital. The *Chronicle* has no information about how long he was kept there but states that he was again arrested in 1975 for "slander of the Soviet system" and was still confined to a special mental hospital as of 1980. In 1982 he was transferred to a general psychiatric hospital,[5] and was still there at the end of 1983.

The next report in no. 39 (1975), of the *Chronicle* concerns a bus drivers' strike in Shauliai (in Lithuania).[6] In no. 42 (1976) there is a report of a sit-down strike at the Kirov Plant in Leningrad. About four hundred workers who showed up for work in fact did not work, fulfilling only 4 percent to 5 percent of the plan. This action was caused by the plant administration's mistreatment of prisoners who worked there.[7] No. 49 (1978) reported a strike at the Kaunas rubber plant.[8]

Beginning in 1980, reports of strikes became more frequent, attributed in some measure to heightened interest after the events in Poland, particularly in Estonia, Latvia, and Lithuania, and to deteriorating economic conditions in the Soviet Union. There were strikes in Sverdlovsk,[9] Tartu and other places in Estonia.[10] On several occasions there were strikes in Kiev.[11] We know that one of the strikes in Kiev was led by the newly elected Party Committee and the union at the factory.[12] But Soviet strikers do not usually make political or general socioeconomic demands, as were the cases in Hungary, Poland, and other East European countries beginning in the fifties. The most frequent causes of strikes in the USSR are unjustified reductions in wages, increases in production norms, failure to pay bonuses, and food shortages.

A commission made up of local Party (or sometimes government) leaders is immediately dispatched to the striking factory. As a rule, the demands of the strikers are met and the superior whose instructions gave rise to the strike is either reprimanded or fired. Recently, demands that local food supplies be improved have increasingly been added to wage and bonus demands. In such cases, more meat or butter is made available for a short while.

The Party or government authorities at the striking plant take on the role of the workers' protectors against factory bureaucrats.

When the initiators of the strike break the rules of the game (that is, if they refuse to believe official claims that in "our workers' government" the authorities are on the side of the workers), then the workers' demands will usually not be met. At that point public criticism and dismissals begin, and sometimes the initiators are even arrested; if so, they are usually declared insane for the purposes of propaganda—in the USSR only those who are insane could be dissatisfied with working conditions. This is what happened to Ivan Greshchuk. Vladimir Klebanov and Aleksey Nikitin, mining engineers from Donetsk, suffered the same fate. In 1968 Klebanov was confined to a mental hospital for a period of five years for trying to organize a workers' group to defend their rights and make sure that labor legislation and industrial safety regulations were observed.[13]

Attempts to formulate more general social and economic demands were made as early as the midfifties. They did not originate with strikers, but came from small underground groups and individuals. Among them were intellectuals who made these demands as an integral part of the Marxist tradition, including the Krasnopevtsev group in Moscow (uncovered in 1957),[14] the *Kolokol* group in Leningrad (uncovered in 1967),[15] a group in Gorky arrested in 1970,[16] and leaflets distributed by Aleksandr Bolonkin in Moscow in 1972 that were signed "The Civil Committee."[17]

Some underground groups included both workers and intellectuals. There were such groups in Alma-Ata, Ryazan, Sverdlovsk, Krasnoyarsk, Kerch, Voroshilovgrad; others appeared in the late sixties and early seventies.[18] The programs and leaflets they distributed expressed both general democratic demands (freedom of speech, freedom of the press, the release of political prisoners, and so forth) and social demands (increased wages for workers and increased stipends for students, improved housing conditions). But the fact that these groups were underground prevented them from establishing contacts and made these groups ineffective. Information on violations of social rights and protests against violations known to the underground groups did not reach the general public and did not go beyond the actual cities and villages in which they occurred.

Recently there have been attempts to inform the public about difficult working conditions in the Soviet Union. Leonid Sery, a worker from Odessa, and the human rights activist Anatoly Marchenko wrote open letters on this issue, appealing to foreign labor unions.

Aleksey Nikitin, an engineer from Donetsk, invited American correspondents to his town and managed to organize a meeting for them with mineworkers, who told the reporters about their difficult life. For this activity Nikitin was sent back to a special psychiatric hospital and died there in 1984.[19]

The first human rights association to publish documents on socioeconomic conditions in the USSR was the Moscow Helsinki Watch Group. In a supplement to document no. 7 (August 1976), the group wrote about the arrests of workers in connection with the strike at the port of Riga in May 1976.[20] In December the group published document no. 13: "Workers' Demands to Emigrate on Political and Economic Grounds." This document consists of statements to the group from workers, with a request for help in emigrating to any capitalist country because the workers are unable to feed their families by honest labor in the USSR. This document emphasizes the powerlessness of Soviet trade unions to protect workers' rights.[21] The Moscow Helsinki Group returned to this theme in document no. 85, a survey entitled "Violations of Socioeconomic Rights in the USSR: The Right to Work":

> The greatest violation of workers' rights is the denial to them of a viable means of defending their interests. There is no right to strike in the Soviet legal system, and any attempt at collective action is harshly suppressed. The trade unions that do exist are in fact government and Party organizations, and not associations for ameliorating working conditions or raising the workers' standard of living. In the USSR trade unions concern themselves with problems of production, fulfillment of production plans, strengthening worker discipline and with educational or ideological work. . . . Only an insignificant portion of their activity is concerned with protecting the interests of the workers.[22]

Beginning in 1978, socioeconomic issues began to be well represented in the Moscow Helsinki Group documents: they appeared in nine out of the thirty-two documents for 1978–79. Document no. 36 is a response to the creation of the Free Trade Union, in which the complete legality of that organization is stressed.[23] Document no. 37, devoted to compensation for illness or injury, points out that pensions are dependent on the length of time worked and that most workers receive miserly pensions, especially those who lose the ability to work early.[24] Document no. 85 discusses: the existence of unemployment and the lack of any unemployment compensation, low levels of pay for the general population, the use of women employees for heavy physical labor, different forms of compulsory or quasi-compulsory labor, the use of overtime work to fulfill plan quotas, *subbotniki* or required volunteer work on days off, the practice of sending urban employees to work on *kolkhozy*, and the strict limitations on choosing one's place of residence, resulting from the system of work passports and residence registration.[25]

Certain documents note the existence of discrimination between different groups of workers: invalids (no. 38), religious believers (no. 23), former political prisoners (nos. 6 and 46), those who have applied to emigrate (nos. 47 and 159), and members of independent organizations (nos. 47, 75–77, 96).[26] Some documents of the Moscow Helsinki Group contain information on the existence of large-scale compulsory labor in the USSR. In addition to the system of compulsory labor for the majority of workers treated in document no. 85, there is a system of compulsory labor connected with the articles in the criminal code on "parasitism" (document no. 47).

Anyone who lives on unearned income may be accused of parasitism. The question of "unearned income" is not taken up in court practice, and this law is often used against dissidents who may be fired from their jobs and prevented from finding another before being accused of parasitism.[27]

Grigory Goldshteyn, a member of the Georgian Helsinki Watch Group and a Ph.D. in cybernetics, was sentenced to one year in prison on March 20, 1978 for parasitism.[28] After applying to emigrate to Israel, he lost his job and lived on his savings. Cases like this are not rare. In order to avoid being prosecuted for "parasitism" after being fired, specialists with high qualifications must look for any kind of work, even low-paying menial labor.

Document no. 63 raises the question of compulsory labor for *kolkhoz* workers who are not allowed to leave their *kolkhoz*. Document no. 85 brings up the particularly difficult conditions of *kolkhoz* work, including nonstandard working days and the lack of paid vacations.[29]

Document no. 87, prepared by political prisoners from labor camps in the Urals, occupies a special place among these documents. The leader of the Moscow Helsinki Group, Yury Orlov, served a sentence beginning in 1978 in a camp for politicals near Perm. In his introduction to this document, he estimates the total number of prisoners in the USSR on the basis of his own observations and those of his fellow prisoners. He sets the number of prisoners of every category in the USSR at 5 million, or 2 percent of the total population. All of them are obliged to do compulsory labor. Orlov concludes that, with their families, these people "are just as visible a part of the labor force as unemployed workers and their families in the West."[30]

The Free Trade Union and Other Groups

The first public association to advocate social demands was the Free Trade Union, founded in February 1978. The impulse leading to the creation of the trade union arose from a special group of individuals known as "the complaint writers"—people who spend long periods of time, sometimes amounting to several years, trying to persuade the authorities to satisfy their grievances. They visit Moscow frequently and spend many long hours in the waiting rooms of the Supreme Soviet, the Communist Party Central Committee, the Procurator's Office, the Central Council of Trade Unions, and so forth. It was in such a place that the future founders of the Free Trade Union became acquainted with each other.

Vladimir Klebanov created this first independent labor union in the USSR. After his discharge from a mental hospital, he was not rehired at his former place of employment and so began to complain to various government departments. In this way he met the "complaint writers." Their first joint action was collective letters to various government offices with descriptions of each particular case, as well as general observations on the unresponsiveness of Soviet bureaucrats to the needs of workers. At the end of 1977 twenty-five people signed an "Open Letter to the World Public About the True Situation of Blue and White Collar Workers on the Eve of the 6oth Anniversary of the USSR." They wrote: "We are Soviet people from various strata of society . . . of various nationalities and from various corners of the country . . . we are the vast army of the Soviet unemployed, thrown out of the gates of factories for demanding the right to complain, the right to criticize, the right to free speech. . . . How many of us are there? We think there are tens of thousands, hundreds of thousands. . . . Today it is we who suffer—tomorrow any citizen of the USSR could become a member of our collective and think as we do."[31]

Klebanov and some of the most active complaint writers organized a press conference for foreign correspondents in Moscow. Each described his own case, and then asked the correspondents to give the letter to the United Nations and to the signatories of the Helsinki accords at the Belgrade conference.[32] Because the complaint writers appeared to speak in the name of the Soviet worker, they acted as human rights advocates. But they did not have firm contacts with dissidents and were even prejudiced against them. Klebanov and his friends kept emphasizing that they "had nothing in common with dissidents," that their goal was "to help in the successful construction of communism and to combat bureaucracy and red tape."[33]

Although to some extent, these statements were a naïve attempt to protect themselves from persecution, which, as they knew, awaited "dissidents," they also reflected the complaint-writers' self-awareness. Yevgeny Nikolayev, who had helped Klebanov and his associates meet the foreign corespondents through his dissident friends, described the press-conference participants who later founded the Free Labor Union: "The people who signed the letters were not dissidents in the usual sense of the word. They were ordinary Soviet people trying to reenter the mainstream of normal Soviet life, from which they had been ejected by the arbitrary actions of local authorities."[34]

These persons possessed neither the psychology of human rights advocates nor their experience. According to Nikolayev, shortly after the press conference, twenty to thirty of the signatories, with Klebanov at their head, asked for an appointment with the KGB. They tried to explain that they were not fighting the Soviet system, but that each of them was seeking a solution to his own case, and that for these rea-

sons they should not be punished. KGB officials talked to them politely and individually, not to all of them at once. All were promised
that their problems would be solved, and they were asked not to take
any further steps, such as calling a press conference. The complaint
writers went home. The KGB, however, was in no hurry to fulfill its
promises. These people began returning to Moscow and made the
rounds of the KGB and other government offices in small groups trying
to satisfy their grievances. Then repressions began: they were rounded
up; some were sent to mental hospitals; others were jailed for fifteen-
day periods, allegedly for minor hooliganism; still others were sent
home under guard; and the rest were required to sign statements
promising to leave Moscow.

Klebanov was confined to a mental hospital for a short time. Upon
his release, he suggested to his friends that they organize a trade union
to fight for their rights collectively. He had already lost all hope in the
KGB. In January 1978 he distributed the Constitution of the Association of the Free Labor Union for the Defense of Workers and sent a
copy to the International Labor Organization asking for support.[35]
Here again Klebanov's lack of experience was evident. To give greater
weight to the new association, he tried to attract as many people as
possible. He assured everyone that the creation of the union was not
illegal, therefore they had no reason to fear persecution.

About two hundred complaint writers joined.[36] The majority were
unprepared for the difficulties inevitably encountered by the founders of independent public associations under the Soviet system. As
soon as Klebanov and two of his closest aides were arrested,[37] the
union fell apart. Nevertheless, the founders of the union had said out
loud what many were evidently thinking or talking about in whispers.
The crackdown did not put an end to the process its members had
begun. Western radio stations broadcasting to the Soviet Union also
had an effect by giving a lot of attention to Klebanov's efforts.

In April 1978 another attempt was made to create an independent
union. Several human rights activists, including Vsevolod Kuvakin,
Yury Grimm, Aleksandr Ivanchenko, and others, sent to the Presidium
of the Supreme Soviet of the USSR, the Council of Ministers, and the
Communist Party Central Committee a statement demanding that
their Independent Trade Union of Workers in the USSR be registered
in accordance with existing laws. Copies of the statement were sent
to the International Labor Organization and the International Con-
federation of Free Trade Unions. No answer was ever received.[38]

Then Vsevolod Kuvakin, a lawyer by profession and one of the
founders of the "legal" trade union, organized a small unofficial Working Group for the Defense of Labor and Socioeconomic Rights in the

USSR. It consisted of five persons. The group did not call a press conference, nor did it make any official announcement. Instead it began to prepare and publicize surveys of violations of the right to work, disparities between social benefits in the USSR and international standards, discrepancies between Soviet labor legislation and appropriate international treaties and agreements signed by the Soviet Union. Some of these documents were published in the *samizdat* journal *Poiski* (Quest) and some in the *samizdat* collection *In Defense of Economic Freedom,* published by Viktor Sokirko under the pseudonym of Konstantin Burzhuademov (he revealed his identity in 1981).[39] The Kuvakin group carried out the preparatory work for the creation of a trade union, but it was in no sense a trade union itself.[40]

The idea of a trade union was heatedly discussed for some time among human rights advocates, and especially among the members of the social-democratic wing. After long discussions, they decided not to put any political limitations on the already faint possibilities for such an organization and to create a human rights organization that would unify people of different professions and different convictions. Thus was formed the Free Interprofessional Association of Workers known as SMOT. Its goal was to give its members legal, moral, and financial help. In order to do this, "cooperatives" would be created in SMOT: mutual aid funds; real estate groups to buy and rent houses for joint use in suburban areas; groups to organize kindergardens where there were either none or too few; and even barter groups (for example, to send tea and condensed milk from Moscow to other cities where these goods were in short supply in exchange for canned pork, which is available in some regions of eastern Siberia, but not in Moscow). In addition, special working groups were to collect and summarize information on violations of socioeconomic rights in informational bulletins.

Structurally, SMOT was to be a union of independent groups of at least five members—residents of a city or village, employees of a single plant or institution. Each group was to determine its own "sphere of activities" in accordance with local conditions and its own capabilities. Each was to elect a representative to the coordinating committee, and only the names of these representatives would be made public. They were not to reveal the names of members of their group or to explain who they were, but could only mention the number of members in their group.

The names of eight representatives were announced when SMOT was formed: Lyudmilla Agapova (engineer), Vladimir Borisov (electrician), Lev Volokhonsky (worker), Aleksandr Ivanchenko (engineer), Yevgeny Nikolayev (geographer), Valeriya Novodvorskaya (librarian), Vladimir Skvirsky (geologist), Albina Yakoreva (student expelled from university). Six others soon joined them: Vadim Baranov (driver), Nikolay Nikitin (driver), Valentin Samoylov (pensioner), and Nikolay Rozanov (engineer). Several months later, Natalya Lesnichenko (typist) and Vsevolod Kuvakin (lawyer) also joined. Three were soon arrested (Vladimir Skvirsky, Nikolay Nikitin and Lev Volokhonsky), and two emigrated (Yevgeny Nikolayev and Vadim Baranov), and several persons left SMOT subsequently without any particular pressure from the authorities. Only Volokhonsky and Nikitin transferred their groups to other representatives.[41]

The other representatives either quit or their groups fell apart (if they had existed at all). The principle of keeping the names of the participants secret made it impossible to record the number of union participants and created opportunities for irresponsible statements.

None of the goals of SMOT were realized, with the exception of the informational bulletin;[42] however, the *Bulletin* turned out to be different from the way it had been planned. The first issues were almost entirely devoted to the harassment of the founders of SMOT, and in that sense they were similar to information publications produced by human rights activists, although unlike those activists they launched sharp attacks against party and state agencies and initiated "disloyal" characterizations of the Soviet system. This eased the persecution of those who took part in SMOT, and scared away potential supporters.

Later, information on socioeconomic issues began to appear in the *SMOT Information Bulletins* (about the interruption of supply lines to various cities; price rises in market goods; the introduction of rationing in various places, and so on),[43] demonstrating the effort of the publishers of the *Information Bulletin* to get closer to the interests of the average reader and at the same time, their success in establishing some of their own information channels.

On June 17, 1982 in Moscow, the authorities arrested three publishers of the *SMOT Information Bulletin:* Valery Senderov (a mathematician who worked as a security guard after expulsion from school), Vladimir Gershuni (a worker and former political prisoner), and Ilya Geltser (a student at the Institute of Steel and Welding). Their homes were searched and *SMOT Bulletins* and materials for them were confiscated. From Geltser's apartment were seized SMOT flyers on the Communist party's food program, calls to boycott *subbotniki,* and an appeal in defense of Andrey Sakharov. Also confiscated from Senderov's apartment were flyers produced by Narodno-trudovoy Soyuz/ Popular Labor Alliance (TS), a political emigré organization which advocates changing the government and social system of the USSR. At the moment of his arrest, Senderov announced that he was a member of the NTS. Numerous searches were carried out in connection with these arrests, in Moscow, Kiev, and in Leningrad, where on June 13, writer Vyachelsav Dolinin was arrested and on June 22, philologist Rostislav Yevdokimov, who said that he considered himself a member of the NTS.[44]

Thus the founders of the Free Trade Union, headed by Klebanov, emphasized their loyalty and dissociated themselves from "dissidents." However, some of the members of SMOT—an organization politically neutral in intent—did associate with the NTS and made no effort to hide their disloyalty to the Soviet system. True, joining the NTS was a private decision of two members of SMOT, but others (as with Volokhonsky) publicly declared their negative attitude to the NTS or, as with Skobov, their neutrality to the organization. Apparently there were heated arguments about this within SMOT.

Meanwhile, harassment continued. On September 11, 1982, searches were held in several towns in the Novgorod region where Lev Volokhonsky, who had been released from labor camp, and some of his friends were working in a logging camp. On December 8, Volokhonsky was arrested. The next day came the announcement of new membership for SMOT's Council of Representatives: Nikolay Ukhanov of Moscow, Tatayana Pletneva, Aleksandr Skobov, Irina Tsurkova, Vladimir Sytinsky, Rusakova, and Pavlov of Leningrad (the last two names are pseudonyms). In Leningrad, the slogans "Freedom for Volokhonsky!" and "Freedom for Political Prisoners!" appeared on walls in several places. In Perm and Ivanovo leaflets signed by SMOT were distributed, calling for a boycott of the December 18 *subbotnik*. On December 20 in Leningrad there was another series of searches and Aleksandr Skobov and Irina Tsurkova were arrested.[45] On June 12, 1983, Nikolay Ukhanov was arrested, and thereafter the Council of Representatives of SMOT issued a statement that they would not announce names of future new members.[46]

Despite all of these arrests, the *SMOT Information Bulletin* continued to come out; after issue no. 35, issues were dated but not numbered.[47]

Another attempt to create an association for the defense of socio-economic rights was more successful. This was the Initiative Group for the Defense of the Rights of Invalids in the USSR. Its existence was announced on October 25, 1978 at a press conference of the Moscow Helsinki Watch Group. The Initiative Group of Invalids was founded by three people from different cities: Yury Kiselyov (Moscow), Valery Fefelov (Yuryev-Polsky), and Fayzulla Khusainov (Chistopol).[48] The group collects and disseminates information on the condition of invalids in the USSR, appeals to the appropriate organizations for improving social benefits and aid to invalids, and also appeals to international organizations when Soviet organizations fail to respond. Its major goal is the creation of an all-union association of invalids. The Initiative Group of Invalids has been harassed by the authorities from its inception (searches, interrogations, slanderous and threatening articles in the local press, revoking of drivers' licenses, damaging means of transport for the handicapped, and so on), yet its activities have not been reduced to mere self-defense. The group publishes an informational bulletin of documents and materials on the condition of invalids.[49] It has prepared and distributed among invalids a sociological questionnaire. All those questioned unanimously support the creation of an association of invalids that would operate without the window dressing of official social-welfare organs, and would have its own journal for discussions of urgent problems and dissemination of information of interest to invalids.[50] The Initiative Group was accepted as a branch of the International Society of Invalids. It informs world opinion of the situation of invalids in the USSR and receives periodicals from abroad on conditions of invalids in other countries and the prospects for rehabilitation through the use of artificial aids and technical devices. Apparently, the path of the Initiative Group for the Defense of the Rights of Invalids is the most practical one advocating socioeconomic rights under the Soviet conditions. At any rate, until the present the most effective groups have not been large associations on the order of trade unions, but rather groups whose aims are to collect information and publicize the situation of different groups of workers. The movement for socioeconomic rights in the USSR in both the theoretical and practical sense has taken only the first steps. In January 1982 a group analogous to the Initiative Group for the Defense of the Rights of Invalids was formed in the Ukraine. Nine people joined it, but soon four members left the Ukrainian Group, unable to withstand the blackmail and threats. The authorities actively fought against the spread of the influence of the Initiative Group; there are reports that the KGB held "chats" with invalids in Moscow, Odessa, Chernigovskaya region, Moldovia, and Kazakhstan, employing threats and promises to stop contacts with the Initiative Group.[51] In 1981, Nikolay Pavlov, a handicapped individual, was arrested and sentenced to five years of strict-regimen labor camp for publicizing through the Initiative Group testimony about the shocking conditions in the labor camp for handicapped prisoners.[52] Vasily Pervushin, a wounded war veteran from Novosibirsk, was forcibly confined in a psychiatric hospital for an appeal demanding that the status of invalids be improved by reducing spending on armaments and redirecting the funds saved to help invalids.[53] In 1983, Valery Fefelov, an invalid, and his wife Olga Zaitseva, members of the Initiative Group, were forced to emigrate under threat of arrest.

Along with the open associations to defend socioeconomic rights, there were, during these same years, several anonymous appeals to the workers to fight for their rights. Leaflets distributed by SMOT and by others called on people not to take part in the *subbotniki*. In April 1983 on Krasnaya Presnya Street in Moscow, similar flyers appeared from "the leftist opposition group, New Path." In Estonia in 1981–1982, leaflets urged a half-hour demonstration and strike with political and socioeconomic demands. The leaflets were signed, "Democratic National Front of the Soviet Union." In mid-1983 in Voronezh three workers were arrested, lathe operator Aleksandr Vysotsky, loader Vladimir Panteleyev, and Matveyeva Tatyana, on charges of twice distributing in Voronezh factories leaflets signed "Voronezh Helsinki Committee," that called for strikes and "silent demonstrations" on the model of those sponsored by the Estonian workers.[54]

The level of education of knowledge of rights of the masses of Soviet workers is now immeasurably higher than it was in the 1930s, when the foundations were laid for the present socioeconomic system. All levels of the Soviet population are clearly aware of the violation of the rights of workers; violation is such a constant and universal phenomenon that it could be called a norm. Trade unions do not protect the rights of workers: most who are reinstated in their jobs by court decision are dismissed with the approval of the trade unions. The National Central Council of Trade Unions had not proposed a single piece of legislation that would improve working conditions or raise wages, yet it has agreed to proposals that limit benefits for long periods of continuous employment and to other constraints on workers.[55] Under present conditions, only independent trade unions can protect workers' rights.

Nevertheless, to assert that the mass of Soviet people recognize the necessity of defending their rights in the face of the "bosses" (some equate them with "Communists") would be to mistake the desirable for the real. Social despair has resulted in general drunkenness as a means of escape from reality. Alcoholism has become a national affliction. The more energetic try to find a way out in isolation: they make a career for themselves or somehow adapt by adjusting relations with their immediate superiors, by earning extra money or stealing on the job. Those who search for spiritual values are led to the church, and usually to nationalist sentiments among both Russians and non-Russians. With the former, low social self-esteem is often compensated for by imperial ambitions. In spite of the almost universal condemnation of Soviet penetration in Cuba, Africa, and other areas considered exotic by the average Soviet ("What are we feeding them for when we have nothing to eat ourselves?"), a significant number of Soviets approved of the invasion of Czechoslovakia in 1968 ("We liberated them and look what they turn around and do!"). There is evidence that Polish Solidarity does not evoke general sympathy, even among workers. At the end of 1980, the following joke appeared: "What is international solidarity?" "That is when there is nothing to eat in Tula, and they strike in Gdansk!"

In an open letter written in 1981 Nikolay Alekseyev, a Moscow worker, reports the following dialogue:

"Have you heard what the Poles are up to now," a friend of mine asked on the way home from the factory. Without waiting for an answer, he added with irritation, "We should have crushed them long ago!" "How can you talk like that?" I asked. "They are workers just like us. They are fighting for their rights. Who taught you such dribble?" "No one taught me, that's what I think. We don't live any better than they do, but we're not on strike; we don't weaken our national defense. They are influenced by outside agitators, that's for sure."[56]

Yet Alekseyev is not alone in his sympathy for Solidarity. The human rights movement in the Soviet Union has succeeded in disseminating its ideas primarily with the help of foreign radio broadcasts. This is reflected in cases of public support in various parts of the country for Klebanov's trade union and Free Interprofessional Union of Workers and for Solidarity. About twenty such cases are known, but we know very little now about the provinces. The vice-chairman of the KGB, Semyon Tsvigun, discussed this support with astounding candor in the September 1981 issue of *Kommunist*. He writes in a style peculiar to Soviet bureaucrats, that, whereas before, foreign intelligence services placed their bets on the dissident leaders, they now attempt to exert a corrupting influence on the masses, playing on the "questions of supplying the population with a variety of foodstuffs and also with individual shortcomings in the organization of medical care and services for the workers." Tsvigun complains that some irresponsible people organize all manner of "unions"—apparently he means trade unions although in the Soviet press even Tsvigun cannot utter this.[57]

The results of an unofficial survey of 618 persons (excluding dissidents or related groups) conducted in Moscow and environs in the spring of 1981 are as follows: Of 163 workers questioned, 1 out of 3 knew nothing about events in Poland or about Solidarity; half of those questioned responded negatively; and only 1 out of 5 (20 percent) expressed sympathy for Solidarity. Only 2 out of 163 people questioned spoke of the events in Poland as something closely affecting them and were concerned for the success of Solidarity. Of the students questioned, 25 percent were sympathetic to Solidarity, and 75 percent were hostile. Among the 10 industrial managers questioned, all reacted negatively to Solidarity. One out of three engineers and technical workers and one out of two humanists supported Solidarity.[58]

Another unofficial survey conducted almost simultaneously with the first in Moscow, but using more detailed questions, confirms that those who support Solidarity rely on information other than that from official Soviet sources, usually foreign radio broadcasts.[59]

However, the authorities are afraid that workers may act on their own initiative, a fear no doubt reinforced by events in Poland.

The authorities fear any initiative in defense of socioeconomic rights, a fear that has increased with the events in Poland and the worsening economic situation in the USSR. The authorities deter people from any attempt to demand these rights, first, through harsh repression of any efforts of initiative, and second, if necessary, by assuming for themselves the role of defender of workers' rights against lower-ranking managers, even sacrificing the authority of these managers and firing individual representatives of the *nomenklatura* in order to preserve social peace. (It has already been noted that even now judges fairly frequently take the side of the person fired, and not his boss.)

Nevertheless, a movement for socioeconomic rights has a potential basis in the Soviet Union as wide as that of the human rights movement. All Soviet citizens are workers and all have one employer, the state (or *kolkhozy*, which are completely subject to the state). Relations between all workers and the state are regulated by the same labor code. The authorities' violations of the code are, in general, the same for all workers, and so are the methods of repression. Consequently, the fundamental social interests of all types of workers are similar, a fact that explains the variation of social backgrounds among participants of independent trade union organizations.

Among 43 founders of the Free Trade Union, the social status of 31 is known: 14 are blue-collar workers; 8, white-collar workers; 9, professionals (engineers, teachers, medical workers).[60] SMOT has even fewer workers. Even in the structural sense the socioeconomic movement will follow the same course as all other dissident movements: not differentiating by class, it will expand and include new strata of Soviet society, developing the scope of its demands as it grows. In essence and in methodology the movement for socioeconomic rights is a human rights movement. This is the platform the nationalist and religious movements have accepted; it is quite likely that the movement for social rights will adopt it as well.

The Socialists

After the Twentieth Party Congress in 1956, dissent, including political, heretofor hidden, burst into the open and began to grow. This process is evident even in analysis of the Soviet press (at this time censorship was somewhat lighter) and from *samizdat*. The memoirs of Pyotr Grigorenko, Yury Orlov, Vladimir Bukovsky, Revolt Pimenov, Boris Vayl, and Raisa Orlova depict the mood in Soviet society of those years.[61]

Those who wished to subvert the Soviet system were rare among dissidents, actually an isolated few. Almost all of the diverse criticism—both in official literature and in *samizdat*—could be termed "democratic socialism." Some emphasized democracy; others stressed socialism. A socialist world view, however, was the predominant trend from the early days of dissent until the end of the 1960s.

The socialists of those days did not all agree on theory. One can distinguish several basic ideological trends in dissident socialism. The most representative, and the best known, was the view of the informal group for which the Moscow historian Roy Medvedev became the informal spokesman.

In his *Book on Socialist Democracy* (1972) Roy Medvedev examines this movement in a chapter entitled: "Internal Party Trends and the Issue of Party Unity." He calls this movement, to which he belongs, "Party-Democratic."[62] He describes its social composition this way:

The Party-Democrats are at present almost completely unrepresented in the highest reaches of the party. However, it is likely that at that level there are some who understand contemporary problems better than others and who in different circumstances and in another environment would be an important source of support. There are a good many sympathizers among officials of the party and state apparatus at all levels—particularly those relatively young ones who came into the apparatus after the Twentieth and Twenty-second Party Congresses. At present the Party-Democrats can also count on considerable support from the scholarly community—philosophers, sociologists, historians—as well as from a section of the scientific and technical intelligentsia, some writers, and other people engaged in cultural activities. There are also certain groups belonging to this trend among the old Bolsheviks, particularly those who returned from prison and exile after the death of Stalin.[63] The author notes that this trend is close to the position of the Italian, Spanish, Australian, and certain other communist parties. The Party-Democratic concept calls for "correct" Leninism and for the Bolshevik policies under Lenin—in other words, from the time of the establishment of the Party and at least until the beginning of the 1920s—and for rejection of "Stalinism"; it blames Stalin and his closest cohorts for the distortion of the socialist essence of the Soviet regime. The Party-Democratic movement sees the contemporary Soviet system as socialist in essence—in its foundation—but denies that the USSR is a society of developed socialism as official ideology insists that it is.[64]

According to Medvedev, if Soviet society is to enter into the phase of developed socialism, it must alter those things in its foundation "which, for various reasons, are outmoded, decayed and even rotten . . . with alacrity but also with the necessary caution."[65] The basic direction of these changes must be democratization of the Soviet system. The point of disagreement among supporters of the Party-Democratic movement was basically the degree of democratization necessary. Opinions ranged from freedom of expression at Party meetings until a decision has been reached (after which the minority must fall into line), to a multi-party system like those of the free world.

Medvedev proclaimed himself to be a supporter of broad socialist democracy for all of society; he believed that such democratization was necessary because of the demands of economic and technological progress, because of the scientific technical revolution and changes in the social structure of Soviet society.[66] Such democratization, he thought, comes about not by itself, but only as a result of a political struggle and political pressure on the "autocratic" regime. Specific strategies for democratizing Soviet society suggested by Medvedev were: elaboration of a fitting theoretical platform; development of Marxism-Leninism for contemporary needs; and the search for constructive ways to democratize economics, education, and the structure of authority. Democratization must be achieved by a peaceful struggle within a constitutional framework, by the dissemination of these ideas through means available in a Soviet-type society—through *samizdat* and, if possible, in the official press, and by organized pressure from the people and the intelligentsia on the conservative and reactionary elements in the ruling Party. Medvedev hoped that such pressure would gradually lead to changes in the apparatus of authority and to the formation in it of influential groups that would support the Party-Democratic program and the democratization process.[67] In this way, a union would be formed "between the best and most active part of the intelligentsia supported by the common people, and the most forward-look-ing individuals in the governing apparatus."[68]

What, more specifically, Medvedev means by pressure from the peo-ple and the intelligentsia within the constitutional framework, can be seen in his positive evaluation of the petition campaign of 1966–1968 and his unfavorable reaction to the human rights movement, even though it saw itself, as Medvedev acknowledged, as an attempt to pressure the authorities within a constitutional framework. Neverthe-less, Medvedev calls the human rights movement "an extremist opposi-tion." He points to the extreme diversity of the views of participants in this movement, which includes "both Party-Democrats and those who openly proclaim their opposition to Leninism and the Communist Party." Medvedev asserts that "the programmatic documents" consist of clearly anarchist proposals."[69]

The dissemination of the ideas of the Party-Democratic movement was made possible by the broad contacts of its participants—both through friendship and in professional life. Their ideas were spread in private conversations and through the 1964 publication of Medvedev's *Political Diary*—"a secret edition, it is assumed, something along the lines of *samizdat* for high-ranking officials," as Sakharov put it.[70]

The humanitarian elite, sympathetic to democratic transformation, at least had access to the special closed archives in research libraries that allowed familiarity with the communist press of other countries. Personal contacts with foreign communists contributed to such famil-iarity. Among those who supported the Party-Democratic movement were persons who had been permitted to travel abroad, and those who met communist visitors to the USSR from other countries. There were particularly close ties with Czechoslovakia, as can be seen in the mate-rials in *Political Diary*, and also in this note in the *Chronicle of Cur-rent Events:*

In the summer of this year Len Vyacheslavovich Karpinsky, head of the Scientific-Communism Department of the publishing house Progress, was expelled from the party.

L. V. Karpinsky is the son of V. A. Karpinsky (1880–1965), the well-known revolutionary, who worked with V. I. Lenin and later served as a member of the All-Union Central Soviet Executive Committee.

At the beginning of the 1960s L. V. Karpinsky was secretary for ideology of the Central Committee of the Komsomol [Communist Youth League], and later served on the editorial board of *Pravda*, as his father had done in his time. After the publication in *Komsomolskaya Pravda* of his article 'On the Way to the Première' (written with F. Burlatsky), on the subject of censor-ship in the theatre, he was removed from the *Pravda* editorial board and worked in the secretariat of *Izvestiya*, then in the USSR Academy of Sci-ences' Institute of Sociology, and, finally, in the Progress publishing house.

Karpinsky was expelled from the party after a pile of typed scientific articles, notes, and essays on sociology, political economy and economics was discovered in his desk. This material included 11 copies of a letter sent from Prague and addressed to Karpinsky. The author of the letter was Otto Lacis, who was working on the journal *Problems of Peace and Socialism*. Lacis had expressed his views on some acute problems in the social sciences. Both the letter and the other material discovered were written from a Marxist point of view and were loyal in tone. One of the main accusations levelled at Karpinsky concerned the number of copies he had of the letter.

Lacis has been expelled from the party and dismissed from his job.

Karpinsky was also dismissed from his job after being expelled from the CPSU.[71]

In the 1950s and 1960s Roy Medvedev's influence, and that of his brother Zhores and their circle, was a major factor in the social life of the Moscow intelligentsia. Andrey Sakharov, at that time at the very top of the Soviet hierarchical pyramid, was a frequent guest of Roy Medvedev. Sakharov wrote in his autobiographical note of 1973: "However our relations may have turned out, and whatever my subsequent disagreements with the Medvedevs on matters of principle, I cannot minimize their role in my own development."[72]

In 1970, Sakharov and Medvedev and Valentin Turchin wrote a letter to the Soviet leadership in which they asked for a democratization of the Soviet system.[73] Aleksandr Solzhenitsyn was also admitted to the Medvedev circle in the 1960s and also was under the influence of these types of ideas. (See his reflections about ethical and Christian socialism in *The Cancer Ward*.)

However, the charm of the Soviet variant of "socialism with a human face" faded in the late 1960s. The distance increased between Medvedev and his supporters, who had not moved from their earlier positions, and those who at this time began to be called human rights activists. The views of most human rights activists were formed "by the rumble of tanks on the streets of unsubdued Prague."[74] These events destroyed the hope of a softening in the Soviet regime and assisted in re-examination *en masse* of the positions of former supporters of the Party-Democratic movement, particularly in its view of the Soviet system as socialist. Some dropped that view altogether, others no longer saw socialism as a positive phenomenon.

The Move Away from the Party-Democratic Movement

The move away from the Party-Democratic movement was quick. In 1972, Medvedev wrote that this movement "is evidently the weakest trend both within and outside the Party."[75] The most noticeable trend at that time became the "Westernist" one, connected with Sakharov's "Thoughts on Progress, Peaceful Coexistence and Intellectual Freedom."[76] The greatest loss to the Party-Democratic movement was Sakharov himself—and not only Sakharov. Year after year Medvedev lost those who had held views similar to his. These people either stopped their social activity or joined the human rights movement, having moved their emphasis from socialist views toward democratic-legal concerns. (Raisa Lert, Pyotr Abovin-Yegides, Valentin Turchin and others).

Differences in points of view between Medvedev and his long-time close supporter, who wrote under the pseudonym Aleksandr Zimin, also came to light in the 1970s. In 1981, the New York Russian-language publishing house, Chalidze Publications, published Zimin's book, *Socialism or NeoStalinism?*, written in 1976–1977. Zimin asserts that the present Soviet structure, which he calls neo-Stalinist, is not an elemental completion of attempts at a socialist structure begun by Lenin and the Bolshevik Party after the October Revolution, but rather a conscious departure from it, initiated by Stalin. In the USSR today everything "is permeated by the interests and aspirations, traditions, ambitions and mythology of the Russian state, inherited from the capitalist and even pre-capitalist past."[77] In the contemporary world capitalism is the democratic alternative to the monstrous outcome of Stalinism. Zimin writes: "The social structure of the USSR, which now calls itself real socialism, is far from the original idea of socialism. . . . That structure . . . not only does not take into account objective laws or head in the direction of socialism, but its political ruling elite is not even interested in such a development. But this is not even capitalism. This is a society that has gone into a blind alley."[78]

Although most of Medvedev's non-Party and Party supporters left him, they were preserved in the Soviet bureaucracy and among establishment humanitarian intellectuals. This is evident in Medvedev's publications in the 1970s and 1980s in which he reveals he is conversant with details of Soviet foreign and domestic policies and with events in the world of the ruling elite.[79] Medvedev preserved his belief in the Party-Democratic ideology. In 1972, despite the continuing departure of supporters, he wrote that the Party-Democratic movement had the potential to change from a "mood" into a mass social movement, receiving support from students and youth in general.[80] In the event of such a development, Medvedev proposed "serious programs of democratic reform" which could be carried out in about ten or fifteen years.[81]

This society of developed socialism could be created in the USSR during the 1970s,[82] and classless communist society could be achieved by the end of the twentieth or beginning of the twenty-first century.[83]

Medvedev had some basis for optimism in regard to the potential of the Party-Democratic movement, since even after the mass disenchantment with the Soviet regime, the idea of democratic socialism held charm for more than a fraction of the Soviet and Party bureaucracy. Dissatisfied individuals and small informal groups who studied Marxist classics and pondered their contents in search of "real" socialism were numerous in the 1950s and 1960s, and continued into the 1970s. Such truth-seekers comprised a significant proportion of political prisoners under Khrushchev and Brezhnev. In his autobiography, Yury Orlov describes one such group of army officers in the early 1950s—fortunately, none of them was arrested. The members of this group came to the conclusion that in the USSR "the dictatorship of the proletariat" had been replaced by a "dictatorship of the bureaucracy."[84] Among the organized socialists were underground and semi-underground groups and organizations which consisted almost exclusively of young people. In most cases each such group was closed in upon itself; only a few had contacts with two or three more groups, and even these contacts did not go beyond joint meetings. These youths of the new postwar generation were sincere Marxists, socialists, and patriots. They did not want to subvert the existing order. Rather, they wanted to better it by a return to "true Leninist socialism" or to a reform "along the Yugoslav model."

In Moscow, the largest and most active such group was Lev Krasnopevtsev's, which was comprised of graduates of the Moscow University History Department. It was founded in May 1957 by seven History Department graduates; their aim was to achieve consistent de-Stalinization and liberalization in politics and economics. The members of the group conducted theoretical work to examine the historical roots of Stalinism and Bolshevism in general. They established contacts with the Polish "revisionists" and attempted to make contact with the Berlin "Gartvig group." They prepared a leaflet calling for a struggle for socialist renewal in the spirit of the Twentieth Party Congress and distributed 500 copies of this leaflet in various regions of Moscow. In August 1957 nine members of this group were arrested. In addition to these activists, twelve other people were acquitted in this case.[85] Similar to this group were the Leningrad groups of Viktor Trofimov and Mikhail Molostvov.

Another similar group was comprised of graduates of the Technological Institute in Leningrad. As students, members of this group had patrolled the city streets together in a Komsomol anti-crime brigade. Their program became a book, *From the Dictatorship of the Bureaucracy to the Dictatorship of the Proletariat*, written by two group members, Valery Ronkin and Sergey Khakhayev. This book was written in 1962 and was very close to the ideas of Milovan Djilas in *The New Class*, although its authors could not have read it before 1965. After their arrest, the investigation uncovered eighty-eight people in ten different areas who had read Ronkin and Khakhayev's book (which had been photocopied). In addition, the group had distributed leaflets. In 1965 it began to publish a journal, *Kolokol* (The Bell). While they were preparing the third issue of their journal, the members of this group were arrested.[86]

A similar fate awaited the following organizations: a group of students and teachers in Gorky, who wrote *Socialism and the State* with a general consideration of issues from a Marxist perspective;[87] a new type of Marxist party in Ryazan in 1968,[88] which had approximately ten members; a similarly small True Communist Party in Saratov;[89] and a Democratic Union of Socialists in the Odessa region, comprised of students from the Kishinev Institute of Art and young schoolteachers. The Union members rigged up a printing machine and ran off 1300 copies of a newspaper, *The People's Truth*, and distributed it in 1964 in Kishinyov and Odessa.[90] The Party for the Struggle for the Realization of Leninist Ideas was broken up in Voroshilovgrad in 1970.[91] A Union for Struggle for the Rebirth of Leninism was formed in 1963 among members of the military in the Far East. Its founder, General Pyotr Grigorenko, wrote leaflets critical of Soviet reality for its deviation from "true" Leninist socialism. Standing in the full uniform of a Soviet general, Grigorenko handed out leaflets to workers arriving at the Moscow "Hammer and Sickle" factory.[92] By the late 1960s, however, Grigorenko, still a convinced communist, had become a human rights activist, and by the mid-1970s he had become a passionate anti-communist.[93]

During the period when the human rights movement was active, underground activities almost stopped. In Moscow, there were no socialist circles. Secret organizations were fewer in the provinces, but socialist sympathizers were active in Leningrad.

On February 24, 1976 the opening day of the Twenty-Fifth Party Congress, four youths threw about one hundred leaflets from the gallery of the Gostinny Dvor department store on Nevsky Prospect. They contained hand-written slogans: "Long Live the New Revolution! Long Live Communism!!"

College students, Andrey Reznikov, Aleksandr Skobov, Arkady Tsurkov, and tenth-grader, Aleksandr Fomenko, were detained. All were expelled from the Komsomol and from their schools.[94] In April 1976 a group calling itself the "Leningrad School," which these students had also joined, announced a platform of activities "directed towards the transformation of existing society" on a Marxist basis in order to achieve true Communism. The group referred to the Soviet system as a government monopoly of capitalism. Their projected transformation of society was quite specific: it consisted of "the removal from power of state bureaucrats" after a class struggle of workers led by intellectuals.[95] In 1976, the group organized a youth commune and rented half a house on the outskirts of Leningrad, where they held discussions, exchanged *samizdat* materials, and entertained friends from various other cities.

In the spring of 1978, the group, which by then called itself the "Left Opposition," began publishing the journal *Perspectives*. Two issues appeared. A conference to which fellow-thinkers from Moscow, Gorky, and other cities were to come was planned for October 1978, but before then searches and interrogations affecting forty people were conducted by authorities.[96] In October Aleksandr Skobov, a history student at Leningrad State University, and Arkady Tsurkov, a physics student, were arrested; a little later Aleksey Khavin, a student-medic, was arrested.[97] Tsurkov, who received a term of five years in a strict-regimen camp and two years of internal exile, stated that he would continue the struggle after his release, and on leaving the court, he shouted to his friends, "Long Live the Democratic Movement!" After the breakup of the commune, members Irina Tsurkova and Aleksandr Skobov joined the unofficial labor union SMOT. When two groups of the Council of SMOT Representatives were arrested, they joined the third group. Both of them were imprisoned.[98]

December 1979 saw the trial of members of a youth group called the Union of Revolutionary Communards (worker Vladimir Mikhaylov, artist Aleksey Stasevich, and student Alevtina Kochneva). The Communards, who also lived communally in a rented house, wrote slogans on building walls, such as "Democracy—Not Demagoguery!" and "Down with Government Capitalism!" They also distributed leaflets explaining that all the evil in the world is embodied in government, private property, and the family; they admonished people to unite in a world-wide organization to eradicate anti-humanitarianism. The defendants in this trial were charged with "hooliganism"; they declared their solidarity with the French students who staged massive demonstrations in 1968.[99]

In the second half of the 1970s, after a twenty-year hiatus, a new union of socialists was formed in Moscow, arising out of the same social milieu as the Party-Democratic movement of the 1950s and 1960s. The three leading activists of the new union were: Andrey Fadin and Pavel Kudyukin, researchers at the Institute of World Economics, and Boris Kagarlitsky, an expelled graduate student at the Institute for Theatre Arts. Due to their family backgrounds, they and their fellow activists had contacts with the Soviet and government establishment, and with the humanitarian elite. Fadin's father was an expert on Norway for the Communist Party Central Committee; Kagarlitsky's father is a well-known literary critic who specializes in English and American science fiction. These activists, who were thirty years old or younger, are the second generation of the post-Stalinist socialist opposition.

In effect, the first real action of this group was the publication of a samizdat periodical journal, Variations, which first appeared in 1977.[100] At first, this journal, like Medvedev's Political Diary, was intended for a small circle, for "our people." Not an informational journal such as Political Diary, it was rather a theoretical publication. Variations, according to the informational human rights publication Bulletin V, contained discussions on "the Marxist heritage and socialist ideas in the contemporary world, first of all in Russia, about the experience of Western social-democratic parties, and on the experience of the drawing together of the intelligentsia and the working class."[101]

The state of mass consciousness in the USSR in the 1980s made this task extremely difficult. A correspondent of the French journal Alternatives in the fall of 1980 surveyed the opinions of the representatives of various social layers of Soviet society on the issue of Soviet dissent. One of his questions was, "What does it mean to be a socialist in the Soviet Union today?" The answers were as follows: A thirty-two-year-old stevedore: "A real socialist is an idea from a film. I have never in my life met one"; a former worker, a lumpenproletarian, thirty-three: "I have never encountered that idea"; a nineteen-year-old female student at a technical institute: "I don't know"; a thirty-five-year-old journalist: "A socialist is a very vague and totally abstract concept, drawn from an ideal realm like many other 'socialist' ideas—particularly 'socialism with a human face.' For some reason, the sixty-year history of a country in which Marxist ideology prevailed and communists are in power, has not taught anything to admirers of these larger-than-life schemes"; a thirty-one-year-old Russian Orthodox publicist: "After sixty years of Soviet power, the word 'socialism' has become so discredited that as a rule it evokes only negative emotions."[102]

In order to inculcate the idea of socialism into the mass consciousness Pavel Kudyukin and Boris Kagarlitsky created in 1979 the samizdat journal, The Left Turn, later renamed Socialism and the Future. Unfortunately, not a single issue of any of the socialist samizdat journals have reached the West. Only by reading a review of the fifteen issues of The Left Turn and Socialism and the Future can one learn about these journals.[103]

The anonymous author of the review says that Variations is the political cousin of The Left Turn, but thinks that the views presented in

Variations are somewhat broader. The reviewer writes that *Variations* supports "democratic socialism so that it will be economically effective." The basic idea of *Variations* can be summarized as "reform from above through pressure from below." The reviewer, who is also a socialist and Marxist, thinks that *The Left Turn*'s emphasis on an appeal to "the silent majority" is justified, as is the creation of an organized base for the movement—independent labor unions, a journal, a secret library, etc—but he is critical of the editors for their "excessive enthusiasm" for Western "leftists" and for "leftist rhetoric."

The Left Turn, as well as *Socialism and the Future*, appeared in about one hundred copies and both were distributed, at least until 1982, in Moscow and in three other cities. The people who worked on *Variations* and *Socialism and the Future* tried to set up an underground printing press to increase the number of copies of their journals.[104]

One gets an impression of the views of this group from its choice of name: "Eurocommunists" and from the lengthy work by Boris Kagarlitsky (under the pseudonym of V. Krasnov), *The Dialectic of Hope,* completed in May 1981. Kagarlitsky's book is a history of the development of socialist ideas in Russia, how they were put into practice from the time of the foundation of the Social-Democratic Party and the triumph of the October revolution until today.[105] The book is evidence of the author's close reading not only of Marx and Lenin, but also of Western literature, *samizdat,* and *tamizdat.* It is obvious that Kagarlitsky and others in his group do not consider the Soviet system to be socialist and are ready to struggle for "true" socialism. In its joint response to the questions of the French journal, *Perspectives,* the editors of *Variations* staunchly announced that "there cannot be any rapprochement with the powers-that-be." But in the distant future they hoped that, given a major crisis, the ruling bloc would split and a certain faction would agree to cooperate with the opposition (the experience of Czechoslovakia in 1968–1969, Spain after 1976, Brazil after 1978, Poland in 1980–1981, etc.) They hoped for the growth of new forms, possibilities, and the dimensions of opposition activity in the 1980s. They hoped that, alongside traditional dissidents (as they called the human rights movement), semi-legal independent organizations would develop, such as clubs, labor unions, etc., together with a socialist underground. They saw themselves as the organizers of the underground, facilitating the development of the previous dissident arrangements under the changed conditions.[106] For this purpose, the Federation of Democratic Forces of Socialist Orientation was planned.[107]

On April 6, 1982, Andrey Fadin, Pavel Kudyukin, Boris Kagarlitsky, Yuly Khavkin, Vladimir Chernetsky, and, a little later, Mikhail Rivkin, were arrested in Moscow, while Andrey Shilkov was arrested in Petro-zavodsk.[108] They were accused of "anti-Soviet propaganda" and of creating an anti-Soviet organization. In an almost unprecedented instance, however, due to a struggle at the top of the Soviet bureaucracy, an agreement to "confess" led to everyone's release before their trial—except Shilkov and Rivkin, who refused to recant.[109]

It is not known how many groups had joined the Federation, or how many such groups there were nation-wide. But the idea of the Federation did not fall on fallow ground. In the late 1970s, approximately at the same time as the journal *Variations*, a neo-Marxist journal, *Perspectives*, appeared in Lithuanian *samizdat*. Vytautas Skuodis, Gintautas Esmantas and Povilas Peceliunas were sentenced for their involvement with this journal.[110] At the same time, in Latvia, Juris Bumeisters re-established (of course, underground) the Latvian Social-Democratic Party.[111] In Moscow, in Leningrad, and in the Russian provinces, graffiti on walls and leaflets testified to the presence of underground socialists in the early 1980s. Several such groups were discovered: the "New Path" group which distributed leaflets in Moscow in the Krasnaya-Presnya district,[112] a socialist group in Vyborg,[113] and Vetrov's Initiative Group in Kuibyshev.[114] A group of socialists is known that formed around the *samizdat* collection, "Socialist-82."[115] (The pseudonym of its editor is Mark Bolkhovskoy.) Most of the eleven articles in this collection (also signed with pseudonyms) focus on evidence of the non-socialist nature of the Soviet system. The type of action favored by this group can be seen in Ya. Vasin's article on the Polish events of 1980, which the author calls "on the whole, a socialist revolution" and which he describes as "the optimal path to mass non-violent resistance and to class organization." He approves of the call not to destroy the committees of the Polish United Workers Party, but rather to create one's own committees.[116]

Yet another collective work by socialist authors that appeared in *samizdat* in late 1983 is the article "The Electoral System in the USSR and the Moral-Political Unity of Soviet Society," signed by the "Marxist-Research Group 68 80." The numbers show the ideological orientation of the group: to the "Prague Spring" (1968) and to the Polish Labor Union, "Solidarity" (1980).[117]

In the *samizdat* of the 1980s, there is a noticeable increase in works of a Marxist or socialist content compared to the 1970s. The literary talent and broad knowledge in the works of Mark Bolkhovskoy are evident.[118] N. Arguni's work, "Russian Socialists and the Future of Russia," belongs to a socialist tradition.[119] Those of the Marxist tradition are the following: Viktor Artsimovich's criticism of Marx's works from a Marxist position in his "Contradictions on Contradiction";[120] the work of physicist Yevgeny Andryushin, "The Situation of the Working Class in the USSR," which is an analysis of problems from a Marxist position;[121] German Obukhov's work, "The Extinguished Dawn," a critique of the foreign and domestic policies of the Communist Party of the Soviet Union;[122] the research of the geologist Georgy Khomizuri in his "History of the Politburo of the Central Committee of the Communist Party of the USSR";[123] and the article by Malinin, a student at the philosophical faculty at Moscow State University, "Marxism-Leninism in the Face of its Chief Prophets."[124] The socialist orientation in the USSR has a clearly democratic coloration. The socialists, along with human rights activists and pacifists oppose the anti-democratic tendencies of dissent: Stalinism, chauvinism, and fascism.

PART SEVEN

THE RUSSIAN NATIONAL MOVEMENT: CONSEQUENCES OF THE HUMAN RIGHTS MOVEMENT

CHAPTER 19

The Russian National Movement

The official ideology of pre-revolutionary Russia, embodied in the slogan, "orthodoxy, autocracy, and nationalism," was transformed in revolutionary Russia to "Proletarians of all countries, unite!" The expectation of an imminent world revolution and the necessity of preserving the integrity of the multi-national composition of the former Russian Empire dictated the official Soviet ideological emphasis on internationalism. But even in the years before the Second World War, the policies of the central Soviet government, in contrast to its ideology, were determined more by the interests of strengthening and expanding the Soviet state and increasing the centralized power within that state. The slogan of internationalism was adapted to the exigencies of "the first government of workers and peasants in the world" to "what is good for the USSR is good for the world proletariat and the future of world revolution."

The revival of the idea of Russian nationalism occurred spontaneously during the war with Nazi Germany. Stalin was the first to give official expression to this idea. During the war, he discarded the doctrine of internationalism and appealed directly to the people, eulogizing the victories of the great Russian warriors of the past. After the war, Stalin made a famous toast to "the Russian people," indicating that he fully intended to exploit national Russian feelings in the future. Official propaganda has since then changed course to adapt current goals to national Bolshevism.

The leaders of the Soviet Union cannot afford to be consistent Russian nationalists. Any emphasis on the special, historical role of the Russian people triggers a negative reaction among the many other nationalities and furthers the growth of separatist tendencies. Therefore, for a while, the authorities support Russian nationalism in the media and then restrain Russophiles who, in their eyes, "go too far." In spite of such occasional counterreactions, a nationalist current is growing stronger in Soviet propaganda and official culture. There are quite a few officially recognized authors of talent who support Russian nationalism, including Andrey Tarkovsky, Vasily Shukshin, Vladimir Soloukhin, Pyotr Paliyevsky, Viktor Chalmayev, and others.

The nationalism of the central authorities and their representatives creates dissatisfaction not only among the non-Russian peoples of the USSR, but also among the Russian educated classes, especially the older generation, which was brought up on the spirit of internationalism of the early days of Soviet power. On the other hand, inconsistencies in the official policy create dissatisfaction among the chauvinistic Soviet establishment and those educated segments of the society that have joined forces with the establishment.

National Bolshevik *Samizdat*

The group centered around A. Fetisov was the first to express national Bolshevik ideas in *samizdat*. In Fetisov's writings, the history of humankind is presented as a struggle between the forces of order and chaos. Chaos is personified by the Jewish people, who were said to have created disorder in Europe for two thousand years. The totalitarian regimes of Hitler and Stalin represented a Teutonic-Slavic intervention that put an end to these disorders. Fetisov saw these forces as positive factors in European history. His economic program called for the de-industrialization and the de-urbanization of the European part of the Soviet Union and a rebirth of the old peasant communal way of life. He proposed that all industry and all workers be relocated in Siberia. The *Chronicle of Current Events* confirmed that Fetisov's program found staunch supporters among the technical specialists who supported the idea of technocracy among those in the humanities, and also among poorly educated people who were desperate for a simple and sure way of changing the world. Extreme antidemocratism was the primary characteristic of Fetisov's group. He believed, for instance, that the writers Sinyavsky and Daniel, whose public defense initiated the human rights movement, ought to be executed. In 1956, Fetisov left the Communist Party in protest against the de-Stalinization which seemed likely to begin at that time.

In the spring of 1968 Fetisov and his three supporters—the architects V. Bykov, Mikhail Antonov, and P. Smirnov—were arrested and confined to mental hospitals.[1]

Similar views were expressed in "Word of a Nation," an anonymous *samizdat* document in the late sixties that bore the signature, "Russian patriots."[2] The authors accused Russian liberals of advocating ideas that would, if realized, lead to the impotence and ruin of Russia. The

"Russian patriots" were concerned with "purity of race," which could be damaged by "random hybridization"; they also pursued "the revival of a great, single and indivisible Russia," with Russian Orthodoxy as the state religion.

The principles enunciated by Fetisov and in "The Word of a Nation" are now continued by Gennady Shimanov, a Moscow intellectual who works as an elevator operator. A prolific *samizdat* writer, he has written a considerable number of articles in which he develops his solution for overcoming the present spiritual crisis of Russia.[3] In Shimanov's view, the causes of this crisis are as follows: the collapse of the Communist utopia; the barrenness of the Western way of life; the industrial-ecological crisis; the Chinese military threat; the internal process of "bourgeoisification"; and the spiritual and moral degradation of the Russians.[4] Shimanov mourns the degeneration of Russia: the complete disorientation of Russians in their everyday life, the disintegration of family life, psychic instability, drunkenness, demoralization, and a feeling of complete hopelessness.[5] Russians must revive spiritually and regain the power and glory that once belonged to Russia if they are to fulfill their historic mission. For this purpose, God has imposed terrible ordeals on the Russian people: the reforms of Peter the Great, the October Revolution, the Gulag labor-camp system, and the Soviet regime. All these ordeals can be justified if they become steps toward the great goal—the realization by the Russian people of their preordained mission to bring the ascetic and spiritual civilization inherent in the Christianity of Russian Orthodoxy to the rest of the world.

Shimanov is less concerned with unmasking the flaws of the Soviet regime—a concern of Solzhenitsyn's, for example—than in making use of the religious and totalitarian qualities of the Soviet regime to achieve an organic fusion of Leninism, in particular, Lenin's Party doctrine, and Russian Orthodoxy: "If the Soviet government would accept Orthodoxy, it would be able to initiate a great transformation of the world."[6] Soviet power could become an instrument for the creation of a thousand-year kingdom of Christ on earth because of its unprecedented totalitarian concentration of political power.

Like the present USSR, the future Russian state is to remain ideocratic, that is, to maintain a single ideology, excluding even the slightest dissidence, and "a highly developed nerve system in the form of the Party, which includes the entire social organism down to its smallest molecule." Shimanov writes that future transformation of the Communist Party into an Orthodox Party of the Soviet Union would result in an ideal state.[7] "This ideal state would fulfill the historic mission of the Russian people. The matter is of the entire world being Orthodoxized and, as a result, somewhat Russified."[8]

Shimanov resolves the problem of nationalities within the borders of the Soviet Union in a similar fashion: "The Soviet Union is not a mechanical conglomerate of separate nations . . . but a mystical organism composed of nations that complement each other and form, with the Russian people at their head, a miniature replica of humankind. It is a spiritual detonator for humankind as a whole," which would multiply in the process of Orthodoxification.[9] Extreme views like this version of national Bolshevism are not widespread.

The national Bolshevism of the Soviet establishment does not promote the Orthodox religion, as Shimanov does, rather it promotes the imperial idea of a great power. Inside the country, this turns into an attitude of discrimination and Russification of the non-Russian nations, through the subjection of economic and other interests of individual nationals to the interests of the whole—the USSR, where the Russian people are proclaimed, according to the official formula, "the first among equals." With regard to Soviet foreign policy, national Bolsheviks in the Soviet establishment favor the maximum extension of the Soviet Union's influence throughout the world by any means (military interventions, propaganda, blackmail, terrorism, and so forth) that would support the growth of the USSR's military power or universal deterrence. This ideology is sharply anti-Western and anti-democratic—chauvinism combined with frustration at the achievements of the West and fear of falling into dependence on the West, as well as the conviction that democratic transformations in the USSR would weaken the dynamism of Soviet foreign policy, and spark successful separatist tendencies in the non-Russian Soviet republics and in the East European countries of the Soviet bloc.

Russian patriotism of a more ordinary kind coexists with this dangerous and ugly manifestation of nationalist feeling. This patriotism of course never died out, and during the war years it naturally grew more passionate. Stalin played upon this nationalist sentiment in appealing to the lessons of Russian history. In the post-war years, a gradual ebbing of official Marxist doctrine was accompanied by a strengthening of nationalist ideology—this was a natural way to fill a spiritual vacuum. The intelligentsia, particularly its most humanitarian members, turned toward traditional, nationalist values.

The practice of spending one's vacation visiting old Russian cities in the north of Russia has become very popular. People appreciate the old Russian countryside and its architecture; they collect icons and folk art such as spinning distaffs. It has become fashionable in Moscow to decorate one's apartment with such objects. Sometimes behind this there is a serious interest in national culture, which extends to philosophy and Orthodox religion, as well as to the history of art. When the Russian intelligentsia began to doubt Marxist interpretations of Russian and world history, they turned to the writings of prerevolutionary historians such as Vladimir Solovyov, Nikolay M. Karamzin, Vasily N. Tatishchev, and Vasily O. Klyuchevsky, as well as Russian philosophers who emigrated after the Revolution. The most popular among the latter was Nikolay Berdyaev.

The All-Russian Social Christian Union

The only known attempt to form an organization for the transformation of the USSR along nationalist and Russian-Orthodox lines occurred in Leningrad in 1964. An underground organization called the All-Russian Social Christian Union for the People's Liberation was formed from the friendships of a few students at Leningrad University.[10] It was led by Igor Ogurtsov, a specialist in Japanese studies. Ogurtsov is an exceptional person, judging from the love and respect he has won not only among his friends in the union, but also among all those he met in prison (in 1967 he was sentenced to fifteen years in camp and five years of internal exile).

The ideology of the union was a reworking of Social Christianity. Its members wanted to use Christian ethics to transform the social and economic structure of Soviet society; their intention was to eliminate totalitarianism and restore a healthy balance between the individual, society, and the state. Emphasis was placed on the development of the individual. The ideas of Berdyaev, the early Vladimir Solovoyov, and Fyodor Dostoyevsky played an important role in the formulation of this ideology.

According to union members, the system of social upbringing had instilled the idea of revolution in the minds of Soviet citizens since childhood. Thus, it is enough to become aware of the compulsory nature and the duplicity of the Soviet system for the revolutionary values of the system to be turned against it. Proceeding from this premise, the union perceived its major goal as one of charting a course of spiritual regeneration and planning a model of the future state, which would be national and Christian in nature. This model is described in the platform of the organization.

The church, which is conceived of as a free community of believers, would play a very important role in the government, as in society. The Christian character of the state would be realized in the Supreme Council (*Sobor*), one-third of whose members must come from the upper hierarchy of the Orthodox church and two-thirds of whom must be "outstanding representatives of the nation, elected for life." The Supreme Council would not have administrative functions or legislative power, but would have the right to veto any law or action contradicting the principles of Social Christianity. The head of the future state would be elected by the people and responsible to Parliament. The economy of the future state would be based on self-regulating national corporations and individual farms. The land would belong to the state, but would be parceled out for use by individuals. Major industries, such as electronics and transportation, would be state property. Wage labor would be permitted only on the basis of parity.[11]

Ideas like these were unusual for the midsixties. At that time, the majority of people who speculated on the future of the USSR stayed within the limits of a Marxist framework; all their ideas bore the stamp of Marxist thought. However, the difference between the Social Christian Union and other underground groups of young people in the sixties and early seventies was not limited to a rejection of Marxism. Although, like many Marxist circles, they collected, typed, and distributed books, the rules of their Union specified that members were not only propagandists and organizers, but also soldiers. In other words, the union considered itself a sort of militant order that must be prepared to lead the anti-Communist forces in Russia in a violent revolution against the existing order. This consideration determined the extreme conspiratorial character of the Social Christian Union. It was divided into three-member units, and each member knew only the second member and the supervisor of his own unit. However, strict secrecy did not save the organization from exposure.

In the camps and prisons where members of the Social Christian Union were sent after their trials, almost no one shared their views. The anti-Semitism of some members and their common goal of preserving a "unified and indivisible Russia" created many enemies.[12] The majority of political prisoners had come from non-Russian national movements (Ukrainians and Baltic peoples), religious movements (Protestants, Baptists, Pentecostalists, and Seventh-Day Adventists for the most part), the human rights movement, and those who had tried to escape to the West. While some prisoners were attracted by the ideas of the Social Christian Union, it was the union members who were most affected by the experiences in the camps.

Shortly after his release from prison in June 1974, active union member Leonid Borodin said at a press conference for foreign correspondents that all of the union members, each for his own reasons, had ceased to accept fully the program of the Social Christian Union. As a result of their contact with the participants of non-Russian national movements, the members realized that their program was seriously limited. Their concentration on formulating a model of a Russian national government with Christianity as the state religion ignored the fact that the Soviet Union is a multi-national state whose people practice religions other than Russian Orthodoxy, or even Christianity. But their platform had only one sentence concerning non-Russian peoples: "Christian culture bears an inherently supra-national character which will play a decisive role in our era in the task of bringing peoples together into one pan-human family."[13] The program included the following additional point: the countries in which Soviet forces are temporarily located can be given aid in national self-determination on the basis of social-Christianity."[14] Consequently, this right does not extend to the peoples inside the USSR.

But what if lack of unity is not overcome? What is supposed to occur while this process—admittedly a slow one—of integration is taking place? Yevgeny Vagin, a Social Christian leader who now resides in the West, continues to defend the notion of a multi-national future state, and in a questionnaire from the Ukrainian journal *Suchastnist*, refused to answer a question about the status of non-Russian peoples.[15]

The Social Christians have learned from contacts with human rights activists in the camps that an open organization has advantages over an underground organization. Experience has proven that secret groups are uncovered relatively quickly: no group was able to operate in secrecy any longer than two years.

The founders of the Social Christian Union realized that conspiracy does not make it possible to survive, but instead increases the difficulties of communicating with sympathizers and reduces effectiveness in general.

Of course, openness was possible only for those dissident activities that do not sanction violent methods. Even former members of the union are no longer exceptions in this respect. L. Borodin, in a statement in January 1977, when authorities tried to blame an explosion in the Moscow subway on dissidents, acknowledged, "Today, all those who call themselves independent thinkers—be they liberal-democrats or religious nationalists—are negatively disposed even to less radical methods."[16]

The Social Christian Union itself was uncovered after only one year, when its membership was roughly ten. A new member, Aleksandr Gidoni, had denounced the union to the KGB. (Gidoni now lives in Canada, where he publishes a Russian journal, *The Contemporary*.) Gidoni was advised by the KGB to continue his contacts with union members. Only after two years, when the union's membership had tripled and then ceased growing, were its members arrested.[17] At the time the union consisted of 26 members, plus candidates for membership. This figure while small is quite high for an underground organization operating under Soviet conditions.

The Journals *Veche*, *The Earth*, and *Moscow Collection*

After liquidation of the All-Russian Social Christian Union for the People's Liberation, the national religious movement joined the mainstream dissident movement in that it was open and peaceful. Unlike the non-Russian national movements, which continue efforts to organize to realize their programs for the transformation of national life, the Russian national religious movement has made no such attempts since the liquidation of the Social Christian Union in 1967. People who share the views of the Russian nationalists cultivate national sentiments and explicate their theoretical basis but they do not take part in any concrete actions. None of their activities is designed to further specific views; they consist entirely of advocating human rights. For example, at the Writers' Union Congress in May 1967, Solzhenitsyn called on the participants to renounce the practice of censorship.[18] In 1970 he became honorary member of the Human Rights Committee, founded by Andrey Sakharov, Valery Chalidze, and Andrey Tverdokhlebov. *Pochvennik* Igor Shafarevich also joined this committee and delivered a paper about Soviet legislation concerning religion. Solzhenitsyn valued Sakharov's human rights activity highly and emphasized its "purifying" role in present Soviet life. Solzhenitsyn was among those who proposed Sakharov as a candidate for the Nobel Peace Prize in 1974.[19]

Other participants of the Russian national religious movement expressed their solidarity with human rights advocates by signing letters in defense of the victims of political persecution—both those who shared their own views and human rights activists. Such signatures were many until 1978.

From 1971 to 1974, activists of the religious wing were grouped around the journal *Veche* (*Popular Assembly*).[20] The editor of *Veche* was an historian Vladimir Osipov. He was one of the activists of meetings in Mayakovsky Square and in 1960 published one of the earliest *samizdat* journals, *Boomerang*. In 1961 he had been arrested for "anti-Soviet propaganda," together with Eduard Kuznetsov, later an activist in the Jewish Movement for Immigration to Israel, and with Ilya Bokshteyn and Anatoly Ivanov. Osipov served a seven-year term.[21] While in a camp with dissidents of various movements (sharply differentiated from each other at the time), Osipov came to the conclusion that "the salvation of the Russian nation is more important than civil rights." By the time he finished his term, he was a staunch supporter of Russian nationalism.

In 1971, ten years after his first arrest and three years after his release from camp, he began to publish *Veche*. Osipov declared in an editorial that the journal would have a "Russian patriotic" orientation. Its major task would be "to turn our faces toward the Motherland . . . to resurrect and preserve the national culture, the moral and intellectual heritage of our ancestors . . . to perpetuate the guiding line of the Slavophiles and Dostoyevsky."[22] Nine issues edited by Osipov discussed various problems of Russian cultural life, religion, the preservation of historical monuments, and the preservation of the environment.

Veche's credo differed radically from that of "Word of a Nation," which preached racism, state despotism, and imperialism. *Veche*'s nationalism was presented not so much as a political ideology as a specific perspective on Russian history, culture, and Orthodoxy, an attitude perfectly compatible with democratic principles.

In April 1973, Osipov wrote an open letter to Gennady Shimanov: "Personally, I am not a 'democrat,' but I have great respect for the best and most sincere among them. . . . It seems to me that the behavior of the Russian patriot is today exemplified by: speaking out openly, taking action against abuses and violations of the Constitution, defending the state against external threats, and loyalty."[23]

In an article condemning an "insidious habituation to Stalinism," Osipov wrote: "With the Initiative Group, the Human Rights Committee, our open letters, and our journals, we are, thank God, gradually beginning to overcome fear. We are inspired by the courage of people like Grigorenko, Ogurtsov, and Bukovsky."[24] The list of names here is representative: Grigorenko, a staunch Communist; Ogurtsov, a Christian and a Russian patriot; and Bukovsky, a human rights activist.

Osipov stated in another article that "freedom of opinion must be given to everyone. Believers and atheists, nationalists and democrats, Zionists and anti-Semites, conservatives and Communists—all must have the right to voice their views."[25]

Osipov applied this pluralism to his fellow-thinkers, seeking to make *Veche* a tribune for all the nuances of Russian nationalist and Russian Orthodox currents of thought. Sometimes the political views of *Veche* contributors did not coincide with his own. One such contributor, Anatoly Ivanov, who published under the pen name, Skuratov, had been a defendant in the trial of 1961, along with Osipov, and had evolved his nationalist ideas in much the same way as had Osipov. However, Ivanov injected Judophobic attitudes and Stalinist sympathies into the journal—sentiments alien to Osipov. Another who differed from Osipov was Mikhail Antonov, a follower of Fetisov's ideas, who wrote an article called "Slavophilism as the Highest Achievement of National Self-Consciousness in Russia in the pre-Lenin Period." He advocated the national-Bolshevist point of view that "only a combination of Russian Orthodoxy and Leninism can give the Russian people a world outlook capable of synthesizing centuries of experience as a nation."

And yet, such diverse authors were able to rally around *Veche* precisely because of a fundamental similarity underlying their ideologies. Aleksandr Yanov mentions five points common to them all.[26]

1. They all believed that the basis of the present world crisis was secularization and a turning away from Christianity. 2. They all referred to the West as the origin and stronghold of secular ideas. 3. They all believed that the Russian people are the mainstay of Russian Orthodoxy, which expresses their inner essence; they hoped that once having liberated themselves from the secular theory of Marxism imported from the West, the Russian people would achieve genuine salvation for themselves and a world that faces the dual threat of secularization from the West and "the Yellow menace" from the East. 4. They all considered the inner freedom of a Christian, indifferent to political regimes and social systems, to be the only true freedom. 5. They were all hostile to the intelligentsia because, in their opinion, Western secularism penetrates Russia through this social stratum, a very thin layer of Russian society, foreign to the majority of Russians, and which diverts the people from their preordained path (Solzhenitsyn referred to this class as the *obrazovanshchina*).

In various combinations, all these provisions are included in the doctrine of the Russian nationalist movement, which unites nationalists from the Soviet establishment and from the dissident factions with nationalist leanings. However, the spectrum of opinions from liberal nationalism to Shimanov's national-Bolshevism was too diverse to be contained in one and the same journal.

Osipov had no real support among the authors or those who collaborated in producing *Veche* and who were still more categorical and less tolerant of the opinions of others. Those hostile to him aired their disagreements and personal antipathies in the journal and also in open letters and statements in *samizdat*. The ambiguity of the position taken by *Veche* and the constant squabbles lowered the prestige of the journal. Eventually, these internal contradictions became irreconcilable. In the ninth issue, Osipov relinquished all editorial responsibility and stated that he would stop publication, whereupon the editorial staff declared that it would continue to publish *Veche* and maintain the same ideological orientation as before. Osipov began to publish a new journal, *The Earth* (*Zemlya*), which was close to *Veche*, but with more pronounced leanings toward Christianity.[27] He managed to publish only two volumes before he was arrested on November 28, 1974.[28]

Not only Osipov's followers (Shafarevich and former members of the

Social Christian Union for the People's Liberation), but also well-known human rights advocates (Turchin, Orlov, Kovalyon, Velikanova, Khodorovich), and Jewish activists (Agursky and Voronel) signed a letter in his defense. Sakharov appealed to all who value freedom of thought to take up Osipov's cause, although he emphasized that he did not share his ideas.[29]

At Osipov's trial, the prosecution based its case on testimony given by the editorial staff of *Veche*. He was sentenced to eight years in a strict-regimen camp.[30]

After Osipov's arrest, Leonid Borodin, a former participant in the Social Christian Union, tried to keep up the tradition of a nationalist-Russian Orthodox journal by publishing *Moscow Collection,* indebted to *Veche* for many of its themes although it did not have the latter's democratic potential. Shimanov was among the contributors, but there was no one to counterbalance his ideas. In April 1975, *Moscow Collection* ceased publication after its third issue was confiscated.[31]

The journals *Veche, Zemyla,* and *Moscow Collection* furthered the formation process of the contemporary Russian Orthodox worldview, but it was Solzhenitsyn who played the definitive role in this process. In September 1973 he addressed his *Letter to the Soviet Leaders.*[32]

Russian Nationalists and the Human Rights Movement

Solzhenitsyn wrote to the leaders of the multi-national Soviet Union about what he held "to be for the good and salvation of our people, to which all of you—and I myself—belong," in other words, as a Russian to Russians, in the supposition that they were conscious of their nationality, and that they, as he, were "swayed by this primary concern" about the fate of the Russian and Ukrainian people. He proposed to the leaders of the Soviet Union "while there is still time, a possible way out of the chief dangers facing our country in the next ten to thirty years." He considered these dangers to be "war with China, and our destruction, together with Western civilization."

Solzhenitsyn wrote that war with China would last at least ten to fifteen years, cause losses of at least 60 million people on the Soviet side, and that after such a war, "the Russian people will virtually cease to exist on this planet." The reasons for this looming danger are ideological, he told the Soviet leaders. "There is the global rivalry developing between you, this claim to be the sole true exponent of Communist doctrine and this ambition to be the one to lead all the peoples of the world after you in carrying it out."

How to avoid this danger? Renounce Marxist ideology, he advised. Solzhenitsyn reminded the leaders that during the Second World

War, Stalin exchanged ideology for "the old Russian banner—sometimes, indeed, the standard of Orthodoxy—and we conquered!" A war with China would require a similar adaptation, but in wartime such a shift could be immensely difficult. "How much wiser it would be to make *this same* turnabout today as a preventive measure." Solzhenitsyn believed that "the savage feuding" between China and the Soviet Union will "melt away, and a military clash will become a much remoter possibility and perhaps *won't take place at all.*"

The second danger is not a military one, he said. An invasion by the West does not threaten; no one intends to attack the USSR from the West; in addition, "the Western world, as a single, clearly united force, no longer counterbalances the Soviet Union, indeed has almost ceased to exist . . . the catastrophic weakening of the Western world and the whole of Western civilization . . . is . . . the result of a historical, psychological, and moral crisis . . . of humanitarian Western culture and world outlook."

But, he wrote, the ecological crisis is an immediate threat to both the West and the USSR, unless we renounce a "civilization of 'perpetual progress' . . . now choked and . . . on its last legs." In order to avert this danger it is once again necessary first and foremost to reject official Marxist ideology. Solzhenitsyn also called on the leaders to escape the "blind alley" of Western civilization; "it is perfectly feasible for a colossus like Russia, with all its spiritual peculiarities and folk traditions, to find its own particular path" and avoid being "dragged along the whole of the Western bourgeois-industrial and Marxist path."

"And herein lies Russia's hope for winning time and winning salvation, in conquering the Northeastern spaces [undeveloped territories]. These spaces allow us to hope that we shall not destroy Russia in the general crises of Western civilization." At the same time these spaces are an outpost against the Chinese threat.

Solzhenitsyn urged the Soviet leaders to stop expending their strength on expansion throughout all the countries of the world: "we need to heal our wounds, cure our national body and national spirit . . . before we busy ourselves with the cares of the entire planet." He proposed reduction of spending on preparations for war, an end to unnecessary space exploration and a redirection of these resources in order to "conquer" the Northeastern territories, to create there a "stable economy" without repeating the mistakes of "uninterrupted progress."

The considerations which guide our country must be these: to encourage the *inner,* the moral, the healthy development of the people; to liberate women from the forced labor of money-earning—especially from the crowbar and the shovel; to improve schooling and children's upbringing; to save the soil and the waters and all of Russian nature; to re-establish healthy cities. . . .

As to the future political system of the Soviet Union, Solzhenitsyn opposed revolutions or armed uprisings. Nor was he an advocate of the "turbulent 'democracy run riot' " he saw as reigning in the West; much less was he an advocate of Russian democracy.

Here in Russia, for sheer lack of practice, democracy survived for only eight months—from February to October 1917. The . . . Constitutional Democrats and Social Democrats . . . turned out to be ill-prepared for it themselves, and then Russia was worse prepared still. Over the last half-century Russia's preparedness for democracy, for a multiparty parliamentary system, could only have diminished. . . . For a thousand years Russia lived with an authoritarian order—and at the beginning of the twentieth century both the physical and spiritual health of her people were still intact. . . . But even the Russian intelligentsia, which for more than a century has invested all its strength in the struggle with an authoritarian regime—what has it achieved for itself or the common people by its enormous losses? The opposite of what it intended. . . .

Thus Solzhenitsyn asked:

So should we not perhaps acknowledge that for Russia this path was either false or premature? That for the foreseeable future, perhaps, whether we like it or not, whether we intend it or not, Russia is nevertheless destined to have an authoritarian order? Perhaps this is all that she is ripe for today?

It is not authoritarianism itself that is intolerable . . . [but] arbitrariness and illegality. . . . Let it be an authoritarian order, but one founded not on an inexhaustible "class hatred" but on love of your fellow men. . . .

Among the political problems in need of immediate resolution, Solzhenitsyn proposed the following: release "captives"; renounce "psychiatric violence," secret trials and labor camps; allow free competition of all ideological and moral currents, particularly all religions; free art and literature, and philosophical, ethical, economic, and social research; cease guarding Eastern Europe and holding the "peripheral nations" within the borders of the country against their will.

Solzhenitsyn did not circulate his Letter in samizdat, but addressed it only to the Soviet leaders, awaiting an answer. The "answer" was his arrest and subsequent expulsion from the country in February 1974. After that event, his letter appeared in samizdat. It called upon all those who cared about the fate of the motherland to "cease living a lie," and to refuse to support the official ideology through participation in the life of official Soviet society.[33] His appeal passed almost unnoticed. Many dissidents of various orientations had already managed to live according to their own moral principles, at peace with their conscience. And those who had not been inspired by the living example of these dissidents remained deaf to Solzhenitsyn's call.

In February 1974, Solzhenitsyn's *Letter to the Leaders* circulated through *samizdat*. People of the most diverse views took part in the wide discussion it evoked. Soon an anthology of fourteen articles responding to the *Letter* appeared in *samizdat*,[34] but these articles were only a small portion of all the materials that appeared on this subject.

Solzhenitsyn's thesis about Soviet society's unpreparedness for democracy attracted the most attention. In his *Letter*, he had stated this idea only as a supposition, in the form of a question, as if to leave it open for discussion. But adherents to the Russian nationalist idea, grouped around the journal *Veche*, wrote that for Russia an authoritarian regime was preferable and that democracy was undesirable and alien. "To a Russian, the distrust which lies at the base of the election system is agonizing; so is the calculation and rationalism of democracy. A Russian feels the need for a whole truth and he cannot conceive of truth as being made up of Social Christian, Social-Democratic, Liberal, Communist and other "truths" stuck together."[35]

The *Letter* became a sort of platform for the entire Russian nationalist movement, from the most democratic to the most conservative participants. The program Solzhenitsyn proposed was accepted by Osipov and Shafarevich, former participants of the Social Christian Union, and even by Skuratov. Only Shimanov rejected it as "too liberal."[36] The *Letter* brought the Russian nationalist movement solidarity and unified it ideologically. But it also provoked a deep rupture between the adherents of this movement and human rights activists, for whom, in the majority of cases, a just democratic government was the ideal. This division also emerged in the discussion about the *Letter*.

Major divergences of opinion with Solzhenitsyn and his followers were formulated, once again, by Sakharov, in his answer to *Letter to the Soviet Leaders:*

> Solzhenitsyn argues that our country may not yet be ready for a democratic system, and that an authoritarian system combined with legality and Orthodoxy cannot be all that bad if Russia managed to conserve its national vitality under such a system right into the twentieth century. These assertions of Solzhenitsyn's are alien to my way of thinking. I consider a democratic mode of development the only satisfactory one for any country.

In response to Solzhenitsyn's call for isolationism, Sakharov wrote:

> I object to the notion that our country should be fenced off from the supposedly corrupting influence of the West. . . . I am quite convinced . . . that there is no really important problem in the world today which can be solved at the national level. . . . [A] strategy for the development of human society on earth, if it is to be compatible with the continuation of the

human species, can only be worked out and put into practice on a global scale. Our country cannot live in economic, scientific, and technical isolation.

Sakharov maintained that:

the nationalist and isolationist tendencies of Solzhenitsyn's thought, and his own patriarchal religious romanticism, lead him into very serious errors. . . . Among the Russian people and the country's leaders are a good many who sympathize with Great Russian nationalism, who are afraid of democratic reforms and of becoming dependent on the West. If they fall on such well-prepared soil, Solzhenitsyn's misconceptions could become dangerous.[37]

Solzhenitsyn's exile and Osipov's arrest seriously undermined the national-Orthodox movement. Although the usual restrictions of official neo-Slavophiles (or "legal" Slavophiles as they preferred to call themselves) started, they did begin to win firm positions in the censored press. This was particularly notable with regard to the celebration of the 600th anniversary of the Battle of Kulikov (1380), when populist *pochvennik* and chauvinist motifs began to dominate the pages of many Soviet journals (*Ogonyok, Oktyabr,* and others). From that period to the present, the liberal wing of the movement has failed to express its views in any regular publication. The last collection of articles to appear was *From Under the Rubble,*[38] circulated in *samizdat* shortly after the *Letter.* The collection was prepared with Solzhenitsyn's participation and it advanced the ideas of the liberal *pochvenniks.*

It demonstrates that even the "liberals" are not monolithic in their views; the diversity of opinion expressed is quite broad, ranging from Yevgeny Barabanov, who called for an active restructuring of Soviet society in the spirit of Christian ethics together with human rights activists, to the author designated by the initials A.B., who condemned the human rights movement as a vain intrusion into secular affairs.

After *Moscow Collection* ceased to publish in April 1975, the nationalist-Russian Orthodox movement was invisible in systematic publishing activity, except for Shimanov's journal *Many Years,* which began to be issued in Moscow *samizdat* in November 1980. In the years 1974 and 1975, the disagreement between the participants of the Russian nationalist movement and the human rights movement was demonstrated in theoretical arguments alone; joint practical activities for human rights continued.

Beginning in early 1977, the Christian Committee for the Defense of the Rights of Religious Believers became the center of the Russian nationalist movement. Its founder, Gleb Yakunin, is not under the influence of nationalist emotions. His efforts have been directed toward the liberation of the Russian Orthodox Church from the debilitating pressures of an atheistic state. Since belonging to the Russian Orthodox church was by then a prerequisite to participation in the Russian national movement, it was only natural that people for whom Russian Orthodoxy was inseparable from their national identity were attracted by the Christian Committee.

The split between the Russian nationalist-religious movement and the human rights movement dates from 1978, when repressions against human rights advocates intensified. The increased level of repression was not the major cause; it was only the catalyst for a disagreement that was political in nature. By that time the Russian religious nationalists had made quite explicit their negative view of a lawful form of government and democracy, which they believed undesirable for a future Russia. This view was the real cause of their rejection of human rights activities.

In a 1978 interview with a correspondent of *Frankfurter Allgemeine Zeitung*, Shafarevich, while describing the currents he distinguished among dissidents, proposed a new definition of the concept of "he who thinks otherwise," or "dissident":

The concept "dissident" is very diffuse and undoubtedly needs a more precise definition. . . . It seems to me that . . . in our country all people are primarily divided into two types. The first are those who feel that their destinies are inextricably bound with the fate of their country, who feel themselves responsible for its future. The second type are all the rest. I do not want to say that the first type are dissidents. . . . Only those whose position in life has led to a clear clash with the power apparatus fit under the Western definition of "dissident." . . . And yet what seems to me to be fundamental is not the fact of the clash with the authorities, which is most noticeable, but the *motive* for this clash—not the outward action but the inner reason.

Shafarevich's lack of concern with "outward action" is demonstrated again in his answer to the question: "What social and political alternative to the current system would you favor?"

What we need are maximum spiritual changes with a minimum of outward changes. . . . A return to God is needed and a return to our people, a sense of the overall national purpose and a feeling of reponsibility before history and the future of our country. . . .

Despite the lack of practical activity, the nationalist religious worldview not only survived, but the number of its adherents increased. The dissemination of these views and emotions continued, chiefly in discussions in homes among friends. This passive position triumphed, if not in theory, then in practice. It is possible that this rejection of "outward actions" and the striving toward "inner changes" facilitated the growth of the number of advocates of the Russian nationalist movement, particularly in the 1980s.

As harassment of all types of opposition activity intensified, the hopes for their success in the foreseeable future died. People were forced to withdraw into themselves, and into a circle of friends. This was the extent of the position of the *pochvenniks,* as adherents of the Russian nationalist movement began to call themselves.

The theoretical development of the nationalist religious doctrine has occurred both at the level of official propaganda, in private discussions, and in *samizdat,* where, as in other areas, the initiative was taken by the spiritual leader of the Russian nationalists, Aleksandr Solzhenitsyn.[39] The most important writings by other authors include *Open the Door for Me* by Feliks Svetov and articles by Vladimir Trostnikov and Boris Mikhaylov.[40] The publishing activity of this movement was chiefly concentrated in *tamizdat.*

After Solzhenitsyn arrived in the West, the support for the Russian nationalist movement by first- and second-wave emigrés became stronger, and was reflected in the Russian emigré press. That press is represented by the *Herald of the Russian Christian Movement;* it is supported by the Popular Labor Alliance (NTS) journal *Possev,* published in West Germany, and by the journal *Veche,* edited by Yevgeny Vagin, a former member of VSKhSON, and even by *Kontinent,*[41] published in Paris, which was intended to serve as a forum for all dissident movement in the USSR and Eastern Europe.

Russian nationalists have formulated their design for Russia's future government almost exclusively in negative terms: in both *samizdat* and *tamizdat* efforts are concentrated on criticizing the weak aspects and faults of democracy—both American and all forms of West European democracy, as well as the short-lived (eight months in 1917) Russian democracy. Thus among *pochvenniks* it is already fairly clearly determined that all of this is not right for a future Russia and thus there are no disagreements among them. However, searches in a positive direction for a specifically Russian government have not, so far, yielded unanimous results. Some of the adherents of the nationalist movement are inclined toward monarchism as a traditional Russian method of rule, but the majority have accepted the idea of "authoritarian power," not defining what this means. Apparently this acceptance has not yet crystallized into a preference for one of the concrete forms of authoritarianism known today, or even a new form.

The shift of the liberal wing of the Russian nationalist movement to the right lessened the gap between it, the "legal Slavophiles" and national-Bolsheviks. At the time, the gap widened between the democratic human rights movement, the national movements of non-Russian peoples and the non-Russian Orthodox religious movements, on the one hand, and the Russian nationalist movement, on the other.

Conclusion

The history of dissent in the USSR is a tragic one. It is an endless chain of crippled and ruined fates. The movement never became a mass movement and the immediate demands of dissidents were almost wholly frustrated.

Does such an unequal struggle make sense? Orwell gave an answer to that question in his book *1984*. It is possible that Soviet society would have become like that of Orwell's novel—even by the year 1984—without individuals in the Soviet Union who risked this struggle.

Orwell was reflecting on tendencies inherent in the Soviet system that he had observed in 1948—five years before the death of Stalin. Fortunately, that period represented the peak of opportunity for Big Brother to penetrate the souls and lives of the people under his control. After Stalin's death, there was an inevitable hitch in the realization of the destiny of the Soviet system as Orwell had predicted there would be. A mass paroxysm of unbearable fury shook the cemetery which Soviet society then was, in the sense of the absence of an independent social life. The authorities recovered very quickly—instantly, from a historical perspective—but the momentary weakening of their grip was sufficient for the birth of dissent. Throughout all of the succeeding years, up to 1984, the year this book was completed, the authorities have struggled against incipient discontent. Yet it does not disappear; it simply changes its form and appearance. Discontent may die down in one place, only to reappear in another. Like ever-widening circles in water, it moves ever farther from Moscow, where its center once was.

And so the gloomy predictions of Orwell have not been fulfilled. To some degree, *1984* assisted this process. I can testify to the direct influence of Orwell's book on the awakening of Soviet society. This book was one of the first to appear in *samizdat*—even before the word was invented. Sometime in 1957 or 1958 a typewritten copy began to circulate from hand to hand. The translation was amateurish and even illiterate—it was a literal translation. But the impression it made was stunning.

Soviet readers of Orwell's books were the very double-thinkers he had described. Yet they had only been vaguely aware of the phenomenon of double-think, until they read about it in *1984*. This awareness hastened the appearance of dissidents (or those who think differently) among the double-thinkers. Recognizing in *1984* their yesterday, which had not yet become just history, and observing the efforts of the authorities to return to that yesterday, some would not come to terms with the prospect of turning back into trembling creatures. Their dissent, however, was unlike the opposition that Winston Smith, in *1984*, was prepared to face. In 1948, there was no opposition in the USSR. Orwell based his image on the only one then known in Soviet history: the Inner Party opposition of the 1920s and 1930s. These oppositionists differed from the ruling party on some issues, but in their morality and methods they did not differ. Nothing in history is mechanically repeated: the dissidents of the post-Stalin era were different from any who had gone before.

During the years of Stalinism, all forms of dissent were so carefully blotted out that there was no person one could join with—everyone went his own way. Everyone did what he could and looked for allies. People were drawn together in small groups of acquaintances—both underground and in public—which they created at the spur of the moment. Someone put *The Book* in Winston Smith's briefcase; Soviet dissidents, on the other hand, had no system of views that had been worked out by someone else. Still they had a major advantage: they did not swear to anyone that they were ready to tell any lie, to perform any cruelty or mean act for the sake of the general cause. Indeed, the opposite was true. One of the early indications of this particular feature of the then incipient human rights movement was the article "Think!" written by Lev Ventsov (Boris Shragin's pseudonym.) Ventsov wrote about the revealing conflict of society with the powers-that-be. He wrote that this conflict was one not of:

political doctrines, not ideology, not party and classes . . . rather, it was something completely different, something more profound: truth versus lying-on-command; honesty versus profit of the vilest sort; a feeling for justice, the warmth of human participation versus cruelty mired in cowardly vengefulness; the consciousness of rights versus lawlessness; finally, a feeling of self-worth versus a sense of one's own insignificance. The historic collision was locked in personalities. . . . The conflict was transferred to the most basic morality. . . . The elementary humanitarian values—truth and kindness—were revealed. They are easily distinguished today if only because the regime as a whole is not even capable of pretending to claim that it partakes of these values.[1]

Now it is obvious that there could not have been any other kind of opposition to the claims of Big Brother. Everyone must start from the very beginning to liberate himself from lies and violence, to strengthen his hostility to them, which inevitably is forfeited in spiritual integration and in official Soviet life. This may sound like a moralizing digression, but this is precisely how the social instinct operated when one had to begin at the very beginning—so that righteous persons and not politicians emerged at the surface of social life. Until 1984, these righteous people were the only visible force in a country that restrained those tendencies which, according to Orwell, would otherwise have been victorious.

In the USSR, a moral, and not a political, opposition arose. The closest analogy to the Soviet human rights movement is less the present human rights movement in the West, than the resistance of the early Christians in the Roman Empire, of the populists in Russia, of Gandhi's movement in India and of Martin Luther King, Jr.'s civil rights movement in the United States. These movements have quite different cultural-historical roots, but all were moral oppositions. Closest to us in time, the movements in India and in the United States, from the historical perspective, represented the first, prepolitical stage of the struggle for political rights for those who had had none. In this sense, Soviet society—all its layers, including the intelligentsia, who began the human rights movement—is comparable to Indian society during the Raj and the black followers of Martin Luther King. The Soviet human rights movement shares common ideals and goals with other contemporary human rights movements, but the different groups operate not only in different political climates, but almost as if in different epochs.

The moral climate of the Soviet human rights movement is closest to that of the early Christian era. The basis of the juridical principle of human rights, as is known, is the Christian idea of freedom and the value of the human personality, the philosophical approach to personality that arose from Christianity. In Soviet society, the Christian tradition as a whole, particularly its interpretation of personality, had been undermined by official collectivist ideology and the entire anti-personality practice of the Soviet system, which imposed itself on the collectivist traditions of the patriarchal Russian peasantry, not yet dissolved by the time of the revolution. Official Soviet ideology appeals to the social unit, not, as a rule, to the individual. To initiate and conduct practical efforts in defense of the sovereignty of the personality would be impossible without liberation from the influence of Soviet ideology and appeals to the ideology of a society based on law—European, Christian. In this sense, the present Soviet intelligentsia revives the tradition of social service of its predecessors, the Russian intelligentsia, and returns to the values of the European-style democracy to which the prerevolutionary intelligentsia adhered, although the present intelligentsia rejects its God-battling. The ideal and moral Christian-European foundation of the human rights movement formed a natural alliance of the human rights activists with the religious and national-religious movements in the USSR, on the one hand, and with the West, on the other. The unification of these previously scattered forces under the human rights banner was the achievement of the human rights movement of the 1960s and 1970s.

By 1984, however, Soviet authorities had achieved a considerable success in suppression: by that time, at the cost of many victims, the public voice of oppositional criticism had been stifled; the human rights movement had been broken up; and the fledgling unity of Soviet dissent had fallent apart. The first period prepolitical dissent in the USSR was concluded. What were the consequences?

Despite the small visible gains of the opposition during the preceding twenty-year period, governmental control of society by 1984 had not attained Orwellian dimensions, but neither had it been proven by the year 1948—the date of Orwell's writing. Of course, dissent is not the only reason for this, but the other reasons are beyond the limits of my theme. Still, without a conscious and self-sacrificing moral opposition inside the system, none of the other factors would be operative.

By 1984, previously amorphous political dissent had crystallized into several trends, including political ones, a majority of them transitional between those that are political and those that lead away from it. As a result of the physical removal from social activism of the activists of the early phase of dissent, and as a result of its own politicization, the moral potential of dissent was lowered. The dispersal of the human rights movement led to an accentuation in the national movements of egoistic, chauvinistic, and xenophobic moods, and, in the religious movements, of a move away from concern about social problems. Among the masses, the cult of Stalin and the general cult of "the strong ruler" spread; fascists and fascist sympathizers appeared; more dissidents confessed under pressure from the authorities; furious attacks by one dissident on another increased. Attacks from all sides on human rights activists—because of their disinterest in any political perspective or organization, for their pro-Western orientation, and for the small gains of their sacrifices—led to a weariness and cynicism that overcame those who supported the human rights movement. This is a regrettable, yet inevitable given of the transition to a new period of social opposition to the government.

What is this new period and what will the future be of Soviet dissent?

Predictions are risky, in any case, especially predictions on the future of the Soviet Union, where special socioeconomic relations exist, without any direct analogies to previous periods of human history. The future development of this socioeconomic formation can be clarified through the personal experience of present and future generations.

Some possible variants of the future development of dissent in the USSR can be seen in the experience of countries with analogous socioeconomic systems: Hungary, Czechoslovakia, Poland. But no possible combination of these other models, or deviation from them, or, furthermore, any temporary frameworks for their realization in the USSR can be defined. It is, however, already evident that, despite the proliferation of the instruments of punitive repression and the increased rage of the authorities, the government cannot draw back to the fold of official ideology those people for whom it has lost its attraction—and those, I think, number in the tens of millions. But this does not mean that there are millions of dissidents in the USSR; there are far fewer. According to my calculations for the fifteen-year period from 1968 until 1983, about half a million Soviet citizens have publicly declared their dissident opinions. (I have in mind the participants in independent social associations, demonstrators, signatories of all types of protest letters, activists in the independent church and national movements, the authors and distributors of *samizdat*, and so on.) This is not a small number considering Soviet conditions, which are too severe for the mass expression of dissent, and considering the Russian tradition of sociopolitical inertia of the majority of the population. (I recall that just before the October revolution there were fewer than 50,000 members of the Bolshevik Party.)

Dissent, having once appeared, will spread in one or another form in the future. Various political orientations will somehow be organizationally grouped. With no possibility of total suppression of dissent, the authorities will regulate it by bringing the weight of repression to bear against the strongest and, in their opinion, the most dangerous, sparing those others with which they can live, and encouraging those they hope to use for their own purposes. Among trends clearly discernible in the early 1980s is the favored treatment of those with antidemocratic tendencies. Testimony to this trend is the defeat of the human rights movement, the decisive steps taken against the national-democratic movements, compared to mere isolated arrests of Russian nationalists. Evidence of this can be seen in the substantial difference in how the authorities have decided the personal fates of the spiritual head of the Russian nationalists, Aleksandr Solzhenitsyn, on the one hand, and of the advocate of democracy and liberalism, Andrei Sakharov, and the participants in the Helsinki groups, on the other. It can be seen in the slight pressure on the "socially close" activists of democratic socialism compared to the sentencing to long camp terms of other activists of this movement; in the markedly soft relationship to the adherents of the apolitical, less socially concerned Orthodox church, contrasted with the unrelenting pressure on the unregistered churches of Baptists, Pentecostalists, Adventists, and even Catholics; in the cautious attitude toward fascists, Stalinists, and other supporters of strong rulership in the USSR compared to the rapid rooting out of the slightest efforts to stand up for socioeconomic rights.

The authorities' political calculation to a significant degree is determined by the increased specific gravity of the antidemocratic trend in dissent in the 1980s. It does not follow, however, that the efforts of the authorities make the decisive difference. They simply regulate those processes in society that develop spontaneously and beyond their control, although directly connected to their general political course. The appearance and growth of an antidemocratic mood during the 1980s can be explained by the bankruptcy of hopes—widespread during the 1960s and still surviving in the 1970s—in the democratization of the Soviet system or, at least, in a major softening of the regime. The failure of the "Prague Spring" of 1968, followed by the policy of re-Stalinization; the invasion of Afghanistan, and the rejection of détente; the reprisal against Sakharov and his fellow-thinkers in 1979–1980; the defeat of public opposition in 1983–1984—these are the landmarks in the extinguishing of hope for democratization. Economic failures, corruption, the deteriorating standard of living, and the fear of war, all have stimulated favorable conditions for popular dreams of a strong ruler, a traditional way out for Russia in times of crises. But during a century of scientific-technical revolution, this traditional formula may have the opposite effect—after all, the present troubles of the USSR are not at all due to the insufficient toughness of its leadership, and the "middle level" has been far surpassed; the troubles are precisely in those areas in which a democratic model could be effective.

Soviet society is in great need of a new George Orwell to delineate present trends and to look again into the possible future, another thirty-five years from now, as 1984 was from 1948, when Orwell wrote his *1984*. Perhaps the horror of a vision of such a future would bring maturity to those living in the USSR. It could mobilize the best spiritual and mental powers of the country. It could help to discover a way out of the approaching nightmare, or at least push it farther away, as earlier the authorities had had to reject their own attempt to re-Stalinize the country in the late 1960s in the face of public pressure.

A positive note can be found in the fact that, as in *1984*, the opposition in the USSR now has its Book. This book is personal experience, as recorded and gathered in *samizdat*, in knowledge that penetrates from the outside through *tamizdat*, through foreign radio broadcasts beamed to the USSR, and the infrequent, but nevertheless recurring, contacts with people from the free world. It is already obvious in what direction one should act: by peaceful pressure from below for reforms from above. This is the general strategy of all orientations—human rights and pacifist, political (all types of socialists, Stalinists, and even fascists) and national and religious. No one in Soviet society espouses a violent revolution or *Putsch* or external aggression. Generations in the USSR have now lived through two world wars, a civil war, and the Stalinist terror. Among these people there are no advocates of violent methods—either external or internal—to achieve goals. No one wants war or a violent revolution; no one believes in the possibility of improving the present situation in this way, except possibly fascists—no one knows what fascist young people want or what they are capable of. Otherwise, dissent still represents a comforting contrast to the violent nature of Soviet totalitarianism.

Independent social life, now no longer visible on the surface because of the forcible suppression of publicity, is discovered in various guises whenever the authorities loosen their grip briefly. Then there is a spontaneous increase in the activity of all dissenting movements, which rapidly develop new organizational forms; there is a burst of interest in social and political problems among the generally inert mass of the Soviet population, first of all among the peoples of the non-Russian republics and in the large cities of the Russian areas of the USSR. It is impossible to discern what the correlation now is between democratic and antidemocratic forces in dissent, on whose side one or another social force is. But there is some data on the present mood of the "silent majority."

In early 1981, a group of sociologists conducted a survey (of course, unofficially and secretly) among Muscovites and people from the Moscow area on the question: "What is your attitude toward Sakharov?" Eight hundred and fifty-three individuals were asked. (Excluded from the survey were dissidents, their friends and families, since the aim was to ascertain the mood of people outside dissident circles.) In September of 1981, another survey was conducted, on the question: "What is your attitude to the Polish labor union, Solidarity?" For this survey, 618 people were interviewed. The proportion of positive answers in both surveys was approximately the same: a little over 20 percent. (The proportion of negative answers in the second survey was higher; more people surveyed were insufficiently informed to reach their own opinions or were indifferent to the topic of the survey.)[2]

Furthermore, the results of an official but unpublished survey conducted in 1981 became known. This survey was conducted among military recruits. Because the USSR has obligatory military service, the survey covered most eighteen- and nineteen-year-old men. The question was: "Do you believe that the USA might be the first to attack the Soviet Union and begin a nuclear war?" Eighteen percent answered negatively. (What percent of those surveyed responded "yes" or "I do not know, I have no opinion" is unknown.)[3] Although the question about the military threat is somewhat removed from the other two, under Soviet conditions anyone who does not believe that the USA will attack does not believe in official Soviet propaganda, for which this has been a basic theme since the early 1980s. It demonstrates also a sympathetic view of the West and evidence of some individual efforts to attain information about the West. It is particularly interesting that this result virtually coincided with the results of the surveys about Sakharov and Solidarity. These three corresponding results permit one to estimate that the potential reserve of democratic orientation includes about one-fifth of the population of large cities; in the non-Russian republics, most likely more. On the results of the Sakharov survey, one can conclude that an approximately similar percentage of 20 percent is of antidemocratic orientation, while the remaining 60 percent is indifferent. If this balance is to be preserved into the future, what citizens among the inert 60 percent prefer depends on which trend in Soviet dissent the West will support, on whether the West will be sufficiently consistent in its support, and on the activity of democratic forces. The West is the only ally of dissidents in the USSR. Western support may play a decisive role.

Notes

(The samizdat human rights publication *Chronicle of Current Events* (*Khronika tekushchikh sobytiy*) (abbreviated as *CCE* in notes) is edited and distributed in Moscow by hand and published in typeset form in the West in both Russian and English. Different issues have been published by different publishers; some issues have not been published at all. The Russian editions are: *Khronika tekushchikh sobytiy,* issues No. 1–27, Amsterdam, A. Herzen Foundation, 1979; *Khronika tekushchikh sobytiy,* issues No. 28–64, New York, Khronika Press, 1974–1984. The English editions are: *Chronicle of Current Events,* issues No. 1–11 in *Uncensored Russia: The Annotated Text of the Unofficial Moscow Journal, The Chronicle of Current Events,* edited by Peter Reddaway, London, Jonathan Cape, 1972; *Chronicle of Current Events,* issues 12–16, have not been published in English; *Chronicle of Current Events,* issues 17–64, London, Amnesty International Publications.)

Introduction

1. Document No. 24, Moscow Helsinki Watch Group, *Reports of the Helsinki Accord Monitors in the Soviet Union and Eastern Europe: Documents of the Public Groups to Promote Observance of the Helsinki Agreements in the USSR* (edited and published by the Staff of the Commission on Security and Cooperation in Europe, Congress of the United States, Washington, DC), vol. 3, p. 13.
2. Ludmilla Alexeyeva, "The Evolution of the Dissent Movement from Underground Cells to Open Associations," in *Chronicle of Human Rights in the USSR* (*CHR*) (New York: Khronika Press), No. 31 (July–September 1978), pp. 41–46.
3. Vladimir Bukovsky, *To Build a Castle: My Life as a Dissenter* (New York: Viking Press, 1979), p. 141.
4. My own calculations, made on the basis of Yury Maltsev, *Volnaya Russkaya Literatura* (Frankfurt-am-Main: Possev, 1976).
5. *Sintaksis* (Paris), no. 1 (1978), pp. 3–5.
6. Bukovsky, *To Build a Castle,* p. 140.
7. Anatoly Levitin-Krasin, *Rodnoy prostor* (Tel Aviv: 1982); Bukovsky,

To Build a Castle; Andrey Amalrik, *Notes of a Revolutionary* (New York: Alfred A. Knopf, 1982); Pyotr Grigorenko, *Memoirs* (New York: W. W. Norton, 1982).

8. Mihajlo Mihajlov, *Leto moskovskoye* (Frankfurt-am-Main: Possev, 1967), p. 48.
9. S. Cohen, ed., *An End of Silence* (New York, London: 1982); Abstract in *Chronicle of Current Events (CCE)*, no. 21, pp. 294–95.
10. Cohen, *End of Silence*, pp. 17–18.
11. *moskov-skoye*, p. 30.
12. *Khronika tekushchikh sobytiy (KTS)* (issues 1–15 and issues 16–27) (Amsterdam: A. Herzen Foundation, 1979); ibid., issues 28–64 (New York: Khronika Press). English text, issues 1–11, "The Annotated Text of *A Chronicle of Current Events,*" in Peter Reddaway, ed., *Uncensored Russia* (London: Jonathan Cape, 1972); issues 16–64, *Chronicle of Current Events (CCE)* (London: Amnesty International Publications); see also Mark Hopkins, *Russia's Underground Press: The Chronicle of Current Events,* foreword by A. Sakharov (New York: Praeger, 1983).
13. "The Formation of the Initiative Group for the Defense of Human Rights" from A. Grumberg, ed., *The Quest of Justice* (London: Pall Mall, 1970), pp. 458–61.
14. *KTS,* 16, pp. 41–43; Valery Chalidze, *To Defend These Rights* (New York: Random House, 1974), Appendix: *Documents of the Human Rights Committee in the USSR,* pp. 199–204.
15. *Vol'noye slovo* (Samizdat, Izbrannoye) (Frankfurt-am-Main: Possev, 1977), vol. 28 (Khristyansky Komitet zashchity (vershchikh v SSSR,
16. See documents of Helsinki Groups in *Reports of Helsinki Accord Monitors in the USSR; The Human Rights Movement in the Ukraine: Informational Bulletins of the Ukrainian Public Group to Promote the Implementation of the Helsinki Accords* (Toronto-Baltimore: Smoloskyp, 1981); *The Violations of Human Rights in Soviet-Occupied Lithuania* (Glenside, PA: The Lithuanian Community of the USA, 1978), report for 1977.

1. The Ukrainian National Movement

1. Testimony of Nadiya Svitlychna, eyewitness of demonstration.
2. *The Economy of the USSR, 1922–1982* (Moscow, 1982), pp. 18, 11, 35.
3. "Ethnocide of Ukrainians in the USSR," *Ukrainsky visnik* (Ukrainian Herald no. 7/8), Baltimore, 1976, p. 39.
4. Ibid., pp. 26–27.
5. Ibid., p. 26.
6. *Results of the All-Union Census,* 1970 (Moscow: Statistika, 1973), vol. 4, pp. 9, 152–58; *Vestnik statistiki* (Statistics Herald), 1980, no. 8.
7. *Results of the All-Union Census,* 1970, vol. 4, pp. 152–53; *Vestnik statistiki,* 1980, no. 8.
8. *Results of the All-Union Census,* 1970, vol. 4, pp. 475–76; vol. 3, p. 358.

9. *Ukrainsky visnik*, no. 7–8, p. 53.
10. "Register of Persons Convicted or Detained in the Struggle for Human Rights in the USSR," *Arkhiv samizdata* (*AS*) (Radio Liberty, Munich), 1971.
11. *CCE*, no. 33, pp. 176–78.
12. *CCE*, no. 51, p. 105.
13. M. Kheyfets, "Zoryan Popadyuk: dissident bez strakha i upryoka," *Forum*, no. 4 (Munich: Suchasnist, 1983).
14. "L. Lukyanenko to the Procurator General of the USSR: Ferment in the Ukraine," ed. M. Browne (London: Macmillan, 1971), p. 37.
15. Leonid Plyushch, *History's Carnival: A Dissident's Autobiography* (New York: Harcourt Brace Jovanovich, 1979), p. 75.
16. Valentin Moroz, *Report from the Beria Reserve* (Chicago: Cataract Press, 1974), p. 90.
17. Ivan Dzyuba, *Internationalism or Russification?* (London: Widenfeld & Nicolson, 1968).
18. Vyacheslav Chornovil, "The Misfortune of Intellectuals," in *The Chornovil Papers* (New York: McGraw-Hill, 1968), pp. 80–81.
19. Moroz, *Report from Beria Reserve*, p. 91.
20. Mikhailo Osadchy, *Belmo* (Cataract) (Munich: Suchasnist, 1980), pp. 66–67.
21. Pavel Litvinov, ed., *The Trial of the Four* (London: Longmans, 1972).
22. *CCE*, nos. 5 and 6, in Reddaway, *Uncensored Russia*, pp. 288–90.
23. Ibid., pp. 295–96; on Gorskaya, testimony of Nadiya Svitlychna.
24. "On the Trial of Pogruzhalsky," in *The National Question in the USSR: A Collection of Documents* (Munich: Suchasnist, 1975), pp. 37–45.
25. Ibid., pp. 45–61.
26. *The Youth of Dnepropetrovsk in the Struggle Against Russification* (Munich: Suchasnist, 1971).
27. Leonid Plyushch, *Na karnavale istorii* (London: Overseas Publications, 1979), pp. 486–89.
28. *Ukrainsky visnik* (1971–72), nos. 1–6.
29. Ibid., no. 7–8, p. 125.
30. *KTS*, no. 14, pp. 440–41; *CCE*, no. 17, pp.
31. *CCE*, nos. 25–27.
32. *CCE*, no. 28, pp. 28–35; no. 29, pp. 56–60; no. 30, pp. 90–91.
33. *Ukrainsky visnik*, nos. 7–8, pp. 122–23.
34. Ibid., pp. 131, 134.
35. Ibid., p. 134.
36. Ibid., p. 134.
37. *CCE*, no. 30, p. 123.
38. *CCE*, no. 60, pp. 52–69.
39. *CCE*, no. 53, p. 71.
40. *CCE*, no. 55, pp. 3–5; Yury Badzio, "An Open Letter to the Presidium of the Supreme Soviet of the USSR" in *New York Foreign Representation of the Ukrainian Public Group to Promote Implementation of the Helsinki Accords*, 1980.
41. *CHR*, 1974, no. 11, p. 28.
42. V. Yasen, ed., *The Human-Rights Movement in the Ukraine: Documents of the Ukrainian Helsinki Group, 1976–1980* (Baltimore: Smoloskyp, 1980), pp. 19–23.

43. Mykola Rudenko, *Monologues on Economics* (New York: Suchasnist, 1978).
44. *Reports of Helsinki Accord Monitors*, vol. 3, pp. 130–157.
45. See *The Human-Rights Movement in the Ukraine.*
46. CCE, no. 8, in Reddaway, *Uncensored Russia*, pp. 290–91; CCE, no. 48, pp. 164–66; CCE, no. 51, p. 105; CCE, no. 61, p. 206; CCE, no. 64, p. 117.
47. CCE, no. 53, pp. 73–74.
48. CCE, nos. 53–63; *USSR News Brief*, (1984), 5, no. 1; 10, no. 1; 19/20, no. 1; (1985), 17, no. 1.
49. CCE, no. 62, pp. 50–55; CCE, no. 63, pp. 68–71.
50. CCE, no. 56, p. 139; CCE, no. 60, pp. 51–52.
51. AS 45/80, and issue 32/80.
52. CCE, no. 61, pp. 158–59; no. 62, pp. 55–59.
53. "Polozheniye tsarkvi v SSR (Ukraina)," AS 8, no. 4850 (1983); CCE, no. 64, pp. 135–37; *USSR News Brief*, (1985), 5, no. 1; 10, no. 1; 14, no. 6; 22, no. 4; AS, 40, (1984) nos. 5371–5373; (1985), 8, nos. 5405–06; 10, nos. 5410; 11, no. 5413; 12, no. 5414.

2. The Lithuanian National Movement

1. Laisves Sauklys, "Herald of Freedom," nos. 1–3, 1976; CCE, no. 45, pp. 320–21.
2. *Violations of Human Rights in Soviet-Occupied Lithuania*, report for 1977, p. 57.
3. Ibid., p. 55.
4. CCE, no. 22, p. 8.
5. *Violations of Human Rights in Soviet-Occupied Lithuania*, p. 57.
6. Bukovsky, *To Build a Castle*, p. 408.
7. CCE, no. 47, p. 55.
8. Bukovsky, *To Build a Castle*, p. 408.
9. CCE, no. 27, pp. 310–11.
10. T. Zenklys [pseud.], "Proshchayas s Antanasom Sneckusom," *Kontinent* (Paris), no. 14 (1977), pp. 229–50.
11. Eitan Finkelshtein, "Old Hopes and New Currents in Present-Day Lithuania," in *Violations of Human Rights in Soviet-Occupied Lithuania*, 1978, pp. 229–50.
12. Zenklys, "Proshchayas s Antanasom Sneckusom."
13. CCE, no. 32, pp. 40–42.
14. CCE, no. 26, pp. 448–50; no. 27, pp. 298–300.
15. CCE, no. 26, p. 251.
16. *The Bell* (*Varpas*), no. 1 (1975).
17. CCChL, no. 23, pp. 49–50.
18. CCE, no. 47, pp. 50–51; no. 48, pp. 113–14.
19. Tomas Remeikis, "Dissent Activity in Lithuania During 1977," in *Violations of Human Rights in Soviet-Occupied Lithuania*, report for 1977, p. 24.

20. *Ibid.*
21. *CCE*, no. 51, p. 226. Tomas Remeikis, ed., *Opposition to Soviet Rule in Lithuania, 1945–1980* (Chicago: n.p., 1980), pp. 411–16.
22. *CCChL*, no. 19, pp. 4–6; no. 28, p. 14.
23. Remeikis, *Opposition to Soviet Rule in Lithuania*, pp. 501–10.
24. *CCE*, no. 22, pp. 27–28; no. 23, pp. 79–84; Remeikis, *Opposition to Soviet Rule in Lithuania*, pp. 511–21.
25. *CCE*, no. 25, pp. 198–99.
26. *CCE*, no. 55, p. 34; *AS* 27, no. 4367 (1981).
27. *AS* 17, no. 632.
28. *CCE*, no. 53, p. 129.
29. *CCE*, no. 37, p. 206.
30. *CCE*, no. 37, pp. 33–35: Remeikis, *Opposition to Soviet Rule in Lithuania*, pp. 593–602.
31. *CCE*, no. 53, p. 129.
32. *CCChL*, no. 28, p. 16.
33. *CCChL*, no. 9, p. 9.
34. *CCChL*, no. 28, p. 13.
35. *CCE*, no. 46, p. 43; Remeikis, *Opposition to Soviet Rule in Lithuania*, pp. 632–35.
36. *CCE*, no. 38, pp. 80–91.
37. *CCChL*, no. 28, p. 18.
38. *CCChL*, no. 19, p. 14; no. 28, p. 13; *CCE*, no. 56, p. 160.
39. "Declaration of the Lithuanian Helsinki Group," in *Reports of the Helsinki Accord Monitors*, vol. 1, p. 122.
40. *Ibid.*, vol. 3, pp. 158–76.
41. *CCE*, no. 47, pp. 46–47; *Violations of Human Rights in Soviet-Occupied Lithuania*, report for 1977, p. 91.
42. *CCE*, no. 54, p. 140; Remeikis, *Opposition to Soviet Rule in Lithuania*, pp. 659–63.
43. *CCE*, no. 54, pp. 140–41; Remeikis, *Opposition to Soviet Rule in Lithuania*, p. 664.
44. *CCE*, no. 56, p. 152.
45. *AS* 6, no. 3857 (1980).
46. *CCE*, no. 56, pp. 153–55; no. 62, pp. 67–69; no. 63, pp. 83–84.
47. *CCChL*, no. 49, pp. 53–55.
48. *CCChL*, no. 48, pp. 43–44; *CCE*, no. 61, pp. 170–72.
49. *CCChL*, no. 49, pp. 16–22; *USSR News Brief*, 4 (1982), no. 22.
50. *CCE*, no. 60, p. 68.
51. *CCE*, no. 62, pp. 67–69.
52. *CCE*, no. 60, pp. 65–68.
53. *CCChL*, no. 56, pp. 9–14; no. 61, pp. 7–15.

3. The Estonian National-Democratic Movement

1. *Nakhoditsya li estonskiy narod i ego kultura pod chuzhezemnym igom?—Pis'mo 15 estonskikh intelligentov* (perevod s estonskogo), *Forum*, no. 3 (Munich: Suchasnist, 1983), pp. 128–45.

2. Ibid., p. 131.
3. Ibid., p. 132; *Vestnik statistiki* (Moscow: Statistika, 1980), no. 11, p. 64.
4. Ibid., pp. 133–34.
5. According to testimony by Boris Mikhalevsky, a scientific researcher at the Institute of Economics of the USSR Academy of Sciences.
6. *Pis'mo 15 estonskikh intelligentov*, p. 134.
7. Ibid.
8. Ibid., p. 139.
9. *CCE*, no. 33, pp. 145, 157.
10. *CCE*, no. 36, pp. 169–70; no. 38, pp. 91–95; "Sudebny protsess po delu estonskogo demokraticheskogo dvizheniya, oktyabr 1975 g." (New York: Khronika, 1976).
11. *CCE*, no. 57, p. 62; no. 62, p. 66.
12. *CCE*, no. 57, p. 61; no. 60, pp. 62, 228; no. 62, p. 60; no. 63, pp. 210–12.
13. *USSR News Brief*, 5 (1983), no. 6; 11, no. 8.
14. *CCE*, no. 57, p. 61; *USSR News Brief*, 1 (1983), no. 3; 7, no. 5; 13/14, no. 3.
15. *CCE*, no. 52, pp. 145–46.
16. *CCE*, no. 55, p. 57.
17. *USSR News Brief*, 19 (1980), no. 32; 20, no. 1.
18. *Pis'mo 15 estonskikh intelligentov*, p. 143.
19. *Vesti iz SSSR*, 1980, 20, no. 1.
20. Ibid.
21. *USSR News Brief*, 19 (1982), no. 4.
22. *USSR News Brief*, 10 (1981), no. 8.
23. *CCE*, no. 54, p. 152; Remeikis, *Opposition to Soviet Rule in Lithuania*, pp. 659–63.
24. *CCE*, no. 56, pp. 151–52; AS 6, no. 3857, Radio Liberty (Munich, 1980).
25. *CCE*, no. 56, pp. 150–52; no. 57, p. 62.
26. *CCE*, no. 64, p. 42.
27. AS 6, no. 4570 (1982).
28. *CCE*, no. 61, pp. 164–69.
29. *CCE*, no. 62, pp. 1–2.
30. *USSR News Brief*, 21 (1981), no. 34; 3 (1982), no. 1; 8, no. 6; 14/15, no. 14; AS 47, no. 4503 (1981).
31. *USSR News Brief*, 23/24 (1982), no. 4.
32. *USSR News Brief* (1981), 12, no. 10; (1985), 7/8, no. 10; 9, no. 3.

4. The Latvian National-Democratic Movement

1. *Istoriiya Latviyskoy SSR*, abbreviated version, second revised and expanded edition (Riga: Latvian SSR Academy of Sciences, 1971), pp. 706–07.
2. *Istoriiya Latviyskoy SSR* (Riga: Latvian SSR Academy of Sciences, Institute of History and Material Culture, 1958), vol. 3, p. 644.
3. Ibid.

4. "The Register of Those Convicted or Imprisoned for the Human Rights Struggle in the USSR from March 5, 1953, to February 1971" (Munich: Radio Liberty, *Samizdat* Archive division, 1971), pp. 211–18.
5. *CCE*, no. 11, in Reddaway, *Uncensored Russia*, p. 404.
6. The testimony of many eyewitnesses—residents of Engure in personal conversations.
7. *CCE*, no. 15, p. 491.
8. *CCE*, no. 17, p. 75.
9. *AS* 2432, Radio Liberty (unpublished).
10. *AS* 2433 (unpublished).
11. *AS* 2434 (unpublished).
12. *AS* 2435, 2692 (unpublished).
13. *CCE*, no. 42, p. 256.
14. *CCE*, no. 41, p. 144; no. 42, pp. 206–07.
15. *CCE*, no. 11, in Reddaway, *Uncensored Russia*, p. 215.
16. *CCE*, no. 17, pp. 77–79.
17. "Narodnoye Khozyastvo SSSR v 1970 godu" (Moscow: Statistika, 1971), p. 20.
18. *CCE*, no. 32, pp. 15, 85–86; *CCE*, no. 34, pp. 8–11.
19. *CCE*, no. 41, p. 144.
20. *AS* 2435, 2692 (unpublished).
21. *CCE*, no. 47, pp. 45–46.
22. *CCE*, no. 54, p. 140; *AS* 3755, 39/79.
23. *AS* 3875, 6/80.
24. *AS* 4570, 6/82.
25. *USSR News Brief*, 10 (1982), no. 35.
26. Ibid., no. 36.
27. Ibid., 13, no. 25.
28. *Forum*, social-political journal, ed. Vladimir Malinkovich (Munich: Suchasnist, 1983), no. 4 (interview with the chairman of the LSDRP Foreign Committee, Bruno Kalnins), pp. 67–74.
29. *USSR News Brief*, 10 (1981), no. 1.
30. Ibid., 8, no. 41; 10, no. 1.
31. Ibid., 11, no. 7.
32. Ibid., 17, no. 4.
33. Ibid., 2 (1982), no. 2.
34. Ibid.
35. Ibid., 22 (1981), no. 8; 23/24 (1983), no. 26.
36. Ibid., 8 (1982), no. 25.
37. Ibid., 22 (1981), no. 8.
38. Ibid., 21, no. 3; 23/24 (1983), no. 2.
39. Ibid., 3 (1983), no. 3; 15, no. 1.
40. Ibid., 2, no. 29; 3, no. 3.
41. Ibid., 3, no. 3.
42. Ibid., 23/24 (1983), no. 2; 3, no. 3; 13, no. 15.
43. Ibid., 18 (1983), no. 1.
44. Ibid., 8, no. 1; 10, no. 15; 16 (1983), no. 3.
45. Ibid., 5, no. 15 (1984).
46. Ibid., 23 (1982), no. 7; 7 (1983), no. 40.
47. Ibid., 4 (1984), no. 5.

5. The Georgian National Movement

1. *AS* 41, no. 1830 (1974).
2. *AS* 28, no. 2581 (1976), p. 15.
3. *AS* 23, no. 2583 (1976); 19, no. 4638 (1982); *CCE*, no. 42, pp. 270–71.
4. *CCE*, no. 49, pp. 85–87; no. 57, p. 120.
5. *AS* 28, no. 2581 (1976); 39, no. 1821 (1974).
6. *CCE*, no. 34, p. 72; *AS* 10, no. 2053 (1975).
7. *CCE*, no. 34, pp. 57–59; no. 35, p. 143; *AS* 39, no. 1821 (1974).
8. *CCE*, no. 34, pp. 57–59; *AS* 2, no. 1961 (1975).
9. *CCE*, no. 38, p. 131; no. 42, pp. 270–72; *AS* 16, no. 2444 (1976); 12, no. 2580 (1977).
10. *CCE*, no. 36, pp. 183–86; no. 38, p. 129; no. 43, p. 86; no. 45, pp. vol. 2, pp. 34–36.
11. *CCE*, no. 41, pp. 175–76; *Reports of the Helsinki Accord Monitors*, vol. 2, pp. 34–36.
12. *CCE*, no. 45, p. 309; *AS* 4, no. 3116 (1978).
13. *CCE*, no. 45, pp. 236–39; no. 46, pp. 29–30.
14. *CCE*, no. 50, pp. 20–27; no. 53, p. 167.
15. *CCE*, no. 38, pp. 158–59; no. 45, pp. 319–20.
16. *CCE*, no. 45, p. 320.
17. *AS* 11, no. 2869 (1977).
18. *CCE*, no. 61, p. 162.
19. *AS* 1, no. 4167 (1981).
20. *CCE*, no. 61, p. 163.
21. *AS* 19, no. 4638 (1982).
22. Ibid., nos. 4639–40; *CCE*, no. 63, pp. 79–80.
23. *AS* 19, no. 4639–40 (1982).
24. *AS* 34, no. 4415 (1981).
25. *CCE*, no. 63, pp. 79–92.
26. *USSR News Brief* 2 (1982), no. 7.
27. *CCE*, no. 63, p. 82; *USSR News Brief*, 13 (1982), no. 11, 14/15, no. 17.
28. Ibid. (1983), 15, no. 21.
29. *CCE*, no. 63, p. 174.
30. *AS* 25, 4682 (1982).
31. *USSR News Brief*, 10 (1983), no. 11.
32. *AS* 11, no. 4871 (1983).
33. *USSR News Brief*, 12 (1983), no. 8.
34. Ibid., 23/24, no. 5.

6. The Armenian National Movement

1. *AS* 24, no. 1214.
2. *AS* 45, no. 3798 (1979).
3. *AS* 24, no. 1217; information given to the author by eyewitness Aleksandr Malakhazyan.
4. Ibid., no. 1216.

5. Information supplied by Aleksandr Malakhazyan.
6. *AS* 24, no. 1216.
7. *AS* 4, no. 3119 (1978).
8. *CCE*, no. 16, pp. 11–13.
9. *CCE*, no. 34, pp. 11–14; *Delo Ayrikyana* (New York: Khronika Press, 1977).
10. *AS* 4, no. 3119 (1978).
11. Ibid.
12. *AS* 41, no. 2285 (1975); *CCE*, no. 43, p. 15; *AS* 32, no. 3075 (1977).
13. *CCE*, no. 46, p. 92; *Reports of the Helsinki Accord Monitors*, May 1978, pp. 106–12.
14. *CCE*, no. 48, pp. 28–33.
15. *CCE*, no. 44, pp. 127–31; no. 48, p. 41.
16. *CCE*, no. 52, pp. 1–10; no. 56, pp. 222–30.
17. *CCE*, no. 52, pp. 9–10.
18. *AS* 32, no. 3712 (1979).
19. *CCE*, no. 53, p. 80.
20. *CCE*, no. 56, pp. 143–45.
21. *USSR News Brief* (1983), 6, no. 1; (1985), 2, no. 1.
22. *CCE*, no. 57, p. 60; no. 62, pp. 64–65.
23. *CCE*, no. 62, pp. 65–66.
24. *USSR News Brief* (1982), 23/24, no. 5; (1983), 15, no. 2.

7. The Crimean Tartar National Movement

1. *AS* 12, no. 630; *Yemel': Sbornik statey i dokumentov*, vol. 1 (New York: Crimean Fund, 1978), p. 33.
2. *Shest' dney: Belaya kniga* (New York: Crimean Fund, 1978), p. 427.
3. *Yemel'*, vol. 1, pp. 43, 6; *CCE*, no. 31, pp. 147–48, 157–58, 160–61.
4. *AS* 12, no. 379.
5. "Pis'mo Mustafy Dzhemileva Petru Grigorenko," in *A kogda my vernyomsya* (New York: Crimean Fund, 1977), pp. 11–25.
6. *AS* 2, no. 137, p. 2.
7. *CCE*, no. 31, pp. 139–43; *AS* 12, no. 1877.
8. *AS* 2, no. 137; *CCE*, no. 31, p. 153.
9. *CCE*, no. 8, in Reddaway, *Uncensored Russia*, p. 250; *AS* 2, no. 137, pp. 2–3.
10. *AS* 2, no. 137, pp. 3–4.
11. *Yemel'*, vol. 1, p. 50; *Shest' dney*, pp. 336–37.
12. U.S. Congress, Commission on Security and Cooperation in Europe, *Documents of Helsinki Dissent from the Soviet Union and Eastern Europe*, 1978, pp. 81–85.
13. *AS* 2, no. 137, p. 5.
14. *AS* 12, no. 630, pp. 24–25.
15. Ibid., no. 379, pp. 38–39; *CCE*, no. 7, in Reddaway, *Uncensored Russia*, pp. 264–66.
16. *AS* 12, no. 397, p. 5.
17. *CCE*, no. 8, in Reddaway, *Uncensored Russia*, pp. 86–88.
18. *CHR*, no. 29, p. 53.
19. *AS* 1, no. 45.

20. Ibid.
21. *AS* 12, no. 638.
22. *CCE*, no. 8, and *CCE*, no. 10, in Reddaway, *Uncensored Russia*, pp. 134–37, 160–61.
23. *KTS*, no. 12, pp. 344–50.
24. *Shest' dney*, pp. 336–66.
25. *CCE*, no. 40, pp. 21–33; *Reports of the Helsinki Accord Monitors*, 1977, pp. 57–61; *CCE*, no. 52, pp. 95–96; no. 53, pp. 6–11; *USSR News Brief*, 1 (1984), no. 1; 4, no. 3.
26. *CCE*, no. 38, p. 128; *CCE*, no. 47, pp. 65–66.
27. *CCE*, no. 47, pp. 76–77.
28. *AS* 137; *CCE*, no. 31, pp. 144, 148; no. 38, p. 128; no. 53, pp. 111–12.
29. *CCE*, no. 38, p. 128.
30. *CCE*, no. 31, p. 145.
31. Ibid., p. 141.
32. *CCE*, no. 47, pp. 65–66.
33. *CCE*, no. 51, p. 122.
34. Ibid., p. 124.
35. *CCE*, no. 52, pp. 79–80.
36. *CCE*, no. 53, pp. 120–21.
37. *CCE*, no. 51, pp. 125–26.
38. *CCE*, no. 51, p. 120.
39. Ibid.
40. *CCE*, no. 52, pp. 88–95.
41. Ibid., p. 93.
42. *CCE*, no. 51, p. 123.
43. *CCE*, no. 60, pp. 3–16.
44. *CCE*, no. 51, p. 128; no. 56, p. 204.
45. *Yemel'*, vol. 1, pp. 57–58.

8. The Meskhi National Movement

1. *CCE*, no. 7, in Reddaway, *Uncensored Russia*, pp. 270–73.
2. Ibid., pp. 273–76.
3. *CCE*, no. 9, pp. 277–78.
4. *CCE*, no. 19.
5. *CCE*, no. 34, pp. 93–94.
6. *CCE*, no. 41, pp. 175–76.
7. U.S. Congress, Commission on Security and Cooperation in Europe, *Documents of Helsinki Dissent from the Soviet Union and Eastern Europe*, 1978, pp. 85–87.

9. The Soviet German Emigration Movement

1. *Re Patria*, in *Vol'noye slovo*, 16 (1975), pp. 54–57.
2. Ibid., p. 9.
3. Ibid., pp. 84–86.
4. *AS* 16, no. 2811 (1978), p. 8.
5. *Re Patria*, p. 86.

6. Ibid., p. 87.
7. Ibid., pp. 50–51.
8. AS 16, no. 2811 (1978), p. 8.
9. Ibid., p. 22.
10. CCE, no. 41, pp. 174–75; Politichesky dnevnik (Amsterdam: A. Herzen Foundation, 1972), pp. 94–95.
11. Resultaty vsesoyuznoy perepisi (1970), vol. 4, p. 9; Vestnik statistiki (1980), no. 8.
12. CCE, no. 32, p. 31.
13. Ibid.
14. CCE, no. 56, pp. 175–76.
15. CCE, no. 41, pp. 173–74.
16. Ibid., pp. 174–75.
17. Sbornik dokumentov obshchestvennoy gruppy sodeystviya vypolneniyu Khelsinkskikh soglasheniy v SSSR (New York: Khronika Press 1980), vol. 6, document no. 22; vol. 7, document no. 122; vol. 8, document nos. 171, 179, 182, 192.
18. AS 44, no. 4487 (1981).
19. USSR News Brief, 4 (1982), no. 1; 5, no. 4; 6, no. 6.
20. USSR News Brief, 2 (1983), no. 33; (1985), 1, no. 33; 21, no. 35; (1986), 3, no. 34.

10. The Jewish Emigration Movement

1. CCE, no. 16, p. 29; no. 22, p. 30.
2. CCE, no. 17, p. 81; no. 21, p. 284.
3. CCE, no. 39, pp. 194–96; AS 13, no. 2759 (1977).
4. CCE, no. 37, p. 49.
5. CCE, no. 21, pp. 282–83; no. 38, p. 149.
6. CCE, no. 35, pp. 170–71; no. 38, pp. 148–49.
7. CCE, no. 43, pp. 55–59.
8. CCE, no. 48, pp. 163–64; no. 50, pp. 89–104.
9. CCE, no. 51, pp. 213–15; no. 53, p. 184; no. 54, pp. 142–43.
10. Daniel Jacoby, Louis Pettiti, and Roland Rappoport, L'affaire Chtcharansky: Proces sans defense (Paris: Bernard Gresset, 1978), p. 160.
11. KTS, no. 14, pp. 441–42; no. 15, pp. 486–87; CCE, no. 17, pp. 48–66.
12. CCE, no. 20, pp. 214–28.
13. CCE, no. 20, pp. 228–30 (Kukuy, Palatnik); no. 22, pp. 15–16 (Trakhenberg); no. 28, pp. 41–42 (Khantsis).
14. CCE, no. 33, p. 147.
15. CCE, no. 17, pp. 68–70 (Borisov).
16. CCE, no. 30, pp. 89–90 (Feldman); no. 34, pp. 15–19 (Shtern); no. 37, pp. 17–18 (Gilyutin), pp. 8–9 (Roytburg); no. 44, pp. 118–20 (Zavurov).
17. CCE, no. 37, pp. 10–16; no. 38, pp. 140–41.
18. Information provided by Roman Rutman.
19. CCE, no. 36, p. 208.
20. CCE, no. 21, p. 283.
21. CCE, no. 32, pp. 67–68.
22. CCE, no. 43, pp. 60–61.
23. CCE, no. 10, in Reddaway, Uncensored Russia, p. 308.

24. *CCE*, no. 44, pp. 114–16; no. 43, pp. 64–65.
25. *CCE*, no. 44, pp. 113–15; no. 50, pp. 95–108.
26. *CCE*, no. 53, p. 148.
27. *Vesti iz SSSR*, 18 (1981), no. 29.
28. *CCE*, no. 60, p. 76.
29. *CCE*, no. 62, pp. 83–86.
30. *CCE*, no. 61, pp. 176–79.
31. *CCE*, no. 56, pp. 135–36; no. 61, pp. 148–49.
32. *CCE*, no. 60, pp. 97–98; no. 55, pp. 63–64.
33. *CCE*, no. 43, p. 60.
34. *CCE*, no. 60, pp. 95–96; *USSR News Brief*, 4 (1982), no. 26; *CCE*, no. 64, pp. 38–39.
35. *CCE*, no. 47, p. 101, *Vesti iz SSSR*, 17 (1981), no. 3.
36. *Vesti iz SSSR*, 5 (1981), no. 39; 7 (1981), no. 31.
37. *CCE*, no. 63, pp. 115–16.
38. *CCE*, no. 56, pp. 173–75.
39. *CCE*, no. 57, pp. 74–79; no. 60, pp. 183–84.
40. *CCE*, no. 62, pp. 98–99; *Vesti iz SSSR* 13 (1981), no. 5.
41. *CCE*, no. 62, p. 103; *Vesti iz SSSR* 19 (1981), no. 1 (Zukerman and Lokshin); *CCE*, no. 61, p. 141 (Magidovich); *Vesti iz SSSR* 21 (1981), no. 1 (Paritsky); *CCE*, no. 62, pp. 80–83 (Brailovsky).
42. *USSR News Brief*, 20 (1982), no. 3; 19/20 (1983), no. 2.
43. *USSR News Brief* (1986), 3, no. 4.
44. *AS* 23, nos. 4660–64 (1982); *USSR News Brief*, 4 (1983), no. 6.
45. *CCE*, no. 61, p. 179.
46. Ibid., *AS* 23, nos. 4660–64 (1982); *USSR News Brief*, 4 (1982), no. 7.
47. *AS* 20, nos. 4927–28 (1983).

11. The Evangelical Christian Baptists

1. *CCE*, no. 35, p. 111; *AS* 15, no. 871, p. 32; data from Georgy Vins.
2. *AS* 14, no. 770, p. 123; no. 771, p. 18.
3. Ibid., no. 773.
4. Ibid., no. 772, p. 15; no. 770, p. 129.
5. Ibid., no. 770, pp. 4–9.
6. Ibid., pp. 9–18.
7. *AS* 15, no. 880, p. 6.
8. *AS* 14, no. 772, p. 5; no. 770, pp. 142–43.
9. Ibid., no. 662, pp. 4–5.
10. Ibid., no. 771, pp. 57–58; no. 770, pp. 142–43.
11. Ibid., no. 771, pp. 58–62; no. 770, pp. 207–15.
12. Gleb Yakunin, "O sovzemennom polozhenii Russkoy pzavoslavnoy tsezkvi," in *SSSR: vnutrenniye protivorechiya* (New York: Chalidze Publications), vol. 3, p. 191.
13. Ibid., p. 189.
14. *CCE*, no. 45, p. 323.
15. *SSSR: vnutrenniye protivor echiya*, vol. 3, p. 189.

16. *AS* 14, no. 770, pp. 234–36; no. 771, pp. 68–70.
17. *CCE*, no. 34, p. 73.
18. *List of Political Prisoners in the USSR*, 1 May 1982, *USSR News Brief*.
19. *CCE*, no. 54, p. 107; no. 60, p. 73.
20. *CCE*, no. 48, p. 124.
21. *CCE*, no. 51, p. 142.
22. *AS* 15, no. 878.
23. *AS* 15, nos. 871–73.
24. *CCE*, no. 43, p. 79.
25. *AS* 14, no. 771, document no. 31, pp. 67–68.
26. *AS* 15, no. 878, p. 3.
27. *Bulletin of the Council of Relatives of Evangelical Christian Baptist Prisoners*, February 1983, no. 11; *USSR News Brief* (1982), 5, no. 1.
28. *CCE*, no. 34, p. 53.
29. *CCE*, no. 46, p. 45 (Ivangorod); no. 56, p. 164 (Starye Kodaki); *Vesti iz SSSR* 15 (1980), no. 1; (1981) 7, no. 3 (Glivenki); *USSR News Brief*, 5 (1982), no. 1 (Tokmak).
30. *AS* 15, no. 871, pp. 11–18.
31. Ibid., no. 865.
32. *AS* 14, no. 770, p. 124.
33. *CCE*, no. 53, pp. 3–4.
34. Figures are based on data collected by the Council of Relatives of Evangelical Christian Baptist Prisoners (Keston, England: Keston College Archive).
35. *CCE*, no. 34, p. 53.
36. *Reports of Helsinki Accord Monitors in the Soviet Union*, vol. 1, pp. 37–48.
37. *CCE*, no. 44, p. 115.
38. My calculations from statistics provided by the Council of Relatives of Evangelical Christian Baptist Prisoners.
39. *List of Political Prisoners in the USSR, USSR, May 1982 News Brief;* information provided by Georgy Vins.

12. The Pentecostalists

1. *AS* 15, no. 4277 (1981), pp. 3–4.
2. *AS* 14, no. 770, p. 123.
3. *Reports of Helsinki Accord Monitors*, 1979, p. 22.
4. *AS* 33, no. 2684 (1980), pp. 1–2.
5. *CCE*, no. 46, p. 46.
6. Ibid., pp. 45–46.
7. *CCE*, no. 32, p. 30.
8. *CCE*, no. 47, p. 65; no. 49, p. 65.
9. *Reports of Helsinki Accord Monitors*, 1979, p. 77.
10. *AS* 35, no. 4423 (1981).
11. Ibid., p. 7.
12. *CCChL*, 1978, no. 28, p. 13.
13. *Reports of Helsinki Accord Monitors*, 1979, p. 8.

14. *CCE*, no. 32, pp. 28–30.
15. *AS* 33, no. 2684 (1980).
16. *CCE*, no. 44, p. 180; Keston College Archive.
17. *Reports of Helsinki Accord Monitors*, 1979, pp. 65–68.
18. Ibid., p. 24; *CCE*, no. 44, pp. 115–16.
19. *CCE*, no. 51, p. 136.
20. *CCE*, no. 47, pp. 91–92; no. 46, p. 52.
21. *Reports of Helsinki Accord Monitors*, 1979, p. 24.
22. Ibid., pp. 24, 8.
23. *CCE*, no. 57, p. 66.
24. *Reports of Helsinki Accord Monitors*, 1979, p. 23.
25. *CCE*, no. 46, p. 55; no. 47, p. 95.
26. *CCE*, no. 48, pp. 143–44; no. 49, p. 78.
27. *CCE*, no. 46, pp. 54–55.
28. Khronika Press Archive.
29. *CCE*, no. 45, p. 300.
30. *CCE*, no. 48, p. 139.
31. *CCE*, no. 45, p. 281.
32. *CCE*, no. 51, pp. 153–54.
33. *CCE*, no. 46, p. 37; no. 47, pp. 34–38; no. 48, pp. 121–22.
34. *CCE*, no. 49, p. 65.
35. *CCE*, no. 47, pp. 88–90.
36. Ibid., p. 85.
37. *Sbornik dokumentov obshchestvennoy gruppy sodeystviya*, vol. 7, pp. 30–31.
38. *AS* 4, no. 4196 (1981), pp. 3, 5.
39. *CCE*, no. 54, p. 128; no. 55, p. 51; no. 63, p. 146.
40. *CCE*, no. 57, p. 66.
41. *AS* 4, no. 4196 (1981), pp. 7–8.
42. Ibid., pp. 9–10.
43. Ibid., p. 9.
44. Ibid.
45. Khronika Press Archive.
46. "List of Political Prisoners in the USSR," 1 May 1982, *USSR News Brief*.

13. The True and Free Seventh-Day Adventists

1. *CCE*, no. 48, pp. 117–18; *Documents of the Christian Committee for the Defense of Believers' Rights in the USSR*, vol. 1 (in Russian with summaries in English) (San Francisco: Washington Street Research Center 1977), pp. 133–38.
2. *CCE*, no. 56, p. 93.
3. *AS* 17, no. 2439 (1976), p. 1.
4. Khronika Press Archives.
5. *AS* 17, no. 2439 (1976), p. 17.
6. Ibid., pp. 1, 16, 18.
7. "Open Letter No. 8," pp. 13, 16, Khronika Press Archives.
8. *KTS*, no. 14, pp. 433–34.
9. *CCE*, no. 38, pp. 134–35.

10. Ibid., p. 140.
11. *Reports of the Helsinki Accord Monitors*, 1979, pp. 37–48.
12. *CCE*, no. 45, p. 300; no. 46, p. 99.
13. *CCE*, no. 47, pp. 160–61; *Documents of Helsinki Dissent from the Soviet Union and Eastern Europe*, May 1978, pp. 74–81.
14. *CCE*, no. 48, p. 7; AS 17, no. 3216 (1978).
15. Rostislav Galetsky, "Report on the Situation of Religion and Believers in the USSR" (in Russian), p. 1, Khronika Press Archives.
16. Ibid., p. 19.
17. Ibid., p. 21.
18. *CCE*, no. 46, pp. 101–03.
19. *AS* 33, no. 4411 (1981); 19 (1981), no. 4301, pp. 19, 41; no. 4302, p. 7, 29–30, 33.
20. *CCE*, no. 48, p. 118; the complete text is in the Khronika Press Archives.
21. *CCE*, no. 48, p. 118; *List of Political Prisoners in the USSR, 1 May 1982, USSR News Brief.*
22. *CCE*, no. 49, pp. 57–63.
23. Ibid., pp. 63–64.
24. Ibid., p. 63.
25. *CCE*, no. 53, pp. 11–23; AS 19, no. 4301 (1981).
26. *CCE*, no. 56, p. 93; the full text of Open Letter No. 12 is in the Khronika Press Archives.
27. Open Letters nos. 1–14, Khronika Press Archives.
28. *CCE*, no. 62, p. 72; *CCE*, no. 57, p. 70; AS 19, no. 4302 (1981), pp. 3–4, 10–20.
29. *CCE*, no. 57, p. 70; no. 62, p. 71.
30. *AS* 19, nos. 4301–02 (1981).
31. *CCE*, no. 62, pp. 70–71.
32. Khronika Press Archives.
33. *CCChL*, no. 28, pp. 13–14.
34. Figures are based on data in documents of the Council of Relatives of Evangelical Christian Baptist Prisoners and the All-Union Church of the True and Free Seventh-Day Adventists.

14. The Russian Orthodox Church

1. *CCE*, no. 41, p. 126.
2. N. Yudintsev, *Pravda o peterburgskikh svyatynyakh* (Leningrad: 1962), p. 8.
3. Ibid.
4. *CCE*, no. 41, p. 125.
5. *AS* 11, no. 701.
6. *AS* 11, no. 724, pp. 4–6.
7. Ibid., nos. 722–24.
8. Ibid., no. 731.
9. Ibid., no. 734.
10. *AS* 1, no. 58; AS 11, nos. 703, 739, 752.
11. *AS* 11, no. 748.
12. *CCE*, nos. 8, 10, in Reddaway, *Uncensored Russia*, pp. 326–28; *CCE*, no. 18, pp. 141–42.
13. *Vol'noye slovo*, nos. 9–10 (1973), pp. 65–70.

14. *AS* 26, no. 1021.
15. Aleksandr Solzhenitsyn, *Publicistika* (Paris: YMCA Press, 1981), pp. 122–23.
16. *CCE*, no. 27, p. 234; *Vol'noye slovo*, nos. 9–10 (1973), pp. 48–55, 201–17.
17. Solzhenitsyn, ed., *Iz pod glyb* (Paris: YMCA Press, 1974), p. 184.
18. Father Dmitry Dudko, *O nashem upovanii*, 1974, abstract in *CCE*, no. 37, p. 65.
19. *CCE*, no. 38, p. 144.
20. *CCE*, no. 39, pp. 212–14.
21. *CCE*, no. 32, pp. 86–87; no. 38, p. 134.
22. *CCE*, no. 56, pp. 119–21.
23. Solzhenitsyn, ed., *Iz pod glyb*, p. 196.
24. A. Krasnov, *Stromaty* (Frankfurt-am-Main: Possev, 1972); A. Levitan-Krasnov, *Likhiye gody* (Paris: YMCA Press, 1977); idem, *Ruk tvoikh zhar* (Tel Aviv: 1979); idem, *V poiskakh Novogo grada* (Tel Aviv: 1980).
25. Lev Regelson, *Tragediya russkoy tserkvi* (Paris: YMCA Press, 1977).
26. Yakunin, *O sovremennom polozhenii Russkoy pravoslavnoy tserkvi*, in *SSSR: Vnutrenniy protivorechiya*, vol. 3, pp. 149–97.
27. Igor Shafarevich, *Zakonodatelstvo o religii v SSSR* (Paris: YMCA Press, 1973).
28. Emmanuel Svetlov [Aleksandr Men'], *Magizm i yedinobozhie* (Brussels: Zhizns' Bogom, 1971); idem. *U vrat molchaniya* (on the spiritual life of China and India) (Brussels: Zhizns' Bogom, 1971); idem, *Dionis, Logos i Sud'ba* (Greek religion and philosophy) (Brussels: Zhizns' Bogom, 1972); idem, *Vestniki Tsarstva Bozhiya* (biblical prophets of the 4th–8th centuries B.C.) (Brussels: Zhizns' Bogom, 1972); Aleksandr Men', *Tainstva, Slovo i Obraz* (Brussels: Zhizns' Bogom, 1980); A. Bogolyubov [Aleksandr Men'], *Syn chelovechesky* (Brussels: Zhizns' Bogom, 1980); A. Men', *Istoki religii* (guide to reading the Old Testament) (Brussels: Zhizns' Bogom, 1980); A. Men', *Kak chitat' Bibliyu* (Brussels: Zhizns' Bogom, 1981).
29. Bishop Feodosy, Pis'mo L. Brezhnevu, in *SSSR: Vnutrenniye protivorechiya*, vol. 3, pp. 112–48.
30. *Vol'noye slovo* 28 (1977), pp. 3–5.
31. Ibid., pp. 58–78.
32. Ibid., pp. 6–9.
33. *Documents of the Christian Committee for the Defense of Believers' Rights in the USSR*, vols. 1–4.
34. Ibid., vol. 1, pp. 17–19.
35. L. Alexeyeva, ed., *Delo Orlova* (New York: Khronika Press, 1980), pp. 72–73.
36. *CCE*, no. 47, pp. 160–61; *Documents of the Helsinki Dissent from the Soviet Union and Eastern Europe*, May 1978, pp. 74–81.
37. *Vol'noye slovo* 28, pp. 33–37; *CCE*, no. 46, pp. 99–100.
38. *CCE*, no. 54, pp. 4–8.
39. *CCE*, no. 55, p. 22; no. 56, pp. 119–23.
40. *CCE*, no. 57, pp. 38–41.
41. *CCE*, no. 58, pp. 23–31.

42. Ibid., pp. 18–23.
43. *CCE*, no. 54, p. 12; no. 56, pp. 122–23.
44. *AS* 33, no. 5037 (1983).
45. *USSR News Brief*, 22 (1983), no. 23; *AS* 33, no. 5031 (1983).
46. *CCE*, no. 63, p. 210.
47. *USSR News Brief*, 13/14 (1983), no. 23.
48. "Sem'voprosov i otvetov o russkoy pravoslavnoy tserkvi," *Vestnik RKhD*, 1983, no. 137.
49. *CCE*, no. 51, pp. 219–20; no. 54, pp. 25–27.
50. *List of Political Prisoners in the USSR, 1 May 1982, USSR News Brief; CCE*, no. 54, pp. 43–46; no. 56, pp. 123–27; no. 57, pp. 1–4; no. 58, pp. 31–32.
51. *AS* 33, no. 3329 (1978).
52. *CCE*, no. 64, p. 16; *AS* 32, nos. 4725–26 (1982).
53. *CCE*, no. 64, p. 16; Khronika Press Archives; *Byulleten'* V 74, nos. 6, 13; *Byulleten'* V 80, nos. 1, 6; *Byulleten'* V 81, nos. 2, 6.
54. *USSR News Brief*, 23/24 (1982), no. 12.
55. Ibid., 17 (1983), no. 5; 1/2, (1984), no. 11.
56. *CCE*, no. 64, pp. 6–12.
57. Solzhenitsyn, ed., *Iz pod glyb*, p. 197.
58. *CCE*, no. 1, in Reddaway, *Uncensored Russia*, pp. 79, 86–88.
59. *CCE*, no. 20, p. 234.
60. *CCE*, no. 5, in Reddaway, *Uncensored Russia*, pp. 329–30; *CCE*, no. 56, p. 90.
61. *CCE*, no. 38, p. 154.
62. S. Zheludkov, *Pochemu i ya khristianin* (Frankfurt-am-Main: Possev, 1973); abstract in *CCE*, no. 56, p. 219.

15. Emergence of the Human Rights Movement

1. Andrey Amalrik, *Notes of a Revolutionary* (New York: Alfred A. Knopf, 1982), p. 26.
2. Chalidze, *To Defend These Rights*, p. 60.
3. Nikolai Arzhak [Yuly Daniel], *This Is Moscow Speaking and Other Stories* (New York: Colliers, First Books Edition, 1979).
4. Mihajlov, *Leto moskovskoye*, p. 51.
5. Yury Orlov, *Autobiography* in *CHR*, no. 25 (1977), pp. 85–88.
6. Grigorenko, *Memoirs*, pp. 237–61.
7. Sara Babyonysheva, "Tsena prozreniya," *SSSR: Vnutrenniye protivorechiya*, vol. 2, pp. 255–83.
8. Bukovsky, *To Build a Castle*, pp. 142–54; Vladimir Osipov, "Ploshchad Mayakovskogo," in *Tri otnosheniya k rodine* (Frankfurt-am-Main: Possev, 1978).
9. *Grani* (Frankfurt-am-Main: Possev, 1966), no. 61, pp. 14–15.
10. *AS* 8, no. 552.
11. Revolt Pimenov, "Odin politichesky protsess," in *Pamyat'* 2 (1979), pp. 160–62; 3 (1980), pp. 7–119 (Paris: YMCA Press).
12. R. Rozhdestvensky, "Materialy k istorii samodeyatelnykh politicheskikh obedineniy v SSSR," in *Pamyet'* 5 (1983), pp. 226–83; Boris Weil, *Osobo opasny* (London: Overseas Publications, 1980).

13. Pavel Litvinov, comp., *The Trial of the Four* (New York: Viking Press, 1972), pp. 5–9; Bukovsky, *To Build a Castle*, pp. 142–54.
14. Rozhdestvensky, "Materialy k istorii," p. 229.
15. Grigorenko, *Memoirs*, pp. 262–314.
16. Abram Tertz [pseud.], *The Makepeace Experiment* (New York: Pantheon Books); idem, *The Icicle and Other Stories* (London: Collin & Harris, 1963). See also note 3.
17. A. Ginzburg, comp., *Belaya kniga po delu A. Sinyavskogo i Yu. Danielya* (Frankfurt-am-Main: Possev, 1967), p. 61.
18. A. S. Yesenin-Volpin, *A Leaf of Spring* (New York: Praeger, 1961).
19. Bukovsky, *To Build a Castle*, p. 229.
20. Ginzburg, *Belaya kniga*, pp. 80–81.
21. Ibid.
22. "Judgement on Pasternak: The All-Moscow Meeting of Writers," *Survey*, July 1966, p. 138.
23. AS 2, no. 116 (L. Chukovskaya); A. Solzhenitsyn, "Letter to the Fourth Congress of Soviet Writers," in *Critical Essays and Documentary Materials*, ed. John Dunlop, Richard Hough, and Alexis Klimoff (Belmont, Mass.: Nordland Pub., 1973), pp. 463–71; "Letter of Grigory Svirksy," in *The Political, Social, and Religious Thought of Russian Samizdat*, ed. M. Meerson and Boris Shragin (Belmont, Mass.: Nordland Pub., 1977), pp. 283–99; A. Sakharov, R. Medvedev, and V. Turchin, "Appeal for a Gradual Democratization," in *Political, Social, and Religious Thought*, pp. 399–412.
24. Pavel Litvinov, comp., *The Demonstration in Pushkin Square* (Boston: Gambit, Inc., 1969); AS 4, no. 273.
25. Litvinov, *Trial of the Four*, p. 227.
26. Litvinov, *Demonstration in Pushkin Square*.
27. Litvinov, *Trial of the Four*, p. 227.
28. Ibid., pp. 228–82.
29. Andrey Amalrik, *Will the Soviet Union Survive until 1984?* (London: Harper Colophon Books, 1970), pp. 22–23.
30. Amalrik, *Notes of a Revolutionary*, p. 23.
31. CCE, in Reddaway, *Uncensored Russia*, pp. 80–86, 88–91.
32. Litvinov, *Trial of the Four*, pp. 225–27.
33. *Times* (London), 11 January 1968, p. 1.
34. Karel Van Het Reve, ed., *Dear Comrade: Pavel Litvinov and the Voice of Soviet Citizens in Dissent* (New York: Pitman Publishing Corp., 1969).

16. The Communication Network of Dissent and the Pattern of Suppression

1. Amalrik, *Notes of a Revolutionary*, pp. 3–5, 52–54.
2. Andrey Sakharov, "Thoughts on Progress, Peaceful Coexistence, and Intellectual Freedom, in *Sakharov Speaks* (New York: Alfred A. Knopf, 1982).
3. Vasily Grossman, *Vsyo techyot* (Frankfurt-am-Main: Possev, 1970); Lidya Chukovskaya, *Opustely dom* (Paris: Five Continents, 1965); idem, *Spusk pod vody* (New York: Chekhov Press, 1972); Venedikt

Yerofeyev, *Moscow to the End of the Line* (New York: Taplan Publishing Co., 1980); Aleksandr Solzhenitsyn, *The First Circle* (New York: Harper & Row, 1968); Vladimir Maksimov, *Seven Days of Creation* (New York: Alfred A. Knopf, 1975); Joseph Brodsky, *Ostanovka v pustyne* (New York: Chekhov Press, 1970); Natalya Gorbanevskaya, *Stikhi* (Frankfurt-am-Main: Possev, 1969); Naum Korzhavin, *Vremena* (Frankfurt-am-Main: Possev, 1970).

4. For example, see the incident concerning Burmistrovich in *Za pyat' let*, Pyotr Smirnov, comp. (Paris: La presse libre, 1972), pp. 125–26.

5. Andrey Sakharov, "Soviet Society," in *My Country and the World* (New York: Alfred A. Knopf, 1965), pp. 38–40; "The Chronicle of Current Events," foreword by Sakharov, in Hopkins, *Russia's Underground Press*.

6. *CCE*, nos. 1–2, in Reddaway, *Uncensored Russia;* nos. 12–15, in *KTS; CCE*, no. 16.

7. *CCE*, no. 5, in Reddaway, *Uncensored Russia*, p. 54.

8. *CCE*, no. 38, pp. 143–44.

9. Orlov, *Autobiography*, in *CHR*, no. 25, pp. 85–88.

10. *CCE*, no. 5, in Reddaway, *Uncensored Russia*, p. 54.

11. *CCE*, no. 7, ibid., pp. 271–76.

12. *CCE*, no. 11, ibid., p. 29; *CCE*, no. 21, pp. 287–88.

13. *CCE*, no. 5, in Reddaway, *Uncensored Russia*, pp. 328–31.

14. See note 3.

15. Natalya Gorbanevskaya, *Red Square at Noon* (New York: Holt, Rinehart & Winston, 1970), pp. 27–41; *CCE*, no. 3, in Reddaway, *Uncensored Russia*, pp. 99–100.

16. *CCE*, no. 4, in Reddaway, *Uncensored Russia*, pp. 112–26.

17. *CCE*, no. 3, ibid., p. 191; for full text of the letter, see Marchenko, *My Testimony*, pp. 392–98.

18. *CCE*, no. 4, in Reddaway, *Uncensored Russia*, pp. 191–94.

19. Ibid., p. 96.

20. *CCE*, no. 9, ibid., p. 108.

21. *CCE*, no. 7, ibid., p. 102.

22. *CCE*, no. 3, ibid., p. 96.

23. *CCE*, no. 6, ibid., p. 104.

24. Ibid., p. 106.

25. *CCE*, no. 201, pp. 255–57.

26. *CCE*, no. 8, in Reddaway, *Uncensored Russia*, pp. 150–51; full text in Brumberg, *In Quest of Justice*, pp. 458–61.

27. *CCE*, no. 8, in Reddaway, *Uncensored Russia*, p. 150.

28. *CCE*, no. 8, ibid., pp. 194–95; *CCE*, no. 10, ibid., pp. 195–97.

29. *CCE*, no. 10, ibid., pp. 154–55, 161.

30. *CCE*, no. 11, ibid., pp. 157–60.

31. *CCE*, no. 14, in *KIS*, vol. 1, pp. 450–51; full text in "Initsiativnaya gruppa po zaschite prav cheloveka v SSSR," in *Sbornik dokumentov* (New York: Khronika Press, 1976), p. 21.

32. Ibid., pp. 26–32, 42.

33. *Proceedings of the Moscow Human Rights Committee* (New York: International League for the Rights of Man, 1972); *CCE*, no. 17, pp. 5–9.

34. *CCE*, no. 17, pp. 11–12; full text in *Political, Social, and Religious Thought*, ed. Meerson and Shragin, pp. 413–14.
35. *Proceedings of the Moscow Human Rights Committee*, pp. 245–52.
36. Ibid., pp. 67–122, 56–66, 125–237, 239–42; *CHR*, nos. 5–6, p. 74.
37. *CCE*, no. 24, p. 157; Chalidze, *To Defend These Rights*, pp. 199–208.
38. S. R. Rozhdestvensky [pseud.], "Materialy k istorii samodeyatel'nykh politicheskikh ob"edineniy v SSSR," *Pamyat'*.
39. Grigorenko, *Memoirs*, pp. 262–314.
40. Rozhdestvensky, "Materialy k istorii"; Revolt Pimenov, "Odin politichesky protsess," *Pamyat'*; Weil, *Osobo opasny*.
41. N. Peskov [pseud], "Delo 'Kolokola,' " *Pamyat'* (Paris).
42. *CCE*, no. 1, in Reddaway, *Uncensored Russia*, p. 441; John B. Dunlop, *The New Russian Revolutionaries* (Belmont, Mass.: Nordland Pub., 1976).
43. *CCE*, no. 46, pp. 111-12.
44. *CCE*, no. 9, in *KTS*, vol. 1, p. 20; *CCE*, no. 33, p. 153.
45. *CCE*, no. 26, pp. 229–30; Valery Ronkin and Sergey Khakhayev, "Proshloye, nastoyashcheye, i budushcheye socializma," *Poiski* (Paris: 1981), pp. 7–30.
46. *Sintaksis*, no. 1, p. 4.
47. Pimenov, "Odin politichesky protsess," pp. 234–40; Weil, *Osobo opasny*, pp. 135–45.
48. Natalya Kononova, "Litso Peterburga," *Kovcheg* (Paris: 1978), no. 1, p. 68.
49. Yefim Etkind, *Zapiski nezagovorshchika* (London: Overseas Publications, 1977), pp. 140–52.
50. Raisa Orlova, "Frida Vigdorova," in *SSSR: Vnutrenniye protivorechiya*, vol. 3, pp. 316–23; for the trial record by Frida Vigdorova, see Etkind, *Zapiski Nezagovorshchika*, pp. 437–66.
51. Etkind, *Zapiski Nezagovorshchika*, pp. 172–81.
52. Peskov, "Delo 'Kolokola,' " pp. 278–80.
53. Litvinov, *Trial of the Four*, pp. 229–31, 265–66, 338–40.
54. *AS 4*, no. 273.
55. *CCE*, no. 11, in Reddaway, *Uncensored Russia*, p. 480; *CCE*, no. 14, in *KTS*, p. 443.
56. *CCE*, no. 3, in Reddaway, *Uncensored Russia*, pp. 380–86.
57. *CCE*, no. 9, ibid., pp. 422–33.
58. Ibid., pp. 101–2.
59. Ibid., p. 106.
60. *CCE*, no. 15, in *KTS*, pp. 479–83; *CCE*, no. 16, pp. 6–10; Weil, *Osobo opasny*, pp. 345–49.
61. *CCE*, no. 18, pp. 105–7.
62. *CCE*, no. 8, in Reddaway, *Uncensored Russia*, pp. 104, 387–89; *CCE*, no. 16, p. 17.
63. *CCE*, no. 8, in Reddaway, *Uncensored Russia*, pp. 405–7.
64. *CCE*, no. 9, ibid., p. 407.
65. *CCE*, no. 10, ibid., pp. 407–8.
66. Ibid., p. 408.
67. From testimony by Vladlen Pavlenkov.
68. *CCE*, no. 6, in Reddaway, *Uncensored Russia*, p. 389; *CCE*, no. 16, pp. 25–26; no. 18, p. 131; no. 19, p. 206.

69. *CCE*, no. 6, in Reddaway, *Uncensored Russia*, p. 390.
70. *CCE*, no. 10, ibid., pp. 390–92.
71. *CCE*, nos. 9–11, in ibid., pp. 390–92; no. 14, in *KTS*, vol. 1, pp. 437–38; *CCE*, no. 16, p. 20.
72. From testimony by Vladlen Pavlenkov.
73. *CCE*, no. 12, in *KTS*, vol. 1, pp. 351–52; no. 14, p. 439.
74. *CCE*, no. 24, pp. 135–36.
75. *CCE*, no. 19, p. 205.
76. *CCE*, no. 12, in *KTS*, vol. 1, p. 352; no. 14, in *KTS*, pp. 431–33.
77. From testimony by Vladislav Uzlov; *CCE*, no. 33, pp. 154–55.
78. *CCE*, no. 24, pp. 140–41; no. 33, pp. 145–46, 154, 155.
79. *CCE*, no. 9, in Reddaway, *Uncensored Russia*, pp. 162–64.
80. *CCE*, no. 11, ibid., p. 167; *CCE*, no. 23, in *KTS*, pp. 384–87.
81. *CCE*, no. 8, in Reddaway, *Uncensored Russia*, pp. 161–62; *CCE*, no. 13, in *KTS*, p. 387.
82. Boris Shragin, "Oppozitsionnye nastroyenya v nauchnykh gorodkakh," in Chalidze, *SSSR*, vol. 1, p. 107.
83. Amalrik, *Will the Soviet Union Survive*, p. 23.
84. Litvinov, *Trial of the Four*, pp. 264–65.
85. *CCE*, no. 2, in Reddaway, *Uncensored Russia*, p. 396.
86. Shragin, "Oppozitsionnye nastroyenya," p. 109.
87. *CCE*, no. 2, in Reddaway, *Uncensored Russia*, p. 396.
88. *CCE*, no. 8, ibid., pp. 408–10.
89. *CCE*, no. 11, ibid., pp. 394–96.
90. *CCE*, no. 6, ibid., p. 102.
91. Shragin, "Oppozitsionnye nastroyenya," p. 119.
92. *CCE*, no. 8, in Reddaway, *Uncensored Russia*, pp. 174–75; *CCE*, no. 9, in *KTS*, p. 206; *CCE*, no. 12, p. 363.
93. *CCE*, no. 10, in Reddaway, *Uncensored Russia*, p. 175.
94. *CCE*, no. 15, in *KTS*, p. 483; *CCE*, no. 33, p. 145.
95. Litvinov, *Demonstration in Pushkin Square*.
96. *CCE*, no. 1, in Reddaway, *Uncensored Russia*, pp. 72–76; Litvinov, *Trial of the Four*, p. 137f.; see notes 15 and 18; Gorbanevskaya, *Red Square at Noon*, pp. 72–228.
97. *CCE*, nos. 8–11, in Reddaway, *Uncensored Russia*, pp. 134–37, 159–60, 169–70; *CCE*, no. 14, in *KTS*, vol. 1, pp. 415–17.
98. *CCE*, no. 13, in *KTS*, vol. 1, pp. 393–95; *CCE*, no. 8, in Reddaway, *Uncensored Russia*, pp. 232–34, 237.
99. *CCE*, nos. 5, 7–11, in Reddaway, *Uncensored Russia*, pp. 102, 106, 126, 128, 148–49, 154–55.
100. *CCE*, no. 8, in Reddaway, *Uncensored Russia*, pp. 150–52; *CCE*, no. 18, p. 1; no. 23, pp. 22–23; no. 26, p. 263; *Initsiativnaya gruppa*, pp. 9–10, 13, 17–19, 26–27, 31, 36, 41.
101. *CCE*, no. 22, pp. 22–23; *Proceedings of the Moscow Human Rights Committee*, pp. 221–32, 236, 237.
102. Bukovsky, *To Build a Castle*, pp. 231–32, 236–37.
103. *CCE*, no. 19, pp. 169–71.
104. *CCE*, no. 23, pp. 55–63.
105. *CCE*, no. 11, in Reddaway, *Uncensored Russia*, pp. 159–60.
106. Ibid., p. 159.
107. *CCE*, no. 24, pp. 119–22.

108. *CCE*, ibid., pp. 123–24, 121.
109. Ibid.
110. *CCE*, no. 26, pp. 226–28.
111. Pyotr Yakir, *Childhood in Prison* (London: Macmillan, 1972); abstract in *CCE*, no. 27, pp. 334–35.
112. *CCE*, no. 25, p. 176.
113. *CCE*, no. 29, pp. 49–50.
114. Ibid., p. 49.
115. *CCE*, no. 28, pp. 23–24.
116. *CCE*, no. 27, p. 297; no. 28, pp. 16–22.
117. *CCE*, no. 30, pp. 87–88.
118. *CCE*, no. 27, pp. 292–93.
119. Ibid., p. 292.
120. *CCE*, no. 28, pp. 14–15.
121. *CCE*, no. 29, pp. 62–65.
122. Ibid., pp. 62–65.
123. *CCE*, no. 30, p. 85.
124. *CCE*, no. 29, pp. 66–68.
125. Ibid., pp. 66–67.
126. Ibid., pp. 56, 76–77, 93.
127. *CCE*, no. 30, pp. 82–84.
128. Ibid., p. 84.
129. Ibid., pp. 85–86.
130. Ibid., pp. 107–9.
131. Ibid., p. 82.
132. *CCE*, no. 27, pp. 323–24; no. 28, p. 43.
133. *CCE*, no. 28, p. 78.
134. *CCE*, no. 27, p. 325.
135. *CHR*, no. 2, pp. 46–48; no. 3, pp. 48–49; no. 4, pp. 36–38.

17. The Human Rights Movement During Détente

1. Bukovsky, *To Build a Castle*, p. 32.
2. *CCE*, no. 30, pp. 110–11; no. 39, pp. 184, 187, 214; no. 41, p. 153.
3. *CCE*, no. 38, p. 109.
4. *CCE*, no. 35, p. 124; no. 37, p. 24; no. 39, p. 169; no. 44, p. 133; no. 52, p. 35; no. 55, p. 23; no. 56, p. 185; no. 64, pp. 86–87.
5. *CCE*, no. 42, pp. 235–36.
6. *CCE*, no. 33, pp. 108–14.
7. *CCE*, no. 30, p. 116; *CHR*, no. 4, pp. 6–8.
8. *CCE*, no. 33, p. 173.
9. *CCE*, no. 32, p. 8.
10. Article by Roy Medvedev, *New York Times*, 7 February 1974.
11. *CCE*, no. 32, pp. 70–77; *CHR*, no. 7, pp. 14–24.
12. *CCE*, no. 29, p. 60; Amalrik, *Notes of a Revolutionary*, pp. 235–47.
13. *CCE*, no. 32, pp. 26–28; no. 46, p. 129.
14. *CCE*, no. 32, p. 71.
15. *CHR*, no. 1, pp. 74–77; no. 7, pp. 23–24.
16. Eduard Kuznetsov, *Prison Diaries* (New York: Stein and Day, Publishers, 1975); abstract in *CCE*, no. 30, pp. 122–23.

17. *CCE*, no. 29, pp. 56, 55.
18. *CHR*, no. 4, pp. 15–17.
19. *CHR*, nos. 5–6, p. 16.
20. *CCE*, no. 29, p. 92.
21. Andrey Sakharov, *Progress, Peaceful Coexistence, and Intellectual Freedom;* introduction to *Sakharov Speaks.*
22. Interview with Olle Stenholm, in *Sakharov Speaks.*
23. Aleksandr Solzhenitsyn, *Letter to the Soviet Leaders* (New York: Harper & Row, 1974).
24. Andrey Sakharov, "On Aleksandr Solzhenitsyn's *A Letter to the Soviet Leaders,* in *Kontinent,* ed. Vladimir Maximov (Garden City, NY: Anchor Press/Doubleday, 1976), pp. 2–14.
25. Aleksandr Solzhenitsyn, *Cancer Ward* (New York: Harper & Row, 1968); idem, *The First Circle;* Roy Medvedev, *Let History Be the Judge* (New York: Alfred A. Knopf, 1971); Zhores Medvedev, *Fruit of the Meetings Between Scientists of the World* (London: St. Martin's Press, 1971); Valentin Turchin, *Inertia of Fear* (New York: Columbia University Press, 1981); Evgenia Ginzburg, *Journey into the Whirlwind;* Nadezhda Mandelstam, *Hope Against Hope: Memoirs* (New York: Atheneum, 1970); Yekaterina Olitskaya, *Moi vospominaniya;* Grigory Pomerants, "The Moral Aspects of Personality," in Meerson and Shragin, eds., *Political, Social, and Religious Thought,* pp. 99–113; Lev Ventsov, "To Think," in ibid., pp. 148–64; Gennady Alekseyev [pseud.], "Obrashcheniye k grazhdanam Sovetskogo Soyuza o vozrozhdenii stalinizma i merakh bor'by s nim," *AS* 1, no. 80 (1968); Valentin Komarov, "Otkrytoye pis'mo o sovetskoy okkupatsii Chekhoslovakii," *AS* 1, no. 69 (1968); *Obshchestvennye problemy,* ed. Valery Chalidze, in *AS* 16, nos. 5–15; Litvinov, *Demonstration in Pushkin Square;* idem, *Trial of the Four;* Gorbanevskaya, *Red Square at Noon;* "Moyo posledneye slovo," *Vol'noye slovo,* 14–15.
26. *CCE*, no. 31, p. 105.
27. *CCE*, no. 14, in *KTS,* vol. 1, pp. 446, 488.
28. *CHR*, no. 2, pp. 5–6.
29. *CCE*, no. 32, p. 11; *CHR*, no. 7, pp. 6–7.
30. *CCE*, no. 32, pp. 98–99; *Initsiativnaya gruppa,* pp. 38–50.
31. *CCE*, no. 33, pp. 108–14.
32. *CHR*, no. 11, p. 30.
33. Andrey Sakharov, Valentin Turchin, and Roy Medvedev, "Manifesto," in *Sakharov Speaks,* pp. 115–34.
34. Abstract in *CCE,* no. 30, pp. 117–18.
35. *CCE*, no. 34, pp. 2–4; no. 36, pp. 164–68.
36. *CCE*, no. 38, pp. 80–91.
37. *Izvestiya,* 25 October 1975, cited in *CCE,* no. 38, p. 72.
38. *CCE*, no. 38, pp. 70–71.
39. *CCE*, no. 38, p. 71.
40. *CCE*, no. 38, p. 70.
41. "Introduction," in *Sakharov Speaks,* p. 37.
42. *CCE*, no. 39, pp. 212–14.
43. *CCE*, no. 40, pp. 4–21.
44. Aleksandr Glezer and Igor Golomshtok, eds., *Soviet Art in Exile* (New York and London: Random House and Secher, 1978).

45. *CCE*, no. 34, pp. 64–65.
46. *CCE*, no. 53, pp. 172–73.
47. *CCE*, no. 40, pp. 95–97; Ludmilla Alexeyeva, "Yury Orlov: rukovoditel' Moskovskoy Khel'sinkskoy gruppy," *Kontinent*, no. 21 (1969), pp. 186–92.
48. Complete text in Alexeyeva, *Delo Orlova*, pp. 201–5.
49. Russian and English text in *Sbornik dokumentov obshchestvennoy gruppy sodeystviya*, vol. 1, pp. 5–7.
50. *CHR*, no. 23/24, pp. 16–18 (Alfred Friendly, Jr., Helsinki Commission).
51. *CHR*, no. 23/24, p. 16.
52. *CCE*, no. 44, p. 116.
53. *Reports of the Helsinki Accord Monitors*, 1977, pp. 32–33.
54. *Sbornik dokumentov obshchestvennoy gruppy sodeystviya*, vol. 3, pp. 52–58 (Lidiya Voronina's account of her trip to Pentecostalist communities); vol. 4, pp. 6–11 (Arkady Polishchuk's report, based on trips to Pentecostalist communities).
55. *CCE*, nos. 6 and 11, in Reddaway, *Uncensored Russia*, p. 71 (for 1969 demonstrations); no. 24, pp. 143–44; no. 35, p. 144 (for 1974); no. 38, p. 144 (for 1975); no. 43, pp. 13–14 (for 1976); no. 48, pp. 162–63 (for 1977); no. 52, pp. 123–25 (for 1978); no. 55, pp. 57–60 (for 1979); no. 60, pp. 96–97 (for 1980); no. 63, pp. 200–01 (for 1981); *USSR News Brief*, 23/24 (1982), no. 25 (for 1982); *USSR News Brief*, 23/24 (1983), no. 24 (for 1983).
56. *CCE*, no. 43, pp. 1–8; Bukovsky, *To Build a Castle*.
57. *CCE*, no. 40, pp. 97–98; Alexeyeva, "Yury Orlov," pp. 189–93.
58. *Sbornik dokumentov obshchestvennoy gruppy sodeystviya*, vol. 4, pp. 42–43; *CCE*, no. 44, pp. 127–28.
59. *CCE*, no. 44, p. 127.
60. "Zayavleniye Gosdepartamenta SShA," *CHR*, no. 25, pp. 8, 11.
61. *CCE*, no. 44, pp. 94–115; Alexeyeva, "Yury Orlov," pp. 195–214.
62. *CCE*, no. 44, pp. 191–93.
63. Ibid., p. 185.
64. *CCE*, no. 45, p. 233 (Marynovich and Matusevych); pp. 236–39 (Gamsakhurdiya and Kostava); no. 46, pp. 1–5 (Landa); no. 47, pp. 45–46 (Petkus); no. 48, pp. 16–23 (Lukyanenko and Vins); no. 49, pp. 3–5 (Goldshteyn).
65. *CCE*, no. 50, pp. 1–20; Alexeyeva, *Delo Orlova*, pp. 123–251, 20–80, 100–02 (Gamsakhurdija, Kostava, Ginsburg, Shcharansky, Petkus); *CCE*, no. 51, pp. 1–10 (Nasaryan); no. 55, pp. 1–3 (Streltsiv, Cichko, Litvin, Berdnyk); no. 56, pp. 95–98 (Landa), pp. 137–39 (Rozumny, Gorbal), p. 140 (Lesiv), pp. 143–45 (Arutyunyan); no. 57, p. 56 (Kalinnichenko), pp. 95–98 (Chornovil); no. 58, pp. 68–69 (Statkevicius), pp. 76–81 (Matusevych, Stus); no. 60, pp. 24–26 (Ternovsky), pp. 65–68 (Skuodis); no. 61, pp. 153–54 (Meshko); no. 62, pp. 7–19 (Osipova), p. 59 (Kandyba), p. 67 (Vaiciunas, Juravicius); "Human Rights," *USSR News Brief*, 7 (1982), no. 1 (Kovalyov).
66. Litvinov, *Trial of the Four*.
67. *Informatsionnyy byulleten' po delu Orlova, Ginzburga, Shcharanskogo*, nos. 1–4; AS 29, no. 3051 (1977); 23, no. 3266 (1978); 41, no. 3399 (1978); 6, no. 4568 (1982); *Delo Orlova*, pp. 53–75; Ab-

stracts: *CCE*, no. 44, pp. 201–05; no. 46, pp. 98, 99, 106; no. 47, pp. 155–62; no. 48, p. 97.

68. See *Sborniki dokumentov obshchestvennoy gruppy sodeystviya*, vols. 1–8.

69. *Informatsionnyy byulleten' Rabochey komissii po rassledovaniyu ispol'zovaniya psikhiatrii v politicheskikh tselakh*, nos. 1–24, in *AS* 28, no. 3045 (1977); 1, no. 3088 (1978); 18, no. 3225 (1978); 24, no. 3270 (1978); 27, no. 3299 (1978); 30–31, no. 3319–20 (1978); 33, no. 3328 (1978); 35, no. 3350 (1978); 2, no. 3448 (1979); 7, no. 3487 (1979); 12, no. 3537 (1979); 36, no. 3737 (1979); 36, no. 2738 (1979); 3, no. 3833 (1980); 15, no. 3946 (1980); 15, no. 3961 (1980); *Vol'noye slovo*, 41–42 (1981), nos. 15, 7–9; see also note 91.

70. *CCE*, no. 41, pp. 129–31; no. 42, pp. 41, 190–91; no. 43, pp. 38–39, 41–46.

71. *CCE*, no. 43, p. 41.

72. *CCE*, no. 45, pp. 274–76; no. 46, pp. 84–85; no. 47, p. 147; no. 48, pp. 91–92.

73. Sidney Bloch and Peter Reddaway, *Russia's Political Hospitals* (London: Victor Gollancz, 1977), pp. 280–340.

74. *CCE*, no. 47, p. 166; Bloch and Reddaway, *Russia's Political Hospitals*, pp. 335–39.

75. *CCE*, no. 50, pp. 81–89; *Informatsionnyy byulleten' Rabochey komissii po rassledovaniyu ispol'zovaniya psikhiatrii v politicheskikh tselakh*, nos. 9, 10. See note 69.

76. *CCE*, no. 50, p. 81; no. 56, p. 102.

77. *CCE*, no. 50, pp. 88–89.

78. *CCE*, no. 51, pp. 179–80; no. 52, pp. 76–77; no. 53, pp. 137–38; no. 54, pp. 30–31; 55, p. 180.

79. *CCE*, no. 56, pp. 103–7; no. 60, pp. 16–17; no. 61, pp. 134–36.

80. *CCE*, no. 58, pp. 13–18 (Bakhmin); no. 60, pp. 24–26 (Ternovsky); no. 61, pp. 131–34 (Podrabinek); no. 63, pp. 1–9 (Grivnina and Serebrov).

81. *CCE*, no. 61, pp. 137–38; no. 62, pp. 19–26.

82. *CCE*, no. 54, p. 112.

83. *CCE*, no. 53, pp. 143–44.

84. *Informatsionnyy byulleten' gruppy 'Prava na emigratsiyu'* (Listy) 1 (1980), in *AS* 15, no. 4274 (1981).

85. Testimony from Vadim Baranov, member of "Elections 79."

86. *Sbornik dokumentov obshchestvennoy gruppy sodeystviya*, vol. 1, pp. 52–55; annotation in *CCE*, no. 41, pp. 163–65.

87. *Hearings Before the CSCE of the 95th Congress: First Session on Implementation of the Helsinki Accords*, vol. 4 (3 June 1971), pp. 39–45; abstract in *CCE*, no. 46, pp. 97–98.

88. *Sbornik dokumentov obshchestvennoy gruppy sodeystviya*, vols. 1–8; *Reports of the Helsinki Accord Monitors*, vols. 1–3, 1977–79.

89. See note 67.

90. *Informatsionnyy byulleten' Komiteta zashchity Tatyana Velikanovoy*, no. 1 (Moscow), 12 December 1979, in *Vol'noye slovo* 38 (1980); see also *AS* 5, nos. 4172, 4555–56 (1982).

91. See note 69; Abstracts: *Information Bulletin* no. 1 in *CCE*, no. 46,

p. 107; *I.B.* no. 9, in *CCE*, no. 51, pp. 197–98; *I.B.* no. 42 in *CCE*, no. 60, p. 117.

92. *Informatsionnyy byulleten' Initsiativnoy gruppy zashchity prav invalidov v SSSR*, nos. 1–16, in *Vol'noye slovo*, 41/42 (1981), nos. 8–10; AS 10, no. 3511 (1979); 40, no. 3765 (1979); 7, no. 4577 (1982); Abstracts: no. 8 in *CCE*, no. 56, p. 218; no. 9 in *CCE*, no. 57, pp. 115–16; no. 24 in *CCE*, no. 60, p. 117.

93. *Informatsionnyy byulleten' Svobodnogo mezhprofessional 'nogo ob'edineniya trudyashchikhsya (SMOT)*, nos. 1–34, in AS 27, no. 3669 (1979); 17, no. 4293 (1981); 27, no. 4370 (1981); 17, no. 4527 (1982); 15, no. 4621 (1982); 17, no. 4628 (1982); 26, no. 4692 (1982); 3, no. 4806 (1983); 5, no. 4824 (1983); Abstracts: nos. 10–11 in *CCE*, no. 61, p. 224; nos. 12–13 in *CCE*, no. 62, pp. 157–58.

94. See note 84.

95. Andrey Sakharov, *My Country and the World;* idem, *Alarm and Hope* (New York: Alfred A. Knopf, 1978); *On Sakharov.*

96. Abstracts in *CCE*, no. 46, pp. 101–3; no. 47, pp. 171–73.

97. *Pamyat'* (New York), 1978, no. 1; (Paris), 1979, no. 2; (Paris), 1980, no. 3; (Paris), 1981, no. 4; (Paris), 1982, no. 5; Annotations: no. 1 in *CCE*, no. 42, pp. 268–70; no. 2 in *CCE*, no. 51, p. 217; no. 3 in *CCE*, no. 52, pp. 142–43.

98. *Pamyat'*, no. 1, pp. V–IX.

99. *Poiski* (New York), 1979, no. 1; (Paris), 1980, no. 2; (Paris), 1981, no. 3; (Paris, 1982, no. 4; Annotations: nos. 1–3 in *CCE*, no. 51, pp. 217–19; nos. 4–5 in *CCE*, no. 52, pp. 140–42; nos. 6–8 in *CCE*, no. 56, pp. 218–20.

100. *Poiski*, no. 1, p. 1.

101. *V zashchitu ekonomicheskikh svobod*, ed. K. Burzhuademov; Annotations: no. 1 in *CCE*, no. 49, p. 105; no. 8 in *CCE*, no. 54, p. 151. See A. Katsenelinboygen, "Tsvetnye rynki i sovetskaya ekonomika," and K. Burzhuademov, "Ya obvinyayu," in *SSSR: vnutrenniye protivorechiya*, vol. 2, pp. 54–132, 223–47.

102. Annotations: *Summa*, 1979, nos. 1–2 in *CCE*, no. 53, pp. 184–86; nos. 3–4 in *CCE*, no. 55, pp. 220–22; 1980, nos. 1–2 in *CCE*, no. 61, p. 224.

103. *Metropol'* (Ann Arbor: Ardis, 1979).

104. *CCE*, no. 52, pp. 119–23; no. 54, pp. 130–31.

105. See N. Kononova, "Litso Peterburga," *Kovcheg*, no. 1 (Paris: 1978), p. 76.

106. 37, nos. 1–6; Annotations: nos. 1–6; in *CCE*, no. 43, pp. 79–80; nos. 7–8 in *CCE*, no. 48, pp. 179–80. See also Kononova, "Litso Peterburga," pp. 77–78.

107. *Khudozhestvennyy arkhiv*, nos. 1–2; annotation in *CCE*, no. 43, p. 80. See also Kononova, "Litso Peterburga," pp. 76–77.

108. *Women and Russia*, ed. Tatyana Mamonova (Boston: Beacon Press, 1984); annotation in *CCE*, no. 55, p. 71.

109. See Yuliya Voznesenskaya, "Kommentariy i pis'ma iz Leningrada," *Possev* (1982), no. 5, pp. 27–28.

110. Vadim Nechayev, "Nravstvennoye znacheniye neofitsial'noy kul'tury," *Poiski*, no. 1, pp. 305–13; Aleksandr Glezer, *Iskusstvo pod bul'dozerom* (London: Overseas Publications, n.d.), pp. 9–43.

111. Glezer, *Iskusstvo pod bul'dozerom*, p. 41; Kononova, "Litso Peterburga," pp. 76–77.
112. *CCE*, no. 32, pp. 26–28 (arrest and trial of Kheyfets); no. 33, pp. 74–77 (Etkind's dismissal); no. 34, pp. 5–8, 22–23 (arrest and trial of Maramzin); no. 35, pp. 112–17. See also Etkind, *Zapiski Nezagovorshchika*.
113. Kononova, "Litso Peterburga," pp. 73–76.
114. *CCE*, no. 38, p. 154; no. 42, pp. 198–99.
115. *CCE*, no. 42, p. 194.
116. *Grani*, 1978, no. 108, pp. 151–64.
117. *CCE*, no. 42, pp. 10–12.
118. *CCE*, no. 43, p. 14.
119. Ibid., pp. 24–28.
120. Ibid., pp. 24–28, 76–77.
121. *CCE*, no. 45, p. 221.
122. Vadim Nechayev, "Istoriya Oskara Rabina," *Kontinent*, no. 21 (1979), p. 336.
123. *CCE*, no. 53, pp. 183–84.
124. Ibid., pp. 63–65, 160–63; no. 63, pp. 31–41.
125. *CCE*, no. 51, p. 175.
126. Ludmilla Alexeyeva, "Obzor vazhneyshikh sobytiy," *Khronika zashchity prav v SSSR*, ed. Valery Chalidre (New York: Khronika Press, 1979), no. 36, p. 42; *List of Political Prisoners in the USSR, 1 May 1982, USSR News Brief*.
127. Litvinov, *Trial of the Four*, pp. 340–42, 344.
128. Amalrik, *Will the Soviet Union Survive*, p. 23.
129. *CCE*, no. 30, p. 98.
130. *CCE*, no. 8, in Reddaway, *Uncensored Russia*, pp. 306–7.
131. *CCE*, no. 11, ibid., pp. 70–71.
132. *CCE*, no. 32, pp. 11, 86.
133. *CCE*, no. 34, pp. 63–64.
134. *CCE*, no. 32, pp. 25–26.
135. *CCE*, no. 38, pp. 99–104.
136. *CCE*, no. 40, pp. 42–56.
137. *CCE*, no. 36, pp. 208–9; no. 38, pp. 95–97.
138. *CCE*, no. 37, p. 21.
139. *CCE*, no. 43, p. 14.
140. *CCE*, no. 44, p. 23.
141. *CCE*, no. 41, pp. 143–44; no. 42, pp. 208–10.
142. See note 141; also *CCE*, no. 44, pp. 120–21.
143. *CCE*, no. 42, pp. 208–10.
144. *CCE*, no. 47, pp. 153–54.
145. *CCE*, no. 56, p. 140.
146. *CCE*, no. 63, p. 77; no. 64, pp. 37–38.
147. *USSR News Brief*, 20/21 (1982), no. 6.
148. *CCE*, no. 53, p. 52.
149. Ibid., pp. 52–53.
150. *CCE*, no. 51, pp. 36–38.
151. *CCE*, no. 53, pp. 53–55.
152. *CCE*, no. 55, pp. 15–18; no. 57, p. 46.
153. *CCE*, no. 58, pp. 92–95; no. 62, pp. 34–35.

154. *CCE*, no. 51, p. 38.
155. *CCE*, no. 51, pp. 20–25.
156. *CCE*, no. 56, p. 200.
157. *CCE*, no. 52, pp. 125–26.
158. Ibid., pp. 26–27.
159. *CCE*, no. 45, p. 318; *CCE*, no. 58, pp. 86–92.
160. *CCE*, no. 40, pp. 106–7.
161. Ibid., p. 106.
162. *CCE*, no. 51, pp. 39–41.
163. *CCE*, no. 53, pp. 55–59.
164. *CCE*, no. 51, pp. 42–43.
165. Ibid., pp. 17–18.
166. *CCE*, no. 54, pp. 1–8.
167. *CCE*, no. 55, pp. 11–14.
168. Ibid., pp. 176–77.
169. Ibid., p. 22.
170. Ibid., p. 21.
171. Ibid., pp. 18–19.
172. Ibid., pp. 15, 18.
173. *CCE*, no. 56, pp. 74–93.
174. *CCE*, no. 56, pp. 112–14.
175. *CCE*, no. 55, pp. 11–14; no. 56, pp. 108–12.
176. *CCE*, no. 51, pp. 179–80; no. 52, pp. 76–77; no. 53, pp. 137–38; no. 54, pp. 30–31; no. 56, p. 180; no. 58, pp. 13–18; no. 60, pp. 24–26; no. 61, pp. 131–34; no. 63, pp. 1–9.
177. *CCE*, nos. 4 and 6, in Reddaway, *Uncensored Russia*, pp. 112–19 (Larisa Bogoraz); *CCE*, no. 6, ibid., pp. 197–202 (Irina Belgorodskaya); *CCE*, no. 11, ibid., pp. 109–10, *CCE*, no. 13, in *KTS*, vol. 1, pp. 379–81 (Valeriya Novodvorskaya); *CCE*, no. 15, ibid., pp. 159–60 (Natalya Gorbanevskaya); *CCE*, no. 23, pp. 63–65 (Nadezhda Emelkina); *CCE*, no. 29, pp. 61, 84 (second trial of Irina Belgorodskaya); *CCE*, no. 46, pp. 1–5 (Mal'va Landa).
178. *CCE*, no. 58, pp. 2–10.
179. *CCE*, no. 56, pp. 95–98.
180. See, for example, the cases of Aleksandr and Kirill Podrabinek, Aleksandr Bolonkin in *CCE*, no. 61, pp. 131–34, 186–93; *Khronika zashchity prav v SSSR*, 1982, no. 45–46, in *SSSR: vnutrenniye protivorechiya*, vol. 5, pp. 270–71.
181. *CCE*, no. 62, pp. 2–3; *Khronika zashchity prav v SSSR*, nos. 43–44, in *SSSR: vnutrenniye protivorechiya*, vol. 3, pp. 352–53.
182. See, for example, the trial of Yury Orlov (*CCE*, no. 50, pp. 14–16) and the trial of Tatyana Osipova (*CCE*, no. 62, p. 14).
183. *CCE*, no. 61, p. 138 (Koryagin); no. 55, p. 20 (Nekipelov); no. 61, pp. 135–36 (Serebrov); no. 62, pp. 40–41 (Kuvakin).
184. The trials of Yury Orlov, Anatoly Shcharansky, Viktoras Petkus, Vladimir and Mariya Slepak (*CCE*, no. 50), Vladimir Sichko (*CCE*, no. 60, p. 60), Aleksandr Podrabinek (*CCE*, no. 61, pp. 131–34).
185. The trials of Ida Nudel (*CCE*, no. 50, p. 99), Yosif Begun (*CCE*, no. 59, p. 107), Anatoly Koryagin (*CCE*, no. 62, p. 20).
186. The trials of Tatyana Velikanova (*CCE*, no. 58, p. 10), Bakhmin (*CCE*, no. 58, p. 14), and Grimm (*CCE*, no. 58, pp. 66–67).

187. *CCE*, no. 62, p. 113 (Kazachkov and Balakhonov), p. 116 (Morozov), p. 118 (Podrabinek).
188. *CCE*, no. 63, p. 66.
189. *CCE*, no. 51, pp. 29–30.
190. *CCE*, no. 63, p. 208.
191. Ibid., p. 141.
192. *USSR News Brief*, 19/20 (1983), no. 5; 23/24 (1983), no. 4.
193. Ibid., 2, no. 22.
194. Ibid., 1/2 (1984), no. 20.
195. Ibid., 14 (1984), no. 25
196. Anatoly Marchenko, "Posledneye slovo," *Possev*, January 1982, pp. 14–16 (incomplete text). Complete text in *AS* 20, no. 4646 (1982).
197. *Kommunist*, Moscow, 1981, no. 14, p. 98; in English: *CHR*, no. 44, p. 32.
198. *CHR*, no. 47–48, p. 30; *USSR News Brief*, 17 (1982), no. 1.
199. "Special Statement on Chronicle No. 59 and Turnover of Chronicle Editors," *CCE*, no. 60; no. 61, pp. 146–47.
200. *USSR News Brief*, 17, (1982), no. 2; 11 (1983), no. 3; *AS* 28, no. 4989 (1983); *USSR News Brief*, 22 (1983), no. 1; 1/2, (1984), no. 8; 6 (1984), no. 4.
201. *USSR News Brief*, 6 (1983), no. 33; *AS* 17, no. 4905 (1983); 24, no. 4973 (1983); 27, no. 4983 (1983); 40, no. 5060 (1983); 42, no. 5072 (1983); *CCE*, no. 64, pp. 1–5.
202. *USSR News Brief*, 5 (1983), no. 1; 22, no. 2; 12, no. 30; *AS* 1, no. 5125 (1984).
203. *USSR News Brief*, 6 (1984), no. 4; *AS* 17, nos. 5220, 5223 (1984).
204. *CCE*, no. 53, p. 166.
205. *Poiski i Razmyshleniya* (Paris), 1980, nos. 1–4; Abstracts: no. 1 (9), no. 2 (10) in *CCE*, no. 57, pp. 116–17; nos. 3 (11) 8 (16) in *CCE*, no. 61, pp. 223–24.
206. *CCE*, no. 56, p. 99; no. 57, p. 29; no. 61, p. 221.
207. *USSR News Brief*, 2 (1982), no. 40.
208. *Sakharovsky sbornik* (New York: Khronika Press, 1982); in English: *On Sakharov*, ed. Aleksandr Babyonyshev (New York: Vintage Books, 1982).
209. "From the Editors," *On Sakharov*, p. ix.
210. Ibid.
211. Ibid.
212. Andrey Sakharov, "The Responsibility of Scientists," ibid., pp. 205–22.
213. Andrey Sakharov, "How to Preserve World Peace," ibid., pp. 262–69.
214. *CCE*, no. 56, p. 222; *Women and Russia*, ed. Mamonova.
215. See, for example, responses to questions by the French journal *L'Alternative*, "Whither Dissent?" in *CHR*, no. 46, pp. 5–11; no. 48, pp. 5–16; *SSSR: vnutrenniye protivorechiya*, vol. 7, pp. 37–166; vol. 8, pp. 139–96; vol. 9, pp. 5–85; *Kontinent*, no. 18, pp. 183–202.
216. *CCE*, no. 62, p. 156.
217. Ibid., p. 49.
218. *CCE*, no. 62, pp. 156–57; *AS* 34, no. 4413 (1981).
219. *CCE*, no. 64, pp. 15–20.
220. *CCE*, no. 58, pp. 86–93; no. 62, pp. 33–38; no. 63, p. 48; no. 64, pp. 6–12.

221. *CCE*, no. 64, pp. 11–12.
222. *CCE*, no. 62, pp. 47–48; no. 64, pp. 6–7; *USSR News Brief*, 19 (1982), no. 3.
223. *CCE*, no. 60, pp. 38–39, 92–93; no. 61, p. 147; no. 62, pp. 47, 144; *USSR News Brief*, 7 (1983), no. 1; 23/24 (1984), no. 4.
224. *CCE*, no. 63, pp. 48–49, 203; *USSR News Brief*, 10 (1983), no. 3.
225. *CCE*, no. 56, p. 211.
226. Ibid., pp. 89–90.
227. *CCE*, no. 60, pp. 96–97.
228. See note 55.
229. *CCE*, no. 63, pp. 200–1.
230. *USSR News Brief*, 9 (1982), no. 31.
231. Ibid., no. 32.
232. *AS* 32, no. 4070 (1980); 45, no. 4164 (1980).
233. *Vesti iz SSSR* 21 (1981), no. 34; 23/24 (1981), no. 35; *Possev* (December 1981), pp. 1–3. The complete text is in *AS* 47, no. 4503 (1981).
234. *Vesti iz SSSR* 21 (1981), no. 35. Complete text is in *Possev*, January 1982, pp. 19–24.
235. *CCE*, no. 60, pp. 29–30.
236. Yevgeny Kozlovsky, "Krasnaya ploshchad'," *Kontinent*, nos. 30–31 (1981); "Dissident i chinovnitsa," *Kontinent*, no. 27 (1981).
237. *USSR News Brief* 23/24 (1981), no. 4; 13 (1982), no. 14.
238. *USSR News Brief* 13 (1982), no. 12; 23/24, no. 8.
239. *Khronika zashchity prav v SSSR*, no. 40, p. 47.
240. *CCE*, no. 61, p. 216.
241. *Khronika zashchity prav v SSSR*, nos. 45–46, in *SSSR: vnutrenniye protivorechiya*, vol. 5, p. 272.
242. See note 214.
243. *CCE*, no. 55, p. 71.
244. *CCE*, no. 60, p. 35.
245. *CHR*, no. 41, p. 22.
246. *CCE*, no. 62, p. 42.
247. Tsvigun, in *CHR*, no. 44, p. 33.
248. Andrey Sakharov, "Trevozhnoye vremya," *Khronika zashchity prav v SSSR*, no. 38, pp. 14–15.
249. "O gruppe doveriya," *Forum*, 1983, no. 4, pp. 8–12; Sergei Batovrin, "Za ochelovechivaniye otnosheniy mezhdu SSSR i SShA," ibid., pp. 13–20.
250. Documents of the Trust Group, ibid., pp. 22–34; *AS* 6, no. 4838 (1983); 21, nos. 4942, 4943, 4945 (1983); 44, no. 5090 (1983).
251. *The Independent Peace Movement in the Soviet Union*, U.S. Helsinki Watch Committee, New York, February 1984.
252. Ibid.
253. *AS* 8, no. 4851 (1983); 10, no. 4869 (1983); 44, no. 5090 (1983).
254. *USSR News Brief* 20 (1982), no. 2; 22 (1983), no. 3; 23/24 (1984), no. 6; *AS* 9, nos. 5176–78 (1984).
255. *USSR News Brief*, 1/2 (1984), no. 9; 4 (1984), no. 36.
256. "O gruppe doveriya," *Forum*, p. 10.
257. *USSR News Brief*, 10 (1983), no. 2.
258. Sergey Grigoryants, "Razgromleno li pravozashchitnoye dvizheniye? *Byulleten' V*, no. 94/95, in *AS* 17 no. 4905 (1983), p. 4.

259. Viktor Nekipelov, "Stalin na vetrovom stekle," *Kontinent,* no. 19, pp. 238–241.
260. n.a., *Fashizm v SSSR (samizdat), Strana i mir,* ed. Kronid Lyubarsky, Munich, no. 1/2 (1984), p. 54.
261. *USSR News Brief* 8 (1982), no. 9.
262. *Pravda,* May 22, 1984; *Komsomolskaya pravda,* August 1, 1984, and many others.
263. Solomon Volkov, "Rok-muzyka v Sovetskom Soyuze," *SSSR: vnutrenniye protivorechiya,* vol. 5, pp. 44–50.
264. *USSR News Brief* 19 (1980), no. 32; 20 (1980), no. 3.
265. *CCE,* no. 60, p. 95; *USSR News Brief* 4 (1983), no. 32; 19 (1984), no. 7; 8 (1984), no. 1.
266. Ibid., 22 (1983), no. 27.
267. *CCE,* no. 20, n.p.
268. *USSR News Brief* 4 (1984), no. 32.
269. Ibid., 5 (1983), no. 7; 23/24 (1983), no. 25.
270. Ibid., 21 (1984), no. 4.
271. *CCE,* no. 41, pp. 178–80; no. 42, p. 258; no. 45, p. 294.
272. *CCE,* no. 8, in Reddaway, *Uncensored Russia,* pp. 405–8.
273. *CCE,* no. 64, p. 22; *USSR News Brief,* 18 (1982), no. 17.
274. *CCE,* no. 64, pp. 20–26.
275. *Byulleten' V* 76, nos. 22–25 (from Khronika Press Archives).
276. *CCE,* no. 25, n.p.
277. *CCE,* no. 49, pp. 85–87; no. 57, p. 120; *CCE,* no. 63, pp. 79–80; *AS* 34, no. 4415 (1981); *USSR News Brief* 2 (1982), no. 7; 13/14 (1983), no. 2; 23/24 (1983), no. 5.
278. *CCE,* no. 52, pp. 145–46; *USSR News Brief,* 19 (1980), no. 32; 20 (1982), no. 1; 19 (1982), no. 4; "Nakhoditsya li estonskiy narod i ego kul'tura pod chuzhezemnym igom?" *Forum,* no. 3, pp. 143–44.
279. *USSR News Brief* 18/19 (1979), no. 14.
280. *AS* 19, no. 4638 (1983).
281. *USSR News Brief,* 22 (1982), no. 29.
282. Ibid.
283. N. Peskov, *Pamyat',* vol. 1, pp. 269–284; S. R. Rozhdestvensky, *Pamyat',* vol. 5; Ludmilla Alexeyeva, "The Dissident Movement," *CHR,* no. 31, pp. 41–46; Weil, *Osobo opasny;* Revolt Pimenov, *Odin politichesky protsess, Pamyat',* vol. 2, pp. 160–260.
284. Bukovsky, *To Build a Castle,* pp. 234–40; Pimenov, *Odin politichesky protsess,* pp. 234–40; Weil, *Osobo opasny,* pp. 135–45.
285. *USSR News Brief,* 9 (1982), no. 31.
286. Ibid., no. 32.
287. *CCE,* no. 61, pp. 158–59; *USSR News Brief,* 14/15 (1982), no. 3; 6 (1983), no. 14; 21 (1983), no. 4.
288. *AS* 32, no. 4070 (1980); 45 (1980), no. 4164; *USSR News Brief* 21 (1981), nos. 34, 35; 23/24 (1981), no. 35.
289. Ibid., 8 (1982), no. 23.
290. Ibid., 19 (1982), no. 39.
291. "Fashizm v SSSR" *(samizdat), Strana i mir,* ed. Cronid Lubarsky, Munich, no. 1/2 (1984), p. 49; *USSR News Brief,* 8 (1982), no. 23; 11 (1982), no. 24.
292. Ibid.

293. Ibid., 11 (1983), no. 34; 4 (1984), no. 44.
294. "Fashizm v SSSR," p. 51.
295. Ibid., p. 53.
296. CCE, no. 64, p. 113.
297. "Fashizm v SSSR," p. 52.
298. USSR News Brief 22 (1982), no. 33.

18. The Movement for Social and Economic Rights in the Soviet Union

1. Ludmilla Alexeyeva, "Quantitative and Qualitative Characteristics of Soviet Dissent," Russia (New York: Foundation for Soviet Studies, 1983), no. 718, pp. 114–35.
2. Sakharov, My Country and the World, pp. 13–30; Anatoly Marchenko, "The Life of Soviet Workers," CHR, no. 29, pp. 46–51; Valery Chalidze, "A Worker Movement in the Soviet Union," CHR, no. 29, pp. 40–45; idem, "Lektsii o pravovom polozhenii rabochikh v SSSR," in SSSR: rabocheye dvizheniye? comp. Valery Chalidze (New York: Khronika Press, 1978), pp. 81–140; Yury Orlov, "Vozmozhen li sotsializm netotalitarnogo tolka?" Samosoznaniye (New York: Khronika Press, 1976), pp. 280–83.
3. Marchenko, My Testimony, p. 90 (Aleksandrov and Murom); Aleksandr Solzhenitsyn, Gulag Archipelago, 3 (New York: Harper & Row, 1974), pp. 506–14 (Novocherkassk); AS 25, no. 1437 (Dneprodzerzhinsk).
4. CCE, no. 8, in Reddaway, Uncensored Russia, pp. 290–91.
5. List of Political Prisoners in the USSR, 1 May 1982, USSR News Brief.
6. CCE, no. 39, p. 205.
7. CCE, no. 42, p. 256.
8. CCE, no. 49, p. 51.
9. For example, the Washington Post, 14 June 1980.
10. Vesti iz SSSR 20 (1980), no. 1.
11. Ibid., 12 (1981), no. 29; 22, no. 33; Possev, 1981, no. 10, p. 3; Visnik represiy v Ukraine, External Representation of the Ukrainian Helsinki Group, New York, 1981, vol. 8, p. 11.
12. Vesti iz SSSR (1981), no. 29.
13. CCE, no. 48, pp. 165–66 (Klebanov); no. 61, pp. 206–7; Washington Post, 10 February 1981 (Editorial); CHR, no. 41, p. 13 (Nikitin).
14. S.R. Rozhdestvensky, in Pamyat' (Paris: YMCA Press), vol. 5, pp. 231–49.
15. N. Peskov, in Pamyat' (New York: Khronika Press, 1978), vol. 1, pp. 269–84.
16. CCE, no. 6, in Reddaway, Uncensored Russia, p. 389.
17. Vol'noye slovo (Possev, 1973), no. 7, pp. 95–106.
18. CCE, no. 33, pp. 145–46, 154–57.
19. See note 2; Chalidze, SSSR: rabocheye dvizheniye? pp. 31–33; USSR News Brief, (1984), 7, no. 24.
20. Ludmilla Alexeyeva, comp., Thematic Survey of the Documents of the

Moscow Helsinki Group, U.S. Congress, Commission on Security and Cooperation in Europe, 1981, pp. 19–21; *Sbornik dokumentov obshchestvennoy gruppy sodeystviya*, 1977, vol. 2, pp. 19–20.

21. Ibid., pp. 39–54.
22. Ibid., 1977, vol. 6, pp. 77–81.
23. *Reports of the Helsinki Accord Monitors in the USSR*, 1978, pp. 41–42.
24. Ibid., pp. 42–43.
25. *Sbornik dokumentov obshchestvennoy gruppy sodeystviya*, vol. 6, pp. 77–81.
26. *Reports of the Helsinki Accord Monitors in the USSR*, vol. 3, documents 38, 46, 47; *Sbornik dokumentov obshchestvennoy gruppy sodeystviya*, vols. 6, 7.
27. Ibid., vol. 5, pp. 36–39.
28. Ibid., p. 38.
29. Ibid., vol. 7, pp. 5–7; vol. 6, p. 79.
30. Ibid., vol. 6, pp. 84–105.
31. *CCE*, no. 48, pp. 164–65; *SSSR: rabocheye dvizheniye?* pp. 55–78.
32. Gleb Vysotin and Sereda Velentin, "Independent Trade Unions," *CHR*, no. 39, p. 28.
33. Ibid.
34. Yevgeny Nikolayev, "K istorii voznikonoveniya Svobodnogo profsoyuza," in *Khronika zashchity prav v SSSR*, ed. Valery Chalidze (New York: Khronika Press), no. 35, p. 30.
35. Vysotin and Sereda, "Independent Trade Unions," p. 28.
36. *SSSR: rabocheye dvizheniye?* pp. 61–64.
37. *CCE*, no. 48, p. 165–66.
38. Vysotin and Sereda, "Independent Trade Unions," p. 29–30.
39. Ibid.
40. Ibid., pp. 30–35.
41. *CCE*, no. 53, pp. 49–52 (Volokhonsky); no. 51, pp. 186–87 (Skvirsky); no. 54, pp. 46–50 (Nikitin); no. 51, pp. 31–32 (Morozov); no. 62, pp. 39–41 (Kuvakin).
42. Vysotin and Sereda, "Independent Trade Unions," pp. 30–35.
43. *Informatsionnyy byulleten' Svobodnogo mezhprofessional'nogo ob"edineniya trudyashchikhsya* (SMOT), nos. 1–29; AS 27 no. 3669 (1979); 17, no. 4293 (1981); 27, no. 4370 (1981); 17, no. 4527 (1982); 15, nos. 4621–22 (1982); 17, no. 4628 (1982); 26, no. 4692 (1982); 30, no. 4711 (1982); 3, no. 4806 (1983); 15, no. 4824 (1983); Abstracts in *I.B.* no. 8 in *CCE*, no. 56, p. 218; *I.B.* no. 9 in *CCE*, no. 47, pp. 115–16; no. 24 in *CCE*, no. 60, p. 117; *CCE*, no. 61, p. 224; no. 62, pp. 157–58; no. 63, pp. 205–6; no. 64, pp. 133–34.
44. *CCE*, no. 64, pp. 20–24; *USSR News Brief*, 7 (1983), no. 4.
45. *USSR News Brief*, 23/24 (1982), no. 1; 2 (1983), no. 31.
46. Ibid. 11 (1983) no. 1.
47. Ibid. 18 (1983), no. 42.
48. *CCE*, no. 51, pp. 164–67; Document no. 134 of the Moscow Helsinki Group, *Sbornik dokumentov obshchestvennoy gruppy sodeystviya*, vol. 8, p. 25.
49. *Informatsionnyy byulleten' Initsiativnoy gruppy zashchity prav invalidov v SSSR*, nos. 1–16, in: *Vol'noye slovo*, 41/42, nos. 8–10 (1981),

and *AS* 10, no. 3511 (1979); 40, no. 3765 (1979); 7, no. 4577 (1982); Abstracts: no. 8 in *CCE*, no. 56, p. 218; 9 in *CCE*, no. 60, p. 117; no. 62, p. 157; no. 63, pp. 204–5; no. 64, p. 133.

50. *CCE*, no. 51, pp. 164–67.
51. *CCE*, no. 63, pp. 59–60.
52. A. Zelyakov [pseud.], "Pamyati zabytykh i pogibshikh zekovinvalidov," *Khronika zashchity prav v SSSR*, no. 42, pp. 61–64; *USSR News Brief*, 7 (1982), no. 9.
53. *USSR News Brief*, 18 (1983), no. 17.
54. Ibid., 16, no. 2.
55. Vysotin and Sereda, "Independent Trade Unions," p. 38.
56. *AS* 34, no. 4413 (1981); *CCE*, no. 62, pp. 156–57.
57. Semyon Tsvigun, "The Intrigues of Foreign Intelligence Agencies," *CHR*, no. 44, pp. 30–34.
58. S. Pukhov, "Ob otnishenii moskvichey k profsoyuzu 'Solidarnost'," *SSSR: vnutrenniye protivorechiya*, 1981, vol. 2, pp. 248–54.
59. Response to questions posed by the Paris journal "L'Alternative" to the Moscow philosopher in *CHR*, no. 46, pp. 5–12.
60. "*SSSR: rabogheye dvizheniye?*" p. 61.
61. Grigory Svirsky, *Na Lobnom Meste. Literatura nravstvennogo soprotivleniya.* (1846–1976) Novaya literaturnaya biblioteka (London: Overseas Publications, 1979); Abraham Rothberg, *The Heirs of Stalin: Dissidence and the Soviet Regime, 1953–1970* (Ithaca-London: Cornell University Press, 1972); Grigorenko, *Memoirs;* Orlov, *Autobiography* in *CHR*, 1977, no. 25, pp. 85–88; Bukovsky, *To Build a Castle;* Revolt Pimenov, *Odin Politichesky Protsess, Pamyat'* (Paris), 2 (1979), pp. 7–119; Weil, *Osobo opasny;* Raisa Orlova, *Memoirs* (New York: Random House, 1983).
62. Roy Medvedev, *On Socialist Democracy* (New York and London: Alfred A. Knopf and Macmillan, 1975), p. 56.
63. Ibid., pp. 57–58.
64. Roy Medvedev, *Kniga o sotsialicheskoy demokratii* (Amsterdam-Parizh Herzen Foundation 1972), p. 400.
65. Medvedev, *On Socialist Democracy*, p. 399.
66. Ibid., p. 311.
67. Ibid., p. 312.
68. Ibid., p. 313.
69. Ibid., pp. 80–81.
70. Sakharov, Introduction, in *Sakharov Speaks*, ed. Harrison Salisbury (New York: Alfred A. Knopf, 1974).
71. *CCE*, no. 37, p. 41; Cohen, *An End to Silence;* full text: *Politichesky Dnevnik*. 1964–70. Amsterdam, Fond im Gerzena. t. I, 1972; t. II, 1975.
72. Sakharov, Introduction, in *Sakharov Speaks*.
73. A. Sakharov, R. Medvedev, and V. Turchin, "Appeal for a Gradual Democratization (Manifesto II)," in *Sakharov Speaks*, pp. 115–34.
74. Sakharov, Postscript to Memorandum, in *Sakharov Speaks*, p. 152.
75. Medvedev, *On Socialist Democracy*, p. 57.
76. *Sakharov Speaks*, pp. 55–114.
77. Aleksandr Zimin, *Sotsializm ili neostalinizm?* (New York: Chalidze Publications, 1981), p. 157.

78. Ibid., pp. 170, 173–74.
79. Roy Medvedev, *Khrushchev* (Garden City, NY: Doubleday, 1983); Roy Medvedev, "Brezhnev: A Bureaucrat's Profile," *Dissent*, Spring 1983; Roy Medvedev, "Whither Dissent?" *CHR*, no. 48, pp. 13–16.
80. Medvedev, *On Socialist Democracy*, p. 58.
81. Ibid., p. 313.
82. Medvedev, *Kniga o sotsialisticheskoy demokratti*, p. 400.
83. Medvedev, *On Socialist Democracy*, p. 308.
84. Orlov, *Autobiography*, p. 86.
85. S. R. Rozhdestvensky, "Materiali k istorii samodevatelnikh politicheskikh ob"edinenii v SSSR posle 1945, goda." *Pamyat'*, vol. 5, s. 231–249.
86. N. Peskov. Delo "Kolokola" *Pamyat'*, vol. I, pp. 269–284.
87. *CCE*, in Reddaway, *Uncensored Russia*, pp. 389–92.
88. *CCE*, no. 12; no. 14, in *KTS*, pp. 352, 431–33.
89. Ibid., pp. 351–52, 439.
90. S. R. Rozhdestvensky, in *Pamyat'*, vol. 5, pp. 276–83.
91. *CCE*, no. 33, p. 155.
92. Grigorenko, *Memoirs*, pp. 274–76.
93. Ibid.
94. *CCE*, no. 40, p. 105.
95. *CCE*, no. 51, p. 34.
96. Ibid., pp. 33–36; *CCE*, no. 53, pp. 33–38.
97. *CCE*, no. 53, pp. 167–69.
98. *USSR News Brief* (1982), 23/24, no. 1; (1983), 2, no. 31.
99. *CCE*, no. 55, pp. 6–7.
100. Otveti nezavisimogo almanakha "Varianti" (Moskva) na voprosi zhurnala "Alternativa" (Parizh) . . . —*Forum*, no. I, p. 33.
101. *Byulleten' V*, 74, no. 49, Khronika Press Archives.
102. Otveti sovetskikh grazhdan na voprosi zhurnala "Alternativa," *Forum*, no. 1, pp. 3–32.
103. *AS 26*, no. 4694 (1982).
104. *Byulleten' V*, 83, no. 48, Khronika Press Archives; *USSR News Brief*, 20/21, (1982) No. 7.
105. V. Krasnov, *Dialektika nadezhdi* (arkhiv "Problemi Vostochnoi Evropi," F. and L. Silnitsky.
106. *Forum*, No. 1, c. 44, 42.
107. *USSR News Brief*, 20/21 (1982), no. 7; 21 (1983), no. 1; V. Krasnov, *Dialektika nadezhdi, Predisloviya*, 1981, p. 1.
108. *CCE*, no. 64, pp. 15–16; *USSR News Brief*, 1982, 10 no. 1, 12 no. 3.
109. *AS* no. 5072, 42/83; *USSR News Brief* (1983), 21, no. 1.
110. *CCChL*, no. 46, pp. 21–35.
111. Intervyu s predsedatelem Zagranichnogo Komiteta Sotsial-Demokraticheskoy partii Latvii Bruno Kalninsshem, *Forum*, no. 4, pp. 67–74.
112. *USSR News Brief*, 16 (1983), no. 32.
113. Ibid., 17 (1983), no. 8.
114. Ibid. (1982), 18, no. 12; (1983), 17, no. 7; (1984), 5, no. 5; 7, (1984), no. 7.
115. *Sotsialist-82* (samizdat), *Forum*, no. 3, pp. 60–80.
116. Ibid., p. 77.
117. *AS* 48, no. 5712 (1983).
118. Mark Bolkhovskoy, "Sudba revolyutsionno-sotsialisticheskoy intelligent-

sii v Rossii," *SSSR—vnutrenniye protivorechiya*, vol. 5, pp. 192–235; "Kataev i revolyutsiya" *AS*, 34, no. 4412 (1981); "Utopii v kosmichesky vek," *AS*, 30, no. 4391 (1981).
119. N. Arguni, "Russkiye sotstialisty i budushcheye Rossii," *Forum*, no. 4, pp. 156–76.
120. *CCE*, no. 64, p. 6.
121. *USSR News Brief*, 6 (1983), no. 16.
122. Ibid., 19/20 (1983), no. 6.
123. Ibid., 9 (1983), no. 4; 15 (1983), no. 1; 7 (1984), no. 8.
124. Ibid., 5 (1984), no. 7.

19. The Russian National Movement

1. *CCE*, no. 7, in Reddaway, *Uncensored Russia*, pp. 431–33.
2. "Slovo natsii," *AS* 8, no. 590; *Veche*, no. 3, 1982; Abstract: *CCE*, no. 17, p. 92.
3. Keston College archive, Keston, England, *AS* 22, no. 1132; 43, nos. 1801, 1846; 2045–46, 2218, 2466, 2086 (1982).
4. Gennady Shimanov, "Kak ponimat' nashu istoriyu i k chemu v ney stremit'sya," *AS*, no. 2086, p. 9.
5. Shimanov, "Protiv techeniya," p. 62, Keston College archive.
6. Shimanov, "Kak ponimat' nashu istoriyu," p. 10.
7. Shimanov, "Ideal'noye gosudarstvo," *AS*, no. 2218, p. 14.
8. Shimanov, "Moskva—tretiy Rim," Keston College archive.
9. Shimanov, "Kak ponimat' nashu istoriyu," p. 14.
10. *CCE*, no. 1, in Reddaway, *Uncensored Russia*, pp. 376–80; John B. Dunlop, *The New Russian Revolutionaries* (Belmont, Mass.: Nordland Publishing Co., 1976).
11. Dunlop, *New Russian Revolutionaries*, p. 280.
12. Andrey Sinyavsky, "Ne nazyvaya imena," *Sintaksis*, no. 2 (1978), pp. 57–62.
13. Dunlop, *New Russian Revolutionaries*, p. 247.
14. Ibid., p. 293.
15. *Prolog*, New York, Suchasnist', no. 7/8 (1980), p. 107.
16. *CCE*, no. 44, p. 127.
17. Testimony of Leonid Borodin.
18. Aleksandr Solzhenitsyn, *Letter to the Fourth Congress of Soviet Writers*, in *Solzhenitsyn: Critical Essays and Documentary*, ed. John Dunlop, Richard Haugh and Alexis Klimoff (Belmont, Mass.: Nordland Publishing Co., 1973), pp. 463–71.
19. Solzhenitsyn, "Mir i nasiliye," *Publitsistika*, p. 133.
20. *Veche*, ed. Vladimir Osipov, Moscow, 1971–74, nos. 1–9 (*samizdat*); *Veche* no. 5, *Vol'noye slovo* 9–10; *Veche*, nos. 7–10, *Vol'noye slovo* 17–18; Abstracts: *Veche*, no. 1 in *CCE*, no. 18, pp. 139–40; no. 2 in *CCE*, no. 20, pp. 257–59; no. 3 in *CCE*, no. 22, pp. 42–43; no. 4 in *CCE*, no. 24, pp. 163–64; no. 5 in *CCE*, no. 26, pp. 265–66.
21. On Osipov see Mikhail Kheyfets, "Russkyy patriot Vladimir Osipov," *Kontinent*, no. 27/28 (1981).
22. *Veche*, no. 1 in *CCE*, no. 18, p. 139.

23. Vladimir Osipov, "Otkrytoye pis'mo Gennadiyu Shimanovu," *Vol'noye slovo*, no. 17/18, pp. 16, 18.
24. Vladimir Osipov, "Trus ne igrayet v khokkey," in *Tri otnosheniya k rodine* (Frankfurt am Main: Possev, 1978), p. 111.
25. Vladimir Osipov, "Sekret svobody," in *CCE*, no. 24, pp. 149–50.
26. Aleksandr Yanov, "Ideal'noye gosudarstvo Gennadiya Shimanova," *Sintaksis*, no. 1, pp. 50–51.
27. *Zemlya*, no. 1/2 in *Vol'noye slovo*, vol. 20, Possev, 1975.
28. *CCE*, no. 34, pp. 28–30.
29. *CCE*, no. 34, p. 30; *CCE*, no. 37, pp. 7–8.
30. *CCE*, no. 37, pp. 5–7. See also Mikhail Kheyfets, "Russkiy patriot."
31. *Moskovskiy sbornik*, ed. Leonid Borodin, Moscow, 1974–75, nos. 1–3 (*samizdat*) in *AS*, no. 2050; *CCE*, no. 36, p. 167.
32. Solzhenitsyn, *Letter to the Soviet Leaders*.
33. Aleksandr Solzhenitsyn, "Live Not by Lies," in *A Documentary Record*, ed. Leopold Labedz (Harmondsworth, England: Penguin Books, 1974), pp. 375–79.
34. *What Awaits the Soviet Union?: A Collection of Articles on the Theme of A. Solzhenitsyn's "Letter to the Soviet Leaders,"* Moscow, 1974 (*samizdat*); Abstract: *CCE*, no. 34, pp. 77–85.
35. *CCE*, no. 34, p. 80.
36. Ibid., pp. 81–82.
37. Andrey Sakharov, "On Aleksandr Solzhenitsyn's *Letter to the Soviet Leaders*," *Political, Social and Religious Thought*, ed. Meerson and Shragin, pp. 291–301.
38. Aleksandr Solzhenitsyn et al., *From Under the Rubble* (Boston: Little, Brown, 1974).
39. Solzhenitsyn, "A. Sakharov i kritika 'pis'ma vozhdyam,' " *Publitsistika*, p. 196.
40. Feliks Svetov, *Otverzi im dveri* (Paris: Les Editeurs Reunis, 1978); V. Trostnikov, *Mysli pered rassvetom* (Paris: YMCA Press, 1980); B. Mikhaylov, "O sovremennom estetizme," *Vestnik RkhD*, no. 134, pp. 246–70.
41. *Vestnik RKhd*, ed. Nikita Struve, Paris; *Possev*, Frankfurt-am-Main; *Kontinent*.

Conclusion

1. *Political, Social and Religious Thought*, ed. Meerson and Shragin, p. 153.
2. Maksudov, "What Do You Think About Sakharov?" in *On Sakharov*, pp. 11–16; S. Pukhov, "Podkhod moskvichey k profsozyuzu 'Solidarnost,' " *SSSR: vnutrenniye protivorechiya*, no. 2, pp. 248–54.
3. *SMOT Bulletin*, no. 29, in *AS* 37, no. 4752 (1982).

Index

Page number in italic indicates a photograph follows that page.

495

About the Author

Ludmilla Alexeyeva, once a member of the Communist Party of the USSR and editor for government publishing houses, left the party and became a leading activist in the *samizdat* movement (underground publishing) in the late 1960s, and a founding member of the Moscow Helsinki Group, of which she is now Western representative. In 1977 under threat of imprisonment, she left the Soviet Union with her husband Nikolai Williams, a mathematician, and her two sons. She lives in Tarrytown, New York, and is a script writer for Radio Liberty and Soviet consultant for the U.S. Helsinki Watch Committee.